PRAISE FOR

ℛ *The Peabody*

"A stunning work of biography and intellectual history. Deftly weaving material from the letters and journals of all three sisters, Ms. Marshall, who spent nearly twenty years researching and writing this book, performs the intellectual equivalent of a triple axel."
— *New York Times*

"This monumental biography answers every question about its subjects but one: Why aren't the Peabody sisters famous?"
— *People*, four-star review

"Excellent . . . By painting so colorful and sympathetic a portrait of these remarkable women . . . Marshall has given us so much that it seems ungrateful to ask for more."
— *New York Times Book Review*

"A commanding intellectual biography."
— *Boston Sunday Globe*

"Through Marshall's beautiful book, we can taste the flavor of three remarkable lives and pay tribute."
— *Washington Post*

"Ignored by history, the brilliant Peabody sisters . . . finally get their due."
— *W*

"The best kind of biography, blending subtle psychological portraiture with astute intellectual history. . . . a fascinating story, too."
— *Slate.com*, Best Books of the Year

"Skillfully paced and richly observed . . . a fascinating, sprawling story that its author commands with finesse."
—*New Republic*

"Heroically researched and beautifully written."
—*Ploughshares*

"This book reads like a novel but is a model of scholarly, feminist biography unmatched by previous works."
—*Library Journal*, starred review

"An engrossing account, replete with both penetrating insights and interesting details."
—*Booklist*, starred review

"Outstanding . . . Marshall has distilled twenty years of research into a book that brings the sisters to life."
—*Publishers Weekly*, starred review

"The sisters themselves would most likely think this book has done them justice . . . one of the best literary biographies to come along in years."
—*New England Quarterly*

"I can't think of any contemporary biographer who has succeeded as well as Megan Marshall in getting so thoroughly inside the heads of her subjects."
—Deborah Pickman Clifford, author of
Mine Eyes Have Seen the Glory: A Biography of Julia Ward Howe

"A splendid achievement . . . an enthralling story, impossible to put down. It is the most satisfying group biography I know."
—Robert D. Richardson Jr., author of *Emerson: The Mind on Fire*

❧ The ❧
Peabody Sisters

THREE WOMEN WHO IGNITED AMERICAN
ROMANTICISM

Megan Marshall

MARINER
BOOKS
An Imprint of HarperCollins *Publishers*
Boston   New York

First Mariner Books edition 2006
Copyright © 2005 by Megan Marshall

Mariner Books
An Imprint of HarperCollins Publishers, registered in the United States
of America and/or other jurisdictions.

Visit our Web site: www.marinerbooks.com

Library of Congress Cataloging-in-Publication Data

Marshall, Megan.
The Peabody sisters : three women who ignited American romanticism /
Megan Marshall.
p. cm.
Includes bibliographical references and index.
ISBN 0-395-38992-5
1. Peabody, Elizabeth Palmer, 1804–1894. 2. Mann, Mary Tyler Peabody,
1806–1887. 3. Hawthorne, Sophia Peabody, 1809–1871. 4. Massachusetts—
Intellectual life—19th century. 5. Women intellectuals—Massachusetts—
Salem—Biography. 6. Sisters—Massachusetts—Salem—Biography.
7. Salem (Mass.)—Biography. 8. Romanticism—Massachusetts—History—
19th century. 9. United States—Intellectual life—19th century.
10. Romanticism—United States—History—19th century. I. Title.
F74.SIM225 2005 974.4'03'0922—DC22
[B] 2004060927

ISBN-13: 978-0-618-71169-7 (pbk.)
ISBN-10: 0-618-71169-4 (pbk.)

Book design by Lisa Diercks
The text of this book is set in Clifford Eighteen.

Printed in the United States of America

23 24 25 26 27 LBC 17 16 15 14 13

For the Sedgwick sisters,

Josio and Sara,

and my own sister, Amy

❧ CONTENTS ❧

❧ LIST OF ILLUSTRATIONS ❧

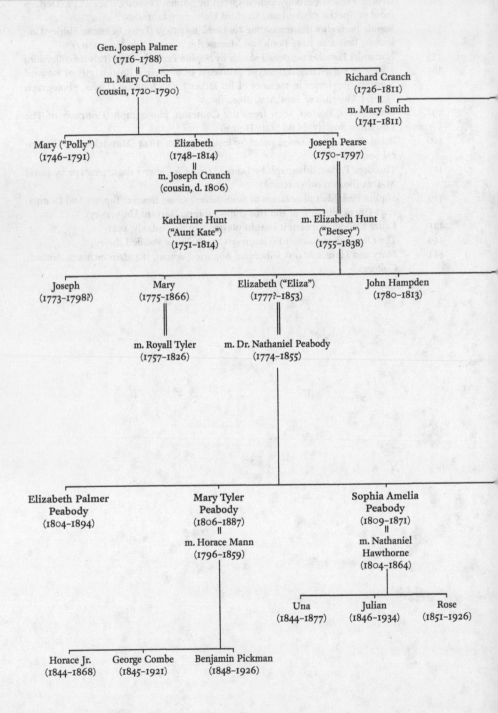

Gen. Joseph Palmer
(1716–1788)
=
m. Mary Cranch
(cousin, 1720–1790)

Richard Cranch
(1726–1811)
=
m. Mary Smith
(1741–1811)

Mary ("Polly")
(1746–1791)

Elizabeth
(1748–1814)
=
m. Joseph Cranch
(cousin, d. 1806)

Joseph Pearse
(1750–1797)

Katherine Hunt
("Aunt Kate")
(1751–1814)

m. Elizabeth Hunt
("Betsey")
(1755–1838)

Joseph
(1773–1798?)

Mary
(1775–1866)

Elizabeth ("Eliza")
(1777?–1853)

John Hampden
(1780–1813)

m. Royall Tyler
(1757–1826)

m. Dr. Nathaniel Peabody
(1774–1855)

Elizabeth Palmer
Peabody
(1804–1894)

Mary Tyler
Peabody
(1806–1887)
=
m. Horace Mann
(1796–1859)

Sophia Amelia
Peabody
(1809–1871)
=
m. Nathaniel
Hawthorne
(1804–1864)

Una
(1844–1877)

Julian
(1846–1934)

Rose
(1851–1926)

Horace Jr.
(1844–1868)

George Combe
(1845–1921)

Benjamin Pickman
(1848–1926)

GENEALOGY ℘

This genealogy is limited to family members who played a significant role in the Peabody sisters' lives. In some cases, as with the Smith, Adams, Hunt, Pickman, and Putnam families, some siblings' names have been omitted.

Abigail Smith
(1744–1818)
‖
m. Pres. John Adams
(1735–1826)

Elizabeth Smith
(1750–1815)
(1) m. Rev. John Shaw
(1748–1794)
(2) m. Rev. Stephen Peabody
(1741–1819)

Abigail ("Nabby")
(1765–1813)

Edward
(1782–1797)

Amelia
(1784–1855)
m. Abel Winslow
Curtis (d. 1816)

Sophia
(natural daughter
of Royall Tyler)
(1786–1862)
‖
m. Dr. Thomas
Pickman (son of
Benjamin Pickman,
1740–1819)
(1773–1817)

Love Rawlins
Pickman
("Miss Rawlins")
(1786–1863)

George
(1788–1855)

Catherine
(1791–1869)
m. Henry Putnam
(1778–1827)

Mary Toppan
("Mary Top")
(1816–1878)

George Palmer
Putnam
(1814–1872)

Nathaniel Cranch
Peabody ("Nat")
(1811–1881)
‖
m. Sarah Elizabeth
Hibbard ("E. Nat")
(1814–1899)

George Francis
Peabody
(1813–1839)

Wellington
Peabody
(1815–1837)

Catharine Putnam
Peabody
(April 26–June 11, 1819)

Ellen Elizabeth
(1836–1906)

Mary
(1837–1917)

ᴼᴿ PREFACE ᴼᴿ

DURING THE FIRST DECADE OF THE NINETEENTH CENTURY, THREE sisters were born into a New England family down on its luck. Like the young American nation, their roots stretched back to a time of colonial upheaval; their future beckoned with opportunity for self-invention.

The three sisters would come of age in an era now known as the American Renaissance, when arts and ideas flourished in an environment of intellectual freedom made possible by the new Republic and its visionary Constitution. Boston, still a close rival in prosperity to New York, was the hub of this universe. The wild nature that inspired the best work of its leading writers— Emerson and Thoreau—was to be found just beyond the city's limits in what are now the tame suburbs of Newton and Concord.

It was here in New England that America experienced a second "more interior revolution," in the words of Elizabeth Peabody, the oldest of the sisters and a leader in the movement. This revolution would transform the nation from a parochial theocracy, in which governors still declared statewide "Fast Days" for religious observance and towns taxed their citizens to support a parish minister, to a modern, secular democracy, in which the lecture platform replaced the pulpit as the source of wisdom and revelation.

The Peabody sisters—Elizabeth, Mary, and Sophia—were fortunate to arrive on an American scene in which women moved freely in intellectual circles and women's ideas were welcome in conversation, if not always in print. Social life for men and women had not yet split into rigidly "separate spheres," and the authority of such institutions as had already taken hold in American soil—centuries-old Protestant denominations, or universities like Harvard, Yale, and Princeton—was hotly contested in ways that, for this brief historical moment, put the sexes on roughly equal footing. Freethinking men and women alike had little use for bastions of male privilege. Thanks to the electrifying sermons of William Ellery Channing, America's first nationally prominent liberal theologian, "knowledge," "love," and "activity" became the watchwords of the era. These imperatives brought America's first cultural awakening: a time of exuberant national self-discovery that would come to define the American character as both fiercely independent and fervently social.

The sisters were luckier still to have been raised by an unconventional mother who cared more that her daughters grow up to achieve "a decent independence" than that they learn to "sew a shirt and bake a pudding": the conventional measures of feminine achievement. Although too poor to attend any of the new female academies flourishing at the time, the Peabody sisters were educated by their schoolteacher mother and through their own determination as fully as most college men. When it was time to find work in their late teenage years, all three wanted to do their mother one better. They became not just teachers—the only white-collar profession open to women—but added to this occupation writing, editing, translating, publishing, bookselling, and, in the case of the youngest of the three, painting and sculpture.

But at heart, the sisters' energy was their own: magnetic, stimulating, nurturing. We all know sets of sisters who draw men to their households. Feminine attraction multiplies exponentially as these women—beautiful, vivacious, or seductively withholding—consider their suitors and pass them from one to the other. The stories are as old as the biblical tale of Rachel and Leah. The Peabodys themselves knew such women and taught them as girls in their schools: the Marshall sisters, Emily and Mary Ann of Boston, who neglected their studies and "coquetted" until they caught rich husbands, like Mayor Harrison Gray Otis's son William; or the Hathaway twins and the Sturgis girls, who married importers, bankers, and doctors.

The Peabody sisters were too poor—and too principled—to coquette. They rarely received invitations to parties or dances, and often varied their dress from one day to the next only by changing to a fresh collar. When they wore jewelry, or lace in their hair, it was borrowed. As Horace Mann noted of the middle sister, Mary, all three were "without wealth, & without property" and had "no *éclat* in the fashionable world." But the same could be said of most of the men in their circle—Mann included, who, for several years when the sisters first knew him, was forced to live in his one-room law office because he couldn't afford the rent in even a modest boarding house. These men had "come down from our back woods . . . having conversed alone with the powers of nature," as Elizabeth described them in a letter promoting her friends to the English poet William Wordsworth, to "fill our first rank of society." Horace Mann and Theodore Parker were farm boys; Nathaniel Hawthorne was the son of a ship captain who died before he could make his fortune; Ralph Waldo Emerson, who also grew up fatherless, reached adulthood with scarcely enough money to pay Harvard's then minimal tuition.

The sisters' magnetism was of the mind and the spirit. Their household was not a hothouse or a hive, but a "Caravanserai," as Nathaniel Hawthorne termed the disparate collection of reformers and literary lights to be found at the Wednesday-night open houses the Peabody sisters held in Boston during the 1840s. In this "Transcendental Exchange," as another visitor called the Peabodys' West Street house, ideas were born, opinions shaped, causes argued, fought, and sometimes won. The sisters' conversation and wide-ranging interests fired the imaginations and captured the affections of the era's most gifted men—Mann, in politics; Hawthorne, in literature; Emerson, in religion and philosophy. Rivalrous themselves, none of the three men trusted or even much liked one another. But all three were comfortable in the Peabody sisters' front parlor and found inspiration there. In the back parlor, two of them married Peabody women.

Marriage was never a prime goal, however. Indeed, to all three sisters, it seemed at times a prime obstacle, a fate to be avoided for its risks and restrictions. The sisters were uniformly disparaging of women whose "principle desire . . . is to get married" and pitied them as lacking "resources." For such women, "life must be one long wearisome burden," Mary once wrote. The problem the sisters posed themselves was one that could only partly, and perhaps never satisfactorily, be answered by marriage: what could women of fierce energy, intellect, and determination do with their talents when they could not enter the public realm by any conventional means? Although the bonds were loosening, it was still a time when, in the words of their friend Emerson, a "woman in our society finds her safety and happiness in exclusions and privacies" and "congratulates herself when she is not called to the market, to the courts, to the polls, to the stage, to the orchestra." Gaining proximity to powerful men, and with it the potential for influence—yielding to the temptation, as the youngest sister, Sophia, put it, to "shine by borrowed light" —was one choice. But it was not the only one, and not the best one for a woman who wanted, as Elizabeth ultimately vowed, to "be myself and *act.*" For such a woman, talent was as much a torment as it was a gift, and ambition was an outright curse. The Peabody sisters struggled with the dilemma, and each one found her own set of answers.

This is not a conventional biography, no cradle-to-grave story of solitary genius rising to accomplishment and renown. It tells the story of three intertwined lives of sisters who both welcomed their group identity and resented it as they strove for independent self-fulfillment. And my story ends at the midpoint— when, after nearly four decades of sometimes empowering, sometimes suffocating togetherness, marriage finally separated them. As I gradually assembled the documentary evidence of their lives—a vast store of private family letters and journals—it became clear to me that the Peabody sisters' story was located here, in the expressions of faith, trust, and love, as well as in the accusations, recriminations, and efforts to influence and to outdo which filled their daily lives during the years when all three were seeking a place in the world.

My first awareness of the Peabody sisters came from a book written more than a half century ago. *The Peabody Sisters of Salem* appeared in 1950 and told a story palatable to readers of the time. In that book, the three sisters seemed a bit like Louisa May Alcott's *Little Women*, a feisty but nonetheless quaint trio, easily typed as "the brain," "the beauty," and "the invalid." The book was wildly popular. Even as late as 1985, when I started my own work, the Boston Public Library still had a shelf full of faded copies purchased thirty years before to accommodate the demand.

Reading the tattered volume I had picked up in a secondhand bookstore, I quickly realized that Louise Tharp, an author who made a specialty of writing about New England's "grandes dames," as they once were called, had never read any of the extensive published writings of the brainy Elizabeth and had little sense of the larger intellectual world the sisters inhabited. Tharp skipped over the youngest sister, Sophia's, career as an artist, failing to appreciate the extent of her accomplishment as a woman with few examples to follow and limited access to training, and instead played up Sophia's invalidism, which she considered the product of a sick symbiosis between domineering mother and dependent youngest daughter. Typically for the 1950s, Tharp painted Mrs. Peabody as an overprotective virago and didn't bother to look up any of the published writing and few of the diaries and letters of that truly grand, if flawed, woman. Yet I was glad Tharp's book had kept the sisters in the public mind, and that it was still there to motivate me to find out more.

When I decided to write the Peabody sisters' story, I set out to read everything they ever wrote in letters and diaries and in print, along with most of the books they read and cared about. I wanted to know who they were on the inside, what they wanted to be, and who they became. Fortunately, because of their connections to famous men, their papers had been preserved; some of their letters were even well known for the "borrowed light" they shed on a particular man's life. But no one since Louise Tharp had attempted to read all three sisters' private papers to see how they illuminated the lives of the women themselves.

I guessed that many more letters and diaries than Tharp had found in the 1940s would surface, once I started looking. And indeed, halfway through the project, I discovered a cache of private journals that dramatically altered the way I viewed these women—and that provided startling new information about the triangular relationship of Elizabeth and Sophia Peabody and the man they both loved, Nathaniel Hawthorne.

In the end, my work took most of two decades. There were many thousands of manuscript pages to track down and decipher, and obscure books to retrieve. In some cases, I found multiple letters and journal entries describing the events of just one day. I realized that the sisters lived in a web of lives, and inevitably I turned to the private papers of their circle of associates as well. These manuscripts were scattered across the country in more than a dozen major archives from Maine to California, where I spent many hours, and sometimes weeks and months, reading and taking notes. I discovered stories that had been waiting more than two centuries for a hearing; and after laborious searching, I was able to set other apocryphal tales, recycled in biographies of Mann, Hawthorne, and Emerson, to rest. There were astonishing finds, as well, that came from smaller collections or from letters still in the hands of descendants. In one case, I traveled to a small-town library to read a single letter and discovered in it the identity of one sister's first suitor—a doomed lover about whom Louise Tharp had speculated wildly (and well off the mark) in *The Peabody Sisters of Salem*.

I became expert in deciphering the sisters' handwriting, and that of their ancestors, parents, and friends. Each era and each correspondent presented different challenges. Some hands were sprawling, some spindly, some cramped; *t*'s went uncrossed at the ends of words, and *f*'s and *s*'s were interchanged; spelling, capitalization, and punctuation could be erratic or idiosyncratic. Often, to save paper and postage, the sisters turned a single sheet ninety degrees and wrote back across a page already covered with handwriting. I learned to be especially attentive to these cross-written lines, in which the sisters invariably confided their deepest feelings in the last hurried moments of closing a letter. Here I would find the urgent personal message that had been put off for the sake of dispensing news or settling business. In one such postscript, I discovered Elizabeth's account of a conversation with Horace Mann in which the two spoke frankly of their love for each other and finally settled on what it meant.

Once I mastered the handwriting, I began to feel that I was reading an entirely new language that spoke of an almost alien sensibility. I noticed, for example, that *disinterested*, a word virtually always misused today when it is used at all, appeared again and again in the sisters' letters and journals as a term of highest approbation. This nearly archaic word opened up the Peabody sisters' world to me: one in which acting without self-interest was a supreme goal, where a premium was placed on friendship, on benevolent acts large and small, and where the sisters truly did have standing, if not *éclat*. As Horace Mann wrote admiringly of Mary, after noting her lack of wealth and property: "whenever within her circle, there has been good to do or evil to remove," she was there to do it, with an unwavering sense of "the true dignity & the true objects of life." This was foreign territory to me. Imagine a time when teenage girls described their best friends not as "cool" or "awesome," but as "disinterested." I felt privileged to inhabit this world, even vicariously—and I wanted today's readers to know about it too.

Women of the nineteenth century have been pitied by American historians in recent decades for suffering under a "Cult of True Womanhood" that held women to exacting standards of piety, purity, and submissiveness. But I found little to pity and a great deal to admire as I read the Peabody sisters' words and pondered the choices they made as young women. The three sisters went on to lead long lives, stretching nearly to the end of the century; they experienced motherhood and widowhood, and they championed new causes with every decade. But I remained fascinated with the years when the sisters were starting out in life, when American Romanticism was born of a widespread yearning for spiritual and intellectual transcendence, and certain women and men of Boston and Concord, the Peabody sisters among them, banded together to create what was then called "the newness": the movement that startled our young nation into a vibrant maturity. These were the years when Elizabeth, Mary, and Sophia Peabody grew up and fell in love—with books, art, ideas, and men.

MEGAN MARSHALL
Newton, Massachusetts
April 2005

ℛ PROLOGUE: JULY 9, 1842 ℛ

SUMMERS IN BOSTON WERE JUST AS HOT IN 1842 AS THEY ARE TODAY. A building boom in the past decade had changed the seaport town, incorporated as a city only twenty years before, into a metropolis of brick and stone. Sea breezes didn't stand a chance of reaching beyond the granite market buildings and warehouses that now fronted the docks, let alone the brick row houses that crowded every street up to the Common and the massive copper dome of the State House. Tightly packed neighborhoods that seemed pleasantly intimate in winter grew unbearable as several days of rising temperatures and mounting humidity turned the city of nearly 100,000 into a furnace with few sources of relief. The Frog Pond on the Common was one oasis: there, near sunset on days when the thermometer refused to drop below ninety, strolling couples could enjoy an accidental splashing from the dogs that capered among the small boys with their toy sailboats at the water's edge. Elsewhere in the city, the air was stifling, tempers flared, and sleep was difficult, until the inevitable thunderstorm cooled the cobblestone streets and brick sidewalks for a night and a day, and the whole process started over again.

It was on a Saturday morning in July, when bright over-hot skies seemed destined to turn thick with storm clouds by midafternoon, that a small wedding party gathered in the upstairs parlor of a modest three-story brick row house (no bow front, no bay window) on West Street, a half block from the Common and the splashing dogs in the Frog Pond. The bride was a small woman, just under five feet tall, whose size and childlike manner belied her thirty-two years. Dressed in a gown she and a friend had stitched together hastily the previous month and trimmed with borrowed cuffs, her light brown hair braided and decorated with pond lilies, Sophia Peabody, the youngest of three remarkable sisters, was about to become the first to marry.

The three Peabody sisters—Elizabeth, Mary, and Sophia—had scarcely been lacking for offers of marriage. Indeed, Elizabeth and Mary each secretly

1

prided themselves on having turned down perfectly eligible, admirably persistent suitors who, to their minds, simply weren't good enough: men of fortune or of intellectual promise, but not men of genius. If the Peabody sisters were to marry, they would not make the same mistake as their mother, who had married young for security, only to be disappointed in the man she had chosen. It was largely thanks to their mother, however, that the sisters had been able to maintain their high standards, despite the family's relative poverty. Mrs. Eliza Peabody had deliberately raised her daughters to discover and develop their own talents in order to become "independant & useful," as she wrote in her unconventional spelling, so that they need never rely on men. It was no accident that she had named her daughters for an English queen, the Holy Mother, and the Greek word for wisdom. Mrs. Peabody was a firm believer in woman's "destination for a sphere of action infinite in duration and boundless in extent"—even if this destiny lay in the far distant future. And her three girls, "so linked in heart, in opinions and in talents," in her view, had done their best to hasten the day.

The house at 13 West Street, where the family now gathered, was itself a monument to Mrs. Peabody's ambitions for her daughters. True, it was on the wrong side of the Common, as far as residences were concerned. West Street wasn't Beacon Hill, nor was it close enough to the small enclave of comfortable houses still clustered around Church Green, the last vestige of fine living near the waterfront, to be considered fashionable. The house itself faced a livery stable. But the Peabody women had no intention of maintaining a conventional household.

The oldest daughter, Elizabeth, now thirty-eight, had chosen the building in 1840 for its location just around the corner from Washington Street—Boston's "publishers' row"—as an ideal spot from which to launch a foreign-language bookstore and her own publishing business. And she had managed to persuade a wealthy backer to loan her the money to stock the shelves. Since then, Elizabeth had succeeded in making the "atom of a shop" that occupied the first-floor parlor famous well beyond city limits as the in-town gathering place for New England's Transcendentalist ministers, writers, and reformers. Elizabeth's bookstore, crammed with hundreds of books and journals imported from Germany, France, Italy, and Spain—many of them circulating as part of a subscription library—brought an erratic income for the Peabody family but provided steady intellectual sustenance for a diverse group of devotees to what was beginning to be called "the newness": men and women, Elizabeth wrote in an article published in the Transcendentalists' journal *The Dial*, "who have dared to say to one another . . . Why not begin to move the mountain of custom and convention?"

On Wednesday evenings at West Street, the sisters held open house, where an invited cast of freethinkers met to lay plans for projects ranging from the utopian community at Brook Farm in nearby West Roxbury to new churches led by the radical Unitarians James Freeman Clarke and Theodore Parker. On Thursday mornings, Margaret Fuller held her "Conversations" for women in the book room, drawing out the voices of the wives, daughters, and sisters of the movement's founders on matters of philosophy, religion, art, and politics. The future abolitionist Lydia Maria Child and the suffragist Elizabeth Cady Stanton were among the women who fell into Fuller's web of influence by way of the weekly Conversations. But Elizabeth Peabody, who often held the floor, needed no prodding to enter the marketplace of ideas. Already the author or translator of a half-dozen books, founder of her own magazine, and contributor to the liberal journals of the day, Elizabeth had now also become the publisher of many of the region's literary lights—Nathaniel Hawthorne, William Ellery Channing, Theodore Parker, and Margaret Fuller—under her own imprint, "E. P. Peabody, Publisher." In October 1841, Elizabeth had taken over as publisher of *The Dial* to work in tandem with the new editor, Ralph Waldo Emerson.

Business at 13 West Street was by no means limited to the ground floor. In the upstairs rooms, Mary Peabody, the middle sister at thirty-five, taught a girls' school on weekday mornings, tutored schoolboys and young women in French, German, and Latin in the afternoons, and wrote textbooks on subjects ranging from elementary grammar to geography and botany in her spare time. Mary's most successful book, *The Flower People*, a children's horticultural guide, was in its third edition, published by her sister Elizabeth. Upstairs, too, Sophia Peabody, the sister who everyone agreed possessed the greatest spark of genius, maintained an art studio in her bedroom, where she painted landscapes and modeled busts and bas-reliefs in clay to be cast later in plaster—or perhaps, one day, in marble. Although her output was slim, limited by the severe migraines that had plagued her since she was a teenager, Sophia was one of just a handful of women artists in New England whose work was shown or sold with any regularity.

Mrs. Peabody was never far from any of this activity. A schoolteacher herself for most of her forty years of marriage, she now kept watch over Sophia when she was ill, ran the bookshop when Elizabeth was around the corner in her publishing office on Washington Street, and joined Mary in translating German tales for publication by Elizabeth's press. Her husband, the constitutionally timid Dr. Nathaniel Peabody, who had struggled—and failed—to keep the family afloat first as a general practitioner, then as a farmer, and finally as a dentist, hovered nearby as well, experimenting in retirement with homeopathic medicines, which he offered for sale in Elizabeth's shop.

But now Sophia Peabody, the youngest and most fragile of the sisters, the daughter apparently most dependent on her "dearest mother in the world," was about to leave this vibrant household to start one of her own. The wedding on the morning of July 9, 1842, seemed the culmination of a Transcendentalist fairy tale. After a three-year secret courtship, Sophia was at last to marry the increasingly famous—and famously handsome—author Nathaniel Hawthorne. She would ride with him that afternoon to Concord, Massachusetts, where the couple would take up residence in a house selected for them by Ralph Waldo Emerson, dine on the produce of a garden planted for them by Henry David Thoreau, and spend their first night together on a maple bedstead hand-painted by Sophia herself with "exquisite light figures and horses and youths and maidens flying through the air," according to one contemporary admirer, in the style of Guido Reni's celebrated Roman fresco *Aurora*.

Yet even Transcendental fairy tales have their dark sides. United as the sisters seemed to outsiders, and "linked in heart" as their devoted mother believed them, the three had always been prone to covert rivalries and shifting alliances. The July wedding was the result of Sophia's having set her cap for a man her oldest sister had loved first, and whose genius Elizabeth Peabody had been among the first in New England to recognize and promote. The dark-haired, moody Hawthorne had entered the Peabody household first on Elizabeth's invitation, been declared "handsomer than Lord Byron" first by Elizabeth, and had confided his fiercely guarded ambitions and private torments in intimate conversation first—to Elizabeth.

How must Elizabeth have felt this Saturday morning in July as she watched her youngest sister glow with anticipation for her marriage to the man Sophia gushingly called "the very king and poet of the world"? Or Mary, for that matter, whose own heart was preoccupied by love—so far unreturned—for a man who had, like Hawthorne, once been Elizabeth's nearest companion?

Only four days earlier, on July 4, the Independence Day parade had passed the Peabodys' West Street house with Mary's beloved Horace Mann at its head, leading a procession of elected officials, ministers, schoolteachers, Sunday school children, and Revolutionary War veterans through the streets of Boston to the Odeon Theater, where Mann would give the most important speech of his life. After an exhausting five-year campaign as secretary of the state's first-ever board of education, Mann had succeeded in persuading the Massachusetts legislature to vote him a lavish budget to reform the Commonwealth's school system. Until he met Elizabeth Peabody ten years earlier, Mann had not taken the slightest interest in the cause of education. Now the six-foot-tall silver-haired reformer was exhorting his listeners to "pour out light and truth, as God pours out sunshine and rain . . . *go forth,* and TEACH THIS PEOPLE" in a speech so instantly popular that 20,000 copies would be in print by summer's end. Yet it was Mary Peabody who had become Mann's confidante in recent years, editing his manuscripts, even contributing anonymously to his *Common School Journal*. Still, Mann's heart remained a mystery to both sisters as they attempted to reconcile themselves to life at West Street with the breakup of the "sisterhood." Although Mary had done her younger sister the favor of setting up the house in Concord during the last weeks of June, she too was beginning to tire of Sophia's self-congratulatory effusions. By the end of the summer she would be chiding the still euphoric newlywed, "You know, dear, there are different kinds of beautiful lives."

And Sophia? On the morning of her wedding day, she turned to two close friends rather than to her sisters to help her dress for the ceremony, an event that itself had been much postponed. Originally planned for mid-June, and finally set for June 30, the wedding date had to be pushed back again by over a week—to the dog days of July—as Sophia was repeatedly overcome by mysterious fevers and palpitations. After three years of secrecy, the month preceding the wedding, when the whole world knew at last that Sophia Peabody and Nathaniel Hawthorne planned to marry, had been fraught with tensions. Sophia's friend and mentor Margaret Fuller had written a peculiarly brief note of congratulations, closing with the ambiguous excuse that "great occasions of bliss, of bane—tell their own story, and we would not, by unnecessary words, come limping after the true sense." Of *bane*? Was Fuller jealous as well? For Nathaniel Hawthorne himself, Fuller's feelings were strong and undivided: "If ever I saw a man who combined delicate tenderness to understand the heart of a woman, with quiet depth and manliness enough to satisfy her, it is Mr. Hawthorne," Fuller had written, leaving Sophia to wonder how she had come by this understanding.

Sophia's prospective in-laws, Nathaniel Hawthorne's widowed mother and two unmarried sisters in Salem, had done little to welcome her into the family. Perhaps the last in all of New England to learn of the wedding—due to Hawthorne's obsessive need for privacy—all three refused to attend, citing insufficient time "to prepare [their] feelings." Congratulations had come only after the writer had traveled to Salem and urged the Hawthorne women to reconsider. His older sister, Elizabeth, nicknamed Ebe, once a close friend of Sophia's, had at last conceded grudgingly that the match might prove a good one. Still, she pressed Sophia, "have you no dread of the cares and vexations inevitable in married life?" Ebe could have been voicing Sophia's own doubts when she wrote of her preference for "situations"—unlike marriage—in which women retain "the power to withdraw," and of her reluctance ever to "feel as if much depended upon me."

And what of her "husband," as Sophia had referred to Nathaniel Hawthorne since their engagement at the New Year 1839? In the past month, the writer seemed no less flighty than Sophia, the woman he liked to call his "little Dove." At times he badgered her in letters, complaining about this worthless "species of communion" and refusing to "write my feelings" any longer (he'd already delivered her well over a hundred passionate love letters, some 70,000 handwritten words, in three years' time). He vowed to take up his pen now only to convey "external things, business, facts, details" and insisted that the wedding take place in June as first planned, counting off the remaining days in the month. He teased her with playful accusations—had she begun to "tremble, and shrink back"?—and mock threats: "Ah, foolish virgin! It is too late; nothing can part us now." But for the most part, Hawthorne tolerated the delay, confiding in his journal that he could think of no more pleasant way to spend his summer afternoons than watching the passing scene at the Frog Pond. Like Sophia, he had been born and raised in Salem, Massachusetts, but to a family long associated with the sea. His father, a sea captain, had died of yellow fever in Surinam when Nathaniel was three years old; the sad news took weeks to reach the young family waiting for him at home. Hawthorne himself had never shipped out as anything other than a passenger, but perhaps it was fitting that, as he was about to embark on married life, he became fascinated with the miniature sailing vessels "all perfectly rigged . . . tossing up and down on the mimic waves" and their small captains, so "well acquainted with all the ropes and sails." What was it about "the whole effect," he puzzled, "that kindles the imagination more than the reality would"?

Although capable of periods of intense work, Hawthorne was at heart a lover of indolence, ready to admit his own "idle nature." Like his bride-to-be, he had suffered from numerous undiagnosable complaints as a child, permitting him to stay home from school and lie in bed reading for months at a stretch. When Sophia's dallying carried over into July, he insisted they put off the wedding until after his thirty-eighth birthday, July 4, so that he could watch the fireworks on the Common. Hawthorne would not have been among the sober patriots who trailed Horace Mann to the Odeon Theater on the morning of the Fourth. But he was there in the crowd of nearly 100,000 residents and revelers from surrounding towns to witness a display the newspapers called "the most splendid" ever seen in New England. The region had been the first to emerge from the shadow of financial panic that overtook the young nation in 1837; Boston bankers had shrewdly steered clear of the machinations of the Bank of the United States, which still hobbled New York City and Philadelphia, and the construction of railroads connecting Boston to inland markets had recently made it the leading port city of its size in the Union. Now some of the city's new wealth had been put into an Independence Day extravaganza. At 8:30 P.M., two bands started to play, and, as darkness fell, a series of illuminations began—Italian Suns, Revolving Pyramids, Persian Flowers—interspersed with flights of pigeons and culminating in a 110-foot-long "Magnificent Temple . . . dedicated to Liberty," which burned with silver fire. The evening's brilliant spectacle ended in a "grand *feu de joie*," as a hundred rockets exploded in the smoky night sky, releasing "colored Stars, Gold Rain, and Serpents" over the heads of the assembled multitudes.

In the final weeks of June and early days of July, the nervous couple reassured themselves with the notion that they had been "married" since the day they agreed to an engagement. "The ceremony is nothing," Sophia wrote one close friend, "our true marriage was three years ago." Hawthorne joked that, rather than unite them, the minister would "thrust himself between us" when he made the marriage legal at last. The two hoped, after a summer's honeymoon, to continue their creative lives together. Sophia had "many visions of great deeds to be wrought on canvass and in marble, during the coming autumn & winter," and Nathaniel expected the contentment he achieved by finally marrying his "blessedest" Sophia to offset the financial pressures that came with taking a wife. He planned to support the two of them with the sale of stories he had already begun jotting down in his notebooks. Yet how could they be sure it would all work out? Clearly, nothing could have been more frightening than marriage for two people so accustomed to exercising the "power to withdraw" whenever they wished—Sophia in her spells of illness or artistic inspiration, Nathaniel by retreating to his study to write or simply leaving town on long summer rambles, keeping his whereabouts a secret so that he could not be reached, even by letter.

Since their engagement in 1839, the two had rarely even lived in the same city. The Peabodys were still based in Salem when Hawthorne took up his job as measurer in Boston's Custom House that same year—the job Elizabeth Peabody had found for him, meant to provide a steady income and minimal obligations so he could write without financial worries. Instead he'd become a wage slave, too tired to write after his days spent among the "brawling slang-whangers" on the waterfront. He carried Sophia's love letters in his breast pocket as tokens of his imaginative life and lived for her rare visits to Boston and his rented rooms on Beacon Hill, which she'd decorated with two fantasy landscapes of Lake Como, an idealized vision of the engaged couple painted as tiny figures into the foreground of each one. Hawthorne found the paintings so redolent of private meaning—"sacred" in his terms—that for a time he had hung black curtains over them, to be parted only when he was in the room alone. Then there had been the six months during 1841 that Hawthorne had spent at Brook Farm, after Sophia had moved to Boston with her family. The couple had hoped to make the fledgling commune their first home together until the reclusive Hawthorne lost patience with his fellow utopians as well as with the hours of hard farm labor required of the residents. This was a man who had spent most of the decade following his college graduation closeted in an attic room in his mother's house writing stories, most of which he tossed aside as unpublishable. It was a testament to the strength of his love for Sophia that he would consider taking up the communal life at Brook Farm in order to give his bride a home. And even now, after three years, how could such a man hurry into marriage?

Yet there was an undeniable yearning toward each other, as perhaps there could only be for two so alike in their simultaneous wariness and longing for connection. Sophia, whose innermost dread was to be consigned to a life "utterly destitute of imagination," was more than willing to offer Nathaniel Hawthorne the adoration he still lacked from his public. At thirty-eight, he had produced just one volume of stories—*Twice-told Tales*—more of a critical success than a commercial one. His set of three children's books, brought out by E. P. Peabody, Publisher, had done little to expand his reputation. And so when Sophia wrote him that "the world's admiration" for him centered in her own adoring heart, called him "King by divine right," and offered "reverence" along with her love, the lure was too powerful to resist. "Being pervaded by your love," he told her, "I . . . would write beautifully, and make myself famous for your sake." He needed this woman who "gets into the remotest recesses of my heart, and shines all through me." For Sophia, who had struggled to find her place in a family of strong-willed women—succeeding most by retreating into illness—it was both a relief and a revelation to fall in love and find her love answered. "Words cannot tell," she wrote Nathaniel a year before the wedding, "how immensely my spirit demands thee. Sometimes I almost lose my breath in a vast heaving towards thy heart." She had come to believe that "for me there is no life without a response of life from thee."

So the hour came on. The young minister James Freeman Clarke, a frequent guest at the sisters' Wednesday-night gatherings, arrived promptly at 11:00. Clarke had never met Nathaniel Hawthorne before, and he admitted to Mary afterward that he'd been so stunned by the writer's "kingly looks"—his perfectly sculpted features, dark eyes, high brow, and shock of black hair—he'd had trouble performing the ceremony. Sophia's friends—Clarke's sister, the painter Sarah Ann Clarke, and the mesmerist Connie Park—joined the Peabody family as witnesses. Downstairs in the book room, the sisters' aunt Sophia Pickman, one of Mrs. Peabody's three younger sisters, arrived too late from Salem. She glanced around at the latest journals and, reluctant to "agitate" the two skittish lovers, left before offering her congratulations.

By noon, the "execution" had taken place, Hawthorne wrote his sister in Salem, "We made a christian end, and came straight to Paradise." The actual journey was a little less than straight. Seven miles outside Concord, as the

Sophia and Nathaniel Hawthorne as newlyweds, silhouette by Auguste
Edouart

couple rode west in the ninety-degree heat, they were halted by "low thunder . . . like celestial artillery" followed by a "driving rain," Sophia wrote her
mother the next day. Taking refuge in a roadside tavern, the newlyweds
waited a full hour until "a silver gleaming in the west called us to proceed."
The delay allowed Sophia the chance to take note of the change in her own

internal weather. After the past weeks of headaches and fevers, she noticed now that "with every step the horses took, I felt better and not the least tired." Her husband, scarcely believing he had Sophia to himself at last, "looked upon me as upon a mirage which would suddenly disappear."

The Hawthornes reached Concord at 5:00 and entered their new house—the one-time parsonage known locally as the "Old Manse"—where they found vases of cut flowers arranged for them in every room. The next day, the couple woke early to find "a perfect Eden round us," and walked through the "fresh" green countryside to Concord's newly erected Battle Monument, feeling like "Adam and Eve," with no one else in sight. Sophia felt certain that "a clear new life" was beginning for her. It had been three years since Nathaniel Hawthorne had written to her, fancifully, "how sweet would be my sleep, and how sweet my waking, when I should find your breathing self in my arms.... What a happy and holy fashion it is that those who love one another should rest on the same pillow." Now, in Concord sharing a pillow with his wife at last, he felt he was beginning to live "as if this world were Heaven."

Back in Boston, however, the thermometer stood at ninety-one degrees at sunset, and there was no sign of rain. At 13 West Street, Mrs. Eliza Peabody began to think about how she would get along without her invalid charge. Soon Sophia's empty studio would be given over to a boarder, following the economies Mrs. Peabody had first learned as a girl in Revolutionary times and then practiced throughout her married life. She studied the faces of her two remaining daughters. Certainly she knew there had been tensions, but nothing to compare with that of her own childhood. "Very different is the affection felt by sisters, who love from a conviction of each other's real worth," she had once written to her oldest daughter, from "that mere animal attachment arising from being nurtured in the same house." *Nurture* was scarcely the word for Mrs. Peabody's own disjointed upbringing. She had told the story—or parts of it—many times over to her three daughters, careful to impress upon them the lessons she had learned. It was ironic that Sophia had chosen a literary man for a husband, exactly the sort Mrs. Peabody had come to fear. But then, Sophia—always sensitive and easily upset—was the one of her three daughters to whom she had never confided the most shocking tale of her childhood. She had never expected Sophia to marry, anyway. No one had.

PART I

Origins

1746–1803

❧ 1 ❧

Matriarch

ASIDE FROM ONE STIFFLY POSED SILHOUETTE, THE ONLY SURVIVING likeness of Mrs. Elizabeth Palmer Peabody is a small pencil drawing Sophia made in one of her sketchbooks in the early 1830s. By this time Sophia and her sisters were all in their twenties and their mother was approaching sixty. Eliza, as she was known to her family, had given birth to four daughters (one died in infancy) and three sons, moved her family in and out of nearly a dozen different houses, never owning one of them, and devoted most of her waking hours to augmenting her husband's meager income by teaching or tutoring young girls. There are hints of that life of hard work in the set of Mrs. Peabody's jaw, in her tired eyes. But the "Mamma" Sophia chose to depict is a woman apparently free of daily burdens. We see her in profile, settled happily at a table, hair tucked back into a lace-trimmed cap, reading a book, with a vase of flowers to complete the tableau.

A hint of a smile plays about Mrs. Peabody's face, reminding us that she was not alone in the room. Was the affectionate look intended for Sophia or her sisters? Sophia manages to suggest a parlor scene with, perhaps, the rest of the family gathered outside the frame, reading or talking. The drawing could have been captioned with Mrs. Peabody's words of advice, written about the same time the sketch was made, when the family had come to believe that Sophia would never be well enough to marry or to leave home. "The love which settles down upon the household circle tho' more quiet, is deeper, steadier, more efficient than any other love," she counseled Sophia. "Anchor your soul on domestic love."

Sophia liked to draw spare, almost stylized sketches of her friends and family inspired by the English artist John Flaxman's illustrations of Greek myths, then popular with the Boston intelligentsia. She gives us just the out-

13

Sophia's sketch of her mother, Eliza Peabody

lines of her mother's short cape—it must have been a chilly New England spring day—and a long sleeve. But the simple props she selected for her mother's portrait were as significant as Diana's arrows or Pandora's box in a Flaxman line drawing. Both book and flowers were signs of high culture and feminine refinement. Yet Mrs. Peabody was no dilettante. She was a published poet and read widely and critically all her life, passing along her passion for literature to her daughters, who made books and learning the central focus of their own lives. She prized flowers and—when she had the time, when she had a garden, and when her husband's ridicule didn't stop her—took long walks in search of unusual specimens to transplant to her own flower beds.

Sophia sketched her mother as she wanted to be seen, and as Sophia wanted to remember her: at peace and surrounded by the elements of her favorite occupations. A decade after she drew this sketch, a month after she left home with her new husband, Nathaniel Hawthorne, Sophia was still trying to think of her mother this way. "I could see in you the image of a perfect woman," she wrote to her mother, recollecting her years at home. But she couldn't keep herself from adding: "through all the shadows of the world over you."

There were shadows. The family's longtime physician and friend Dr. Walter Channing, brother of the celebrated Unitarian minister William Ellery Channing, once wrote of Mrs. Peabody that "in memory I always see her smiling," yet "her smile was always to me like the shining out of an angel's face from behind a mask where brave struggles with heavy sorrows had left deep imprints of mortality." Sophia and her sisters were called on throughout their lives to puzzle out and then to soothe their mother's heavy sorrows, to vindicate her defeats with their accomplishments, to compensate for her troubled marriage with grand passions of their own. Like many American women who extolled the virtues of female domesticity during the first half century following the Revolution, Mrs. Peabody sought to "anchor" her soul on "domestic love" because it had always been elusive.

For Mrs. Peabody there were private troubles to contend with, but these were also years when men and women jockeyed for power in households throughout the thirteen states after independence was declared. During the 1780s, the decade of Eliza Peabody's childhood, families were reunited and women took control of the home as their "sphere." But for some women, authority in the home seemed a good deal less than the reward American men had given themselves for wartime service: the exclusive right to rule in public life. It was possible for a woman to convince herself that raising the sons of the Republic was a worthy task; and women used the ideology of "Republican Motherhood" to win new privileges, particularly the right to an education, and later the opportunity to work as teachers and reformers. But for some daughters of independence—girls who, like Eliza, grew up as the children or sisters of soldiers, who had helped run farms and businesses while the men of the family fought the war—power at home was never quite enough, and the very domestic tranquility they later espoused as wives and mothers proved hard to come by.

Mrs. Peabody once wrote to her daughter Mary, "I long for means and power . . . but I wear peticoats and can never be Governor . . . nor alderman, Judge or jury, senator or representative—so I may as well be quiet—content with intreating the Father of all mercies." Yet Mrs. Peabody could never silence her longings, and she passed them on to her daughters in the form of stories about her ancestors—stories intricately entwined with the early history of the nation, told and retold until they became touchstones for the three girls who would grow into women of extraordinary energy and influence. Through her "patriotic mother," her oldest daughter, Elizabeth, liked to say that she had been "educated by the heroic age of the country's history." Not a little of that heroism was her mother's, as she struggled to overcome a family heritage of betrayal and loss.

❧ 2 ❧

Legacies

LIKE THE SMILE ON HER FACE IN SOPHIA'S DRAWING, THERE WAS A surface history, a tale of brave deeds in grander times, that Mrs. Peabody recited proudly, usually omitting the sorry ending. She even wrote a novel adapting and improving on the events of her family's past. The novel was never published, but it remained part of the Peabody family's treasured papers for a century after it was written, keeping alive for each new generation the stories that guided this embattled family of women through the early decades of the American Republic.

She was born Elizabeth Palmer, the third of nine children of wealthy Massachusetts colonials. The wealth came from her grandfather, General Joseph Palmer, whom she remembered from early childhood as "more like an old fashioned English country gentleman, than any one" of his time and place. The general was so beloved by all who knew him, even animals, it was said that when he was away from home his cat tried to climb onto the shoulder of the John Singleton Copley portrait of him that hung in his library.

Yet Eliza scarcely knew the luxury she might have inherited. Family life was so fractured by the time she was born that neither birth nor baptism, if there was one, was ever recorded. The month was February, but the year might have been 1776, 1777, or 1778, according to conflicting family documents. These were the war years—soon to be the dark years of the war for the Palmer family—when town records were unevenly kept.

In sunnier times, the Palmers lived in a large square house made of oak and stone, with four enormous chimneys rising up at each corner, perched on a hill above a pretty cove known as Snug Harbor in Germantown, thirteen miles south of Boston. Not quite a mansion, the house nevertheless became known as Friendship Hall in the decades at midcentury when the benevolent

17

General Joseph Palmer, engraving from the Copley portrait

General Palmer oversaw "a settlement of free and independent artisans and manufacturers" who operated his chocolate mills; spermaceti, salt, and glass works; and a factory for weaving stockings. In fact, Palmer owned all of Germantown, which occupied a small peninsula jutting out into Boston Harbor at the northernmost corner of Braintree, a town that would later become famous for its native sons John Hancock and John Adams.

Emigrating from England in 1746, the visionary Palmer had seen fit to house his workmen and their families—most of them newly arrived from Europe as well—in several stone buildings near his factories, making the Germantown settlement a commercial version of the Puritans' earlier "city upon a hill." And he realized his plan nearly a century before the founding of New England's model industrial towns at Lawrence and Lowell. Although she never lived there, Eliza would remember Friendship Hall best of all the Germantown buildings, with its polished mahogany floors and banisters, its wallpaper painted with scenes of classical ruins, its hillside planted with fruit trees leading down to Snug Harbor. There, she knew, "Grandpapa Palmer" had once entertained an emerging local aristocracy made up of Adamses, Palmers, and Quincys—the family that would produce three mayors of Boston, one of whom went on to become a president of Harvard College, and for whom this portion of Braintree was later renamed.

Women were a powerful presence at Friendship Hall gatherings as well. Palmer's brother-in-law Richard Cranch, a fellow emigrant who was also his cousin, had married one of the three talented Smith sisters of nearby Weymouth, and settled in Braintree, where he eventually became a judge. Cranch's bride was Mary, the oldest; the middle sister, Abigail, married John Adams; the youngest, Elizabeth, would later play a pivotal role in Eliza Palmer's life. The Friendship Hall circle was a close-knit group of practical idealists: intellectuals with solid financial underpinnings and multiple kinship ties. Even as dissatisfaction with British rule crept into conversation, Friendship Hall seemed sure to remain a reliable sanctuary.

General Palmer raised three children in Germantown: two daughters, Polly and Elizabeth, and a son, Joseph Pearse Palmer, Eliza's father. When young Joseph graduated from Harvard in 1771 and married Betsey Hunt, one of the famously beautiful daughters of a preacher turned distiller in Watertown, just west of Cambridge, General Palmer set him up with an importing business in Boston. Eliza's oldest brother, the third Joseph Palmer, was born there in 1773. But her father had little enthusiasm for business ventures, preferring to be known chiefly as a man of high principles and keen intellect. And Boston in the mid-1770s was a difficult place for a man of principle to pay attention to anything besides the increasingly tense relations between New and Old England. Joseph Pearse Palmer's ideals led him, even though he was only a first-generation American, to join the Patriot cause.

Eliza's mother, Betsey, liked to tell about the December night in 1773 when she was home alone "sitting rocking the baby when I heard the gate and door open." Betsey looked up, expecting to find her husband returning from a night at his club, only to find "three stout Indians" standing in her front parlor. The young mother "screamed out and would have fainted of very fright" had she not recognized her husband's voice as one of the Indians, saying "Don't be frightened, Betsey, it is I. We have only been making a little salt water tea." Betsey was calmed by her husband's words, but within days Joseph Pearse

Palmer and his fellow Indians were found out and declared traitors for their part in the Boston Tea Party. In retaliation, British soldiers looted and burned the Palmer warehouses on Boston's Long Wharf, and the young family fled to Watertown to take refuge with Betsey's family, the Hunts.

Both Joseph Palmers, the father then almost sixty and the son in his twenties, continued to protest British rule, first serving in the Provincial Congress and then assisting at the Battles of Lexington and Concord, where the first shots were fired in the Revolution, and later at Breed's Hill. For his active role in the Congress—he was president of the body for a term and helped organize the tea boycott—for his donations of money and supplies to the Patriot army, and for his assistance in key battles, the senior Palmer was eventually made brigadier general, and his son quartermaster general. But if the Battle of Lexington marked the birth of a new nation, it also signaled the decline of the Palmer family fortune. General Palmer's Boston warehouses had already been plundered, and after war broke out one of his ships carrying a valuable cargo of spermaceti candles from Germantown was captured by the British. As more men joined the cause, the senior Joseph Palmer was forced to close his factories for lack of workers, and he continued to spend on the Patriot cause. In the first two years of the war, Palmer contributed as much as 5,000 pounds sterling, nearly $750,000 in today's currency.

Then came the disastrous Rhode Island campaign—or "Burlesque," as it was later called. General Palmer proposed the surprise attack on Newport, Rhode Island, in the fall of 1777, but he never expected to serve as chief commanding officer for the invasion. In his sixties and a man of business, Palmer had largely confined his military service to mustering troops and overseeing the construction of fortifications. Still, his new superior officer, General Joseph Spencer, approved the plan and then left Palmer to lead the attack, promising him a militia of 9,000 to confront the 3,600 British and German soldiers camped near Newport.

A comedy of errors ensued. Spencer promised "boats and everything ready" in Newport, but Palmer and his troops arrived to find only a motley collection of dories and fishing vessels greatly in need of repair. The few skilled carpenters among his Patriot recruits refused to turn "artificers," and quit rather than help with the repairs. Angered by the delay, a handful of soldiers defected and revealed Palmer's plans to their new British officers. Mishaps followed in rapid succession: reconnaissance parties lost their way, heavy rains further delayed the attack, and then a bright moonlit sky exposed the Patriot forces to the enemy. Finally Palmer was forced to recommend a retreat. Comedy turned to tragedy when General Spencer, anxious to escape blame, ordered Palmer to face a court-martial on charges of "Neglect and Disobedience" for failing to carry out the attack as planned.

Already regretful of his own part in the botched invasion, Palmer was devastated when he learned that his honor had been called into question. He appealed to his one-time Braintree neighbor John Hancock, now president of the Continental Congress, to provide him with a copy of the charges filed against him. Hancock refused, putting the older man in the untenable position of being tried—possibly for his life—with no chance to prepare his own defense. Ultimately the case was thrown out of court, but a congressional commission then spent six months collecting testimony and studying the evidence before clearing Palmer of all charges; he remained the unofficial scapegoat for what turned out to be one of the Continental army's more notable blunders. Palmer had appointed his son, Eliza's father, to lead one of the Rhode Island battalions, and both men seem never to have recovered from the humiliation.

By the time the war was won, the disgrace that shadowed the Palmer men was compounded by financial losses. Like many members of the colonial gentry, the Palmers had fallen deeply into debt. With currency values fluctuating wildly, General Palmer was forced to pay off his creditors by selling his Germantown land and Friendship Hall. Within three years of the war's end, the aging general was begging for credit from the same neighbors and friends who had once been his houseguests, and his son was suffering the first of many depressions that would ensure his continued business failures. The Revolution so crippled the Palmer men that when Eliza turned her grandfather's hard luck into fiction in her novel, she described his downfall as the result of an outright attack by the British on Germantown and Friendship Hall. "The sun rose on a scene of havoc indescribable," she wrote. "Every house & cabin was level with the ground. Chocolate, glass, salt, candles, were scattered along the beach and spread over the extensive grounds and pastures. . . . In a few hours, the friend and benefactor of all who lived near him was thus made a comparatively poor man." Of course the truth was more complex and disturbing. The Palmers had been betrayed by their own countrymen even as they gave all they had to the Patriot cause.

It was into this period of decline that Eliza Palmer, Joseph Pearse Palmer's third child, was born in Watertown, where her parents had fled in the wake of the Tea Party reprisals. Soon after, Eliza moved with her mother and older brother, Joe, and sister, Mary—born in 1775 during the Battle of Lexington—to a vacant workman's cottage on General Palmer's estate. These early war years, though marked by the frequent absences of her father and grandfather, seemed to Eliza "the spring time of existence," she later confided in her journal. She clung to the memory of this brief interval of freedom and noblesse oblige, when she roamed the hillsides and beaches of Germantown with her brother and sister, the two small girls dressed in the best "pink frocks and red morocco shoes and white stockings" available in wartime. It was to be the only time in her life when her family's financial adversity did not weigh on her mind.

In Germantown, Eliza was allowed to tag along to school with Mary and Joe, to a small class taught by their aunt Elizabeth Palmer in a sunny upstairs room in Friendship Hall. Eliza proved the best student of the three, and once she learned to read, she was given the run of her grandfather's library. Many years later, Eliza recalled for her own three daughters the happy days spent stretched out on the highly polished floor of the library, poring over General Palmer's collection of Shakespeare folios. According to family legend, Eliza read through the entire set when she was only four. Occasional visits home from her grandfather provided Eliza with the vision of domestic harmony she would try to recapture throughout her life. "We were the happiest group imaginable when collected around [my grandparents'] table to read in turn some interesting parts of the Bible, or some short catechetical lesson or little hymns," she wrote nearly fifty years later, and "the Smiles and Caresses of the dear old people and our no less cheerful younger relatives [were] our rich reward." Living on the fringes of Friendship Hall society, itself on tenuous ground, Eliza learned early to calculate wealth in terms of intangibles: piety, domestic affection, learning.

During the war years, the big house was filled with women: young ones not yet married, including Eliza's aunts Polly and Elizabeth Palmer, and older ones, widowed, sick, or simply lonely, on whom the general had taken pity. A household of talented and productive women facing adversity as a unit would be another of Eliza's lifelong ideals. In her novel, she described the group as a vigorous, self-sufficient "Sisterhood." "We had no drones in our hive," she wrote of these women who before the war had spent their days reading, drawing, and doing fine needlework, and now happily sewed shirts for soldiers, taught at the local school in place of a schoolmaster gone to war, raised chickens, and knitted shawls, stockings, and caps in exchange for groceries. "The highest culture and refinement," Eliza wrote proudly, "did not prevent this admirable family from undertaking the humblest employments in order to preserve their independance." The young Eliza could not fail to notice that the household functioned just as efficiently when the men were off at war.

Yet the stories she began to hear around this time from the women in her immediate family all spoke of a woman's need to secure the attention of a man—as well as of the perils of failing to do so. The history of the Hunt women of Watertown, her mother's line, was an unambiguous endorsement of education as a means of social ascension through marriage. The men of the Hunt family were, like Eliza's father, Joseph Pearse Palmer, Harvard-educated, but the Hunt women had been deliberately kept ignorant. Eliza's mother,

Betsey Hunt, and her sisters—dubbed the "Watertown beauties" by their brothers' classmates at Harvard—were known for their good looks. To their father's way of thinking, his girls needed only to acquire a few domestic skills to make themselves marriageable. Squire Hunt, as he was called by the regulars in his Watertown general store and tavern, had chosen his own wife on a summer's walk when he passed a bevy of girls playing at rolling down a hill; he took a fancy to the "exposed shoes, stockings, and underclothes" of his future wife before he even met her. According to family legend, Hunt's interest was not actually prurient: the girl's undergarments were so dainty and neat that he knew he'd found himself a good housekeeper. Hunt then raised his own daughters on the maxim that it was "quite enough if they could make a shirt and a pudding."

By the time his girls were ready to marry, however, it took more than good looks and housekeeping abilities to win a marriage proposal from a man of property and high standing in the colonial cities along the North Atlantic coast. In prosperous circles, a woman's character was judged by skills she cultivated at leisure: conversation, letter writing, fine needlework. Betsey Hunt was just fourteen when she met Joseph Pearse Palmer at a party given by Harvard men for Watertown ladies, but she was canny enough to put the encounter to good use. Likely she was flattered at first when one high-spirited youth bet another man a bottle of Madeira that he didn't dare kiss Miss Betsey Hunt. But Joseph Palmer was affronted on Betsey's behalf, all the more so when he saw the young man publicly embarrass Miss Hunt by successfully planting a kiss on her cheek. Palmer interceded, speaking his first words to his future wife: "What books have you read?" he asked. As Betsey later told her daughters, the conversation that followed from that question "was so wholly different from anything I had ever heard or expected, that I was quite pleased with him."

At fourteen, Betsey Hunt had to admit that she had never read a book; she could scarcely get through an occasional issue of *The Spectator*. Palmer offered to remedy the problem by lending her books from his own shelves at the college, and he proposed regular tutoring sessions in composition. The young girl eagerly agreed. The first book Palmer brought Betsey Hunt was Samuel Richardson's novel *The History of Sir Charles Grandison*, the tale of a supremely honorable gentleman who rescues an innocent beauty from a brutish seducer, and then wins her for himself with his kindness. Having delivered Betsey Hunt from her tormentors, the young Palmer no doubt fancied himself as a New World version of Richardson's hero. Betsey Hunt must have seen her suitor the same way, for long before their course of study was complete, she had decided to marry the gallant, well-spoken Joseph Pearse Palmer—as soon as he asked her.

But a marriage proposal would have to wait. When General Palmer heard that his son was courting a tavern keeper's daughter, one of eleven children, he tried to break off the match. Still, young Palmer persisted; he would not give up the pleasant task of educating Betsey Hunt. For the rest of his years at Harvard, he continued the weekly lessons, and the couple branched out from romantic novels to arithmetic, geography, and history texts, discussing them while walking or riding. Each week he left books with Betsey, which she hid away in her attic to read whenever she could escape the notice of her father and sisters. At last young Palmer decided that his fiancée had added sufficient polish to her native beauty to impress his family, and he brought her home to meet his parents and older sisters. Now Betsey, at nearly seventeen, could answer the kind of questions that had previously left her speechless. She charmed her prospective father-in-law and soon found herself celebrating her marriage to Joseph Pearse Palmer, scion of Friendship Hall and the Germantown manufacturing fortune. According to family lore, the wedding party included Paul Revere along with Palmer's future Tea Party comrades. On their wedding day, in November 1772, the couple's future looked eminently rosy.

By contrast, Betsey's older sister, Eliza's aunt Kate Hunt, fared dismally in the marriage market. She never learned to read or write, and—as Betsey later told the story to her own daughters—Kate lost her lover because of it. The young man was Elbridge Gerry, one of Joseph Pearse Palmer's comrades in the Revolutionary cause, and afterward a key figure in the framing of the Constitution. Along with Palmer and his wife and infant son, Gerry came to board with the Hunt family in Watertown at the time of the Boston Tea Party retributions. There he was smitten by Kate's looks and courted her for several months. When Gerry left Watertown to serve in the Provincial Congress, he wrote frequently, attempting to maintain the connection. Kate asked her younger sister, Betsey—now well versed in literary matters—to read Gerry's letters out loud to her, but she was too proud to allow Betsey to write back for her, and too ashamed to admit her ignorance to her suitor. His letters went unanswered, and Gerry took Kate's silence to mean that he'd been jilted. In the end, Gerry married another woman; Kate never found another lover.

Aunt Kate's story became a cautionary tale for her niece Eliza, a spur, if she needed one, to the avid young reader. But Eliza's Palmer aunts—her father's sisters, Polly and Elizabeth—struggled with an opposite problem. A woman, Eliza also learned, had to be careful not to flaunt her education and to restrain the impulse toward self-assertion that seemed to come with it. Eliza would attempt to teach her own three girls this lesson too.

General Palmer gave his daughters an education equal to his son's, and he fostered their independence of mind. Eliza was old enough to witness the results firsthand. As a child attending school and occasional dinners at Friendship Hall, Eliza knew her aunt Polly Palmer as the family's invalid, a "trembling and feeble" woman in her early thirties, so sensitive to noise that she shut herself in a closet during thunderstorms and so easily frightened that her family treated her as a "timid infant." But in her youth, Eliza was told, Polly—General Palmer's first and best-loved child—had been renowned for her beauty and "literary genius," and, above all, for her courage. The general made Polly his confidante in business, and by the time she was sixteen, Polly was making important transactions for him on her own, riding the thirteen miles to Boston through the woods alone. On errands that required her to carry money, Polly armed herself with the gun her father had taught her to use.

But this pre-Revolutionary idyll could not last. One afternoon, General Palmer returned from a hunting expedition with his neighbor Colonel Josiah Quincy, who had begun to take a romantic interest in Polly. They spotted the girl "reclining on the grass . . . deeply absorbed in a book." The general boasted to Colonel Quincy of Polly's fearlessness and skill with her gun, prompting Quincy to lay a wager that *he* could find a way to frighten her. The general was so sure of his daughter's "wondrous strength of nerve" that he consented to the prank, and stood by as Quincy crept up behind Polly and fired a gun over her head. As Eliza retold the story in her novel, Polly sprang up, then fainted, and "fell as if shot by a cannon-ball." After a night of alternating "fits" and collapses, "her boasted nervous system was ruined forever." Even Polly's literary talents were wasted: for many years her hands shook too hard to hold a pen. From that day on, according to the tale told and retold in the Palmer and Peabody families, Polly Palmer stayed inside the house, venturing out only to visit Colonel Quincy to assure him "she bore no malice."

The misfortunes of General Palmer's talented daughters did not end here. In the wake of his financial losses in the early 1780s, Palmer moved his family out of Friendship Hall to a smaller house in Dorchester. Hoping to repeat his earlier success as a factory owner, Palmer had persuaded investors to speculate in a saltworks on Boston Neck, the narrow peninsula connecting Dorchester and Roxbury to the fist of land that was Boston proper in the days before landfill created the current Back Bay and South End. In the Dorchester house, Eliza's aunt Elizabeth Palmer began a stormy love affair with Nathaniel Cranch, a distant cousin who had emigrated from England before the war to practice law in Boston. Eliza had first known her aunt Elizabeth as an exacting and difficult schoolteacher, easily angered by the inevitable restlessness of her small charges. Now she saw that Elizabeth Palmer was just as demanding of her suitor; the romance progressed from quarrel to quarrel over the course of several years. A final argument took place one winter night in the parlor of the Palmers' Dorchester house in which, the family later agreed, Elizabeth had "provoked" her lover. Nathaniel Cranch walked out into the cold, and the next morning his "mangled" body was discovered washed ashore on Boston Neck, an apparent suicide.

Now it was Aunt Elizabeth's turn to collapse into "a long and severe fever." In Eliza's version of the story, recorded in her novel, Aunt Elizabeth realized too late that she was to blame for all those quarrels, with "her own wilful reliance on her romantic notions of the respect due to women." Like her older sister, Polly, Elizabeth Palmer emerged from her sickbed a changed woman, her spirit broken, her "selfish sorrow . . . subdued." When General Palmer died of a stroke several years later, his saltworks never completed, leaving his two unmarried daughters with no means of support, Elizabeth married Nathaniel's younger brother Joseph Cranch, a munitions manufacturer. She moved with him to West Point, New York, taking along her invalid sister, Polly. There Polly lived scarcely more than a year, most likely deliberately wasting away. Polly's letters, written in a shaky hand, tell of her torment in living next to a field used for drying gunpowder, of her frustrated ambition to become a writer, and of her increasing despair and ultimate refusal to eat. Not long after Polly's death, Joseph Cranch fell ill of liver disease and was unable to work; Elizabeth became a schoolteacher once more, no longer as a favor to a handful of young nieces and nephews, but this time for an income she desperately needed.

The examples Polly and Elizabeth Palmer set for young Eliza may have been extreme, but they were not unique. When Alexis de Tocqueville visited America in 1830, he noticed a pattern in American women's lives that had its origins in the years leading up to the Revolution when women confronted the contradictory social imperatives of independence and domesticity. When he described the remarkable freedom of the American girl, who "has scarcely ceased to be a child when she already thinks for herself, speaks with freedom, and acts on her own impulse," he might have been describing Polly Palmer in her youth. But, he also noted, "In America the independence of woman is irrecoverably lost in the bonds of matrimony . . . [which] require much abnegation on the part of woman, and a constant sacrifice of her pleasures to her duties." Polly Palmer may have been resisting this seemingly inevitable self-sacrifice when she took to her bed, although the control over her own life she achieved as an invalid brought its own set of restrictions. Elizabeth Palmer, too, refused to accept submission in marriage until she found herself with no alternative. Neither woman, it seemed, had developed the attentiveness to male needs and demands that appeared to be as essential a survival skill as literacy.

Accounts of the Palmer sisters' tragedies were passed down through generations of female descendants because of the deep resonance they held for these women of education and ambition. Growing up in the literary atmosphere of Friendship Hall, the precocious Eliza Palmer instinctively mistrusted her shirt-making, pudding-baking Hunt relatives and admired the superior education of her Palmer aunts and the Adams, Cranch, and Quincy women who were their friends. Indeed, as her family's fortunes slid, Eliza came to believe that education—whether as the first step toward a teaching career or as the means of attracting a husband in the social class from which she was rapidly falling—was her only form of deliverance from poverty. But the sobering counterlessons of Polly and Elizabeth Palmer were not lost on her. Early on, Eliza learned to play down her desire for independence—what she once called "my greatest fault." She also learned to expect that, like her Palmer aunts, she would one day have to surrender her literary ambitions and pay a price for her strivings, most likely when it came time to marry.

And there were other hard truths embedded in these stories as well. Was Polly Palmer made a permanent invalid because of her inability to withstand the single shock of a gun fired over her head by a man who had taken a romantic interest in her? Perhaps. But more significantly, the accident foreshadowed setbacks for the entire family. Polly Palmer grew up with wealth and privilege and independence; then, on the brink of womanhood, she lost it all. She saw her beloved father humiliated as he tried to aid his country. The "shot heard round the world" that liberated the American colonies dealt an internal blow to the Palmer family. Little wonder that Polly, registering her own wound, should refuse, thereafter, to go out into a world so changed. Similarly, Elizabeth Palmer's imperious treatment of Nathaniel Cranch simply could not be supported in the years after her older sister's collapse and her father's reversal of fortune. She could not afford to toy with suitors. Eventually she had to marry, or find herself homeless. While her story was told in the family primarily as a lesson in proper feminine behavior, the true lesson was one in the harsh economics faced by a single woman of no means in the years following the Revolution. Her niece Eliza Palmer would learn the same lesson at a much younger age.

CR 3 SO

Seductions

THE DRAMA OF THE PALMER SISTERS' STORIES PALED IN COMPARISON to the fate of their younger brother and his children, Eliza Palmer's immediate family circle. General Palmer survived the Revolution by just five years. As Joseph Pearse Palmer watched his father fail, he gave up all hope of recovering the family fortune. Eliza's once chivalric father became "a man of almost feminine delicacy of mind." The boldness that had brought him to Betsey Hunt's rescue and then to the Boston Tea Party vanished, to be replaced by long bouts of depression during which he could do no work. Eliza's mother was forced to take the lead in family affairs.

Betsey Palmer's first solution was to move the family to a house on School Street near King's Chapel in the center of Boston where she took in boarders, hoping to cover living expenses and take some profit by keeping house for other families. Even less experienced in business matters than her husband, however, Betsey never managed to make ends meet. The family moved nearly every two years during the 1780s, first to a grand house with a cupola on Fort Hill overlooking Boston Harbor, and then to a succession of smaller houses in increasingly less prestigious locations. The last of these was in an alley in Cornhill, Boston's business district. Living there, Eliza's older sister, Mary, recalled, felt like "being caged." Every two years as well, Betsey gave birth to another child, to whom Eliza, old enough now to care for infants but still too young to go out to work, became the chief nurse.

As the situation became more desperate, Betsey Palmer found ways for her children to leave home. When her oldest son, Joseph, reached fourteen, he shipped out from Boston as a cabin boy, never to return. She encouraged her second child, Mary, to spend long stretches of time with her Cranch relations in Quincy, where she avoided child-care duties and continued to enjoy some of the luxuries of the Friendship Hall days. When Mary reached her teens, however, she was sent to New York City as nursemaid to the family of her aunt Kate Hunt's former beau, her father's one-time comrade in the Patriot cause, Elbridge Gerry. Mary remembered bitterly the humiliation of moving into the household of family friends, expecting to be treated as an equal, only to be given a room in a dark closet off the nursery and told to eat her meals with the kitchen help. Not long after Mary found her way home, Betsey Palmer agreed to part with one of her younger children when Aunt Elizabeth Palmer Cranch wrote to ask for a girl to help out in her West Point household. Little Amelia Palmer was just seven when she made the long trip by wagon, carriage, and boat alone; her family could afford only a single one-way fare. In the end Amelia was adopted by her aunt Elizabeth and never saw her own large family again until she was grown.

Eliza was the oldest daughter regularly living at home during the fall of 1785 when her father traveled to Maine to look for work in the lumber trade, leaving his family in the care of one of his boarders at School Street, a handsome younger friend from his Harvard days named Royall Tyler. It was the start of a year that, despite all the misfortune that had come before, would culminate in what Eliza Palmer would always consider the "first tragedy in the family's history"—a tragedy for which she was the chief witness and, judging from its lasting impact on her, also the chief victim.

Royall Tyler would win fame later in the decade as America's first playwright with his comedy of New World manners, *The Contrast*, which played to audiences from Boston to Charleston; later still he would build a career as a lawyer and judge in Vermont. But now, in the mid-1780s, he was a witty and glamorous family friend, blessed with an inherited fortune such as the Palmers had recently lost, and touched by romantic sorrow: in September 1785, Tyler had been jilted by Nabby Adams, the only daughter of John and Abigail Adams.

Ready to be distracted from her miserable lot, and increasingly disappointed in her husband, Eliza's mother became Royall Tyler's chief comforter in the months after Nabby Adams cut off their courtship with a terse letter from Europe—months that happened to coincide with Joseph Pearse Palmer's absence in Maine. Betsey listened to Tyler weep and moan, and she refused to hear anything against the man whom her in-laws in the Cranch and Adams families had come to believe was an insincere, albeit charming, flatterer. Betsey may never have heard the stories about Tyler's Harvard days which had resurfaced to influence the Braintree intelligentsia against him: he drank, he gambled, and he had fathered a child, Royal Morse, by a charwoman at the college. Joseph Pearse Palmer himself had been willing to overlook all that. Not only was Tyler a reliable lodger, but he interceded on at least one occasion when a policeman came to the house with a writ demanding immediate payment of the grocer's and baker's overdue bills. Betsey Palmer had collapsed in tears on the doorstep when, responding to the commotion, Tyler pounded down the stairs with a handful of silver coins.

Betsey Palmer may have been enjoying Royall Tyler's company during the winter of 1785 to 1786, or at the least willingly accepting his attentions in exchange for his financial support, but the nine-year-old Eliza was horrified by what she saw taking place between her mother and this "polished man of literary eminence" while her father was away. Decades later, when she could finally bring herself to write obliquely of the experience, Eliza could still "recollect with almost incredible vividness the shudder of terror and disgust" she felt when Royall Tyler "enter[ed] the sanctuary of sleeping innocence, of absolute childhood, for the basest purposes." Betsey shared a bedroom with her young children in the house on School Street, and it was there that, as a means of escaping the notice of other boarders, her affair was consummated. But Eliza was not sleeping that night: she lay awake and watching as Royall Tyler "seduced the woman, whose children he would have corrupted."

Almost certainly, Tyler laid hands on Eliza herself that winter. Royall Tyler had a fondness for young girls. He had taken up with Nabby Adams when she was just sixteen. And, unbeknownst to Eliza, he had paid a visit to her ten-year-old sister, Mary, in Braintree at the same time that he was romancing their mother, dropping in on the girl when she was alone in her great-aunt's house, taking her by the hand and seating her on his knee. Ignorant of the situation back home on School Street, young Mary Palmer was won over by Tyler's "cheerful, musical voice" and impressed by his "scarlet broadcloth coat, white vest, ruffled shirt and knee-length breeches," as well as by his good looks and his fine manners. "I had never seen anything so beautiful," she would later recall. The attraction was strong on both sides. But Eliza would not be taken in by the "polluted wretch," as she called him afterward, "who enters a worthy family and leaves it not, till some victim falls a prey to his designs." Eliza had seen Tyler seduce her mother; she could feel only "terror and disgust" when his attentions turned her way. We will never know whether Eliza managed to ward off Tyler's predations, but the revulsion with which she writes about him suggests that she did not.

Joseph Pearse Palmer returned home from Maine in April 1786. His wife gave birth to her seventh child five months later, claiming that the infant, Sophia Palmer, had been born prematurely, after a fright. But Sophia was fully formed, the largest at birth of Betsey Palmer's children so far. Everyone who knew the family's circumstances felt certain that the real father was Royall Tyler.

There followed a time of remorse and recrimination in the Palmer house-

Royall Tyler

hold. Joseph Pearse Palmer and Royall Tyler had coexisted amicably in the house on School Street for the several months before Sophia was born. But once the baby arrived, gossip traveled from Boston to Braintree and back again. Joseph Pearse Palmer's aunt Mary Cranch made a rare trip to School Street to examine the baby, the object of "so much Speculatin that I was determin'd to see it," she wrote afterward to her sister Abigail Adams, then in Europe. "You may laugh," she continued, relaying Betsey's story with amused incredulity, but "we live in an age of discovery," when "a full grown, fine child may be produc'd in less than five months . . . provided the mother Should meet with a Small fright a few hours before its Birth." Eliza had led her great-aunt upstairs to her parents' bedroom, where Mary Cranch found all three adults sitting in "the most perfect harmony," Betsey suckling her child, Palmer playing the proud father, and Tyler lounging at the bedside with his shoes off, in what must have been a charade enacted for Aunt Mary's benefit.

While visiting the house on School Street, Mary Cranch pretended to accept Betsey Palmer's explanation, but she knew full well, both from her own experience and from those "learned in the obstetrick Art," that it was "not possible" for a fully formed infant to be born after a pregnancy of just five months. In a second letter, she wrote Abigail Adams of her astonishment that Royall Tyler "should be continu'd in the Family and no notice taken." How could Joseph Pearse Palmer "suffer the enemy of [his] peace to be under the same roof," she wondered. She could only presume that "they have made a bargain." Palmer must have consented to take the child as his own, and possibly even agreed to tolerate an ongoing affair, if Tyler would continue to pay the family's bills. But most of all, Mary Cranch worried about "the disgrace which will forever attend even the Innocent" Palmer children if news of the affair traveled beyond the extended family. If she had known of Tyler's advances on Palmer's two oldest daughters, she would have worried still more.

Bargain or not, the situation soon became intolerable. Tyler and the Palmers may have been able to present a facade of "perfect harmony" to visitors like Mary Cranch, but Eliza herself recalled the "deep-seated agony" felt by her "betrayed, insulted" father. Not long after Sophia Palmer's birth, Royall Tyler left the Palmer boarding house, ushering in an era of even greater "distress and privations" for the family. Eliza's sister Mary, who had been living in Braintree much of this time, remembered only that Royall Tyler, the dashing man she had met at her great-aunt's house, "left town and ceased to let us see him, we never knew why." Possibly the traumas of the previous year had rendered Eliza speechless on the subject. In any case, as young as she was, Eliza knew she must keep the details of the past winter's seductions a secret, even from her own older sister.

Genteel poverty was something that young Eliza Palmer was prepared to bear; she had known little else. She was proud of the self-sufficient Sisterhood of Friendship Hall, and she felt no shame for her grandfather's business and military failures. Nor would she mourn the lost luxuries of her early childhood, except perhaps for the luxury of time to read and write. But she could not overcome the humiliation and fear she felt in the wake of her mother's affair with Royall Tyler, the revulsion she had felt in her own encounters with the man. She tried hard to see her mother as a "martyr," the victim of a morally corrupt predator. But she could recall, too, long-ago days in wartime when her mother had spent hours dressing for the French soldiers who sometimes visited Friendship Hall when her father was away. Had her mother, despite the long tutorial with Joseph Pearse Palmer, always remained a "Watertown beauty"? Or was Betsey Hunt Palmer a woman so desperate, financially and personally, that she willingly played her part in this "basest" of crimes? Both were possibilities Eliza would hereafter school herself to avoid in her own life. She had already learned to mistrust men of wealth and political power, like the villains who brought about her grandfather Palmer's downfall, General Spencer and John Hancock. Now a disdain for men who traded on their personal magnetism would grow in her as well, strengthening the desire for independence that may have been her saving grace as she became accustomed to life as an outsider—even within her own family.

· · ·

Without Royall Tyler's generous handouts to tide her over, Betsey Palmer despaired of life in Boston. In 1790 she made arrangements with two of her Hunt brothers to move the family to a farm they owned in Framingham. Twenty miles west of Boston into the relatively primitive interior of the state, Framingham was more distant from city ways than Germantown had been. Little more than a collection of farms and market centers, and linked to no major port city by river or canal, Framingham had remained a more insular community than towns closer to the coast. Perhaps this was why it had such a long history as a refuge for undesirables. During the Salem witch trials of the previous century, the families of the convicted witches Sarah Clayes and Rebecca Nurse settled on the west side of Framingham in a neighborhood still known in the Palmers' time as "Salem End."

In a sense, the Palmers had gone into hiding also. On the Hunt farm, there were no other houses in sight, and mail came only once a week to a post office two and a half miles away. The Palmer children, once accustomed to spending their mornings in a schoolroom, were set to milking cows and repairing fences. According to one local history, the Hunts kept a tavern on their Framingham property and required Betsey and Joseph Palmer to run it for them. Chiefly, however, Palmer was expected to farm the land he soon discovered to be worn-out, and to share the profits with his brothers-in-law.

Completely unsuited to farming, Palmer was forced to "change work" in order to make ends meet. In summer he hoed corn and raked hay for neighboring farmers in exchange for their plowing and mowing his fields. In the winter, Palmer worked on his neighbors' account books in exchange for firewood. The first winter, Palmer also ran a small school in his front parlor for his younger sons and several neighborhood boys. The thirteen-year-old Eliza was allowed to attend, and although this classroom experience was her first formal schooling in seven years, according to her sister Mary, "she shone conspicuous as a grammar scholar, and also in speaking pieces."

But mainly Eliza set her mind to acquiring more practical skills. By her own account, she "knew nothing of the art of manufacturing flax, cotton or wool" when she arrived in Framingham, and she "felt a far greater inclination to read Shakespeare than turn the spinning wheel, which was now almost our only means of gaining necessaries for the family." But Eliza taught herself to spin all the same, and "wholly suppressed the almost unconquerable desire I had for literary improvement." Only at night, while the rest of the family slept, could Eliza pursue her studies, reading over and over the volumes of Shakespeare and the English poets that were all that was left of her grandfather Palmer's library. She was discovering in herself "an irripressible desire" for learning, and on those late nights she allowed herself to dream of one day becoming a teacher or, better still, a writer.

By the winter of 1791, Joseph Pearse Palmer was too depressed to teach school and even to stock wood to heat the house. Eliza took over this duty as well, often on an emergency basis. She remembered checking the woodbin as the sky clouded over for a storm and finding little left to burn. She would run "to a wood lot half a mile distant from the house, bring home wood in my arms, and cut it up myself" as the snow swirled around her. Still, her sympathy would always be greater for her father than for her mother. Difficult circumstances continued to bring out the worst in Betsey Palmer. Eliza remembered being "whipt, shut up—sent supperless to bed," simply because her mother was out of patience. "Well do I remember how my freeborn spirit revolted, not at the punishment, but at the injustice," she wrote. Possibly Betsey Palmer sensed her young daughter's now instinctive disapproval and struck out at her. Eliza's father, on the other hand, "never spoke harshly, never called me names, never beat, never raved. . . . When I erred, he reproved, reasond, convinced, touched every feeling of tenderness."

Yet as the family sank deeper into poverty over the next two years, many of Palmer's refined manners began to seem increasingly out of place, even to his older daughters. According to one account, he insisted that Mary and Eliza finish off their long workdays by dressing for tea each afternoon, although their best clothes were worn-out hand-me-downs, and tea itself was scarce. Each morning, during those still frequent months when his wife was nursing an infant, Palmer heated a cup of hot chocolate and carried it to her himself, sacrificing necessities for the price of Betsey's cocoa, possibly in an effort to win back his wife's affection.

And infants there continued to be. In Framingham, Eliza had five younger brothers and sisters to look after, and neglect would not have been too strong a word for her parents' treatment of them. Little Sophia was left so much to herself that she had difficulty learning to speak. Her older sister Mary recalled that Sophia "had a vocabulary of her own, which was very new and amusing while she was little, but caused her some trouble to rectify as she grew up." On one winter morning in Framingham when the family awoke to find that the fire had died out, five-year-old George was sent to a neighbor's house with a pair of tongs to bring back a live coal. On his way home, cinders from the hot ember set his clothing on fire, severely burning the child.

Into this scene of destitution, Royall Tyler entered once again. Although Mary and Eliza could not have known it, Tyler had continued to write to their father during his long, unexplained absence. The younger man had traveled to western Massachusetts, where he took part in the effort to quell Shays's Rebellion. But his letters contained more than news from the front. In one he mentioned having seen "some very pretty girls," and in all of them he asked Palmer to give his love to Mary, referring to the adolescent girl as "my little wife." The fall that Mary turned eighteen, Tyler suddenly appeared at the Palmer farm in Framingham "with a fine span of black horses." In Mary's view, his arrival was a miracle of deliverance. Eliza, however, was stunned to find the villain of her childhood welcomed again into her home. Soon she would be forced to play witness to yet another seduction.

Tyler arrived with the news that he had begun a law practice in southern Vermont—now the fastest-growing state in the Union—and he had found Palmer work as a tutor for a family in Vermont as well, in a town sixty miles distant from his own Guilford. He then took Mary aside and made a formal proposal of marriage. Her parents, by Mary's account, were "little less rejoiced than myself," presumably because Tyler would now resume his generosity to the entire family. His proposal was accepted. But Joseph Pearse Palmer was the first to leave Framingham for Vermont. We can only imagine what Betsey Palmer must have thought of this turn of events, especially when she was left husbandless once again, with Royall Tyler in residence—unless, of course, this marriage was part of the "bargain" the three had struck almost ten years before in Boston.

With Mary's father away, Tyler evidently felt he could make free with his fiancée. By Mary's account, Tyler announced that "he was about to put my love and confidence in him to the test." He asked Mary to consent to a secret marriage immediately, although he would not tell her why. And he told her he could not bring her back with him to Vermont until the following winter, when he would "come for me in a sleigh, travelling otherwise for me and baggage being impossible," Mary wrote in a memoir many years later, attempting to excuse Tyler's erratic behavior.

In these early days of the new Republic, it was not uncommon for couples to marry and then "go to housekeeping" some weeks after the wedding. But a full year was well beyond the norm. Mary asserted in her memoir that the marriage took place in the spring of 1794, but she gave no details of the wedding. Perhaps this secret marriage—and even Tyler's impulsive marriage proposal—was Mary's own fiction, a post facto defense of an illicit affair with Royall Tyler that all too closely resembled her mother's. In any case, married or not, their connection had become sexual; as soon as Tyler returned to Vermont, Mary discovered that she was pregnant. For months she kept her pregnancy a secret from everyone but her sister Eliza, suffering "intense" anxiety. But at last, and perhaps as a strategy to secure Tyler's affections, Mary began introducing herself around as Mrs. Tyler. When the baby was born, she named him for his father, Royall Tyler, Jr.

Now it was winter; Mary's trunk was packed, her baby swaddled. Eliza tried to comfort her older sister as Mary watched anxiously for the snow to pile deep enough for her husband to come for her by sleigh. Tyler did return to admire his child. He brought his bride a black satin cloak with an ermine collar and took her into Boston to the theater. But again he left for Vermont without her, this time not bothering to give a reason. In her memoir, Mary explained that Tyler's "reputation as an author was high, and his genius covered a multitude of faults." But this second period of waiting was almost more than Mary could bear. She made the teenage Eliza her only confidante; somehow Mary sensed that "my mother would not understand me." Eliza also took over the care of the infant Royall as Mary grew increasingly despondent, tormented by guilt over her "sinful nature." It may have been at this time that Eliza, seeking consolation herself, joined the Framingham First Parish Church of Reverend David Kellogg, a man who preached a reassuringly orthodox gospel of sin and repentance.

Another year passed before Tyler returned for his child and young wife, who was by now pregnant with their second son. This time, Tyler seems to have reconciled himself to married life, and he arrived with a sleigh large enough to carry off Mary, Royall Jr., and two other Palmer children: Eliza's younger brother Hampden and her sister Sophia, the girl who, Eliza and her parents knew, was Royall Tyler's daughter. Tyler promised to take care of them all. For Mary it was a happy ending. Eliza must have been relieved that Tyler no longer had reason to visit the Palmer home. But the knowledge that this "betrayer of innocence" was now a member of the family would never cease to distress her.

Her sister's experience as a single mother made Eliza more determined than ever to become, as her own daughter later phrased it, "personally independent by undertaking some trade." With the numbers in the Palmer household drastically reduced, at last she had the opportunity to make her first effort at opening a school. Sometime before her eighteenth birthday, Eliza began taking young neighborhood children into the family parlor to teach them reading and composition as her father had during his last energetic winter at home. She launched her experiment on an ambitious scale. Imitating the most rigorous academies, she held an exhibition at the end of the term and invited the town's prominent citizens to hear her pupils recite their lessons. Best of all, she managed to pay off the overdue tax bill on the Framingham farm. But this season of triumph was to be brief.

During the two years that Mary and Eliza waited for Royall Tyler to make good on his promises, they had scarcely heard from their father, and he had sent his family no money at all. Now, little more than a year after Mary had finally left home, in the summer of 1797, word came that Joseph Pearse Palmer had died in a fall from a bridge. He had been touring a construction site, the family was informed, and lost his footing; but the nature of the accident suggested a more desperate act, as did his last letter. Mary had been the one to receive it, and the letter showed Palmer still tormented by his business failures, which he blamed for his estrangement from his wife. He had chosen to write to Mary rather than to his wife because "I can see no good it can do," and he asked his daughter to smooth things over with her as best she could. Then he recalled the days when he had wooed Betsey Hunt. "Your mother was sure that my conversation and address was very different from common gallantry," Palmer wrote. "My principles were good, I had read much, I had a retentive memory; by these means I gained her love and unbounded confidence." But his sensitive nature had not served him well in the difficult years following the war. He concluded: "If I had not suffered more in my feelings for ten years past than, I believe, ever man suffered before, I should have been as agreeable a companion as your mother thought me when we were first acquainted."

As far as Eliza was concerned, however, her father was the wronged party. She would always favor him, in memory perhaps even more than during his lifetime. And when it came time to choose a husband, she would look for a man of learning, and then hold him up to her father's standards of gentlemanly behavior—standards that rose the farther she was from that long-ago time at Friendship Hall when the Palmers were the center of an ideal society.

The years during which Eliza Palmer came of age saw a loosening of sexual mores in young Americans that would not be equaled again for more than 150 years. In the post-Revolutionary late eighteenth century, one out of three first children was conceived out of wedlock, compared with less than one of ten in the Puritanical seventeenth. The first generation of independent Americans lived by its own rules in a time of experiment and upheaval. The extramarital dalliances of Eliza's mother and older sister were not really so scandalous, as the Cranch and Adams families' amused tolerance of the breach in the Palmer marriage confirms. Yet Eliza's trauma as witness and victim was profound. And once Eliza herself was grown and raising daughters of her own, the prevailing morality had changed direction again. Americans were turning away from the relative promiscuity of the late eighteenth century and moving toward the more repressive Victorian morality of the nineteenth. The shift in social conventions only strengthened the abhorrence Eliza felt when she considered what happened to the women of her family in the Revolution's aftermath.

Eliza kept her silence for many years, and ultimately confessed the story of Royall Tyler's predations only to her two oldest daughters, Elizabeth and Mary, who in turn would keep her secret as best they could. Mary Peabody once hinted darkly that her mother had "suffered much, not only for herself but for others." But "what she has borne and what she has conquered" is "a history that cannot be told." In the presence of her sons, and of her invalid daughter, the child Eliza named after her own sister Sophia, possibly in an effort at continued concealment, the incident remained "of a nature that repels speech." Yet the less she spoke of the episode, the larger it loomed in her imagination. Eliza Palmer could not rid herself of her fear of predatory men, and she began to form her own private vision of romantic love, made up of elements of Spenserian chivalry and Christian piety: a vision that would prove almost impossible to realize in the chronic state of economic distress that was her Palmer legacy.

❧ 4 ❧

"Belinda"

BY THE TIME ELIZA PALMER WAS TWENTY, HER ONCE PROUD FAMILY
had collapsed. In 1797, she moved from Framingham with her widowed
mother and youngest brother and sister into the Hunt household in Watertown, an environment even more alien than Framingham had been. Watertown was closer to Boston, but the social life that centered on the Hunts' general store and tavern in the town square was a far cry from the literate
Friendship Hall "Sisterhood." Her mother worried about the gang of boys that
nine-year-old George played with at the nearby bridge over the Charles River,
but she had no time to supervise him or his little sister, Catherine. Nor, for
once, did Eliza. Betsey Palmer had started a dressmaking business with Aunt
Kate Hunt, and Eliza was expected to take an equal share in the work. But
here, surrounded by the conventionally domestic Hunt women, Eliza was no
longer so willing to do anything that was asked of her. In Eliza's assessment,
"the whole W[atertown] concern looked no higher than the Almighty dollar,"
and she became "very much disgusted with the ultra-fashionable life of Watertown in those days."

Eliza could not hide her feelings for long, and at last her literary ambitions
drove her to defiance. She carried pen and paper with her at all times, and,
her mother recalled with a mixture of pride and frustration, "I have known
her frequently when standing at the Wheel—set down on the stairs—take out
her pen—and write an ode." The Hunts felt differently about poetry than the
Palmers did, and soon they were accusing Eliza of "mispending her time at her
pen and books." Well aware that "*this* of all families is the most improper to
form the Mind of a . . . girl," Betsey Palmer agreed to help the daughter who
had guarded the family's secrets for so long find a way to leave home.

Betsey wrote to her late husband's aunt Mary Cranch—the same woman who had amused herself by visiting the Palmers' promiscuous Boston household ten years before—to ask for help. Mary Cranch had never let on to Betsey that she knew about her affair with Royall Tyler, and she had maintained her concern for her now fatherless grandnieces and -nephews. In letters to her younger sister Abigail Adams, recently installed in the President's House in Philadelphia, she routinely passed on news of the Palmer children when it came her way. Now she invited Eliza to stay with her in Quincy while she helped her find employment.

When Betsey Palmer sent Eliza to Mary Cranch in May 1798, she wrote a letter of introduction describing her daughter as "a good girl" whose childhood had been "repleat with woes—such as rend the heart." It was Eliza's greatest wish "to gain for herself a decent independence" and, her mother promised, she would "not be backward in adopting any plan for future subsistance" that Mrs. Cranch might propose. Eliza herself was eager to return to the vigorous intellectual climate of her Germantown childhood. She knew that escape from the downward spiral of poverty depended on educating herself for teaching or on making a good marriage. More than anything, she wanted to avoid the compromising sexual entanglements she had seen her mother and sister enter into out of desperation.

Yet Eliza remained with the Cranches for only a few weeks before beginning work as a shop clerk in Boston during the late spring of 1798. This first effort to gain "a decent independence" was a brief one. By summer a yellow fever epidemic had shut down commerce in the city. Eliza's employers fled Boston, leaving the young woman to fend for herself in a city where many houses were empty of all but the sick and dying. Eliza volunteered as a nurse for as long as her own health remained good. She may also have stayed on in Boston because of a romantic possibility. Betsey Palmer wrote to Mary Cranch of a surprise visit from her daughter in July 1798, when Eliza must have hinted at an attachment. Betsey wrote, "My heart glows with delight at the pleasure she feels," and added, "while I tremble for her unsuspecting heart—I feel a confidence in her prudence." Evidently Betsey Palmer had ceded all responsibility for Eliza to Mrs. Cranch, for she asked Eliza's great-aunt to exercise "every necessary caution" in guiding Eliza through this incipient romance.

By the end of the summer, however, Eliza was back in Quincy with the Cranches. She had fallen ill from exhaustion, not yellow fever. Perhaps disappointment played a role in her collapse as well, for nothing more was said or written about that summer's "pleasure." By the time Eliza recovered, her employers had returned to Boston, but they had hired a man in Eliza's place.

Next, Mrs. Cranch appealed to her youngest sister, Elizabeth Smith Peabody, whose own eighteen-year-old daughter, Elizabeth, had died suddenly in early autumn. Elizabeth's second husband (her first had died in 1794), the Reverend

Elizabeth Smith Peabody, by Gilbert Stuart

Stephen Peabody, ran a farm and a renowned preparatory school in addition
to meeting his pastoral duties in the small New Hampshire farm community
of Atkinson, just across the Massachusetts border from Haverhill, a bustling
mill town on the Merrimack River. Elizabeth Smith Peabody was fully the
equal of her older sisters in wit and learning, and probably superior in intelligence to her burly, jocular husband, "Parson" Peabody. She played a large role
in the Atkinson Academy, which had recently become coeducational, teaching
composition to both boys and girls and serving as housemother to a dozen or
more boarders at a time. Over the years, Abigail and Mary had tried many

ways to help Elizabeth along in what they saw as a difficult and isolated existence in Atkinson. Abigail sent her young grandsons to the academy to be educated, paying generous tuitions. Now Mary offered Eliza Palmer's services as
an assistant in the busy household. Abigail, who must have met Eliza on a visit
to Quincy, also approved of the idea. "Miss Palmer," she wrote in a letter to
Elizabeth that expressed both older sisters' hopes, "will prove to you the companion of your leisure hours possessing taste to entertain, and to receive improvement, whilst her care and assiduity will I trust relieve you from the too
great burden of a large Family."

To the Palmers, Mary Cranch hinted that Mrs. Peabody might adopt Eliza
in her own daughter's place. But Mary Cranch had not counted on her sister's
mounting grief over the loss of her cherished daughter. The household that
Mary Cranch imagined would serve as a refuge for Eliza proved to be the last
and most precarious way station on her road to "a decent independence."

On her arrival at the Atkinson parsonage in late December 1798, Eliza
Palmer impressed Elizabeth Smith Peabody as "a most amiable person . . . exactly the gentle, kind, helpful companion my full heart required." For her part,
Eliza was awed by her new guardian who, she later wrote, possessed "all the
mental acquisitions you could covet." In her eagerness to please, Eliza presented herself as a far more worldly and self-assured young woman than she
actually was. Elizabeth Smith Peabody wrote to Mary Cranch that she was
afraid Eliza "will not be contented—It is very different here from Boston,
amid scenes of gaiety and all her youthful companions." She imagined that
Eliza had always known the life she lived for a few short months in Quincy,
and wrote that "I believe [Atkinson] is a perfect contrast with any situation
she was ever in before." She couldn't have been further from the truth, but
Eliza was too proud to mention the hardships of her childhood. From the
outset, Elizabeth viewed Eliza's presence as an emotional burden, even if it
was also a practical relief. "I am sensible I cannot be the companion I was formerly," she wrote to her sister Mary Cranch. All she could think of was the
other Elizabeth who "lies there under yonder cold sod."

The indifference Eliza sensed in Elizabeth Smith Peabody contributed to
her feeling that she had been brought to Atkinson not as a surrogate daughter but as a "maid of all work." The disappointment was severe. Eliza saw little
of her guardian, and she took orders instead from the family's longtime servant, Lydia Springer. Eliza wrote to Mrs. Cranch that she was required to
"assist in preparing the usual meals, take care of the chambers, scour all the
floors, excepting the kitchen and a little bed-room adjoining, wash, iron . . .
mend and make mostly for all." Aside from the Peabody family, there were
eight boarders in the house under the age of fourteen that winter whose frequently torn clothing became Eliza's special province of care. Elizabeth Smith

Peabody even conscripted Eliza for the duty of making up shirts for the Adams grandsons, who had arrived at school without the requisite wardrobe.

Despite her many chores, Eliza must have found time to befriend the Atkinson Academy students, for she soon gained the nickname "walking dictionary." It was a distinction she came to regret, however, for although she was neither teacher nor student, her obvious talents brought her the worst of both roles. "In the midst of my laborious employments," she wrote to Mary Cranch, "the boarders will come with pen and ink and paper," clamoring: "do write my piece off, do compose me a poem to speak next Saturday, do write me a letter to carry into school today, do correct my composition, do look over my figures in rhetoric, or make me some, and pray hear me say my lesson in geography." She felt she must comply with "all these requests . . . or they will think me unkind."

Although these demands weighed on Eliza, she gained confidence in her literary and teaching abilities once she saw how well they served in a rigorous preparatory school. She continued to write poetry in spare moments, and Parson Peabody, who had heard the results of Eliza's efforts in his students' recitations, encouraged her to publish them. He passed several of her poems on to friends in Haverhill who had begun a weekly newspaper, and soon Eliza's pieces were appearing as a regular feature in the *Haverhill Federal Gazette* under the heading "Apollo's Lyre." She signed the seven ambitious poems she published during the spring and summer of 1799 with the pseudonym "Belinda," a name borrowed from Alexander Pope's comic heroine of *The Rape of the Lock*. But Eliza's poetic statements were far from humorous.

As Belinda, Eliza Palmer emerged as an advocate for women, giving voice to some of the pent-up anger of the past decade and discovering a surprising idealism as well. In a poem published in March 1799, titled "Some Thoughts Occasioned by the Present Juncture," Eliza argued that America's politicians should listen to the women of the Republic before going to war with France in the wake of the infamous XYZ Affair. She wrote in rhymed couplets reminiscent of Pope, and she began with some forceful questions:

> . . . First I ask: who has the bounds assign'd,
> Which hold in humble awe the female mind?
> Has man the soul prerogative to feel
> His Country's wrongs, and guide the public wheel?

Eliza conceded that women may "shine in the domestic sphere." Yet, she wrote, God "Has giv'n to both" men and women "the same immortal mind." She insisted that women "have pow'rs" equal to men, "If called to action." Drawing on her personal knowledge of predatory males, she claimed women had achieved moral superiority: they could point out the "sad degen'racy of *man*" that all too often led nations into war.

In a poem published the following month, Eliza described the character of "A True Lady." Once again she took men, particularly literary men—she listed Rousseau, Milton, and the popular British essayists Fordyce and Gregory—to task for their view of women as frivolous inferiors:

> This is the language all their writings speak,
> That woman, to be *lovely,* must be *weak!*
> That she was born *all powerful man* to bless;
> For him must think, must act, must move, and dress!

Then Eliza went on to describe her ideal woman, a combination of Hunt domesticity and Palmer intellectuality, darkened by her own bitter experience of the world. It was a statement of the philosophy that would later guide her in rearing three daughters:

> Thus must the woman I esteem most fair,
> Disdain false modesty's affected air;
> Must know no feelings that she dares not speak;
> Must rev'rence virtue, for true virtue's sake. . . .
> And oft she must one sacred hour devote
> To useful study and to serious thought;
> And thus her high immortal mind prepare
> For that hereafter, which we all must share.
> She must be gentle, in her person neat;
> Be in domestic knowledge, quite complete;
> Be firm in friendship, and in love sincere,
> Steady in purpose, and yet not severe;
> Nor let her mind severest sorrows bend,
> But nobly bear the ills which heaven may send.
> A course like this, her much wrong'd sex would raise,
> Honor her god, and gain 'unflattering praise.'

Compared to her provocative opening lines, Eliza's requirements of a "true lady" seem modest. But her underlying message was a powerful one. The Belinda of Pope's poem was a vain and foolish girl who spent hours at her mirror; *The Rape of the Lock* refers to a drawing room dispute over a lock of her hair. In "A True Lady," Eliza Palmer, who knew firsthand that seduction and sexual abuse were lurking just beyond the drawing room, was taking Belinda's side against her creator. Eliza's Belinda spoke up for the intellectual and spiritual dignity of women in language not so different from that used by Mary Wollstonecraft in her 1792 *Vindication of the Rights of Women*, just beginning to gain a following in the United States. Wollstonecraft, too, was concerned with releasing women from charges of vanity and ignorance. In her poem, Eliza echoed Wollstonecraft's directive that women reject the low standards for female behavior that men held for them and instead aspire to honesty, intelligence, and virtue. Eliza's belief that, in the new era of independence, American women *could* reform their sex gave her poem an urgency and optimism. Her poem set British feminism in a major key.

At first Elizabeth Smith Peabody joined her husband in encouraging their young assistant's literary efforts. She held many of the same views on women, and she may even have suggested the pseudonym "Belinda" to Eliza. (Pope was Elizabeth Smith Peabody's favorite poet.) She also sent several of Eliza's poems to her son, William Smith Shaw, who had taken a post as special assistant to his uncle, President John Adams. "Did you hear my Son," she wrote, "that Apollo had mistaken the heights of Atkinson for Parnassus"? She went on to praise Eliza's writing: "The *gentle Belinda's* notes are in perfect Unison with his Lyre." And she recommended that her son pass on the poems to the president, who she expected would be "pleased, especially with the piece upon the present Juncture of Affairs." Elizabeth Smith Peabody knew that Eliza's pacifist sentiments in regard to war with France would please her brother-in-law, and she may also have been carrying on a campaign, begun by her sister back in 1776, to persuade John Adams to "Remember the Ladies."

President John Adams seems to have read and liked Eliza's poems. The following autumn, Elizabeth Smith Peabody was still sending her son "the effusions of Miss Palmers pen" to pass on to the president, this time a prose work that one of the Adams grandsons had used as a recitation piece. But around the Peabody parsonage, Eliza's poetry was earning her another kind of attention: not the "unflattering praise" she wrote about, but the romantic interest of the Reverend Peabody's ministerial students who taught in the academy. This response was not the one that Mrs. Parson Peabody wished for her charge, especially when she learned of the jealous anger it aroused in her already disgruntled housekeeper, Lydia Springer, who, Eliza wrote to Mary Cranch, "feels hurt and dissatisfied with the attentions I receive from those who pay not the same to her."

To a young ministerial candidate in a rural parsonage, Eliza Palmer must have been an appealing figure: she was a published poet whose works described a powerful feminine ideal, yet she was forced to earn her keep as a maid of all work. It is easy to imagine that Eliza's lines in "A True Lady" describing the moment when a woman of good character meets a correspondingly virtuous man might have tempted one or more members of the Atkinson Academy faculty to declare their affection:

> 'Tis then sweet friendship knows no base alloy,
> But proves the source, and spring of every joy;
> Then in each breast the same emotions rise;
> Soul speaks with soul, and into union flies.

It is also easy to imagine Eliza's anger when her brief experience of literary fame was followed almost immediately by a threatened dismissal from the Peabody household. There is no record of the accusations made against Eliza Palmer, but she wrote about the incident to Mary Cranch in words that show she still had Belinda—both hers and Pope's—on her mind. "It is a received opinion that a poet is good for nothing," she wrote to Mary Cranch, "and a person may throw five hours away at the toilet and yet be loved and admired, when she would be condemned if she spent one hour at the pen." But it was time spent on housework, not in front of a mirror, that was being measured in the Peabody parsonage. Lydia Springer, who clearly resented Eliza's efforts to vault out of the servant class, seems to have directed her jealousy into charges that Eliza was again "mispending" her time on literary pursuits.

A letter from Abigail Adams to Mary Cranch shows that the two older Smith sisters had plenty of sympathy for Eliza Palmer's plight. Abigail worried that "Sister Peabody" was "too hard" on Eliza, and tended to forget "that she herself was once young, and possesst a heart as . . . susceptable to the tender passions as any body I can recollect." Of Eliza, she wrote, "Her heart is good," and—perhaps recalling what she knew of Betsey Palmer's impulsive sexuality—she "has a hereditary spice of the Romantic in her constitution." Eliza needed guidance, but not repression. "A cold youth would be a frozen Age," Abigail warned.

But her sister's opinions do not seem to have reached Elizabeth Smith Peabody, who remained mournful and self-absorbed. She complained to Abigail that her own "round of duties" and "unremitted exertions" prevented her from "devoting a large portion of time, to literary improvements" and that "infirmities of body, disappointments, and *afflictions* of *various kinds,* have damped the ardor of youth, depressed my genius, and extinguished almost every latent spark." Little wonder that Elizabeth Smith Peabody shared her housekeeper's resentment of the energetic Eliza Palmer, whose "abilities, and manners are too fascinating, for the repose of others."

By now Eliza knew she was unwelcome in Atkinson, but she had no place to go. She was twenty-two years old. She had exhausted Mary Cranch's gen-

erosity, and she could not return to the Hunts in Watertown. When her
mother heard of Eliza's latest troubles, she sympathized. "O! she has sufferd
from *envy* and malice," Betsey Palmer wrote to Mary Cranch. And she wished,
not for the first time, that her daughter's "ideas had been surcumscribed as her
circumstances." But she could not provide a home for Eliza.

Eliza must have felt that her only choice was to give in. "I mean to do all I
can to keep peace," she wrote to Mary Cranch. She was "determined never to
write anything again, excepting letters, and as few of them as possible; never
to touch a book, except upon the Sabbath, and to devote every moment to
work of some kind." Driven from her earliest childhood to pursue a life of the
mind, Eliza Palmer would not be able to keep these prohibitions for long. But
she would turn her ambitions away from literature and toward what must
have seemed to her now the only remaining route out of poverty and dependence: marriage.

Flight into Union

THE TWENTY-SIX-YEAR-OLD NATHANIEL PEABODY WAS NOT AMONG THE men whose attentions caused Eliza Palmer so much trouble in the summer of 1799. She met the Dartmouth student, then in his last year at college, in early 1800 when he paid a weekend visit to his former teacher and distant relation, the Reverend Stephen Peabody.

Born in 1774, Nathaniel Peabody was just a few years older than Eliza Palmer, but he had considerably less experience of the world. His childhood in the southern New Hampshire town of New Boston was scarcely touched by the events of the Revolution, and his early home life could not have been more distant from the genteel intellectual atmosphere of Friendship Hall. Nathaniel was the second of eight children, the oldest son born to Isaac Peabody, then a tailor in Topsfield, Massachusetts, and his wife, Mary Potter Peabody. The boy was nine years old when his father moved the family across the not-too-distant state line to take up farming in New Boston. He was to remember vividly the hours spent clearing the forest and building the family homestead with whatever materials lay at hand. It was Nathaniel who "placed every stone in the cellar & in the underpinning & squared every stick of timber."

Nathaniel's father, Isaac, was, like the Reverend Stephen Peabody of Atkinson, a member of the fifth generation of Peabodys born in America. But he was as reticent as the Parson was talkative, and he never learned to read. Once when Nathaniel sent him a hand-carved cane as a gift, he had to enclose a note to be read out loud to his father explaining that the cane was inscribed with "all the letters of your own name." Nathaniel Peabody inherited Isaac's taciturn nature, but, like Eliza Palmer, he determined early on that education would be his means of escape from a harsh rural existence. His was no desperate flight, however. He left home to prepare for college later than most boys, and with trepidation. He would always remember the day when he crossed the brook that ran past his New Boston home and turned back for a last look only to feel the tears start, knowing that "I was launching out into the ocean & could not divine where I should land." As difficult as it was, Nathaniel's choice turned out to be a lucky one. The brothers and sisters he left behind on the farm were hard-pressed to make a living off the land; during the first decades of the new century, two of them served time in debtors' prison.

Just how this first son of an illiterate farmer became enough of a scholar to find his way into the Reverend Stephen Peabody's academy, most likely earning his keep by teaching younger students, is not known. But by the time Eliza Palmer met Nathaniel Peabody in the early months of 1800, he had earned a solid reputation among the Atkinson Peabodys as a bright student with a promising future and as a man of "virtue," possessing "merit, good sense," and even "something original in his genius." His election to Phi Beta Kappa at Dartmouth seemed to confirm this assessment. Even before their meeting, Eliza had heard enough about him to become convinced that Nathaniel Peabody would be a worthy object of her affection. "I beheld you," she wrote in one of her first letters, "as I should one of the planets in the canopy of heaven; as something which I ought to admire but never hope to call mine." Sometime during his visit an understanding was reached that a "connexion" between the two had been "suddenly formed." Perhaps it was when Eliza read Nathaniel her poem "A True Lady." Afterward she wrote of the moment, paraphrasing her verse: "I flattered myself, that every pleasing sentiment affected us equally; that 'In either breast the same emotions rose, / Soul spoke with soul, and into union flew.'" Yet somehow, through an entire weekend of outings and hours spent reading to each other, Eliza Palmer seems to have overlooked the sort of man Nathaniel Peabody really was.

By all accounts, Nathaniel Peabody's rise from rural poverty had come at some cost to his nerves. Small in stature and slightly stooped as if in resignation, he was a determined but fearful man, as cautious as he was ambitious. The two qualities, present as early as his courtship with Eliza Palmer, warred in him constantly, compromising his every action. Eliza may have been attracted, at first, to Nathaniel's prudent nature. As unrefined as he was, the young man had more in common with her gentlemanly but passive father than with the rakish Royall Tyler. Nevertheless, she quickly sensed her fiancé's tendency to stall—what she later called his "constitutional timidity"—which, combined with his fondness for "raking up objections for argument's sake," so often stymied his efforts. Eliza soon found herself acting as the aggressor in the nearly three-year period of negotiation following the weekend that marked the beginning of their "connexion."

After Nathaniel's return to Dartmouth in the spring of 1800 to complete his college course, the courtship became almost entirely epistolary. Although only Eliza's side of the correspondence survives, her letters show that she often wrote two to Nathaniel's one. Hers were long, carefully crafted pieces of persuasion in which she attempted to set the terms of their romance and future marriage. The reticent Nathaniel may have needed Eliza to define feelings he could barely express; yet he may also have shrunk from Eliza's directive eloquence.

Eliza herself knew that she would have to mask her determination. Perhaps unconsciously mimicking her parents' tutelary courtship, Eliza posed Nathaniel Peabody in these letters as her "Instructor." She claimed that she had never expected "my humble virtues should attract the attention of one whose character, and education entitled him, to the favour of the favourites of fortune." She sent him a copy of "A True Lady," calling it a *"very poor poem,"* and she asked his advice on improving it. Yet if anyone was doing the instructing, it was Eliza. Her poem, already polished enough to have found its way into print, told Nathaniel Peabody about the kind of woman she was, and about the "union" of sympathetic souls she hoped to achieve in marriage.

As in her poems, she wrote of her efforts "to endeavor to persuade the generality of mankind, that a woman can feel the ennobling passion of love, in all its purity, without its weakness." Was her mother in the back of her mind as she wrote? In any case, Eliza told Nathaniel that her love for him was of an elevated kind: more spiritual than earthly, an ideal made real. Indeed, she argued that their union was predestined. Otherwise, she wrote, why would she not have felt the same way for their mutual acquaintance—a "Mr. R"? She could "account for the decided preference my heart instantly felt for you, in no other way, than by indulging the dear Idea that our souls 'were cast in the same mould, were lighted at the same taper.'"

On the subject of women, she was insistent. She paraphrased a line from her poem condemning Milton's definition of women as "fair defects in Nature," and then asked, in words that let Nathaniel know there was only one proper answer: "Do you think, with the world at large, that [women] are . . . *an after-thought of creation?*" She felt "confident that a rightly educated woman, is capable of so much greatness of mind." Not only would an educated woman make an ideal mate, Eliza argued, she would also make a superior mother. "The necessity of cultivating the female mind, is a subject upon which I am almost enthusiastic," she wrote to Nathaniel. And she outlined the philosophy that had permitted her to shift her ambitions from literature to motherhood:

> Though *they* move in a different sphere of life, from the other sex;
> yet the duties they have to fulfill are not less important. In no instance are [their] duties more important than in that of a Mother.

In that character, they have perhaps the charge of a numerous family. And they ought to be capable, to teach the lisping infant to speak with propriety, and as the tender mind expands to fill it with virtuous principles—Early impressions are hard to be obliterated. And the man who is, from the very morning of existence, taught to think justly, to reverence virtue, and cultivate benevolence, will, in all human probability, be an ornament to human-nature. In this view, the fate of our Country, is in some degree dependant, on the education of its females.

Although Eliza ended this last discourse, as so many others, with an apology —"Pardon my dwelling so long on a subject, with which you are far better acquainted than I am"—clearly she was selling Nathaniel Peabody on the idea of raising a family with her as his wife.

If written arguments were not enough to convince, Eliza began mending Nathaniel's clothes and bedding, which she returned to him by mail along with handmade gifts. She would always work to offset her Palmer intellectuality with Hunt domesticity. But Eliza would never allow the domestic to become mundane. She hoped that the fob she had embroidered with an olive branch as an "ornament" for Nathaniel's watch would "prove emblematical of our future lives. May the knot which shall unite our hearts be fastened by purity, and innocence, and may the olive branch ever flourish near us," she wrote.

All of this activity on Eliza's part—the mending, the embroidery, the letter writing—could not escape the notice of Elizabeth Smith Peabody. Once again she became alarmed by what she saw as Eliza's forward nature. Another flurry of letters passed between the Peabody and Cranch households, and Betsey Palmer was alerted to her daughter's impropriety. "I think she has been a little too premature in everything," Elizabeth Smith Peabody wrote to Mary Cranch, "and I find her Mother was of the same opinion as well as you." Eliza's elders seemed more aware than she of Nathaniel's potential liabilities as a provider. Late to graduate from college, he was, at twenty-six, still "in the infancy of his education," and, Elizabeth Smith Peabody knew, her husband's protégé was "not wholly determined what profession to follow." She regretted that Eliza had interfered far enough to propose that Nathaniel study for the ministry. Whatever career the young man decided on, Eliza's elders were united in the belief that a "sudden marriage" would be a terrible mistake. Eliza's mother especially endorsed this view, writing from her own bitter experience that "there was nothing more dreadful, than Poverty, to those who had flattered themselves with high expectations." Elizabeth Smith Peabody told Eliza that she would have to wait to marry, "perhaps many years," until Nathaniel Peabody "had a permanent support, and a good prospect for a genteel maintenance."

Considering that the usual period of courtship in these times was one year at the least, and more often many, Eliza may well have been "premature" when she wrote to Nathaniel scarcely two months after their first meeting that "my heart is unreservedly yours." In this letter, she defended herself against charges from an "accusing spirit"—perhaps Elizabeth Smith Peabody—who claimed that Eliza had erred in her conduct toward Nathaniel. She had been told that she should not have revealed her feelings so soon, and Eliza admitted that "prudence would have dictated more reserve." But she was "unused to dissimulation," and the immediate certainty that she had felt on that fateful weekend seemed to her confirmation that their union was preordained. This inward conviction in turn proved the "innocence" of their love, and of her impulsive declaration. Eliza had allowed the Atkinson Peabodys to crush one early ambition; she would not let it happen again.

But, given Nathaniel's instinctive wariness, delay was inevitable. Poverty was the great leveler that had brought the daughter of a Harvard-educated gentleman together with the son of an illiterate farmer. Eliza liked to say that both she and Nathaniel had been "early tutored in the school of adversity." But hardship also worked to keep the two apart. Both were eager for a way out of their present circumstances. For Eliza, marriage was that escape. For Nathaniel, however, the prospect of supporting a wife and children made him increasingly fearful about making his "connexion" with Eliza permanent.

Perhaps the marriage would never have taken place if it weren't for the helpful intervention of the Reverend Peabody. In the fall of 1800 a proposal came, through the Parson, that seemed to solve both Eliza's and Nathaniel's problems. Several prominent citizens in the nearby town of Andover, Massachusetts, had decided to open a school—to be called the North Parish Free School—that would be the first incorporated academy in the state to offer classes for both sexes. Two "preceptors" were needed to run the school, and the Reverend Peabody recommended Eliza Palmer and Nathaniel Peabody. Eliza worried that she was not qualified for the position, but she could not refuse the opportunity to work alongside her fiancé in the profession to which she had long aspired. Perhaps she also expected Nathaniel to take this joint job offer as a sign that it was time to propose marriage. But although he took the job as boys' preceptor, Nathaniel did nothing to advance the progress of his courtship. By January 1801, the two were installed in separate wings of the school building where Eliza had fifty-one "young ladies" to care for, both as teacher and as housemother.

Andover was a larger and wealthier town than Atkinson, and its first coeducational academy drew as pupils the sons and daughters of successful merchants and landowners from twenty-five neighboring towns. According to one town historian, Andover was at the turn of the century a "remarkably social town." The young women who were Eliza Palmer's charges were more accustomed to rounds of parties than to the hours of solitary study and meditation that she thought suited "A True Lady." Female literacy was higher in New England than in other regions, but, like the Hunt women of Watertown, many of the mothers of Eliza's students were themselves illiterate. They sent their daughters to school because it had become fashionable. To her fifty-one pupils Eliza gave lessons in "needlework, grammar, geography, arithmetic, reading, writing and composition." But their mothers were far more interested in Eliza Palmer's success in teaching needlework than in the other subjects, and some evidently were interested most of all in gossiping about Eliza's apparent attachment to the young man who was her colleague at the school.

Eliza soon proved herself capable as a teacher. She wrote to Mary Cranch that she had earned the love of her charges and that "no school consisting of so large a number could be more orderly. They follow all my directions with promptitude and, I think, with pleasure." But the embarrassment of being made the subject of rumors, combined with the enormous labor of preparing lessons for so many pupils, soon wore her down, and she developed a painful cough. After a year of teaching, Eliza withdrew from her job for several months of rest and study, and to take stock of the progress of her courtship with Nathaniel Peabody. She retreated once again to the south shore of Boston, this time to the Milton home of her aunt Elizabeth Palmer Cranch, who had recently returned from West Point with Eliza's younger sister Amelia to start a school of their own.

Eliza's first letter to Nathaniel from Milton betrayed her impatience with him. She asked Nathaniel outright whether he would be "content to begin *life* in [a] plain economical manner" and challenged him to ignore "the sneers of a few in 'higher stile of living.'" She did not "wish to hasten anything—contrary to your wishes." But she also informed him of the rumors being spread about her presence at "the A[cademy] with one so nearly connected." Even her supporters "thought it must give rise—if I was ever so prudent, to melicious observation." One woman had suggested, Eliza reported, that if she and Nathaniel "were *one*"—that is, married—"it would shortly stop every one's tongue—and relieve Miss P. from an embarrassing situation."

But Eliza's pressure tactics only put Nathaniel off. In her next letter, she wrote to assure him that "no friend of yours, *does* wish you to risk it!—Let it be another summer—another year or *years* if necessary." She had hoped to "silence the tongue of Scandal . . . but not by the sacrifice of your repose." She turned her efforts instead to a piece of needlepoint that she intended to present to one of her accusers. She was studying grammar, arithmetic, and geography as well, but it was for her decorative sewing—the symbol of refinement for women of leisure—that she had received the sharpest criticism from the mothers of her students. She resented spending her time on such frivolous work, but she poured into this needlepoint project all the energy she had previously given to pressing her suit with Nathaniel. She visited schools all over Boston to compare her piece with others, and at last felt satisfied that hers, a portrait of George Washington—whose death in 1799 had made him a popular subject for memorials in thread—was as well done as any she saw. She could return to teaching with full confidence in her abilities, if not in her clean reputation.

Her last letter to Nathaniel from Milton took up once again the theme of modest aspirations, and this time she phrased her argument in language more likely to please her reluctant suitor. "Some place happiness in possessing much wealth, in having a finer house than their neighbours, riding in a fine carriage, and faring sumptuously every day," she wrote, "but my heart and disposition are such, that to be happy I must be quiet, rather retired than otherways, and be employed in the humbler but respectable circle of domestic duties, with those I love around me." She had heard that Nathaniel's younger brother planned to seek his fortune at sea, and she hoped Nathaniel would not fall prey to such schemes. "It is a business which often brings abundance of wealth," she wrote with considerable firsthand knowledge of the subject, "but it often throws families from the height of opulence to the Depth of poverty." Not only had her father and grandfather lost an enormous fortune based on overseas commerce, but her own older brother, Joseph, who had shipped out at an early age, had not been heard from in years and was now presumed dead. "I should rather be the possessor of one farm, that would afford me food and raiment," she wrote, "than of the best ships that sail out of our harbour, if any of my near friends must sail with them."

This time Eliza's persuasions worked. In the summer of 1802, she returned to the North Parish Free School in Andover and resumed her tasks at the side of her fiancé. In early October, Eliza wrote to her mother of their "determination of going to Houskeeping this winter." On November 2, Eliza Palmer and Nathaniel Peabody were married in Andover. No family members from either side attended; the expense of travel was too great. Honeymoons had not yet become customary in America, but the newlywed Peabodys took a two-week leave from teaching during which they visited Palmer relatives and friends in Watertown and Boston. Their chief object was to buy furniture and make up linens for the student boarding house Eliza planned to run when they returned to Andover. She would also take her two youngest siblings—fourteen-year-old George and eleven-year-old Catherine—into her new family.

Eliza Palmer had at last maneuvered Nathaniel Peabody into marriage. But she was to find Nathaniel no less stubborn a husband than a fiancé. Eliza once confided to her eldest daughter that during their first week of marriage

Nathaniel announced to her: "You must not expect that my love for you is to oblige me to yield my opinion, or alter my habits, or that I shall go to bed or rise a moment earlier or later—because I am married." She told her daughter that "it was a queer speech, and on my heart produced an effect I never could remove."

Eliza had not yet written her novel of Revolutionary times in which she described the disastrous effects of her aunt Elizabeth Palmer Cranch's "wilful reliance on her romantic notions of the respect due to women." But she was being forced to reckon now with the consequences of her own idealism, of what she termed "forming too romantic notions of married life." She held Nathaniel Peabody up to the standards of chivalry set by her father and grandfather, who, she once wrote, "would match any lovers in romance through their whole lives." And already she was disappointed. Compared to her father's "watchful tenderness, his delicate attentions" to her mother, Nathaniel's declaration seemed stingy. She tried to remind herself of the "great difference in our educations" and "early associations." She knew that Nathaniel had been raised in a family with "strong prejudices against expressing much feeling." But what troubled her was the growing awareness that, in his speech, her husband had revealed his "jealousy of my assuming power."

Evidently Eliza soon learned to work her way within the marriage, however. In little more than a year, the couple had resigned their posts in Andover and set up housekeeping on a farm in neighboring Billerica, where Eliza would start her own smaller school. There Nathaniel began an apprenticeship in medicine; he had settled, at last, on a profession. And the couple's first child, named for her mother—Elizabeth Palmer Peabody—was born.

PART II

The Family School

1804–1820

❦ 6 ❧

"My Hopes All of Happiness"

ELIZA PEABODY WAS TWENTY-SEVEN YEARS OLD AND EIGHT MONTHS
pregnant with her first child when she moved to Billerica in April 1804 with
the plan of starting her own school. She was exhausted from the effort of running a student boarding house in Andover (she had economized by doing all
the laundry and cooking herself) as well as from teaching more than fifty
girls through so many months of her pregnancy. Her cough had returned.
Still, she was to remember these early years of motherhood in Billerica as a
time of great optimism. She later recalled that her first child had been "born
and nursed while my heart was at rest, and my hopes *all* of happiness." She
believed that a mother's state of mind as she nursed her baby helped to form
the child's character: blue-eyed Elizabeth, born in Billerica on May 16, 1804,
with a mass of curly fair hair, was to have the "firmest constitution" of all her
children. Elizabeth herself would later recall her good fortune at being the
"first-born child in a home where the atmosphere was love."

The tension resulting from Nathaniel's "jealousy" of his wife's forceful
nature lessened when he signed on as a medical apprentice to Dr. Pemberton
of Billerica. At the turn of the eighteenth century, teaching was the highest
calling a woman could respectably aspire to, but it was near the bottom of the
scale for a college-educated man, generally a prelude to a career in law, medicine, or the ministry. There is nothing in Nathaniel's letters to indicate
whether he was pleased with the decision to become a doctor, or indeed
whether the idea originated with Nathaniel or Eliza, although the practical
work of a physician may have seemed the most suitable choice for a farmer's
son. Certainly he never displayed the passion for his work that his wife had
once showed for literature and now devoted to her teaching; throughout the
nearly two decades that he practiced as a physician, his correspondence is

scattered with sardonic complaints about the lack of illness in town or the arrival of younger competitors. But in 1804 all these trials lay ahead, and simply to have reached a decision that would take him out of the poorly paid teaching profession was a relief for both Nathaniel and Eliza. To the guardedly ambitious Nathaniel Peabody, doctoring was a safe and honorable way to accumulate wealth.

Eliza's spirits rose with her expectation that her own teaching days would end once Nathaniel completed his training. She looked forward to writing poetry again, and as she nursed the infant Elizabeth, she made plans for a small, select boarding school that she could run in a spare room of the farmhouse—a "family school." She hired a young woman to cook and mind the baby during school hours in exchange for board and lessons. Eager to give her namesake a more official welcome into the world than she had received, Eliza had her first daughter baptized when she was four days old in the First Church of Billerica. There her name—Elizabeth Palmer Peabody—was duly entered in the church records on May 20, 1804.

That year the town of Billerica itself was alive with new hopes. Thirty miles inland of the great port towns of Boston and Salem, Billerica was embarked on what then seemed a steady progress from farm village to commercial center. Billerica lacked the settled aristocracy of nearby Andover, and the Peabodys might well have worried about how they would find enough "young ladies" to fill Eliza's school. But in the past ten years the town had grown in population from almost 1,200 to nearly 1,400, swelling with a new class of residents lured by novel business prospects. In 1803, the ambitious Middlesex Canal project had just been completed, and now this twenty-five-mile-long man-made waterway—the first traction canal in the nation—promised to speed farm goods and lumber from upper New England to the port of Boston, avoiding the rocky seacoast and passing straight through Billerica. Then, shortly after the Peabodys arrived, the Middlesex Turnpike received its charter; early plans called for this first direct wagon and stage route from the north to pass through the center of Billerica on its way to Cambridge, attracting business to the town along with the new canal. Billerica, indeed all of New England, was beginning to feel that prosperity had arrived with the new century to chase away memories of the war and its chaotic aftermath.

The first year of Elizabeth's infancy followed the steady rhythm of her mother's teaching: six-hour schooldays, five days a week, except for half days on Fridays, interrupted by three-week recesses every quarter throughout the year. And soon another maternal rhythm resumed: early in 1806, Eliza was pregnant again. But it was to be a brief season of optimism for the family, and for the town. As Eliza planned for the arrival of a second child, she was forced to acknowledge that Billerica's rosy prospects had dimmed. In three years of operation, the Middlesex Canal had failed to draw sufficient business to turn a profit, and its sister project, the turnpike, was rerouted to the outside of town under pressure from a group of wealthy Billerica landholders. The town's once mounting population began to decline, and the Peabodys joined the migration in the fall of 1806, leaving Billerica for Cambridge.

The family gave Nathaniel's medical education as the reason for relocating: he would attend lectures at Harvard's Medical Institution, as any doctor's apprentice could for the price of an admission ticket. And he would finish off his training under the supervision of the eminent Boston surgeon Dr. John Jeffries, a move designed to add luster to his résumé. Jeffries was one of just a handful of New England physicians who had trained in European universities and received medical degrees.

It was now possible to earn an M.D. at Harvard, but only after expending considerably more scholarly effort than Nathaniel Peabody could afford. He was not alone in making this choice: Harvard had awarded fewer than five M.D.s since first offering them in 1788. Fewer than fifty men had earned Harvard's basic bachelor's degree in medicine, offered since the institution's founding in 1782 and requiring the completion of a two-year course of lectures (actually just one yearlong course that was meant to be repeated). It was a time when medical training was only minimally regulated, and the majority of New England's physicians called themselves doctors without the benefit of an academic degree. That Nathaniel Peabody considered it important to take the Harvard course was a sign of his ambition to serve a class of patients who valued the European-style classroom training offered at Harvard; the fact that he had no concrete plans to complete it was a sign of his increasing financial distress.

For Nathaniel was now borrowing money from his seafaring younger brother; in the months before the move to Cambridge, he made at least one trip back to the family farm in New Boston to inquire about his share in the meager profits. Once again Eliza worked through until the eighth month of her pregnancy and planned only her customary three-week recess to cover the move and the birth. This time when a second daughter was born in Cambridge, on November 16, 1806, the family was too hard-pressed to go through with the ritual of baptism.

The birth of Mary Tyler Peabody—named for Eliza's romantically adventurous older sister—was never recorded in town or church records. Eliza's state of mind while nursing her second child was anything but tranquil, and Mary was to suffer ever after from a sense of anonymity within the family: a feeling of being lost in the shuffle of moves that was soon to be exacerbated by finding herself the middle sister in a powerfully emotional trio. Mary's dark beauty, even as an infant, was striking. But her looks also set her uncomfortably apart; as she grew older, Mary sometimes felt as if she were no more than an attractive face and form, with a hidden self that went unrecognized by those who should have known her best.

The Peabodys may never have intended to settle permanently in Cambridge. But once again they had selected a community that was at the peak of a boom, and they would stay just long enough to see it go bust. Their house stood at the easternmost edge of town near the new bridge in Cambridgeport, "in a pleasant but retired spot," as Eliza wrote to one prospective student. For Nathaniel Peabody, the location midway between Dr. Jeffries's examining rooms in Boston and the medical school at Harvard couldn't have been more convenient. But the spot was too retired to support a successful school.

The new bridge, known as the West Boston Bridge, had opened for travel in 1793, becoming only the second to span the Charles River since the smaller Great Bridge was built three miles upriver near Harvard College more than a century before. The West Boston Bridge was the first to reach the commercial center of Boston directly, and speculators quickly bought up the marshland on the Cambridge side, drained it, and laid it out in commercial lots, certain that business would spill across the river. But by 1800 scarcely any lots had sold. Eager to make good on their investment, the speculators in Cambridgeport became the chief backers of the Middlesex Turnpike project (the road that was to have enriched Billerica), hoping to bring goods from as far north as New Hampshire down to market near the new bridge, bypassing Harvard and the old town center entirely; in 1805 a port of delivery was established on the banks of the Charles River adjacent to the bridge, giving the new section of town its name.

When the Peabodys arrived in 1806, Cambridgeport was nothing like the Cambridge of colonial mansions, green commons, clapboard churches, and brick classroom buildings that clustered around the old town center at Harvard College. Nor was it yet the crowded workers' quarter it would become at midcentury. Old Cambridge had just voted to make Cambridgeport a separate parish—perhaps a measure of how distasteful this new commercial venture was to much of the town. But Cambridgeport's citizens had not yet raised the money to build their own meetinghouse, possibly another reason Mary's birth went unrecorded. A few of the original investors built houses in the area, including the wealthy Judge Francis Dana, father of the influential editor and poet Richard Henry Dana, who owned most of the land along the river between Harvard and the bridge. Yet Judge Dana would eventually lose most of his fortune in his Cambridgeport speculations. New England's farmers had little interest in a through route to a hypothetical market; and Yankee ship captains cared even less for a port with no goods to fill their holds.

Eliza tried hard to advertise the attractions of her new school, which opened in the winter of 1806, shortly after Mary's birth. She planned to take in only four or five students, all of them as boarders in order to help defray living costs for the family. Eliza wrote to a pair of sisters who were considering the school that although "our number of pupils will be small, of course their advantages will be much greater than in a large public school"—where, she might have added, girls were generally allowed lessons for only two hours each day after boys were dismissed. But the plan that had worked for a time in Billerica was harder to realize in Cambridge, with several well-established private girls' academies across the river in Boston to compete with. Whether because Nathaniel decided against the required repetition of the yearlong Harvard course, or because Eliza had been unable to fill her school, the Peabodys were on the move again within the year. In 1807, Eliza took over the directorship of a girls' academy in Lynn—the fledgling shoe-manufacturing town a few miles up the coast from Boston—where her husband at last began to practice medicine, without the benefit of a Harvard degree.

And then Lynn, too, proved another way station for the family. After a year, Eliza resigned her post, overwhelmed again by supervising the education of so many girls. On Elizabeth's fourth birthday, May 16, 1808, the Peabodys left Lynn for neighboring Salem, the old port town to the north, in hopes of finding a steadier clientele among the wealthy merchant class, both for Eliza's home school and for Nathaniel's medical practice. So far Eliza had been able to provide little more stability for her two daughters than she had known as a child. Running a girls' academy while raising small children was unlikely to produce the intimate family circle devoted to intellectual pursuits that she had yearned for since Friendship Hall days. Salem, with its elegant brick mansions and its sleek sailing ships, its well-stocked Athenaeum library and its many churches, beckoned—and it would hold the Peabody family for the next decade.

ॐ 7 ॐ

Salem Girlhoods

TODAY THE TOWN OF SALEM IS ALMOST INSEPARABLE FROM THE PEABODY name, with a museum and numerous local institutions named for the midnineteenth-century banker and philanthropist George Peabody, only a distant relation of Nathaniel Peabody. But in 1808, the one Peabody of significance to Eliza and Nathaniel already living in Salem was Nathaniel's younger brother John, recently made Captain John Peabody, the only one of Dr. Peabody's seven siblings to leave rural New Hampshire. The year before, John had married Elizabeth Manning of Salem (the first cousin of another Elizabeth Manning, also of Salem, who had married Captain Nathaniel Hathorne in 1801). The two wandering Peabody brothers banded together, now that they both had families of their own. Nathaniel could act as protector to his sister-in-law during the long months of John's absences at sea; John could be counted on to lend Nathaniel money on occasion, until the older brother had established his medical practice.

Eliza Peabody also wanted to raise her daughters in a more cosmopolitan town than Lynn, a mere fishing village compared to Salem, the second-largest city in New England with a population approaching 12,000. Boston, nearly three times the size of Salem, had been too daunting a city for the young family, and too painful a reminder to Eliza of her parents' failures. Salem offered a fresh start, and its small but well-established aristocracy could be expected to appreciate Eliza's intellectual talents, without inquiring too closely into her fall from grace. According to the memoirs of one Salem resident, "there was a decidedly aristocratic element in Salem society then, but ... if a candidate for its favor could show an undoubted ancestry, no question was asked as to his or her wealth. The aristocracy was purely of descent, though intellect and scholarship were always acknowledged and respected." Eliza could present herself as the granddaughter of General Joseph Palmer to any who cared to ask, and rely on her wits to carry her into the social circles she needed to enter for the sake of gathering pupils for her school. It now seemed evident that she would continue teaching indefinitely. Soon after the Peabodys arrived in town, Salem—the port that had long dominated the China and East Indies trade—began to feel the disastrous financial effects of Thomas Jefferson's Embargo Act, passed by Congress in December 1807.

If four-year-old Elizabeth Peabody had been allowed to wander along the waterfront the year her family moved to Salem, she would have come across a scene of devastation nearly as shocking as those her mother had witnessed as a little girl during the Revolution. The Embargo Act, which prohibited any ship bound for a foreign destination from leaving port in the United States, had been designed to strike back at France and Britain for an escalating series of trade restrictions that encouraged the capture of American cargo by privateers. When American captains began to resist the seizures, the result was an undeclared war at sea. But rather than force the hands of the French and the British, the 1807 Embargo Act abruptly decimated commerce in all the major ports along the Atlantic seaboard. According to one eyewitness account, by the summer of 1808, "the harbors were filled with dismantled vessels, which lay rotting at the wharves. Thousands of seamen were thrown out of employment . . . and the spirit of desolation seemed to be spreading her dark wings over the land." In Salem, virtually all of the 225-vessel merchant fleet was tied up at dock until the embargo was lifted a year later for all trade but that with Britain and France. Even then, although merchants rushed to send their ships on voyages to the Caribbean, the Baltic, and the Far East, their ships and sailors remained in serious jeopardy from French and British privateers.

Jefferson's successor, James Madison, declared war on England in 1812 in an effort to put an end to the hostilities and gain Canada in the bargain— much to the chagrin of Salem's shipowners, who had long held France accountable for the worst of the damage. Reluctantly Salem dedicated 40 of its fleet to the cause, losing 26 ships before the war ended in 1815, in a peace agreement that did not include the annexation of any Canadian lands. By then, of the 225 vessels registered in Salem at the start of the war, only 57 were left, the rest becoming the casualties of harsh economics. Salem would never regain its leadership position in foreign trade, ceding it to the deeper harbors of Boston and New York. Salem's merchant class shrank to an aristocracy that lived on past glory and interest income—and that was never able to provide more than a passing sense of security to its new doctor, Nathaniel Peabody, and his young family.

Before war was declared, the Peabodys had settled on Union Street, a mostly residential side street crowded with clapboard houses, leading down to

Crowninshield's Wharf, Salem, by George Ropes, 1806

the waterfront. The Peabodys lived near the corner of Union and Essex streets, Salem's main thoroughfare, in a brick row house connected to a new commercial block. It was in the Union Street house that young Elizabeth Peabody formed her first impressions of the world, many of which centered around her mother's schoolroom.

At ages four and five, when she was still "so very young that my fancy clothed her words" with fabulous images, Elizabeth loved to listen to her mother's tales of the more glorious moments in her family's Revolutionary past and to her classroom accounts of the British settlement of New England. As Mrs. Peabody repeatedly evoked their Pilgrim "ancestors," Elizabeth began to imagine a "procession of fair women in white robes" who were "streaming along" from their boat and onto Plymouth Rock. Elizabeth had mistaken her mother's term "ancestors" for one of her own devising, "Ann Sisters": a group of *"sisters,"* who "strangely enough were all named *Ann.*"

In her mind's eye, Elizabeth saw "these holy women kneel down in the snow under the trees of the forest, and thank God for their safety from the perils of the sea; and then go to work . . . and gather sticks to make a fire, and build shelters from the weather with the branches of trees." Her mother em-

phasized that "among those first rude buildings . . . [was] a schoolhouse where all the children were to be taught to read the Bible." So attractive was this "self-created mythology," Elizabeth recalled many years later, that she cherished her vision of the "Ann Sisters" long after she learned the correct definition of the term—and learned that there were Peabody *men* among her colonial ancestors as well. These lessons were her first on "personal freedom and independent action" for women. She would not forget them.

The "Ann Sisters" story must have seemed entirely credible to a young girl who had watched her mother establish a new school in nearly every year of her own short life. By the time Elizabeth was five years old, the Peabody household had become almost exclusively female, with Dr. Peabody an increasingly distant star in the family constellation. Every spare room in the house was filled with Eliza's "young lady" boarding students or housekeepers who worked for the family in exchange for training as teachers. For as long as Elizabeth could remember, at least one of her mother's younger unmarried sisters had lived with the family: first Catherine, the youngest Palmer sister, had stayed until her marriage to the Boston lawyer Henry Putnam in 1807; and now the beautiful but uneducated Sophia Palmer had left the Tyler farm in Vermont for Salem in hopes of finding a husband. Then there were the Peabody sisters themselves: Mary was now old enough to trail along wherever Elizabeth might lead her, and on September 21, 1809, a third sister was born, named Sophia Amelia Peabody after two of her aunts. It was little wonder that Elizabeth could believe her country had been settled by hardy, self-replicating females.

But as Elizabeth strove to take her place at the head of her own small band of sisters, tensions were inevitable. "My sister Mary was very small & very beautiful," Elizabeth once remembered in a journal, and "I constantly heard of her beauty." Elizabeth claimed not to have felt jealous—"it never entered my head that I might have been made equally beautiful"—but only to have become dissatisfied with her own appearance. "I did not like my own looks," she wrote. If she could not—or would not—allow herself to feel jealousy, she could choose not to care about her own physical attributes. Her curly hair was a particular "torment," along with the bother it took to "keep it looking nice." One morning, as her mother was brushing out tangles, Elizabeth reached for a pair of scissors in a nearby sewing basket and cut off most of her curls before her mother could stop her. Elizabeth was beginning to define herself as the sister least interested in her appearance. The scissors incident became a story she would tell with increasing pride as the years passed, as a sign of precocious asceticism and a preference for the life of the mind.

For her part, Eliza struggled to offer her daughters the maternal devotion she had never experienced. She still felt bitterly her own loss of "nearly all the advantages of that kind of parental care, which forms the heart." If she brooded over how to manage the cautious yet stern man she had chosen for a husband, she had no such ambivalence about how she meant to raise her three girls. She vowed to provide "the gentle influence of tenderness & encouragement" she had missed in her own childhood, and often she succeeded. Already she had inspired her oldest daughter with a vivid image of female enterprise. "Any other mother I have ever known," Elizabeth once wrote, "would have been a calamity" for the headstrong child she became.

But inevitably there were mistakes. Eliza tried to teach Elizabeth to read at the same early age that she herself had learned, giving her a seat in her classroom at age four. Elizabeth was slow at first and began to sense that her mother thought of her as "a dull little girl." The situation worsened when Eliza invited a bright young neighbor child, Ebe Hathorne—a notorious "bookworm," whose reclusive widowed mother frequently kept her out of school—to read two hours each day with Elizabeth and spur her on. The experiment backfired. Elizabeth only became further discouraged as she compared her own limited abilities to the "astonishing learning" of Ebe, a girl two years older than herself. So fixed was she in her "youthful admiration" of Ebe, that she took little note of Ebe's younger brother Nathaniel, just her own age.

Elizabeth would later recall only once catching sight from a rear window of the sturdy-shouldered boy with a "head of clustering locks," playing below in the adjoining yard. Within two years, the Peabodys had moved to another neighborhood, and the two families lost contact.

A second painful incident in the schoolroom was to stay with Elizabeth much longer, driving a wedge between her and her mother. After classes one day, an older student took Elizabeth on her lap, "caressing me, and calling me sweet, beautiful, darling, etc., when all at once she seized me into a closer embrace and exclaimed . . . Who made you?" Elizabeth did not understand that her questioner was simply rehearsing a standard Sunday school quiz, to which the correct answer was "God made me." Instead she searched her imagination and "a Face arose," she later recalled, "close to me, and looking upon me with the most benignant smile." Elizabeth answered: "A man."

The older child was horrified and pushed Elizabeth from her lap, unaware that the little girl was innocently describing her private vision of a benign God rather than speaking scandalously of her own conception. Elizabeth ran to her mother for comfort, only to have Eliza take her student's side and give her daughter a lecture in Calvinist theology. "I came out of it with another image of God in my mind," Elizabeth recalled. This one was of an "old man, sitting away up on the clouds, dressed in a black silk gown and cocked hat, the costume of our old Puritan minister . . . spying round among the children to see who was doing wrong, in order to punish offenders."

Eliza might have preferred not to answer Elizabeth so severely. Indeed, within a few years, Eliza would publish her first textbook—*Sabbath Lessons*—in which she aimed to combat the tendency of "young people . . . to attach an idea of gloom to every thing of a religious cast." But Eliza had not yet begun to question the orthodox Calvinism she'd learned as a lonely teenager in Framingham's First Parish Church. On this occasion, she felt the need to impress her sorely needed pupil with a properly orthodox account of divine creation. The hard, hidden lesson here was not actually theological; rather it was that Elizabeth had to share her mother with the students who crowded the house virtually twenty-four hours a day. Already aware that her mother had found her a disappointing student, Elizabeth's "confidence in my own mind was shaken." It was not just the "benignant smile" of her imaginary God that was crowded out by her mother's failure of sympathy, but also the Ann Sisters in their streaming white gowns. Elizabeth was more on her own, now, than she wanted to be.

Despite her wish to attend to her daughters more closely than her own mother had, Eliza was forced to adopt her mother's practice of sending her children to live with relatives for long stretches of time when finances were tight, or when childbirth or illness in the family meant that she could not adequately care for them. At least six-year-old Elizabeth, the first to be sent away, was lucky in her mother's choice of a surrogate parent. For most of a year, she lived with her widowed great-aunt Elizabeth Palmer Cranch, enjoying a quiet household where she was finally left to read as she pleased. She became fond of her aged aunt, the same woman who had taught her mother to read forty years before in a sunny upstairs room in Friendship Hall. Soon Elizabeth was picking up any book she could find, chiefly children's fables that she read over and over again.

Elizabeth returned home as much a bookworm as Ebe Hathorne. She rejoined her mother's schoolroom, where she began to show an astonishing capacity to absorb information with a nearly photographic memory, as well as a propensity for philosophical and religious dispute. She was readying herself to take on her mother in the very spiritual matters that had driven them apart. What may have begun as a means of paying her mother back for her yearlong banishment would turn into a lifelong passion for Elizabeth as she found herself drawn to the hotly contested issues of Christian theology that were at the center of intellectual life at the time.

Debates about God's nature—whether benign or vengeful, unitary or trinitary—were raging in New England, and with a particular vehemence in Salem. Whole families, including the Palmers and Peabodys of Eliza and Nathaniel's generation, were split apart by the controversy, which ultimately led to the separation of New England's town churches into liberal Unitarian and orthodox Congregational. New to the city, the Peabodys had the infant Sophia baptized in Salem's South Church, whose minister, Daniel Hopkins, was the sole graduate of Yale's orthodox divinity school in a town dominated by a proto-Unitarian Harvard-trained pastorate. This was the religion of Eliza's mother, Betsey Hunt Palmer, and the Hunt women of Watertown—the religion Eliza had grown up with and never yet questioned.

Soon, however, the Peabodys began to attend Salem's North Church, a congregation made up of families aspiring to mainstream prosperity, and led by the moderate Thomas Barnard. There, shortly after Elizabeth returned home from her great-aunt's house in August 1811, she heard a guest minister preach: the Reverend William Ellery Channing of Boston. Ironically, it was her mother who insisted that seven-year-old Elizabeth come along. Having heard that Channing was a brilliant preacher, Eliza decided to test his ability to affect a young child. Elizabeth would always remember her mother saying to her father, as they set off for North Church that morning with Elizabeth in tow, "It takes genius to reach children."

Elizabeth never forgot, either, her first sight of the small, pale man who arrived "dressed in a traveller's great-coat," strode immediately to the pulpit, and, "lifting up his large, remarkable eyes, with the expression of *seeing something*,"

The Reverend William Ellery Channing, by Washington Allston, 1811

began to recite a prayer. Elizabeth was "thrilled as never before" by the spectacle of a man "communing with God, face to face." Watching Channing, Elizabeth was reminded of the forbidden image she had conjured up all on her own of a benign deity who could be visualized and almost touched. Here was hope that her mother's version of a stern, punishing God might not be the only choice.

The thirty-one-year-old Boston minister, just eight years into his career, had not yet openly declared himself a Unitarian, and there is no transcript of this Salem sermon. But Channing was already preaching an unorthodox gospel that was swelling the pews of the once languishing Federal Street Church with a new breed of New Englander eager for a more personal religion based on divine forgiveness and spiritual inquiry rather than on arbitrary

authority. A year before, Channing had told his Boston congregation that "perfection" was man's proper goal, an end toward which all could strive. It was a
radical statement, directly rebutting the orthodox Calvinist notion that all humanity was born "depraved" and that "grace" was meted out to a handful of
the "elect" by a spiteful God. "Do you ask in what this perfection consists?"
Channing had persisted. "I answer in *knowledge,* in *love,* and in *activity.*" No
one could have stated more concisely the aims that would propel Elizabeth
into adulthood.

Sophia Peabody may have been baptized in an orthodox church, but there
was nothing conventional about her, even as a baby. By all accounts, Sophia
was born with a "rebellious spirit" and soon grew into a "very wilful, obstinate
child." From the start, Eliza's attachment to Sophia was fiercely protective as
she refused to discipline her youngest daughter overtly. Eliza sympathized
with Sophia's independent streak, recognizing something of herself in the
child, and she was determined to rule her with "the gentle influence of tenderness & encouragement," rather than with the beatings her own mother had resorted to out of anger and frustration. In the end, she found subtler ways to
bend Sophia's will to her own, for much as she might sympathize with
Sophia, Eliza could not, in a household devoted to the education of young
ladies, afford to give her free rein.

As Eliza wrote to Sophia many years later, when the country-bred
Nathaniel and even her younger Palmer sisters had urged punishment, "I
firmly resisted all coercion in your bringing up. When you shreiked, I soothed
& comforted till your affectionate heart melted and to save me from suffering,
you made an effort to subdue the rebellious spirit within." Eventually, Sophia
herself recalled, all her mother needed to do was whisper the cautionary
words "my love" in her ear to end a tantrum: they communicated her mother's
"sorrow for any thing amiss," and "very early I perceived that the influence of
that silent regret was far more powerful with me than any rebuke from any
other person." The emotions of mother and daughter became deeply intertwined; Sophia grew up to feel "my soul is knit to hers." It was a mutual dependence that Sophia would break only with great difficulty.

As early as Sophia's infancy, Eliza concluded that the girl's passionate
nature was the result of extreme sensitivity—what she called the "delicacy" of
Sophia's "organization"—rather than simple "bad temper," as her Palmer relatives would have it. Sophia herself became convinced of this appraisal, writing in adulthood that "ever since I saw the light [I have been] an instrument
out of which the greatest amount of pain or joy might be extracted." But
Sophia's delicacy may not have been constitutional; well before she was a year
old, Eliza and Nathaniel had unwittingly done their best to ruin their

youngest daughter's health when they tried to cure her of what they believed was a dangerous bout with teething.

Throughout the nineteenth century, indeed until recently, a profusion of early childhood illnesses were attributed to teething. Fevers, diarrhea, or chronic fretfulness such as Sophia must have been prone to, were all put down to "difficult dentition." The elegant phrase masked a real fear. Because teething was thought to be the source of so many ailments, it was often listed in New England town records as a cause of infant death, and infant mortality was alarmingly high. In some parts of the Northeast, it was estimated that as many as one in four children died before age one, and according to one American doctor practicing early in the century, as many as one in six of these deaths was the result of teething or its complications.

As a result, the full weight of the heroic system of medicine, so called because of its advocacy of extreme measures, such as bloodletting and blistering, as well as high dosages of medication, was brought to bear on a teething infant, frequently causing greater harm than the "disease" itself. Many fatal fevers ascribed to teething were likely the result of infections brought on by lancing inflamed gums, a procedure usually carried out by parents at home with unsterile kitchen knives. Sophia may not have been subjected to lancing, but when her parents decided to medicate her for the irritability that must have been disrupting the Peabody household, she was treated with a more insidious "cure": regular heroic doses of mercury in solutions made from calomel powder.

Ironically, it may have been Dr. Peabody's medical training that consigned his third daughter to a lifelong struggle with illness. During the early years of his practice, the Harvard-trained Nathaniel Peabody was firmly on the side of the heroic medical establishment; in 1811, the year Sophia turned two, he was granted membership in the elite Massachusetts Medical Society, presumably because of his training under Dr. Jeffries, as well as his completion of five years of practice on his own. Dr. Peabody was well versed in the standard treatment of teething and its presumed complications with "purges" or emetics, based on the theory that ridding the body of fluids gave the disease less to feed on. But even popular child-rearing manuals, such as one written by Eliza's older sister, Mary Palmer Tyler, in 1810, endorsed the twofold attack of lancing and purging in cases where extreme irritability, high fever, or other symptoms seemed to require swift intervention.

Calomel, the strongest of the purges available, was Dr. Peabody's choice in treating Sophia's illness. Commonly, children were dosed with calomel until they began to salivate, now known to be a sign of acute mercury poisoning. Their tongues swelled to several times their normal size as saliva drained from their mouths. Some infants died from dehydration after treatment with calomel, although parents and physicians never suspected medication as the culprit. Children who recovered were sometimes doomed to lives of recurrent "trembling, anxiety, weakness, rheumaticlike pains, chills, restlessness, delirium, and a host of varied debilities," the result of the drug's attack on the central nervous system. But none of these ill effects were linked to mercury by the medical establishment—or by Sophia's family—until midcentury.

Attending to Sophia became so complex and fraught that Eliza was forced to give up her school for most of a year, making finances even tighter in the Peabody household (this was the year Elizabeth spent with her great-aunt). And in the end, Sophia emerged from the treatment as excitable as ever and prone to nervous exhaustion. (It is now known that mercury lodges permanently in many organ systems in the body, with neurotoxic effects ranging from motor tremors and seizures to chronic fatigue, personality changes, and psychoses.) Never one to insist that her daughters master household skills, Eliza exempted Sophia from domestic chores as she grew older, and even from regular attendance in the schoolroom. A pattern was set that would permit Sophia to use illness or fatigue as an escape, even as her high-pitched emotions served as a vicarious release for her overburdened mother and more dutiful older sisters.

Yet despite such special dispensations—or perhaps because of them— Sophia continued to struggle against restrictions wherever she met them. Sometime before her sixth birthday, probably after the birth of one of her three younger brothers, born between 1811 and 1815, Sophia was sent to her grandmother Betsey Hunt Palmer's dressmaking establishment in Watertown for an extended stay. The arranged visit, a mark of how desperate finances had become in Salem, turned out to be nothing like the blissful interlude Elizabeth spent with her great-aunt Elizabeth Cranch.

By contrast, Grandmother Palmer was a "severe disciplinarian," Sophia wrote many years later, who sent her to bed alone in a dark attic room each night at 6:00. Worse still was her grandmother's "unenlightened religious zeal," which combined with a passion for fancy dress to torment Sophia on Sunday mornings. Betsey Palmer evidently viewed the visit from her little granddaughter as an opportunity to advertise her skills as a seamstress. On Sundays in Watertown, Sophia was "elaborately dressed in very tight frocks" by her grandmother, then marched off to the orthodox church and made to sit still through the "infinite weariness" of the sermon. Finally she was led away to Sunday school "with other unfortunate babies [to be] tortured with catechism, not a word of which I understood."

Her grandmother's insistence on finery caused further misery when Sophia was dressed up for presentation at a party. "Oh shall I ever forget the torture of the little satin boots and of the pantalettes, to which I was doomed?" she

wrote in her memoir. They produced in her "a general sensation of utter dis-
comfort and bondage," and after being introduced to the women of Watertown, who passed her around "like a toy," Sophia escaped to her room, where
she untied the "cruel strings that fastened the pantalettes" to reveal "a bright
scarlet line round my wretched little ankles, where the strings had cut into the
tender flesh." Happily unfettered, Sophia returned to the party barelegged,
where one of her aunts "swooped" down on her "like a broad winged vulture
on a most innocent dove" and sent her off to bed in the middle of the afternoon for her disobedience.

In the Watertown household, when beyond the reach of her strict aunts
and grandmother, Sophia faced outright bullying at the hands of her older
and rougher Hunt cousins. "My sensitiveness doubtless incited them to ingen-
ious devices to mortify and frighten me," Sophia later wrote. Annoyed that the
young girl seemed to expect special treatment, the older children played tricks
on Sophia, once promising to show her a beautiful garden and then shoving
her through a cellar door and locking her in. On another occasion, they led
her into a courtyard full of turkeys and drove them toward her, "gobbling like
so many fiends," Sophia recalled.

Sophia's instinctive rejection of the fashion-conscious Hunts must have
masked the embarrassment and fear she felt at joining the household of her
widowed grandmother in the heart of working-class Watertown. The entire
Peabody household was devoted to teaching young women the refinements
they would need to marry well or to become teachers in order that they might
never need to work as "mantuamakers," the derogatory term for dressmakers
Eliza often used. The religious orthodoxy and hoydenish attention to clothes
Sophia witnessed in her grandmother and aunts represented the downward
mobility of the Hunt-Palmers in contrast to the spartan intellectuality of the
upward-striving Peabodys. In Watertown, Sophia sensed the thin line that separated her own genteel poverty from her grandmother's gaudy squalor. And
Sophia must have made it plain to her mother how much she had suffered in
exile, for this extended stay away from home was her last until she was grown.

Yet even at home in Salem such fears were never far off. In her memoir,
Sophia wrote of a day when she wandered up the street on what she called
her "first independent stroll . . . out of the garden gate at home." In truth, the
still rebellious child had run away. "It was glorious," she remembered. "My
steps were winged, and there seemed more room on every side than I had
heretofore supposed the world contained. The sense of freedom from all
shackles was intoxicating—I had on no hat, no walking dress—no gloves—."
What put an end to her delicious disobedience this time, however, was not a
family member, but a street urchin, a little girl of about Sophia's own age.
Sophia had climbed a steep hillside until she felt she "stood on the top of the

earth," when she was accosted by a "beggar girl, the first ragged, begrimed human being I had ever seen." The girl grabbed Sophia's hand and ordered her to curtsy. Sophia refused and ran back home, frightened, but unable to tell her mother because she couldn't admit that she had run off in the first place. For a time after that, the beggar girl seemed to haunt her, passing the Peabody house while Sophia was standing in the doorway, muttering threats, promising to return and kidnap or "maul" her.

Was Sophia preoccupied by fears that attached themselves to her hobgoblin double? Sophia seemed not to mind being poor—up to a point. She was just as happy in her plain dresses as in the finery her grandmother concocted. But the prospect of being on the absolute bottom of the heap, forced to curtsy to a beggar girl, terrified her. It was a fine thing to run away once, but what if there had been no home to run from at all? Yet Sophia seems also to have been fascinated by the girl, perhaps as an embodiment of the rebellious self she and her mother had collaborated in repressing: a grimy, poorly dressed child who nonetheless was free to go where she pleased, order other children around, and answer to no one but herself. The power this penniless beggar held over Sophia was both frightening and enviable. Was the only way to achieve such power to give up all trappings of upper-class femininity?

Even as a young child, Sophia well knew that certain symbols of social status were necessary in order to maintain the illusion that the Peabodys were not about to fall even from genteel poverty. A little girl running about town without hat and gloves could easily be seen by the rest of Salem as a little girl who simply didn't have them. Yet Sophia never lost her inborn willfulness, the rebellious spirit that experienced tight frocks as "bondage" and hats and gloves as "shackles." As she grew older, if she was not going to be a runaway, where else but in an invalid's day bed could she avoid such restraints?

Sophia's delicacy may have emerged as a means of securing the marks of feminine gentility she benefited from—the luxury to indulge in high sentiment; the leisure to read, write letters, and, later, to paint—without entirely giving in to convention. Illness "controlled her without making her feel that her liberty was invaded," a close relative once wrote. And Eliza, distressed as she was by Sophia's frailty, may have felt inwardly pleased to have one daughter who lived her life beyond the reach of daily cares—costly as that was to the rest of the family. Yet illness would turn out to be its own kind of prison.

In the Peabody household, filled with girls and young women, Mary, the middle sister, learned to play the fugitive. While Sophia was becoming the family's "hot-house plant" and Elizabeth the shining star of the classroom, Mary used the excuse of her own "delicate nerves" to run "in and out of the school-room at my own sweet will" and to "dwell more in trees and skies"

Benjamin Pickman

than in the cramped quarters of home. Like Sophia, Mary was a sickly child, and she too was dosed with calomel and kept "in a state of salivation a great deal of the time," she wrote in a memoir of her childhood. But she found a better means of escape than illness in her rambles through the woods on the outskirts of town. And when the growing family moved away from Salem's waterfront to rented rooms in a large brick house on the corner of Essex and Cambridge streets, she also found a benefactor who made her outdoor existence possible.

The elderly Benjamin Pickman, a new neighbor of the Peabodys in a more fashionable section of Essex Street, was the patriarch of one of Salem's foremost mercantile families. He was also a Tory who had spent the Revolutionary War years in London, a fact that was not held against him on his return by Salem's Anglophile aristocracy. Ordinarily, because of differences in station and politics, the Peabodys and the Pickmans would never have become acquainted. But Benjamin Pickman's brilliant and best-loved son, Thomas, was a doctor who must have befriended Dr. Peabody. Not long after the Peabodys' arrival in Salem, Dr. Pickman was spending enough time in the Peabody household to develop a romantic interest in Eliza's younger sister Sophia Palmer, who had joined the family since the move to Salem. Somewhat to the Peabodys' amazement, the two were married in 1815. Sophia Palmer, after all, was the sister Eliza knew to be Royall Tyler's child, the girl who had been so neglected in her youth that she had had difficulty learning to talk. Her inferior education still showed in her preference for playing cards over reading books. Yet she managed to marry into Salem's monied elite. Then, once ensconced in her own Salem mansion, Sophia Palmer Pickman seems to have done her best to avoid the company of her older sister's family.

Well before that marriage took place, however, old Benjamin Pickman had taken a fancy to "little Mary P.," as he called her. Mary lacked the verbal precocity with which Elizabeth was already beginning to dazzle her elders, but she shared Benjamin Pickman's love of flowers, and her childish beauty was undeniable. Over seventy years old and comfortably retired, Benjamin Pickman had the time for Mary that no one could give her at home. She recalled that from the age of four, she spent parts of "almost every day for many years . . . in [his] arms, and by [his] side." In good weather, the two would stroll through his extensive flower gardens, with the elderly gentleman pausing to pluck a sprig and explain its name and method of cultivation. Benjamin Pickman's own diary records that beginning in 1812, when she was five years old, until his death in 1819, Mary was a frequent visitor at dinner in his Salem mansion or on his four-hundred-acre farm on the south side of town. In winter, he often sent one of his servants down the street to the Peabody house to carry Mary back over the snowdrifts for a visit. Afterward, Mary looked back on her years of friendship with the "kind and partial" Benjamin Pickman as "the most beautiful chapter of my life."

Mary loved the Pickman farm "with its forty cows and consequent calves, [and] the model piggery where those animals were actually kept clean." There was a goose and duck pond lined with water lilies, a hillside covered with violets in the spring, and a poultry yard with "turkeys and guinea-[fowl], peacocks and parrots," all of whom became Mary's "beloved companions." Benjamin Pickman gave Mary a small plot in his formal Essex Street garden and taught her to plant and tend it. Her favorite book became one they studied together: the French botanist Bernardin St. Pierre's *Harmonies of Nature*, which envisioned the world as a paradise of plants cultivated by benign human gardeners. When she grew older, Mary spent whole summers on the Pickman estate in Andover, where Benjamin's unmarried daughter, Rawlins Pickman, took over her care. There, she once wrote, "the hills took possession of me, and I scoured the country . . . with a troop of children behind me, who had never before had courage to 'take walks,' but who under my leadership climbed hills, waded through brooks, hunted wild flowers, and went to the tops of trees and barns, risking necks in pursuit of swallows' nests."

But Mary's outdoor life barely made up for the anonymity she felt at home. While Elizabeth's precocity soon became famous in Salem, Mary recalled only that she "learned to read so early that I have no recollection of the process." Like her mother, Mary was a very young reader of Shakespeare, but she came to it by chance as she stood in a chair behind her father's, looking over his shoulder and trying to make out the words. When, during a family reading of *King Lear*, she burst out in a childish lisp—"Bwow winds and cwack your cheeks!"—she received laughter rather than encouragement. Several years later, Elizabeth was given the privilege of studying Latin with her father, a subject rarely taught to girls and so one of the few in which Nathaniel's knowledge surpassed Eliza's. Mary, just two years younger, was told that she was not strong enough to attempt such concentrated study; but, hiding her interest from Elizabeth and her parents, she carried off Elizabeth's Latin grammar as often as she could to "study it in the garret when no one knew it."

Mary simply had trouble standing up to Elizabeth's overpowering personality—everyone did. When the two girls were together, Mary became Elizabeth's "satellite," hanging back while Elizabeth talked astronomy or geography with Dr. Nathaniel Bowditch, Salem's eminent astronomer who had heard that Elizabeth was a "studious child" and invited her to look through his telescope whenever she wished; or theology with the Reverend John Emery Abbot, North Church's new minister, who offered to loan Elizabeth any book in his extensive library. Elizabeth liked to bring Mary along for company on such excursions, probably to ease her own initial shyness, but inevitably she forgot about her younger sister as she became engrossed in conversation, leaving Mary feeling abandoned and resentful.

Just as Elizabeth channeled her envy of Mary's good looks into a studied disregard for her own appearance, Mary struggled to hide her mixed feelings about Elizabeth's intellectual conquests in a show of sisterly friendship. "My existence has never been a separate one from hers since I can remember," Mary once wrote to Miss Rawlins Pickman. "Some one said once that neither E. or I were complete without the other—and that is the way I feel about it." But the truth was, Mary often sensed that Elizabeth gained more from having a satellite than Mary did from basking in Elizabeth's reflected glory. She developed the middle child's classic tendency to withdraw. Mary would not compete openly with Elizabeth for friendships, achievements, or possessions. She

View of Salem from Gallows Hill, by Alvan Fisher, 1818

would not even let Elizabeth—or anyone else—know she cared about these things. "I used to think that never to any human being would I show the inward workings of my soul," Mary once recalled, "and to wish that I had the power of disguising every emotion." She cultivated "the habit of preserving a calm exterior" even when she felt anything but calm inside. Remarkably, she managed to keep Elizabeth from meeting her Pickman friends until both girls were grown, for fear that Elizabeth might win them away from her.

Mary withdrew into a vivid imaginary world, one that provided room for feelings every bit as passionate as her sisters'. More than for either Sophia or Elizabeth, Mary's fantasies took the form of infatuations with Salem boys. From early childhood, perhaps inspired by her companionship with the courtly Benjamin Pickman, Mary "imagined" herself "the wife of the best of men." At seven, she formed what she later called a "baby passion" for an older neighbor child, Charley Pickering, "the noblest, the purest, the most delicate & refined little boy" she knew. As she watched Charley assemble and sort his collection of shells and stones, she developed a "reverence" for him as a "blue-eyed & fair haired ideal." When he went on to play a leading role in a wave of farcical student rebellions at Harvard, getting himself expelled the week before commencement for supporting his classmates' right to get drunk the night before final exams, Mary simply detached her love from that "earthly object" and waited to find another embodiment of her "ideal perfection."

Yet in truth, Mary and Elizabeth had a great deal in common. Through her teaching and with her own example, their mother inspired in all three girls "a taste and enthusiasm for genius," as Elizabeth once wrote. From an early age, they were taught that "education, the cultivation of the intellect," was the "only foundation of permanent rank" in American society. They hoped to discover and nurture talent in themselves, and to recognize and support genius in others. With Elizabeth's glimpse of the Reverend Channing in the pulpit, and Mary's attraction to men of wealth and influence, both girls were beginning to look beyond the limits of home. Indeed, they got along best out-of-doors by themselves on walks, such as their annual springtime trek to Gallows Hill to gather early snowdrops. There, on the "bare and rocky height where the poor witches were hung" over a century before, Mary later recalled, they could stand together, looking "far out upon the blue ocean," feeling the "spirit-stirring" atmosphere, each absorbed in imagining her future life.

ℭℛ 8 ℛⅅ

The Doctor and His Wife

LIFE AT HOME WAS BECOMING INCREASINGLY "CLOUDED WITH SORROWS and cares," Elizabeth later wrote, for Eliza's dominance in the household was nearly as much the result of her husband's inadequacies as of her own strengths. Even something as routine as the family's nightly prayers was an arena for tension and faultfinding. Dr. Peabody led them, but in a way that made his wife and daughters cringe: he always used the same prayer, Elizabeth complained, and as he recited it he seemed to "shrink from the sound of his own voice." *Meek* was a word that all his daughters came to apply to him. Only singing, which he did regularly in the North Church choir, seemed to draw him out of his shell. Yet Dr. Peabody could also be stubborn, prone to fits of temper if he was crossed, as Elizabeth discovered when she studied Latin with him. Although she eventually learned enough to teach the language herself, her lessons with her father were a frustration. Dr. Peabody assigned her passages to translate, then left her alone to "find out the language by grammar and dictionary, without any oral help." As a matter of principle, "he never answered a question by telling me what I wanted to know." Dr. Peabody may have decided to give Elizabeth a taste of what public schooling in rural New Hampshire had been like for him, but she had already spent several years studying under Eliza, who, Elizabeth remembered, "followed her motherly instinct" in teaching. She resented her father's impersonal, harsh discipline; she knew there was no need for it.

In contrast to her husband, Mrs. Peabody ran her classroom on a stimulating mix of dramatic readings, lively conversation, and inventive writing exercises. Her aim was to "make [her] Pupils happy, to have them delight to crowd around ... for information and for aid." She "did not *talk down*" to children "but rather drew them up to her own mental and moral level," Elizabeth re-

called. To teach geography, she had her students write imaginary letters home
from destinations of their choice after researching each location with gazet-
teers and guidebooks (maps were a rarity in turn-of-the-century American
classrooms). Her pupils read histories by the New England writer Hannah
Adams, novels by Maria Edgeworth, and political essays by Madame de Staël
with the result that, Elizabeth wrote, "the idea that women were less capable
of the highest education in literature and science, and of authorship on any
subject, truly never entered my mind." Dr. Peabody's willingness to teach Elizabeth Latin probably meant he shared his wife's views about women's intellect. But Elizabeth was not, like other girl savants of her time who went on to
become prominent intellectuals—Margaret Fuller or Catharine Beecher—the
pet pupil of a devoted father. There were benefits to the lack of paternal guidance: at least at home Elizabeth was never made to feel that intelligence conflicted with femininity, nor was she singled out as an exception among her
sex, as Beecher and Fuller were by their ambitious fathers, leaving them to
feel at odds with other girls and women.

Instead, Dr. Peabody was a preoccupied and increasingly bitter man. It
didn't help that the economy in New England, particularly in Salem, had
soured during the embargo and war years. Virtually any man without family
wealth to fall back on was in financial jeopardy. Nathaniel's younger brother
John, who had done so well at sea in the first decade of the century with his
bold "nothing venture nothing have" attitude, had suffered heavily. Now, as
the war drew to a close, Nathaniel was loaning money to John in hopes of a
handsome payback once commerce resumed. Both turned to the family farm
for shares of any profits, but there was little to spare. Then, during 1816 and
1817, Nathaniel's brother Moses and older sister Lydia suffered business failures, and both were threatened with debtors' prison. Moses and Lydia looked
to the family for aid as well. Yet, as the oldest son, Dr. Peabody indignantly refused to allow the family to pay off Moses's and Lydia's debts. Moses, he felt,
should go to jail and stay there to contemplate his errors; in Lydia's case, the
family could pay the lower cost of bail.

In the wake of the bankruptcies, Dr. Peabody worried obsessively that the
farm itself was in jeopardy and advised his youngest brother, Francis, who
now managed the property, to "look out for enemies." Dr. Peabody counseled
Francis with characteristic distrust: "No doubt there are some who would delight to see you lose your hearts blood—especially if you appear to be getting
along well." Nevertheless, to all moneymaking ventures proposed by Francis—
brick-making, investing in a spinning jenny—Dr. Peabody urged caution and
delay. "Deliberate well before you strike a stroke" was a favorite admonition,
which usually meant that nothing was accomplished.

Dr. Peabody himself was not above devising get-rich-quick schemes. Although he sometimes tried to persuade himself that "it may be for my good that I have nothing," he also believed that "rich men are the ornament & support of any country," and he wanted very much to become one. In 1817, the year Elizabeth was twelve, he opened a singing school, which he expected would yield $80 a quarter. He tried selling butter churned on the family farm at market in Salem, and he arranged to serve as an accountant for Mary's friend, the elderly Benjamin Pickman. He developed elaborate plans for a sawmill that Francis could operate on the creek that ran through the family property; from the scraps, Francis would construct small storage boxes to sell to the pharmacists whom Dr. Peabody dealt with in his medical practice. But most of his plans to pick up extra money failed: the singing school attracted too few pupils and the price of butter fluctuated too rapidly for either scheme to turn a profit. Despite numerous letters filled with design specifications for the apothecary boxes and repeated harangues—"I wonder! wonder! wonder! wonder! at you!!!!!!" he raged when he discovered that Francis had left the mill idle during one January thaw—nothing came of that project either.

The chief result of all this plotting was to undermine Dr. Peabody's credibility in his chosen profession. Recording a brief encounter with him during the summer of 1815, the great Salem diarist of the era, the Reverend William Bentley, dismissed him as "half Physician & Schoolmaster & perhaps half of something else." In more than a decade in Salem, Dr. Peabody never developed a steady clientele of healthy patients. He was, instead, the doctor of last resort, called in when the more established physicians failed to produce a cure. When the nine-year-old Nathaniel Hathorne became mysteriously lame after a slight injury during a ball game, Dr. Peabody was the third to be consulted. Beyond such cases, his earnings were tied to outbreaks of disease. In a good "sickly" month in Salem, he might collect $200, but he spent over half that on household expenses. Simply keeping his growing family supplied with flour cost $15 a month. By the spring of 1817, Dr. Peabody was writing to Francis, "I never was more put to it to collect money to purchase necessaries of life."

The arrival in the Peabody household of three sons—Nat in 1811, George Francis in 1813, and Wellington in 1815—strained the budget further and did nothing to tip the balance of power away from the women of the family toward Nathaniel. After nearly a decade in Salem, a pattern had been set, no doubt fostered by the social snobbery of the old port town. Dr. Peabody led the family prayers (however feebly), held the copyright for the textbooks his wife began to publish in 1810, and occasionally brought the household to cowering submission in one of his rages. But the entire family privately recognized Eliza, with her greater learning, more refined manners, and noble ancestors, as its highest authority. It was Eliza who declared that the Sabbath should be spent as "a day of quiet but constant enjoyment," Elizabeth recalled, "letting us paint, and cut paper, with other little amusements, devoting herself to making us happy, while the rest of the week she was busy." When Mrs. Peabody asked her children "to refuse to eat sugar because it was the fruit of slave labour," they obeyed. The oldest son, Nat, who grew up to become the family genealogist, recalled that his father had always seemed to acknowledge Eliza's superiority. Indeed, Nat considered his father so far inferior to his mother that he believed Dr. Peabody "never fully perceived . . . the length, breadth and depth of her character."

But neither Eliza nor Nathaniel was content with this state of affairs. Having chosen her husband in a time of desperation for his caution and respectability, Eliza still longed for a man with at least some of the qualities of her beloved father and grandfather: charm, literary taste, and what Eliza called "watchful tenderness." As she once wrote of her husband, Nathaniel had grown up "accustomed to see the female part of his family labour hard, dress coarsely & think themselves happy to be allowed a decent garment for holidays." Eliza could not "conquer my aversion to telling him of wants"—a new bonnet, for example, when the old one had become frayed—that she felt a husband should anticipate and offer to supply. As she grew older, Elizabeth became the one to notice her mother's needs and offer to replace the worn-out bonnet or slippers with her own money. Elizabeth also urged her mother to take short vacations to escape family pressures, but Nathaniel jealously guarded Eliza's time away from home and refused to permit visits of more than a few days to her more prosperous older sister, Mary Tyler, who had moved with her own large family to Vermont's resort town of Brattleboro. Worse still, different as he was from her father in manner, Nathaniel was not immune to the kind of depression that had crippled Joseph Pearse Palmer. As Eliza watched Moses, Francis, and her own husband suffer financial setbacks, she began to see it as a "family malady" with the Peabody men "to despond, to think they shall come to want, & cease all effort from a belief that effort is vain."

With each successive pregnancy, Eliza felt increasing despair, until at last, with the birth of Wellington in 1815, she entered "the most agonized period of my life." Under the strain of hard work, the cough that had troubled her since she kept a student boarding house in Andover grew worse; she began to treat herself with small quantities of opium, readily available in apothecary shops. The opium freed her of symptoms for twenty-four hours at a time but left her with irritable nerves and "stupyfying" headaches. By this time Dr. Peabody's temper was often at the flash point.

As Eliza saw it, Nathaniel's irritability was incurable, the result of "suspicion . . . arising from the union of families not exactly on equality in relation to mental culture." Not surprisingly, Nathaniel was acutely sensitive to any hint that he might be thought inferior, and he quickly turned defensive. Eliza tried to be understanding. "This is almost always the case," she once wrote Elizabeth, with "those who have been taken out" from "a family so uneducated as his." To keep the peace, Eliza struggled to show deference and attempted to rein in Elizabeth's criticisms, vowing, "I would rather a thousand times have my own pride & delicacy wounded than have his." She kept her own reservations to herself as best she could, even as she cultivated in her daughters a decided preference for a different sort of man.

All her children remembered Mrs. Peabody as "averse to contention" and possessing a "dread of violent emotions," but only Sophia ever recorded an outbreak of her father's "excessive violence." The incident occurred after Sophia was grown, but it was so familiar in its outlines that she could remind Mary when she wrote of it, "you know [how] he will always go through with the matter in hand when his blood is up." On this occasion, during an argument between Eliza and Nathaniel over a proposed move, witnessed by Sophia and young Nat, Dr. Peabody was "perfectly insane": "He continued to blurt out his displeasure so angrily & fiercely that finally Nat said he thought he would leave the room for the sake of putting an end to the conversation. . . . Several minutes afterwards, he was astonished to hear father going on in the same violent way, & he heard poor mother's tremulous voice making an effort to appease him. . . . When [father] is angry he forgets every body & thing & only remembers to wreak his passion till it is exhausted." Sophia concluded that her father "should not live where there is a child" in the house. Yet for many years he was surrounded by six of his own.

There was little Eliza could do to protect her children from her husband's outbursts, nor could she afford to give much of her own time to her three young boys. She paid scant attention to their early education, leaving her daughters to experiment with teaching them the basics of reading and writing and anything else they cared to attempt. She counted on Salem's public schools, which offered a far more substantial curriculum to boys than to girls, to prepare them for college, in hopes the family could one day spare the tuition. (There was no college for women in the United States for another half century.) Eliza railed against the regimentation and severity of these schools, particularly when one of her boys was sent home with bruised hands after a caning for failure to prepare his lesson, but there was no affordable alternative. She would later have cause to regret her inattention to the boys, but she could not give up her school to teach them at home, and she could not include them in her own classroom as she had her daughters. The families who sent their girls to Mrs. Peabody's school would not have welcomed an experiment in coeducation.

As an adult, Nat would come to despise the kind of broad cultural educa-

tion his mother had given his sisters at home, claiming it only created romantic notions and false hopes in young girls' minds. But as a child he formed
vivid impressions of his mother's second-floor schoolroom, with its "raised
platform in one corner ... occupied by my mother, seated at her desk." Plainly
he felt envious as he looked in on the bevy of young ladies crowding around
his mother in conversation, or sitting at their needlepoint as Mrs. Peabody
read aloud tales from Spenser, Milton, or Shakespeare. From his position at
the doorway, Nat had no way of knowing that his oldest sister, often the most
outspoken in the classroom, was locked in a struggle with her mother for intellectual freedom.

❧ 9 ❧

"Heretical Tendencies"

ALTHOUGH ELIZA HAD BEEN THE ONE TO TAKE SEVEN-YEAR-OLD ELIZA-beth along to hear the liberal-minded William Ellery Channing preach that August day in 1811, religion became a sparring ground for mother and daughter early on, and it would take many years and many quarrels for that to change. Eliza's determination to offer her oldest daughter more maternal guidance than she had known as a child meant that she was reluctant to give up control of Elizabeth's spiritual development. For Elizabeth's part, while she sided with her mother in domestic disputes, she would find herself fighting tenaciously for permission to form her own beliefs.

Mothers and their adolescent daughters have always struggled for control. But in early-nineteenth-century Salem, for the Peabodys, this struggle took on the themes of the religious controversy that caught up so many New Englanders at the time. As young progressive Harvard-trained ministers began to preach sermons questioning the fundamental tenets of Calvinist faith, the more conservative—"orthodox"—clergy and congregants dug in their heels. The points of contention were basic. Was Christ a divine being, part of a holy Trinity, set on earth to enact a drama of atonement for the sins of mankind? Or was he human, a teacher whose moral example could be followed by anyone who chose to do so? The essential nature of humanity was at issue. In the Calvinist view, children were born "depraved" and could achieve salvation as adults only after admitting their sin and seeking evidence of God's forgiveness in a conversion experience—or face eternal damnation in hell. The religious liberals held an opposite view: children were born innocent and with an innate spirituality that could be maintained and perfected over the course of a lifetime by following Christ's example. What might seem an abstract theoretical question—was there a Trinity?—had enormous practical consequences in the daily lives of believers.

Elizabeth found herself joining heated arguments with young children her own age over the same complex issues of theology that divided their parents. In particular, she remembered tussling verbally at age ten or eleven with one "remarkable little girl [who] . . . was precociously an adept in the dialectics of Calvinism." The girl maintained that no one could escape "everlasting punishment" who would not first admit to having hated God and then beg His forgiveness, the usual terms of a Calvinist conversion. Elizabeth would not budge from her own early vision of a benign, human-faced deity and "vehemently protested that I did not hate God." Just as precocious as her sparring partner, Elizabeth went on to attack the doctrine of the Trinity: Christ, she insisted, was not divine but human. Furthermore, she argued, all people had the same "freedom to be good" that Christ displayed. "Salvation was a moral growth under the universal Father's eye," she protested, not "an arbitrary gift" from a vengeful God. The two girls could not be reconciled.

But the chief battleground for Elizabeth was at home, within her own family. There the issues were not as straightforward as on the streets among the schoolchildren of Salem. The entire Peabody family was embarked on a spiritual quest. The question was, whose revisionist view would win out?

Elizabeth clearly remembered the day when Dr. Peabody brought home Noah Worcester's *Bible News of the Father, Son, and Holy Spirit*. Although she was less than ten years old when she overheard her parents discussing the Bible in light of Worcester's mildly anti-Trinitarian volume, "it gave me relief," she later wrote, to find that religion was "a subject of enquiry and dispute" and that "it was not quite a settled thing that we must believe the popular system of theology." (Worcester himself found little relief from setting down his views in print; after the publication of his book in 1810, he was forced out of his New Hampshire pulpit, never to preach again.) Next Elizabeth listened as her parents read aloud the Quaker William Penn's *Sandy Foundation Shaken*, the anti-Trinitarian tract that had landed Penn in the Tower of London over a hundred years before. By the time a family friend brought the ideas of the eighteenth-century Swedish mystic Emanuel Swedenborg into the house, Elizabeth was ready to join the debate.

Swedenborg's teachings, which had been gaining currency since 1810 when a society was formed to disseminate his works in English, had several points in common with Noah Worcester's *Bible News* and the murmurings of Unitarianism that had drifted into Salem with the Reverend Channing's 1811 sermon. Swedenborg compressed the Trinity into a unified "Godhead" and flatly rejected the doctrine of inborn depravity. Like many mothers at the time, Mrs. Peabody had long been troubled by the Calvinist dictum that children who died before they were old enough to have experienced "conversion" could never reach heaven, and she eagerly "plunged into" this new system of belief, Elizabeth recalled. Her father was sympathetic as well. But on her own, Elizabeth read further in Swedenborg's works and became "disgusted" with his fantastical visions of heaven and hell. What had captured her interest in the anti-Trinitarian cause was the historical argument for Jesus's humanity. She had no patience for religious mysticism. For a time, she tried to talk her mother out of her new views, but "in vain." Eventually Mrs. Peabody became "so excitable upon the matter," Elizabeth later wrote, that the subject of religion was "entirely dropped between us."

Coincidentally, as part of the liberal advance, a young divinity student of the Reverend Channing's became minister of Salem's North Church for a time. Channing preached at John Emery Abbot's ordination service in 1815, the year Elizabeth was eleven, and she made sure to hear him. This time Channing spoke out explicitly against Calvinist orthodoxy as an "unreasonable religion" dependent on "terror, that passion which more than any other unsettles the intellect." True religion, he told the Salem congregation, should be "addressed at once to the *understanding;* and to the *heart.*" Having earned Channing's endorsement, the Reverend Abbot immediately became the object of Elizabeth's religious inquiries. She sought him out after church on Sundays and won him over with her intense questioning. He invited her to borrow and discuss with him any books that interested her from the library he had accumulated as a divinity student at Harvard. But Abbot was an invalid, and after little more than a year, he retreated full-time to his sickbed. Elizabeth now lacked even "one friend to whom I might turn for advice." Already disappointed by her father—whose failure to be either reliably kind or effectively authoritarian must have been a disturbing reminder of the larger debate over the kind of "father" God could be—and unable to confide in her mother, Elizabeth was left feeling that she "had no pilot."

Meanwhile, Elizabeth's aunt Amelia, the Palmer sister who had left home for West Point at age seven, had surfaced in Salem, where she too opened a school. More conventionally religious than her older sister and impressed by her niece's intellectual precocity, Amelia offered Elizabeth a piano and music lessons if she would promise to read only Calvinist works and study them with the Reverend Samuel Worcester, minister of Salem's orthodox Tabernacle Church and one of Channing's staunchest opponents. Tempted by the offer of the piano, which represented a world of feminine accomplishment otherwise unattainable by the Peabodys, Elizabeth nevertheless "revolted" from her aunt's proposition, knowing that it was intended to "divide" her from Channing's and Abbot's influence. The proffered bargain worked only to "strengthen a resolution I had already made" to "examine the claims of the different sects ... and judge for myself," Elizabeth wrote in her journal.

At twelve, Elizabeth began to teach herself Hebrew in order to read the

Old Testament in its original language "and find out the *truth*." She dreamed of one day making her own "new and perfect translation of the scriptures and writing a commentary on every verse." She borrowed books from a circulating library frequented by Salem's clergy and discovered the work of the British Socinians, the most extreme supporters of the notion that Christ was human, not divine. In England, and especially in New England, even self-admitted Unitarians feared being labeled "Socinian," and so it was that it felt to Elizabeth "like taking hold of hot coals" to pick up a Socinian book. But even as her mother looked on "with horror," Elizabeth found that reading the Socinians left her "with a feeling of strength in my mind, a sense of clearness in my ideas." It had never seemed credible to her that Christ's suffering on earth was a mere "pageant" enacted by an immortal being—she wanted to believe that his martyrdom was real, and to take inspiration from his human example. Reading the Socinians, Elizabeth found what seemed to her confirmation in both historical evidence and scriptural analysis of "the literal humanity of Christ & the original freedom of man from total depravity."

Yet it was no comfort to Elizabeth to feel that "my relations were all against me" and to hear herself spoken of as "one who had '*degraded*' in my ideas." Religious discussion within the family, which had once come as a relief to Elizabeth, was now "painful" to endure. She felt "alone and unhappy" and found herself clinging to her new ideas "with desperate feeling." Opposition to her views caused her to "fly into a passion, the strength and bitterness of which shook my frame & overwhelmed me." Elizabeth's parents became "much alarmed" and ordered a stop to her studies, which Elizabeth vehemently protested. At last they struck a bargain: Elizabeth would read only the Bible for an entire summer; all commentaries, particularly Socinian ones, were banned. "At the end of the time, if I continued in my present desire I should be perfectly free," Elizabeth recalled, to read any books she wanted and to follow whatever beliefs she chose.

And so, at thirteen, Elizabeth proceeded to read the New Testament through thirty times in three months, each time in reference to a different disputed point of doctrine. The plan worked brilliantly, at least from Elizabeth's point of view. As she copied out relevant passages and compared them to one another, she became more certain than ever that "the distinctive doctrines of orthodoxy" were "corruptions" of true Christianity. And she later wrote, "the more deeply I studied, the more was I satisfied, enraptured." She felt "as if I had gone astray & come home."

That same summer, Elizabeth met a visitor to Salem who had recently joined Channing's Federal Street Church. Mrs. Davis was astonished by Elizabeth's learning, and her words of praise for the studies that Elizabeth's own family considered "heretical" reassured Elizabeth that she "had talents" that were "worth something." Mrs. Davis invited Elizabeth to visit her in Boston in the fall and to stay until she could meet Channing when he visited the house for his customary pastoral call on a new church member. Elizabeth traveled the twenty miles to Boston and stayed six weeks, listening to Channing's sermons each Sunday, unwilling to leave without the bonus of a personal encounter with her hero.

The man Elizabeth finally heard preach in his home pulpit was now, at thirty-seven, among the most prominent ministers in New England. William Ellery Channing's popularity derived from quite different qualities than those of the Calvinist revival preachers whose fire-and-brimstone conversion sermons were beginning to draw crowds across New England. As young as he was, Channing's health was said to have been broken during two years of intense study while he prepared for the ministry. Sickly, short, and slight, Channing suffered visibly in the pulpit—both physically and spiritually—in a way that drew the sympathy of his parishioners, particularly the women. Elizabeth once described his strangely seductive voice as having been "weakened and narrowed by consumptive complaints until it has no great power of expressing any thing but pathos and persuasion." The passionately cerebral Channing seemed instinctively to know how to inspire a generation of New Englanders raised on Yankee self-denial but ready for a new age of religious seeking.

Although Channing had been a brilliant student orator at Harvard, where he gave the commencement address for his graduating class at eighteen, he had nonetheless doubted his ability to lead a congregation. After completing his divinity studies, he was offered two churches in Boston and chose the smaller, shabbier Federal Street Church, where the pay was lower and the prestige considerably less, fearing he might not succeed even there. Yet his popularity soon forced the once dwindling congregation to construct a new church building to house its swelling numbers. From the start, Channing used the pulpit to share his private doubts with his parishioners, which had the paradoxical effect of shoring up both their faith and his own. In the pulpit, he was the most intimate and confiding of ministers, and he made a habit, throughout his career, of using personal experience—the baptism of his own child, the death of a beloved relative—in his sermons. Channing was the first in a line of influential American rhetoricians to recognize the power of bringing private experience into public discourse, and this may have been his greatest gift to the generation of writers that followed him: Emerson, Thoreau, Whitman, and others.

Yet Channing could be intimidating in person, if unintentionally so. Mrs. Davis brought Elizabeth to Channing's gospel discussion meetings for women of the congregation, where Elizabeth was impressed with Channing's willingness to "take the position of fellow-inquirer." More striking, however, was the sight of adult women struggling to speak their thoughts in public. Even when Channing put forward the most gently phrased questions, "the silence was appalling," Elizabeth later recalled. She was tempted to break the silence herself, "but, though I was not afraid of Dr. Channing, I was so of the silent ladies." Reminding herself that "I was a stranger and interloper, hardly thirteen years old," Elizabeth held her tongue. The image of the "silent ladies" would stay with her for many years to come, prompting a twofold ambition: to be different herself, and to help other women learn to speak their minds.

At last, the long-awaited meeting took place. "When word was brought to me that Dr. Channing was in the parlor," Elizabeth recalled, "I almost flew to the interview," at which the minister greeted her "with a gracious, beaming smile, and both hands stretched out to take mine." This time nothing kept Elizabeth from answering all of her hero's questions, most of which concerned the activities of Sunday school children in Salem. "I need not say how happy I was to be talking with him," Elizabeth wrote later. Channing seems to have been equally delighted. He went home and told his sister, "I have had a genuine pleasure and surprise to-day; a child ran into my arms and poured out her whole heart in utter confidence of my sympathy!" If Elizabeth had outlined her past several years' reading, Channing would have been even more astonished. All on her own, and by the age of thirteen, she had followed a good portion of the course of study he recommended for his graduate students in divinity at Harvard.

The two would not meet again in private for more than a decade, but Elizabeth had now gained the certainty that she could hold her own in conversation with a man of genius. She would never be satisfied simply to enjoy the ideas of the great thinkers of her day from the audience, or between the covers of a book. She must write letters, visit, talk, argue, persuade. Already by the age of thirteen, Elizabeth had achieved the confidence in her powers of thought and speech that would continue to carry her across the boundaries of propriety that held most adult women in check, both intellectually and socially. What she did not yet realize was that those boundaries were much looser for a child in the progressive circles of Salem and Boston, where a young girl who "poured out her whole heart" would be kindly received by adults eager to see proof of the innocent wisdom of childhood. As she grew older, Elizabeth would have to reckon with the fact that others began to find that same forthright manner disturbing in a young woman.

For now, however, Elizabeth returned to Salem exultant, as full of conviction about her religious views as ever. All the time she had been reading and studying the Bible, "nothing had been said at home about my heretical tendencies," Elizabeth recalled. "But this brought the matter to the carpet again." Now "my father & mother found that what they had left me inclining to . . . had become a part of my creed. They expressed strongly their dissent, but seeing I was not to be moved, they gave me full freedom to read what I pleased." Elizabeth had won.

❧ 10 ❧

"Beginning to Live"

THE YEAR 1819 WAS A TURNING POINT FOR THE PEABODYS. AFFAIRS IN the outside world combined with household crises to bring about a reformulation of the family structure. In the spring, the liberal wing of the ministry staged an event intended to transform religious debate in New England. The time was ripe for a bold statement of the new views, and William Ellery Channing was chosen for the job. In May, he traveled to Baltimore to give an ordination sermon for another Harvard protégé, Jared Sparks, in which he outlined what it meant to be a Unitarian and emphatically welcomed the term for himself. It is hard to overestimate the importance of Channing's "Baltimore Sermon." Presses worked overtime throughout the Atlantic states to publish rebuttals and rejoinders, including a virulent attack from Salem's Samuel Worcester. But the controversy only spurred the demand for copies of Channing's sermon itself, which quickly became the most widely published piece of literature in America, a place it held for over a decade. Defections to Unitarianism by clergy and congregants became rampant, leading to a historic court battle that, within the year, put an end to the Calvinist hold on Massachusetts churches.

In the Peabody household, the family relaxed its strictures against the fifteen-year-old Elizabeth. Indeed, Eliza began to see her oldest daughter as leading the way—"before the age in Salem," in Eliza's words—a view she held through the years to come. Elizabeth now asked to take charge of Sophia's spiritual education, determined that her youngest sister "never should hear of any of the terrible doctrines." Mary was already too old for such an experiment and too much Elizabeth's peer. Elizabeth's plan was to turn Sophia into an example of "a child growing up ... innocent and forever improving, with the simple creed that everything that can happen to a human being is either for enjoyment in the present or instruction for the future." Eliza gave the plan her blessing, in no small measure because her own life seemed increasingly beyond her control.

In the spring of 1819, Eliza was due to deliver her seventh child. Some premonition of disaster caused Eliza to write a letter of advice to Elizabeth, who was visiting the Davis family in Boston again, listening to Channing preach. Eliza was now past forty, and it had been four years since her youngest child, Wellington, was born. She considered the outcome of this birth "doubtful," and feared that she would not survive. Characteristically, she cautioned her opinionated oldest daughter to be more guarded in expressing herself outside the family circle and recalled the hurtful blows that she had been dealt by Elizabeth Smith Peabody, her guardian from Atkinson days. Even when facing the possibility of death, it was her daughter's difficulty in maintaining proper feminine decorum—a difficulty Eliza well understood—that concerned her most.

But instead of Eliza it was the new infant, Catharine, who died. Born on April 26, 1819, Catharine Putnam Peabody lived only seven weeks, to die of lung fever in mid-June. And it was Sophia, not Elizabeth or even Mary, who witnessed the death and then bore her mother's grief that summer. Elizabeth had stayed on in Boston, and Mary was spending the summer on her aunt Mary Tyler's farm in Brattleboro. When Mary returned to Salem that fall, she discovered "a tall little girl sitting in the doorway dressed in mourning calico . . . so altered that I did not know her." It was the ten-year-old Sophia, whose customary good cheer was replaced by a "weary & worn expression . . . and from that time [she] was an embodied headache." This summer marked the first appearance of the migraines that would torment Sophia for the next two decades, causing her increasingly to seek refuge in the sickroom.

Perhaps it was during this same summer of 1819, when Elizabeth and Mary were away from home, that Eliza began to treat Sophia's headaches with the opiates she herself was using. Opium was freely available without prescription in pills, powders, and alcohol-based elixirs, such as the commonly dispensed ruby-colored laudanum. Although its effects were milder than those of pure morphine, which later in the century would be extracted from opium to be injected by hypodermic, opium was still addictive. Like mercury, it caused more problems in Sophia than it cured. Many years later she recalled having taken the drug "in my young girlhood . . . to stop my headaches," and by her late twenties she was using it daily. Still the headaches came, perhaps as a *result* of her opium use, for as one writer on nineteenth-century opium addiction has noted, it was impossible to tell which symptoms were brought on by the opium dose itself and which emerged as the drug wore off.

Early in the century, few Americans understood opium's addictive properties or linked the nightmare visions, severe headaches, and hypersensitivity to

light and sound that were its side effects with the miracle drug that could replace pain of all sorts with a calm euphoria—if only one used it steadily. Even
after Thomas De Quincey's sensational *Confessions of an English Opium Eater*
appeared in 1821, describing the pleasures and pains of opium addiction—as
well as the excruciating stomach cramps, fevers, and insomnia that accompanied withdrawal—English and American physicians continued to administer
the drug. To both doctors and their patients, opium seemed more attractive
than the old "heroic" cures: emetics, blisters, and bloodletting. Addiction was
presumed to be rare, the result of taking opium for pleasure rather than to al-
leviate pain. By the 1830s opium was the most widely prescribed drug in
America. With a doctor for a father, Sophia grew up with opium as a household staple.

Illness had joined Sophia and her mother from earliest infancy. Perhaps
the headaches that began to plague Sophia after Catharine's death allowed
Eliza to care for another daughter in place of the lost baby. The opportunity
to nurse Sophia might also have helped ease the guilt that so often tormented
women after the death of a child. Even as she had welcomed the more forgiving theology of Swedenborg and now the Unitarians, Eliza had been reared
on the Calvinism that taught a mother that a young child's death was punishment for her own sins. Eliza's inward struggle to accept the hardships of her
marriage often seemed to her a battle with sinful egotism. If God were punishing her in this way now, why would He stop after taking just one child? Although Sophia's illness at this time amounted chiefly to migraines, in Eliza's
accounts of her daughter's suffering there was always a note of fear that the
girl was in danger and might not survive. Sophia quickly learned to give her
ailments the same serious scrutiny that her mother did.

And when Mary returned home in the fall, she too began to suffer—not so
much from physical ailments as from a loss of spirit, perhaps brought on by
the dark mood in the household, or by the recent death of her elderly benefactor, Benjamin Pickman, in May 1819. She could no longer escape to his farm
and gardens, or walk by his side. And her second-best friend in the Pickman
household, Miss Rawlins, was now preoccupied with another Mary, little
"Mary Top," the Peabody sisters' three-year-old cousin, Mary Toppan Pickman,
who had moved with her mother, Aunt Sophia Palmer Pickman, into the Pickmans' Essex Street mansion after her father's sudden death in 1817. Mary
would not complain, but Miss Rawlins remarked on her "change of character
from extreme talkativeness to reserve." And Sophia noticed, as she wrote to
Mary many years later, that "a shadow fell upon your gayety . . . you gradually
became paler & dimmer."

In an effort to economize, the Peabodys were on the move again, first to a
smaller but "pleasant" house on Court Street, and then to what Mary de-

scribed as "a brick tenement in Essex Street that stood behind a shop." It was "a dark, dismal abode where I came to a sense of many privations and much sorrow." Dr. Peabody had been taking in several hundred dollars less each year from doctoring and was desperately seeking other sources of income. Most recently, he had persuaded the town school board, of which he was a volunteer member, to pay him for the time he spent supervising the building of a new grammar school. Possibly Dr. Peabody's temper was raging again, for in September 1819 Mrs. Peabody took special note in her diary of a sermon she'd heard on "the indulgence of unbridled temper" within marriage. "The husband," she quoted the minister, "then becomes the *scourge*, the *tyrant*, not the ruler of the house. . . . If sometimes a truce is made and open hostilities cease for a time, it is only to gather fresh strength for increased rankour and malignity."

Elizabeth responded to the mounting family tensions by entering an "excited state of sensibility" provoked by her idol, Channing's, return to Salem in October 1819, this time to preach the funeral sermon for the young Reverend Abbot. Elizabeth had lost Abbot as a spiritual adviser several years earlier when he had become bedridden through illness, but his death marked the end of Elizabeth's hope that Salem might ever become an intellectual haven. She looked increasingly toward Boston as the source of her ideas as she rushed to prepare herself for the profession she must soon enter. Teaching was to be the end result for all the Peabody sisters of the years of study and observation of their mother and aunts in their Salem schools. As family finances shrank, the need for Elizabeth to begin work became an imperative. But she was eager for the task. Propelled since early childhood by her "self-created mythology" of the Ann Sisters, and remembering vividly her own "suffering from want of clear ideas," Elizabeth looked forward to the opportunity to "bring forward the minds of the young." If she was just barely old enough to begin teaching, she was also young enough to remember what she had longed for in a teacher.

In the spring of 1820, Elizabeth was once again staying in Boston with friends who belonged to Channing's congregation, ready to call on her "vast deal of *impudence*" to approach the great man and draw him into conversation. While in the city she also engineered a meeting with the sixty-five-year-old Hannah Adams, author of the texts on American history that most New England schoolchildren, including Elizabeth herself, had been raised on. At the time, Adams was the most celebrated woman writer in Boston, the first woman in America to earn a living by her pen. To Elizabeth, however, in her present mood of high confidence, the formidably accomplished Miss Adams seemed no more than a "poor lady," and the fifteen-year-old girl recalled the meeting "without much pleasure."

But even as her excitable emotions and growing ambitions seemed ready to carry Elizabeth spinning out of Salem's orbit, she recognized that the loss of the fourth and youngest Peabody sister had been "a common calamity" for the three surviving daughters. It was during this period of mourning, depression, and, for Elizabeth, a sort of frenzied activity, that "we three were first drawn together," she later recalled. She took seriously her charge to supervise Sophia's religious instruction, and when away from home sent long letters full of reading lists and study schedules. From this time on, the three sisters were in many ways on their own.

There were still good times in Salem, but they were mainly manufactured by the girls themselves. They led their younger brothers on excursions around the town's stately common, where one day tiny Wellington vowed to be rich enough to own all the houses surrounding the green. And on pleasant Sunday afternoons, they walked up Paradise Hill, the nearest open land, to gather wildflowers and watch the ships in the harbor. Elizabeth had befriended several of the more intellectual young women in town—the three daughters of a Quaker family, the Chases; and Mary and Elizabeth White, the daughters of a Salem widower, Judge Daniel Appleton White. The girls formed a group they called the Social Circle to read and discuss one anothers' writing. Thirteen-year-old Mary was too young to contribute, but she tagged along and later recorded the system the group instituted in order to encourage participation and avoid hurt feelings when criticism was offered. "All the members used to put their hands, on entering, into a box," she wrote, "and either deposit or pretend to deposit an original article, poetry, story, review of a book." Then one member read out the pieces anonymously, and the group debated each work's merits. The best pieces were copied over into one large volume. Whether the girls knew it then or not, it was the kind of literary club that women were forming throughout the young Republic, one that offered a private audience to support the fledgling ambitions of writers like Harriet Beecher Stowe.

Elizabeth's first written efforts were, like her mother's, poetry. But she soon began to favor essays, which could lead the group into the kind of intellectual dispute she enjoyed. She introduced books of theology or philosophy for discussion, often writing abstracts of the more esoteric volumes, which the other girls found easier to read than the originals. Above all, she delighted in drawing out and challenging her friends' views. She would not countenance ideas expressed by members of the Social Circle simply "because they have heard [them] from their parents or instructors." During one series of meetings she presented her own critiques of works by Martin Luther and William Penn, whom she had read during her years of solitary study. "Both these men I venerate," she wrote, "not for their speculative opinions, for I do not agree with either, but for their principles of enquiry which are also mine." Based on her own experience, she had come to believe that "every person who has talents, time and opportunity should not rest contentedly with any creed however simple till they have fully discussed every article of it," as she wrote to one of the Chase sisters in continuation of an argument begun in the Social Circle. "To sit still and pray for light is farcical when we have opportunity to search," she insisted.

But the Social Circle would soon have to do without Elizabeth's hectoring. Her father's tenuous finances had at last forced him to look for a more likely place to make a living than Salem. By December 1820, Dr. Peabody's only steady job was as physician to the local almshouse, a position reserved in most towns for novices. He thought of opening an apothecary shop, but "the time has gone by for making great profits," Dr. Peabody wrote his brother Francis. "All sorts of business is crowded," he explained, "and underselling has got to be such a trade, that many sell themselves out of property & their creditors are obliged to whistle for their dues." It wasn't entirely Dr. Peabody's fault that his medical practice had failed. All across New England, there were more skilled professionals than there was work to be done.

Young doctors, lawyers, and ministers were leaving Massachusetts in search of greater opportunity in the west—Ohio and Kentucky. But Dr. Peabody was no longer young. His family was too large to move a great distance, and too rooted in New England. He considered returning to New Hampshire, where the town physician in New Boston had recently left a vacancy, but he could not make up his mind. Then he began to hear about the inland Massachusetts town of Lancaster, a small village forty miles to the west along the banks of the Nashua River, where some of Salem's wealthier residents were building summer homes. A doctor there was giving up his practice and offered it along with a house and farmland if the Peabodys would move before summer, warning Dr. Peabody to keep quiet about the deal, or competitors would rush into town. It seemed an attractive opportunity. He could try his hand at farming, the old trade of his boyhood, once again; add a few hours of doctoring; and do better than he ever had in Salem. There would be enough space in the farmhouse to open a full-scale academy for young ladies.

Through the winter and spring of 1821 he vacillated. But when he learned that Salem's town council had refused to pay him for his work on the new schoolhouse, claiming the school board had not first asked its approval for the expenditure, Dr. Peabody's feelings for Salem finally soured. He brought suit against the town for the $150, arranged for a loan in the same amount to cover the costs of the move, and in early May loaded his large family and few possessions into a wagon to leave the port town, they all supposed, for good. The girls would miss their friends—the Chases, Whites, and Pickmans—but they shared their parents' hopes for a better life in Lancaster.

After a week in the new town, Dr. Peabody wrote his brother Francis, "We hope we are now beginning to live." And in a rare mood of optimism, he placed an advertisement in the *Massachusetts Spy* on behalf of his wife and oldest daughter:

LANCASTER BOARDING SCHOOL

Mrs. PEABODY and Daughter

Will open a Day & Boarding School for Young Ladies, the 3d Monday in May instant, in Lancaster, about half a mile north of the Meeting-House.—Instruction will be given in all the Branches of English Education, together with Ornamental Needlework, Drawing and Painting. Particular attention will be paid to Composition and Polite Literature.

Terms for Board and Tuition, $28 per Quarter—Ornamental Needlework, Drawing and Painting will be an additional charge of $2 per Quarter

Mrs. Peabody flatters herself that she can give satisfaction to those who may favour her with their patronage, as she has been employed in the business nearly all the time for twenty years past; and has been in the habit of preparing Young Ladies for instructing Schools and Academies. She intends her School shall be equal to any Ladies Academy in the State.

Lancaster, May 11, 1821

Elizabeth would soon celebrate her seventeenth birthday. And although the notice didn't explicitly say so, this school would be her own.

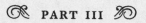

PART III

Elizabeth

1821–1824

❧ 11 ❧

Lancaster

PERHAPS IT WAS BECAUSE THE FAMILY ARRIVED IN LANCASTER DURING the spring that all three Peabody sisters came to love the place so well. As in every other town where they had settled, financial hardships soon emerged. But for the girls, Lancaster and its surrounding countryside became, in Sophia's words, "the brightest spot on the globe," a place of unequivocal happiness against whose physical beauty all later experiences in nature would be measured. And it was to be the last place in which all three sisters would live together for nearly a decade. In retrospect, the rambling white Lancaster farmhouse became the girls' own Friendship Hall.

The town center was nestled in a triangle of land just north of "the meeting of the waters," the familiar name for the spot where the south and north branches of the gently meandering Nashua River converged. In virtually any direction the sisters walked across Lancaster's rich meadowland they came to the river. Barely twenty yards wide and, in late summer, shallow enough to wade across, the Nashua was spanned by twelve bridges, providing endless vantage points for viewing the landscape. The sisters made hobbies of botanizing and sky watching, recording in their letters and journals the colors of sunsets, rainbows, and storm clouds, the intensity of moonlight, and the names of rare trees and wildflowers. Nature became their chief nonliterary entertainment, a theater of sorts, and the one luxury they could nearly always afford. Along with the rest of New England's cultural avant-garde, the Peabody sisters were learning to appropriate the natural world as a subject for observation, discussion, and ultimately transformation into art and literature.

The Peabodys' farm was among the oldest in town, their house one of a collection of white clapboard buildings lining the town's main street, which ran roughly parallel to the Nashua's north branch. The "mansion," as the girls playfully called it, was large enough, particularly when compared to their most recent Salem lodgings, but the first floor was beginning to wander from its foundations. Still, the property stretched all the way down to the river and faced west toward the region's single eminence, Mount Wachusett. Ever hopeful of increasing his income, Dr. Peabody put in long days plowing and sowing hay that first summer; he planned to pick up extra money by pasturing the livestock of his wealthier neighbors. But his daughters used the land differently.

On hot summer afternoons, Sophia and Mary, now eleven and fourteen, dragged the little boys' outgrown highchairs down from the house and set them in the shallow river to study their Latin *Liber Primus* as the water swirled around them, shaded by the large elms that lined the riverbank, the topmost branches meeting to form a canopy overhead. More physically adventurous than Sophia, Mary often couldn't be bothered to bring a chair; instead she carried her books with her out onto the low branches of a favorite weeping willow from which she could dangle her feet in the water as she read. So intermixed were study and outdoor pleasures for the younger Peabody girls that when, one afternoon, Sophia proposed that her five-year-old brother, Wellington, run down to the river "for exercise," he assumed she was asking him to retrieve a forgotten book of grammar exercises.

Although Lancaster now appeared as tame as any New England village on the cusp of the industrial age, with its well-tilled farms and scattering of cotton, lumber, and grist mills along the river, the town had a history that would have placed it in the sisters' minds as part of the wilderness. In the seventeenth century, Lancaster was one of the Massachusetts Bay Colony's westernmost outposts. During King Philip's War, the last and most brutal struggle over Indian lands in New England, it was also one of the most exposed. After a surprise attack on the town in February 1675, the casualties were so high and the wreckage so severe that the town was not resettled for five years. But even this tragedy might have been forgotten by 1821 were it not for Mary Rowlandson, the minister's wife, who was taken captive in the raid, along with her infant daughter. Both mother and child had been wounded by the same rifle shot, which struck Mary as she nursed her baby. Only Mary survived the next several months as prisoner, camping all winter with Quabaug Indian war parties as they skirmished with the colonists. Finally ransomed to freedom, she published a narrative of her experiences that became so popular for its grisly details, pious soul-searching, and surprising flashes of sympathy for her captors, that it was still in print in a dozen pamphlet editions when the Peabodys arrived in Lancaster. Like Salem, the town was one of the few in New England with histories that featured women. From Salem came the witch trials; from Lancaster, Mary Rowlandson's account of her torments: all tales of women victimized by frontier justice, yet whose passionate voices were still remembered centuries later.

By 1821, Lancaster had become an outpost of a quite different sort. The parish was presided over by a Unitarian, Dr. Nathaniel Thayer, so well respected in Cambridge that renegade Harvard students were "rusticated" with him, in hopes that under his influence they would return to college ready for serious study. Dr. Thayer's rusticants, along with the pupils of a first-rate boys' academy (whose past teachers included the Reverend Channing), filled virtually every spare room in town, a fact that would severely compromise the success of Elizabeth's own school. Few parents of young ladies, it turned out, wished them to board in such a town. But the presence of so many relatively unsupervised young men, some of them badly in need of reform, made the sisters' experience there unexpectedly lively. Mrs. Peabody had coaxed her daughters to Lancaster with the prediction that "social enjoyments are always greatest in the country," where it was not necessary to have money "enough to command the best of fashionable life" in order to be welcome in society. And she was correct. For the three girls on the brink of adulthood, the years in Lancaster were a time when intellect, social station, and femininity were in rare conjunction. The Peabody sisters became popular.

Rather than ride with the family to Lancaster from Salem, Elizabeth had come on her own, by way of Boston. Anxious about taking over her first school, she had spent six weeks there in intensive study, emerging on Sundays to attend the Reverend Channing's services, Sunday school meetings, and Bible study groups. She arrived in Lancaster by stage in late May, and with the aid of her first pair of glasses, she later wrote, "my eyes . . . were opened to the beauties of nature displayed there so . . . touchingly in that enchanting valley." Her delayed arrival, perhaps a conscious effort to separate her fortunes from her father's and to make her own impression on the people of Lancaster, resulted in her receiving a hero's welcome.

Dr. Thayer walked up Main Street to the Peabody house to greet Elizabeth on her first morning in town and, after talking with her for several hours, promised his own daughter as one of her pupils. Then Mrs. Dorcas Cleveland paid Elizabeth a rare visit. An accomplished musician and essayist who had settled in Lancaster with her Salem shipping magnate husband while their sons attended the academy, Mrs. Cleveland was proprietress of the town's intellectual salon. At once Elizabeth was caught up in her spell. Mrs. Cleveland seemed to fulfill her feminine ideal. "Highly cultivated and interesting[,] she never says any thing unmarked with deep thought," Elizabeth wrote of her new acquaintance to a Salem friend, "and yet her manners are so unaffected [and] so elegant that you do not think of her being a *professed literary lady.*" Elizabeth herself had been struggling to manage her own outsized intellect in polite company, and Mrs. Cleveland seemed to point the way. She was, however, both wealthy and married and did not need to push herself in the marketplace of ideas or take a socially subordinate role as a teacher of young ladies. These conflicting requirements would keep Elizabeth in turmoil for much of her young adulthood as she sought to put her own intellectual powers to effective use.

She was invited to attend Mrs. Cleveland's "symposia," as Elizabeth termed the informal nightly gatherings at the Cleveland estate, and while they may not have equaled Boston's in brilliance, they far surpassed anything she had known in the more tightly sex- and class-segregated Salem. During the summer of 1821 she met teachers in the academy, old and new: the current headmaster, Solomon P. Miles; the versatile minister, editor, and historian Jared Sparks, who later became president of Harvard College; and the educational reformer George B. Emerson, headmaster of Boston's English Classical School. Dr. Thayer was a frequent attendant, as was the brilliant mathematician Warren Colburn, soon to be named superintendent of the new mills at Lowell. The talk was of European educational theorists—Pestalozzi and Rousseau—and of how to implement their ideas in the New World. And Elizabeth wasn't the only promising young woman to find her way into Mrs. Cleveland's parlor. She became fast friends with the witty Caroline Whiting, who offered to join Elizabeth in studying Latin during her after-school hours. Just a few years older, Whiting wrote poetry that had already been published in a Salem newspaper. A gentleman friend had submitted the poems, Caroline was careful to tell Elizabeth, and "without her knowing it." Whiting went on to become a prolific novelist in later years, publishing under her married name, Caroline Lee Hentz.

Elizabeth Peabody herself cut quite a figure. She made a vivid impression on William Henry Channing, a nephew of the Reverend Channing and then a student at the Lancaster Academy, who recalled meeting her on the street around this time, possibly in the company of Caroline Whiting and Dorcas Cleveland:

> It was a bright May sunset! Walking westward into the light, between two older friends, with eyes downcast on the ground as she listened earnestly to their counsel, appeared a young girl of sixteen. She was fair and bright-cheeked, with brown hair neatly parted on her forehead, and rather slight and graceful in form and movement, so that I remember thinking how good and pure and gentle, and even beautiful, she looked, with the soul shining all through her, and the light pouring all over face and figure as she moved.

Elizabeth had, in fact, turned seventeen the month she arrived in Lancaster. The blond hair of her childhood may well have darkened to brown, but it would have been the exceptional evening when it was neatly parted, for

Elizabeth continued to disregard the curls that she had once cropped in a fury. Her mother's letters had already begun to contain frequent admonitions to attend to her wardrobe and reminders that "neatness is a duty" or that "purity of mind must be exhibited to the world by purity in dress." But Channing's phrase "even beautiful" hit the mark.

Elizabeth was slim and small, fair and blue-eyed, pretty in all the standard ways. And she had magnetism: the aura of intellectual and spiritual vitality that Channing described. Yet there was something off-putting about Elizabeth to a young man. Once her eyes were raised to meet his, her manner could be so forthright that he might instantly forget what had drawn him to her in the first place. Face-to-face with her demanding intelligence, Elizabeth's looks suddenly seemed beside the point. Hers was an attractive force not easily reckoned with, even by men whose ideas on other matters were less than conventional. Men could, and did, fall in love with Elizabeth. But whether they would stay in love, and whether Elizabeth wanted them to, were quite different questions.

Elizabeth's disregard of conventional dress and manners may have been her way of avoiding the ultimate consequence of feminine beauty—a romantic involvement—just at this juncture, when she was "on the eve of entering upon the vocation for which I had been educated from childhood," as she later wrote. Her plans were ambitious: what she hoped to accomplish in her school was not merely "teaching" but "educating children morally and spiritually as well as intellectually from the first." Knowing she must teach, Elizabeth was determined to improve on her mother's example, to make teaching a profession worthy of the far-ranging studies she had carried out on her own and would continue to engage in with ceaseless energy. The girl who had hoped, at thirteen, to make her own translation of the Bible would not at seventeen give herself over to just any man, or to just any schoolroom.

Ambitious on his daughter's behalf, Dr. Peabody constructed an ell adjoining the kitchen for her first classroom, with a raised platform at one end for Elizabeth, scarcely five feet tall, to stand on as she conducted lessons. He wanted to provide an academy-style schoolroom to justify the relatively high tuition that Elizabeth planned to charge. For a first-time country schoolmistress, $28 per quarter was a lot to ask. One of her Vermont cousins, Amelia Tyler, who was teaching in Salem at about this time, earned just $24 a term for teaching an entire class of children. Into the new schoolroom, Elizabeth gathered her first paying pupils: a half-dozen daughters of the farmers and traders of Lancaster, aged ten to eighteen, two of them older than their teacher. She filled out the class with her five brothers and sisters. For the sometime invalids Sophia and Mary, Elizabeth's school became the only regular classroom education they would ever receive. But Elizabeth's methods were so unusual that little more than the six-hour schoolday she adhered to could be called regular.

In Elizabeth's school there were no grammar books or spellers, no slates for reckoning sums, no multiplication tables to memorize. She taught history with the liveliest texts she could find: a translation from the French of Rollin's chronicles of Greece and Rome; the Scottish divine William Robertson's account of the discovery and settlement of the New World; and Hannah Adams's histories of New England. She queried her pupils on the comparative merits of the statesmen and warriors in Plutarch's *Lives,* and she remembered later how eleven-year-old Sophia had become "intensely interested" in "summing-up their heroic deeds." She taught reading by asking her students to bring in their own favorite books of poetry or prose from which they read aloud to the class, inspired to clear, expressive reading by the desire to entertain their schoolmates. Spelling lessons followed the readings; Elizabeth chose several sentences the child had read and asked her to spell each word. Common repeated words were easily memorized this way, and her students enjoyed the challenge of spelling the more unusual ones.

Elizabeth taught the principles of mathematics by a method Warren Colburn had described to her at Mrs. Cleveland's. From him she learned that "arithmetic is the exercise of powers of calculation, and never a matter of memory, at *any* stage." Children, she believed, could "discover and make the rules of arithmetic" on their own and understand them better in the process. Her students worked with piles of dried beans, adding, subtracting, multiplying, and dividing them until they had mastered all the mathematical functions. (A similar system, using plastic chips, is now widely used in American grade schools.)

Elizabeth's method of teaching grammar was all her own, and her enthusiasm for words and their uses lay at the heart of her success as an innovative teacher. As she later wrote in a summary of her methods, the study of language "touches into life the whole spiritual nature." She called her lessons "examinations of words," omitting the tedious label *grammar* altogether, and began by persuading her students of the importance of words as "the signs of our thoughts and feelings in all their minutest shades and variations." As in their spelling lessons, her students analyzed sentences, one word at a time, taken from a beloved story or poem. Parts of speech were identified by their functions—as signifying objects, actions, ideas. Tense was discussed as "time" and person as "speaker." The lessons were "always in the form of a conversation," Elizabeth wrote, "which they saw that I was as earnestly engaged in as they were." Her aim was to make the exercise "*social,*" in order to emphasize the "*study* of the lesson, not the recitation of it," as was common practice in most schools. The analysis of one word could raise deep philosophical questions: what was the difference between an object and an idea, for example? Conversation became so compelling to both teacher and pupils that, after some experiment, Elizabeth determined always to hold these sessions during the hour before lunch or the lesson might take up an entire morning. Aside from her school's low enrollment, and the occasional minor insurrection from Mary, who could sometimes be "a thorn in her flesh," Elizabeth's debut as a teacher was a success.

Elizabeth's methods would have been extraordinary in any school setting in post-Revolutionary America. But she had inherited a disposition toward experiment from her mother, and indeed it has been observed by historians of education that "many of the most important curricular innovations of the nineteenth century were the products of women educators who were free to 'experiment' in their schools for girls." It was in boys' schools, both private and public, that rote learning, competition for class rank, and corporal punishment went largely unquestioned. Still, Elizabeth's innovations were the result of her own particular and passionate interests in history, theology, and human nature. For now she was tilling these fields alone in her country classroom; one day she would have the company of a wider circle of social reformers equally determined to remake New England's institutions. But she could not know that yet.

Elizabeth's own mornings began well before the start of school with a walk down to the parsonage to talk with Dr. Thayer as he worked in his garden from 5:00 to 7:00. They filled the hours discussing the books she was reading, many of them borrowed from Dr. Thayer's own collection. During the summer of 1821, they argued over all of William Paley's works, beginning with *Natural Theology* and *Principles of Moral and Political Philosophy,* as well as Jared Sparks's recently published *Letters on the Ministry, Ritual, and Doctrine of the Protestant Episcopal Church.* Elizabeth was an anomaly to Dr. Thayer: although younger and female, she was far more dedicated to study than his Harvard charges, and not afraid to challenge his ideas. Like the Reverend Channing, he accepted her company and endless questions readily; his greater age, his marriage, and his role as minister all permitted an intimate intellectual friendship. Had she been a young man, he would have helped her prepare for the ministry. Instead, all he could do was make Elizabeth his "catechumen" and prepare her for membership in his church.

For the seventeen-year-old Elizabeth the offer of church membership was no small gift. She was not in the habit of mourning what might have been hers, had she been a man. Indeed, through her mother came the subliminal message that women might have superior powers—moral, spiritual, even intellectual—because of their gender. She preferred to believe, as she later wrote, that "women could take and were allowed to take any course they were fitted for, if they chose." But Elizabeth was never one to accept the status quo when her private ideals were challenged. She had not expected to find a church whose creed allowed her enough freedom of thought to accept membership. She refused to join any congregation that required its members to take communion—a ritual she considered a mockery of Christ's humanity—as the Unitarian North Church in Salem had. (In this view she was somewhat in advance of Ralph Waldo Emerson, who resigned his ministry a decade later over the requirement that he perform communion services at Boston's Unitarian Second Church.) Even the Reverend Channing's Federal Street Church in Boston still required a profession of faith that Elizabeth disputed. Dr. Thayer's church made no such requirements, and it was the only established church she ever joined.

Aside from theology, another favorite subject of Elizabeth's morning discussions with Dr. Thayer was the company of Harvard students under his care. These young men, close in age to both Mary and Elizabeth, increasingly filled the sisters' after-school hours. There was Russell Sturgis of Harvard's notoriously rowdy class of 1823, the same one in which Mary's once beloved Charley Pickering had enrolled—and from which over half the students would be expelled before graduation. The 1820s were a time of recurrent strife between administration and students at Harvard, as its fourteenth president, John Kirkland, attempted to reform the college, then little better than a plush prep school for boys in their midteens, into a serious university. The class of 1823 was the first to encounter—and to resist—Kirkland's ban on the traditional dinners held the night before final examinations. The dinners took place in taverns at some distance from the college and included games of billiards, bowling, and countless rounds of toasts lasting far into the night. Not only had Russell Sturgis helped to organize one such dinner, but he also distributed the class drinking song, improvised on the occasion, to all his classmates the following morning as they gathered to take their exams.

Found guilty of entering into a "combination against the authority of the College," Sturgis was instantly suspended. Yet his actions were considered the height of class loyalty by his fellows and led to all manner of protests once he'd been disciplined: walkouts, bonfires, even one incident in which a student dropped a cannonball from his fourth-floor window "with an insulting note attached to the Proctor, breaking the stone steps and endangering the life of Professor Downing," according to the college's disciplinary records. The few students who had informed on Sturgis became part of a "black list" group that was heckled throughout their years on campus, although they became favorites with the faculty. Returning to college after his suspension, Sturgis disrupted an important lecture being delivered by the Reverend Channing when he walked in late and his classmates rose to applaud him. This transgression brought him a full nine months' suspension, most of which he took in Lancaster. Yet Sturgis was one of the top scholars in his class. So self-assured that flouting the Harvard authorities meant little to him, Sturgis was instantly appealing to the Peabody sisters; Sturgis himself took a particular fancy to Mary.

Then there was John F. Brown, who started his freshman year at Harvard in 1821. A native of Charleston, South Carolina, Brown was ill suited to college life in New England. So handsome the sisters called him "beautiful," and something of a dandy besides (he wore gray satin suits in springtime), Brown lasted only a few months before he was dropped from the class. Like many students, he smoked and drank and spent altogether too little time in study. One Saturday, he'd driven into Boston with a friend and returned to find his room on fire, resulting in considerable damage to college property. Brown was "consigned for negligence." The faculty determined, as well, that he'd fallen hopelessly behind in his classwork and would have to catch up before returning to college. Several months with Dr. Thayer was his best hope.

Elizabeth agreed with Dr. Thayer that failure to study was, as she wrote to a Salem friend, "the worst crime ... of college life ... for if college studies will not excite the mind to diligence, what will?" Unable to attend college, Elizabeth could hardly imagine why anyone would waste such an opportunity. Still, her horror didn't preclude an active sympathy with Sturgis, Brown, and the half-dozen other young probationers she and her sisters encountered in Lancaster. Suspension from college put these young men in exactly the same position in which the girls found themselves, pursuing college-level studies outside a university. By now, study had become more than a habit to them; it was a way of life. Why couldn't the men share their enthusiasm? Brown became a pet project for the sisters, who referred to him as "the Knight of the fiery spirit," one of several epithets borrowed from the legendary Gaelic poet Ossian which they attached to their more intriguing gentlemen callers. Whether or not they knew of the Harvard dormitory fire, the title fit the charming, passionate southerner with the alluring drawl—a man unlike any they'd met in Boston or Salem. The sisters invited Brown to tea, to Thanksgiving dinner, coached him in his studies, pleaded with him to take his life more seriously, and brought him along to the impromptu dances held on winter evenings in the neighboring farmers' kitchens or even, on occasion, in Elizabeth's schoolroom.

It may have been through the delinquent Brown that Elizabeth met her first suitor. The young man's identity has long been a subject of speculation. Elizabeth referred to him only once in writing, more than ten years after the "affair" was over, and then only by the initials "L.B." Yet, when combined with evidence from her letters of the time, that clue is enough to confirm that Lyman Buckminster, a former schoolmaster "paid a liberal salary" as a tutor for Dr. Thayer's renegades and other college-bound Lancaster boys, was the young man who courted Elizabeth with such persistence the year she turned seventeen.

Older than the college men she knew, Lyman Buckminster had recently completed his graduate studies in divinity at Harvard. In June of the year that Elizabeth arrived in Lancaster, he had received the approval of the Boston Association of Ministers and was ready to embark on a career as a preacher—as soon as he could find a church. Lyman Buckminster should have been a promising candidate for a husband: at twenty-five he had a bright future ahead. Yet he lived in the shadow of his brilliant older half brother, the late Reverend Joseph Stevens Buckminster.

The older Buckminster boy had been born with an extraordinary gift for the pulpit. At five he led his large family—parents, siblings, and household servants—in daily prayers. He had begun to study Latin and Greek at four, and by age twelve was ready for Harvard. He took over Boston's prestigious Brattle Street Church in 1804, at age twenty-two, where his sermons were greeted with "delight and wonder," according to one contemporary account. By the time he was Lyman's age, Joseph had already delivered a stunning Phi Beta Kappa address at Harvard's commencement, the most prestigious speaking engagement in town. He was rewarded with the first lectureship on biblical criticism at Harvard. Were it not for his early death from epilepsy at age twenty-eight, Joseph Stevens Buckminster would likely have won the place in Elizabeth's pantheon of preachers that the Reverend Channing held. For Channing, it was said, had filled the void in Boston's Unitarian leadership created by Buckminster's tragic death in 1812.

Much less can be discovered about Lyman Buckminster than about his "ever-lamented" brother. One can only read him into the history of his large family and fill out that hazy picture with a few details from his Harvard days. Lyman's father, Joseph Buckminster, D.D., a popular minister in his Portsmouth, New Hampshire, parish, was given to serious depressions and may have been stricken with one at the time that little Joseph Jr. took over the family prayers, after the death of his mother. Lyman's mother, Joseph Sr.'s second wife, became an invalid soon after her son's birth. She died when Lyman was just nine years old, sending his father, who, it was said, loved her "with a passion fond almost to idolatry," into another period of despondency. Lyman and his three younger brothers and sisters were left in the care of two older half sisters. His father filled in as a "strong and tender" parent when his spirits improved, yet he often fell victim to attacks of "a nameless depression, an apparently causeless anxiety."

Such a mood "was beginning to gather in dark clouds over his [father's] mind" during the spring of 1812, Lyman's first year at Harvard. Lyman may have learned from his sisters of the obsessive doubts his father suffered at home, repeating over and over to anyone who would listen his "fear that he had sinned beyond the reach of mercy; that his ministry had been only a hypocritical exercise of sinful or insincere experiments, and that he had ruined all with whom he had ever been connected." Traveling in Vermont in an effort to shake off his depression, the elder Buckminster received a premonition that his son Joseph had died. Hours later word arrived confirming his fears, and during the night Joseph Sr. "followed" his son. Now an orphan, Lyman Buckminster left Harvard for the remainder of the term. There is no further record of the boy until the June day in 1821 when he was examined by the Boston Association of Ministers to determine his worthiness to fill a pulpit. His text was Timothy 1:15: "This *is* a faithful saying, and worthy of all acceptation, that Christ Jesus came into the world to save sinners; of whom I am chief."

This was the background of the young man who paid suit to Elizabeth during the fall and winter of 1821 and 1822 in Lancaster. She was still just seventeen, perhaps too young to marry, but not too young for courting. Was it her youth, her ambition, or, most likely, something not quite to her liking about Lyman Buckminster that caused Elizabeth virtually to laugh him off? He had become enough of a familiar in the Peabody household to earn the term of endearment "*our* friend Lyman." He had even presented Elizabeth with a small volume of Virgil. But when he "came to the point," proposing marriage in the early spring of 1822, her answer was a flat no. Elizabeth evidently felt he should have known better than to have asked. She would not forget his proposal, however. She stored it in her memory as a badge of her femininity, a tribute that would increase in value as the years passed.

Many years later Elizabeth would tell the story a little differently, insisting that she had been "sought and all but *won*." And evidence suggests that Buckminster continued to press his suit even after her abrupt rejection, if only by letting her know how painful her refusal had been. But for now, Elizabeth continued to take a greater interest in the wayward Brown than in "*our* Lyman" and to inquire closely of her Salem friends about "Alonzo," a young poet she had met before her move: "When did you see Alonzo? Has he written any more poetry? *Has he received any more letters from me?*" She pretended not to mind that, while she was away in Lancaster, Alonzo married a Frenchwoman; instead, she suddenly declared unpublishable the same poems she had once been so eager to see "go into the world."

Although Elizabeth wasn't ready to marry, marriage itself was never far from her mind. How could it be for a young woman whose only sure route out of poverty would be a good marriage? The news of Alonzo's wedding was just the first of many announcements of friends' engagements she would hear over the next several years. Then, too, her reading in 1821 and 1822, besides

Paley and Sparks, included a number of popular didactic novels on the subject of marriage, which she discussed heatedly with her female friends.

One that earned Elizabeth's close scrutiny was the British novelist Hannah More's *Coelebs in Search of a Wife*. More's message was about the importance of education for women—not for their own use, but to make them better wives. Her protagonist, Charles—"Coelebs" of the title—seeks a woman who will be "a directress for his family, a preceptress for his children, and a companion for himself." His parents warn him off women whose educations run to showy accomplishments—music, drawing, even classical languages. "You will want a COMPANION," his father chides him, "an ARTIST you may hire." Charles eventually finds his ideal in Lucilla Stanley, a woman who "may rather be said to be a nice judge of the genius of others than to be a genius herself." Lucilla has studied Latin, but it takes Charles some time to ferret out the information, for Lucilla has the good taste never to display her learning in public. In Elizabeth's view, however, Lucilla's "modesty and diffidence" were "very much over-strained." She preferred the character Phoebe, a virtuous, plainspoken young woman who has trained to be a governess yet sells paper flowers for a living because she cannot bear to be parted from her invalid mother. Disguising her intelligence was unacceptable to Elizabeth. Compromising her ambitions to meet family obligations, however, could seem a worthy sacrifice.

Coelebs raised questions that Elizabeth would have to answer whether or not she married. Should she put forward her own genius, or simply cultivate talent in others? Should she leave home to pursue her ambitions, or stay behind with her impoverished family, accepting only the work she could find close at hand? As it became plain that her school would never expand beyond the handful of local girls she had initially attracted, Elizabeth had to consider her alternatives. Moreover, she was beginning to sense that the Lancaster move would prove a financial disaster for her father. The community had remained "remarkably healthy" during the family's stay, according to Dr. Peabody, except for one profitable outbreak of smallpox in a neighboring town. He now saw that his predecessor's insistence on secrecy during the sale of the farm and medical practice had been a ruse: there was no real need for another doctor in Lancaster. Reduced to dependence on the meager income from his pasturelands and from Elizabeth's school, Dr. Peabody decided to switch from medicine to dentistry, in those days the last resort of a failed physician. Yet a dental practice could hardly survive in a rural village like Lancaster. Elizabeth would have to decide whether to follow her family wherever her father might take them—most likely back again to Salem—or to pursue her own ambitions in a city like Boston that could support them.

These were questions more often faced by oldest sons than by daughters in the New England of the 1820s. For Elizabeth, the decision to leave home would go against every convention of daughterly behavior she'd seen around her as she grew up. All the girls she knew in Lancaster or Salem would stay at home until they married. And those who never married would continue to live with their parents, caring for them in old age. Yet her relative poverty may have seemed a blessing to her now, when her inmost desire was to further her education, to experiment as a teacher, and then, perhaps, to write. Financial necessity was a good mask for a woman's ambition or even for simple wanderlust. Although *Coelebs* failed to offer Elizabeth an attractive model of marriage, or of a working life, it did deliver another tantalizing vision—one that Hannah More quite likely did not intend her female readers to receive. When Charles's search takes him to London, he comforts himself with the notion that, even if he does not find his beloved, he will surely revel in "the feast of reason and the flow of soul" available there, a phrase borrowed from Alexander Pope. Ever after, when one of the Peabody sisters experienced delightful intellectual company—and often that one was Elizabeth—she would use those words to describe it. The awareness that such feasts awaited her in Boston helped tip the balance as Elizabeth made up her mind about whether to stay or go.

By the winter of 1822, Elizabeth was reading an author more suited to her professional dilemma: Madame de Staël. Like others in New England's intellectual avant-garde, Elizabeth was finding her way to the European Romantic philosophers and poets, whose ideas became known to Americans in the early 1820s largely through de Staël's writings on Germany. (Few could read German, even if the works of Kant and his followers had been available for purchase, while de Staël's writings were more easily accessible both in their original French and in recent English translations.) In Boston, men like Channing and Emerson were reading de Staël systematically, critically, and so too did Elizabeth in Lancaster. She dismissed the "high wrought romance" of *Corinne*, de Staël's novel about a charismatic poetess in Rome, allowing only that it contained the "best account of Italy extant," as she wrote her friend Maria Chase. *Ten Years' Exile*, de Staël's memoir of her banishment from Paris under Napoléon Bonaparte, was "merely a collection of papers thrown together . . . and not designed to be published until revised." It was *De l'Allemagne* that won Elizabeth's profound respect, with its extensive analysis of the "new" German philosophy and its place in German literary and political life. And, despite her inclination to criticize anything that wasn't purely intellectual in de Staël's writings, Elizabeth had something more to learn from de Staël than the men did. Bonaparte had banished the writer as an outspoken critic of his regime. De Staël's uncompromising nature, her politics, her salon, and her literary career all captured Elizabeth's imagination. As she read, Elizabeth was strengthening her resolve to leave home.

In the end, an unexpected encounter with Mrs. Cleveland forced the issue.

There is no precise account of the incident, but evidently Mrs. Cleveland had grown impatient with Elizabeth and criticized her sharply in public. It was the first of several painful dressings-down Elizabeth would receive at the hands of older women she admired, and the seventeen-year-old suffered intensely. Elizabeth believed herself innocent of the charges—accusations of unladylike behavior, capped off with the prediction that Elizabeth "would be good for nothing"—yet she had so idealized Dorcas Cleveland for her sense of propriety that she could not wholly discount her opinion. Nor could she see that Mrs. Cleveland, a gifted woman hemmed in by the conventions of married life, might have lashed out at Elizabeth in envy of her youth and relative freedom.

It was not a happy frame of mind in which to leave Lancaster, yet Elizabeth's fall from favor with Mrs. Cleveland made the town seem less enchanting. Ambivalent about the move, Elizabeth may have preferred to feel that she had been ejected from "this little Paradise," as she still termed Lancaster after her departure. Paradoxically, the charges may even have supported her instinctive choice to appear to the world as an intellectual above all else—and to remove herself from the influence of socially powerful women whose "unaffected" elegance belied inner malice. Still, she was beginning to see how precarious life could be for a single woman. Unlike the Harvard men she knew in Lancaster, whose rowdy behavior at college had landed them in Paradise, Elizabeth suffered for her errors.

Encouraged by Russell Sturgis's father, who offered her a schoolroom in his Beacon Hill mansion and his youngest children as pupils, and by the Reverend Channing, who wrote that he had four students waiting for her, Elizabeth left Lancaster for Boston in the spring of 1822, as she later declared, "in a high heroic mood, intending to get money to educate at College my brothers." Or at least that was the reason she gave, one that would appease her family as she followed her own ambitions, cloaking them in the more appropriate desire to help advance her brothers' careers. For even in the matriarchal Peabody family, hopes for better times lay with the boys. The sisters took the slightest sign of academic talent in their brothers as evidence that one or another would someday become "a great man." And if Elizabeth or her sisters couldn't earn the money, there would be little chance of a college education for the boys. No one liked to think of a future for the boys without college. For all his failings, at least Dr. Peabody had his degree, by now almost his sole claim to membership in the professional class. Nat, the oldest of Elizabeth's brothers, would one day accuse her of selfishness when she left home to start her own school in Boston, arguing that the entire family would have been better off financially if Elizabeth had consented to marry Lyman Buckminster. But in 1822, at ages six, eight, and ten, the boys were too young to object, and too young, yet, to show the signs of trouble that would result from growing up in a family where brilliance was a female virtue and failure virtually a heritable male trait.

It was Eliza Peabody who had the most trouble letting her oldest daughter go. Mrs. Peabody knew far better than her husband the impulse that took Elizabeth to Boston in May 1822, just a few days after her eighteenth birthday. She envied Elizabeth, as she wrote in an early letter, the Johnsonian "mental feasts" and "flow of soul" she would encounter among the "literati" in Boston, the "seat of Science." But she also remembered her own difficulty defending her reputation during her years as an unmarried schoolmistress. And she would always be haunted by memories, from far back in her childhood, of the ways powerful men could take sexual advantage of vulnerable women. She cautioned Elizabeth that although "with youth health talents and friends you have reason for strong hopes," unforeseen events "will sometimes render abortive these and even additional advantages." If the new school failed, Elizabeth would always be welcome at home "till some other opening appears." Mrs. Peabody could not help admitting that she felt a "tightness about my heart," as she wrote Elizabeth, whenever "the little table at which you have studied so many days & nights meets my eye." She found it hard to be optimistic when so little had gone well in her own life. Yet in the end, Eliza bid a fond goodbye to her firstborn and namesake, the "child of my hopes & prayers."

❧ 12 ❧

Boston

ELIZABETH SPENT HER FIRST WEEKS IN BOSTON, DURING LATE MAY AND
early June 1822, in the home of a distant relative, the lawyer Augustus
Peabody, whose family summered in Lancaster. His was one of several new
townhouses built at the summit of Beacon Hill near Bulfinch's spectacular
copper-domed State House. According to Elizabeth, the Peabody house's five
stories "towered" above the old Governor Hancock house, previously the highest building in Boston, where her maternal great-grandfather General Palmer
had once pleaded for leniency. She was given a fifth-floor room with an eastern exposure that more than repaid the effort of the climb. The lush gardens
of the Bowdoin estate were directly below, Elizabeth wrote her Salem friend
Maria Chase, and beyond lay "all of Boston ... a perfect view of the beautiful
harbour with its islands and vessels."

The city that Elizabeth looked out on that spring was in the midst of
changes far greater than any since the Revolutionary era. During the 1820s,
Boston transformed itself from a harbor dependent on foreign imports to one
rich in exports from the rising inland mill towns of Lawrence and Lowell. Independent proprietors built new wharves and bridges. A toll road stretching
west across swampland between Boston and Brookline was laid out atop an
ambitious system of dykes that provided waterpower for scores of new mills.
Known as the Mill Dam, this last project served as the underpinnings for
future expansion into the Back Bay. In the next decades, Boston, once just a
tight fist of land thrust into the Atlantic, would nearly double in landmass: its
seven hills were razed and its riverbeds dredged for landfill to support a population swelling past 50,000.

Culturally, too, Boston was poised for renewal. Its most ambitious artist,
Washington Allston, had returned to the city in 1818 after two decades as an

View of Boston Harbor

expatriate in Rome, Paris, and London. Allston's enormous Rembrandtesque allegorical paintings had been exhibited widely in Europe, where he became a favorite of the literary establishment. (He counted Coleridge as one of his closest friends.) Yet after the death of his wife in 1815 and a lucrative sale of a painting to the Pennsylvania Academy of Fine Arts, Allston became persuaded that the New World could offer him as good a home as London. To him, Boston was America's capital. He returned to find a new library—the Boston Athenaeum—which was commencing construction of a building that would include lavish exhibition space for artworks, a flourishing historical society devoted to establishing Boston as the nation's birthplace, and several important artists' studios, including Gilbert Stuart's. With Allston's much-heralded arrival, Bostonians woke up to the richness of visual art. During Elizabeth's first week in Boston, she visited a landmark show of paintings, fifty-two copies of European masterworks, the closest any American could come to experiencing high culture without crossing the Atlantic. She peered so "long and intently" at the pictures in the dim light of Doggett's Repository, a framing gallery that doubled as Boston's largest exhibition space, she wrote her mother, that she strained her increasingly myopic eyes.

In 1822, Boston was a magnet for single women seeking a living. Some of these were among the region's earliest Irish immigrants, who took up the several occupations available to them: household servant, laundress, dressmaker, milliner. Most were native New Englanders, however, many of them widows or abandoned wives who, like Elizabeth's Grandmother Palmer in the previous century, turned their rented homes into boarding houses to make ends meet. Still other women worked as nurses or midwives, and a handful sold English goods, groceries, or toys in small shops near the wharves.

Yet in the 1820s, virtually all trades and professions were segregated by sex. Only men could become lawyers, merchants, ministers, surgeons, booksellers, musicians, cordwainers, rope makers, goldbeaters, bricklayers, housewrights, victuallers, masons, bakers—just a small portion of the occupations men listed alongside their addresses in the Boston city directories of the time. Teaching was the single profession open to both sexes, and even that had its hierarchy. Men taught Boston's public, or "common" schools. They ran academies for boys preparing for college, and for boys "preparing for mercantile professions who may want education superior to common schools," as one school's prospectus read. They offered special classes, mainly for boys, in drawing, music, languages, writing, and dancing. Women, by contrast, taught small classes of girls, or sometimes groups of young children of both sexes, in their homes or rented rooms. In 1822, there were more than fifty such "schoolmistresses" listing their services in the Boston directory, and probably just as many women teaching school without bothering to register their addresses. Girls in these "primary schools" learned little more than the basics of reading, writing, geography, arithmetic, and needlepoint.

Only a few female teachers could provide as challenging or innovative a course of study as Elizabeth Peabody. But Elizabeth was still just eighteen years old, and she knew almost nothing of the business of operating a school on a larger scale than her mother's "family" schools. Moving to Boston by herself took courage, but her plan to gather a class larger than she'd had in Lancaster, in a city where she was virtually unknown, was impossibly bold. The truth was, few parents even in Boston wished their daughters to follow a demanding curriculum. And most of these families preferred the new academies begun by college men trying to capitalize on the growing demand for a systematic education for girls. Within a year of her arrival in Boston, the same George Emerson whom she had met at Mrs. Cleveland's, the headmaster of the boys' English Classical School in Boston, would leave his post to found a large and lucrative academy for girls. As Dr. Peabody noted with some frustration, "the gentlemen [teachers] are all turning Ladies-men." Until at least a core of Boston families knew of Elizabeth's extraordinary intellect, her sex would count against her in the fierce competition for students: she would be just another schoolmistress.

Perhaps because she knew her reputation as a scholar would be her chief asset, Elizabeth devoted her first weeks in town to an ambitious round of visits to the first families of Unitarian Boston, and to the more influential families of intellectual Cambridge, the town across the Charles River she called "the focus of all that's bright." She plainly thrived on the competitive atmosphere she found in the parlors and dining rooms of Cambridge, where, she wrote to her Salem friend Maria Chase, "there is a constant stimulus to improvement . . . [and] even if you do know today more than some others they may sit up all night and put you down tomorrow." During her six-week stay in Boston the year before, she had already met a handful of Harvard's most celebrated professors: Levi Frisbie (natural religion), George Ticknor (modern languages), Henry Ware (theology), Andrews Norton (sacred literature), and John Farrar (mathematics). Farrar was married to an older half sister of Lyman Buckminster who impressed Elizabeth as "a woman of masculine mind and acquirements . . . full of wit, vivacity and elegance." In fact, Lucy Buckminster Farrar and the women of Cambridge intrigued Elizabeth as much as the men. As she wrote to Maria Chase, "you will not find any ladies there whose business is dress and visiting."

During the winter in Lancaster she had met Sophia Dana, the granddaughter of a former Harvard president and cousin of the future novelist Richard Henry Dana, Jr., whose brother Frank was in school at Lancaster Academy. Now Elizabeth was invited for a weekend to the Dana household in Cambridge, which, she wrote to Maria Chase, "has ever been the resort of the government of College, and the first literary men and women in N[ew] England." Here she met the "perfectly graceful and elegant" painter Washington Allston, who planned a second marriage to Sophia Dana's aunt. She became better acquainted with Harvard president John T. Kirkland—"a man more generally beloved I scarcely know." Kirkland offered Elizabeth the use of his private library and spoke to her about the "history and the characteristics of families" in Boston whose children she would be teaching, in order to "facilitate my beneficent activity among them." But getting to know Sophia Dana was an education in itself for Elizabeth. An exact contemporary, she knew Latin, French, and Italian, had studied history and modern literature, and had "paid not a little attention to metaphysics," Elizabeth's own area of expertise. Most impressive was her manner, the result of "being from her earliest youth brought up in immediate and daily intercourse with the choicest of Cambridge society."

Elizabeth worked hard to catch up to her new friend in mastery of languages and literature, but she feared she might never acquire the polish that a childhood spent with the Cambridge intelligentsia bestowed. Indeed this quality in Sophia Dana and her friends continued to both fascinate and disturb Elizabeth. On a later occasion, she was invited to attend a session of Sophia Dana's Italian class, along with a young Italian traveler with whom

Elizabeth discussed the Cambridge women. For some time they both watched the six female students, "the most animated set," in Elizabeth's view, recite their lessons to Harvard's Italian instructor, Mr. Folsom. The Italian guest was astonished, however, at the stark contrast between the female students and the language they were attempting to master. He confided in Elizabeth his opinion that New England women were like *"talking statues,"* so *"composed"* and "restrained" were they even in their most lively conversations. It was a composure that Elizabeth herself would never achieve, although it would be many years before she gave up the effort.

Yet Elizabeth's eagerness, intelligence, and strong opinions earned her a place in Cambridge society—she was a welcome houseguest of the Danas, despite her inability to return the favor—and won her a good deal of attention from young men. At a musical evening at Professor Farrar's, she danced with George Emerson, her Lancaster acquaintance, while Farrar's sister-in-law Mary Buckminster played the piano. And on the first morning of her weekend stay with the Danas, Solomon Miles, headmaster of the Lancaster Academy, and Mr. Folsom took Elizabeth on a tour of Harvard College. Elizabeth's interest in the outing was more scholarly than recreational, as she described it to her mother. "We looked over the library very thoroughly," Elizabeth reported, then went to the "philosophical room" to see Professor Farrar, and ended with a call on the Reverend Abiel Holmes, whose son Oliver Wendell Holmes would soon enter Harvard. If she felt envious of the Holmes boy's opportunity, or frustrated by her own lack of access to the libraries and classrooms she visited, Elizabeth did not say so. She preferred to be taken as the intellectual equal of the college graduates who were her guides, and she was quick to engage the professors they met in conversation as a means of establishing her qualifications. Precisely how the college men saw Elizabeth is hard to determine. In the afternoon, however, the same gentlemen took her through Harvard's botanical garden and hothouse and presented her with a "superb" bunch of flowers—a gift she happily accepted.

That evening she attended a party with the Dana girls, the Holmes daughters, and "a half a dozen Divinity students, among whom was our friend Buckminster." It was the first party Lyman Buckminster had been to, Elizabeth learned, since she'd refused his offer of marriage. He'd even stayed away from his sister Lucy Farrar's musical soiree, because he suspected that Elizabeth would be there. Sophia Dana's mother told Elizabeth that she had been Lyman's "counsellor" in *"that affair"* and had advised him against his proposal. Now Mrs. Dana wished he'd taken her advice: Lyman had not been able to recover from his disappointment, and she feared he never would. Mildly flattered and a little disturbed, Elizabeth passed the news along to her mother. She had enjoyed the party, she confessed, "all but the sight of him. He looked very melancholy."

Taking pity on Buckminster, Elizabeth walked with him and the Dana girls into Boston the next morning to hear the Reverend Channing preach. They set out in the early-Sunday stillness, crossing the "green carpet" of Cambridge Common and passing the buildings of Harvard before most students were awake. During the week, the main road to Boston was heavily traveled with cartloads of farm goods and building materials. But on this Sunday morning it seemed just another country lane with pastureland and marshes blooming with wild azaleas on either side. They walked most of the four miles in silence.

Reaching the West Boston Bridge in Cambridgeport, near where Elizabeth had lived for one year as a child, they stopped to admire the "broad beautiful bason" of the Charles River, which "reflected the statehouse and steeples of Boston in softened beauty on one side, and then Roxbury, Brighton, [and] Brookline . . . with their green hills and elegant country seats, and fine rich orchards" on the other. It was a view that, the great Allston pronounced one evening during Elizabeth's Cambridge visit, "rivals if not excels the Bay of Naples." Knowing nothing more of Italy than what she'd read in books, Elizabeth happily agreed. On this day, with the dejected Lyman Buckminster standing beside her, she knew that the intellectual challenges of Boston drew her much more powerfully than marriage, or even romance. But could she manage on her own?

The group hurried over the bridge as church bells began to ring, then across Boston Common to Channing's Federal Street Church. Elizabeth knew that Channing would soon be leaving Boston on a tour of Europe for his health. But she had not realized what effect, after a year in Lancaster, seeing her hero looking now "like the shadow of a shade" would have on her. He was almost too weak to walk, and he leaned against the desk as he spoke in little more than a whisper. Next Sunday he would deliver his farewell sermon, and many in his congregation believed he would not live to return.

In Boston that day, Elizabeth suffered what almost seemed a sympathetic breakdown: her eyes began to fail her. By the end of the afternoon, they had become so weak that it was "painful to look at any thing steadily," she wrote her mother. The Dana girls persuaded her to return with them to Cambridge by carriage, leaving Lyman Buckminster to find his way home alone. It was a hasty parting and, although she didn't know it then, a final one. At the Danas', Elizabeth sat in near blindness, waiting for a doctor to give his opinion. She identified the source of her problems as the day spent looking at pictures in Doggett's Repository. Besides that, whenever she was not talking or teaching, she read almost constantly, often in dim light; and the crudely fashioned spectacles she used for distances might have strained her eyes further.

Yet this episode of debilitating eyestrain was to be the first of several that Elizabeth would suffer at times of high tension—and overwhelming stress is probably the best explanation for the otherwise mysterious ailment. Arriving in Boston with nothing but the promises of Sturgis and Channing to go on as she opened her school, Elizabeth was instantly reminded by the sight of the melancholy Buckminster of the past winter's hasty decision: turning down a bright young divinity school graduate's offer of marriage was not the choice most young women would have made. Worse still, she had allowed her family to stake their hopes for financial relief on her own quixotic plans. Elizabeth may not have known the full extent of her father's debts, but she felt the pressure. As her Grandmother Palmer wrote to the Tylers in Vermont shortly after Elizabeth moved to Boston, "nothing but the success of Elizabeth['s] school in Boston can keep them from the most serious trouble."

That morning in church Elizabeth had been handed a note informing her that the Sturgis family expected her to begin teaching at once. The time she had allotted for visits had come to an end, but her temporary blindness won her a respite in the care of a family who could afford to coddle her. Elizabeth's stay at the Danas' stretched to a week, on doctor's orders. Her eyes were bandaged, and she spent most of every day in a rocking chair while her friends read or talked to her. Twice a day, a doctor provided by her hosts examined her eyes for signs of improvement.

On the Sunday following, the day of Channing's farewell sermon, the Dana girls led her into Boston across the same beautiful route, this time blindfolded. Only when she was seated in the church was she allowed to open her eyes, and the effect must have increased Elizabeth's identification with her invalid hero when she found that her eyes had cleared. She was able to gaze freely on the frail man who would soon be "breaking the tenderest ties of nature and social life," Elizabeth wrote to her mother, unconsciously summing up her own predicament. Channing had "spent strength and perhaps life itself in search of truth." Yet at this "moment of deepest agitation," she wrote, he proclaimed himself "satisfied" with the course he had taken. As she contemplated a year of Sundays without Channing's reassuring presence in the pulpit, and the more dreadful possibility that he might not survive his European voyage, Elizabeth vowed to remember his "calm beauty" as he spoke, as an inspiration "how ever great may be my trials."

The next day Elizabeth moved from the Augustus Peabody house on Beacon Hill down to a rented room on High Street near the waterfront and began a working life that temporarily put an end to the pleasant times in Cambridge and Boston. Her view was "not so varied" now, she wrote to her family in Lancaster, but it featured handsome merchant ships with their "white sails spread to the fresh wind." She was reading Byron, and she managed to find something in the harbor scene to remind her of his lines from *Childe Harold's Pil-*

The young Ralph
Waldo Emerson

grimage, beginning, "There is a rapture on the lonely shore." She had never
lived in the city before, and she had never felt so alone. Her own home had
often functioned as a boarding house, filled with her mother's students, yet
Elizabeth herself had never been a boarder. Worse, her new room was just a
block from Channing's Federal Street Church. The proximity of his empty
pulpit made his absence all the more painful.

Elizabeth walked across the Common each morning to teach her small
class in the Sturgis family's Beacon Hill townhouse, and back again six hours
later, stopping to watch teams of small boys play cricket in the late-afternoon
sun. But she allowed herself little free time. She plunged instead into projects
for self-improvement. First she found herself a Greek tutor to carry on the
study of classical languages that she had begun with her father in Salem. By
chance, a nineteen-year-old Harvard graduate with a good knowledge of
Greek, Ralph Waldo Emerson, was teaching that year in Boston at his older
brother William's academy for young ladies, around the corner from Elizabeth's High Street room. The two were introduced by young Waldo's cousin,
Elizabeth's dancing partner George Emerson. So began a series of awkward
lessons, with teacher and pupil seated "opposite each other at the study table,"

as Elizabeth later wrote, "not lifting our eyes from our books—I reciting the poems of the 'Graeca Majora,' and he commenting and elucidating in the most instructive manner." Even in this formal setting, "we were quite too much afraid of each other to venture any other conversation." Neither of the two future Transcendentalists were aware that a five-year-old named David Henry Thoreau (later Henry David) was taking his first lessons in reading at another new school opened by his father just across town in Cornhill—nor that a twelve-year-old Margaret Fuller was crossing the bridge daily from Cambridgeport to study Latin, French, and Italian (but not Greek) at Dr. Park's Lyceum for Young Ladies on Mt. Vernon Street.

Elizabeth also joined a group of Boston women who gathered in the late afternoon to read aloud the lectures on French literature that Professor George Ticknor had delivered to his Harvard students the previous quarter. It was the closest any of the women would come to attending a college class. Although Ticknor was not present at the readings, Elizabeth knew and admired this "very ugly" yet "most popular" professor, who had recently returned from a lengthy tour of Europe full of tales of Elizabeth's revered Madame de Staël. Ticknor had become a regular in de Staël's salon "crowded by all the literary men in Europe," Elizabeth learned, "where all subjects were discussed and political rivals and enemies became personal friends." He had even attended de Staël in her sickroom during the last hours of her life. Back in America, Ticknor had become engaged to a woman of "immense fortune," Elizabeth told her friend Maria Chase, whose inheritance would permit him to accept a low-paying Harvard professorship, a means of leading the academic life that would become almost customary in Boston during the coming century.

Intellectual men were so much admired in New England that wealthy fathers happily married off their daughters to them, provided that they taught at Harvard, preached from an influential pulpit, or produced certifiable works of genius. Professor Andrews Norton had married the sister of Ticknor's fiancée, an Eliot worth $150,000 (roughly $2 million in today's currency), according to Elizabeth's sources. And the Reverend Channing had won the hand of a China trade heiress, his first cousin Ruth Gibbs. Washington Allston, whose first wife was Channing's sister, planned to marry into the prosperous Dana family of Cambridge now that he was back in the United States and in need of commissions. In the next two decades, the new Harvard president Jared Sparks and Professor Henry Wadsworth Longfellow would follow suit: Sparks married the Salem socialite Mary Silsbee, and Longfellow an heiress to the Lowell Mills, Fanny Appleton. But it was a path to financial security that was generally closed to women of superior intellect. Elizabeth might attract an up-and-coming ministerial candidate like Lyman Buckminster, but never an heir to an "immense fortune." Her intelligence was more an obstacle than an aid to marrying up, and she knew it.

At least once a week Elizabeth wrote home to her mother and sisters, telling of the "feasts of reason" she'd experienced in Boston. But the news that came by return mail was hardly encouraging. Mary wrote that while their mother was managing to teach five of Elizabeth's former students, the Peabody boys were too much for her, particularly six-year-old Wellington, the brightest of the three, who was "literally *ruining* at home. He is idle, lazy, & grows more uneasy at restraint every day." Little Welly had developed an unfortunate habit of allowing his tongue to loll out of his mouth, deliberately maddening his parents and older sisters. Even after several falls, in which he'd bitten deeply into his tongue, Welly persisted in the habit. Perhaps seeing the attention their sisters lavished on reprobate Harvard youths, the three brothers had begun to cultivate dissipation early.

Mary's eyes were beginning to trouble her as well. She had accepted the gift of an old pair of glasses from Mrs. Cleveland, but the spectacles only caused her more problems. When she wore them in public, the sisters' Lancaster beaus found her ridiculous, laughing at her when the "spectacles shone so that her eyes looked like two stars." Sophia reported that Mary "looked so cross that I should have thought the ten furies had stationed themselves in her face." Only much later did the romantically inclined Mary admit that she wasn't so much angry as "sick at heart," her faith in her good looks shaken by the taunting.

Sophia's headaches had worsened. Although she was exempted from most housework, Sophia found it difficult to study and prepare for what her mother hoped would be her "future usefulness as an Instructress." Both Elizabeth, who continued to regard Sophia as her intellectual property, and Mrs. Peabody viewed Sophia's intelligence as potentially equal to Elizabeth's. She was a good writer, with "many fine ideas and elevated sentiments in her pieces," her mother wrote. Only the "frequent and severe headaches" had managed to "retard her progress." What would become of Sophia if she could not teach? Would she be one more burden for Elizabeth?

Headaches or no, Elizabeth heard from Mary that the twelve-year-old Sophia was turning into a flirt, playing kissing games with the academy boys and wandering into the woods with Frank Dana, the younger brother of Elizabeth's Cambridge friend. Sophia claimed, in her own defense, that she had pushed young Thomas Allston down "when he came on his hands and [knees] to kiss me." As for the walk, she'd gone alone with Frank only because she believed Mary was following behind them. All spring Mary and Sophia had wandered the woods and streams together, carving their names in "every smooth tree we came to." But, with Elizabeth away, their ramblings had attracted gossip, and Mrs. Peabody no longer allowed the girls to walk in the woods unescorted. "If we do not have him to go with us we shall just have to stay at home," Sophia complained. "Do *you* think it is wrong for both of us to walk with *Frank Dana?*" she asked Elizabeth.

Elizabeth herself had to reckon with the social constraints her mother attempted to impose on her long-distance. Mrs. Peabody urged her to maintain the "delicacy of your situation and . . . the circumspection necessary to support your respectability," by asking her landlady's permission to entertain gentlemen callers in the downstairs parlor. Eliza Peabody knew how swiftly her oldest daughter could befriend any acquaintance, male or female, who shared her interests and warned her of the "impropriety of [men] being in your apartment." She worried that Mrs. Cleveland and the "Harpies of Envy" were "on the watch." After her own youthful experiences, Mrs. Peabody may well have feared that worse harm than gossip would come to Elizabeth if a man should visit her room unsupervised.

But Mrs. Peabody needn't have worried. Elizabeth had no interest in allowing Lyman Buckminster to call on her, and her friendship with the shy Waldo Emerson was safely confined to his brother's schoolroom. Most of her evenings were spent in writing letters, many of them to Sophia, who increasingly looked to Elizabeth as her spiritual guide. Perhaps this reliance evolved because, unlike Mrs. Peabody, who tended to coddle Sophia, Elizabeth wrote to the girl "not as a *child* to be advis'd—but as one who like myself; is *seriously* engaged" in a course of study. Elizabeth recalled that "it has been my feeling since the time I was as old as you now are, that *life* was a serious thing." She sent reading lists including many of the theological texts she had read during her years of solitary study in Salem, and in return Sophia took to addressing letters to her oldest sister as "Miss Elizabeth P. Peabody, D.D."—only half in jest.

Elizabeth told Sophia that although the sisters' "lot" was one of "many privations," Sophia possessed "the eye & the heart of a poet." She ignored Mrs. Peabody's warnings about Sophia's headaches and applied pressure instead. "*I hope from my inmost heart,* that these means will not be neglected by you," she wrote, "that the studies in which you are now engaged will be pursued with unremitted industry." And she proposed that Sophia use "the *leisure* you at present enjoy, for obtaining a classical education," by which she meant learning Latin and Greek, for "if it is best for the minds of boys—it is best also for the minds of *girls.*"

As Elizabeth wrote to Maria Chase later that year, she had developed a "fondness for dwelling upon the subject" of "the intellectual capacity of the female sex," and she had "sought for all the ideas of authors upon this subject." She had formed her own theory, one that allowed for greater independence of mind than Hannah More permitted women in *Coelebs,* but with some qualifications. She firmly believed that "mind has no sex": there was no limit to what Sophia or any girl might learn. Yet gender did affect the uses of knowledge. A woman's education was not for the purpose of professional advancement, but neither was it merely ornamental. Sophia must remember "that you do not study for the sake of having acquirements to display, for the sake of being admired, for the sake of attracting attention." In Elizabeth's view, woman's more circumscribed role in society actually freed her to study for deeper, more personal reasons: for the "*pleasure* . . . derived from the feeling of energy that arises in the mind from the keen exercise of its powers in metaphysical, scientific or mathematical reasoning."

So far Elizabeth had been unable to envision an active role for herself as a female intellectual beyond that of teacher. De Staël's example seemed unnervingly foreign, derived from the European system of aristocracy. But Elizabeth's theory of study for its own sake—for "pleasure" and a "feeling of energy"—put her on a par with her wealthier female students, conferring dignity on her work by framing it as a collaborative effort with her pupils. Ironically, this same justification for study would be taken up in the near future not just by intellectual women like Elizabeth, to whom most professions were closed, but by men rebelling against the constraints placed on them by the professions. The most notable examples would be Elizabeth's Greek tutor, Waldo Emerson, who, within the decade, gave up a prestigious Boston pulpit to become a freelance lecturer and essayist; and Henry Thoreau, a Harvard graduate who relied on odd jobs to support his chief occupation, journal writing. Self-education would become the common path for both men and women of the Transcendentalist movement, leading them to innovative self-expression in literature, religion, and politics.

But for now, isolated as she was from family and Cambridge friends, Elizabeth's efforts to make progress in her own studies while teaching long hours each day were exhausting her. In late August, at the end of her first quarter, Elizabeth returned to Lancaster with a severe case of dysentery—only to learn that her father faced bankruptcy. The Tyler nephew who had advanced him money on the farm was calling in the mortgage because his own Boston business had failed. Until Dr. Peabody could pay back the $150 he owed, John Tyler laid claim to the family's "horse & chaise, sleigh, & furniture." Even as Elizabeth attempted to rest and regain her health, her father pressured her to turn over more of her earnings to him.

Elizabeth had arrived in Lancaster intent on climbing Mount Wachusett. Instead she suffered two relapses and spent most of September in bed. Yet she hid her illness so successfully from anyone outside the family that one of the Dana girls, who had not seen her since early June, wrote afterward, "we knew nothing of your sickness. . . . I never before thought of you, but in a state of perfect health and as you say 'on horseback.'" Sophia Dana joked that "the disease with which you ... are afflicted is obstinacy, or a strong opposition to the wishes of those older and more experienced than yourself." The truth was just the opposite: Elizabeth's desire to ease her parents' financial woes was consuming her. She returned to Boston at the end of the month nearly as worn-out as when she'd left.

In the end, Dr. Peabody managed to avoid bankruptcy by some fast talking and what he called "one of my old tricks, *borrowing*." But as Elizabeth had foreseen, the failure of her father's medical practice forced the family to return to Salem, trailing a string of debts, overdue tax bills, and threatened lawsuits. Worse still, Dr. Peabody's "very industrious" and "worthy" brother John, the sea captain, had died in far-off Java. John Peabody's death meant the loss of the only sibling to whom Dr. Peabody had been close, as well as the end of a financial partnership. Dr. Peabody assumed responsibility for his brother's widow and two young daughters in Salem; although he could rarely spare them cash, he was tireless in his efforts to secure them the share in the late captain's voyage that was their due.

Dr. Peabody assured his own creditors that he was "honestly straining every nerve to pay," and if they would only wait for gradual disbursements, they would certainly get their full sums rather than the fraction they might receive by settling in bankruptcy court. But the feeling of being deeply in debt at the meridian of his life, with his family obligations increasing, was a "dead weight hanging upon me," he wrote his lawyer in Lancaster. It would be many years before he was no longer required to send any small extra sums he gained to "pacify Lancaster folks," and his schemes for tending to those "afflicted with the *suing mania*" absorbed him till the end of the decade. He later confided in his son George that after Lancaster he no longer hoped to become a wealthy man and merely looked for ways to "get along."

In Salem, the little boys' lives were further disrupted when they arrived too late to enter their old school. Nat and George started instead at Mr. Eames's, where lessons were tedious, and disobedience was punished by floggings. Sophia held out hope of attending her aunt Amelia's school and studying Latin following Elizabeth's advice, but Dr. Peabody could not come up with the cash for tuition. Only Mary was pleased to be back in Salem, where her Pickman friends had hired her a French tutor.

Back in Boston, Elizabeth was attempting to learn French on her own in after-school hours, working from a dictionary. But she feared that the boarding house diet and constant strain had cost her the "firmness of constitution" she once possessed. Her moods swung from elation over the progress of her studies to acute anxiety about the prospects of her still tiny school. Her mother warned her in November to "be cautious about over excitement of mind or body. . . . To have a soul too big for ones body is as destructive of usefulness" as having no soul at all. "Your countenance has lost that healthy, florid glow which it wore when you lived at home upon our simple regular fare," Dr. Peabody wrote Elizabeth early in 1823. In his judgment, Elizabeth's "constitution" had "received a severe shock" through overwork, and "it will require very regular living & regular habits to reinstate it." But her parents' warnings were not enough. In March 1823, Elizabeth strained her eyes again and had to suspend her school for the month.

Despite his concern for his daughter's health, Dr. Peabody did little to ease the pressure she felt to succeed with her school. Late in March, while Elizabeth was still recuperating, Dr. Peabody told his lawyer that he hoped she would help pay his debts at the end of her next quarter. And he hinted to Elizabeth that she should speak to the dashing John Brown of Lancaster days about whether he might have any outgrown clothing to pass on to the Peabody boys. While he was on the subject, Dr. Peabody advised Elizabeth to "replenish" her own wardrobe as soon as her quarter bills came in. "It is a little more necessary than you may imagine to be nice in your personal appearance," he wrote. "Realy I do not see why you should be behind any other lady in your way in Boston—and if you do not succeed I shall not know what to ascribe it to unless to carelessness in your person."

Then Elizabeth's Grandmother Palmer, who had joined the Peabody family after their return to Salem, asked Elizabeth to shop for supplies for a hat-making venture. She wanted Elizabeth to send the dimensions of her own "turban" and to locate customers in Boston. Well into her seventies, Betsey Hunt Palmer still felt an "impatience for a *degree* of independence," she wrote Elizabeth, for now "truly I am reduced to *very begerry.*" Perhaps the last hopeful member of the Salem household, Grandmother Palmer confided, "I work all the time and expect to make my fortune."

At last Elizabeth's Cambridge friend and mentor, Harvard president John Kirkland, took pity on the overburdened eighteen-year-old. Kirkland told Elizabeth he knew of two families in Maine looking for a schoolteacher for their children and others in the neighborhood. Two dozen pupils were promised, and, with living expenses lower in Maine, Elizabeth would surely turn a profit. Kirkland had already recommended Elizabeth to his friends, writing that "few young men when they leave college could pass as good an examination as she might, in Mathematicks, latin, English grammar and history."

Elizabeth had begun to sense that the time wasn't right to gain a firm hold on Boston. Still, the town of Hallowell, Maine, was so distant from any city— more than 40 miles up the Kennebec River from the Maine coast, 180 miles from Salem—that Elizabeth would feel more governess than teacher, dependent on her employers for social and intellectual stimulus if she was lucky enough to be treated as an equal. Kirkland assured her that the Vaughan family, strong Unitarians devoted to literature and philosophy, would welcome Elizabeth as one of their own. The Gardiners—Episcopalians—he could not vouch for.

It was not an easy choice. Many years later, a friend of the Peabodys would comment on the sisters' fascination with Boston and their determination to make a home there "in spite of fate." Elizabeth was the first to move to Boston, and the city's lure would always be strongest for her. In the end, however, Elizabeth was so anxious to change her circumstances that, without consulting her parents, and without meeting her future employers, she accepted the job.

Elizabeth would miss her weekly lessons with Waldo Emerson, all the more so now that the two had dropped some of their instinctive reticence. "I sent for his bill, through his cousin George B. Emerson," she wrote of their final encounter. "He came with that gentleman to say that he had no bill to render, for he found he could teach me nothing. It was then that, protected by his cousin's presence, he ventured to speak freely; and he poured out quite a stream of eloquence." The two fell into an animated discussion of the popular orator Edward Everett and his recent lectures on ancient Athens.

Elizabeth must also have felt apprehensive when she received a parting letter of advice from President Kirkland. Usually so full of compliments, Kirkland took a different tack this time, echoing the criticisms of her appearance she had received from so many others. "If any [woman] is raised by genius and knowledge above the level of her sex," the Harvard president cautioned Elizabeth, "her neglect of attention appropriate to that best half of the creation, attentions called femininities[,] will more than counterbalance all her advantages and reduce her below other women." There is no record of how she responded to what was now becoming a chorus of disapproval from her elders.

Perhaps Elizabeth paid more than usual heed to the state of her wardrobe as she packed her bags shortly after her nineteenth birthday in May 1823. She spent most of three days making the trip by packet to Portland and then by barge up the river to Hallowell, escorted by her father. There would be no Thanksgiving visits home, no brief appearances of friends or family from Lancaster or Salem. Only now could she realize just how distant she would be from the "focus of all that's bright."

❦ 13 ❧

Maine

HALLOWELL, MAINE, WAS LITERALLY A BACKWATER TOWN, BUT FOR MOST of the two years she spent there, Elizabeth refused to let it feel like one. Maine had just earned its statehood in 1820, separating from Massachusetts under the infamous Missouri Compromise. The debate over separation—and over the terms of the Compromise, which pinned Maine's admission to the Union to Missouri's entrance as a slave state—had been especially bitter along the shores of the Kennebec, where enormous tracts of land had been held since colonial times by descendants of the nine-member Plymouth Company, all originally Boston men. The campaign for statehood had kept the political fervor of the Revolution alive and fostered a radical spirit in Maine's women as well. The future abolitionist Lydia Maria Child spent her adolescence just a few miles up the Kennebec from Hallowell; and, as Elizabeth soon discovered, even the least intellectual of young women in small Maine towns were enthusiastic members of Blue Stocking clubs.

But it was with the descendants of two of the original Kennebec Proprietors that Elizabeth had cast her lot. The life she came to know in the sister towns of Hallowell and Gardiner—named for the Plymouth Company landholders Benjamin Hallowell and Silvester Gardiner—had all the trappings of a pre-Revolutionary British aristocracy, much like the Germantown of her Palmer ancestors. Her employer, the septuagenarian Benjamin Vaughan, whose grandchildren she would be teaching, was a direct Hallowell descendant, and had been born and raised in England. His personal history, however, could not have been better suited to Elizabeth's taste.

A Unitarian by upbringing, Vaughan had studied as a boy with Joseph Priestley, the theologian whose *Corruptions of Christianity* was a source of inspiration for Elizabeth in her Salem girlhood. As a young man he taught mathe-

Benjamin Vaughan,
by Thomas Badger

matics to William Enfield, who went on to write *The History of Philosophy*, another formative text of her youth. Suffering religious prejudice in England, Vaughan traveled to the University of Edinburgh for medical training, where he fell under the influence of the Scottish commonsense philosopher Thomas Brown, whose explanation of human behavior as a series of rational choices contingent on circumstance had found favor with British Unitarians. But Vaughan was no armchair philosopher. In London during the Revolution, he put his considerable talents and wealth to work for the cause of American independence and, as a protégé of Benjamin Franklin, helped negotiate the peace between England and the United States. His subsequent diplomatic efforts to keep England from going to war with France during the French Revolution did not endear him to the governments of either nation, however, and at one point landed him in a Paris prison. It was more as a political refugee than as a feudal lord that Vaughan arrived in the United States to claim his Kennebec properties in 1797.

In the two decades since, Vaughan had built an enclave of manor houses and manicured gardens for himself and his children as they grew up and married. "An English family cannot submit willingly" to "privations," Vaughan had written to his brother as he contemplated settling in America. His own gracious white clapboard mansion, the Homestead, became the centerpiece of his plan to "live humbly, but in comfort and plenty." The house stood on a bluff above the Kennebec, with a commanding view of the river. A smaller tributary, lined with towering virgin pines, ran through a steep ravine behind the property, and a dramatically cascading waterfall could be reached by a short footpath leading from the Homestead's topiary garden. But Elizabeth was more taken by the intellectual environment than by her picturesque surroundings.

Benjamin Vaughan invited her to join his "metaphysical class," a group of local clergy, college men from Bowdoin, and other town professionals who met nearly every night of the week to discuss Thomas Brown's *Cause and Effect* and *Philosophy of the Human Mind*. Elizabeth was the only female member. Vaughan had not neglected the education of his own daughters, but their interests ran in a different direction. The women of the family had all visited England, where they had befriended the writers Maria Edgeworth and Anna Barbauld. Elizabeth's letters home were often full of transatlantic literary gossip. And Vaughan was yet another New England patriarch who valued the intellectual in his daughters' suitors. He had happily married off one daughter to the tutor, John Merrick, he'd brought from England for his sons. Merrick's was a story of upward mobility through pedagogy, which Elizabeth could ponder as she taught the Merrick girls each day in school. Once again, however, the beneficiary was male.

Vaughan arranged for Elizabeth to use Hallowell's newly constructed Town House for her school, which she soon filled with a larger class than any she'd taught before. There were twenty-two children enrolled and the prospect of a dozen more in the future. But the high numbers didn't faze her. Instead, eager to gather in the remaining twelve, she wrote home advising her protégée Sophia to join Mary in her French lessons with the aim of coming to Maine as an assistant teacher. Elizabeth also expected to save enough to hire a Latin tutor for Sophia and urged her to begin by studying her brothers' homework assignments. Although Sophia complained of the little boys' slow pace, by her fourteenth birthday in September 1823, she was translating whole chapters from her French texts each morning and nearly an equivalent amount of Latin in the afternoon six days a week. To this ambitious schedule she added drawing lessons on Wednesdays and Saturdays, she wrote Elizabeth, all with the hope of joining her sister in that "little white lyceum" in the Maine woods.

By the close of the summer term, Elizabeth's school had done so well that she expected she would take in $600 that year, more than twice the amount she would need to cover living expenses. She decided to use some of her earnings for a trip to Cambridge at the end of August to attend graduation exercises at Harvard. The 1820s saw the likes of Ralph Waldo Emerson, Charles

Sumner, and Oliver Wendell Holmes reciting original poetry, giving dissertations on literature and politics, or delivering Latin orations at Harvard commencements. And the class of 1823 was the one Elizabeth had come to know so well through Russell Sturgis at Lancaster. Yet Mrs. Peabody was stung when she learned that Elizabeth woudn't visit her family in Salem *en route*. Elizabeth enjoyed her display of independence. On the packet from Portland to Boston, she boasted in a letter to Sophia, she easily managed to befriend several young collegians who served as her escorts.

Back in Hallowell, Elizabeth joined the local Blue Stocking Club, a group of fifteen young women devoted to literary and philanthropic pursuits. After just one meeting, however, she concluded that the Hallowell "Blues" couldn't measure up to her old Salem Social Circle. She complained that although the Blues met once a week to "work for the poor and read, I cannot say they accomplish so much of the latter as *we* used to, for they generally all talk and talk loud." Elizabeth was more taken by the young men who were invited in at the close of business—as she wrote in one of the doggerel verses she began to compose at the time: "Haggard students from their cells . . . To sport a season with the Belles." She favored Sylvanus Robinson, a man with "bright, penetrating and expressive" blue eyes and "a deep tide of feeling flowing thro' his heart." Elizabeth hastened to add that the young man, a member of the Hallowell aristocracy, was already engaged to "a fair Methodist enthusiast of Bath, [Maine]." Robinson was safely off limits, so Elizabeth felt free to make him a "particular friend." If she had any romantic interest in him, she concealed it even from herself by establishing a correspondence with this "fair Methodist."

It was to Robinson that Elizabeth turned when she discovered during the winter that word of her discontent with the Blue Stocking Club had gotten out, and she had been "accused of indifference to the society of Hallowell." On Robinson's advice she tried to save the situation by convening her own meeting of the club. Elizabeth begged the use of her landlady's best parlor for the event, and, she wrote to Sophia, "laid myself out to buy 'golden opinions.'" First, she explained, "I never took so much pains with my person." With President Kirkland's admonitions on "femininities" in mind, she "rigg'd" herself in a black bombazine gown trimmed with crimson and black merino at the sleeves and hem, fastened three square handkerchiefs at her waist, and arranged her usually straggling light brown hair "more tastefully than it ever was before." After her guests arrived, as Robinson suggested, Elizabeth made a point of talking with "each who had formerly considered themselves neglected by me—& made myself as agreeable as possible." But she could not resist trying to impress the Blues with her erudition and her Harvard connections by reading aloud an "Essay on Moral Taste" by the late professor Levi Frisbie,

The Vaughan Homestead, Hallowell, Maine

one of her Cambridge acquaintances before his recent death at age thirty-nine. For once, Elizabeth wrote Sophia, "there was no noise, no romping—every thing was gentle quiet & perfectly proper," although she admitted that the "beaux seemed to be under a little restraint."

When Dr. Peabody heard about Elizabeth's party, he congratulated her on having "reinstated" herself, but he admonished her to "make *favorable* impressions at first, & save the trouble of removing *un*favorable ones." Mrs. Peabody, who had repeatedly warned Elizabeth to observe "the decencies of dress," was happy, at least, to hear about her daughter's attempt to appear fashionable. But when she learned by the next mail that Elizabeth had abruptly resigned from the Blue Stocking Club in order to study Greek on Tuesday evenings with the new Unitarian minister in Hallowell, she grew concerned. Now every night but Sunday was given over to scholarly pursuits. Was Elizabeth burning her bridges with Hallowell society?

As if this were not enough, Elizabeth was planning to teach herself German as well. She was determined to read the Romantic philosophers in their original texts, and she had made a ten-mile trip into Augusta to consult the region's only expert in German literature, the Calvinist minister Benjamin Tappan, on how to study the language. Her "precious apparatus for learning German," a dictionary and exercise book recommended by Tappan, had arrived in the mail from Boston, and she was eager to begin. Mrs. Peabody worried that Elizabeth's late-night studies would bring on another breakdown of health or spirits. "Let me urge you to moderate the ardour of your mind," Mrs. Peabody wrote. Her oldest daughter, who was "capable of such high acquirements," must learn to protect herself from "tumult from within and from storms from without." Both, it turned out, were on the horizon.

Elizabeth's first setback was minor: Sophia began to resist the notion of moving to Maine to teach. During the fall of 1823, she hinted in a letter to Elizabeth that Mary "wants to go *very much*," while Sophia herself felt too diminutive in both "acquirements and height." Sophia wondered what the "young ladies will say to see such a pigmy as *I* come to teach." At fourteen, she had yet to reach five feet. In another letter, she gave Elizabeth a better reason to pass her over in favor of Mary: her migraines. "The demon in my head is twisting every feeling muscle in it—with his rage," she wrote. The pain had become so relentless that Sophia worried she might be "tormented with such a headache always—Instead of growing better it grows *worse*." While Elizabeth had assumed that Mary would eventually start her own Salem school, and looked forward to having Sophia under direct supervision, she saw the wisdom of taking Mary in Sophia's place. Once the decision was made, Sophia revived. She resumed the fast pace of her studies, and her letters ceased, for some months, to mention headaches.

When Mary arrived in Hallowell in the late spring of 1824, Elizabeth greeted her at the dock with shouts and hugs. She had not seen any member of her family for nearly a year. Yet she had to report to Mary that the prospects for their school's expansion had suddenly dimmed with the appearance of a rival teacher in nearby Augusta. Charlotte Farnham, a twenty-one-year-old "*real blue*" who could read Latin, French, and Italian with perfect ease, had siphoned off the expected dozen pupils. In order to make any profit at all, Elizabeth now planned to leave Mary in charge of the Hallowell school and move five miles downriver to serve as governess for the Gardiner family in the town of the same name. Elizabeth had another reason to be annoyed with Miss Farnham. When the two met for the first time in Hallowell, Elizabeth had shown off her precious German texts. Not only had Charlotte Farnham sent for the same books herself, but she had also arranged for tutoring with the Reverend Tappan, who lived near her in Augusta. "She will *beat* me out and out," Elizabeth complained.

But Elizabeth should have been more concerned with the problem of leaving her school under the care of her seventeen-year-old sister, a novice teacher, than with competing to see who could learn German the fastest. While the two sisters spent their first month together in vacation, it was to be the last tranquil interlude of the Maine sojourn. They took moonlit walks

Robert Hallowell Gardiner, by Chester Harding

through the wooded glen behind the Vaughan estate in the company of the Hallowell beaus, Sylvanus Robinson and his friend John Otis, and the older Vaughan and Merrick girls. And they joined the Blue Stocking Club in mounting a July Fourth celebration. Elizabeth was assigned the oration, Charlotte Farnham would recite a poem, and Mary was asked to assist Harriet Merrick in composing an ode to the tune of "Hark the Goddess Diana." Elizabeth spent days refining her speech, but Mary had to beg her mother for help, for "we never did such a thing in our lives." Mrs. Peabody, who had just published her first poem in almost twenty-five years, happily obliged by return mail with a half-dozen stanzas beginning with the lines: "Rise Genius of Freedom! . . . High, high, let the standard of excellence rise!"

The next week brought the start of Mary's Hallowell school, and of Eliza-

Oaklands, the Gardiner estate

beth's employment as a governess. Although Elizabeth welcomed the move to Oaklands, the Gardiner family's Greek Revival mansion, she had no idea how temperamentally ill suited she would be for her new situation. With the Vaughans in Hallowell, Elizabeth had succeeded by impressing her male companions and mentors. But the Gardiner line was dominated by its women. Robert Hallowell Gardiner, a man who had taken "Gardiner" as his last name on reaching adulthood in order to retain ownership of his mother's Kennebec properties, was Elizabeth's nominal employer. His wife—a "most elegant" woman whom Elizabeth almost immediately began to compare to Dorcas Cleveland of Lancaster—was her boss. Although Mrs. Gardiner had praised Elizabeth's July 4 address—the manuscript had been circulating among the Vaughan and Gardiner families—telling her "you think profoundly upon human nature and may do something with your pen," she made certain Elizabeth understood it was a privilege to be "appointed" governess of her children. Elizabeth quickly saw that "Mrs. G." was even more exacting than "Mrs. C." had been. "Her eye is caught . . . by any deficiency," she wrote her mother, "and her disappointment is greater in proportion as the defect is small." While "Mrs. C." was merely "stern," "Mrs. G." was "very cold." Elizabeth feared there could be no pleasing such a woman.

Mary, meanwhile, was floundering under her new obligations. Elizabeth returned to Hallowell on Sundays to "wind" her up for the week's teaching, yet

Mary felt terrified by the large group. She was more relieved than discouraged when, after a few days, a twenty-five-year-old student, whom Elizabeth had taught successfully for a full year, walked out of class vowing "not to go to school to that little girl!" Mary managed to make friends with her remaining pupils, who were mostly "too young and all too ignorant to note the disparity" between their teachers, Mary hoped. Still, Mary felt she learned more from her weekly "windings" with Elizabeth than her students did in her classroom, except in French.

As a reward for her efforts, Elizabeth sent Mary down to Harvard's commencement in August 1824 to hear the Marquis de Lafayette speak at the outset of a yearlong American tour. Elizabeth took her own vacation at Bowdoin College, where she heard graduation exercises, which, she wrote Maria Chase, were "an injury to the public from their extreme stupidity." Still, she managed to engage the "celebrated Tutor Smith" in a "flow of soul" on Brown's philosophy.

Both sisters were back in Hallowell by September for the preaching of the thirty-year-old Reverend James Walker of Charlestown, Massachusetts, who had come to perform the installation of Elizabeth's Greek tutor, the Reverend Everett. Walker, a future Harvard president whose commanding presence as a speaker had been likened to Daniel Webster's. He was one of Channing's closest allies, and Elizabeth engineered several long conversations with him. Mary witnessed them all, watching Elizabeth swiftly become "more acquainted with him than I did." As Mary wrote to her mother, "you know . . . she has a remarkable facility," whereas "I am very hard to get acquainted." Plainly envious, Mary boasted nonetheless that "I do not know as she understands [Rev. Walker's] character better than I do." This encounter marked the beginning of a pattern of triangular friendships in which Mary would hope to best her older sister by maintaining a more conventionally feminine demeanor, playing the observer, and waiting to be noticed.

Perhaps Mrs. Gardiner also felt some envy of Elizabeth's intellectual conquests. When "Mrs. G." ran out of faults to harp on, she began to criticize what she saw as Elizabeth's overzealous nature. Her employer was annoyed, Elizabeth learned, by the way the upstart governess did not "learn French, but *jumped into it*," as she did "into everything." It was true that, during the fall and winter at Oaklands, Elizabeth took up several causes with a passion. With the Reverend Everett's arrival, the Unitarian controversy struck Maine, in one case literally dividing a congregation in half down the center aisle over the question of Christ's humanity and the doctrine of original sin. Elizabeth devised a plan for sending "missionaries" of the liberal religion into the remote parts of the state and spent much of her spare time composing a long letter arguing her case to the Reverend Channing, now back in Boston and in improved health. Then, as a substitute for the Hallowell metaphysical parties, she enrolled in a series of chemistry and physics lectures given by Bowdoin professor Benjamin Hale. Elizabeth took copious notes to use in her own teaching and sent synopses home to her brothers, hoping to interest them in science. She reported, to the boys' amusement, that during his lecture on sulphur Professor Hale had released some of the gas in the room, explaining only afterward that if any ladies in the audience had been wearing face powder—in New England a scandalous sign of feminine vanity—their cheeks would have turned black.

Elizabeth also had private worries that she kept from Mrs. Gardiner, but that must have visibly preoccupied her. As the snows arrived in winter, Mary's spirits dipped. She had moved from her room at the Vaughan Homestead to a household that included a chronic invalid, a young woman of about Mary's age, who required absolute quiet. Mary wrote her mother that a "death-like stillness" pervaded the house, where for more than three years "the family have accustomed themselves to moving and speaking almost in a whisper." Even the townspeople complied with the restrictions by avoiding the house.

On one of her visits to cheer up Mary, Elizabeth learned that her Cambridge dancing partner George B. Emerson had married Olivia Buckminster, an older sister of "*our* friend" Lyman. The newlyweds were visiting Emerson's family on the southern coast of Maine, and shocking news of Lyman Buckminster's mental state had traveled upriver. Wounded by Elizabeth's refusal and still unable to find employment as a minister, Buckminster had become "dejected and melancholly," his mind "deranged." He was tormented by thoughts that "his friends and the publick expected from him the exhibition of talents and devotion equal to those of his brother." Buckminster had been sent from Lancaster into the care of an orthodox Congregational minister, the Reverend Pitt Clarke of Norton, Massachusetts. Elizabeth relived the scenes in which she had so blithely rejected Buckminster's offer of marriage, and now "horrid feelings" of guilt began to "agonize" her. Yet she could not undo the damage.

At Oaklands, Mrs. Gardiner's faultfinding increased. First there was the usual indictment for "neglect of externals," causing the exasperated Elizabeth to charge that Mrs. Gardiner placed "outward order & neatness above . . . the inward purity of the heart." As Elizabeth wrote to one of her Boston friends, she hated the "tedious toils of vanity." But soon there were other accusations from "Mrs. G.": Elizabeth was conceited, pedantic, selfish, and wanting in tenderness. Yet Elizabeth was also chided for becoming overly familiar with the girls; Mrs. Gardiner had become jealous of the influence Elizabeth was gaining over her daughters.

The charges had a "paralysing effect," Elizabeth wrote, because she believed her success in teaching grew out of her ability to form close ties with her students and their families. Now she felt "ridiculed" for "exercising affection," which in the Gardiner household "must be expressed in perfect taste." When Elizabeth had suffered Dorcas Cleveland's scorn in Lancaster, she had been able to retreat to her own home. Now there was no escaping Mrs. G's censure, and she worried that in such an atmosphere, her naturally openhearted spirit would be crushed.

The greatest blow of the winter, however, had nothing to do with the Gardiners. Sometime in February 1825, Elizabeth learned that Lyman Buckminster had killed himself. On January 22, the desperately depressed would-be minister had walked into the woods behind the Reverend Clark's house in Norton, held a pistol to his mouth, and fired. He was twenty-eight, the same age at which his celebrated older brother had died of an epileptic seizure.

To most nineteenth-century New Englanders, suicide was a dark crime, not to be spoken of. The death of this young divinity school graduate, the son and brother of illustrious preachers, rated no obituaries and only a terse report in the town of Norton's *Vital Records*. Elizabeth mentioned Buckminster's suicide only once in writing. Almost ten years later she allowed herself to recall, in a letter to Mary, how "poor L.B. found his way in such a horrid way out of the world." To a liberal Unitarian like Elizabeth, taking one's own life was not a sin. She could even sympathize with the tangled emotions that might have led to her suitor's death. Like Buckminster, she measured herself against impossibly high standards and often found herself wanting. She had also experienced periods of acute loneliness. Yet a self-protective instinct had so far enabled her to resist the chronic despair that had afflicted the men of her family over several generations. Elizabeth would not give up the struggle to achieve a faith that would help her accept life as it was, and death when it came.

While Elizabeth knew she was not responsible for Lyman Buckminster's suicide, the memory of his despondent mood the last time they'd met, the direct result of her refusal to marry him, lay "like a dead weight on my heart." From this time on, Elizabeth's letters contained no offhand remarks about "steamboat beaux" or mock serious portraits of gallant young men like Sylvanus Robinson. Although she may never have considered marriage to any of the men she'd met so far, Elizabeth had enjoyed her share of the entertainments for young men and women that might lead to courtship: moonlight walks, musical evenings, well-chaperoned dances. Now that she had seen where misplaced affection could lead, she became wary of casual friendships with unmarried men.

Enduring her sorrow and regret over Buckminster's death alone at Oaklands, Elizabeth found that she could no longer withstand her employer's criticism. By now Mrs. G's "blasts" had become routine. "How perfectly she understands how to torment me," Elizabeth confided to the journal she began keeping in 1825, the year she turned twenty-one, and she wondered at Mrs. Gardiner's "power over my mind." It was galling to endure such tyranny from a woman who "never experienced a calamity in her life" and whose "infinite indolence" seemed to be spent in criticizing those around her. Elizabeth was beginning to realize that many of the attributes she had admired in women like Mrs. Gardiner—the graciousness and elegance—were mere affectations of the idle rich. "There are some things the prosperous cannot learn," she told herself, "and one is to value affection, without extreme decoration."

Elizabeth always had difficulty letting such barbs go unanswered, although, she wrote, "I wish I had the blessed faculty of holding my tongue at least until I am aware of what I am going to say." She knew she suffered from an "impetuosity of feeling." The effort to "say everything in a breath" caused her only to "begin at the end, or dash into the middle" of her argument when she felt the pressure to defend herself. The same pressure "gives my voice a tone, which those around me mistake for anger with them; and thus I leave the impression of having a confused head & a bad temper." She vacillated between concern about how she appeared to the worldly Gardiners and the growing awareness that the stay at Oaklands had become a "misery," causing her to feel as if "steeped in a fountain, deadly, lethean & cold."

Her letters home grew shorter, and she began to complain of fatigue. Mary's school, Elizabeth knew, had not turned a profit this winter, even though the Vaughans had supplied her with stove wood free of charge. When the daughter of a Unitarian family from the Boston suburb of Brookline visited Oaklands, and Elizabeth learned that the girl's father—a member of the Reverend Channing's congregation—needed a teacher for his girls, she easily persuaded Mary to move south with her to open a school together.

Elizabeth did not quite consider her Maine venture a failure. "Had I lived two years more in Boston" instead of moving to Maine, she once told Mary, "I should have been in the Insane Hospital or the grave at the end of it." Now Elizabeth would be facing the big city from the safe distance of suburban Brookline, and she would have her younger sister as a partner and support. To Elizabeth's surprise, Mrs. Gardiner announced that she would send her daughter Lucy to board in Brookline so she could attend Mary and Elizabeth's school. With the Reverend Channing back in Boston and preaching at the Federal Street Church, her own health revived, and her store of wisdom increasing, Elizabeth was ready for a new start, one that would mark the beginning of "an era in my life."

PART IV

Mary and Elizabeth

1825–1828

ॐ 14 ॐ

"I Am Always My Own Heroine"

MARY PEABODY LACKED THE INTENSE THEOLOGICAL FOCUS OF HER older sister, yet she was also a voracious reader, chiefly of fiction. She had heard her mother complain that her pupils' minds were "weakened by light reading," but Mary felt instinctively that the popular novels she cherished provided a key to her future every bit as useful as the Unitarian doctrinal works Elizabeth devoured. Among her favorite novelists were the Scottish writers Mary Brunton, the author of *Discipline* and *Self-Control*, and Susan Ferrier, whose *Marriage* and *Inheritance* featured intelligent young women of humble origins or ruined fortunes struggling to move up in the world by winning a worthy husband. Mary read each new novel by Walter Scott as it came out, but she preferred a fictional women's world of heroines who "contended with obstacles & either conquered their fate or were swept away by the merciless tide of circumstances." One treasured book asked the question: "What is life, if not a vast desire, a great attempt?" As she read, Mary drew inspiration for her own break from poverty, which she sensed would come in a different way from Elizabeth's.

Daydreaming about romantic adventure also insulated Mary from the uncertainty of daily life in the Peabody household and allowed her to withdraw from competition with her brilliant older sister and delicate younger one. In "delicious" moments of "reverie," Mary retreated to an "imaginary world," she later wrote, where "all things present fade from my vision" and "I am always my own heroine." Perhaps Mary found it easy to imagine taking a part in romantic tales because she possessed something that neither of her two sisters did—the sheer physical beauty of a novel's heroine—a fact that sometimes made her sisters jealous. By contrast to the dark-haired Mary, pale Sophia felt her own "plainness." But the younger Sophia's attitude was more often one of adoration. In her late teens, Sophia wrote, Mary's complexion took on a "rich damask bloom." Three years younger, Sophia loved to sit and watch her sister dress, memorizing the forms of "your shoulders & arms & the turn of your head & the curved mouth."

Mary herself was well aware that she was "called beautiful," as she once wrote. Yet, in the self-deprecating domestic culture of nineteenth-century New England, this difference did not make her feel vain so much as marked for a special destiny. While the distressing example of their parents' troubled marriage had determined Elizabeth to become financially independent, it made Mary, sure of her winning looks, romantically ambitious.

Already Mary's reading seemed to have prepared her to negotiate parlor intrigues better than her sisters. She was never confused about her feelings for the opposite sex, and she readily perceived men's feelings for her. She was fully aware, even proud, of her childhood crush on Charley Pickering. Later, in Lancaster, she easily sensed that the Harvard renegade Russell Sturgis had fallen in love with her. Mary felt flattered by Sturgis's interest but knew she was too young, at fifteen, to respond. The Reverend Thayer's son Christopher also paid Mary some attention while in town on a college vacation. But when the young man returned in summer and never called at the Peabody farmhouse, Mary resolutely stayed away from all the Thayers, unwilling to have Christopher "think I came to see him." Mary knew better than to put herself forward where she was not wanted. Besides, her sights were set higher; she would wait for someone more serious, more intellectual, more heroic than either Sturgis or Thayer.

With her dreamy nature, Mary was also more forgiving of her parents than Elizabeth, particularly concerning their father. She may have felt that Dr. Peabody resembled the heroine's guardian in one favorite novel, a chemist who was "careless, kindly, improvident," yet "the only being on earth to whom her heart clung." Mary stayed out of her mother's schoolroom as a young teenager, instinctively avoiding what had become Elizabeth's arena. Instead, the talent she cultivated seriously—singing—was one she shared with Dr. Peabody. After the family returned to Salem from Lancaster, Mary sang soprano and her father tenor in the North Church choir. It was in her father's company that she experienced through music "the highest moments of a contemplative kind," when "I seemed to see the relations of things . . . and my soul was rapt to enthusiasm to live & be what I ought." Because of their essential sympathy, Mary could even appreciate Dr. Peabody's dry wit and increasingly black humor. The long weekly letters that Mrs. Peabody sent to Elizabeth after she left home often concluded with caustic postscripts from "Molly" and "N.P."

For Mary also shared her father's grim sense that everyday life was frequently beyond control. From the ramshackle "mansion" on Main Street in Lancaster, the family had retreated in 1822 to Court Street in Salem, where Dr. Peabody rented what his oldest son, Nat, later described as "one half of a large, old-fashioned, unattractive house . . . having the reputation of being haunted." It was several hundred yards from the broad North River and a few short blocks from the Howard Street Cemetery, where the family had buried the infant Catharine three years before. Mary maintained that "we had no fearful associations" with the house, yet she was not pleased to learn that she would have to share a bed with her Grandmother Palmer, who now rotated her residence among the families of her grown daughters.

There had been changes in Salem beyond her own household that caught Mary off-guard. From Court Street she could still walk to the Pickman mansion on Essex Street, but now she went chiefly to entertain Miss Rawlins Pickman, the unmarried daughter who had nursed Benjamin Pickman, Mary's childhood benefactor, through his final illness. There Mary was forced to confront the fact that her young cousin Mary Toppan Pickman, daughter of Mary's aunt Sophia Palmer Pickman, had taken her place in the affections of the wealthy family. Now six years old, "Mary Top," whose father had died the year she was born, was the sole heir to her father's share of Benjamin Pickman's estate. With a portion of the inheritance, little Top and her mother had moved into a handsome Essex Street house all their own. Both households were intently focused on the fledgling talents of the rich half-orphan girl.

It is not possible to determine precisely who in Salem knew that Mary Top's mother, "Aunt Pickman," as she was called by her three Peabody nieces, was not a real Palmer. Perhaps, at this moment, it was only Mrs. Peabody, the witness to her mother's seduction by Royall Tyler, and victim, herself, of his advances. It is possible that Aunt Pickman herself knew nothing of her tangled parentage. But a frostiness existed between the sisters—Mrs. Eliza Palmer Peabody and Mrs. Sophia Palmer Pickman—that intensified as the misbegotten Sophia's fortunes rose and Eliza's sank. There was little communication between the houses besides that generated by Mary Peabody. Gallingly, Aunt Sophia Pickman refused to allow the younger Peabody boys, whom she viewed as social inferiors, to spend much time in the company of their cousin, her precious Top.

At sixteen, Mary Peabody knew only that she was too old to remain a surrogate child in the Pickman family. With no firm bond between her mother and aunt to unite the households, the chasm of wealth that separated Mary from the Pickmans could no longer be ignored. But it was humiliating to feel the outsider even with her own near relations, and an object of charity besides. Soon after the Peabody family returned to Salem, Miss Rawlins Pickman hired Mary a French master, not so much for the girl's enjoyment, but because the ability to teach French would give Mary an advantage over other young schoolteachers just starting out.

Monsieur Louvrier, a rare French national in Royalist Salem, took his charge seriously. The tireless Frenchman often allowed Mary's daily one-hour lessons to stretch to four. At Elizabeth's insistence from far-off Hallowell, Maine, Sophia joined in, and the girls were soon translating entire chapters from Pascal or Voltaire at night, then suffering under M. Louvrier's "merciless . . . exactions" the next morning as he examined their work sentence by sentence. All corrections had to be memorized and recited along with drills in irregular verbs. By noon, if they were not overcome by exhaustion, the sisters arranged the chairs in the dining room, where M. Louvrier conducted lessons, into a set of hurdles and ran races to break the tension. But frequently Mary was in tears at the end of the morning, and Sophia had entered one of the "long trances" that led to her "unmentionable headaches."

Mary was of two minds about the experience. After eighteen months of the regimen, M. Louvrier had succeeded in "engraving the language upon my soul," Mary later recalled. She even dreamed in French. After a spotty and unconventional education in her mother's and older sister's schools, she was grateful for this first taste of disciplined study and pleased to have acquired a method for learning other languages swiftly and efficiently. In this field she would always surpass Elizabeth. But Mary also blamed the lessons for her younger sister's broken health. She developed an intense hatred for "cramming" and hoped to find a way to teach her own future students to "love the very act of study."

With Elizabeth out of the house, Mary became a more assertive young woman. She enjoyed the first-daughter's status that had been Elizabeth's for so long, and the crucial French lessons exempted her from cooking and sewing duties, including the mending she had been doing for Elizabeth long-distance. During the year before her move to join Elizabeth in Maine, Mary produced several issues of a "literary paper" she called the *Salem Recorder*—or, in lighter moments, "the Spinster's Review." The paper contained "poetry, essays, reviews, *anything*," she wrote to one of her Tyler cousins in Vermont soliciting material, and "I expect it to vie with the North American," she joked, referring to the prestigious journal edited by Edward Everett in Boston. Sophia wrote poetry for the paper, Elizabeth sent down her analysis of Thomas Brown's philosophy, and Mary organized the entire effort, copying out the articles by hand. Emboldened by her editorial role, Mary began dispensing opinions in her letters, including her views on "the equality of the female sex," after her cousin William Tyler dared raise the question "whether ladies *ought* to do anything but darn stockings!"

Yet when Mary left home for Maine in April 1824, she was not nearly so eager for adventure as Elizabeth had been. The journey came at a time when all three sisters were reading *Clarissa*, Samuel Richardson's story of a virtuous young woman, estranged from her wealthy family, who dies a martyr's death in a lodging house after being raped by a rejected suitor. The tale carried a different lesson from the novels Mary usually read. *Clarissa* was the relic of a not-so-distant era when literary heroines paid dearly for any move toward self-sufficiency and were more often passive victims to cruel seducers than agents of their own romantic destinies. More distressing for Mary, *Clarissa* was a powerful reminder of the family secrets her mother seems finally to have confided in each of her two older daughters as they left home. Judging from her letters, Mary now knew about "all the heart-rending and almost unparalleled sorrows you have endured," as she wrote Mrs. Peabody after she'd read the book.

Indeed, Mrs. Peabody, who felt painfully "the hard duty of sending from me two so dear and so lovely," had worried about whether *Clarissa* was suitable reading for a young woman like Mary, who cared for "novels more than any other books." She hoped *Clarissa* would underscore the importance of female "purity of character." Yet simply reading such a book could be no inoculation. Mrs. Peabody knew firsthand "so much of the wickedness and villainy of man," she wrote Elizabeth the day after Mary set out for Hallowell, that she could not help but fear for her younger daughter's safety, "safty I mean, from moral evil, compared with which no physical ill is worth a thought." Perhaps she considered the beautiful Mary a more likely target of male depredations than the rumpled, garrulous Elizabeth.

Elizabeth, who had practice traveling on her own, advised Mary to go straight to Patten's Hotel in Portland, Maine, on her one-night stopover there: "take a chamber to yourself and lock yourself in, and have your meals brought up to you." Even these precautions did not guarantee an entirely smooth passage. Riding by stage on the final leg of her journey, Mary found herself the only female in the coach, listening in as her four male traveling companions traded ribald stories. Trying to make herself inconspicuous, she succeeded almost too well. The joking escalated around her until one man told of Jonathan Swift "riding along in a stage coach just as we are doing now" and witnessing "a man and a woman under a hedge actually engaged Sir, yes! by God sir! actually engaged in the act of copulation!" At this, another passenger remembered Mary—"a young and extremely pretty girl" sitting in embarrassed silence—and kicked the heedless raconteur on the shin, provoking him to shout out, further humiliating Mary, "By God! Sir, I forgot the gal."

Painfully aware of the delicacy of her situation, and especially vigilant after her mother's recent revelations, Mary was intensely distressed by "the horrors" of the day's ride, she wrote to her parents. She compared "the extent of my courage" to that of Diana Vernon, the heroine of Walter Scott's *Rob Roy*. Fortunately, "every terror" was "lost in the pleasure of seeing Elizabeth" again after a year's separation. "How she screamed!"

Yet the Maine sojourn failed to produce the partnership both sisters had envisioned, as Elizabeth moved downriver to cater to the "over-refined and unapproachable" Mrs. Gardiner's daughters and Mary stayed behind to teach the large Hallowell class by herself. Indeed, while Mary depended on Elizabeth for long-distance guidance, she could not help but resent the fix her older sister had put her in. Mrs. Peabody's letters of instruction, following on her cautionary tales of the "villainy of man," only made matters worse. "You must forego almost everything that constitutes the happiness of girls of your age—frequent visiting, gay company, light reading," her mother wrote in her first letter. "Literary enjoyments are the highest enjoyment, but they cannot occur in the every day walks of life," she counseled. Instead, Mary should take an interest in the "details of domestic life" in order to make herself useful to her hosts and guard her reputation by taking care never to offend even "the humblest domestic."

Mrs. Peabody's advice on teaching—"twine yourself round the hearts of your scholars by gentleness"—was more palatable, and Mary came close to accomplishing it, once the older and more rebellious students had resigned from the class. But for a young woman who had once loved the outdoors so much that "walls were oppressive to me," and who preferred daydreaming to book learning, running the Hallowell school by herself was a hard sentence.

Mary Peabody turned eighteen in November 1824, teaching alone in a snowbound Maine village. She would soon spend her first Thanksgiving away from home in a household of strangers. Little wonder that when Elizabeth suggested the two sisters leave the Kennebec River valley the following spring to teach school together in Brookline—where, she was told, "all the people are prepared to like us"—Mary was more than happy to go along with the plan.

ᏚᎡ 15 ᏚᎠ

"There Is No Scandal in Brookline"

IT TOOK SOME TIME FOR BOTH SISTERS TO REGAIN THEIR EQUILIBRIUM after the Maine ordeal, and at first it seemed they could hardly have chosen a better place for it than picturesque Brookline, Massachusetts, with its "serpentine paths ... grand avenues ... [and] copses of pine and hemlock," as Mary described their new surroundings. When the sisters arrived in May 1825, there were scarcely more than a hundred houses in Brookline, the first town west of Boston, and a fair portion of them were expansive Roman classical style "cottages" built as summer homes after the turn of the century by Boston businessmen. The girls who would be Mary and Elizabeth's students were daughters of bankers and importers who had begun to find year-round residence in the suburbs attractive now that the new Boston–Worcester Turnpike provided a through route to the city. Perhaps it was because of the relative youth of the community that one neighbor was able to assure Mary, on their first meeting, "there is no scandal in Brookline." Deeply wounded by the malicious faultfinding of women like Mrs. Gardiner and Mrs. Cleveland, and still grappling with the shocking news of Lyman Buckminster's suicide, Elizabeth could only feel relieved.

Now twenty-one, Elizabeth had moved every spring since her seventeenth birthday, first to Lancaster, then Boston, Hallowell, Gardiner, and finally Brookline, each time in search of a way to earn her own living and help pay off her father's debts. Prospects for financial success were far better in Brookline than they had been during the past year in Maine: Elizabeth found room and board for both sisters at just $4 a week, and the Brookline families promised a minimum of $500 a year in salary. They boarded with a shoemaker's family, taking a large room on the top floor of a house next to the blacksmith's shop in the center of town. Despite the heat and noise in late spring

153

Elizabeth and Mary's Brookline house and school

and summer, the sisters were pleased to find a front yard so filled with flowering shrubs that the house seemed to float on a cloud of lilac and eglantine.

Yet all through the summer months Elizabeth's moods swung wildly. On one of their first free weekends, the sisters walked a twelve-mile circuit from Brookline to Cambridge, where they spent the night with friends, then into Boston for Channing's sermon the next day, and back to Brookline. On the last leg of the journey, Elizabeth was so exhausted that Mary "proposed being a horse" and dragged her older sister home hanging on to a corner of a kerchief she slung over her back. Even as Elizabeth clung to Mary's scarf, she would not cede authority to her younger sister. "We struck up a bargain to be husband and wife on the road," Mary wrote afterward, only slightly amused, "but E. insisted upon being husband, not considering that she was violating all rules of chivalry" by turning her "wife" into a beast of burden. At eighteen and twenty-one, struggling to make their way in the world, both Mary and Elizabeth must have had marriage at the back of their minds as an alternative to itinerant school teaching.

By mid-June, Elizabeth appeared to have "revived amazingly," Mary wrote to a Salem friend. "She says she begins to have *feelings* again." On June 17, Elizabeth rode into Charlestown for the ceremony commemorating the fiftieth anniversary of the Battle of Bunker Hill. Two hundred Revolutionary War veterans, many of them bent with age or crippled by war, marched in slow procession up Bunker Hill past hundreds of spectators. She heard Daniel Webster, "his arms flung over his head, his robe floating in the wind," deliver an impassioned speech on free government and then introduce the Marquis de Lafayette, now near the end of his triumphal yearlong American tour. Elizabeth watched a somber, aged Lafayette lay the cornerstone of the new monument. Along with many of the women at the scene, she pressed forward toward the venerable Frenchman to shake his hand. She saved the glove she wore that day, "which I had not time to take off," for the rest of her life.

The following Sunday, when Elizabeth heard that Lafayette was taking tea in Brookline and "nobody but gentlemen were invited," she walked out to the street corner and waited several hours to flag down his carriage when it passed. A crowd of women and children gathered, but Elizabeth, having reached "the tip-top of excitement," sprang forward to become the first to kiss the hand of the great man, who returned the favor. "When he was gone," Elizabeth wrote afterward, "we were all trembling and shaking—like the sea after a storm—and everybody congratulated *me* who had 'kicked up the row.'"

Mary watched helplessly as Elizabeth's elation at the encounter with Lafayette, and her near ecstasy through much of June at once again seeing "the ineffable light" beam from Dr. Channing's eyes as he preached on Sundays, evaporated with Channing's departure for Newport on a two-month summer holiday. "If I could put in a letter," Mary wrote to a Salem friend, "the tone and gesture and expression of face with which E. says 'he is gone!' when anybody asks her about [Channing], you would feel instantly the whole extent of the evil." The highs and lows of Elizabeth's spirits were sometimes more than Mary could tolerate at close range.

Aside from the month's vacation in Hallowell the previous summer, Mary and Elizabeth had not lived together since Lancaster, when the two sisters were fifteen and seventeen years old. In Elizabeth's memory, the Lancaster year was a "gracious time in our lives," when Mary had at last grown up enough to become a real companion. There Elizabeth first recognized what she called the "beauty" of Mary's "individuality" and felt the strength of Mary's "*belief in me*"—a devotion that, in retrospect, Elizabeth would be forced to admit had its "culmination" in Lancaster as well. In that time, now four years distant, Elizabeth felt as if "we *married* each other," achieving a "spiritual communion" that countered the authority of their parents' acrimonious marriage. Even Sophia agreed that in Lancaster days Elizabeth and Mary had been "intimate," enjoying the "fulness" of "friendship," while the twelve-year-old Sophia was relegated to "a secondary object of regard, a playmate only."

Yet what had seemed "belief" and "communion" to Elizabeth, and "intimate . . . fulness" to Sophia, was the result of a youthful adoration on Mary's part that she was beginning to outgrow. There were still moments of mutual contentment, as when Mary passed along a favorite Susan Ferrier novel to Elizabeth, who instantly devoured it, stretched full-length on the bed, "roaring" over the dialogue. But at other times Mary hardly knew what to make of her older sister. With Elizabeth's books, papers, and articles of clothing strewn about, their shared bedroom seemed to Mary "a little chaos." There were mornings when Elizabeth woke at dawn "quite crazed," Mary wrote to a friend only half in jest, her "faculties ... dancing jigs," and rushed out to discuss her latest enthusiasm with whoever might be up. Mary, by contrast, usually woke slowly, with the fragments of pleasant dreams hovering about her. And there were far too many days when Elizabeth's early-morning brilliance would dissolve into depression and self-doubt. Then Elizabeth could turn on Mary, laying siege to her character, applying the same blistering scrutiny to her younger sister that she did to herself—and expect Mary to appreciate the attention.

In the face of such criticism, Mary nearly always held her tongue. She knew that for now, at least, her fate was linked to Elizabeth's. Frustratingly for Mary, the sisters were often seen as indistinguishable: two young women in eyeglasses, the elder speaking almost uninterruptedly for both of them. Wherever they went together, Elizabeth's reputation as an intellect preceded them and drew attention away from Mary, whose inclination to withdraw became ever more powerful. At times Mary was grateful that, as she once wrote, "E[lizabeth] has spirit enough to keep herself and me feelingly alive to all that it is necessary to be interested in." Yet it also pained her to hear Elizabeth spoken of within the family as "that favorite of fortune—our Liz." Inevitably a recitation of the list of influential men with whom Elizabeth had become acquainted would follow: the Reverends Abbot, Walker, Thayer, and Channing; Harvard president Kirkland; Washington Allston; Nathaniel Bowditch; and more. Aside from the jealousy this stirred, Mary knew firsthand how much such excitement cost her older sister, and she worried about the risk Elizabeth took in seeking even purely intellectual intimacy as a single woman with married men.

Besides, Mary had her own troubles to contend with. It was Mrs. Peabody, no stranger to such restlessness, who guessed that Mary was not enjoying teaching. "A mind like yours cannot stand still," she wrote in an attempt to boost Mary's confidence and help her make the best of her situation. She counseled Mary to find her duties in the schoolroom "a source of daily improvement to yourself," to develop "your thirst for useful knowledge," and then "you will be happier than you ever anticipated, in the line of life, which providence has marked out for you."

Sometimes Mary tried to follow an Elizabeth-inspired regimen. For a month or more in Maine she had risen early to study Italian or translate Virgil before breakfast; in the evenings she read Brown's philosophy or de Staël's *De l'Allemagne* until bedtime. She was seized by the same fervor to learn German, and, once the sisters were settled in Brookline, Mary arranged to study each day with a next-door neighbor, a wealthy German-speaking importer, until she was the one translating the Romantic philosophers aloud to Elizabeth. But what Mary retained of de Staël, she confessed in a letter to Miss Rawlins Pickman, had more to do with "her sentiments and the progress of her character than [with] any events that distinguished her life." She took to heart de Staël's pronouncement that "no woman of sensibility ever lived to be twenty six without feeling the sentiment of love." In Brookline, as she turned nineteen, Mary believed she still had plenty of time to "redeem" her own character for "sensibility" and fall in love.

For even as she dutifully followed her family's plans for her, Mary resisted the notion that teaching would be her "line of life." She had enjoyed the smaller children in her class in Maine, and she was pleased to become the confidante of their fantasies and fears. But during the summer in Brookline, it seemed all too often that "dry French and Latin verbs . . . mangled recitations of poetry, and tangled composition were the order of the day." Unlike Elizabeth, who was always actively engaged in conversation when in a room full of people, whether children or adults, Mary would sometimes set the class to studying a lesson, then steal a few moments to herself for reading or writing a letter. As each new term began, "time seem[ed] to droop its wing," and she counted the weeks to be endured until the next vacation. Elizabeth's stormy moods were no help.

Elizabeth claimed to have recovered from the wounds inflicted by Mrs. Gardiner and Mrs. Cleveland, yet toward the end of the summer she still found herself crying uncontrollably whenever she was reminded of the painful scenes. Perhaps in an effort at exorcism, she undertook what she termed a "fearful experiment" when the sisters closed the Brookline school for a late-August vacation. Mary must have been appalled when she discovered that Elizabeth had written letters to each of their pupils, "telling them in black & white what [she] thought of their characters—both in school and out."

Elizabeth told some girls they were "unfeminine and indelicate"; others had "acted without principle" or were vain or overly passionate. As she passed out the letters on the last day of school, each one stamped with a wax seal bearing a lancet, signifying "I wound to heal," her hands shook as she saw the "sparkle" of eagerness with which the girls received them. Even if they hadn't always behaved well, Elizabeth acknowledged now with some regret, the Brookline students had been "exceedingly affectionate" toward their teachers. Although she might have harbored some resentment toward the girls, many just a few years younger than she, Elizabeth knew they were not themselves to blame for the wealth and leisure that sometimes spoiled their manners. She asked them not to read the letters until they returned home.

While Mary took the stage to Salem, Elizabeth left for a short vacation in Lancaster, consumed with anxiety and with a "presentiment of coming evil." She admitted to herself that she had not been able to shake off the "wretched state of mind" she had been in "for a very long time," and she was beginning to fear that she might never be able to "rally my spirits." If she failed to enjoy her visit to Lancaster, wouldn't that prove she had permanently lost "the susceptibility of happiness"? Perhaps the awareness that Lyman Buckminster had ended his life in such despair preyed upon her.

To Elizabeth's great relief, however, the opposite proved true. In Lancaster, she was restored to "my former rational self" after "four days continual conversation" with Dr. Thayer, who had "by a sort of sympathy entered into my mind and arranged all the discordant elements." She even recognized what a trial she had been to Mary and promised to make amends. When she returned to Brookline and learned that Mary had caught the mumps from Sophia in Salem, forcing her to miss the start of the fall term, Elizabeth wrote home impatiently, "I long to have Mary here. . . . Tell Mary if *she* can live without *me*—I cannot without her—*now.*"

When Elizabeth opened school again, she was thrilled to discover that her letters had actually succeeded. The girl with whom she had been most severe handed her a note of thanks. The entire class was now "quiet & grave—but affectionate," and one student, considered "incorrigible" by Elizabeth's predecessor, burst into tears when she saw Elizabeth and offered a sincere apology for her behavior. Elizabeth took up her fall's work with new confidence, full of plans for the school and for her own studies. Yet she vowed to avoid the fever pitch of "ecstasy" she'd felt during Lafayette's visit, "that rapturous sensation which if indulged in too long, causes a reaction of dullness." As she wrote in her journal, "may I be preserved from extremes!"

That fall, Mary and Elizabeth moved their school from the boys' Classical School building on the turnpike (vacant during the summer months) into their boarding house. Oddly, the new arrangement—in which the sisters slept in the attic at night and taught in the large room below each day—seemed a happier one. The knowledge that their twenty pupils would arrive every weekday morning forced Elizabeth to keep her books and papers in order, and a neighbor loaned them a broad, brilliantly colored Turkish carpet that made the sunny classroom seem "in itself a summer."

Now the sisters could sometimes spell each other during the schoolday, leaving Elizabeth free for several hours of study or conversation and Mary to indulge in the "laziness" she often could not resist. They enjoyed each other's company more than when they had been forced together through every long schoolday. When their students left for the afternoon, Mary wrote, "I take my [needle]work & E. a book, & here we sit for the hour together especially on a rainy day," Elizabeth reading aloud. The system solved the problem the two sisters faced when they got hold of James Fenimore Cooper's latest—*The Last of the Mohicans*—and both were so eager to read the book that they could not decide who should have it first. Like many independent-minded bookish young women, the sisters were inspired by Natty Bumppo's naive courage and honesty—the same characteristics that made Cooper's hero seem an unlikely frontiersman to male readers and critics.

But it was the Reverend Channing's return from Newport that secured Elizabeth's recovery and ushered in what she would one day call "an era in my life." In September 1825, Elizabeth began to make weekly trips to Channing's Federal Street Church, where she listened so closely to his sermons that, with her powerful memory, she was able to return home and write them down almost verbatim. Then one Sunday morning in early October, Elizabeth walked into Boston in a fog so dense she couldn't see three yards in front of her, only to find that Channing would not be preaching. She lingered for the afternoon service, and although Channing didn't take the pulpit, he rose from his seat in the congregation to make an announcement. "His voice so unexpectedly coming upon me," Elizabeth later wrote in her journal, "fluttered me to my very hearts core." She managed to shake his hand as she left the church with her friend Eliza Cabot, one of Channing's Sunday school teachers.

As the two women walked up Winter Street, Channing followed and joined them on the Common, where all three stopped—a diminutive trio, the charismatic minister scarcely taller than his women friends—to watch the sunset through the thick fog. "The sun shorne of his beams by the smoky atmosphere," Elizabeth recorded melodramatically, "rolled unshining along of a bloody hue." Channing was reminded of classical accounts of the skies following the "burning of towns in wars & conquest." As darkness fell, he turned to Elizabeth and invited her "to go home with him, promising to give me his ideas upon the suggestions I had made to him in my long letter from Gardiner with respect to missionaries into Maine. Of course I went."

It was a short walk to Channing's house on Mt. Vernon Street, where, Elizabeth wrote in her journal, Channing led her to the sofa in his study, seated her beside him, and began to discuss her letter. Elizabeth spoke freely, and to her surprise, so did Channing. It seemed that the minister no longer regarded her as the child who had "poured out her whole heart" to him at age thirteen. He was treating her as an equal. Soon the two were exchanging spiritual records of their childhoods: Elizabeth confided her first image of God as a smiling man, and her mother's scolding when she'd confessed it to an older student; Channing told of the gloom cast over his childhood by the brimstone rhetoric of a revival preacher he'd heard at an early age.

Such tales of personal progress from a repressive Calvinist upbringing to the freedom of liberal religion often helped deepen acquaintance into friendship for this first generation of American Unitarians, many of whom went on to become Transcendentalists. "Each of us felt that we had one case of development that we thoroughly knew, and that was our own," Elizabeth explained many years later, "and we offered ourselves freely as diagrams for demonstration of principles." The result, quite often, was an intense platonic friendship that seemed to defy categories. Passionate connections could be formed between members of the same sex, between married men and single women, even between unmarried men and women (usually the most formally choreographed of all relationships), all in the name of spiritual enlightenment. For some—usually women—these relationships could be a setup for heartbreak. For Elizabeth, reluctant to marry, yet eager for intellectual companionship, such friendships were a boon. She could hold regular intercourse with the Reverend Channing—which, in her circle, meant simply exchanging ideas—alone in his study or even in the presence of his rather grim wife, Ruth Gibbs Channing, who was also his first cousin and the heiress to a shipping fortune, without risking censure.

Not long afterward, on a Friday in late October, Channing rode out for a midday dinner with a Brookline family who invited both Peabody sisters to join them. Mary now had her own opportunity to observe Channing firsthand. The abstemious minister paid little attention to his food, but the dinner hour stretched into a long afternoon and evening of conversation on "religion, manners, dress, [and] his travels in Europe," Mary recorded. Pale and slight of stature, Channing could still be animated, even witty, and had "the sweetest smile imaginable." Yet, Mary wrote, "when he turns his full eye upon you, it seems as if it would search into the innermost recesses of your soul." More disconcerting to Mary was Channing's tendency to consider questions at length before answering them—sometimes leaving as many as ten minutes of "appalling silence," which only then was "amply rewarded . . . by the depth and beauty of his thoughts."

From this meeting, Mary concluded that Channing had "a most exalted opinion of women," whom, she explained, he "has a fine opportunity of judging, for he has the confidence of many." Whether because he revered women or because he simply felt more comfortable with them, Channing was, unlike the later Transcendentalists—Emerson, Thoreau, Alcott—drawn more to the company of women than of men. Indeed, it seemed the forty-five-year-old Channing used the minister's prerogative to mingle with his female parishioners more freely than any clergyman the sisters had encountered before. He would not, like the late-century Boston preacher Henry Ward Beecher, exploit the women he gathered around him. Channing had an androgynous quality, the result of his physical frailty as well as his genuinely empathic nature. It was the reason so many in his congregation had compared him to Christ. Women felt safe with him, even as he aroused their "highest" spiritual passions.

The next morning, Mary and Elizabeth rode into Boston with Channing, who had stayed the night in Brookline, at last "having him all to ourselves for a whole hour." Mary returned to Brookline alone in the carriage, but Elizabeth remained, continuing the conversation of the previous day—on Pestalozzi, Rousseau, Maria Edgeworth, the Christian miracles, and "*beauty*," which, to Elizabeth's delight, Channing distinguished from "mere neatness." On the following Saturday, when Channing knew he would not be preaching the next day, he sent for Elizabeth to spend the afternoon with him again. Mary reported that her sister returned to Brookline that evening looking "her very beautifullest and as if she had just come from the seventh heaven." And so, Elizabeth's "long apprenticeship" with the minister began.

Elizabeth began to hear from others that Channing had been impressed by her conversation, "spoke of me affectionately," or "expressed a wish to see me when I arrived in town." Gradually, Saturday-afternoon visits became a habit. Channing liked Elizabeth's candor, and her readiness to interrupt when she disagreed with him. She quickly recognized Channing's impatience with "persons . . . of a timid disposition or of an anxious temperament"; Channing could sympathize with such people, Elizabeth later wrote, but he "did not think their opinion about religious doctrine of any importance; because he thought these weaknesses inclined them to dependence on the . . . common creed." As Mary recorded at the time, Elizabeth "talked to him as none else ever dared to do, for she has none of that fear of him which most who approach him have in a greater or less degree." Elizabeth herself had begun to realize that it was "my peculiarity to sound [those] with whom I have intercourse to their depths."

If Elizabeth gave Channing an enthusiastic and challenging audience of one, Channing gave Elizabeth the attention and guidance she had craved since childhood. The years after she left home had been "so filled with painful moral experience that I had become depressed in hope," she wrote years later. Channing "gave me back my childhood's faith." All on her own, Elizabeth had read and studied her way out of the Calvinist doctrine of original sin. But she had merely substituted her own "Unitarian discipline," holding herself responsible for her "personal transgressions and sins" and never allowing herself "any relief from self-reproach."

Channing was able to assure her that such painful self-scrutiny was not the intent of the Unitarian faith, that "our life is woven into a social web" and that it is useless to attempt to "conquer fate by agonies of naked will." In short, she need not blame herself for her clashes with Mrs. Cleveland and Mrs. Gardiner, or for Lyman Buckminster's suicidal depression. It was Channing who released her, for a time, from self-doubt, advising her to "forget this bitter experience ... except so far as to learn to avoid making those mistakes in your turn." She should, instead, pursue self-examination of the sort that would "bring the mind to a consciousness of [its] highest" capacities. "The proof that our hour of self-examination is profitable," he told her, "is that we come from it stronger, more hopeful."

During their weekly conversations, Channing introduced Elizabeth to the work of the British Romantic poets—especially Coleridge and Wordsworth, who had befriended Channing as the apostle of a new American spirituality during his 1822 tour of Europe. He loaned Elizabeth a volume of Coleridge's essays, and they discussed the poet's use of the word *transcendental*. Channing was grappling with the concept in his own theology, and he confided to Elizabeth that he now believed "the idea of God, sublime and awful as it is, is the idea of our own spiritual nature, purified and enlarged to infinity. In ourselves are the elements of the Divinity." Channing never tried out these thoughts on his congregation; it was far too radical to suggest, even to liberal Unitarians, that God was an idea originating in man. In less than a decade, the young minister Ralph Waldo Emerson would resign from his prestigious Boston pulpit because he could not hide his own similar beliefs. Now, however, Emerson was still a student at Harvard Divinity School following, along with his fellows, a reading list drawn up by Channing and listening to the eminent preacher's sermons from the pew. It was Elizabeth who had gained an audience—and on a regular basis—with the man.

What did she learn? On one memorable day, Channing sat Elizabeth down and asked her to read Wordsworth's "Intimations of Immortality" out loud to him. Elizabeth would never forget the feeling of his eyes "gazing on me as if he would have read my inmost soul" as she spoke each word. Her mentor was "desirous not to lose a particle of the fact of its first impression on me." In 1825, Wordsworth's poetry was less than a generation old. Elizabeth was among the first Americans to read the phrases that are now so well known: "The child is father of the man," and "Nothing can bring back the hour / Of splendour in the grass, of glory in the flower." Elizabeth was captivated by Wordsworth's merging of themes that resonated so deeply with her own most cherished beliefs: the significance of early childhood impressions, the presence of God in nature. Not long after, she spent much of her earnings on a set of Wordsworth's collected works. Channing was at first shocked: he'd have gladly loaned her his own. But he could also understand that "one would prefer to possess" such books.

The Reverend William
Ellery Channing, by
Spiridone Gambardella

The influence of Coleridge and Wordsworth set Elizabeth writing again, at
first mainly in her journal. Inspired by Wordsworth's example of self-recollec-
tion and Channing's injunction to remain "hopeful," she began to analyze incidents from her youth: the scenes of disillusionment with her mother, the
shearing of her hair, the year spent with Aunt Elizabeth Cranch, the struggles
over Swedenborg, her parents' proscriptions on her reading. Elizabeth was
reinventing herself by searching her past for sources of a personal theology,
one that might sustain her through troubles worse than the petty carping of
wealthy patronesses.

Mary was relieved to see Elizabeth so steadily engaged. "She has been
living this winter upon Coleridge, Wordsworth and Dr. Channing," Mary
wrote to a Salem friend early in 1826. Mary often watched Elizabeth at her
work, unaware of what she wrote, but awed and daunted by her energy and
dedication. "She sits with a ream of paper at her elbow," Mary wrote the same
friend on another occasion, and "looks for all the world as if she was going to
write up all the thoughts there are about, and leave nothing for her contemporaries or posterity to do."

Elizabeth would afterward count the year 1826 as "the first year of my intellectual life," a year during which the self-doubt she had lived with for so long began to fade and she learned to trust her own thoughts. Starting in on a project she had dreamed of as a thirteen-year-old, Elizabeth wrote her own loose translation—a "free paraphrase," she called it—of the Gospel according to Saint John, in which she interpreted the famous opening verses, "In the beginning was the Word ... and the Word was made flesh," to mean that "moral truth-speaking" was a divine gift to man, empowering each individual to search for meaning in life. She was drawing on her earlier studies of the Greek language (*logos* was the Greek term, commonly translated as "the word," which Elizabeth was exploring in the original text) and Socinian and Unitarian theology, and grafting them to a Wordsworthian Romanticism, imbibed from Channing, that emphasized personal freedom.

Elizabeth showed her paraphrase to Channing, who was astounded by her "original thoughts." The "foundation of their intimacy" was secured, Elizabeth later wrote, when her hero told her, "God has given you a deeper insight into these high subjects than others have." Yet Channing also cautioned Elizabeth to "devote your powers to the service of your fellow creatures, and not use them to make yourself distinguished." Was Channing concerned that Elizabeth's views might arouse controversy of the sort he was reluctant to instigate in his own church? Or was he simply enforcing a code that required women to serve rather than to seek distinction? Whatever the reason, Channing was not now going to encourage his young disciple to make her "original thoughts" public by putting them into print.

As a twenty-one-year-old schoolteacher feeling grateful for a growing "intimacy" with the man whose mind she most admired, Elizabeth contented herself with Channing's praise. Indeed, she was "startled with mingled terror & delight" by his words, she wrote. She did not stop to question his instructions to employ her "deeper insights" in service to others. Elizabeth was ready to dispute orthodox theology, but not to challenge the social orthodoxy that told her teaching school was the single suitable occupation for a woman of intellect, especially when Channing himself upheld the convention.

Yet Elizabeth continued to write. She started work on an essay that ultimately stretched to six parts and nearly 40,000 words on the meaning of the Old Testament in the present day, "Spirit of the Hebrew Scriptures." Under the sway of the Romantic poets, she defied orthodox literalists and wrote that it is "in the poetical vein" that we "find the key" to interpreting the Bible. Beginning with the first of the essays, on Genesis, she set out to prove that "man is created imperfect" not because he is innately sinful but so that "he may have a share in building the edifice of his own happiness ... and that he may make and see himself *good*."

Elizabeth expanded on the notion she had introduced in her paraphrase of Saint John: that "every one of us" is free to cultivate an "inward soul" by searching for spiritual meaning, or "inward revelation." Each of us is an "*inalienable, absolute being,*" she wrote, asserting as well the "moral equality of woman and man." The individual's quest for meaning was balanced by what she called "the social principle"—a sympathy for others "spontaneous in every human being" and "rooted" in the human heart. "It is the consciousness of our nature which gives us moral power, and this alone," she wrote. The "recognition of personal identity" enables "our power of choosing"—the power of choosing for the good of others, she meant. Elizabeth was arguing something quite radical for her time and place: that personal choice and individual freedom were innate, and fully consistent with social responsibility and a "Godly" way of life. Following from the discussion she'd had with Channing about Coleridge's term *transcendental,* she called her new philosophy "*transcendentalism.*"

Elizabeth completed these essays, she later recalled, "with no view of ever being an author," but simply as an attempt to express "thoughts of my own." If Channing's advice to serve others had crept into her thinking by way of "the social principle," it continued to dampen her ardor for publication. She stored the articles away and showed them to no one for almost ten years.

But Elizabeth's growing intimacy with Channing may have inspired another of her projects in 1826: a letter to their mutual hero, Wordsworth. The audacity of her plan was impressive. At about the same age, Elizabeth's future colleague in Transcendentalism, Margaret Fuller, would write a long passionate letter to another Romantic icon, Ludwig van Beethoven—but Beethoven was already dead, and Fuller was addressing her hero imaginatively. Elizabeth's letter was a real one, and it contained a real-world business proposition —a further effort to follow Channing's advice and turn her "original thoughts" to the service of others. Still, she wrote to Wordsworth in a poetical vein, hoping to convey "what is in my heart with fervour and simplicity." She identified herself as "an American girl of twenty two," although she was still several months shy of her birthday, who had been "for five years . . . an instructor of youth." She began by describing her childhood, a distillation of much that she had explored in her journal and expressed now as a Romantic conceit. "I often felt a want of reality in everything around me," she wrote, "and experienced a thrill of terror inexpressible at the sense of loneliness amid the universe." In her own schooling, although it was "said to be a very fine one," she had sensed that "the whole theory of education was essentially defective." It seemed to her that "the soul was neglected." She recalled that, as a child, "I found old people hardly ever knew how young people felt," and she had vowed "to keep in remembrance how *I* felt & when I grew up to inform the world,—perhaps to lay out a better system."

Elizabeth then put forward her proposal: would Wordsworth write a volume of poetry specifically for children? "If this use of the divine art to which you have devoted yourself should strike you as feasible," she wrote, "it would be widely & rapidly circulated and perhaps a new & deeper tone given to the art of education." She closed by saying that if the poet wished to answer—and she "craved" the favor of a reply—he could write to her "care of John T. Kirkland—President of Harvard University—Cambridge—or of Rev. William E. Channing—Boston—Mass." She may have hoped that the stature of her protectors would influence the poet to respond. Yet she was careful to add that "no one knows that I have written—I fear it is taking too great a liberty and dare not ask advice." And then, as with her "free paraphrase" of Saint John and the essays on the "transcendentalism" implicit in the Hebrew scriptures, Elizabeth put the letter away. It would take two years for her to gather the nerve to send it.

A book of poetry for children by Wordsworth might have saved Elizabeth from the trouble she soon faced in Brookline. Instead, she embarked on her project to originate a "better system" of education on her own, using the instruments she had at hand—not poetry, but Unitarian theology.

Inspired by her weekly conversations with Channing, Elizabeth began to hold Saturday-morning discussion classes for the "older young ladies" in her school. Elizabeth and the girls "freely conversed upon some principle of life," which became the subject of the coming week's exercise in composition. In November 1825, the topics included "the Development of the Religious affections" and "our Savior as he actually was." Elizabeth tried to draw out the girls' own ideas, never "taking children out of their childhood," as she felt had been done to her once her precocious grasp of theological texts became evident. She believed she could help them discover an intuitive spirituality—the child's natural connection with the divine, which she felt her mother had severed from her back in Salem when she took a pupil's side against her daughter. But Elizabeth was testing out some of the most controversial ideas of her time on a class of young ladies; the simple notion that children might be able to derive their own religious beliefs was supreme heresy in most New England households. Elizabeth would soon learn why her mother had made the choice she did.

Channing listened eagerly to the results of these Saturday-morning conversations when Elizabeth arrived at his house for their weekly midday dinners. Years later she was startled to recognize, after reading over her Brookline diary, the convergence of their ideas. "In every instance," she wrote in a memoir of Channing, "the subject of composition I chose for my class on Saturday proved to be the subject of Dr. Channing's sermon the next day." She refused to consider that her own views might have influenced Channing's. The closest she would come was to credit Channing with making her a colleague in his own efforts at "self-education": "instead of subjecting my mind, he gave it liberty to grow with his," she wrote in her memoir. Channing often told her, she recalled, that "we were studying together—teacher and preacher—the high art of education." The notion flattered Elizabeth, and helped her believe she was accomplishing important work in her school.

Elizabeth so revered Channing, then near the pinnacle of his career, that it never occurred to her that ideas generated by the two of them would meet opposition in her own classroom. But Channing was preaching to the converted. While several of the girls in Elizabeth's class came from Federal Street Church families, others were reluctant to take part in exercises in liberal religion led by a twenty-one-year-old schoolmistress—no matter how brilliant she was said to be. One girl insisted, Elizabeth recorded in her journal, that "the view of the mind she had been taught was essentially different from what I represented it." Elizabeth assured the girl that she did not intend to discuss the "peculiarities of sect" and that "the ground I had taken I believed was common to all sects." She argued that all sects agreed that true religion was something to "strive after . . . hence all sects imply men have a capacity for it. This capacity is all I contend for."

But this was precisely the ground on which Elizabeth most risked the ire of the orthodox. Her student, becoming tearful, replied that "the Bible told her men were totally depraved, the heart desperately wicked." Elizabeth's sympathies were aroused. She could not resist trying to persuade the girl of her essential goodness, telling her that "self-knowledge is the foundation of Religion," not self-hatred. But she could not win. In short order, the girl asked to be excused from composition assignments, and her father summoned Elizabeth to his house to rebuke her for tempting his daughter to stray from her beliefs. A certain amount of religious instruction was expected in schools, especially small private schools for girls, if only as a means of instilling discipline. But by suggesting that religion was a matter of inquiry rather than rote learning, Elizabeth had made a radical departure—even as she hoped to stimulate in her students the questioning frame of mind that she believed underlay all genuine learning.

In December, Elizabeth shifted her discussions to less controversial topics: the "Domestic affections," memory as "the parent of the virtues as well as of the muses." But the damage was done. At an afternoon tea with one of the Brookline mothers, four of her students stopped in. Listening to their conversation, Elizabeth wrote afterward in her journal, "I heard from them so many of my own observations repeated in totally different coloring, such curious constructions put upon my innocent and meaningless actions, and received such an impression that all was going wrong that I became perfectly nervous."

Evidently her pupils, some of them several years older than Elizabeth had been when she had entered her own period of intense spiritual questioning, were far less open to self-examination than she ever expected.

She wondered how it could have happened. Had resentment over the past summer's letters of criticism been smoldering, only to be inflamed during her Saturday-morning discussion classes? Elizabeth learned that one of her Brookline neighbors, Lewis Tappan, had joined with the angry father to stir public opinion against her, augmenting attacks on Elizabeth's liberal religious views with rumors that "my word and conduct were unprincipled and unkind and ungenerous." Tappan was the same man who carried the sisters' mail in from Boston and drove them into town whenever he passed them in his carriage on the road. Yet Elizabeth had never entirely trusted him. She recalled now his "coming to me with that catlike familiarity which is so peculiar to him," causing her to "shrink from" his attempts to befriend her. Could he have been a seducer, the sort of man her mother had warned her against? Was he punishing Elizabeth for the times she had rebuffed him? Or were her attempts to engage a handful of teenage girls in religious inquiry really enough of a scandal to turn the whole town against her?

At night in bed, the same dark thoughts that had tormented her the previous winter returned "with tenfold force." She worried that Tappan's malicious talk would "destroy all the good effect I fancied myself to have produced upon my scholars." Were such whispering campaigns to be her perpetual undoing as she sought her living "unprotected by home"? She feared that this new crisis in a Boston suburb might leave her "injured in that reputation which is my family's chief wealth." She could not afford to be smeared as a corrupter of young girls' souls. When she learned from her Brookline allies that word of her troubles had reached the Reverend Gannett, Channing's new assistant minister, the news left her "unaccountably depressed," even though her friends assured her they had defended Elizabeth ably to Mr. Gannett.

In May 1826, Elizabeth received a letter from Tappan so "atrocious and contemptible" that she could not think how to answer it. Worst of all, the letter arrived while her students were on holiday, so she could not hope to counter the charges in class. The letter has not survived, but Elizabeth quoted one line in her journal. Tappan closed his attack with: "I have not the slightest confidence in your integrity or your honor." She felt as if the words were emblazoned in "large letters on my forehead." Elizabeth spent her week's vacation writing draft after draft of her reply. In some versions she angrily defended herself as an able guardian of her young charges' souls; in others she attempted to ignore the assault. She even tried humble deference to Tappan's judgment. In the end, she sent her most straightforward self-defense—and lost the students whose parents had allied themselves with Tappan.

In the aftermath of the controversy, Elizabeth decided it was time to move her school into Boston, to the inner sanctum of the religion she was helping to refine and the shelter of its "poet-prophet" Channing. Although she might have viewed the Brookline debacle as another setback of the kind she had suffered in Lancaster and in Maine, Elizabeth was beginning to realize that her own ambitions simply required a larger stage. Her mistake was not in making her attempt, but in failing to gather enough support for it to succeed. Elizabeth's Boston friend Eliza Cabot promised to help gather a school with her own niece as its first pupil. Then Channing himself offered his seven-year-old daughter, Mary. Elizabeth was pleased to find that "my own friends are as wonderfully kind in their interpretation of me, as strangers are uncharitable."

Mary Peabody might have felt differently about the new plan. She was finally beginning to adjust to the classroom routine in Brookline. "I don't think you ever saw so pretty a school in your life," she wrote to her Pickman friends in Salem that summer, "or so many sweet children together." As Elizabeth's sectarian controversy died down, Mary enjoyed new friendships with the older sisters of some of her pupils. There were impromptu musicales in their spacious drawing rooms and moonlit evenings spent singing on the hillsides overlooking Jamaica Pond and Boston. She would surely miss "all the delightfuls" of Brookline.

For Mary it had been enough to make occasional weekend trips into Boston to visit the portrait studios of Gilbert Stuart and Francis Alexander. At Alexander's, the young celebrity writer Lydia Maria Francis, whose novel of Indian life, *Hobomok*, had won instant acclaim, was sitting for a portrait that made her look as "fierce" as a "tiger." Although her most recent roman à clef, *The Rebels*, had angered patrician Boston, Alexander was said to be infatuated with Maria Francis, as she preferred to be called, and was painting the portrait free of charge. Mary enjoyed being privy to such gossip, but she was content to have come no closer to Francis than this glimpse of her portrait session; privately, she judged the young novelist's works harshly as revealing that their author "never was in love." (In this assumption, Mary seems to have been correct: Francis did not marry for another two years. Her choice was the newspaperman David Child; as Lydia Maria Child she achieved even wider fame as an abolitionist and as the author of the best-selling advice manual *The Frugal Housewife*.)

Elizabeth, however, continued to be drawn to the intellectual life of the city, and to the intellectuals themselves. In July, the sisters attended the first public examinations at Harvard's newly chartered theological school in handsome red-brick Divinity Hall. Once there, Elizabeth garnered an invitation to visit Professor Andrews Norton's private library at Shady Hill, his Cambridge estate, after the exhibition. Elizabeth went home with a biography of de Staël, which,

Mary wrote, "we have been trying to procure these two years," and Professor Norton's promise that she could borrow any books she liked in the future.

Elizabeth had made herself welcome in two of the most significant private libraries in New England: first Harvard president John Kirkland's and now that of Andrews Norton, America's leading Unitarian scholar. She could never be a student at Harvard College, let alone a graduate preparing for the ministry in the new Divinity Hall. But she had brought herself closer to these men than many of their young male students would ever come; the clash and collegiality of intellectual friendship Elizabeth hungered for was also her means of acquiring a graduate-school education. As she earned the respect of the men whose minds she most admired—many of whom shared her doubts about the standard education provided by New England's schools and colleges —it hardly seemed to matter that she would never win the degrees that her male counterparts could take for granted.

At the end of the summer term, in August 1826, the sisters' remaining Brookline pupils presented them with a handsome writing desk, filled with paper, pens, penknives, wax, and "a seal with a heart upon it"; its motto read, "You merit it." For Elizabeth, receiving the surprise gift was "one of the pleasantest experiences of my life." That night she wrote in her journal, "how delightful it is, this overflowing heart of the young. How blest is the employment which brings one in such close contact with it."

Yet Elizabeth was still determined to move her school to Boston. When she received word from Eliza Cabot that there were enough students ready to support the sisters in Boston, as well as the possibility of "making a good deal of money over & above tuition" by writing or translating, she was elated. "I never before could say that I had fully succeeded," Elizabeth wrote in her journal, because she had always longed to be "permanently established" in Boston. "This seems a kind of consummating of my plans." Thinking back on her run-ins with various authorities, she concluded now, "perhaps all the suffering I experience in this way is to teach me how to use power, when, as in the course of providence it may be, I gain it myself."

❧ 16 ❧

"Life Is Too Interesting to Me Now"

THE BOSTON THAT ELIZABETH AND MARY MOVED TO IN THE FALL OF 1826 was growing more receptive to women of accomplishment. The young literary lioness Lydia Maria Francis, whom Mary had observed sitting for her portrait at Francis Alexander's studio, was feted at parties throughout the spring; and the painter Jane Stuart had recently "flashed upon the world as a great genius," in Mary's words. Jane's aging father, Gilbert Stuart, had ceded her his studio, where Jane's own equestrian paintings now drew a steady stream of visitors. Mary, who hated to be "a bird of passage," hoped that the sisters would finally achieve "a certain degree of permanency" in Boston. There could be no better place for two young women of ambition to live and work.

For the next several years, the sisters' school was filled to capacity, and Elizabeth—still the head teacher—often kept a waiting list of eager girls. In the beginning, a half dozen of their most loyal Brookline students made the trip into Boston each day with their fathers. One of the Brookline girls was Lydia Sears, an orphaned minister's daughter with a substantial inheritance. Lydia boarded with Elizabeth and Mary in Boston, or in Salem under Mrs. Peabody's care, until her marriage to the scion of a wealthy Dedham family in 1830. All the Peabodys came to view Lydia as an adopted sister—albeit a more fortunate one. Elizabeth's supervision of the girl's education, her maneuverings with Lydia's guardian, and the spiritual counsel she provided in moments of crisis, left her with the conviction that she could succeed in the quasi-maternal role she had first practiced on Sophia.

Along with Lydia, there were other protégées: Fanny Jackson, the sweet-tempered daughter of a prominent Boston judge, and Mary and Sarah Hathaway, the orphaned twin heiresses to a New Bedford shipping fortune. Elizabeth discovered a "new pleasure" in teaching her older pupils, "those on the

Promenade on Boston Common, by George Harvey, 1830

verge of responsible life," as she considered them. She recalled that at their age, she had felt closer to fifty than fifteen, and "it was as much as my head & heart could do to go through the duties that pressed on me connected with the welfare of my family." Reaching her midtwenties, Elizabeth no longer mistrusted the wealthy girls who once seemed not to have "suffered enough to be *charitable*" to their teacher. She still wrote long letters of advice to her older students and required them to write essays analyzing their own character flaws, but she had learned to soften the tone of her assessments and "never to find fault unless circumstances will allow me to be near & watch the result."

Perhaps for the first time in her life, Elizabeth permitted herself some of the carefree manner of a schoolgirl. Still a trim, slight, if somewhat disheveled young woman, Elizabeth could often be found in the after-school hours, as Mary once described her, "extended full length on the floor at my feet . . . studying astronomy at the tip of her voice and ever and anon calling my attention to some beautiful explanation of a constellation." The book she read from, however, was no schoolgirl's text but a French treatise, Jean-Sylvain Bailly's two-volume *Histoire de l'Astronomie Ancienne,* from which she distilled lessons for her class.

In Boston, Elizabeth occasionally encountered resistance to her teaching methods from the parents of her pupils, but now she managed to win over her critics. One of these was her "beloved & revered" mentor, the Reverend Channing, who was astonished one day to find his seven-year-old daughter, Mary, memorizing several densely printed pages in an advanced Latin grammar. He wrote a brusque note chastising Elizabeth for putting Mary to work on "the minutiae of the tenses" when no boy her age would be expected to do the same. Indeed, it was rare for girls to learn Latin in school at all: the study was considered too taxing, and pointless as well, for no woman could enter a profession, such as law or medicine, that required a knowledge of the language.

Elizabeth felt differently, however. She firmly believed, as she had written Sophia several years earlier, that "mind has no sex." Regardless of the use a girl might find for a classical education later in life, Elizabeth saw no reason why women should not achieve intellectual equality with men. Learning classical languages strengthened the mind and supported the analytical approach she took in all her studies; it was a foundation, too, for the study of history. She sent back a letter to Channing informing him that Mary's exercise "was self-imposed . . . and had been perfectly recited." Generally Elizabeth required no homework of her students, she explained, but her method of teaching Latin directly from the ancient texts rather than with grammar books had so piqued the girls' interest that they had begged Elizabeth to be allowed to study Latin grammar by themselves at home. When Channing, at Elizabeth's suggestion, asked Mary why she was memorizing so complex a lesson and saw her genuine delight in mastering tenses, he had to admit, as he told Elizabeth when they next met, "You have triumphed."

"All great acquisitions come from voluntary thought" was Elizabeth's guiding principle. She would not cultivate any motive for learning in her students besides curiosity, claiming that study for the sake of reward or in fear of punishment produced "superficial rather than profound" knowledge. With her infectious enthusiasm, Elizabeth was able to make her theories work and to draw her students into far more challenging studies than most other teachers of young ladies ever attempted. The girls in her beginning Latin class discovered, once they started learning grammar at home, that their two-hour lessons three days a week with Elizabeth had kept them well ahead of their brothers, who studied Latin a half day every day in school and two hours at home each night. By the end of three years in Boston, Elizabeth wrote to friends in Brookline, "I have . . . more feeling of individual power than I ever had before." Teaching had become "*my craft.*"

For a time she employed a partner in her school, William Russell—a Scottish educator, elocutionist, and founder of the *American Journal of Education*—who took Boston by storm the autumn that Elizabeth and Mary moved in from Brookline. The sisters first encountered Russell in a series of weekly reading parties he conducted for the Channing family circle, widened to include several young schoolmasters, a future Harvard instructor of German languages, and occasional celebrity guests, such as the novelist Catharine Maria Sedgwick. At the opening session Elizabeth volunteered to read first and then submit to Russell's criticism. Mary, who wrote a full account of the proceedings in a letter to Maria Chase, remarked on Elizabeth's "courage," and begged off when her own turn came. What drew Mary's attention most, however, was the spectacle of the Reverend Channing "learning to read" out loud. It was "odd," she wrote, to see the spellbinding preacher taken to task for pitching his voice incorrectly. But Russell proved his worth at the end of this and later classes with his dramatic interpretations of English and Greek poetry, including a riveting enactment of Satan's monologue from *Paradise Lost*. For Bostonians mistrustful of staged drama, Russell's parlor recitations— presented as educational—were the ideal entertainment.

Elizabeth had hoped Russell, many years her senior and a minor celebrity in Boston, would take over the business of attracting students to the school, leaving her more time to study and write. But in the end, although he gave rousing performances each day for the girls, Russell, who suffered from respiratory ailments, could do little else after exhausting himself with a recitation. Indeed, for a period of several months when the sisters rented a house with Russell and his family to be paid for out of the proceeds of their school, it seemed that the elocutionist was abusing Elizabeth's generosity. In gratitude, Russell named a daughter born to his family during this time for Elizabeth (the first of several such tributes she was to receive in coming years), but she had to notice that he was not earning his share of the rent.

If Elizabeth's connection with the Reverend Channing was the model for future relationships with influential men, her involvement with Russell foreshadowed a number of disastrous entanglements with brilliant eccentrics. It came as a relief when, after two years' association, Russell was hired away by a male competitor. Financial concerns aside, Elizabeth found that she had "not been able to feel myself an assistant," nor had "the public" been willing to accept her self-demotion. Elizabeth was becoming a Boston personality, her school—experimental though it was—a Boston institution.

Even without Russell's assistance, Elizabeth managed to make time to take part in the intellectual flowering now under way in Boston. Her entrée came through Channing, who made Elizabeth one of a handpicked group of Sunday school teachers from Federal Street Church that met weekly to discuss religious education. Sunday school at Federal Street was no simple matter of singing hymns and quizzing restless youngsters on their catechism lessons. Classes were held only for teenagers or young adults, and they followed a Socratic method similar to the one Elizabeth had employed with her "older young ladies" in Brookline. Elizabeth was by far the youngest of the Channing disciples who made up his faculty. The group included two Harvard faculty members, several future ministers, and two unmarried sisters in their thirties—like Elizabeth, self-educated intellectuals. One of these, Elizabeth's friend Eliza Cabot, was translating the French theologian François Fénelon's essays for publication. The Sunday school meetings brought romance for Cabot, who married her fellow teacher, the Harvard German instructor and future Unitarian minister Charles Follen.

Elizabeth next joined Channing's "education party," an informal group consisting of the Boston philanthropist Jonathan Phillips and a handful of local teachers and Unitarian clergymen who met weekly in Channing's study. Over the course of several years, the discussion topics evolved from abstract issues of educational theory to more practical questions about the best means of assisting Boston's "less favored," in the phrase of minister to the poor Joseph Tuckerman. "No book ever gave me such a treat as these conversations," Elizabeth wrote to Dorothea Dix, another Channing protégée of the time, who would later become nationally known as a crusader on behalf of the mentally ill. Elizabeth enumerated for Dix a "multiplicity of things to do" that were making life "too interesting to me now."

But Elizabeth was more intent on deepening her connection with Channing than on befriending her peers or Channing's less luminous clerical colleagues. Reluctant to substitute Sunday school teachers' meetings or education party gatherings for the regular private encounters with Channing she had come to rely on while living in Brookline, Elizabeth engineered a project that would ensure they could continue—one that may also have followed from Channing's admonishment to serve others rather than make herself distinguished.

It began with Elizabeth's suggestion that Channing prepare some of his sermons for publication. When Channing pleaded that he hadn't the time or strength to copy his rough notes for the printer, Elizabeth volunteered to do the job herself. Channing was reluctant to burden his young friend with the task, but Elizabeth insisted that it was no effort at all; she could do it while "listening to an interesting book read aloud," she boasted. Channing promptly handed Elizabeth his sermon notes and copying paper and began to read from a French edition of Plato's *Timaeus*, translating spontaneously and eyeing Elizabeth to be sure she was taking in Plato as she wrote. In spite of his doubts, Elizabeth supplied an excellent copy after this "severe test"; the job of copyist was hers, along with the privilege of regular evening visits.

Over the next several years Elizabeth copied more than fifty of Channing's sermons, sometimes filling out his notes from her own memory, as Channing read to her, translating into English the books of the French philosophers Victor

Cousin and Baron Joseph-Marie de Gérando, then coming into vogue with for-ward-thinking Bostonians. Her work ensured that Channing would become more than just the most popular liberal preacher of his day. She set down his words—among the first examples of what later would be called "the literary sermon," closer to personal essays than scriptural homilies—for posterity.

For a time in the late 1820s, Elizabeth became a fixture in the Channing household. She served as the reverend's amanuensis, but she was also practi-cally a member of the family. She often walked home with Mary Channing after school, read to her mentor from the latest English newspapers, stayed for supper and then to hear Channing read to his son and daughter at bedtime. After the children were asleep came copying sessions, or, if Channing was unwell, Elizabeth read aloud until the ailing minister nodded off.

Although Channing's wife seems to have attended education party meet-ings, she rarely appears in Elizabeth's accounts of the time, and then chiefly as a manager of household details, concentrated on raising the children and feed-ing her sickly, finicky husband. Perhaps Ruth Channing was grateful to Eliza-beth for providing the intellectual diversion she hadn't the time or inclination to supply for her husband. Or perhaps Mrs. Channing is absent from Eliza-beth's reminiscences because the adoring young schoolteacher preferred to overlook her idol's wife. In either case, Elizabeth plainly could not stay away from this family ruled, unlike her own, by a benign patriarch. As she later wrote, she simply fell into "the habit of spending my evenings with Dr. Chan-ning." In short order, the two had become, in Elizabeth's words, "extremely in-timate." No one seemed to object—not even her sister Mary.

For Mary, meanwhile, was warming to Boston, where she felt free at last to make her own plans and pursue her own friendships. In Brookline she had relied on Elizabeth to beg rides into Boston; once there, she followed in Eliz-abeth's wake. But Mary had begun to tire of playing Boswell to Elizabeth's Dr. Johnson, as she recorded her sister's meetings with Channing and the other celebrated ministers of Unitarian Boston in letters home or to friends in Hal-lowell and Salem. Mary joined Channing's education party for the better part of a year, and she took her own notes on what she considered to be Chan-ning's most "transcendent" sermons, including one in which he advised his listeners to "look within, into their own souls and find heaven there. He made this desire, religion." But Mary never felt compelled to press for membership in Channing's inner circle; she would not compete with her sister for his at-tention. Instead she began to cultivate an interest in a sternly charismatic Methodist, Father Edward Taylor, Boston's waterfront preacher, who would later become the inspiration for Melville's Father Mapple in *Moby Dick*.

In the summer of 1828, Elizabeth received the ultimate sign of acceptance from her mentor: an invitation to spend a month at Oakland, Channing's

Oakland, Channing's summer house in Newport

wife's eighty-acre estate near Newport, Rhode Island. Oakland was purchased by the Vanderbilts later in the century and made into a Gilded Age showplace. In the 1820s, however, it was still a comparatively modest establishment, centered on a plain Federal-style house with a pillared verandah along one side. Still, the house was filled with mahogany furniture, china, and silks collected by Channing's father-in-law, George Gibbs II, one of New England's most successful traders in Europe and Asia, and it was surrounded by exotic specimen gardens.

Elizabeth learned on her arrival at Oakland that Channing had insisted that his wife retain sole ownership of her share in the property, as well as of the entire amount of her inheritance. This arrangement was rare for the time: by law, a woman's property became her husband's when she married. Perhaps Channing was enlightened on the topic of women's rights; just as likely, he may have wanted to keep his distance from the Gibbs fortune, derived from the infamous triangle trade in African slaves—by the 1820s a source of shame to all right-thinking New Englanders. At home in Boston, Channing's family shared the Gibbs mansion on Mt. Vernon Street with his mother-in-law, but the minister insisted that his wife and children live within the bounds of his modest salary. The bounty at Oakland in summertime, however, was too delicious to abstain from. Here, he refused all responsibility for running the estate, with one exception. A pacifist in even the smallest details, Channing had ordered that no game be hunted on the grounds. The result was an almost Edenic quiet, broken only by ocean winds and birdsong.

Each morning at sunrise, Elizabeth joined Channing as he walked the garden paths with his young son and daughter, "inquiring into the aspect of the earth and the sky, into the life of the flowers and of the birds that made their nests in the undisturbed bushes." Then the great man rang a handbell calling family and servants to morning prayers. At breakfast, Elizabeth noticed, Channing consumed only a cup of black tea and a slice of toasted brown bread. Channing told her that he suffered from an incurable "contraction of the stomach," brought on in his divinity school days when he had deliberately starved himself, believing that he could study longer hours if his body had no need to burn off fuel in physical exercise. Now, almost thirty years later, he considered himself unable "to eat enough to support a man's body," and, in the inverse of his student regimen, could do no more than a few hours of strenuous mental work each day.

At Oakland that summer, Channing's craving for fresh air and exercise provided a convenient excuse for him to take Elizabeth on long drives through Newport and the surrounding countryside, recounting tales of his childhood in Rhode Island. With Elizabeth, the ascetic minister could forget that his marriage had lifted him into an echelon of wealth that made him uneasy. By different routes, both Elizabeth and her mentor had arrived at a similar attitude toward New England's landed gentry: they would rather be guests, or even hired hands, than full members of the ruling elite. So it was with recollections of his humbler boyhood as one of ten children of a Newport lawyer that Channing now scanned the skies for signs that the winds and tide were right, then drove Elizabeth and his own children in an open wagon down to the shore. Dressed in "bathing bombasets," they held hands "in a long band" and walked into the surf, letting it "roll over us,—a sport most exhilarating to Dr. Channing," Elizabeth wrote. Ruth Channing did not join these excursions, but she sent along a strong Negro servant—the descendant of Gibbs family slaves—with orders to hold fast to her husband's hand lest the frail minister and his charges be dragged out to sea.

Elizabeth returned from Newport, Mary reported, "perfectly blissified." And she was even further transported by a letter she received from Channing afterward. He told Elizabeth that she had "passed through the furnace of a nearer inspection and daily scrutiny, not only unhurt, but with increased favor." Although he noted that in the matter of "*exteriors*" she was not yet a "faultless model" to children, she had "sensibly improved." She had "a noble mind in its moral and intellectual power," and he asked that she always treat him, in future, as a "fellow-being." She couldn't have imagined a higher reward for her devotion.

ℛ 17 ℛ

An Interior Revolution

SOME OUTSIDERS BEGAN TO FIND THE PEABODY-CHANNING RELATIONSHIP unsettling, however. To a more conventionally modest young woman than Elizabeth, the gossip might have proved daunting. A friend of Channing's warned him, he wrote her, that "I injured you by attention." And a "calumnious" rumor that Channing *exploited* the enthusiasm of an impecunious young friend"—Elizabeth Peabody—by putting her to work copying his sermons for no pay had traveled as far as England. No doubt both Elizabeth and her mentor were aware that, had she been one of his Harvard Divinity School students, such objections would never have been raised. To Channing's credit, he refused to let the talk compromise the friendship, assuring Elizabeth that, far from injuring her, he believed the attention he paid her could only be to her benefit—words Elizabeth rejoiced to hear. In any case, her intellectual infatuation was too intense to break off the connection because of a groundless rumor. As she wrote many years later, her firsthand "knowledge" of Channing "justified all the imagination and faith of my enthusiastic youth."

Most of the talk that went on behind Elizabeth's back now was favorable. After their first meeting at one of William Russell's reading parties, the popular novelist Catharine Maria Sedgwick, whose roots were in western Massachusetts and New York, had been so impressed with Elizabeth that she proposed her as a model for her niece to emulate. Although "Miss Peabody" was younger, Sedgwick wrote, she had already taught for several years in and around Boston, where teachers "are of the first caste—the first order of gentility." Furthermore, Peabody was "a very intelligent and highly improved young woman" who had her own distinct methods. "Her pupils," Sedgwick explained, "do not commit any lessons [to memory]. She reads to them—and talks with them. She begins with Homer as the earliest history, and in order to give them the best notions of mythology—she then follows the stream—reads Herodotus [and] Thucydides—."

Elizabeth's world was expanding rapidly now, taking her farther than ever, in spirit at least, from her provincial Salem girlhood. The distance became painfully obvious during the winter of 1828 when Elizabeth consented—to her parents' distress—to have her portrait painted by Chester Harding, the most famous portraitist in Boston after Gilbert Stuart. Although the bulk of Harding's income came from society portraits, his subjects included nationally recognized celebrities such as Washington Allston, John Quincy Adams, and Daniel Boone. Both Dr. and Mrs. Peabody were appalled to learn that their daughter had joined, even indirectly, the company of such public figures.

This was a time, before photography, when women of Elizabeth's class might sit for painted miniatures or silhouettes that were stored away in pocket-sized cases as keepsakes by family members. Dr. Peabody treasured one such crude likeness of his mother, painted on wood, which measured just a few inches high. But a full-scale portrait in oils meant to be hung on the wall as a work of art was still a relatively new medium, even for women of New England's upper classes. In Elizabeth's case it was not a wealthy husband or father who would pay for the portrait: in a scheme to help support Harding's large family and to enhance her own reputation at the same time, Elizabeth had invited the artist to send his children to her school tuition-free in exchange for the painting.

When Elizabeth sent the finished portrait to Salem as a gift to her family, Mrs. Peabody wrote back brusquely that she was pleased her daughter had not chosen to be "taken with a library of books about you," as the historian Hannah Adams had done for her sittings with Harding. But the truth was, the portrait created a scene. Once it was unwrapped, Grandmother Palmer rushed up to the vivid likeness screaming, "Elizabeth! why Elizabeth!" Neighbors dropped in to gawk, and Mrs. Peabody, mortified by her mother's crude outburst and her daughter's immodesty, gave way to tears and took to her bed. Twelve-year-old Wellington attempted to calm her with the reminder that "Lizzy ... did not spend any money about it." But the high price of such a portrait was not Mrs. Peabody's concern; rather, it was Elizabeth's apparent vanity and ostentation. She confided in a letter to Mary that, while she had once hoped "the good would triumph" in her eldest daughter, making Elizabeth "a blessing in her day & generation," she knew now that she had been "mistaken."

Sadly, the painting—the only likeness of Elizabeth Peabody as a blond, blue-eyed young woman—burned in a New York City warehouse fire late in the century. No copy exists, and we cannot know precisely what disturbed Mrs. Peabody, beyond what she took to be Elizabeth's hubris in having the portrait made. Mrs. Peabody was no conformist. In the wake of Elizabeth's

Chester Harding, self-portrait

Brookline troubles, she had advised her to "judge of herself, and not again suffer . . . from what others say or think." Yet her high ambitions for her daughters collided with exacting notions of female humility derived from her own austere childhood and reinforced by her fear that standing out might attract disaster. To her credit, Mrs. Peabody managed to forgive her daughter this impropriety once she saw that Elizabeth came to no harm. After a week's time, she wrote Elizabeth that the Harding portrait was "doing hurt" only because "it is making us wish for more": Elizabeth in person.

The incident brought a turning point in family dynamics, however. Previously, the Peabodys had merely hoped that Elizabeth's teaching might augment the family income. Now the portrait signaled the prominence that Elizabeth had achieved in Boston. The family began to consider ways of joining Mary and Elizabeth there, with a plan of making their school the foundation of the family's earnings.

The first step was to send fourteen-year-old George to share the sisters' rooms while he attended Boston's English Classical School. George's habitual lethargy had caused his parents to despair of his ever finding a profession. The boy was often sick, and it was Elizabeth's plan that he should withdraw from the college preparatory course at Salem's Latin school and ready himself for an "active life" in business. Boston would be a good place to make his start as an apprentice, once he finished off the less rigorous course at Boston English.

Young Welly needed direction too, in Elizabeth's view. Still the brightest of the boys, and the only one now with the real prospect of a college career, Welly had little self-discipline and a taste for mischief. Dr. Peabody enrolled him for several terms in the North Andover Academy, where he had once served as preceptor, and sent him for a summer on the Peabody farm in New Hampshire in hopes he might "take to farming business." But the boy was already too citified—he had never even ridden a horse—for the experiment to succeed. Only the eldest son, Nat, plodded along in Salem's public schools, an indifferent student, reciting his lessons in a timid whisper, frightened by the canings and floggings he witnessed there.

Mrs. Peabody puzzled over her three sons, so different in ability and motivation from her daughters. "I am sure the mind of a Boy arrives more slowly to maturity than a girl's," she once wrote hopefully to Mary and Elizabeth. She tried to persuade herself that it was too soon to worry, but she had little notion of how to guide her sons away from the downward course that had become the seemingly inevitable fate of so many men in her family. Their father's example of frustrated ambition, all too often surfacing in angry outbursts against his wife and children, compounded the problem—and surely was one of its sources.

The one piece of encouraging news from Salem, soon after Sophia's seventeenth birthday in 1826, came from her drawing teacher, Miss Davis, who reported that the girl had shown signs of "very uncommon talent." But this praise only made Elizabeth eager to bring Sophia to Boston as well, so that she might study art with the masters.

• • •

Perhaps it was her concern with the boys' schooling, along with her conviction of the deficiency of American education generally, that prompted Elizabeth finally to send her letter to Wordsworth. She was also gaining confidence in her powers as a correspondent. When Harvard president John Kirkland retired in the spring of 1828 and left New England for an extended tour of Europe, he made Elizabeth one of his regular correspondents. As she received Kirkland's monthly letters describing the cultural riches of the Old World, and saw how eager he was for her own accounts of the intellectual life he had left behind in Cambridge and Boston, she lost the reservations she once held about writing to Wordsworth. To her delight, the poet answered her letter. He gracefully refused the children's book suggestion but invited Elizabeth to visit him at Dove Cottage and "talk." Although she was forced to turn down the invitation—"I fear I shall never see Europe," she wrote—Elizabeth had received further confirmation that she could be counted as a "fellow-being" with the great men of the age.

Writing back to Wordsworth in March 1829, Elizabeth showed she had moved beyond the sectarian controversies that had preoccupied her for more than a decade and was beginning to sense the cultural shift that would usher in the era of Transcendentalist reform. Indeed her words anticipate Emerson's rallying cry, the "American Scholar" address of 1837. "Everything in the forms of society & almost in the forms of thought is in a state of flux" here, she wrote. It was a productive instability, she believed. Writers and artists in the New World were "unfettered" by what Wordsworth called the "weight of custom." There was possibility for genius to arise virtually anywhere. "The young men come down from our back woods . . . having conversed alone with the powers of nature," she wrote, to "fill our first rank of society." She had seen the careers of the unpolished schoolmen of Lancaster—Warren Colburn, George B. Emerson, Jared Sparks—take root and flourish. Boston's Chester Harding, a farmer's son who'd produced his first work with sign paint and a board, had made himself into a master of portraiture. Even the Reverend Channing, the god in Elizabeth's firmament, had emerged from Rhode Island —"a pale midget with a trembling voice," in one biographer's account—to become one of the most influential preachers of his time.

Elizabeth acknowledged that "political ambition & the spirit of commercial enterprise quench the pure enthusiasm" in some New Englanders. But "there was a time before it was dammed up with paper mills and saw mills," she wrote, and "the soul cannot forget this period of its glory—the stream of romance still flows calm & untouched." She predicted that America would "see *grand souls* indeed, which would do in the republic of letters, in the temple of lofty sciences" what the founding fathers had accomplished "fifty years since in politics." She saw a "more interior revolution" in the making that would "give life to . . . those forms of freedom which Washington & his friends left to us."

And—unlike Emerson, who would later define "the American scholar" as "Man Thinking"—Elizabeth expected to count women among these cultural revolutionaries. She wrote of the "tremendous excitement [that] begins when each takes his own destiny into his hands," and she added that in place of "each" she'd almost written "every woman." Although conventional usage would not allow her to express it, and she dared not venture the outright statement to Wordsworth, Elizabeth herself was beginning to feel that "tremendous excitement" when *a woman takes her own destiny into her hands.*

During the preceding year, Elizabeth had entered "the stream" of literary romance. Two years earlier, she had turned down the job of editing a literary anthology, *The Souvenir,* on the advice of her mentor Channing, who felt she should attend to her new school. But now she took on the editorship of a Christmas anthology for children called *The Casket*—a term meaning a small chest filled with jewels. One of the literary jewels she published in the anthology was her own.

The Casket was among several new "whip syllabubs of literature"—as the Peabody sisters referred to *The Souvenir, The Token, Youth's Keepsake,* and other illustrated gift annuals—that provided an increasingly popular forum for new writers. Americans often published their work anonymously in the annuals, alongside celebrated British authors whose writings could not be copyrighted across the Atlantic and were thus fair game for anthologists. Nathaniel Hawthorne would publish his first stories in this way during the coming decade. Elizabeth's *Casket* selections included poetry by her fellow Sunday school teacher Eliza Cabot, Wordsworth's "To the Skylark," a story by Mrs. Peabody based on Palmer family lore, and more than two dozen other entries whose authors were identified by their initials, if at all.

Elizabeth's contribution, a retelling of the German fable *Undine,* published in 1800 by Baron Friedrich de La Motte-Fouqué, was the centerpiece of the volume. Hers was the first rendering into English of a story that would be widely translated through the century to come, inspiring an opera and a Tchaikovsky ballet, while Hans Christian Andersen wrote his own variant, "The Little Mermaid." Elizabeth's version, which she titled "The Water-Spirit," was so much her own that she sometimes referred to herself as "the author of Undine." It was a tale she frequently summarized in her teaching, and the story as she told it revealed nearly as much about Elizabeth as about the spiritual matters she hoped to illuminate for her students.

Undine is a beautiful but unruly sea nymph, one of a "faery race" of "frolicsome" undersea creatures who lack souls. Undine's father, the Prince of the Mediterranean, wants his favorite child to have an immortal soul. Without one, it is impossible to love and to do good, "to attend and remember" people long enough to care about them. Yet in order to acquire a soul, Undine must marry a mortal and leave the undersea world behind. The prince unleashes a flood that carries away a fisherman's daughter and leaves Undine in her place. Undine grows up in the fisherman's cottage, full of "vivacity, wit, brilliancy," but seeming to "care for nothing but herself"—until a second storm brings a handsome knight, Hildebrand, to shore. Because she has no "maidenly timidity," Undine immediately proposes marriage, something "real women never do." Hildebrand is "excited" by the "strangeness" of her proposal, and he accepts. At her wedding, Undine is "changed from a child to a woman in a moment," Elizabeth writes, "silent, attentive, and tender."

But the reader soon learns that simply possessing a soul is not enough to cause one to act lovingly or to do good. In fact, most of the mortals in the tale are prone to treachery, thoughtlessness, and vanity—the sins of life in a material world "which prefers the things of *show* to the things of *truth*." Undine's freshly acquired soul turns out to be the truest one of all. First, Hildebrand confesses to Undine that at the time of their wedding he was already engaged to Bertha, a young woman of property who turns out to be the fisherman's lost daughter. Undine offers to renounce her marriage in favor of Bertha, but the bewildered Hildebrand refuses. Then Undine attempts to reunite Bertha and her fisherman father—but Bertha angrily dismisses the old man. When Bertha's wealthy adoptive parents learn that she is a fisherman's daughter, they turn her out of their house. The kindhearted Undine invites her to live in Hildebrand's castle, where Hildebrand and Bertha continue to socialize with the town's nobility while Undine devotes herself to helping the poor of the surrounding countryside. Marriage, she tells Hildebrand with gratitude, has made her "a living, spiritual, suffering woman."

Finally, Hildebrand and Bertha persuade Undine to leave off her good works long enough to take a pleasure trip by boat, during which the conflicted Hildebrand turns on his wife in anger. An enormous wave rises up, sent by Undine's father, and threatens to wash Hildebrand out to sea. But Undine steps into the wave and is swept overboard to her death. The grief-stricken Hildebrand tries to overcome his remorse by "employing himself as Undine used to do, in doing kind things for the country people." Yet he soon weakens and dies. Near his grave a "little fountain well[s] up," an earthly sign that the spirits of Hildebrand and Undine now "worship God together in Heaven." At last they can "love without shadow, in the world of souls."

In the simple facts of its plot, "The Water-Spirit" seems to support the notion that women—whether sea nymphs or mortals—have no place in adult society until they marry. Yet Elizabeth's version of the fable reads more like a fantasy of accomplishment by a single woman than like an endorsement of marriage. Married or not, Undine is always a free agent. Unmarried, her wildness is both attractive and forgivable, a rare vision of a girl's life without restrictions. It is easy to imagine that Elizabeth might have realized in the young Undine her own repressed desire to "care for nothing but herself." Married, Undine becomes another of Elizabeth's ideal selves: a teacher of fallen souls by her own example of suffering and self-sacrifice. The pagan sprite becomes a female, domestic Christ.

Marriage in "The Water-Spirit" is a chaste partnership, a chiefly spiritual state, perhaps because Elizabeth wrote the tale for young children. Yet a platonic alliance may also have been the only kind of union Elizabeth could imagine for herself. Elizabeth was well aware of the hardships—what her mother called "the golden toils"—of most marriages. For Undine there are no fleshly delights in marriage, but also no small children to care for. Even Hildebrand is dispensable once the marriage ceremony has taken place and the formerly selfish sea nymph becomes a self-motivated philanthropist. Undine shares her husband with the less-deserving Bertha, leaves the couple to an earthly partnership, and waits for a reunion of souls in heaven. It was to be a pattern Elizabeth followed more than once with her own sisters.

Yet absolute isolation is never Undine's goal. Caring for others is her chief concern, as it had been Elizabeth's at least since the Saturdays with the Reverend Channing in 1826, when she had claimed "the social principle" as "spontaneous in every human being" in her essays on the Hebrew scriptures. As she wrestled with the spiritual questions that would occupy New England's reformers in the coming decade, Elizabeth gravitated toward a communitarian view rather than toward the cult of the self-reliant individual that Emerson and Thoreau would espouse. Whether because teaching was central to her professional identity or because she had grown up accustomed to accepting responsibility for her own large family, Elizabeth would always feel inextricably linked to the human community, even as she sought the inner strength to think "thoughts of my own" and to make them heard. Her clashes with relatives, friends, and mentors had only revealed to her what she considered an essential need: to connect with others. Like Channing and Wordsworth, she was ready to find sources of the divine in the human soul. But what she found there was different, perhaps because she was a woman. "What alone is divine in human nature," she wrote to a friend at about this time, is the "power of being interested to tenderness in others."

"Love is *the end & destiny* of the human soul," Elizabeth declared in the same letter. The question remained: how to achieve that destiny?

PART V

Sophia

1829–1832

✑ 18 ✑

Dr. Walter

FROM THE FALL OF 1826 TO THE EARLY WINTER OF 1828, MARY AND ELIZ-abeth had lived in four different Boston boarding houses—some too noisy, others too distant from their students' homes to stay in for more than a term. Finally, in the spring of 1828, after a year during which the fourteen-year-old George shared their living quarters, Elizabeth persuaded her father to move the entire family to Boston to save paying rent on two households. Dr. Peabody would commute by stage to Salem twice a month to maintain his dental practice. Nat, now sixteen, took an apprenticeship in a pharmacy at the corner of Washington and Winter streets.

At first Dr. Peabody rented a house in Colonnade Row, a new block of elegant brick buildings designed by Charles Bulfinch overlooking Boston Common. With Mary and Elizabeth's school "profitable" and three student boarders helping to cover expenses, the prestigious address seemed affordable. The next year, however, he found a cheaper house a few blocks away on a narrow side street near the Granary Burial Ground, exchanging a "beautiful prospect," Mary mourned, for a view of brick walls, back yards, and gravestones of Revolutionary War heroes. Sophia, awarded a top-floor room of her own, which she quickly dubbed "my *snuggerie*," was lucky to be able to catch a sidelong glance of the Charles River by peering out her window. She claimed, nevertheless, to delight in the golden glow that filled the sky on autumn evenings—"all the glory of sunset without seeing the sun"—and she decorated her tiny attic room with amaranths and peacock feathers. The family would remain at 7 Tremont Place until 1832.

At nineteen, Sophia was entering an uncertain adulthood. A year before she joined her older sisters in Boston, Nat had written from Salem that Sophia was now "never entirely free from headache." Frequently she stayed in her

Colonnade Row, facing Boston Common

room during meals because the clatter of knives and forks had become such "excruciating torture." When she sat with the family for an evening of reading and mending in the parlor, her father was forbidden to rock in his chair because of the dizziness it caused her. More disturbing were Sophia's occasional bouts of what the family referred to as "confusion," when pain and fever kept her delirious in bed for days at a time. Sometimes these episodes were a prelude to a feeling she described as "a floating off of my senses," or, most frightening of all, a "syncope of the brain," during which she briefly lost consciousness. No doctor in Salem had succeeded in diagnosing, let alone curing, her condition.

Sophia's symptoms were a puzzle to which a collection of doctors so numerous she called them "the Faculty" had offered a multitude of remedies, some worse than the illness itself. First, there was her father, whose purgative doses of mercury in Sophia's infancy later came to be considered by the family as the chief reason she seemed destined to become "a life-long invalid." In treating Sophia's headaches, Dr. Peabody favored the painful procedure of blistering the skin with hot plasters to draw off pernicious internal humors thought to be the cause of recurrent headaches. Mary once summarized the theory, in which Sophia's childhood willfulness, first ascribed to teething, had been converted into pain: "I have not the least doubt that the humour from which you used to suffer so much when a child & which was so suddenly driven away to all appearance, is the cause of your headaches." Sophia's best hope for being "cured of the scourge," Mary explained, was in "bringing it out" by "exciting" the skin. In a related effort, Dr. Peabody closely monitored Sophia's diet—insisting on "abstinence from animal food" at one time, bland meals of rice and milk at another—as a defense against humors thought to lodge in the stomach. Yet nothing he tried could tame "my rebellious head," as Sophia termed it, in apparent agreement with her sister's diagnosis.

In Salem, there followed a succession of doctors—Hubbard, Nichols, and Treadwell—who proffered leeches, ammonia, carbonate of iron, and colchicum (an extract made from the poisonous seeds of the autumn crocus, still used today in the treatment of gout). Sophia found only temporary relief in each new remedy. When she first tried leeches in 1826, in a further attempt to draw out the suspected humors, she praised them as "generous, fine, disinterested, excellent, dear, elegant, knowing, graceful, active, lively, animated . . . fascinating creatures" and pronounced them "the very quietest, easiest way of freeing oneself from pain that can be thought of." She had not felt "so essentially better" for six years, she wrote to her sisters in Boston. Yet the headaches returned, and she ultimately dismissed the "little vile imps of darkness."

The family had high hopes for Sophia with the move to Boston, which promised a change of scene as well as the opportunity to make something of the talent for drawing she had begun to display. Sophia looked forward to studying the work of Boston's prominent artists in the city's galleries and studios, and to taking lessons, as Elizabeth had promised. In anticipation, Sophia appeared to be gaining strength. Late in 1827, before the family's move to the city, she spent two weeks in Boston attending lectures on perspective. And in January 1828, feeling more vigorous than in recent years, she took Mary's place in school while her older sister retreated to Salem for several weeks to recover from a brush with rheumatic fever. Suffering only occasional debilitating blasts from the "cannonaders in my temples and forehead," Sophia had managed to teach and to attend a sermon delivered by the newly minted Reverend Ralph Waldo Emerson and a party in the portraitist Chester Harding's exhibition rooms, all the while developing a fondness for Boston, "this capital of my world."

But when the entire family descended on Boston and the Peabodys were at last gathered again under one roof, Sophia's health deteriorated. "Sophia took to her chamber in a few days after our arrival the 19th of March," Dr. Peabody wrote his brother in June 1828, "& has continued in it with a very few days interval ever since." What began as a bad cold swiftly led to "an uncommon degree of intense pain in her head—so that she could not bear the least noise." Mrs. Peabody exhausted herself watching over Sophia as she shuddered through the nights, delirious with fevers and the "terrific visions" she was prone to in her most severe attacks.

After a separation of nearly five years, Mary, who sometimes relieved her mother now at her sister's bedside, was alarmed to see that for Sophia sleep was "no 'sweet restorer' . . . but rather a curb taken from her self government, leaving the elements of her being in a state of wild chaos." The eminent doctors Shattuck and Warren were called in, and a new pharmaceutical arsenal employed: sulphate of iron, arsenic, quinine. Nothing seemed to help. Overcome with anxiety, and helpless to effect a cure, Dr. Peabody confided in Elizabeth that he feared "a speedy termination of her sufferings": he believed Sophia would not survive the summer.

Even as family members and her sisters' students tiptoed through the narrow townhouse, speaking in whispers and shutting doors as gently as possible, Sophia, sequestered in her upstairs room, appeared "bright" in her lucid moments, although too dizzy and weak to walk, and "grateful for every pleasure & every alleviation." As Elizabeth wrote to a friend in Brookline, years of experience had made her fragile sister entirely "submissive to pain." Indeed, in a curious inversion, Sophia ultimately declared her gratitude for the "very great blessing of sickness" that had allowed her to construct an "inner temple whither I can retreat with heavenly Father to say to him '*I am willing* & happy in being so!'" Willing to die is what she meant.

This attitude was expected in an invalid—particularly in a woman. "How fortunate it is," Mary had written of Sophia a year earlier, "that she has so much of that courage which is peculiar to woman—patient endurance." Yet Sophia's surrender to pain went beyond endurance. From Salem, she had written to Elizabeth that she "felt a perfect exhilaration of spirits & exalted in my pains —because GOD saith he chasteneth whom he loveth." She discovered that there could be worldly compensations for such a life. "Blessed be every pain that has rent my head asunder!" she wrote at about the same time. The charismatic Reverend Walker had visited Salem and "inquired for *me!* . . . He asked how my headache did!" In a household where Elizabeth had set the bar high for encounters with influential men, Sophia was finding a way to compete.

Yet during the spring and summer of 1828, Sophia's condition seemed so precarious that even she could find little to be grateful for. It was a sign of the family's desperation that Dr. Walter Channing—Boston's leading doctor of midwifery and the younger brother of the Reverend William Ellery Channing —was called in for consultation. The Peabodys were ready to consider an alternative explanation for Sophia's illness, one prevailing in Philadelphia and

Dr. Walter Channing,
by William F. Draper

Edinburgh, where the independent-minded Channing had trained. In this view, chronic headache was a disease of explosively overactive "sympathetic nerves" emanating, in a woman's case, from the uterus. The family hoped Channing's expertise in women's physiology would provide the answer that the "humoral" diagnosis had not.

But there was more to recommend Walter Channing than his medical training. Sophia had first met "Dr. Walter," as she soon began to call the burly, mustachioed physician—as a means of distinguishing him from the more celebrated "Dr. Channing," his brother William, D.D.—six months before at the party in Chester Harding's studio. As the two stood admiring a copy of a Joshua Reynolds portrait of the young Samuel Johnson, Walter Channing may have spoken of his own childhood hopes of becoming a painter. The ambition was squelched by his family, but it was a sign of what one biographer has called "a romantic flair then still unusual among descendants of New England Puritans"—and never to be extinguished in Walter Channing. Drawn to the literary scene that his older brother had come to dominate in Boston, and marked by sorrow with the death six years before of his young wife from tuberculosis, Walter Channing was nevertheless as robust and worldly as his brother, William, was sickly and ethereal. He may well have had William's case in mind when he wrote, for the 1818–1819 *North American Review*, an article "On the Health of Literary Men," recommending strenuous exercise and a wholesome diet and condemning the practice of "intellectual forcing" that imposed long periods of intensive study on growing boys and young men.

When Walter Channing was called to Sophia Peabody's bedside in 1828, cases like hers were relatively unknown. Much more familiar was the pale, consumptive beauty whose disease claimed her with swift violence in a matter of a few short years. In New England, during the first half of the nineteenth century, as many as one-quarter of all deaths may have been attributable to tuberculosis. Channing's own wife, Barbara, had succumbed at twenty-six, fighting for her life while giving birth to the last of the couple's four children during a delivery overseen by the grief-stricken father.

Sophia had none of the distinctive symptoms of pulmonary tuberculosis, but few who knew her could imagine that her illness was not also a degenerative disease. "It must be expected that every year of such physical suffering will render her nervous system more sensitive," Mrs. Peabody wrote the year Sophia turned eighteen. Even as her husband concealed from her his own worst fears, Mrs. Peabody confided in Mary that Sophia's "loss of consciousness is an evil, for which I endeavour to prepare my mind."

As it turned out, the Peabodys were fortunate in their decision to call in Walter Channing during this crisis. Perhaps because he had witnessed so much female suffering, Channing had taken a particular interest in the chronic invalid, whose cluster of ailments he would later label "bed case" in a pioneering work on the subject. By the time he published his 1860 pamphlet with that title, Walter Channing had observed scores of women whose "morbidly acute" sensitivities had confined them to bed for years despite the absence of any "troubles" that actually "threaten life." In 1860, Channing wrote with assurance that the only risk of death was in patients whose withdrawal from active life was so extreme that they refused food and gradually wasted away, the Victorian era's equivalent to anorexia nervosa. In 1828, he told Sophia's anxious parents the same thing: whatever ailed her, Sophia was not about to die from it.

Channing's term *bed case* never took hold, but he was among the first American doctors to identify a syndrome that was ultimately labeled *neurasthenia* as more women fell prey to it late in the century. Sophia's illness was not classic neurasthenia, defined at the time as a generalized weakening of the nervous system. She suffered from migraines, whose wide range of manifestations was probably not known to her doctors in Salem and Boston: sensitivity to light and noise, dizziness, confusion, fever, insomnia, night terrors, syncope, all of which are now understood to be relatively common, if severe, migraine phenomena when accompanying a headache. Yet in the absence of modern medication, Walter Channing's approach was probably the best one available at the time for migraine, as well as for the more vague maladies of the neurasthenic "bed case."

Although Channing was only beginning to gain an acquaintance with the syndrome in the late 1820s, he instinctively approached Sophia much as he would his later patients. In contrast to her previous doctors' prescriptions, Walter Channing's treatment of Sophia, as recorded in her journals, seems oddly casual, scarcely even medical in nature. In *Bed Case* he wrote, "The great object should be to get the confidence of the patient" by accepting and sympathizing with her complaints. Any dispute over the patient's "beliefs and notions" about her illness would "directly tend to its increase." Only after a bond of trust was formed could family members and physician succeed in persuading the patient "by means so gentle" to take gradual steps toward increased activity and eventual full recovery.

The root of the problem, Channing believed, was the patient's inward focus, an "entire absorption in one's self" that, masked by a host of physical complaints and a disconcertingly compliant and cheerful manner, usually escaped the notice of friends and family as they anxiously strove to make their sufferer comfortable. Almost imperceptibly, he noted, the patient will have constructed for herself "a refuge from a thousand annoyances" in a bedroom filled with books and attractive pictures. She plies herself with opium—as Sophia is known to have done at least occasionally—"with its promises and performances of solace and sleep." Over time, the "effort for cure is gradually given up," with the result that "the bed is the home of the sick."

But rather than blame the patient for a failure of initiative, Channing charged the medical community with neglect: it was the "abandonment of these cases by physicians, and friends" that was "most to be deplored." By 1860, Channing had come to believe that "cure is to be regarded as the rule, not the exception; and . . . it must be found in the use of the mind, both of physician and patient." Sometimes, he wrote, it could be "a new physician" or "some extraordinary, unexpected change in condition" that will "let the *attention* of the patient, the *direction of consciousness*, be detached . . . from *herself*, and given, heart and soul . . . to something *out of herself*." Then "we may find a change produced which we might, under other circumstances, have regarded almost as miraculous." Channing had several times seen patients rise from their couches, fully cured in an instant, leading him to conclude that, while most women took to their beds at first with genuine illness, "habit alone has kept the patient in bed." And habit, Channing believed, could be overcome.

Channing's views were well ahead of his time—and perhaps for that reason were never widely accepted. More popular treatments, like those of the celebrated Dr. S. Weir Mitchell, who accepted "neurasthenia" as a chronic and debilitating illness, involved restricting activity rather than encouraging it incrementally. Channing's prescriptions foreshadow the style of treatment advocated by the modern-day migraine expert Dr. Oliver Sacks in his definitive *Migraine: Understanding a Common Disorder*. Any cure for what Sacks calls the "habitual" migraine patient, who experiences "incessant unremitting migraines," as Sophia Peabody did, first requires the development of a "trusting relationship between physician and patient." Like Channing, Sacks recognizes that this most "deeply incapacitated group of patients—may be *attached* to their symptoms, in *need* of them," and "may *prefer* the migraine way of life, with all its torments, to any alternative which is left open to them." Even modern drugs are likely to bring only temporary relief: it is the situation producing the migraine that physician and patient must work together to identify and change.

Yet even Walter Channing's sympathy for the "bed case" went only so far. Like most nineteenth-century New Englanders, he expected a healthy woman to direct her attention "out of herself," most commonly toward a husband and children, but always in a life of service to others. As he wrote to Sophia a year after he began treating her, "Get all health, and though it be so happy to be ministered to, you will also become then a minister of good and plenty." He did not recognize the desire to focus inward—a requirement for anyone contemplating a career in the creative arts—as legitimate in women. Nor, probably, did Sophia herself. Before Channing tried to persuade her otherwise, illness had been her best guarantee of an "inner temple whither I can retreat." Under his care, she began to reconsider the bargain she had made with her own health for the sake of otherwise forbidden selfishness.

Channing's prescriptions for Sophia were minimal: a few grains of rhubarb mixed with magnesia, morning fasting, shower baths, carriage rides, a trip to the seashore. His visits were impromptu and often purely social—one suspects intentionally so—and he kept them up long after the initial crisis that brought him to her bedside had passed. Perhaps because she never knew precisely when he would be coming, Sophia began to look forward to Channing's visits more than to any other doctor's examinations. He "always leaves me in a glow of delight," she wrote in her journal a year after he'd first appeared at her bedside.

Walter Channing enjoyed reminiscing about his student days at Harvard, where, taking the opposite tack from his dutiful brother William, he was dismissed without a degree for taking part in the famous "Rotten Cabbage" rebellion of 1807—a food fight in protest of the inedible dinners produced by the college kitchen. He could laugh about it now that he had been named professor of obstetrics and medical jurisprudence at Harvard's medical school. He entertained the entire Peabody family with stories about Byron that he'd learned from the poet's tutor, a Mr. Rogers, during his travels in Europe as a medical student. In the 1820s and early 1830s, perhaps hoping to win a place alongside his older brother in Boston's literary pantheon, Walter Channing wrote essays on *Hamlet* and *King Lear* and an article distinguishing authors from mere writers for the *United States Literary Gazette*. He often left manuscripts with Elizabeth, asking her opinion and urging her to pass them on to Sophia. Channing seems to have used his literary efforts as a means to draw out his patient and to tempt her into mental exercise. Sophia, however, preferred to hear Channing read "his productions" aloud to her in the low, gentle voice that, she confided to her mother, "wakes the sweetest echoes of my heart."

Despite Channing's propensity for chatter, his conversations with Sophia were never one-sided. He encouraged Sophia to talk about her symptoms and listened with what may have seemed to her more than a physician's clinical attention. "It is one of the privileges of our profession to learn much of human suffering," he wrote to Sophia when he first began treating her in 1828, inviting full, free confessions of her condition. Once she began to provide them, he flattered her stoicism in the face of pain, calling one account she sent him of a particularly fierce headache "another proof to me, that how ever long, and severe the hours of pain may be, the mind may still remain true to itself."

However Sophia might have interpreted them, it is clear in light of his stated methods that Channing's letters and visits to "my much esteemed friend and patient" were chiefly aimed at finding a cure. His praise of her "perfect submission" to pain always contained a cautiously worded hint that she might one day give up the life of suffering she had chosen. He was not, he wrote, "enamoured of martyrdom in my friends," and he repeatedly assured her that "in your case . . . disease has made no conquest" and "eventually you must do well." For a New Englander, Channing had a touch of the hedonist and was given to issuing statements of his personal philosophy. One observation that Sophia recorded in her journal must have struck her, in the hard-pressed Peabody household, as attractively unthinkable: because the "primary object in every man's mind," Channing told her, was "to live comfortably," he thought it must be "the design of Providence" to do so.

All this gentle prodding began to work. Sophia started to draw again, well enough that her sisters' wealthy students began to commission sketches— some of which she wished could be given instead to *"dear* Dr. Walter." Gradually she emerged from her room to take tea with visitors, especially Walter Channing. And she began to attend church, where, not incidentally, she could hope to meet her physician. On one particular Sunday, Sophia noted in her journal, Walter Channing "looked so *beaming* bright & spoke in such liquid music & shook hands so cordially" that "for a time I felt not my poor weary dizzy body."

By 1830, the relationship of trust Channing aimed for had been firmly established—becoming perhaps even stronger on Sophia's part than he had intended. More than twenty years her senior, and a widower with children aged eight to sixteen, Channing may not have considered that Sophia could develop a romantic interest in him. Yet, early in their acquaintance, Sophia had served as intermediary when Channing arranged to take Elizabeth's protégée, the orphaned heiress Lydia Sears, then boarding with the Peabodys, for a Saturday-afternoon drive. Lydia herself was sickly and no older than Sophia, but she had a handsome income and social standing. After Lydia announced her engagement in 1829 to the Dedham lawyer Samuel Haven, Sophia might, despite her relative poverty, have entertained hopes that Walter Channing would permit himself to become not just the "new physician" who could bring about Sophia's cure, but even, possibly, that "something *out of herself*" to which she would give her attention "heart and soul."

There were times when Sophia "felt shockingly all day & had a longing desire to see Dr. Walter, & as if he understood my wishes intuitively he came— . . . lovely & kind & interesting as usual." Nothing pleased her more than a spring morning when his "chaise came up to the door & the whole entry was filled with the ringing tones of Dr. *Walter,* who ran upstairs, his eyes glowing . . . & his whole countenance reflecting . . . the beauty of the day." Before Sophia had a chance to recite her symptoms, Channing had burst out, "Sophia, how do you do?—you cannot but be well on such a day." Only from Dr. Walter could Sophia tolerate the assumption of improved health; certainly he was the only one of her doctors who was inclined to make it. And no matter how she felt when he arrived unannounced, Channing was the only one of all the "Faculty" whose mere presence "utterly banished all sense of pain and made me sensible only of enchantment."

Her family, pleased with Channing's diagnosis, rendered early in 1830, that Sophia was "without any disease but *the habit of being sick,*" nevertheless noted the attachment with some concern. Mrs. Peabody remarked that "she so loves Dr. C. that if he prescribed decapitation I believe she would feel uneasy not to submit." And how could the family afford the lengthy rest cure in a warm climate that Channing now recommended? Beginning in 1829, a voyage to South America or Cuba was repeatedly considered but had to be abandoned as impractical or too costly. More fundamentally, Mrs. Peabody questioned Channing's advice to Sophia to put aside her artwork and ease herself instead into the domestic sphere with needlework, which he may have considered a less challenging, perhaps even comforting enterprise. Sophia "has resolved to go out every tolerable day & not paint, read or draw so much as she has done," Mrs. Peabody wrote to Mary with some alarm in the fall of 1832. "Why is painting worse than sewing? I, who see more & better, because always with her, how she is affected by different employments than any one can, am certain that sewing of any kind, would be what she could not endure." Mrs. Peabody had always allowed her daughters, whenever possible, to shirk household duties in favor of self-improvement, particularly when the activity might one day bring an income. But Sophia may have been entertaining the notion of another calling entirely.

One Sunday in June 1830, Sophia asked *"kind Dr. Walter"* home after church, only to have him counter with an invitation to visit his own newly renovated house on nearby Tremont Street. There "he enacted the hospitable lord," Sophia wrote afterward in her journal. "He got a book and read some of his own productions, at my request, in a tone that rung through my depths, and then after talking awhile, he accompanied me home." One can only imagine the hopes such a visit might have stirred in the twenty-year-old Sophia. Yet whatever domestic reverie Sophia had concocted involving Walter Channing was almost instantly dispelled.

On the way home, Sophia's youngest brother, Wellington, passed the couple on the street and "did not recognize us at first." When all three met up again at the Peabody house, Channing joked that it was little wonder Welly had missed them in the crowd of Sunday strollers: "two such poor old people— Sophia here—she ought to have a cane—I can but just uphold her." Were these her physician's true feelings for her? Had the outing caused Walter Channing to drop his optimistic bedside manner and reveal his opinion of Sophia as impossibly frail, just when Sophia, for once, wished to be seen as a vital young woman?

Stunned, Sophia refused to permit Channing to examine her, feeling "altogether too sick and tired and nervous to be touched in any way," and, for the first time, glad that her physician "did not stay long . . . for even *he* was one too many for my then condition." Not long after, she spent a night "pursued by horrid visions," dreaming that she was about to be "boiled for some heresy and that Dr. Walter attempted to avert the doom, but died himself before he had rescued me." Walter Channing had failed her.

Sophia recovered, at least in a measure, from this episode, but she was deeply shaken the following year when Channing announced his engagement to Eliza Wainwright, a woman of independent means and nearer his own age. Perhaps sensing the effect the news would have on her, Channing made a special visit to discuss his plans with Sophia, who described the scene in her journal. As on earlier occasions, Sophia had felt sure, when she heard a caller "knock with the greatest animation," that it would be Walter Channing. Although she opened the door for him with "a leaping sensation," she was reassured when "he took my hand in the warmest manner," and "I saw how unreserved he felt." Could Channing, too, have harbored more than the usual feelings of a doctor for his patient? Yet his news was not at all what she wanted to hear. "When he went," Sophia wrote in conclusion, "he took off his glove & in such a sweet way—shook my hand—that not a word could I say." On that day, Sophia claimed to be happy for him, and even wrote Eliza Wainwright a note of congratulations. But she once again refused Channing's visits until she was thrown into what her father called "one of her sickest turns" a month later, requiring nightly watchers for two weeks.

The attack began one morning when "I awoke with fierce pain tearing my brain" and was followed by four days of "inexpressible agonies," during which, Sophia wrote, "for a few hours I very nearly lost the governance of my intellect & felt that if such sensations lasted in full power much longer I should surely *go mad*." Now she felt "obliged" to send for Dr. Channing, who attended her throughout the ordeal with "unwearied solicitude." This time he prescribed hyoscyamus, an extract of henbane, a variety of nightshade from which the modern antispasmodic scopalomine is also derived. "Dear Dr. Walter—have you found the cure at last?" she wrote in her journal. Hyoscyamus, with its powerful sedative effects, became Sophia's favored remedy—"my kind potion"—for the next several years, soothing her nerves, although it could do little to touch her headaches.

Most likely, however, Sophia's greatest relief came in finding that Walter Channing had been "as usual invaluable." She had assured herself that the doctor-patient relationship would not be altered by his engagement to Eliza Wainwright. From then on, his visits continued to be "refreshing," but now the invigorating effects rarely lasted. There seemed little incentive for further gains; indeed, quite the opposite. This may have been the moment when Sophia concluded, as she wrote later of Dr. Walter Channing, "one must be sick to know his *tout ensemble*. That pale angel—*suffering*—alone admits you to the holy of holies of his mind. . . . That pale angel is my dearest friend."

Sophia's connection with Walter Channing faded with time—perhaps as both doctor and patient tacitly acknowledged that any further progress arising from his treatment was unlikely. But her attachment to the "pale angel" of suffering remained firm, as she waited for something, or someone "*out of herself*," to dissolve it.

❧ 19 ❧

"My Soul Steps Forth upon the Paper"

DURING THE SUMMER OF 1829, AS SOPHIA WONDERED IF SHE WOULD ever "lay aside this weary shroud" of pain, Elizabeth met Francis Graeter, a German illustrator and drawing master recently arrived in Boston, at the Reverend Channing's house. Graeter was also a literary man, and Elizabeth had just finished reading his first book in English, a novel titled *Mary's Journey*, which told the harrowing tale of a young woman reared in the German countryside, orphaned by revolution, and beset by lustful barons. Mary's story ends happily when she discovers her talent for landscape painting and joins the household of a wealthy female philanthropist who supports her work. "Whatever is living in nature," Graeter wrote, "its elementary spirits, whether slumbering, smiling, or in majestic wrath, she conjured up by the charms of her inspired mind, her art." No doubt Elizabeth was attracted to this vision of a productive, self-sustaining sisterhood, as well as to the heroine herself: an unreformed Undine whose mind was "free from any slavish imitation" and who had given herself "entirely up to nature." Elizabeth knew she must hire this man, with his singular faith in female potential, to teach drawing in her school.

Soon after Graeter's lessons commenced, Sophia began to drift downstairs into the classroom to hear him talk—Graeter could speak as well on German literature and philosophy as on color theory and perspective—and she finally tried her hand, again, at sketching a landscape. It had been nearly three years since she'd taken lessons with Miss Davis in Salem, an interval spent more in her bed than at the drawing table. In Elizabeth's recollection of the moment, the usually voluble Graeter looked over Sophia's shoulder as she worked, offering no comment. When she had finished, Sophia looked up and asked, "Have you no word of criticism for me?" Graeter answered, "I can only envy you."

This was not the first time Sophia's work had won unexpected praise. Growing up in a family in which fine art was virtually unknown, Sophia had ventured into drawing in a tentative way. At thirteen, seeking to add one more accomplishment to the sisters' collective teaching repertoire, she took a few lessons on Saturday afternoons, several with her aunt Amelia Curtis, who had her own school in Salem. Curtis recognized that drawing was fast taking the place embroidery once held in a girl's education. Several years later Sophia tried again, under the direction of Miss Davis, a more skilled teacher whose school featured daily art lessons. Here Sophia showed the first signs of what her family and friends called her "genius." While the other girls were copying outlines of simple household objects, Sophia insisted on trying a landscape that Miss Davis warned was "much too difficult to imitate." But Sophia succeeded brilliantly in her teacher's eyes, transferring the image in precise, sure lines to her paper and capturing the spirit of the original composition.

Soon Mrs. Peabody had arranged for Sophia to receive drawing lessons each afternoon in exchange for helping Miss Davis teach arithmetic and grammar during the mornings. In Elizabeth's recollection of the first afternoons with Miss Davis, Sophia's work was always "so perfect in each lesson that it looked like a model. She never made a false stroke." Yet from the outset, Sophia herself saw drawing as more than a craft to be mastered for later use in teaching. Art was a higher calling, with a potential for self-expression. After six months, she was still working at landscapes and firmly attached to the process. "I could not possibly express to you the intense delight I experience in every stroke of my pencil," Sophia wrote to her sisters in Boston. "My soul steps forth upon the paper."

A slip of a penknife, slicing deep into the base of her right thumb, for a time threatened this early start. The wound itself healed, but Sophia's forearm swelled up from infection, and Dr. Peabody predicted that the muscles in her thumb might "wither away." In the end, there was no lasting damage, but the accident provided Sophia with an excuse to skip her morning teaching duties; Miss Davis urged her to continue the afternoon lessons as best she could, and Sophia happily complied. As long as her subject was delicate enough, Sophia claimed—she was now copying an intricate etching of a swan—drawing bothered her far less than any other work she might do with her hands, either writing or sewing.

What ambitions could Sophia have formed as a young female drawing student in Salem? In the mid-1820s, aside from the illustrations in travel guides and gift annuals she practiced copying for Miss Davis, and the few works she might glimpse on an occasional visit to one of Salem's more opulent mansions, most of what she knew of painting and sculpture came to her in words. She read the ecstatic descriptions of Italian art treasures in de Staël's *Corinne*

—all of them based on works by men. At sixteen, she copied long passages into her commonplace book from a play about the Italian Renaissance painter Correggio, a high-toned melodrama that emphasized the role the artist's wife, Maria, played in his career. It is impossible to know whether Sophia was inspired more by the painter's dedication to his calling or by the sacrifices Maria was willing to make so that her husband's "fugitive creations" would reach an admiring public. The final scene could have appealed to any sixteen-year-old girl: the painter dies in his wife's arms on a city street amid strangers who take the devoted couple for "lovers still—not married people."

From Boston, in Elizabeth's and Mary's letters, came news of a fledgling art scene, primarily organized around the portrait studios of Chester Harding, Rembrandt Peale (transplanted briefly from his native Philadelphia), and the aged Gilbert Stuart, whose daughter Jane now completed much of his work for him. Elizabeth and Mary, both determinedly self-educating, visited the portrait studios and reported on the images of national and local luminaries they found there, meeting the artists and sometimes the sitters. When Elizabeth's own portrait by Harding arrived in Salem in 1827, causing Mrs. Peabody's tearful retreat to her room, it was among the first oil paintings Sophia had ever seen.

The next fall, Sophia came down to Boston to visit the studios herself. At Peale's, she found George Washington's portrait and a half-finished Mrs. Catharine Gardiner, along with a brilliant likeness of Charles Bonaparte, Napoléon's ornithologist nephew. At Stuart's, Daniel Webster, Nathaniel Bowditch, and Harvard president John Kirkland hung on the walls, and the brilliant young actor Edwin Forrest, in town playing Othello, was sitting for his portrait. But Sophia had missed the signal event of the year, and of the century, for Boston's art world: the opening of the Athenaeum picture gallery in the spring, in which, Mary had written, "all the fine paintings in the city, public & private," were exhibited.

Two decades earlier, Gilbert Stuart had blocked the establishment of an academy of instruction in Boston, arguing that anyone wealthy enough to endow such an institution would certainly compromise its artistic integrity. This lack put Boston at a disadvantage compared to Philadelphia, where the Pennsylvania Academy of the Fine Arts, founded in 1805, was already cultivating a number of the landscape painters who would later gain fame as members of the Hudson River school. But by the 1820s, Stuart was happy to give his nod of approval to a gallery planned as an extension to the Boston Athenaeum's new library building on Pearl Street, near his own and Harding's studios—particularly when the gallery's founders announced that they planned to purchase Stuart's work as the basis of a permanent collection.

Previously, exhibition space in Boston had been scarce and inadequate.

There was Doggett's Repository, a frame gallery where artists displayed large pieces, often singly, in an attempt to raise money on ticket receipts. (Doggett's was where Elizabeth had strained her eyes gazing too closely at a collection of locally owned works.) Occasionally the large hall over Faneuil Market had served the same purpose. Starting in 1825, the Pendleton brothers' lithographic studio had doubled as a modest gallery, selling small paintings on card stock by local artists, along with prints and plaster casts of classical subjects. Goodrich's auction house sometimes held an oil painting or two beyond the usual lacquered boxes and porcelain urns from China, as the fortunes of Boston's ownership class rose and fell.

In 1827, the Athenaeum Gallery became Boston's first and, for the next fifty years, only museum of art. That May, when the exhibition rooms opened, the Athenaeum's permanent collection included just seven works: six portraits (five of them either Stuart originals or copies of Stuart works, two by his nephew Gilbert Stuart Newton) and *Rebecca at the Well,* a biblical scene first supposed to have been painted by Titian, then attributed to Murillo, and now known to be a copy. It was a small start, but the 1827 exhibition itself ran to more than three hundred works on loan from local artists or collectors, hung in long rows stretching all the way to the ceiling. Half were attributed to old masters, although many were known copies or—like the Murillo—fakes. Elizabeth and Mary Peabody, along with other discerning viewers, gravitated to the twelve Washington Allstons and the half-dozen American scenes painted by the newly acclaimed self-taught Philadelphian Thomas Doughty. Both sisters refused to take sides in the debate over which portrait of George Washington—Gilbert Stuart's or Rembrandt Peale's—achieved the better likeness.

Even the Athenaeum trustees were astonished by the show's success. After just one week, 2,000 season passes had been sold in a city with a population under 60,000. By the end of the three-month show, $2,500 had been raised. Yearly exhibitions followed, and within five years the permanent collection had expanded to nearly fifty works.

Along with the rest of Boston, Sophia and her sisters were caught up in discovering visual art. It became a mark of distinction to be able to discuss important artists and their works knowledgeably, to collect art, or, at the very least, to see and be seen at the Athenaeum's yearly shows. Among New Englanders, the ascetic legacy of the Puritan age and the privations of two wars with England had given way to a compelling urge to admire, critique, and, if one had the money, acquire works of art. Elizabeth hoped to turn this wave of enthusiasm to Sophia's benefit. Why shouldn't she make a profession of what one Salem friend called "her darling art"?

The lack of an academy in Boston may have helped Sophia. There was no art school from which she could be excluded, as women were from the Penn-

Athenaeum Gallery, Pearl Street, Boston, 1830

sylvania Academy until 1844. Under Elizabeth's plan, Sophia could learn to paint in oils by apprenticing herself to a master, observing him at work, and then copying some of his productions. She could sell her copies to cover the cost of her materials and, eventually, contribute to family expenses.

The plan had plenty of precedents. Before the opening of the Pennsylvania Academy, American artists like Thomas Doughty and Chester Harding, who could not afford to study in Europe, learned their trade by apprenticeship and by copying works loaned to them by wealthy benefactors. Young painters supported themselves by selling copies until their reputations were strong enough to bring commissions for original work. Even those who trained in Europe's academies found copying instructive. In his student days, Washington Allston copied Veronese and Rubens in Paris and developed his own style through a conscious emulation of both living mentors—Benjamin West, Thomas Lawrence—and old masters, borrowing compositional elements, adapting color schemes, or painting similar subjects as he gained confidence in his own powers.

Luckily for Sophia and other talented young artists, early-nineteenth-century patrons of the arts were nearly as happy with carefully executed copies as they were with the genuine item. Before the invention of photography, which several decades later made European art widely known through picture postcards, the only way Americans could learn about the art treasures of the Old World was by looking at hand-painted copies. Few felt that there was much point in distinguishing. The composition *was* the work, from this point of view: a Salem merchant who owned a copy in oils of a Raphael Madonna could freely state that he owned Raphael's *Madonna*. The Joshua Reynolds portrait of Samuel Johnson that Sophia Peabody and Walter Channing had admired together in Chester Harding's studio was certainly not a Reynolds original. It may have been a copy by Harding himself, yet they both viewed it as essentially Reynolds's work and admired it as such.

Boston's newly eager collectors paid high prices for good copies. Elizabeth encouraged Sophia with the news that a wealthy friend had paid $60 for a copy of a painting by Carlo Dolci, the same amount their brother George, now out of school and clerking for the importer Thomas Searle, earned in two months. By comparison, Chester Harding averaged $100 for his original portraits. Washington Allston, one of the most highly regarded American painters and a member of London's Royal Academy, asked as much as $500 for his paintings at the peak of his career. Unfortunately, Allston worked slowly, taking years to complete a single work; Harding could finish a portrait in a matter of days.

The artists themselves, of course, knew the value of original work. Yet copying was not entirely disparaged by them either. Rembrandt Peale, whose copies made in Italy were highly prized, once wrote that "excellent copies" of the old masters' best works were "in all cases more interesting and useful than inferior originals purchased at great prices."

All of these artists who had made their way from copying to original work, however, were men. Sophia's illness at the time of the family's move to Boston, when it was expected that she would begin to study art in earnest, may have pointed to an internal resistance to Elizabeth's scheme. Even the heroine of Francis Graeter's *Mary's Journey* had flourished only in an ideal world, with a lady bountiful subsidizing her creative life: she was not required to peddle her landscapes to make a living.

Once Sophia began drawing again in 1829, her talent easily carried her into a newly burgeoning women's world of drawing parties, where eager female amateurs gathered in one anothers' parlors to assemble portfolios and exchange sketches. Graeter himself led one such party that met regularly at the Peabodys' during after-school hours. Small plaster casts—busts of Apollo or Hercules—were placed on the table as models for sketching, and in good weather the group moved out into the courtyard to draw a tree or flowering plant "from nature." These young women, Elizabeth's and Mary's former students, the daughters, sisters, and wives of Unitarian ministers or progressive schoolmasters, collected their best work in hand-decorated portfolios and begged the more talented artists among them for drawings to fill out their collections.

Sophia's work was always the most sought after, and her exquisitely drawn landscapes were coveted for copying by her friends. Her superior talent, her illness, and her relative poverty set her apart. In the end, she missed more drawing parties than she attended, and she continued to impress more by her occasional, inspired productions than by consistent effort. Sophia seemed destined for a different path, but could she manage the move that Elizabeth envisioned, from parlor to marketplace?

The idea of painting in oils had appealed to Sophia since she first began to draw, but so far she had held herself to the more severe discipline—and the more feminine pursuit—of sketching with pencil, or pen and ink. Now both Elizabeth and Francis Graeter were urging her forward. First Graeter stunned Sophia with his offhand remark that he thought it "comfortable" to sit at an easel with brush in one hand and palette in the other *because Raphael once sat in the same position doing the same thing.* Perhaps, like Walter Channing, Graeter hoped such comments would ease Sophia into action. Sophia confided in her diary that she had been "quite startled by his bringing *Raphael* so near me." Nevertheless, she rose to the bait, telling Graeter, "I supposed I might humbly aim at perfection, though I should never really expect to reach it." Graeter assured Sophia that "by using every advantage" she naturally possessed, she would surely succeed.

Eager to see Graeter's hopes for her younger sister fulfilled, Elizabeth set to work finding Sophia a teacher—the most prominent one then available in Boston. In the spring of 1830, she learned that the landscapist Thomas Doughty, whose paintings she had admired since they first appeared in the Athenaeum's 1827 exhibition, had moved to Boston from Philadelphia to capitalize on his growing fame in New England.

Unlike most of Boston's well-known painters, Doughty taught classes. But he held them in his studio, customarily for male students only. Doughty's method was to gather his pupils around him to watch as he painted, then leave them to copy his work as best they could—offering no explanation. It would be a rough initiation for someone who had never before held a brush. Even if Elizabeth could persuade Doughty to let Sophia attend, could her younger sister withstand the pressure to perform in public? Instead, Elizabeth used Sophia's illness to her advantage. She persuaded Doughty to set up one of his canvases in Sophia's bedroom, where she could look on from the couch, if necessary. Then she would complete each lesson by herself as her strength allowed.

On the day Doughty was scheduled to give his first lesson, Sophia was so jittery that she was near collapse. She had already had one embarrassing interview with the painter, when the bearded celebrity had arrived only to be

Thomas Doughty

announced by Wellington as "Mr. Dowdy." Now "my whole organization underwent an agitation at the sight of him," she wrote in her journal. "How my heart beat. It seemed as though he embodied art in some way, so that I was in its immediate presence and I felt consequently awestruck." She watched Doughty paint for an hour, then he left her to copy his preliminary sketch, which seemed to hold "the same awful power as he brought with him." As she raised her brush to paint, "I trembled from head to foot." She had "never felt so much about any such thing before," she wrote.

Yet, with two friends from Graeter's drawing party looking on, Sophia set to work and completed the lesson by nightfall. Day by day, Doughty's landscape took form—a mountain scene in full sunlight, with a glowing bank, trees, water, and clouds—and Sophia's did too. Some mornings she was again so agitated that she could barely "keep my eyes upon his creating fingers, though he *was* raising rocks, and flinging out branches of trees in a masterly manner." The sight of his efforts sent her to bed with a "suffocating" feeling, particularly as the June heat descended on Boston. But even on those days, after an hour on the sofa, she rose and "attacked the board with intent to execute."

Between lessons, Sophia repeatedly visited the Athenaeum's fourth exhibition, where Doughty's landscapes dominated the show. By the end of the month, she found herself critically analyzing the works of the same man who had made her whole body shake just a few weeks earlier. Doughty, she now saw, was "rather too purple in his heavenly tastes," an objection most modern critics share.

Perhaps Sophia made adjustments in her copy, for once again she garnered rave reviews for a first attempt. It had taken her little over a month to complete a painting that was instantly admired by all in her circle. The Reverend Channing, who claimed to prefer Sophia's landscape to the original, was among the most enthusiastic. "I cannot possibly take in this notion," Sophia recorded in her journal the day Channing visited. Was it reflexive modesty that caused her to add "I only wish *I* could like it as well as Mr. Doughty's"?

Sophia did not conceal her pleasure, however, when Elizabeth's Cambridge friend Sophia Dana, recently married to the Unitarian minister George Ripley, offered to purchase the first original work she undertook. "What an intense delight it gives me," Sophia wrote that same month, "to think I may ever create too!" Then Chester Harding made a special trip to the Peabody house to see the painting and volunteered to teach Sophia to paint portraits. He even promised to let her copy his portrait of Washington Allston, "which he would not suffer any body else in Boston to do," Sophia recorded proudly in her journal. Harding was also, tacitly, giving her permission to sell her work, for a good copy of his *Allston*—judged "the most capital portrait" in the nation by the critic N. P. Willis—would certainly sell.

But for the twenty-year-old Sophia, the lavish praise, the promised lessons and commission, suddenly proved too much pressure. She spent the month of July watching Harding work while she climbed a chair to fan the large man in the sweltering heat. Next she sat for her own portrait, the second of the three he now owed Elizabeth as tuition for his children. Sophia was never satisfied with the portrait; in later years she would try to alter it herself by touching up the mouth. She may have seen that the somewhat enigmatic smile revealed the self-doubt that was beginning to overtake her during the summer of 1830. Yet most of all she felt in awe of Harding, who was "so quick—so masterly" that he could sketch an entire head in minutes and capture a likeness in less than an hour. In the end, she chose to copy Harding's 1827 portrait of his five-year-old daughter, Margaret, rather than the imposing *Allston* he had initially offered. She never sold the copy, which became a fixture in her sisters' schoolroom.

The ambition Sophia had begun to nurture under Graeter's reassuring praise and in the safety of her "dear little chamber & studio in one" was weak-

Sophia Peabody, by Chester Harding

ening. The further she ventured into the world of working artists, the more reminders she encountered that women were not expected to be a part of it.
One summer day, not long after her month of lessons with Doughty, she
stopped in at his studio to look at his work in progress. Doughty welcomed
her, then became flustered once he remembered his male students were at
work in a corner of the room. His embarrassment quickly spread to Sophia,

who flushed and stammered as her teacher dragged a screen across the room to conceal the offending sight, presumably of men painting in their shirtsleeves: men in training to become "masterly" artists, like Harding and Doughty. The visit was spoiled, and Sophia went home.

These few months, from June to August 1830, were the extent of Sophia's instruction in oil painting. Yet her friends and family now expected her to turn out competent original work. Elizabeth was only too glad to act as her agent, but Sophia had to produce. Perhaps most daunting was the assumption by many who knew her, expressed by one friend after a visit to the workshop Sophia had set up in her bedroom, that "such a studio & such an occupation must surely cure the headache." But was she ready to part with pain as a way of life?

At twenty, Sophia may not have been prepared to commit herself to a solitary profession of any sort. As Ralph Waldo Emerson would write later in the century, possessing creative genius "dangerously narrows the career of a woman." That "career" was the expected one of marriage and motherhood. The same philosopher who celebrated nonconformity in men saw nothing but good in the conventional "woman in our society [who] finds her safety and happiness in exclusions and privacies." Such a woman, he wrote, "congratulates herself when she is not called to the market, to the courts, to the polls, to the stage, to the orchestra. Only the most extraordinary genius can make the career of an artist secure and agreeable to her." Taking a different path from the usual "career of a woman" required unwavering ambition, tremendous reserves of self-confidence, and a willingness to defy convention: the essential underpinnings of what Emerson called "extraordinary genius." Talent alone would never be enough.

It may have been during this time of uncertainty, perhaps after reading over the passages from *Correggio* in her commonplace book, that Sophia put aside her drawing pencil and brushes long enough to write a love poem, addressed "To the Unknown yet known." At least while composing this poem, Sophia indulged the notion that she had a soul mate somewhere in the world, a man who was "an artist & a poet too": a man she hoped to marry. Perhaps she had already met this man, she wrote; she might already have "seen some carved or printed poesy of thine." Or maybe the two were not destined to meet on earth, but only in heaven. Yet, she concluded:

> . . . Though thou find not the way
> To me, this truth we'll rest content to know.
> This truth: All good I do
> For others or myself is done for thee;
> All good thou worked too . . . is done for me.

Sophia was imagining a course even more radical for her times than that of a lone woman artist. She envisioned a joint venture: a man and a woman working together, inspiring each other, dedicating their creative lives to each other. As her interest in art grew stronger, this new ideal began to seem far more appealing than her fleeting fantasy of marriage to a paternal caretaker like Dr. Walter Channing. She knew it might be impossible to realize here on earth—in New England, in 1830. But she could dream.

ℭℛ 20 ℬ𝔇

"First Retreat into Solitude"

AS A CHILD, SOPHIA HAD BEEN THE MOST OPENLY AMBITIOUS OF THE sisters—wildly, improbably so. At twelve she had written to Elizabeth, then away in Boston starting her first school, that reading a book of sermons by the British Unitarian Joseph Fawcett had made her wish "I was a divine and gifted with such powers." Given the chance to be a minister, Sophia believed she would "astonish the *Americans*." She well knew that no one could "look so elevated, so expressive, or so energetic as when in the *pulpit* pouring forth the divine truth," and she wanted to be there herself.

At other times, Sophia wished to be "president of Uncle Sam!!!" so that she could help the Indians, or, as she called them, borrowing James Fenimore Cooper's phrase, "the Sons of the Forest." She wanted to go to school with her brothers so she could learn Greek. She wanted to go to college, where she could study chemistry by working in a laboratory rather than from books. She would have liked to be a night watchman, so that she could roam the moonlit streets of Salem by herself.

As Sophia grew older, unabashed longing turned to envy and an inward struggle to accept the limitations on her life. At age fifteen in Salem, Sophia had only qualified admiration for the newly ordained Reverend Charles Upham's preaching: he looked "like an Adonis," but his manner was "tedious." She felt jealous of "the genius in the young ministry," who, like Upham, were "continually coming from Harvard University" to try out sermons on the Salem congregations. This time her words, "How I wish *I* could be a minister!" were followed by a reminder to herself that, as the past week's ministerial candidate had counseled her, "it is not given to ministers alone to be instrumental to the progression of Christianity. . . . [T]he most humble of human beings can be useful in the example he sets." Joining the ranks of the "most humble" did not come easily to Sophia, however. The afternoon spent in church, as her emotions shifted from inspiration to resentment to attempted humility, had caused her head to ache so much that "I have almost feared I should come asunder."

Just a generation or two later, a handful of women in western New York and Ohio would gain permission to train as ministers, eventually winning an occasional Unitarian, Universalist, or even Congregational pulpit during the second half of the nineteenth century. But in Salem during the 1820s, the only female preacher Sophia could have known was the controversial "New Light" Quaker Mary Newhall of neighboring Lynn, Massachusetts, a woman whose fate was not so different from that of the persecuted Quaker women of the Puritan era: forced to separate from the Lynn Society of Friends, she eventually died penniless of tuberculosis. Newhall's sadly neglected teenage daughter later came to board with the Peabodys, exchanging household help for training to become a teacher.

How different it all could be for a man. In 1825, as Sophia turned sixteen listening to "the genius in the young ministry," Ralph Waldo Emerson, a passionate twenty-one-year-old with his "mind on fire," entered Harvard Divinity School, a course that would place him in an influential Boston pulpit within five years. While Emerson was reading Plato and Montaigne and preparing to write his first sermon, Sophia Peabody was attending church on Sundays "with a fire in my brain," tormented by the impossibility of her aspirations. Like her two older sisters, Sophia continued to educate herself as best she could at home—studying Italian, German, and Hebrew on her own, reading widely in philosophy, theology, history, and literature. But it would not be long before illness virtually ended her churchgoing.

By the time Sophia was twenty, she had constructed her own "inner temple whither I can retreat," a private "sanctuary" that chronic pain allowed her. The summer that Dr. Walter Channing advised her to abandon the habit of being "ministered to" and become "a minister of good and plenty," she wrote in her journal, in rare resistance to his instructions: "I do believe th[at] Sickness and pain are some of the highest ministers of GOD's inexpressible love." If she could not become a minister in a pulpit, and would not *minister to* others in the traditional role of dutiful daughter, she could hold her own interior church. In one of her most emphatic descriptions of her illness, Sophia once explained to Elizabeth, "My heart never moves to joy or grief without sending out a ministry of pain through all my nerves." It was a formulation to which she would return throughout her life: the "silent ministry of pain," as she called it in a late reminiscence, which "has helped me to the perfect, the unshadowed belief in the instant Providence of GOD."

If power was what she wanted, Sophia gained it through illness. Her sensitivity to noise silenced household clatter and cut short the "fussation" between her father and brothers and the "contention" between her parents that might otherwise "craze" her. Sophia may have been the weakest member of the family physically, yet, Elizabeth would later recall, "I never knew any human creature who had more sovereign power over everybody—grown and child—that came into her sweet and gracious presence." Her struggle with pain gave Sophia an authority that nothing else in her life could guarantee.

Elizabeth used Sophia's example to "tame" her more unruly pupils. Her mother held her up as a model, for her sons, of a young person whose religious faith had enabled her to triumph over "trials rarely endured at so early an age." The entire family came to believe that for a "nature" like Sophia's—restless and inappropriately ambitious in childhood—no "better training and restraining power could be devised than pain." Her mother credited Sophia's "years of pain" with developing "a character at once lovely and elevated—correcting, subduing, eradicating self sufficiency, pride, obstinacy." Unlike the ministry, or even painting, invalidism was a career that Sophia could train for within the bounds of expected female behavior. "I have repeatedly felt," she once wrote to Elizabeth, "that I wanted to take all the pain in the world to myself." As a woman, she could not become an ordained minister of Christ, but she could follow Christ's example and become a martyr to pain. In Mary's words, "what partially destroyed the body seemed to purify the spirit."

Sophia's two older sisters were inexorably drawn to ministerial power as well, although neither admitted to envying their preachers. Buoyed by the support of Boston's premier liberal divine, the Reverend William Ellery Channing, Elizabeth made as much as she could of her own omnivorous intelligence. She joined every conversation circle and discussion group available, short of the men-only supper clubs that were an outright impossibility. Starting in 1830, she supplemented her daytime teaching with an afternoon "reading party" once a week in history for women, where she guided a college-level discussion of texts on world history. Close to twenty signed on, eager for instruction from the woman who had earned Channing's respect as a "fellow being." Elizabeth was in her element leading this early all-woman version of what later became a signature Transcendentalist forum: the conversation. She was realizing her long-ago ambition, born among the "silent ladies" of the Reverend Channing's gospel discussion group when she was just thirteen years old, to provide adult women with an opportunity to form opinions on serious intellectual issues—and give voice to them.

During 1829 and 1830, besides writing and publishing an innovative grammar textbook, Elizabeth worked tirelessly on translations of the French philosopher Baron Joseph-Marie de Gérando's *Self-Education* and *Visitor of the*

Poor, both key proto-Transcendentalist texts advocating individual responsibility for the reform of self and society. Mary and Sophia were sometimes conscripted for the work of translating and copying de Gérando for the printer, whose bills Elizabeth paid by selling subscriptions. The baron, whose dictum "the life of man is ... but one continued education" had captured Elizabeth's imagination, became another of her eminent transatlantic correspondents.

None of these publishing ventures turned a profit, but Elizabeth was earning a place for herself in Boston's growing community of freethinkers, many of whom emerged from the ranks of the Unitarian ministry. The newly ordained Reverend Ralph Waldo Emerson, recently installed at Boston's Second Church in the North End, took up Elizabeth's translation of *Self-Education* with a passion during the fall of 1830, and then turned to the rest of de Gérando's work in French, making notes in his journal that he would draw on for his essay "Self-Reliance" a decade later. The Reverend George Ripley, who would one day lead the utopian community at Brook Farm, published a thirty-page defense of *Self-Education* in the *Christian Examiner* after the book had been dismissed as "vague and misty" and lacking in "scientific method" in two separate articles in the *Massachusetts Journal*—an early taste of the charges soon to be leveled against Transcendentalism. By the time *The Visitor of the Poor* was ready for publication in 1832, the Reverend Joseph Tuckerman, the prominent Unitarian who had given up his pulpit to establish a roving ministry to the poor in Boston, was happy to contribute an enthusiastic introduction to Elizabeth's translation.

Mary took a different route toward ministerial power, attaching herself to Father Edward Taylor, Boston's spellbinding waterfront missionary. Father Taylor's biography was the stuff of legend. Born in Virginia in 1793 and orphaned in early childhood, Taylor had shipped out as a cabin boy at age seven, and ten years later experienced a religious conversion in a Methodist chapel while on shore leave in Boston. At nineteen, he began preaching to his fellow sailors when his crew was captured at sea and imprisoned by the British at Halifax during the War of 1812. Supporting himself next as a rag and junk dealer, Taylor continued to preach as he peddled his wares, gaining converts with his energetic sermons studded with seafaring metaphors, delivered in barns and schoolhouses along the New England coast. Impressed with his natural abilities, the Methodists licensed the barely literate Taylor to preach and set him up in his own Seaman's Bethel in Boston, later the model for Father Mapple's Whaleman's Chapel in *Moby Dick.*

With his blunt eloquence, Taylor managed to sidestep the doctrinal issues that had so polarized New England's Protestant sects. "Religion is one thing, and theology another!" was a Taylor aphorism Mary often quoted. Sailors who were hardened to the jeremiads of revival preachers regularly filled his church to the "hatches," Taylor liked to say, and soon liberal Unitarians and other curiosity seekers—Jenny Lind and Charles Dickens in later years—were lining the aisles and back stairs as well. Elizabeth Peabody introduced the Reverend Channing to Father Taylor, but it was Mary who developed a personal connection. She began to linger after Sunday services for the famous group confessions when Taylor descended from the "quarter-deck," as he referred to his pulpit, and joined his "brothers" to hear their sins and pray with them. Out of concern for his congregation, Taylor was an early and impassioned temperance advocate, and he did his best work on the church floor.

Mary befriended Taylor's wife, Deborah, the woman who showed her "what a true and noble wife could be under the most difficult circumstances," Mary later wrote. Mother Taylor brought her home on Sundays to the "small and uncomfortable" house where Mary volunteered to look after the children when Father Taylor returned home "perfectly drenched in perspiration" between morning, afternoon, and evening services, needing Deborah to provide him with freshly pressed clothes. Mary saw that Taylor, too busy to help with household chores, nonetheless "kept himself informed of every detail" about the children and was "mindful" of his wife. He "had the spirit of help and care for her," which "lightened every thing." She watched admiringly as Deborah Taylor demonstrated an equal attentiveness to her husband's concerns, dissuading him from one course of action or urging him to another with a carefully timed shake of her head, a smile, or a brief silence. Here was female influence at work in a marriage, asserted without bitterness or recrimination.

Mary recruited the Taylor children as students in the sisters' school, and she spent full weeks in the Taylor household when Father Taylor toured the state campaigning for temperance. She was there, also, to nurse sick children and sometimes Mother Taylor herself, whose moments of exhaustion seemed to Mary just another badge of her devotion to a good man and, through him, to a good cause. Mary had often coped with family pressures by seeking refuge in another household, and by the early 1830s there was ample reason for Mary to have transferred her allegiance from the wealthy Pickmans of Salem to the family of a working-class hero like Father Taylor. The years in Boston were making a democrat of her.

Certainly cultural opportunities were greater in Boston than they had been in Maine, Brookline, or even Salem. But the possibilities only made the sisters —or Mary at least—more painfully aware of their inferior station. Mary could not afford to attend paying lectures or reading parties except as the guest of her wealthier friends. She had lost her taste for English novels of manners, and when she read Marie Antoinette's memoir in French, she scoffed at the "ridiculous . . . etiquette of the French court," declaring she "would rather be schoolmistress" than a queen in order "to have the privilege of putting on my own chemise." Once provided with a ticket to a performance of *Othello*, Mary wrote to a friend afterward that "*I* would marry such a black man in a minute and just now I think the quicker for being a moor & a black man." Her romantic ideal was shifting, yet so too were her hopes for realizing it. As the sisters' older pupils outgrew school and married or took up lives of leisurely study, Mary began to worry that life in the schoolroom was all she would ever know.

It must have rankled all three Peabody sisters when, in 1831, their fifteen-year-old brother Wellington spent a semester at Harvard only to drop out, becoming the first in his class to leave. There were plenty of boys his age at the college, but few whose relative poverty prevented them from running up gambling debts. Yet Welly showed little interest in anything but gambling. As punishment, his disappointed parents signed him on to a whaling ship, hoping that the rigors of life at sea would improve his character. Before his departure, Mary arranged for a private temperance lecture from Father Taylor. Elizabeth could barely conceal her disgust at Welly, who showed no inclination toward "a steady strong conduct of life."

That same year, Nat's surprise announcement in April that he planned to marry a hat maker's daughter came close to outright betrayal. Now almost twenty, Nat might soon have relieved Mary and Elizabeth of their financial burdens. Instead, without telling anyone, he had made plans to move out and start a family, choosing as his bride a woman with prospects even worse than his own.

To be fair, Nat's fiancée, Elizabeth Hibbard, was, like the Peabody children, just two generations removed from sound social standing: her grandfather had been a minister in New Hampshire. But the Peabody sisters knew only too well that good lineage counted for little in the present moment. The day Nat brought her home to meet the family, Sophia "could not say a word" to Miss Hibbard and "could only look on her as a stranger." Sophia felt, she wrote afterward, "as if a millstone" lay upon her chest. Only Mary "managed excellingly," in Sophia's view, to make Nat's sweetheart feel welcome.

Mrs. Peabody viewed the match as a tragedy and openly mourned her son's lost youth. Although she had been quick to see men as predatory in regard to her daughters, she blamed Elizabeth Hibbard for pursuing her son while he was still just a lowly apprentice in an apothecary shop. She might have felt differently if the girl had an education, but there was no hope that Elizabeth Hibbard could ever "aid her husband in getting support—as some women can," she later wrote. She regretted that "girls in that class are taught by parents & relatives that to get married is the sumum bonum of earthly good." It would take several years for Eliza Peabody to admit that her future daughter-in-law was, at least, "very neat . . . quiet and gentle" and "capable of being improved."

Now in her midfifties, and free of the classroom for the first time in her adult life, Eliza Peabody had started to keep a journal in which she confided her sorrows, sometimes crossing out her darkest thoughts later in heavy ink. In July 1830, she revisited Germantown and Friendship Hall for the first time since childhood. She found the mansion in disrepair but still suggestive of "the social powers, the domestic virtues, the intellectual riches, the moral energies, which once gave [it] life and beauty." When she returned to Boston, Eliza was stricken by the contrast presented by her irritable husband and the mean existence he provided. She could hardly bear the realization, now seemingly inescapable, that "it is *forgotten* that I have a heart to feel and a mind to enjoy." As in the years before her marriage, she consoled herself by turning her anguish into verse:

> Not a joy lives, save
> In quiet scenes of home delight.
> And even there—yes there, where we might hope
> Peace would be ever found; Ghosts of blissful days
> Long since departed never to return
> Haunt the wild heart . . .

Such was the atmosphere at 7 Tremont Place during the late summer of 1830 when Sophia, troubled by the new pressures of a fledgling career in art and still battling her familiar headaches, suddenly made plans to leave home. Unable to travel to Cuba or South America as Walter Channing had recommended, Sophia decided on a "voluntary rustication" in Dedham, a county seat fifteen miles west of Boston, for the fall of 1830. It would be "my first retreat into solitude," Sophia wrote at the start of a journal in which she recorded her efforts to achieve her twin goals: to regain her health and to "create" the original scenes her teachers, family, and friends now expected from her. Sophia would turn twenty-one alone in Dedham. She was on the threshold of a career as a copyist and painter. But did she want to take on all that entailed? Perhaps the retreat into solitude was also a means of delaying her decision.

A town of just over three thousand residents, Dedham was set deep in the countryside west of Boston, and its village center was pure New England: a town green, two white-spired churches, and a new white-granite courthouse in the style of a Greek temple. Lydia Sears, recently settled in Dedham with her lawyer husband, Sam Haven, on his family's estate at "Havenwood," helped Sophia find a boarding house near the outskirts of town. At a rent of $2 a week, covering meals and laundry, Sophia's second-floor room, with deep bay windows facing east toward Great Blue Hill and "a sweep of sky and of earth," seemed ideal. How long she stayed would depend on the success of her experiment.

"Here I am in the holy country," Sophia wrote on the first page of her journal at the end of August 1830, "alone with the trees & birds." Her mood was hopeful, yet the ride from Boston had made "the grasp of *the iron hand* upon my poor brain . . . more excruciating than almost ever." She took refuge in her window seat in an attempt to "forget my agonies in the contemplation of the scene." For the next several days, it seemed that nothing could calm her "raging head." The humming of insects, the buzzing of flies and mosquitoes, the "clishmaclavering among the cows," tormented her, along with her well-meaning landlady, who "cannot believe I can be contented up in my chamber, solitary" and repeatedly knocked on her door with invitations for tea and conversation. Any attempt to draw sent Sophia straight to her couch. Finally, a change from sultry weather to "cool and fresh" brought partial relief, and Sophia could at last "lift up my eyelids without an agony." After four days, she went downstairs to tea "feeling more alive" than she had since her arrival in Dedham.

Sophia's Dedham journal, in which she set down her physical symptoms in detail each day, reveals the full extent of her suffering from migraines. Her episodes followed a classic migraine course, whether they lasted a few hours or, more commonly, several days. They began with a period of arousal, a "singular elation of mind," in Sophia's terms, when "every inch of me was awake." At such times she felt driven by a "supernatural force," and as if "I could study Hebrew or hieroglyphics—or solve the abstrusest problems . . . if my eyes would keep steady and could see." Elation soon gave way to an "excessive agitation," when a "tumultuous heaving and palpitation commoted my whole being." Next came the attack itself: "utter prostration" to the "blinding and annihilating fury" of headache. During this stage Sophia retreated to her bed— or window seat—feeling "powerless" and "bound" by "a coronet of thongs cutting into my brain." At last the intense pain receded, "as if a tempest had passed over," leaving only "a vacuum within." Then came a brief resurgence of energy—as Sophia wrote, "I am always better than usual after such a catastrophe"—before the cycle began again.

Sophia's headaches were so relentless that they fit a rare category defined by Oliver Sacks as "situational migraine." Patients with "incessant unremitting migraines," Sacks writes, are not simply "the victims of . . . physiological stimuli or sensitivities, but are caught in a malignant emotional 'bind.'" Monitoring food intake and limiting exposure to environmental stressors, such as noise and bright lights, along with modern medications (unavailable to Sophia), can ease the symptoms of situational migraine sufferers, but none of these remedies provide a cure. Such patients' migraines "fill a dramatic role in the emotional economy of the individual . . . a task of emotional equilibration," Sacks writes, and can be "summoned to serve an endless variety of emotional ends."

Emotional stresses convert to physical symptoms, and what "starts as a reflex, can become a creation": a way of life.

Sacks's description of the situational migraine patient has much in common with Walter Channing's bed case, who suffered from "the habit of being sick." The cure Sacks proposes is similar, too: identify the "malignant" situation and change it. Migraine, Sacks writes, "is both a friend and an enemy, and will retreat only if radically new choices can be offered to the patient." Yet where would Sophia Peabody find "radically new choices" when the stresses troubling her were built into her daily life and into virtually any choice available for the future? Inevitably, headaches accompanied Sophia to Dedham, "pain clinging to me—like a good friend," as she wrote in her journal three weeks into her stay.

The situation producing Sophia's migraines was clearly more than a chaotic Boston household, or even the dynamics of her family. Her malignant bind had become internal: Sophia had learned as a child to repress her voluble spirits, and as a teenager to suppress her ambitions by submitting to the "training and restraining power" of pain. Frustrated ambition, envy, and the inability to envision a future any more promising than her past, were the origins of her distress. Sophia's head could "rage" or mount an "insurrection" even if she could not. This dynamic would not go away with a move to the countryside, even when the opportunity to realize her desire "to create" as an artist awaited her there.

Sophia's headaches were themselves a form of "creation," in Sacks's term, in which she transformed the intractable problems of everyday life into meaningful suffering. The migraine cycle—which allowed Sophia to make spiritual conquest over earthly affliction—granted her regular access to a transcendent realm not so different from the ecstatic state of mind she sometimes achieved while drawing or painting. "How wonderful is *happiness*," she once told Elizabeth during one of her worst bouts of illness: "the more I suffer—the more I feel it is in my heart of hearts." Pain and painting were in direct competition for Sophia's innermost aspirations. When she retreated to the "inner sanctuary" that pain allowed her, Sophia found "the peace that was nowhere without." Painting was still a relatively untried route to self-revelation.

Sophia's chances of altering her circumstances for the better through marriage, the obvious "radically new choice" available to a woman, seemed no more certain than success as an artist. The unions she had imagined so far—marriage to a man with the money or the disposition to play caretaker, or to a partner who would share her creative life—seemed unlikely. Sophia saw, just as her sisters did, that marrying into wealth required a dowry, such as Lydia Sears possessed. A marriage like her mother's, to a man struggling for a steady income in the crowded professions of New England, could be a bitter experience. Many of the young men Sophia knew were leaving town to find work; those who married either left their wives behind or took them away from friends and family to move west to Ohio or Kentucky. Sophia would not have welcomed either fate. When the results of the 1830 census were published, Sophia and her sisters would learn that New England had become the only region in the United States where women outnumbered men; the marriage market in Boston was truly bleak.

Sophia was wary of marriage in any case. Her Dedham journal mentions the weddings or engagements of three close friends during 1830, the year she turned twenty-one. On the day her friend Eliza Dwight was to be married in Salem, Sophia fell asleep with a headache, only to dream of a sky filled with clouds in the shape of coffins. Perhaps she was mourning the end of a girlhood friendship, but marriage itself had a lethal aspect in Sophia's view. It signaled an end to selfish ambition, and to the small measure of power she had gained through illness. To each of the three friends who married that year, Sophia sent the same wedding gift: a handmade copy of Caroline Southey's "The Ladye's Brydalle," a narrative poem she had found in a rare English volume. In it, the bride dies on the brink of marriage; her "brydalle"—the wedding ceremony—becomes a funeral procession. The scene actually fit the popular view of true love as immortal, finding ultimate consummation in heaven: an ideal marriage might skip the harsh realities of conjugal life on earth in favor of heavenly bliss. Yet genuine fear—of the risks of childbirth, perhaps most of all—underlay this morbid sentimentalism.

As summer drew to a close in Dedham, Sophia walked in the woods when she felt well enough and woke early each day to watch the sunrise from her windows before falling back into a fitful sleep. Her quivering eyes, along with a feeling of being "too trembly to do much," prevented her from drawing. Natural beauty dizzied her, and virtually any stimuli brought on a headache. One Sunday in late September, she was attracted to the view out her window, made unusually bright after a morning rain. Yet "I could not endure my own delight," Sophia wrote. She quickly closed the curtains "from mere inability to look alone upon such loveliness." She had just written to her mother asking her not to send her oil paints.

And then, the decision not to paint freed Sophia. Without the pressure of supplies waiting to be used, Sophia started to draw scenes in her sketchbook which she planned to turn into landscapes in oil when she returned to Boston. And she began to write more expansively in her journal. The sensitivity that migraines had given her to "my whole inward being" released a torrent of sensation in response to the natural world. She quoted the German Romantic writer Jean-Paul Richter, whose work, along with Friedrich von Schiller's, she had been deciphering during the past year with the help of a

German dictionary: "Man has a universe within him, as well as without." Most often in the past, Sophia had felt the inner and outer universe collide painfully, in the form of crushing headaches. Now this same convergence seemed a glorious philosophical truth for which she sought confirmation on her walks in the countryside to "feed upon the air." On one such day, she felt herself enveloped in a "wilderness of melody as I gazed." In response to the "dewy freshness & life" around her, "every faculty sang a hymn."

After writing to her parents in October that she planned to return home at the end of the month, Sophia suddenly found the energy to "draw, draw, draw" and completed a half-dozen sketches that she had promised to her sisters' students. She read Leonardo da Vinci's *Treatise on Painting* in Italian. And she realized that she had been relatively healthy—aside from her customary headaches, she had not experienced "the slightest cold in my head," nor backache, nor menstrual pain—for more than a month. She had gained "a vast deal of strength," she wrote to her mother. One afternoon she climbed a large boulder in the middle of a pine grove and settled down for a nap. To her amazement, after years of avoiding heights, the climb provoked no dizziness.

On the last page of her Dedham journal, Sophia wrote of taking her sketchbook into the woods, where, too overwhelmed by the splendors of nature to draw, "I held my breath to hear the breathing of the spirit around me." It was a perfect utterance of what would become the Transcendentalists' credo a decade later: that a unifying divinity—Emerson called it "the Oversoul"—is present in nature, available to all receptive individuals. Sophia had arrived there already.

Sophia Peabody's "retreat into solitude" took place nearly two full decades before another journalizer—Sophia's one-day neighbor in Concord, Henry David Thoreau—spent two years alone in a cabin at Walden Pond observing nature and writing about it. Sophia's effort to assuage her own "quiet desperation" in solitary contemplation of nature was no less a spiritual quest than Thoreau's, and in many ways a more courageous one. She was a woman. It had taken illness to permit this rare burst of female individualism, art to fuel it, and Sophia's "whole inner being," pulsing to the rhythms of migraine as well as to the rhythms of nature, to experience it. For the moment, at least, it did not seem to matter whether she decided to become a painter. She had lived in delicious independence for the space of two months. How many women she knew could say the same?

⟨℞ 21 ℞⟩

"Scatteration"

RETURNING TO BOSTON, SOPHIA FELT A NEW APPRECIATION FOR THE household at 7 Tremont Place. Soon after her arrival, she wrote to a friend describing a late-December evening in the parlor, which had been transformed into a portrait gallery during her absence. There were now three Harding portraits hanging above the sofas: Elizabeth's, done in 1827; Sophia's from the past summer; and a new likeness of William Tyler, one of the Vermont cousins who had come down to Boston to make his fortune and dazzled the Peabody sisters with his good looks. Alternating with the Hardings were images of Milton, Locke, and the Reverend William Ellery Channing.

Mary never said whether she minded being left out of the Harding trio of portraits. Elizabeth, of course, had earned hers by negotiating the exchange, and Sophia deserved the opportunity as part of her training. Harding had promised a third portrait to complete his tuition payments, and he must have assumed he would paint Mary. How was the decision made to paint William Tyler instead? Perhaps Mary's good looks were a continued source of quiet resentment in her two sisters, her smooth brown hair and fine features quite enough to look at each day in the flesh, let alone in a portrait. Or Mary herself may have conceded her turn to Cousin William out of habitual deference, permitting what was otherwise a glaring oversight. In any case, while Sophia was away in Dedham and William Tyler sat for his portrait in Harding's studio, Mary had turned her attention toward music instead of art and taken up the guitar.

On this winter evening just after Christmas of 1830, all seemed right with Sophia's world. She sat at a desk writing her letter "under the mooney influences of the astral lamp." Elizabeth and a friend huddled together on a sofa "in deep communion over some letters" beneath Locke's portrait, and Mary was "looking her beautifullest & sweeping the lyre." A young boy had joined the family group as well: Frank Rotch of New Bedford, who was contentedly "pouring over" *The Boy's Own Book*. It would have been hard to guess that Elizabeth's involvement with Frank Rotch and his family could prove the Peabodys' undoing in Boston.

In recent months, the sisters' school had begun to suffer along with New England's shaky economy, which experienced a series of shocks in advance of the nationally felt Panic of 1837. In August 1829, there had been spectacular business failures among the "great & mighty rich" in Salem and Boston, leading Sophia to conclude, "Happy are those who have nothing to lose!" Elizabeth mourned along with friends who were forced to sell off most of their household furnishings, including "a perfect jewel of a library—mostly German books" to pay off debts. Inevitably, the effects spread. "People feel poor," Elizabeth wrote in October 1830, as she projected a wintertime drop in enrollment. Even the enlightened parents who had entrusted their daughters to Elizabeth's progressive brand of schooling seemed to feel that a girl's education could easily be suspended as a means of economizing.

To compensate, Elizabeth looked to a greater income from boarders, cultivating several prominent New Bedford families who were summer neighbors of the Channings in Newport. When Frank Rotch, a boy of seven or eight years old and heir to a New Bedford whaling fortune, first came to stay with the Peabodys, it was a simple business proposition. But by winter, scandal had broken out. All of New Bedford—and soon after, all of Boston—knew about "The Great Rotch Scandal," which painted little Frank's father, Francis Rotch, as a sexual predator.

There was no disputing the facts of the case. The senior Francis Rotch had secretly made a mistress of his cousin Elizabeth Rotch Arnold, a girl twenty-one years younger than he. On the eve of her wedding to another man, the tearful Elizabeth Arnold confessed the two-year affair to her father, Rotch's mentor in business, knowing full well that the news would prevent her marrying. The enraged Arnold made the story public and ran Francis Rotch out of town, leaving young Frank's mother a temporary widow and nearly hysterical with grief and shame. Of course Elizabeth Peabody tried to help her.

Elizabeth made trips to New Bedford, where Anna Rotch confided her sorrows and Elizabeth offered the "deepest religious sympathy" she could muster, along with proposals for "reform of the criminal." But Elizabeth knew little about affairs of the heart and even less about the ways of the rich. To Elizabeth's astonishment, within six months Anna Rotch had forgiven her husband and taken her son to join him in upstate New York, where the family began a new life together. Instead of bringing about a climactic reunion in New Bedford, with the penitent husband submitting to the "purifying furnace" of his wife's indignation, Elizabeth was left behind in Boston, accused of "indiscretion" by Anna Rotch and tarnished in the eyes of Channing and his circle as a result of her association, however indirect, with the guilty Francis. Nearly all her students—except for the daughters of Boston's Judge Charles Jackson—were removed from her school.

The cumulative disillusionments of "that terrible winter" left Elizabeth "shattered" in both "mind and nerves" and increasingly unable to teach. Too late, she realized she should have listened to Channing when he counseled her by letter from his winter residence in St. Croix to limit her "exertions in that sad affair." He had doubted that Elizabeth was "equal to this ministry" and warned that "this train of burning thoughts" could "fill your mind too exclusively" and make it difficult for Elizabeth to "perform efficiently your daily task." When Channing returned to Boston in the spring to find his prediction fulfilled, Elizabeth was further stricken as she sensed that her mentor had "got tired of me just at the moment when I needed him most."

As long as she worked as a teacher, Elizabeth would face the temptation to involve herself in the lives of the students and families she served—most often giving in, to her eventual regret. The "New Bedford affair," as she came to refer to the fiasco, proved to have some of the most long-lasting effects. Through most of 1831, Elizabeth struggled to take pleasure in a reduced class of younger girls just learning to read and in the weekly historical course for adult women that had become her major source of income. She refused to believe a rumor circulating that the Reverend Channing had called her a "parasite" and had "tried to shake me off but could not." She knew the rumor's source was Charlotte Farnham, her old teaching rival from Maine. But it was discouraging that such jealousy could reach across a distance of almost ten years. To be safe, she kept her distance from Channing—and she could not help feeling a void.

Mrs. Peabody looked on, helpless, recalling similar crises from years past. She watched Elizabeth become even more careless about her clothes and hair—inattentions that, she knew from her own youthful experience, were among the worst sins of omission a woman could commit. Her oldest daughter, she believed, "had too great a desire to do uncommonly well," as she once wrote to Mary. "She wished to be all and more than all, that those she loved would have her be." In the end, it only caused suffering.

Elizabeth would not scale back her ambitions, but the time had come to revise her strategy. By the spring of 1832, when she was still unable to rally her spirits, Elizabeth concluded that she could no longer "do my duty to my scholars without a change." She was scarcely twenty-six years old, and she had allowed herself to take on the "too great responsibility" for her family for almost four years. She decided, now, to close down her school and implement a "scatteration plan."

Already the feckless Wellington had signed on to a whaling ship that would keep him out at sea for most of the next two years. Eighteen-year-old George, who suffered increasingly from stomach pains and an unaccountable fatigue, made plans for a transatlantic voyage to Smyrna in hopes of finding employment as a clerk in a warmer climate. Nothing could induce Nat to leave Boston and his fiancée, Elizabeth Hibbard; he prevailed upon Dr. Peabody to loan him what spare cash he had to make a start in the apothecary business. Mary and Elizabeth would resume their former boarding house life after a summer spent apart: this time Mary had been invited to the Channing estate in Newport, where she would work as governess and soothe the ailing minister's nerves with the "spirit tones" of her voice and guitar when he called for her. Elizabeth planned to start work on her *Key to History*, a series of textbooks that she hoped would appeal not just to teachers but "to a family of sisters, or a party of friends, or a solitary student" to whom formal instruction in history was unavailable. In her introduction to *First Steps to the Study of History*, Elizabeth might have been addressing her own sorry predicament as she argued that understanding the past was the best means "to deliver the mind from the thraldom of the present, and to prepare it to comprehend the future."

No one took Elizabeth's decision to break up the Boston household harder than twenty-two-year-old Sophia, who was selected to return to Salem with her parents. "For the first time in her life she broke down," Elizabeth recalled, crying "hopeless misery!" It was little wonder. The year since her return from Dedham had been one in which, with the support of Boston friends and fellow artists, she slowly gathered her energies and directed them toward a career as a painter.

At first Sophia had toyed with a number of subjects for paintings—a "soft and misty" sunrise she had sketched in Dedham, a version of a moonlit landscape by Doughty recollected from a visit to his studio, and two lake scenes. Of the four, she may have completed one. Headaches continued to plague her, striking as often as several times a week. In July 1831, she wrote that she now had "no idea" what it felt like to be in "perfect health." After each "revolution ... passed in my head," the pain lingered, keeping "the sensation in vivid memory." Yet she managed to rejoin Francis Graeter's drawing party, and she experimented with making plaster casts from intaglios, venturing toward sculpture. She discovered a new source of ready cash in transferring small ink drawings onto calling card cases to sell to the mothers of Elizabeth's students, and she tutored a young girl in Greek.

Then in December 1831, Elizabeth managed to borrow a landscape by Washington Allston, with the owner's permission for Sophia to copy it. At Christmastime, Sophia hung the painting in her room, where she studied it closely for hours each day, memorizing its crags and clouds. Two weeks later, on January 9, she began to paint. At first she felt overwhelmed, just as on the day she had started work with Thomas Doughty. She experienced an "enjoyment—almost intoxicating" yet "altogether too intense for my physicals." She worked through the day, managing to tolerate an almost "deathly sickness," and went to bed with one of her "pure" headaches, only to be flooded with images of "landscapes & scenes such as never rose upon other than the mental eyes." Sophia was in the arousal stage of migraine when visions—this time extravagantly beautiful ones—sometimes kept her awake all night.

Over the next few days, Sophia painted through her headache "in a perfect rapture." This was "the very first time," she wrote Elizabeth, "I have felt *satisfied* with a copy." Indeed, *copying* hardly seemed the right word for the process. Sophia was "bodying forth the poet's dream—*Creation!*" She felt like a singer performing the aria of a great composer: Allston's genius was flowing through her brush. Sophia managed several hours of work on her Allston each day for the next month, and even before it was complete Miss Rawlins Pickman had purchased it.

Flush with success, Sophia looked for a way to stay on in Boston alone, in defiance of Elizabeth's plans. In May, as her parents searched for rooms to rent in Salem and Elizabeth moved into a boarding house in Somerset Court to work on her textbook, Sophia garnered an invitation to stay with the Rice family on Beacon Hill for as long as it took to copy *Sappho*, a French rococo portrait of the Greek poet much prized by Maria Rice, her hostess. Sophia could then sell her copy and perhaps subsidize a longer stay in Boston.

Thrilled to have an artist in the house, Maria and Henry Rice—the parents of a girl in Elizabeth's reading class—gave Sophia an upstairs room of her own and moved *Sappho* into it so that Sophia might work undisturbed in an "atmosphere of turpentine and paint" all day if she liked. Sophia brought along her Allston copy for inspiration and began work on *Sappho* almost immediately, writing to her mother that she "never sat down to the easel with a more harmonious and tranquil mind." Sappho was known to nineteenth-century Americans not as a lesbian love poet, but as a tragic heroine, a creative genius who threw herself from a cliff after being spurned by a handsome boatman. Sappho's passion for women, like the intense friendships in Sophia's circle, was presumed to be chaste and sisterly. All these perceptions of Sappho—as a brilliant woman, an abandoned lover, and a proponent of female friendship—contributed to making "the sad lady" a subject with enormous appeal and potential for identification for Sophia. Although neither the original painting nor Sophia's copy survive, it is clear from her letters that Sophia's confidence was at a peak as she "sketched the beautiful figure entirely" and "quite to my satisfaction" all in one day. The next morning she began applying color.

It was now Sophia's turn to become a minor celebrity in Boston. Her work

on *Sappho* was interrupted by a steady stream of visitors eager to see her Allston copy. George Flagg, Allston's sixteen-year-old nephew, was one of her
more frequent guests. The boy had come to Boston to study painting for a
year with his uncle, who quickly proclaimed him a genius. In the spring of
1832, Flagg had seven paintings on view in the Athenaeum's sixth exhibition,
and he was selling them off by raffle. Soon he would not need even this
source of income, for benefactors had stepped forward offering portrait commissions and sponsorship for European study, thanks to Allston's endorsement. Sophia found Flagg to be good company, particularly after listening to
him praise her Allston. A "delicate and fragile" boy, as pale as marble, Flagg
seemed sustained by the intensity of his passion for art. He watched Sophia
work on *Sappho* and told her he admired the painting so much that he would
like to finish the color work himself. He envied her "perfectly correct" eye for
form. For her part, Sophia had much to envy in Flagg—only some of it having
to do with his precocious skill as an artist.

Other visitors were more daunting. Catherine Scollay was one of a handful
of women painters who exhibited in the Athenaeum shows, the only well-
known female artist in Boston who was not, like Jane Stuart, the daughter of
an even more famous male artist. Miss Scollay came to inspect the Allston
copy on a day when Sophia was out, requiring her to pay a return visit. The
invitation was an honor, but the encounter with Miss Scollay in her spare attic
apartment, a single woman approaching fifty with her hair wrapped in a
turban, signifying spinsterhood, frightened Sophia. Were Scollay's few paintings of scenes from Walter Scott's novels hanging on the Athenaeum's walls
worth this lonely existence? Another visitor eager to meet Sophia was the poet
Eliza Townsend, who arrived with her "ancient" sister in tow. Townsend admired the painting "extravagantly" while Sophia herself shrunk from this eccentric "specimen of past times," dressed in a highly inappropriate "dazzling
sunflower yellow." The three older women, arriving in quick succession, must
have seemed a macabre vision of the Peabody sisters' own future to Sophia.

Finally Washington Allston himself—"the Tiger of the age," in Sophia's
words—came to see her copy. Sophia watched from the window as the patrician master with his flowing silver mane approached the Rices' house, trying
to suppress the "uncontrollable tumult" she inwardly felt. Once inside, Allston
took down "the poor pic" and looked at it for a long time while Sophia stood
behind him "trembling like a sinner," she wrote afterward to her mother. Although Elizabeth had extracted the owner's permission for Sophia to copy the
landscape, no one knew what the artist's judgment would be.

Mary, who had come to witness the event, urged Sophia to "tell him you
painted it in perfect ignorance," and "like a parrot" Sophia repeated the words.
Allston turned to her and replied, "But you have not painted it ignorantly—It

Washington Allston, by Chester Harding

does you great credit." He found "no fault" in the copy and declared himself "very much surprised," for the painting was far "superior to what I expected, although I have heard it much spoken of." Ignoring the implicit slight, Sophia took the eminent painter's assessment as "the words of an oracle." Elizabeth, also on hand, quickly asked Allston if he minded having his work copied. The great man readily gave Sophia his permission, but urged her instead to "copy nature." Here was more encouragement—and more pressure—to produce original work.

Sophia then led Allston upstairs to see *Sappho*. To her dismay, the oracle detested the French original, calling it "ill drawn, poorly colored, and badly put together." He advised Sophia to continue copying it for practice in applying color, but "whenever I felt inclined to alter, I had better do it." Allston then launched into his prescription for an artist's education: "draw a great deal from fine statues and casts and from life as much as possible." He reminisced about his years spent "fagging"—laboring to master the technical aspects of painting—in London, Paris, and Rome, and spoke of his expectation that a New York patron would send his talented young nephew to art school.

Allston's praise and his advice ran in contrary directions. Clearly he was impressed by Sophia's work, but he felt that she needed a much longer apprenticeship. Had she the means or freedom to undertake one, Sophia would have happily agreed. Allston was not a rich man anymore, but he'd had an inheritance to run through as a youth in Italy and England. Now he was using his influence to find George Flagg a patron. Sophia had no money of her own, and no connections. She was lucky simply to have a borrowed room in Boston for several months.

How could Sophia think of "fagging" anywhere but in Boston or Salem— if she had the strength for it? Where in New England could she find "fine statues" to draw? Allston had in mind the figures in the Capitoline Museum in Rome. Even if Sophia could get there, no American woman had yet traveled alone in Italy and sketched nude statues in public. For that matter, no woman, anywhere, could practice drawing the human figure "from life"—unless, as Francis Graeter suggested on a later visit, Sophia tried sketching her friends' infant children when they were undressed. At the Pennsylvania Academy, where women were finally permitted to study in separate classrooms in 1844, the first Ladies' Life Class wasn't offered until 1869.

Not surprisingly, Sophia was too sick to paint during the week following Allston's visit. When she resumed work on "my fair poetess," it was with a great deal less conviction. It didn't help matters that Graeter, too, "denounced" the painting, telling her that it was "talent wasted" to copy it, for even if she "altered every part" it would still be the same florid portrait.

In Allston, as generous as he was with his praise and encouragement, Sophia had come face-to-face with the male art establishment and its aesthetic. She had encountered it before when she was hustled out of Thomas Doughty's studio while a men's painting class was in session. More recently, at a gathering in the Reverend Channing's parlor, she had been stunned when the minister had quoted the influential British artist Henry Fuseli's sneering observation that there was "no *fist*" in women's painting—and then demanded Sophia's response. Flustered, Sophia had "sunk away into my shell," unable to speak, she confided in her journal. She had enough trouble summoning the confidence to paint each day, let alone defend women artists as a class. Channing's question struck to the heart of Sophia's ambivalence about taking the initiative to create original works of art.

Virtually unopposed, the male aesthetic prevailed. The Rices' fanciful *Sappho* was spurned because it lacked strong, classic lines. There was "no fist," no power or mastery, in it. For Washington Allston, the aesthetic ideal was represented in a simple sculptured fragment of Greek marble that he'd seen in his travels: a nude female torso, headless and "without legs or arms" but more "divinely beautiful," in his words, than the *Venus de Medici*. "In seeing it," Allston once told a young follower, "I became aware that it came nearer the eternal standard . . . than anything my eyes had before beheld. It was a pure gratification of the sense of beauty." Male artists sought out the beautiful, they certified it, and they created it. Women *were* beautiful, and all the more so when, like the marble fragment, they lacked the mind and limbs that could have made them artists.

Unconsciously, perhaps inevitably, Sophia accepted Allston's standard. For Sophia, it had always been Doughty and Harding and Allston who were "masterly." They "embodied" art in a way that the turbaned Catherine Scollay in her attic studio never could. If women had a recognized place in the art world it was as muse or model—or wife. Yet, with the exception of the Reverend Channing's question, no one spoke of art in terms of gender. Because it was unacknowledged, the gap between a young woman with talent and a man of accomplishment could seem an unbridgeable chasm.

It was safer for Sophia to paint covers for ladies' card cases or, at most, copy paintings that offered a thrilling proximity to greatness. Neither would require an open admission of her own aspirations to greatness—aspirations that could easily go unfulfilled in the absence of adequate training. Sophia had seen what had happened to her oldest sister, whose naked desire to become "all and more than all, that those she loved would have her be" had exposed her to disappointment and failure. Sophia would not risk that.

In July 1832, Sophia packed away her paints, leaving *Sappho* unfinished, and arranged to spend the month with Lydia and Sam Haven, who insisted that Sophia "not paint a stroke" while there. Sophia would not return to Boston to live, but instead to the "nutshell" home on Church Street in Salem that had been the only house her parents could afford to rent. Commuting from Boston for the past four years had so diminished Dr. Peabody's income from his Salem dental practice that he was forced to resign his membership in the Massachusetts Medical Society to avoid paying the annual dues; he hoped to donate his medical books to the society's library to settle past "arrearages." Saddened by the departure of two of his sons for distant ports, and by the "distribution" of his remaining four children to other households, Dr. Peabody considered the recent "separations" to be an "epoch in our family." He could not help wondering "whether we shall ever all meet again in this world."

Sophia insisted that she was looking forward to the smaller household circle in Salem and to a winter during which "we will read and paint and talk and think," as she wrote to her mother. But the seventeen friends who gathered to say goodbye to Sophia at the Rices' house on Beacon Hill were an emblem of all she would leave behind in Boston. Catherine Scollay, Francis Graeter, and Thomas Doughty were among them. To her surprise, both Scollay and Doughty admired *Sappho*. Doughty offered to teach her the finicky, time-consuming art of "finishing" a painting—the method by which artists of the time applied multiple layers of lead-based varnishes, bringing the oil paints to a high sheen. But Sophia would soon be gone. She could only take the formula for Doughty's varnish along with her to Salem, and hope to learn by trial and error.

Sophia planned to follow her visit to the Havens with a stay in rural Roxbury with another pair of well-to-do newlywed friends, Connie and Thomas Park, for the month of August. At least Connie was eager to have Sophia continue painting there, and she offered to have *Sappho* shipped out "to receive her last touches." But Sophia suffered miserably from headaches during her stay with the Havens in July. The only pictures she contemplated there were views of nature gleaned on walks in the Dedham countryside, when she felt well enough to take them. She vowed to memorize these scenes "to hang up in my inner gallery"—an exhibition that Sophia was free to judge by her own lights.

PART VI

Somerset Court and La Recompensa

1833–1835

☙ 22 ☜

Chastity

MARY'S SUMMER AT OAKLAND, THE CHANNING ESTATE IN NEWPORT, could not have started in a worse way. When she arrived on a late evening in July 1832, hungry after a full day's journey, the Reverend Channing stood to greet her, then resumed his backgammon game with his son; Mrs. Channing went back to writing letters. No one thought to offer her dinner. Then, hoping to take refuge in her room, Mary was directed to an upstairs antechamber, little more than a hallway leading to Mrs. Channing's bedroom. For the three months she had agreed to work as a governess at Oakland, Mary would have no privacy. She saw immediately that Mrs. Channing intended to treat her as hired help, not as a guest or even as a family friend.

The next morning the Reverend Channing sat down in the schoolroom alongside his children—Mary, aged thirteen, and William, eleven—and asked to hear them recite their Latin lessons. Flustered and self-conscious, Mary Peabody forgot to make her customary opening speech on classroom decorum. Once the great man left the room, his children proceeded to test her with all manner of "bad tricks at school," Mary wrote afterward to Elizabeth. Sensing that the new teacher was on probation, young William reported to his parents any loss of patience on Mary's part—a scarcely forgivable sin in the Channing household—further undermining her authority.

William's favorite prank that summer was to snatch his sister's puppy during her singing lesson with Mary and pull the dog's tail until he yelped and his sister started shouting, bringing the entire household in to witness the commotion. Mary Channing was a masterly tease as well and could easily provoke William into hitting her—the only act that rated the disapproval of their parents. Mary Peabody soon discovered that the liberal Channings otherwise did nothing to discipline their children, who had, by consequence, become de-

SOMERSET COURT AND LA RECOMPENSA

vious, stubborn, and rude. The Channings saw none of this, however. They believed everything their children told them and would hear nothing said
against them. Mary grumbled in letters to Elizabeth that Dorothea Dix—the
past summer's governess—could only have succeeded in the position through
flattery, a strategy that even the conciliatory Mary refused to consider.

Mary was also expected to manage the children outside of school, a task
she found nearly impossible. When William rode his pony through the
kitchen, and Mary Channing let the cows into the corn, Mary Peabody took
the blame. The situation became ludicrous when a younger cousin arrived to
join the class. Little Wolcott Gibbs was well behaved in school and fond of
Mary but showed his affection by pelting her with grapes, green apples, and
gooseberries from the garden as she read on the porch in her few spare moments. The experience filled her with loathing for the position of governess,
which she later described as "the worst of all slaveries."

At twenty-five, Mary now came the closest to exhibiting the conventional
womanly submission to fate that her headstrong mother and sisters all struggled to acquire. She had trained herself, as she once wrote her brother George,
to be "willing to be baffled" in plans of her own, and had almost given up
making any, knowing that Elizabeth would win out in the end. She found it
increasingly difficult to retreat to "my secret mind," the imaginary world of her
daydreams. She had even sworn off reading novels, telling herself "they give
one a taste for romantic situations, and make the every day routine . . . something to be endured." But there was a cost to this self-imposed selflessness.
Mary's energy flagged, and depression lay just below her surface reserve. At
times, in damp weather, she felt as if she were "dissolving" or "evaporating" into
the atmosphere. She wrote Miss Rawlins Pickman that she could understand
why suicide was so prevalent in England during "gloomy seasons of the year."

Although she was never bedridden like Sophia, Mary too was subject to
headaches, intense muscle and joint pains that she classified as rheumatism,
and an annoying facial twitch when she was overly tired. Perhaps the only
thing that saved her from giving in to invalidism—or to a suicidal impulse—
was the small pleasure she took in "physicating," designing her own remedies
gleaned from conversations with other self-appointed "women doctors": bur-
gundy pitch plasters and blisters, bread-and-milk poultices, flannel wraps. A
year before she took the job as governess to the Channings, she confided in
her friend Maria Chase, "I have come to the end of my book education—not
finished it by any means—but I believe I have lost all my energy in regard to
cultivating my mind." Instead, she wrote, "I take the lessons of experience
every day, and some of them are proper hard."

Then one day in mid-August, the Reverend Channing took Mary surf-
bathing in a small cove with the children. At first the power of the waves as

they broke over her in full bathing dress caused Mary, already near despair over her position as governess, to imagine being swept out to sea and becoming one with the surging ocean. But when the Reverend Channing "came down to the rocks where I stood stockingless" and offered to take Mary to see the open ocean, she eagerly accepted. He drove her by wagon across the island to a rocky promontory. There it began to rain, and "he took me under his arm & we went out upon that beautiful point. . . . The waves were . . . oh so beautiful! dashing up among the rocks & breaking . . . & then throwing up spray all round us—and retreating with a murmer . . . and there were the Dr. & the ocean & I all by ourselves!" she wrote to Elizabeth, who had herself experienced a similarly ecstatic moment in Channing's company at Newport several years before.

Mary now summoned the courage to speak to Channing about her difficulties with the children. She was surprised to find that, out of his wife's presence, the reverend sympathized with her views and urged her to say more. Back at Oakland, Channing began to ask Mary to read aloud to him, and to sing to him as she had once done in Boston. His interest in her remained just as strong when, toward the end of summer, he fell ill and had to be confined to his room. Now Mrs. Channing became an obstacle, insisting that her husband could not receive company. Yet whenever Mary managed to poke her head into his sickroom, Channing reprimanded her for not coming more often. On one memorable day, the Reverend made her stay and talk, and confided that he enjoyed being sick—especially the "delicious" laudanum visions that kept him awake at night. "If he had made any advance in his life," Channing told her, "it had been in sickness."

Mary discovered they shared the same reveries, always "fictions" of "heroes & heroines . . . who rose out of obscurity, conquered almost insurmountable obstacles, and achieved great good to their race." Under the Reverend Channing's kind attention, she was finding the resilience to enter her "secret mind" once again. Mary was still just twenty-five; she had most of a year to meet de Staël's deadline for romance. The French writer's pronouncement that "no woman of sensibility ever lived to be twenty six without feeling the sentiment of love" had not been lost on Mary Peabody.

In October 1832, Mary rejoined Elizabeth in a Beacon Hill boarding house run by Mrs. Rebecca Clarke at 3 Somerset Court (now Ashburton Place), near the State House. Their new rooms had a view of Charlestown and the massive granite obelisk still under construction on Bunker Hill: it had been seven years since Elizabeth watched the venerable Lafayette lay the cornerstone of this monument to Revolutionary War dead. But Mary found life in Boston without her family nearly unbearable at first. She particularly missed Sophia, who had stopped in at Somerset Court on her way to Salem after spending the late-summer months in rural Roxbury with her friends Connie and Tom Park. The parting, soon after Mary's arrival from Newport, was "so painful," Mary wrote, "that I did not even care to look at the rooms . . . where we were to keep our little school." Mary knew that Sophia's poor health, along with the expense of travel between the two cities, would keep her almost permanently sequestered in Salem.

Elizabeth was ready to teach again, but her reputation had been tarnished by her miscalculations in the New Bedford affair. Mrs. Clarke later recalled that she had been unwilling at first to rent to Elizabeth—she was "so queer" —although in the end she conceded that she'd "never had a pleasanter winter" than the one during which the Peabody sisters were her boarders. For the sisters, finances were shakier than ever. Elizabeth, Mrs. Peabody noted over the summer, "seems to be unfortunate in her exertions to get money." With no yearly guarantee such as they had received in Hallowell and Brookline, "every mite is of importance to us now," Mary wrote of the several young children whose $25 fees per term were their sole source of revenue. "Miss E. P. Peabody's school" would never again reach the thirty-student capacity that had once supported virtually the entire Peabody family. "If we have just enough to live with I don't care one fig for another cent," Mary confided to Lydia Haven. "[W]e have not quite enough however, for that."

As would be the case through much of the next decade, the sisters made do by wearing the same dresses day after day, washing out detachable collars each night to appear fresh the next morning. Mary proved far more skillful than her habitually untidy older sister at maintaining appearances. But both had long since mastered the art of mending stockings and underclothes until they could no longer be worn. As for room and board, they relied on Elizabeth's credit, which for the moment was still good. An apocryphal story from this period has Mary running up to her landlady with her "apron full of silver half dollars" after Chester Harding paid off an old debt, crying out, "*Now* I can pay you Mrs. Clarke!" True or not, it was Mary who worried most about what she called "our own personal poverty" and once again found herself losing "interest in life itself."

It did not help that Elizabeth's moods fluctuated wildly in the wake of the great Austrian phrenologist J. G. Spurzheim's ill-fated American tour in the fall of 1832. Largely out of concern for Sophia, both Mary and Elizabeth had taken an interest in the new science, phrenology, which analyzed the shapes of subjects' heads for signs of strengths and weaknesses of mind and character. They read George Combe's *Constitution of Man* and Spurzheim's *Outlines of Phrenology*. Elizabeth had even invited the local practitioner Jonathan Barber in to examine the family heads two years before. When Dr. Barber came to tea at the Peabodys' in April 1830 and "set out to examine" Elizabeth's head "with regard to her bumps," Sophia had recorded with astonishment in her diary that the doctor's findings of "Benevolence, Veneration, Causality . . . Determination, & Love of approbation" were *very strikingly true.*" Sophia did not submit to analysis that day, but Mary's was called "the noblest head of all," with causality, veneration, and benevolence all "finely developed." Like astrologers or psychics today, phrenologists won converts by confirming previously accepted truths about their subjects. Elizabeth *did* torment her sisters and herself with her driving ambition and desperate need for approval; Mary was not just the most beautiful of the three sisters, but also the steadiest in temperament.

Far from quackery, however, phrenology was, through the nineteenth century, the most widely credited science of the mind. By 1832 it had been accepted as gospel by the Boston Medical Society and enshrined in the curriculum at Harvard's medical school. Ultimately phrenology held a fascination and influence comparable to that of Freudian psychoanalysis in the twentieth century. Phrenologists claimed that such traits as benevolence, intellectual curiosity (termed *causality*), or aggression (*combativeness*) resided in specific areas of the brain and could be measured in surface bumps. Once analyzed by a phrenologist, the subject could work to improve or mitigate congenital traits. Today phrenology may seem far-fetched, yet modern neuropsychology offers a similar view: that personality derives from genetic predispositions, expressed through the release of neurotransmitters at specific sites in the brain. The phrenologists' intuition that the brain could be studied as a factor in human behavior, subject to influence by environment and circumstance, was prescient.

A figure of controversy in Europe, Johann Gaspar Spurzheim, the world's foremost popularizer of phrenology, was embraced wholeheartedly in America, where his reform-minded disciples believed that whole populations could be made more intelligent and humane if the study of phrenology was taken up universally. Spurzheim's Boston lectures were packed, and consultations with the doctor were highly prized. In September 1832, Elizabeth engineered a private meeting with the doctor in Boston while Sophia was in town. The encounter sent her hopes soaring for a cure to Sophia's multiple ailments. Spurzheim was finishing out a demanding lecture schedule in Boston, but he promised to add a two-week course in Salem in late October that Sophia could attend.

Then Spurzheim fell ill. Elizabeth still planned to smuggle the weakened doctor, who was besieged by admirers, medical men, and the afflicted wherever he went, into Salem to examine Sophia's head. When Spurzheim died suddenly in Boston on the eve of his Salem visit, Elizabeth could not be consoled. Both Mary and Elizabeth joined the thousands of mourners who gath-

ered at Boston's Old South Meeting House, where odes were sung by the
Handel and Haydn Society and a eulogy delivered by the Harvard instructor
of German languages Charles Follen. Then they marched in procession along
with the entire Boston Medical Society and four hundred Harvard medical
students to the new Mount Auburn Cemetery in Cambridge. There Spurzheim
became only the second person to be interred on the artfully landscaped hillside.

As Mary wrote afterward, the outpouring of grief from Boston's intellectual
elite stemmed from the widespread belief that Spurzheim had "discovered a
truth which none thoroughly understood but himself" and that was "absolutely necessary to our well-being as a nation." The Boston Medical Society,
meeting the week after Spurzheim's death, issued a proclamation that "we
view the decease of Dr. Spurzheim and the termination of his labors, as a
calamity to mankind, and in an especial manner to this country." So much was
"left unsaid & unasked," Mary wrote, that his loss was "doubly felt—totally irreparable." Even Mary thought, now that Dr. Spurzheim was gone, "I want to
die more than ever—... I am impatient to be in a better place."

Yet as Elizabeth eventually busied herself collecting anecdotes for a memorial to Spurzheim and set Sophia to sketching his portrait, Mary began to see
the attractions of boarding house life in Boston. Mrs. Clarke's establishment
at Somerset Court was in many ways typical of a new style of living in American cities. Until the 1820s, population growth in rural and urban areas had
remained relatively equal. But between 1830 and 1840, cities gained the advantage, growing by over 60 percent, and in the following decade, by more
than 90 percent. Many of the newcomers were young unmarried men and
women looking for jobs as the workplace began to shift from farm to factory
or office. During the 1830s, there may have been as many as five thousand
single women living in Boston—well over 5 percent of the total population—
and one-third of the adult male population was unmarried, most of them
under the age of thirty-five.

The single-sex dormitory-style boarding house had yet to become widely
available to women, as it would later in the century. In the 1830s, most young
single women still worked as domestic servants and lived with the families
that employed them. Educated women with professional ambitions like the
Peabody sisters were in the minority. They pinched pennies to meet the rent
along with their higher-paid bachelor counterparts in family-run boarding
houses that simply expanded on the home environment. Few of these households were sex-segregated, with the result that, for the first time in American
social life, an emerging class of upwardly mobile single men and women lived
in homes together, sharing daily meals and evenings of conversation with un-
precedented freedom and informality.

Even in the spirited boarding house milieu of Boston in the 1830s, Mrs. Clarke's household at Somerset Court was exceptional. Although the widowed Mrs. Clarke herself was a meddlesome gossip who liked to speculate on the romantic prospects of her unmarried guests, the Peabody sisters found much in common with her twenty-four-year-old daughter, Sarah, a talented landscape painter. Sarah's younger brother, James Freeman Clarke, was a divinity student at Harvard capable of discussing German philosophy and eager to show off his brilliant new friend Margaret Fuller. Jared Sparks, an acquaintance of the Peabody sisters from Lancaster days, had moved his "immense & choice" library into rooms upstairs, and he invited Mary and Elizabeth to borrow any of his books. Sparks had recently resigned the editorship of the *North American Review* to write a biography of George Washington, and his collection included "a dozen shelves of large books containing 20,000 of Washington's letters in manuscript," according to Mary. The completion of his book, along with several edited volumes of Washington's correspondence, would carry Sparks to a professorship and then to the presidency at Harvard. And there was the young lawyer-journalist, George Hillard, soon to enter a partnership with the firebrand Charles Sumner.

The atmosphere at 3 Somerset Court was one into which visitors such as "the two intellectual Mr. Emersons"—Elizabeth's former Greek tutor, Ralph Waldo, widowed at twenty-eight, and his younger brother, Charles, a man of high literary promise—could safely venture without seeming to court the young women living there. Indeed, it was said that both Waldo and Charles were dispatched by their aunt Mary Moody Emerson, herself a disputatious intellectual, to consider Elizabeth Peabody as a bride. Neither one was tempted, but both returned for conversation—"one of those conversations which 'make the soul,'" Elizabeth later recalled, borrowing a phrase from Emerson's aunt Mary. Talk turned to the "free paraphrase" of the Gospel according to Saint John, which Elizabeth had shown to the Reverend Channing when she'd first written it almost ten years before. Like Channing, Waldo Emerson must have been struck by Elizabeth's "original thoughts": he asked for a copy. An intellectual connection, if not a romantic one, was made.

Just before Christmas 1832, the Clarke household expanded to accommodate a new member, the six-foot tall, elegantly mannered, silver-haired lawyer Horace Mann. At thirty-six, after only five years as a Whig in the Massachusetts House of Representatives, Mann was already one of the state's noteworthy reformers, a visionary with a strong pragmatic streak. Mann was among the first lawmakers in the nation to see that state governments could profit from subsidizing the construction of bridges and that newest of technologies, the railroad; thanks to his efforts, the Commonwealth had chartered the first state-sponsored railroad in the country, leading from Boston to Worcester and beyond. He also took a broad view of the state's responsibility toward the poor and the helpless. Mann had persuaded his colleagues to fund a state-run asylum for the insane, among the first in the nation, that would move the mentally ill out of town jails and into a more humane medical environment, where he believed they could be cured and eventually released. But Mann had initially made a name for himself by taking an unpopular stand on an issue close to the Peabody sisters' hearts. His first speech in the legislature had been against the Blandford petition, which, as a last gasp of the Puritan church-state, would have required every Massachusetts town to support "a learned, pious, Trinitarian Congregational minister." Mann was no Unitarian —if he had any belief at all, it was in phrenology—but he objected to this "invasion of Heaven's prerogatives" and spoke eloquently on behalf of every man's right to make his own "inquiries after truth." His argument carried the day.

The boarders at 3 Somerset Court knew that Horace Mann had joined their party in an effort to distract himself from the grief that had overwhelmed him since the death of his young wife, Charlotte, from tuberculosis the previous summer. But even if he had not been mourning Charlotte, the gaunt statesman with the massive brow and hooded, violet eyes would have cut a tragic figure. The smile he flashed in rare moments of levity captivated Elizabeth and Mary Peabody all the more for its suggestion of the depths of sorrow from which it had risen. The sisters would soon learn that Mann's painstakingly correct manners—rare in the reform circles in which the Peabodys traveled—belied his humble origins and a spartan upbringing, marked by other untimely deaths and a grim struggle for subsistence.

Mann's father died when Horace was eleven, leaving his mother with five children to support on the family farm in Franklin, Massachusetts. The next year, Horace's favorite older brother, Stephen, drowned on a summer Sunday morning when he skipped church to go swimming. Young Horace was profoundly distressed when the local Calvinist minister made an example of Stephen and preached that death was a fitting punishment for breaking the Sabbath. The boy endured a crisis of faith that tormented him with nightmares and imagined phantoms for months. At last he determined to abandon the unforgiving creed of his parents, but he could find no substitute beyond the gospel of hard work that he practiced on the farm in long days spent behind the plow since age seven. And even that doctrine had its reprisals. "I believe in the rugged nursing of Toil," he later wrote, "but she nursed me too much." Mann was plagued all his adult life by a weakened constitution—a susceptibility to colds and influenza, and a stomach so sensitive he could sometimes tolerate only spoonfuls of strained currant juice—that he attributed to his early labors.

Mann's route to the Massachusetts State House and beyond, when it was

Horace Mann

recounted in later years, would help shape the classic American success story. He was one of those "young men come down from the back woods . . . to fill our first rank of society" whom Elizabeth had written of to Wordsworth—although she had not known him then. His story began in a one-room schoolhouse in Franklin, where he mastered the curriculum during brief winter terms in a classroom so cold that his ink sometimes froze in his pen. The boy was determined to go to college, yet by age eighteen he had learned none of the Latin, Greek, or higher mathematics he would need to pass entrance exams. He set to work braiding straw on winter nights to sell to hat makers, and eventually he saved enough to hire a tutor. But who could teach him? He'd broken with the town minister who taught other local boys the classics. He tried teaching himself Latin, but ultimately had to walk four miles to the next town to study with a Baptist minister who encouraged Mann to attend his alma mater, Brown University in Rhode Island. Horace Mann was twenty by the time he was able to pass the entrance exams, after cramming much of the necessary information in a six-month crash course that permanently weakened his eyes. Then he did so well that he was granted special dispensation by Brown's president, Asa Messer, to enter college as a sophomore.

At Brown, Mann's relatively advanced age and dogged intelligence set him apart from the other boys, many of whom, like their Harvard counterparts, followed the cycle of rebellion and rustication. In his college essays, which earned him entrance to an elite debating society, Mann began to show the penchant for vituperation that would be his chief weapon in defense of fiercely held democratic ideals. Perhaps thinking of the generous treatment he had received from Asa Messer, he wrote of "American Genius" that it "is elicited from its abode, nurtured and cherished" in the New World, while in Europe talent "is awed into silence, unless some parasite of royalty can call it his own." He gave as examples the rough-hewn statesmen who were his heroes: Benjamin Franklin, Samuel Adams, Thomas Jefferson. Of the arts, he took a dim view. In two separate essays, one "Against Novels" and another "Against Fiction," he classified the novel as "a long series of incredibilities, impossible conjunctures, and sickening interviews." For the reader of fiction, he wrote, "the imagination is continually feasted with lively descriptions," while "the mind has received no improvement, principles no correction, nor ideas enlargement."

If Mann seemed overly serious, it was because his belief in "Self-Improvement," as he titled another essay, was of necessity so powerful. He knew that his own future depended on what he made of himself. Most of Mann's classmates had arrived at Brown with some form of American privilege—money, land, or business connections. He needed to believe that "there is by nature little, or perhaps, no distinction among men, with respect to their original powers of intellect." The difference, he wrote, came about when "perpetual culture" was applied to "those seeds of knowledge," which were the same, "implanted by the impartial hand of nature," in the mind of both "illiterate peasant" and "philosopher." When Mann became class valedictorian, it was on self-education that he lectured his fellow seniors, telling them "the common idea of *completing* an education ought to be expunged from the intellectual world." And, while his classmates reveled in the days following graduation, then bid one another tearful goodbyes, Mann made plans to study law in Connecticut. "'Tis pleasant to form connexions," he wrote his sister matter-of-factly, "but they must be broken." If there was any sadness in parting, the stoic young philosopher, already inured to loss, mused, "we enjoy only while our means of enjoyment are passing from us, as the spark, which shines only while it is consuming."

The one connection Horace Mann retained at Brown was to his mentor, President Asa Messer, and, through him, to his youngest daughter. Charlotte Messer was just ten years old when Mann graduated from Brown. Yet during the next decade, as he made conquests in moot court competitions at Litchfield Law School, returned to his home state to establish a law practice in Dedham, and won election to the Massachusetts House of Representatives, it was to Charlotte that his thoughts turned when he considered marriage. For the ambitious farm-bred lawyer, winning the hand of a college president's daughter must have seemed the ultimate prize. First there were occasional visits, then letters, and finally a carefully worded request that Charlotte allow him to call on her regularly "in the character of an *avowed.*" Yet Mann failed to notice that the girl never quite managed to grow up, so fragile was her health. No one realized that when the couple married at last in 1830, the twenty-one-year-old Charlotte was already dying of tuberculosis, the disease that granted her a pale luminescence even as it inexorably ravaged her lungs.

Indeed, Charlotte's fragility may only have added to her attraction. Mann loved Charlotte's delicate coquettishness and naïve optimism, which contrasted so sharply with his own two sisters' work-weary Calvinism. Perhaps because Mann took for granted his own precarious health, he could not see Charlotte's frequent illnesses as life-threatening, even when she began to cough up blood. And, because he spent so much time in Boston on business, he rarely minded her long absences from their Dedham home to recuperate with her family. She was in Providence on their first anniversary when Mann realized that they had lived together little more than half the year. Mann's chief worry was that loneliness was the root cause of Charlotte's continued attachment to her family. But he could not persuade himself to work any less hard in order to spend more time with his wife. He may also have had reason to believe in her improving health: it is likely that Charlotte became pregnant in March 1832. By July, however, she was too weak to walk, and Mann gave up all his duties to nurse her at home in what he described as "a scene of anxiety, of dismay, of struggling" while Charlotte, delirious with fever, fought for breath. When Charlotte died a month later, less than two years after their wedding, Horace Mann was nearly broken by the loss of his wife and unborn child. The trauma of those final weeks, mutual friends told the Peabody sisters, had turned Mann's dark hair completely white—giving the thirty-five-year-old widower a spectral look.

Charlotte's death released emotions long pent up in Horace Mann. The sober, crusading legislator began writing poetry to comfort himself. His old theological doubts returned. He could not bear to think of Charlotte reduced to cold dust in the Providence cemetery where he had buried her. Yet if he renewed his childhood belief in a Calvinist heaven, must Charlotte's death have been a form of retribution—a consignment to hell for Horace Mann? Tormented by guilt over his neglect of his invalid wife and regret for the domestic idyll he had taken for granted, the habitually guarded man found himself pouring out his grief and doubt to anyone who offered sympathy.

In the boarding house at 3 Somerset Court, the Peabody sisters met a Horace Mann that no one else had known before, and they were both smitten. For Elizabeth, it was a safe love—she was convinced that Mann's devotion to Charlotte's memory was so strong he would never remarry. But Mary's love was dangerous—she was *afraid* he never would.

"He came into my sphere prostrated, scathed, blasted," Mary wrote years later in a short story she composed based on her early love for Horace Mann. Despite his "languid step, the broken accents of his sorrow," she immediately recognized in the tall, violet-eyed politician "a commanding nature born to sway men." At this moment, however, it was twenty-six-year-old Mary Peabody he swayed most of all. "The voice of his complaint penetrated the inmost recesses of my being," she wrote in the highly charged language of the sentimental novels she admired. Mary held her breath when Horace Mann spoke; she was "riveted" the first time he held open a door for her and smiled as she passed through. "I felt the glow permeate every fibre & vein, I knew nothing more till I was seated by the window in my own apartment." Mary had finally found her way into the plot she had been rehearsing in all her "reveries" since childhood. "Here was life and something to do," she told herself: "It was to make that smile perpetual."

So sure was Mary of her feelings, after years of comparing the marriageable men she met with her heroes of romance or of real life—the Reverend Channing and Father Taylor—that she inwardly began to think of Horace Mann as "my husband." Mary knew that Horace Mann was still wedded to his memories of Charlotte, a woman so delicate and pampered that she had once subsisted for most of a month on oysters. Surely he would not consider another match now; she must hold her feelings in check. "I learned to repress all outward signs of emotion," Mary wrote in her story, "for the one grand object of my existence was to contribute to his happiness, and any outward expression of the flame that glowed within me would have marred it." But in her letters home to Sophia, during the winter and spring of 1833, Mary could barely conceal her newfound joy. She wrote of the "corruscations" at teatime in Somerset Court, and the "comical times" at dinner when "Mr. Mann" shook off his gloom and joined the conversation. Best of all were several weeks when Mrs. Clarke, who tended to "spoil many of our talks by her clamorousness," was away, leaving her boarders with "no head to the table or the house."

The "unsettled state" of affairs, without "even the appearance of a married lady" at their communal dinners, delighted nearly everyone. Horace Mann became "intolerably witty," with "an anecdote, a story or a saying for every emergency," and a way of telling them that "well nigh destroys me," Mary wrote to Sophia. Sarah Clarke was "so blushy, and Mr. Sparks so crusty, and

George Hillard so sick and melancholy, and E. so talkative that altogether we form a hodge-podge ... so very agreeable—that I am almost sorry for the necessity which is to bring Mrs. Clarke back to us." That winter, Mary even managed to make light of the muddy streets of Beacon Hill, which some days caused her to slide back down as many steps as she climbed. The only cloudy moments were the several days each month when Horace Mann traveled to Worcester to inspect the state Lunatic Hospital or to Dedham to try cases at the courthouse. "People's ideas get into a strange jumble when he is away," Mary wrote Sophia. "[H]e seems to be a point of union to the heterogeneous mass—all defer to his opinion."

Part of Mary's program for cheering up Horace Mann was reading aloud to him in the evening. She and Elizabeth took turns translating extemporaneously from the French philosophers Benjamin Constant and Victor Cousin, and then Mary tried Anna Jameson's essays on Shakespeare's heroines, *Characteristics of Women*. Mann returned the favor by reading Edmund Burke and Thomas Jefferson. But there were many nights when Mann was moody and silent, unwilling to be distracted. He would pace the small parlor while the other boarders read and talked, or sit in a corner, his face turned to the wall to conceal the emotions that gripped him as he succumbed to painful memories. Sometimes, snippets of conversation would remind him of Charlotte, and, as on one evening when the group had discussed a set of drawings of Adam and Eve, he would leave the room choking back tears. The result, of course, was only to draw the sisters further into his suffering.

One night Mary tried singing, and this time Mann could not control himself. Although there is no record of what was said, many years later Mary recalled, "he poured out his grief with such passionate eloquence that ... I stood awed & ... terror-struck before it. I thought I had sounded many depths of pain, but never this. ... With trembling I listened—speechless I wept—then every power of my soul was taxed to console & finally to cheer." Horace Mann wrote to her the next day, "I regret exceedingly that I had so little command over my feelings last evening as to suffer them to betray me." By chance, Mary had sung a favorite song of Charlotte's, and "I was taken unawares," he explained. "I do not regret the occurrence myself, for I know I must pass through such scenes till feelings are cauterized, if indeed that can *ever* be," Mann apologized, "and it is less painful to me to pass through them with such friends than with strangers." Mary treasured his letter; she now had proof that Horace Mann regarded her as a trusted friend.

In April, Mary wrote to Sophia, "I have felt for the last few months as if the eyes of my heart were open to what they have been shut for a long time." The reason she gave was Horace Mann: "one effect Mr. Mann produces is, to make me feel my connection with human beings more keenly." Although she did not tell Sophia she was in love, she came close to it: "I am some times tempted to ask him where he got that smile that melts away the ice-bergs that enclose some of us poor mortals, and that lingers round the borders of the heart so long after it has passed from his countenance." Did Sophia guess? In later years, Sophia would claim that she "never imagined" such a thing. But in the spring of 1833, Sophia began to wish that she, too, could "comfort" Horace Mann.

By midsummer, when Mary left Boston for a two-week stay in New Bedford to celebrate the marriage of a wealthy former student, she was completely immune to the attentions of a young man in the wedding party, Benjamin Lindsay, who seemed to believe that Mary met *his* ideal. Lindsay let Mary know that he "thought me perfection." But "I was not satisfied," Mary wrote. Now that she had set herself the challenge of winning over Horace Mann, Mary found an easy love such as Benjamin Lindsay's too tame. She thirsted for the love of a man "born to sway men." She would not settle for anything less.

Mary carried with her to New Bedford two vivid memories of her newly beloved Horace Mann. The first was of an early-July excursion to Mount Auburn Cemetery led by the Clarkes. The same hillsides that had, less than a year before, provided the setting for hundreds of mourners at J. G. Spurzheim's burial, had become one of Boston's most popular tourist destinations in the green summer months. Now, in a suddenly "radiant mood," Horace Mann mocked the stone memorials to the dead by swinging his long frame up into a tree and climbing to its highest branches. Mary looked up with delight into Mann's "sublime face" as he exclaimed over the "glorious" views of Cambridge and Fresh Pond from his leafy perch.

The day before, Mary had witnessed a scene that she considered even more glorious. At Elizabeth's urging, Horace Mann had agreed to address a temperance rally of nearly a thousand Sunday school children at Father Taylor's church. Before the event, Mann confided in Mary his worry that he might not know how to speak to children. But Mary found herself in "a sort of little ecstacy" as she saw Horace Mann take an "electrifying part" in the meeting and enthrall his young audience with a retelling of Krummacher's fable of "The Little Dove," a story that Mary herself had translated for him from the original German. The man sitting next to Mary attested that Mann had the same effect in the Massachusetts legislature: "*he* was the man that always *took the ear—he* knew how to hit the nail on the head—*he* was the great man."

Back home at Somerset Court, Mary wrote to Sophia that she should never have doubted that Horace Mann "could do any thing where love & affection had a part." She then set to work composing an article for the Unitarian weekly the *Christian Register* describing the event. Mary commanded herself to refrain from writing "con amore," she told Sophia, even though she planned to publish the account anonymously. This was the first time since her days as editor of the homespun *Salem Recorder* that Mary had taken pen in hand with the intent of publication.

Love was not the only feeling that Mary struggled to conceal during the spring and summer of 1833, however. There was anger and jealousy too. Mary saw instantly that Elizabeth had more in common with Horace Mann than she did. Both tended to live their lives out of books—philosophy books, like Thomas Brown's *Cause and Effect*, rather than the novels Mary favored. And Elizabeth, with her incessant conversation, exceeded only by Mrs. Clarke's nattering at the dinner table, had managed from the start to monopolize Horace Mann's attention with "talk, talk, talk, ad infinitum." Mary felt hopelessly upstaged as she watched the two "hold metaphysical arguments long enough to exhaust all common minds." She wrote Sophia of one hot summer day when "we were all very tired," and Mary, Elizabeth, and Horace Mann "assembled in Sarah [Clarke]'s little painting room and talked about necessity & free will all the afternoon." She had to admit that it was "E & Mr. M." who did most of the talking. In the end, Mary and Sarah Clarke were forced to conclude "that we had not minds capable of taking in the subject." So intent did "E & Mr. M." seem on conversation that year at Somerset Court that Mrs. Clarke had the other boarders speculating on the likelihood of a marriage between the two.

Now qualities in Elizabeth that had once been merely annoying to Mary threatened to demolish the castle she had built in the air. In the short story Mary wrote years later, she sketched a villainess with the same menacing features as her older sister. "She wanted to excel others in every thing," Mary wrote, "having felt the gratification of excelling most people by brilliancy of intellect." This "egotist" managed to appear "kindhearted & sympathetic" as she pursued the hero of the story, a grieving widower who "bore the marks of lofty faculties." But hers was "never a self-forgetting kindness," and she easily dominated all who came into her sphere of influence. "I could not cope with her stronger will," Mary wrote, "she always overpowered me with her logic & silenced me by her authority." Most dangerous of all, "I knew she loved him with all the strength of her nature."

Did Elizabeth love Horace Mann? Perhaps not in the way Mary feared. But her attraction to him was powerful, and her need for Mann's attention intense. "I can get food for my mind in books—in observation of life—in my own reflections," Elizabeth had once written to a friend, but "food for my heart must come direct from others—& *my heart* always craved more than my mind."

During the weeks of Mrs. Clarke's absence from Somerset Court, Elizabeth initiated a subtle contest with Mary to see which sister could outlast the other in the parlor at night with Horace Mann. One evening—the night after the

Adam and Eve pictures had plunged Mann into such a "deep gloom," as Elizabeth wrote to Sophia—Sarah Clarke and the others left the room. Finally Mary rose to go, but Elizabeth lingered. She felt she could not leave Horace Mann, who was lost in one of his abject silences, "without making some sign of my sympathy." She took his hand as she said good night and "he still held my hand till Mary had gone out of the room."

Once the two were alone, Mann "drew me nearer & throwing his arm round me—let the tears flow." Then "he laid his head upon my bosom and begged my pardon for taking such a liberty with his grief." Elizabeth assured him he had done nothing wrong. Indeed, she told Mann, she too *needed a friend to my shattered mind and nerves.* That night the two formed a pact that "he be sincere with me always and let me tell him all my troubles and never flatter me," and "*I* should be the forever obliged and should feel that my sympathy was infinitely overpaid." Horace Mann, by Elizabeth's account, was relieved: "Again, again, and again he pressed me to his heart, and with floods of tears, *thanked me.*"

Elizabeth wrote Sophia of the scene several days later, but when she climbed the stairs to her room that night and took her place on the side of the bed she shared with Mary, Elizabeth said nothing. She claimed afterward that she feared Mary would blame her for drawing out Mann's grief rather than helping him contain it; she expected Mary to accuse her of being "led too far by my feelings." Perhaps Elizabeth did have qualms about the liberties both she and Horace Mann had taken that night. But, in truth, Elizabeth enjoyed the secret bond, just as Mary thrilled to her private fantasy of Horace Mann as her "husband." Elizabeth needed Mann's friendship as much as Mary wished for his love. And, with her willingness to stretch the limits of feminine propriety, Elizabeth could bypass the formalities of engagements and weddings that most men and women required to establish an emotional intimacy, and attain that friendship just by sharing a parlor in a genteel boarding house on Beacon Hill.

Later Elizabeth would write, in defense of her behavior, "I do not know what would have become of me—If Mr M—had not fallen like an angel of comfort & sustaining friendship on my path—received my confidence—& mended my heart with his essential approbation—& unshadowed sympathy." This kind of intimacy may have been the closest Elizabeth wished to come to a man who, nevertheless, she saw as "one of the few—who might die for love because one of the few who knew how to love." If she also admired Horace Mann, with his "Jupiter brow," as "one of Nature's noblemen," then so much the better. Later that same year she would attempt to resolve her confused emotions in a sonnet she titled "Chastity." The poem was no hymn to prudishness. Instead it celebrated "Love-in-the-Eternal-Reason": an energizing passion, divorced from the body and purifying to the soul. Elizabeth's newfound devotion to Horace Mann, and the affection he gave in return, helped to fuel the rapture of her closing line: "Forever more from Chaos' night, in ecstasy I rise!"

Unwilling to admit that she had played the aggressor, or perhaps too accustomed to taking the lead to notice that she had just elbowed her younger sister out of the way, Elizabeth was to recall the first months of 1833 as some of the best in her life. Despite her desire to lay claim to Horace Mann's innermost thoughts, Elizabeth had no interest in winning his exclusive attention. If anything, she felt her connection to Mary, sorely tested in recent years by her own moodiness and financial woes, was being repaired in the process. "I did feel that he drew us together in becoming a common object of affection to us," she once wrote to Mary. In an unconscious reference to the watery threesome, Undine, Bertha, and Hildebrand, she envisioned the connection with Mann as a "new stream of friendship—where we both could drink." She was not dissembling when she wrote, "It is the supreme delight of my heart when one of us has a friend that the other may have the same, and I do not wish to be preferred." The relationship with Mary was the one Elizabeth had always considered fundamental, viewing it, at times, as a kind of marriage. Elizabeth may have needed Mary to ratify her passions, and to make them safe. Now, in the vibrant atmosphere of Somerset Court, she believed that the trio—Mary, Elizabeth, and Horace Mann—had achieved a "happy union" that was "as transparent as Heaven's intercourse will be." She had little expectation, she wrote afterward, that "I shall ever come *so near* happiness again—in human circumstances."

Mary saw things differently. Chastity had never been an inspiring notion for her. Mary *did* want Horace Mann's exclusive attention—romantically, too. Not knowing of his late-night encounter with Elizabeth, or their secret pact, Mary grew increasingly disturbed by Elizabeth's frank discussions with Horace Mann and her tendency to draw him to the brink of despair in order to analyze his feelings when he got there—"to take out his heart & pick it to pieces," as she saw it. Mary had to worry now not only that Elizabeth might detect her younger sister's feelings for Horace Mann and reveal them, but that Elizabeth's own intense involvement with Mann might lead to either of two disastrous results: she could alienate him entirely from them both with her intrusive sympathy, or he might fall in love with Elizabeth instead.

In 1833, however, the truth was that Horace Mann, with his widower's prerogative to entertain single women as if he were still safely married, was equally involved with both sisters, if in different ways. The adoration of two women—sisters, who he sensed were competing for his attention—must have been powerfully reassuring at a time when he felt guilt-stricken and vulnerable. That summer Mann addressed Mary as "my dear friend," and complimented her "nature, composed of affection." With Elizabeth, the attachment was more complicated. Few unmarried women would have willingly received Mann's embrace without at least the hint of a forthcoming marriage proposal. Yet something about Elizabeth—perhaps the same qualities that had caused Mrs. Clarke to call her "queer"—told him he would not be rebuffed by this ardent, bookish twenty-nine-year-old. By keeping their conversation on an intellectual plane, debating necessity and free will or the probability of an afterlife for Charlotte, he was able to receive from Elizabeth the physical consolation he needed even more than talk in the months after his wife's death. In the immediate confusion of his grief, Elizabeth's chaste love, made up of an unorthodox blend of sympathies—intellectual, maternal, sisterly, wifely—was the ideal balm.

Unable, both by nature and in deference to Horace Mann's grieving, to press her case, Mary was forced to play a waiting game. After all, she reasoned, "[H]ad I not given him my whole heart unasked?" Accustomed to letting Elizabeth do the talking for the both of them, Mary could not compete with Elizabeth as a conversationalist. She could only hope that Mann would one day tire of Elizabeth's aggressive intellectuality and come to prefer Mary's brand of sympathy instead. But Mary's ability to hold out was threatened by the sisters' increasingly precarious financial situation.

"Our school has about died out," Mary wrote to Lydia Sears Haven in March 1833. After the summer term, most of their students would move on to one of several prestigious Boston academies run by Harvard men. They could not borrow rent money from Dr. Peabody: their three brothers had already depleted his slim reserves with what Mary and Elizabeth could see only as foolishness. Nat's drugstore in Boston failed at midsummer, costing Dr. Peabody his investment. George had borrowed the fare for his voyage to Smyrna, where he'd heard he could find work as a shipping clerk; his tip was false, however, and he returned several months later having driven his father deeper into debt. And within a year, Wellington would jump ship in Rio, forfeiting his share in the profits of his whaling voyage.

Elizabeth began to hint that one of the sisters should return to Salem. Proud of the reputation she was making for herself as a historian in Boston— with a promising new history class for adult women under way and her three-volume *Key to History* in the works, the first of her books to be published under her own name—Elizabeth pressured her younger sister to retreat. Mary responded by taking on several students to tutor in German; she wrote to a friend, "I intend to live in Boston just as long as I can keep soul and body together here." When the possibility arose that one of the sisters might take Sophia, who seemed to the family "feebler & more easily tired than ever," to Italy to recuperate with the Clarke family in the fall, Mary was elated. She knew Elizabeth would not refuse the opportunity. "If I can get E. & Sophy off to the Southern climes I shall be very happy," she wrote Lydia Haven. Mary, too, could have gone, but she had suddenly developed the ambition to "take a school by myself" in Boston, and "it will be more agreeable to *send E out of the country* first."

Before a decision could be reached, Horace Mann packed his bags and, without any warning, left Mrs. Clarke's boarding house for a single room nearby. It was the end of July, and both sisters were thrown into a panic. Mary worried that her occasional suggestions to the widower that he might be "dwelling too intently" on his sorrows had offended him; Elizabeth feared that she had pressed too far in the opposite direction. Each blamed the other, for both sensed that their rivalry for Horace Mann's attention had spilled out into the open. In after years they would quibble endlessly about "the impressions our manner to each other had caused in his mind": the ill effects of Elizabeth's seeming to "tyrannize" Mary and of Mary's "palpable forbearance" and "distrust" of Elizabeth.

Ever politic, Mann explained his abrupt departure in a letter to Elizabeth, who had come right out and asked if she and Mary were to blame. "I found every female member of the family more agreeable even than I had anticipated," he wrote of the Clarke ménage. Yet so much feminine sympathy had only reminded him bitterly of "that for which I mourned." As the anniversary of Charlotte's death approached, "drawing me into its vortex," he felt overcome by "the most frightful situation of grief, *powerless* but *conscious*" and "more incapacitated for business daily." In hopes that he might "reedify the ruins" of his mind, Horace Mann had determined, as in the days following his graduation from Brown, that "the ties of association must be broken" in order to "reverse this fatal current of thought." And he had not wished to inflict his sorrow on others. He wrote to both sisters telling them his only wish was that they remain happy, and "you will then truly contribute something towards restoring that 'Peace' which you so feelingly supplicate for me."

What Horace Mann really felt about the move is impossible to judge. Perhaps, as one biographer has suggested, he simply wanted to economize. Failed investments in his surviving brother's business ventures had recently thrown him into debt. As his ruined brother, Stanley, succumbed to alcoholism, Mann became the sole support of his mother and sisters. The single room he moved into was his law office. But Mann may also have felt guilty about the kind of "frolic" he had been persuaded to engage in with the Clarke and Peabody women during the outing at Mount Auburn Cemetery earlier in the month. If Mary had caught an inkling then that Mann must once have been "the gayest hearted creature," the self-punishing widower had likely been stricken with remorse afterward.

Elizabeth was more convinced than ever, as she wrote to Sophia on the anniversary of Charlotte Mann's death, that "time will do little if anything" for Horace Mann. On a recent evening visit, Mann had read to her an article from the *Christian Examiner* on capital punishment, and the two had discussed the issue at length. But "his countenance . . . when ever he was not making an effort to be gay—expressed *anguish.*" Nothing could be done, Elizabeth concluded, "but quietly to let him struggle." Even Elizabeth could see that any word of sympathy might upset her new friend's hard-won composure.

Mary was left in her own state of mourning for "the sound of his voice," which she had grown accustomed to hearing at all times of the day. "No music of bird, or of human throat, or of wind or stringed instrument, was so melodious to my ear," she wrote in her fictional account. In idle moments, Mary allowed herself to imagine that Horace Mann might one day return her love with "a love such as mine was for an ideal being—warm appreciation & sympathy, tender regard, ever expecting new joys, love for my possibilities." But she grew increasingly fearful of "betraying myself," now that Mann's visits to the Clarke household were only sporadic. She could feel her face flush "if I saw him unexpectedly or even heard a careless remark about him," she wrote. To Sophia, she confided that since Horace Mann had moved away, life at Somerset Court, once "so very agreeable," had become an "abomination of desolation."

ℭ 23 ℨ

Blind Fair

DURING THE SUMMER OF 1832, WHILE MARY WAS QUIETLY BEARING the indignities inflicted on her as governess to the Channing children, Sophia drifted between her friends' country houses, postponing her retreat from Boston to Salem. She quickly came to regret her month-long stay with Lydia and Sam Haven at their new house on the wooded outskirts of Lowell, where Sam had set up his law practice in the young mill city. Lydia's recurrent illnesses, exacerbated by the birth of a son, had begun to take the distinct form of pulmonary tuberculosis. Listening to her friend cough through the night, sensing the strain Lydia's ill health put on her marriage, and worrying about who would care for the young Foster Haven in the years ahead kept the "hypersympathetic" Sophia in bed through most of July in "perpetual torture."

But Sophia's stay with Connie Park and her husband, the Boston financier Tom Park, was an entirely different matter. The two newlyweds were passionately in love, and when Sophia arrived at their Roxbury house in August, they seemed willing to include her in their bliss. As Mary wrote afterward, aside from Sophia, there was nobody that the Parks had "such a passion for except one another." The Parks' estate was a "retreat of the Arts and Graces," in Sophia's description, with lush gardens on every side and enormous alabaster urns in the parlors, filled with "spicy flowers and eglantine—reminding one of Araby." At night the three entertained one another by winding out extravagantly harmonized melodies on the Parks' new music box. The next day Sophia could sleep until noon, if she wished, and "never hear a rude sound." Tom Park stopped all the clocks each night to prevent them from chiming the hours and would not put on his shoes or speak above a whisper until his guest woke in the morning. For once, Sophia felt entirely at ease and, after a short period of adjustment, free of headache.

A few days into the visit, a drenching rainstorm provoked a bout of rheumatism in Tom Park, who stayed home from his Boston office for most of a week. At first the two women wept in their rooms for the suffering husband. But once the worst of the attack had passed, Sophia wrote to Mary, "we enjoy him imprisoned prodigiously." At Connie's suggestion, Sophia "absconded to the attic" with Tom to paint his portrait. Shaking off the doubts that had crippled her last efforts at painting in Boston, Sophia extended her visit from two weeks to nearly two months, finding one excuse after another to stay and finish Tom Park's portrait, her first from a live subject.

Yet, inevitably, summer came to an end, and Sophia had no choice but to return to Salem. On her way home, she stopped at Mrs. Clarke's boarding house in Boston just long enough to be felled by "a violent toothach—or rather headach in my teeth—caused by overfatigue." Sophia always spelled the word "headach" in the same archaic manner as her mother—the mother who anxiously awaited her in Salem. But Sophia dallied, allowing her toothache to subside, taking tea with J. G. Spurzheim, and completing the finish work on *Sappho* along with a small painting, *Temple of Paestum*, based on a J.M.W. Turner engraving in Samuel Rogers's verse travelogue *Italy*, one of her favorite books. She sent both productions to the Parks as thank-you gifts.

Despite the recuperative stay in Roxbury, Sophia arrived in Salem in early October feeling weaker than she had for the past year, the "natural" result of "unintermitted pain," she supposed. Or perhaps it was Salem itself and the final separation "from Mary and Elizabeth and the treasures of Boston" that caused a relapse. Sophia now implored Mary to write full letters whenever she visited Boston's galleries and artists' studios and "let your pen be my eyes." After the past four years in a Boston townhouse large enough to accommodate her sisters' school, most of the Peabody family, and several boarders, Sophia was dismayed by the "minimum of a house" her parents had rented on Church Street in Salem. At first she found the ceilings so "nearly upon my head" and "the walls so near together" that "upon entering I really felt a slight want of breath." How much compensation was it, as she wrote to more than one friend during the next few months, to find "there was no want of room" in her mother's welcoming arms?

Sophia was well aware of what she called a "peculiar bond" that had "grown up between Mother & me from my invalid state." One link was through opium, the drug Eliza Peabody used to soften the effects of her own chronic cough. "Delicious" laudanum reveries were a refuge for many, not just the Reverend William Ellery Channing, during these years before the addictive properties of opium were understood and when a multitude of concoctions based on the drug were readily available without prescription. Through most of her twenties, Sophia used small amounts of opium at least occasionally and sometimes on a daily basis. But ultimately it was the sheer number of hours that

Mrs. Peabody spent at her daughter's bedside that caused Sophia to write in later years, "my soul is knit to hers." Illness provided mother and daughter with a shared language of "headachs" and remedies, of sensitivities and precautions, as if the "demon in my head" were a creature known only to the two of them. "There is no person living," she once wrote to Elizabeth, "who knows or can know all my pros & cons but Mother."

Perhaps the vocation of nursing Sophia compensated for Mrs. Peabody's own disappointments—her ineffectual husband, her lapsed literary career, the loss of her seventh child, Catharine, in infancy. "We live for our dear invalids," Eliza Peabody had once written to Sophia, "our happiness is to devote time and talents to their comfort." Sophia's invalidism also provided a link with Eliza's Palmer ancestors. During the 1830s, Mrs. Peabody began to write her novel of the Revolutionary era in which she told the story of an earlier family invalid, her aunt Polly Palmer, whose nerves had been shattered by gunfire. In this fictional version, Polly was transformed into the character Mary Lawson, an artist like Sophia whose paintings were "specimens of genius" and "brought a liberal price," even as they were also "valued for her sake." In Eliza Peabody's straitened circumstances, caring for an invalid-artist daughter evoked a small measure of the life of privilege and refinement that she recalled from her early childhood at Friendship Hall.

Yet the "peculiar bond" between mother and daughter was more likely a result than the source of Sophia's migraines. Eliza Peabody had educated all three of her daughters for "future usefulness" as teachers, impressing on them the unconventional notion that "to be independant so far as money extends, of every one, is to be desirable." She never gave up hoping to make Sophia "independant & useful as an Instructress," insisting that she attend to "a certain routine of studies" even when she was sick and seeing to it that the "girls as well as boys" in the family devoted the majority of their time to schoolwork. All of Mrs. Peabody's efforts to identify the triggers of Sophia's headaches—travel, exciting conversation, "fussation" among family members—and to limit Sophia's exposure to them, were aimed at making her daughter as productive as possible, given the "frequent and severe headachs, which retard her progress." Mrs. Peabody's program was no different from Oliver Sacks's first line of defense against migraines: "avoidance of circumstances known to be provocative of attacks."

Sophia's ambivalence about the independence her mother envisioned for her was surely a greater factor in her chronic illness than any unconcious desire on her mother's part to keep her a dependent at home, as previous biographers have suggested. Sophia's headaches first became incapacitating when Elizabeth and Mary went out to work and Sophia glimpsed the conditions of "independant" life for her self-supporting sisters. Headaches had allowed

Sophia to decline Elizabeth's invitation to share teaching duties in Maine when Sophia was just fourteen. Since then she had watched her sisters struggle to attract students, gather fees, and pay their bills. She had seen them settle into a social stratum distinctly below that of the families for whom they worked— families whose daughters had become Sophia's friends.

Sophia may have preferred remaining an invalid in her mother's care to becoming a schoolteacher—or even an artist. How could she be sure that painting, itself dependent on elusive moments of inspiration and on training she might never acquire, would ever be a reliable source of income? She had seen the meager livelihood painting supplied to Catherine Scollay. Why not stay home, instead, and continue to "look upon herself as a little girl," as Elizabeth once explained Sophia's preternatural innocence and optimism? A child, even a sick one, could always hope for the future. A commitment to a profession, whether teaching or painting, might mean closing off an option that Sophia privately entertained: the fantasy of a collaborative marriage to her artist "Unknown yet known."

For the past two months, Sophia had worked well in the companionable opulence of the Park household, full of "love & loveliness." There her paintings had been admired as art and given as gifts, not sold for profit in a marketplace guided by the harsh judgments of strangers. But she could not be a guest forever, and she could only dream of re-creating such an atmosphere on her own. Now that she was back home in Salem, Sophia found herself once again "full of love and headach," and struggling to paint.

Yet Sophia, recently turned twenty-three, received a rude shock when she learned that she would be expected to work as both artist and instructress during the coming year. Elizabeth's tendency to be "unfortunate in her exertions to get money" evidently did not extend to her efforts on her youngest sister's behalf. She had coaxed several Boston collectors into loaning Sophia paintings to copy for sale, and she had arranged for the motherless Quaker girl Mary Newhall to board with the Peabody family while Sophia taught her to paint. Newhall's wealthy guardian—a devotee of Mary Newhall's recently deceased mother, the New Light Quaker preacher with the same name—had agreed to pay a generous portion of the Peabodys' rent and provide art materials if Sophia would allow the girl to paint alongside her, following the Doughty method of instruction. Elizabeth argued that, after two years of practice, the penniless Newhall, now in her late teens, could work as an art teacher herself; Sophia would not have to expend any extra energy to instruct her, assuming she felt well enough to paint. Into Sophia's "sweet little chamber, studio & boudoir (all in one)" came plaster models, brushes, paints and varnishes, the several paintings that Elizabeth had obtained for Sophia to copy, and two easels—one for Sophia and one for Mary Newhall.

After a two-week confinement to her bed with headaches, Sophia seemed spurred on by the requirement to guide a younger painter. Side by side the two women completed copies of *Reichenbach Falls,* a mountain landscape by an unknown artist, and *Contentment,* a Harvard College scene by Washington Allston's nephew George Flagg. This "divine art," Sophia confided with evident satisfaction in her journal, "which two years ago—I knew not of—how much it is to me now!"

Then, in November, the unexpected happened: inspiration struck. "What think you I have actually begun to do?" Sophia wrote to Mary in Boston. "Nothing less than *create.*" She had enlarged a scene of three nymphs and a boy gathered at a fountain from Samuel Rogers's *Italy,* "added a castle in the distance, & mountains—& a winding path." The "coloring will be all my own," she wrote in her journal on November 19. Sophia knew she had one more step to take toward originating "both form & color." Still, she was jubilant: "Mortal man cannot conceive what a bliss it has been to me to plan out this picture." In her letter to Mary, she told of the ecstatic "first night after the first creation": "Do you wonder that I lay awake all last night after sketching my first picture? I actually thought my poor head would have made its final explosion. When once I began to excurse, I could not stop. Three distinct landscapes came forth in full array, besides that I had arranged before I went to bed, and it seemed as if I should fly to be up and doing. All I feared was that I should die on the spot, so completely, so unnaturally was my whole mind, soul, heart, and body awake and busy."

Of course this flood of images also signaled the arousal phase of her migraine. Sophia was experiencing the effects of migraine aura, when kaleidoscopic visions appear to acute sufferers. "Landscape after landscape came past like Shakespeare's line of kings," she wrote in her journal. "Distant mountains—verdant vallies—winding rivers—graceful waterfalls—golden skies—Oh what a troop —I really feared for my senses." The medieval mystic Hildegard of Bingen was the first in a long line of artists and writers whose migraine visions have been considered a source of their extraordinary creativity. But Sophia was not to join their company. Instead, she collapsed. The next day her head was "whirling like a top"; she felt too sick to paint and scarcely able to "command my attention."

Sophia never mentioned "my first picture" again. By December, she was copying another painting, a densely wooded landscape by the Italian baroque artist Salvator Rosa that she considered too complex for Mary Newhall to imitate. She set Newhall to work on a scene depicting the eruption of Mount Vesuvius. In the "minimum of a house" in Salem, Sophia aimed to steady her nerves, grateful now for the "profound quiet" she found there and striving to achieve "peace & possession of soul."

• • •

Early in 1833, Sophia began to hear from both Mary and Elizabeth of their intensifying involvement with Horace Mann—"one of Nature's noblemen," in Elizabeth's earliest description, "intolerably witty," in Mary's. Learning that Mann had lived for the past several years in Dedham, Sophia consulted Sam and Lydia Haven about her sisters' new hero, only to hear dreadful gossip: according to Sam, Mann had romanced his younger sister, Catherine, then dropped her for Charlotte Messer, leaving Catherine heartbroken. Both Elizabeth and Mary angrily defended Horace Mann. "I assure you all your impressions are a wicked lie," Elizabeth wrote Sophia in late February, begging her to "entirely suspend your judgment" about Horace Mann until she had the opportunity to observe his "benevolence and excellence" firsthand. And when Sophia finally met the "benign & sweet & kind & *towering*" widower in June 1833, while Horace Mann was in Salem on state business, she dropped any reservations she once held about the bereaved statesman. Clearly Mann had the knack of winning over a woman on first acquaintance.

Even before he stopped in at the Peabody house in Salem, Horace Mann had inadvertently supplied a new motive to Sophia's work by introducing her older sisters to his friend Samuel Gridley Howe, director of the fledgling New England Asylum for the Education of the Blind. In January, Mann had taken Elizabeth and Mary for a tour of the six-month-old school, then located in Howe's family home on Pleasant Street in Boston. There, in Elizabeth's account, the trio had observed the "half-dozen first pupils" that Howe had "picked up in the highways and byways"—all of them charity cases supported by state funds that Mann had helped his friend procure. They also met Dr. Howe himself, a man widely considered "one of the most romantic characters" of his time. A graduate of Brown, like Mann, and of Harvard's medical school, Howe had never settled down to practice medicine. Instead, quixotically, he joined a group of international partisans who fought in the Greek Revolution in the 1820s, among them Lord Byron, whose helmet Howe brought home to Boston as a trophy, along with the title "Chevalier of the Greek Legion of Honor," bestowed on him by the revolutionary government. More recently, while traveling in Europe to study methods of educating the blind, Howe had survived a month in a Prussian prison after attempting to deliver aid to Polish refugees on Prussian soil.

Howe's was the first school for the blind in the United States, and he aimed to make his outshine another first: Thomas Gallaudet's celebrated American Asylum for the Deaf and Dumb, founded in Hartford in 1815. On their tour, Elizabeth and Mary saw the books Howe had "invented and laboriously executed," as Elizabeth described them, using gummed twine on cardboard to form raised letters, so that his students could learn to read by touch. Although he had no dramatic successes to report as yet, Howe knew that he

Samuel Gridley Howe

could win supporters by showing them a few blind children working together in a schoolroom to master the rudiments of spelling, mathematics, and even geography from specially crafted globes—unthinkable anywhere in the United States until now. The humble conditions of the school on Pleasant Street were intended to gain the active sympathy of visitors like Elizabeth and Mary Peabody, who were instantly impressed by the "economy and self-denial" Howe and his students practiced. By February 1833, two ambitious ladies' fairs were in the planning stages in Boston and Salem—also among the first of their kind in the nation—intended to raise funds for Howe's school through the sale of women's handicrafts.

Elizabeth had an ulterior motive in promoting the cause: she imagined that displaying one or two of Sophia's paintings at the Salem fair would bring "a great advantage" to Sophia, expanding her reputation as an artist while earning good money for the asylum. Unlike most of the women donating lace caps, bombazine bags, crocheted dolls, camphor trunks, or needlepoint ottomans, the Peabody sisters were just as needy of cash as Howe and his students. Elizabeth arranged for Sophia's materials to be paid for, thereby affording Sophia "the luxury of contributing all" the proceeds from the sale of her paintings to the fair.

Yet in significant ways, the impoverished sisters had much in common with wealthier female donors when it came to raising money for a worthy cause. By federal law, married women could not hold property or control their own money, and few single women had the means to support benefactions. The Salem and Boston Blind Fairs represented some of the earliest attempts on the part of American women to join the effort for reform independent of husbands and fathers. If women pooled their resources—the handicrafts that relative leisure allowed them to produce—and charged good money for them, an independent fund could be raised to help support a cause of their own choice. Eighteen months later, in December 1834, the abolitionists Lydia Maria Child and Maria Chapman held the nation's first antislavery "bazaar" in Boston, which would become an annual fundraising event. Craft fairs and bazaars proliferated in the coming decades as a variety of ladies' benevolent associations sprang up throughout the nation to feed, clothe, and house the poor; preserve historic landmarks; build monuments; and ultimately to support troops in the Civil War. Although the goods women manufactured for sale seemed to represent the height of conventional domesticity, the fairs themselves were a first step into the public sphere and gave women confidence that they could work together to change the society around them.

The energy expended on the two Blind Fairs was tremendous, as "Boston and Salem seemed to contend with each other in the race of benevolence," an elated Dr. Howe wrote. For Sophia, the incentive was a perfect one. She could join other women selling handmade goods—not for profit, but to promote good works. Elizabeth, who had arranged for the reissue of her own *Water-Spirit* in a special benefit edition, now worried that buyers she had already lined up for her sister's future paintings might purchase Sophia's donations to the fair instead, depriving the family of desperately needed income. But Sophia never seemed to care. She set aside the demanding Salvator Rosa and quickly completed two copies of landscapes by the Philadelphian Samuel

Scarlett to give to the fair. "I may as well suffer from painting as from a thousand other causes which agonize nerves" was now her "sober and rational philosophy." Gaining confidence, she began to speak again of a time "when I [may] come to originate pictures." Then, with the copies done, she turned to painting a dozen miniature scenes to be fitted onto a pair of ivory-handled fire screens and an eight-sided hand basket.

Sophia painted quickly in the last week before the fair opened in April 1833, and when it came time to finish off the hand basket, she had run out of scenes to copy. Working from her memory of engravings in travel books and from her imagination, Sophia improvised four original scenes—one of Walter Scott's Abbotsford castle, two of Rome, and one of Lake Como. "Four of them I created!!!!!!!" she wrote to Mary and Elizabeth in Boston, describing the "half original" octagonal basket. Miss Rawlins Pickman, who had come to visit Sophia in her studio, had "lavished every epithet upon it in the dictionary," Sophia gloated, and promised to pay Sophia $12 for a basket of her own, once the rush of the fair subsided.

When the Ladies' Fair opened in Salem's Hamilton Hall on April 10, Sophia was one of just two artists whose names were published in an auction catalogue that listed several hundred items. The eminent Salem lawyer and politician Leverett Saltonstall had already proclaimed Sophia's oil-painted copies "too beautiful for the fair." The sale continued for four days as auctioneers solicited bids for large items, and Salem's women took turns presiding over long tables crammed with velvet, lace, and silk goods, or serving drinks in a refreshment room where wine sold for a dollar a glass. Several women paced the exhibition rooms with silk handbags held open to receive spontaneous donations of cash. When it was all over, the "2 splendid Paintings in Oils, of Scenery near Bristol, in England, by Miss Sophia Peabody" had brought the highest price of any items: $60. The two fairs in Salem and at Boston's Faneuil Hall raised nearly $35,000, inspiring the China trade mogul Thomas Handasyd Perkins to match this generosity with the gift of an estate on Pearl Street in South Boston to house a larger, more ambitious school. The Perkins Institution for the Blind was born.

Back in the "nutshell" house on Church Street in Salem, however, Sophia was most proud of the four tiny original scenes she had painted on a hand basket that sold for just $10. The women who visited the Salem fair had found them captivating also. Soon Sophia had more orders for hand baskets than she could accept and she started in on one right away for her most influential new client, Salem's literary hostess Susan Burley. This time all the scenes were original, based on recollections of Como etchings and engravings from Rogers's *Italy*, or settings in Scott's Waverley novels. Sophia was so pleased with the Como she painted on the bottom of Miss Burley's basket that "for

Scene near Bristol, England, by Sophia Peabody

the first time I sat down & entirely admired a production of my own," she wrote to Elizabeth less than a week after the fair.

Sophia's miniatures were far less ambitious than "my first picture"—the landscape that had set her head whirling six months before in such a way that she could scarcely begin work on it. But as with many women of artistic talent, the smaller scope held powerful attractions: the safety of a sure sale, the admiration of other women, and the familiar pride of accomplishment in a handsome object handcrafted for domestic use. For Sophia there was the added satisfaction that her work seemed to outshine the medium itself. Through the coming months, Sophia found it "pleasant" to hear from the husbands and fathers of her female patrons that it seemed "barbarous" to have such fine work as hers wasted on ladies' hand baskets and fire screens when it really "ought to be framed." But she made no moves toward "creating" on a larger canvas.

Instead she returned to work on her copy of the Salvator Rosa forest scene, which Elizabeth hoped to show in the next year's Athenaeum exhibition and to market for a high sum. Visitors to Sophia's studio admired the copy, but in this case their praise only disturbed her. "Everybody who sees [the Salvator Rosa] thinks it is finished excepting myself," she wrote to Mary, "and the only comfort I have from this judgement of others is that they know nothing about it. I yearn for a good tearing, rending critic—For Mr. Graeter I sigh daily."

Would Sophia have made more progress as a landscape painter if she'd stayed in Boston, close to Graeter, Allston, and Doughty? Her Boston friend Sarah Clarke arranged for lessons with Allston around this time and went on to a modest career in the field. But in truth, New England remained something of a backwater in visual art, even as it was to become a wellspring of original literary work in the next decades. The Transcendental view of nature as a divine emanation encouraged painters to seek the ideal in a landscape; Sophia relied on the eye of her imagination to present scenes to her, usually composed of elements she admired in other paintings or lithographs. The pressure to produce the ideal mountain, lake, or forest was too much, and may have overwhelmed not just Sophia but her mentor Allston as well, whose productivity had dropped markedly since his return to Boston. Doughty was soon to leave the city for his native Philadelphia, a working environment he found more congenial. The Hudson River painters, who worked at a greater distance from the new ethos, were in the end better able to capture the natural world that New England's philosophers deified.

So while Sophia tinkered with her copy, she let Elizabeth talk her into a collaborative project that at first seemed easily within reach. Elizabeth had recently become enamored of the English artist John Flaxman's illustrations of Greek myths, done in spare, highly stylized ink drawings modeled after classical statuary. Washington Allston, whose studio Elizabeth had visited with increasing frequency since his approval of Sophia's copy the year before, valued his former London neighbor Flaxman's illustrated books above all others. Elizabeth couldn't help noticing that the few volumes that crossed the ocean sold for as high as $68 apiece. Having just completed her third volume of the *Key to History* texts she began in 1832, Elizabeth now proposed a more substantial work on "Ancient Story—historical and mythological" to be illustrated by Sophia with copies of Flaxman's drawings and sketches of other classical "gems" that Elizabeth would secure. Elizabeth had obtained an estimate on the presswork from Boston's premier lithographers, the Pendleton brothers, and figured that she could sell her book for one-third the price of the imported Flaxman volumes and still earn a handsome sum. Sophia tried a few sketches, found the work "enchanting," and agreed to the task.

But Sophia hadn't counted on transferring the sketches to the lithographic stone herself. Through the summer of 1833 she struggled with the new medium—one that, during the 1830s, would radically transform the appearance of printed books, newspapers, and magazines on both sides of the Atlantic by permitting the easy integration of illustrations and text. First the heavy stones had to be shipped from the Pendletons to Salem. Then Sophia had to paint with special lithographic brushes and ink on the polished stone with a steady hand and fix the completed image with powerful etching chemicals. Sometimes, as she labored over the outlines of Mercury or Apollo, "the idea of being an instrument in bringing these divine creations into the common light for all to see gives me a blessed feeling of serene pleasure," she wrote Elizabeth. But with increasing frequency she succumbed to "deepest despair," "violent headach—& utter lassitude," until eventually a "tide of disappointment swept over me" as she began to consider giving up the project. Sophia's distress may have been compounded by the swift emergence and nearly as swift withdrawal of the offer to accompany Elizabeth and the Clarke family to Italy, where she could have viewed at first hand the beloved marbles, the shores of Lake Como, and the temples and villas she had sketched and painted so many times from engravings. The Clarkes had postponed their trip, and Elizabeth's increasingly strained relations with the meddlesome Rebecca Clarke guaranteed that no later invitation would be issued.

Unfortunately, Elizabeth had already presented some of Sophia's Flaxman drawings to the Reverend Channing, asking for his help in selling subscriptions to support the book's publication. Impressed by Sophia's samples, Channing had endorsed the project as "a great and noble undertaking." He sent Elizabeth's prospectus on to the portraitist Henry Inman in Philadelphia, and offered to tap Washington Allston, Samuel F. B. Morse, and Thomas Sully—the first names in American art—for endorsements. Yet this good news was offset by Elizabeth's discovery that the size of the illustrations Sophia was producing would require larger sheets of a higher grade of paper, as well as the use of twice as many stones, nearly doubling her costs. She was beginning to understand the high price of the imported Flaxman volumes.

By August, Sophia's head had "taken to whirling." She felt "more feeble" and as if "I cannot bear nearly so much as I could last summer." Toward the end of the month, her vision became blurry whenever she tried to draw, and she stopped work altogether. Elizabeth finally quit pestering Sophia for more drawings and began to address seriously the fact that, as Mary phrased it, Sophia had reached "the lowest ebb of declension." Always tiny, and cautious about eating, the exhausted Sophia now weighed less than eighty pounds.

Sophia desperately needed the rest cure in a warm climate that Dr. Walter Channing had advocated for so long, Mary and Elizabeth agreed. The Italy plan had evaporated, but Elizabeth learned of an opening for a governess on a Cuban coffee plantation whose owner, a French doctor, occasionally accepted paying guests for extended stays. In September 1833, Elizabeth negotiated an exchange of Mary's services as governess for Sophia's convalescence on Dr. Morrell's plantation, La Recompensa, forty-five miles southwest of Havana in the fertile San Marcos Valley.

"You and I would be together at least," Mary wrote to Sophia in an effort to sell the plan, "so that it is better than if the three were sundered." Despite her miserable experience as governess to the Channing children just a year before, Mary bravely pretended that she could not "see any disadvantages" to the plan, and "it might do you a real lasting good, for which it is worth while to make a sacrifice." There were only "two dear little boys to teach" and a girl of fifteen in the Morrell family. Horace Mann's abrupt departure from Somerset Court the previous month helped Mary make up her mind to leave Boston; she was not feeling particularly warmly toward Elizabeth. Even the prospect of working as a governess again seemed better than staying in town with her older sister in a boarding house that had been transformed by Horace Mann's absence into an "abomination of desolation."

Once Sophia agreed to the plan in early October, over Dr. Peabody's anxious objections to the expense of outfitting for the journey and the risks of a sea voyage, the period of preparation seemed endless. There were clothes to be sewn—"nothing but *muslin* or *linen*"—and final visits to be paid to family and friends in Salem. Both sisters began studying Spanish. By November, their trunks were packed and they entered what Sophia termed "a dread vacuum of waiting"—for the proper ship, for a reputable escort, for a northeaster to blow out to sea.

Mary found herself in "a tossing condition of mind" as she alternately savored Horace Mann's "*delicious* sympathy" about her impending departure and contemplated the loss she would feel once she was gone. She may have hoped the journey would test Mann's interest. Would he miss her? If he did, would he write and tell her so? Her apparent withdrawal could set Mary in sharper contrast to her domineering older sister—and might even place her in spiritual company with Mann's absent beloved, Charlotte.

At the eleventh hour, Mary's suitor Benjamin Lindsay arrived from New Bedford, hoping to block her departure with a proposal of marriage. Mary made a polite refusal, but Lindsay was heartbroken and vowed he would not give up unless she could tell him for certain whether she was "engaged to any body privately." Was it a "predilection for another person which decided your mind?" he wanted to know. With the unerring intuition of a man in love, Lindsay had guessed the truth. But Mary could not tell him so. Instead she boarded the *Newcastle* bound for Havana in December 1833, still nurturing her secret passion for Horace Mann. "When the ocean rolled between me & the happy land that held him," she wrote years later in her fictional account, "I felt as if I was outside of creation."

Sophia turned her face toward Cuba, admitting no regrets about abandoning the career that had begun to take hold in Salem during the months of work for the Blind Fair. It was from La Recompensa the following spring that she learned that Elizabeth had enlisted Sarah Clarke to apply the finishing varnish to her copy of Salvator Rosa and, with the help of Catherine Scollay, entered the painting in the Athenaeum's 1834 exhibition. There it hung, titled simply "*Landscape* by Miss Peabody," among the Hardings, Doughtys, Stuarts, and Peales, the Veroneses, Guercinos, Poussins, and Claudes—with Sophia too far off to see it, or to capitalize on this astonishing coup. Just four years after she had first taken up a brush, Sophia Peabody had earned the one badge of artistic success Boston had to confer. She never answered Elizabeth's letter bearing the good news.

24

Cuba Journals

AFTER A LATE-DECEMBER SEA VOYAGE, AT TIMES SO ROUGH THAT MARY and Sophia were lashed to beef barrels and water casks to keep them from washing overboard, the sisters reached port at Havana, where they attempted to rest for several days with the Cleveland family, friends from Lancaster and Salem. Dorcas Cleveland's husband now served as the American vice-consul to Cuba, and the couple lived with their grown son Horace in a suite of rooms adjoining the custom house on Havana's waterfront. Sophia slept fitfully there, disturbed by the street cries of fruit sellers and their "squalling" children, the "hammering of coopers & tinkers[,] the screams of macaws & parrots," the "roaring and gibbering" of the Spaniards who occupied the apartment below, and "the bells! the bells!" that rang "from morning till night and from night till morning" through a city nearly half again the size of Boston.

Still as attentive to propriety as when she had clashed with Elizabeth a decade earlier in Lancaster, Mrs. Cleveland lectured the sisters on the "gross immorality and vice" prevalent in the Spanish colony. After a violent, decades-long independence movement had swept through its American territories, Spain retained only Puerto Rico and Cuba, nicknamed "the ever-faithful isle," as the last outposts of its three-hundred-year-old empire. Elite society, in Havana at least, had achieved a decadence hardly imaginable to New Englanders. Mrs. Cleveland warned Mary and Sophia never to leave the house unescorted, for "any woman who walked out alone, even for her health, was presumed headed for a romantic assignation." Mary teased Elizabeth by letter that she would surely "lose [her] reputation in a week" in Cuba.

By comparison, the two days spent traveling forty-five miles by horse-drawn *volante* over deeply rutted roads to the Morrells' coffee plantation near Artemisa, stopping at roadside taverns for drinks of orange water, were pleasantly tolerable. The sisters had found a willing escort in James Burroughs, a handsome forty-year-old Bostonian and fellow passenger on the *Newcastle* with business in Cuba, the younger brother of Sophia's benefactor Maria Rice. Burroughs rode on horseback in advance of the carriage through forests of "lofty and luxuriant" trees draped with flowering vines and "full of birds"— not the noisy ones of Havana's waterfront, by Mary's account. The sisters had entered the "vast garden of the island" southwest of Havana, where most of Cuba's coffee, sugar, and tobacco were grown, according to one recent American traveler, an invalid minister who had himself spent several months under Dr. Morrell's care and afterward published his travel letters.

As the sisters approached La Recompensa, dense forest gave way to coffee and orange groves, until at last the riders turned into a drive lined with mango trees leading to the *hacienda* that would be the sisters' home for almost two years. Sophia slept soundly through the first night in the room she shared with Mary, savoring the fragrance of a rosebush in full bloom outside their window. Soon afterward she met the six-foot-tall Dr. Robert Morrell, a man "with soft dark eyes, and great gentleness" who "has taken my case in hand and determines to cure me," Sophia wrote in her first letter home from La Recompensa.

Life as a recuperating invalid on a Cuban coffee plantation, Sophia was happy to learn, could be spent almost entirely outdoors. All the common rooms in the sprawling one-story house opened onto long galleries leading to wide manicured lawns; windows stretched from floor to ceiling and could be closed against the midday heat or the night air with heavy wooden shutters, but they held no glass. The size of the estate—six miles in diameter—dwarfed anything Sophia had known in New England. One of Dr. Morrell's first prescriptions, a daily morning ride on horseback intended to raise "genial perspirations," could send her meandering down La Recompensa's avenues of "hard, red earth" lined with dense lime tree hedges for over an hour without ever reaching the public road.

Beyond the acres under cultivation lay the *portrero*, where sheep and cattle grazed: vast "plains," to Sophia's eye, which stretched past a bamboo-fringed *laguna* all the way to the shimmering, palm-covered San Salvador Mountains. The scene seemed ideal for a landscape, and as the days passed Sophia memorized the colors and recorded them in a notebook in preparation for the day when she might feel well enough to paint. Back in her room alone, while Mary began her classes, Sophia peeled and ate an orange plucked on her ride, feeling as if she were Eve in a world "just made" that morning at sunrise.

The sisters had arrived at La Recompensa when Cuban plantation society was at its peak. Dr. Morrell's lease from the Spanish government on three plantations—coffee, tobacco, and sugar—dated from the 1790s, when land-

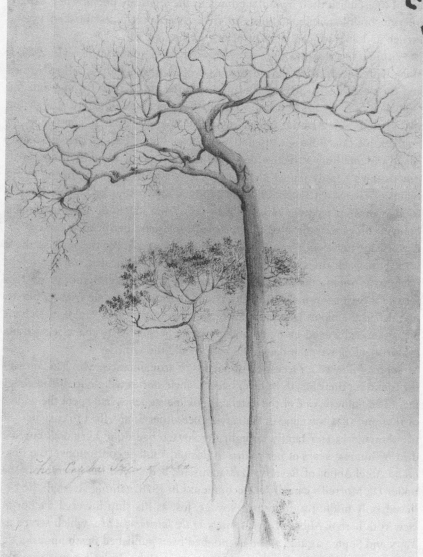

The Ceyba Tree of Cuba, drawing by Sophia Peabody

holders on the neighboring French colony of Haiti, then the undisputed
leader of sugar and coffee production in the Caribbean, had fled Toussaint
L'Ouverture's slave rebellion. The French cultivation of lands west of Havana
had sparked a rise in Cuba's fortunes; by 1830, Cuba's coffee and sugar production was second only to Jamaica's, and American investors flocked to the

island to establish their own plantations in the relatively uncultivated eastern interior, building manor houses to rival those already established by the French and Spanish colonial aristocracy in the west.

Within a few decades, the relative privations of country life on an island, along with the threat of slave uprisings, would send most plantation owners and their families to live in Havana's suburbs, or back to Europe and the United States, where they could spend their fortunes in safety. But in the 1830s, there was a casual intermingling of Spanish, French, and American families for fancy-dress balls and week-long house parties that made the island's plantations attractive destinations for wealthy invalids from North America, who easily joined a circle of guests already in place. In the grand rooms of estates with names like La Gloriata, La Content, or La Providencia, young women played the harp and sang arias from Italian operas after dinner. Long evenings were devoted to sewing costumes and performing *tableaux vivants*, featuring scenes from history or popular novels. For the restless, there were horseback rides after dark when a classically educated traveler might imagine, as Sophia Peabody did, that the long rows of eighty-foot palm trees formed a "vast colonnade" with their "symmetrical trunks almost as white as marble" in the moonlight. Here even the most industrious Yankee merchant or banker, exhausted by overwork, could be persuaded to make leisure his business; ailing wives or daughters happily did the same.

Sophia followed a succession of friends or acquaintances who had come to the island for their health in recent years. Their stories were not all encouraging: Eliza Sullivan, one of the sisters' Brookline students, had spent the winter of 1831 and 1832 traveling in Cuba with her father in an effort to cure herself of tuberculosis. Her family thought the voyage had done her good, but she died within two years of her return to Boston. Another consumptive, the Reverend Abiel Abbot of Beverly, Massachusetts, had stayed for several months under Dr. Morrell's care at La Recompensa in 1828, gaining strength, he believed, only to die on the return voyage, just as his ship lowered anchor at New York harbor. Abbot's *Letters Written in the Interior of Cuba*, which served as Mary and Sophia's guide to the island, had been published posthumously.

Yet no one blamed the attempt at a cure in Cuba. Indeed it was thought that the stay might well have extended the lives of these sufferers and was their only chance for a complete recovery. As Dr. Walter Channing presented it to Sophia's anxious family, "What are two or three years of exile ... to a life of suffering?" The key was to give the experiment long enough to work. "My old tired feeling hangs on," Sophia wrote home early in 1834, and her headaches lingered. But Dr. Morrell assured her that "after I have been here & my blood grows thinner," the cure would begin.

Mary, who arrived at La Recompensa resigned to a year or more of that "worst of all slaveries," the work of a governess, was as horrified by the life she found on the hacienda as Sophia was enchanted. Mary had been right about the two young Morrell boys, Eduardo and Carlito: they were no trouble to teach. But Mary's democratic spirit, along with her near-servant status, made her far more sensitive than Sophia to what she quickly called "the incubus of slavery": the real slavery of the African men and women who worked the plantation, savagely oppressed by the last minions of a crumbling Spanish empire. While Sophia liked to be waited on by the Morrells' house slaves—Zepherino, who waved a bamboo fan at table to keep flies off the guests; Urbano, who helped her mount the gentle nag she rode each morning; and Thekla, the "enthusiastic, devoted . . . genius domi" who "will not let me breathe for myself when she is near"—Mary was shocked to learn that the broad lawns surrounding the manor house were designed to allow surveillance of these same loyal servants' thatch-roofed cabins by a pair of armed guards.

Mary could never "get used to" the sight of those cabins, as Elizabeth, concerned chiefly with Sophia's recovery, counseled her from a safe distance in Boston. Elizabeth was no proponent of slavery, and at least some in Boston were already playing leadership roles in the American antislavery movement: in 1831, William Lloyd Garrison had started publication of *The Liberator* from an African-American neighborhood just blocks from the Somerset Court boarding house where the sisters had lived. But, at thirty, Elizabeth's preoccupations were the same causes she had always found compelling: progressive education, spiritual and philosophical inquiry, and the recognition and promotion of genius. The Boston she cared about in the mid-1830s was populated with a loosely affiliated band of like-minded men and women as devoted to soul-searching as they were to reform. With Mary's departure, Elizabeth's circle expanded to include not just Horace Mann, Washington Allston, and the Reverend William Ellery Channing, but a "transcendental company" of newcomers like Margaret Fuller, Bronson Alcott, and Waldo Emerson's erudite fiancée, Lydia Jackson.

It was Mary who encountered an island with a population of more than 700,000—larger than the entire state of Massachusetts—on which slaves and free blacks vastly outnumbered whites. Laws against the slave trade were flagrantly disregarded in Cuba's port cities, with the result that captured Africans arrived at a rate of 15,000 a year in the early 1830s to be sold into slavery on the island's ever expanding sugar and coffee plantations. Cuba's population of more than 100,000 free blacks, slaves who had purchased their freedom by raising crops on the small plots of land guaranteed them under Cuba's relatively liberal slave laws, combined with outlaw bands of escaped slaves, surviving easily in Cuba's mountain regions, to produce an unusually volatile situation. Starting as early as 1812, Cuba experienced periodic slave uprisings,

A Cuban coffee plantation, circa 1834

checked only by brutal public torture and executions. But Mary knew it didn't have to be that way. A slave revolt on the British colony of Jamaica during 1831 and 1832 had been unsuccessful. Yet news of the bloody rebellion energized an English antislavery movement that swiftly brought passage of the British Emancipation Act of 1833, abolishing slavery throughout the British Empire.

At La Recompensa, whenever Mary could excuse herself from her multitude of duties—teaching, nursing Sophia, or the obligation to socialize with her host family—she worked alongside the house slaves assigned to the flower gardens. She asked for a tour of Dr. Morrell's sugar plantation, where she saw black men and women put to work "like brutes" under the direction of a whip-brandishing Spanish *mayoral*. From dawn to dusk, through the heat of the tropical day, the slaves worked cutting cane or feeding the fires of the sugar refinery with dried husks that burned so rapidly there was no chance for rest. Mary understood now why so few Cuban planters built their homes on sugar plantations. But even the *cafetal* slaves, who were allowed the comparative luxury of sitting as they sorted coffee beans, did their work under close supervision by men who believed, as the Morrells themselves did, that "nothing but fear" would keep the slaves in order. When the doctor's wife, Laurette Morrell, confided in Mary that the only slave she could trust was a "perfectly servile" one, Mary nodded in agreement, but privately reached a different conclusion. Laurette Morrell's opinion only proved its opposite: "A slave should be perfectly servile," Mary wrote Elizabeth after the conversation, "therefore there should be no slavery."

In the early days of her stay on the island, Mary learned that Dr. Morrell's *volante* had overturned on the severely rutted road from Havana to La Recompensa, sending the doctor to bed with bruised ribs. As punishment, the black coachman had been "whipped in a savage manner for his carelessness," then "put in irons for a month in a dark prison house." All this had been "done in passion" by the vicious *mayoral*, Mary wrote to Elizabeth in disgust, and "out of sight" so as not to disturb Dr. Morrell's family and their American guests. Risking her own good standing in the household, Mary took the opportunity to propose to the doctor's wife that a master should witness all punishments meted out to his slaves. Like many New Englanders opposed to slavery in the 1830s, Mary naïvely imagined that the sight of such brutality would influence slave owners to reject the institution of slavery itself. But instead, Mme. Morrell chided Mary for expressing such foolish hopes, explaining that her husband, who had been made "perfectly sick" the one time he witnessed the lashing of a favored servant, still believed he had "as much right to his slaves" as Mary did to "her gown."

In the end, to keep her job, Mary confined her efforts at reform to the Morrell boys; she made sure to include instruction on democratic principles and the fundamental liberty of all human souls with their lessons in grammar and mathematics, in the hope that they might grow up to renounce slave ownership. On Sundays, the day off she shared with the more fortunate *cafetal* slaves, Mary listened in distress to their beating drums and watched their wild dances with anxiety, not because, like the Morrells, she considered them dangerous heathens. Rather, she privately suspected that "there is as much religion in Africa as in this country, only of a different kind." She could not help but note the cruel irony that on the "ever-faithful isle," ruled by a distant Spanish monarch, two African kings were enslaved. Mary and Sophia had been taken to see them as curiosities on a neighboring plantation: one of these men, a towering "majestic figure," was set to work pacing on a waterwheel; the other, a much older man, sat impassively in the doorway to his cabin, a bamboo pole in one hand in place of a scepter. To assuage her guilt at finding no better means of protest, and as an outlet when even Elizabeth no longer welcomed her indignant accounts of slave life, Mary began making notes for a novel she planned to write one day, exposing the evils of slavery in "this land of bondage."

As on her first "voluntary rustication" at Dedham four years earlier, Sophia devoted a part of each day to writing in her journal, which she kept, following the Reverend Abiel Abbot's example, in the form of letters home. Once the letters started to arrive in Salem, Mrs. Peabody urged Sophia by return mail to "pour everything—the whole mingled tide of feelings" into them. Sophia did her best to oblige by giving a full account of her "*innere,*" the term all three Peabody sisters, now ardent Germanophiles, had begun to use as a shorthand when they wanted to speak of their interior lives. For Sophia keeping a journal meant a great deal more than chronicling the headaches and fatigue that continued to limit her activities for much of the stay, even as she eventually boasted of gaining color in her cheeks and reaching ninety-eight pounds. Sophia never did find the strength to paint her Cuban landscape, although she became adept at sketching likenesses of the Morrell family and their friends, which she freely gave away.

Instead, steeped in the writings of the English and German Romantics, and attuned to the landscape as an artist, Sophia worked to perfect the style of nature writing she had begun to develop in Dedham. If her "Cuba Journal," as the family came to call it, had been published at the time of its writing, Sophia would have been counted among the earliest practitioners of literary Transcendentalism. "How beautifully nature educates the soul," Sophia wrote after one early-morning ride, in a formulation anticipating both Emerson and Thoreau. Like the later Thoreau, Sophia described flowering plants, trees, and wildlife in precise detail, often sketching them in the margins of her journal; but she was even more alert to what Emerson would call the "Spiritual Laws" made manifest in the natural world. Nature was teaching her that "intuition is the unerring truth"; a moonlit walk could bring a clear "revelation of Unity."

In Boston, Elizabeth and her friends were groping toward these same principles: that true religion derived from a personal intuition of the divine, and divinity itself was the unifying force of nature. These tenets would be among the few that Transcendentalists agreed upon. But in Cuba, where she woke some mornings feeling "consecrated by the breath of flowers," Sophia had already absorbed what Emerson would one day term the essential "optimism of nature." She was awed by the "determination upward to the sun and air all vegetable nature has in this tropical world." And as she contemplated her return to New England after more than a year of easy access to wild nature, Sophia expected that she would now "see more in a blade of grass" than she ever had before. Elizabeth's project, begun when she took over Sophia's religious education in childhood, to ensure that her little sister "never should hear of any of the terrible doctrines" of Calvinism and would learn instead "the simple creed that everything that can happen to a human being is either for enjoyment in the present or instruction for the future" was bearing fruit. Even before there was a name for it, Sophia had become an instinctive Transcendentalist.

Perhaps Sophia's initial motivation in keeping a journal was to entertain her mother, who complained of the lack of variety in her life in Salem, where "to day is as yesterday the week through." Mrs. Peabody was busy as always:

Night-blooming Cereus, page from Sophia Peabody's Cuba Journal

tutoring Mary Newhall in Sophia's place, writing her own stories of Pilgrim life, teaching herself Spanish, and studying botanical specimens with a newly acquired microscope. She visited her sister Mary Tyler in Brattleboro, Vermont, reestablishing a tie of kinship after the death of her brother-in-law Royall Tyler, that villain of her childhood whose "horrors of . . . mind" during his last "lingering disease were the dreadful fruits of sin," Mrs. Peabody believed. Still, she missed Mary and Sophia profoundly. Nothing delighted her more than reading Sophia's journal letters, which she eventually bound into three volumes numbering 785 pages.

To her mother, Sophia modestly described her Cuba Journal as "only a record of my uprisings and down sittings." Yet from the start she understood that back home her mother and sister were reading portions of the letters to interested neighbors and passing them among friends—not just the Pickmans, but the prominent Saltonstalls in Salem, and even the Reverend Channing's family in Boston. During the summer of 1834, Elizabeth began holding evening reading parties for a circle of women in Boston who, she wrote Sophia, were "ravished" by her descriptions of the Cuban landscape, and "all are in love" with the young men of the de Layas family, friends of the Morrells who appeared to be courting Dr. Morrell's teenaged daughter, Luisa.

Sophia pretended anger at Elizabeth for making her letters public in this way. She felt, she wrote with indignation, "as if the nation were feeling my pulse." Yet she never asked Elizabeth to stop, and she continued writing as expansively as before. Sophia took pride in her mastery of the "black art" of letter writing, and when Elizabeth defended her reading parties by telling her youngest sister that she could not possibly estimate the pleasure her journal gave to "Northers," Sophia must have been pleased. "I doubt ever such a picture of the tropics was put on paper," Elizabeth continued, and pleaded that "it would be wicked of us to hoard it." Sophia was well aware of a tradition of circulating highly prized women's journals and letters among female friends and relatives over many decades. Through her mother, Sophia knew of a shipboard journal kept by Abigail Adams in 1784 and passed among generations of Adams, Cranch, and Smith women; the Peabodys themselves treasured the deathbed correspondence of Eunice Paine, one of the cherished sisterhood of Friendship Hall, whose graceful acceptance of her fate profoundly affected all who read the letters.

Sophia may have taken as a model the recent *Diary of an Ennuyée,* published anonymously by the British writer Anna Jameson, which appeared in its first American edition in 1833, the year before Mary and Sophia traveled to Cuba. This fictional diary of a young woman seeking consolation in Italy's museums and churches after rejection by her lover had broken her health was embraced by Boston's literati with the same enthusiasm as had greeted Madame de Staël's *Corinne* a few years earlier. But *Diary of an Ennuyée,* like the Reverend Abbot's *Letters Written in the Interior of Cuba,* was purported to have been published posthumously: only after death was it proper to expose this "real picture of natural and feminine feeling" to the reading public, Jameson wrote in her preface.

Although Elizabeth urged Sophia to revise her journal letters for publication in the *American Monthly*, Sophia wished for that no more than she wished for her own death. Sophia preferred to be seen as an ailing traveler writing for a private audience, rather than as a traveling journalist writing for profit, like several British women writers just becoming known in the United States. Frances Trollope had published her *Domestic Manners of the Americans* in 1832; and Harriet Martineau was in Boston gathering material, with Elizabeth's aid, for her own *Society in America* at the same time that Sophia was writing her journal in Cuba. But Trollope was a married woman in her fifties writing to pay off family debts, and her "gossipy pages" had been received angrily in America; Martineau was a single woman in her thirties who had famously refused marriage to become a journalist. At twenty-five, Sophia found neither example appealing. Perhaps, too, she did not see—or *want* to see—in her own writing the sparks of literary talent that Elizabeth knew were there. Sophia was already burdened enough by Elizabeth's efforts to extract works of genius from her brush.

Significantly, there was one episode Sophia never wrote about in her Cuba Journal. Instead the news reached Elizabeth in Boston by way of the meddling Mrs. Cleveland and was later confirmed by Mary in reports to Elizabeth. This was the story of Sophia's dalliance with the sisters' escort James Burroughs. Sophia had written about Burroughs in a letter from the *Newcastle* on the voyage south in December 1833. After the fierce Atlantic storms had subsided, Burroughs appeared as a constant and "devotedly attentive" presence at Sophia's side: spotting porpoises and flying fish, praising the captain's navigational skills, helping Sophia find a comfortable perch atop a water cask to observe the moonlight, and manfully taking a "complete drenching" to save Sophia's clothes when a wave crashed over the deck. But once on shore, Sophia never mentioned him again in her letters home. It was Mary who reported that Burroughs had been the sisters' guide on a sightseeing tour of Havana and their escort through the forests to La Recompensa, before the gallant Bostonian traveled east on the island to pursue his own business prospects.

Yet soon afterward, Sophia began to receive letters from Burroughs at La Recompensa, attracting the notice of Mme. Morrell. To Mary's chagrin, Sophia refused to show her either Burroughs's letters or her own replies, citing Elizabeth's private correspondence with Horace Mann as a precedent. Sophia could not be persuaded that writing to a bachelor was any different from corresponding with a grieving widower, and Mary was forced to initiate a correspondence of her own with Burroughs to cover for Sophia. She became alarmed when Burroughs's affection for Sophia surfaced in a letter in which he puzzlingly remarked that the word "marry" was not in his vocabulary. Was he angling for some form of shameful Cuban alliance? Mary began to fear, as she later wrote Elizabeth, that Burroughs expected her to "befriend" a "match."

When James Burroughs arrived at La Recompensa in the spring of 1834 to deliver the sisters' mail from Boston, and Sophia rose to greet him with a kiss, Mme. Morrell's suspicions of "*la belle passion*" were inflamed. They were all but confirmed when Sophia cheerfully offered to mend Burroughs's trousers and, to Mme. Morrell's horror, allowed him to rest his foot in her lap as she worked. A scene that might have passed without notice in the slapdash Peabody household was shocking at La Recompensa. Mary, as Sophia's chaperone, was called on the carpet for an explanation. She could give none.

Back in their room, Mary quizzed Sophia, who belatedly confessed that Burroughs had proposed marriage to her onboard ship and that she had refused him. Sophia explained that although she had no wish to marry James Burroughs, she had wanted to protect his feelings by keeping his proposal—and her refusal—a secret. Maintaining a "sisterly" fondness for Burroughs, she had tried to soothe his wounded feelings by way of a correspondence. Sophia despised any rules of etiquette that would not support such kindness on her part, she told Mary.

Yet subsequent events caused even Sophia to change her mind. Dorcas Cleveland sent word sub rosa to Mary from Havana that Burroughs had been bragging of a connection to a young lady at La Recompensa and reading affectionate passages from her letters aloud in his boarding house. Mrs. Cleveland instantly knew the woman in question must be Sophia and feared others would soon guess as much. Now that the sisters were out of earshot, Burroughs felt free to declare that everything about the voyage to Cuba—the food, the captain, the accommodations, the company—had been "execrable." All except "two traveling Ps."

When Mrs. Cleveland returned to Massachusetts for several months that summer, she told the full story to Elizabeth. To cap off her tale, Mrs. Cleveland reported that while Mme. Morrell "admired" Mary "to the last degree," her "impressions" of Sophia were quite different. If it hadn't been for Mrs. Cleveland's arguments to the contrary, Laurette Morrell would have been "*completely* ... convinced" that Sophia was carrying on an affair with James Burroughs.

Elizabeth immediately fired off an "infinity" of letters to both Mary and Sophia about how to handle the "rascally dolt." She had been informed—too late—by James Burroughs's sister Maria Rice that his own family thought him "ignorant, sensual, selfish," and a "brute in his habits." Far from considering him a proper escort, the Burroughs family had hoped the dissolute James might be reformed by the trip south with Mary and Sophia Peabody. Maria Rice now declared her brother "a perfect Cain" and admitted that she was not surprised to learn he had "beguiled" a young woman in "the transient era of passion."

Elizabeth preferred to accept Sophia's explanation that it was James who was beguiled, not Sophia. But Sophia had been wrong to answer Burroughs's letters once she had turned him down. Elizabeth's instructions to Sophia were explicit, and no doubt informed by her own painful experience with Lyman Buckminster. It was "most delicate—& most considerate of the gentleman's feelings," Elizabeth wrote, "to drop acquaintance after a refusal. . . . There should never be free and any thing like affectionate communication." She advised Sophia to return Burroughs's letters and ask him to do the same with hers; then she must burn them all. Mary should write also and in the plainest terms forbid James Burroughs to visit La Recompensa again. Elizabeth hoped that, properly maneuvered, Mme. Morrell would "admit" Sophia's "goodness & innocence." But Sophia "must not draw on that bank in future."

The several weeks it sometimes took for mail from Boston to reach Cuba did not help matters. Sophia returned Burroughs's letters, but her own never arrived; then she learned that he had sailed for Boston still in possession of them. Mary had to send her letter of dismissal to Elizabeth in Boston to pass on to Burroughs. And before Elizabeth received it, she had already met with the man and decided on a different course.

Maria Rice had warned that her brother might take retribution if he felt wronged. When Burroughs told Elizabeth that he planned to return to Cuba immediately and go into business as a fruit exporter, she feared that he meant to do Sophia's reputation further damage. "There is a kind of love which turns to *hate*," Elizabeth wrote to Mary. On the spot, she improvised a story of some unspecified "embarrassment" that prevented Burroughs from seeing Mary and Sophia at La Recompensa in the future, and, mollified for the moment, Burroughs handed over his packet of letters. In the end, however, it took virtually the entire stay to resolve the case, and even then Burroughs held back two of Sophia's letters. Sophia's relations with Mme. Morrell were never entirely repaired. In a letter to her friend Maria Chase, not included in her Cuba Journal, Sophia wrote obliquely that she had been "sadly bruised and commoted" by what she'd learned of human nature during her stay in Cuba; to another friend, Mary Wilder White, she confessed to a sudden longing for New England, with its "aristocracy of cultivation talent & virtue."

The episode may have provided the best resolution for Elizabeth. It was no small thrill for Elizabeth to realize, on reading the letters Burroughs left with her to destroy, that the man was "really *in love*" with Sophia and had been "making love" to her in every one of them—only to be turned down by her willful little sister. Further, Burroughs's letters persuaded her all the more that Sophia had been right to refuse him. Elizabeth saw no "indications of any thing interesting" there, aside from the passion he expressed for her sister. "Some things are to be excused in a man who was in love," Elizabeth concluded, once she sensed that disaster had been averted, "and many things in one who is so intellectually weak."

Elizabeth was obviously pleased to be able to say now, as she wrote to Mary, "all three of us have been compelled to reject" offers of marriage: no Peabody woman would ever marry simply to gain the status a wedding band conferred. Here the sisters' relative poverty worked to their advantage, relieving them of the pressure, felt by women whose dowries were bargaining chips in a highly competitive marriage market, to "make a match." Yet the list of disappointed suitors—Lyman Buckminster, Mary's Benjamin Lindsay, and now James Burroughs—seemed confirmation that all three Peabody sisters had achieved an important measure of adult femininity. Although the sisters were separated by over a thousand miles of ocean, Elizabeth could view their chosen singleness as a commitment that might bind them together for life. It had been Elizabeth's plan from the start that, after Sophia's cure was complete, "we may *all three* commence business together." Now Elizabeth felt confident that "the future is our own," as she wrote to Mary in September 1834. She preferred to overlook signs that Mary was simply waiting patiently for Horace Mann to leave off his widower's weeds, or that Sophia, as eager for unfettered male companionship as Elizabeth, was ready to fall in love as well. As the Burroughs affair proved, the youngest Peabody sister had learned to use her illness as Elizabeth did her intellect, to cultivate intimacies that were otherwise forbidden to single women.

Elizabeth had not nearly so high an opinion of the journal letters she wrote to Mary from Boston as she did of Sophia's from Cuba. But her output more than equaled Sophia's, and, as her pages mounted up in the sisters' room at La Recompensa, Mary and Sophia began to refer to Elizabeth's record of daily life in Boston as her "Cuba Journal" as well. Elizabeth's Boston was exotic in its own way; some of the news she delivered was so shocking that Mary took to reading only snippets of the letters to Sophia for fear of alarming her.

Elizabeth was privy to all kinds of confidences: engagements broken off or reconsidered, the secret pregnancy of a student's older sister who became "a *mother* before she was a wife." During the eighteen months that Mary and Sophia lived in Cuba, two men involved in a love triangle had dueled; a minister's young wife slit her throat; two friends' babies died, one after being sent out to a wet nurse; and another friend's husband—the painter Gilbert Stuart Newton, Gilbert Stuart's nephew—became insane while traveling in Europe and was institutionalized in London. The tragedies that struck closest to home were the deaths of Dr. Walter Channing's second wife, Eliza, in childbirth, and her infant. Channing himself had presided. "He took away a beautiful boy," Elizabeth wrote. This information could not be kept from Sophia, who fell into one of her speechless trances and found herself unable to write to Walter Channing throughout her stay in Cuba.

The news that Elizabeth sent of the Peabody boys was disturbing as well. With the failure of his pharmacy in Boston, Nat, now twenty-two, returned home to Salem unrepentant. There he pleaded with Dr. Peabody to permit him to marry his fiancée, Elizabeth Hibbard, and move her in with the family. Elizabeth wrote that Sophia was lucky to be in Cuba, far from the turbulent scenes when "Father rips out" at Nat for his "lack of order, preciseness and tact" in conducting business. Nat took the abuse in silence, then offered to leave New England to try farming in the west, out of range of his creditors. Elizabeth cheered this decision and began to borrow books on agriculture for Nat to study. But Dr. Peabody, full of his own "wild schemes," refused to hear of it.

Instead, Dr. Peabody set up Nat as the agent for another druggist on Salem's fashionable Essex Street. Under this plan, little capital would be risked. But Aunt Sophia Pickman, having risen, improbably, to the top of Salem society through her marriage to Dr. Thomas Pickman, warned that "public sentiment in Salem is so strongly against" the Peabody boys that Nat would fail in any occupation that "depended on public patronage." She was right. The best Nat managed to do was "rub along," in Dr. Peabody's words, taking in a dollar a day. His $1,100 debt to Boston creditors only swelled by the amount he now owed in Salem for advertising and outfitting the new shop. Even Mrs. Peabody, who liked to point out that Nat was "honest, industrious," and "fond of good books," had to agree that her oldest son could "never be made a man of the world." Elizabeth was more severe, pronouncing Nat "destitute of all kinds of get-a-long-ity."

Elizabeth reported that eighteen-year-old Wellington, too, seemed to have a "mania for spending other people's money," but he went about it in an entirely different style. Despite the ragged shoes he'd worn home from Rio after deserting the *Hector* and sacrificing his share of the ship's hefty profits in whale oil, Wellington still managed to cut a "dandyish" figure. When he turned up in Boston, Wellington complained to Elizabeth that he'd been whipped when he was too sick with scurvy to get out of his bunk and was revolted by the "lowlived, blackguard conversation of the men" with whom he was "compelled to associate." He'd jumped ship and charmed his way back to Boston, via New York, borrowing his passage from strangers or distant relatives, along with the lesser sums he required to keep himself in "cegars" and to escort women to the theater.

Wellington's debts were smaller than Nat's, but only, Elizabeth suspected, because he had not yet entered into any serious business. The memory of his semester at Harvard, when he'd distinguished himself in "dissipation, drinking," and "extravagance when his family was poor," was still fresh in her mind.

Debt, she worried in one of her journal letters, had become "the evil genius of our family." She had to wonder whether Welly's tales of his seafaring life were not just so much "palaver." When he told Elizabeth that he planned to write a book about his voyage and had applied to the Duke of Wellington for employment, she was aghast at his "extravagant *sottise*"—and told him so.

Nonetheless, Elizabeth loaned Wellington money to cover the fare from New York and to buy new shoes, counting herself lucky that she had no more than $10 on hand when he stopped to see her on his way home to Salem. Wellington promised to pay her back as soon as their cousin George Palmer Putnam made good on his offer to appoint him head clerk in a New York publishing venture. It was several months before Elizabeth learned that this story, too, was a lie. By then, Wellington had gone into business with Nat, moving the Essex Street drugstore to South Salem and adding groceries to the shop. The two brothers had joined forces to their "mutual benifet," their mother hoped, even as her Pickman relations derided the new plan as simply a case of the boys "supplying each others' deficiencies."

With Nat and Wellington now both living at home, Mrs. Peabody struggled to understand "what can have made my boys so different from my girls," who seemed to her so wonderfully "linked in heart, in opinions and in talents," she wrote to Mary and Sophia in Cuba. She was inclined to blame the public schools, where her boys had been "bored . . . under leaden headed teachers—mothers being thought unfit to manage their 'masculine progeny.'" She brooded, too, over the cool treatment her sons received from her own sister, Sophia Palmer Pickman, who seemed all too ready to see them fail when she might have helped sway public opinion in their favor. With two of her daughters out of the country, Mrs. Peabody had grown painfully aware of her own lack of "those sweet sympathies" she had seen her girls supply to one another out of "sisterly interest."

Knowing nothing of the Burroughs escapade, Mrs. Peabody took pride that "my three beloved girls have so much moral power," as she wrote to Mary and Sophia early in their stay, warning them against the "villains in the world, who seek the young and lovely and virtuous, as the roaring lion does his lawful prey." Yet even had she known of Sophia's indiscretions, or of the shifting alliances within "the sisterhood," Mrs. Peabody was right to identify their mutual concern as a mainstay for all three. Each of her daughters had grown into an accomplished woman and, like stars in a constellation, their combined talents worked to magnify their individual attractions.

Only her middle son, George, seemed to have acquired some measure of the "moral power" Mrs. Peabody credited to her daughters—and that was getting him into trouble. Elizabeth wrote to Mary that twenty-one-year-old George was working now as a clerk in a Boston import firm, earning $9 a week and putting aside enough to cover the debts he'd accumulated on his ill-advised trip to Smyrna the year before. But George had taken sides in a boarding house dispute that for a time threatened to drag down both him and Elizabeth. Mary Ann Dwight, a twenty-eight-year-old drawing teacher and free spirit who lived in George's boarding house, had been accused of "having an improper intercourse" with a fellow boarder—a married man whose wife charged Dwight with allowing her husband "all sorts of privileges in her room." When Mary Ann responded to the accusations with her own charges of slander, George came to her defense.

Elizabeth and George knew Mary Ann Dwight as an artist and one-time boarder in Mrs. Clarke's "hodge-podge" household, where she had followed the same casual rules that allowed Elizabeth to embrace the weeping Horace Mann in a common parlor late at night. They both believed the gregarious Mary Ann was simply carrying dinner table conversations over into her private room, a practice that would have gone unnoticed at Mrs. Clarke's. The rest of the boarders sided with Mary Ann's accusers, however, and demanded that both Mary Ann and George be turned out. Word of the scandal spread so rapidly that no landlord in Boston would rent to Mary Ann.

Elizabeth decided to step in and help salvage her young friend's reputation. The result was an improvised court convened in Elizabeth's rooms, at which all parties presented their claims in front of an impartial arbiter. Elizabeth supplied a letter from the novelist Catharine Maria Sedgwick, a distant relation of Dwight's, attesting to Mary Ann's good character and endorsing the freedom allowed to single women in New England which "occasionally exposes a young lady to calumny," yet is still "the expression and best safeguard of purity of manners." In the end, Mary Ann's honor was restored, and both George and Mary Ann were allowed to keep their rooms—but not before George had received a challenge to a duel, which he wisely ignored. The whole "blow up," he wrote afterward to Mary, had turned him "misanthropic," showing how much "treachery, falsehood, deceit, coldness, selfishness, revenge & hatred" there was in the world. He assured Mary, however, that "women I still hold in adoration." In a family like the Peabodys, George could hardly have said otherwise.

Yet Elizabeth's journal letters also painted a picture of the New England economy suggesting that it was not only their place in the matriarchal Peabody family that made life difficult for her brothers. The boys—and Elizabeth herself—had been unlucky in the decade in which they reached adulthood. As their father readily pointed out, it was not just in his Salem dental practice that business had become "quite slack." In 1834, what Dr. Peabody called "this Jackson crazy experiment on the currency" had begun to "affect every fibre in the country." In an effort to secure reelection in 1832, Andrew

Jackson had vetoed the renewal of the privately held United States Bank's charter, and then withdrawn all federal monies, although the charter wasn't due to expire until 1836. Despite popular support for the veto, Jackson's move had the result of destabilizing the young country's fragile economy, introducing a period of rapid inflation and unchecked speculation, punctuated by panics in 1834 and 1837, as local wildcat bankers rushed in to fill the place of Nicholas Biddle's monolithic U.S. Bank. Particularly in the Northeast, long-standing fortunes were eroded or lost, and new business ventures foundered.

Elizabeth's Cuba Journal was dotted with reports of friends who had "failed" in these "dreadful times." Perhaps the saddest case was Tom and Connie Park, whose Roxbury house, where Sophia had spent several happy months two years before, had to be sold, and their Oriental carpets and Chinese urns auctioned at Goodrich's. Now the couple were part of the Boston boarding house set, and Tom was making plans to sail for California to seek a second fortune, leaving Connie behind to wait for a summons to the west. Yet for the Peabodys, who had so little to lose, there was a silver lining. These same economic pressures made it possible for Dr. Peabody to bring Nat's creditors, eager for cash in almost any amount, to a compromise, reducing the $1,100 debt to $400. He borrowed the lesser sum from his nephew John Tyler in Boston, and Nat agreed to pay back the $400, with interest, in yearly installments of $50, although the loan had to be taken in Dr. Peabody's name.

"Raising money here . . . is harder work than ever," Elizabeth wrote to Mary in the spring of 1834, as she discovered that she could no longer support the rent of a room at the Clarke boarding house. She took a part-time job as governess for the Rice family in exchange for room and board, hoping to cover further expenses with the fees from her increasingly popular women's "Historical Conferences," as she had begun to call them. Elizabeth now held sessions twice a week for a term of six months, during which each class member studied a separate country or ancient civilization and prepared to address the group. On presentation days, Elizabeth's method was to ask her student to "put into my hands a few questions . . . to guide me in bringing out from her what proved to be a lecture to the rest." The sessions, begun at 10:00 in the morning, often stretched well into the afternoon, "so interesting were the conversations." Word of Elizabeth's extensive knowledge of historical texts written not just in English, but in Greek and German as well, had even spread to the "brothers and friends of my scholars" at Harvard, who "came to me sub rosa . . . and asked my advice as to their historical reading." There was, at the time, no professor of history at Harvard or any other American college, and Elizabeth happily filled in—"sub rosa," and for no pay.

Elizabeth hoped to earn still more by publishing articles and textbooks. She had the promise of steady work from Andrews Norton, the editor of the

Unitarian bimonthly the *Christian Examiner.* Norton, who as Harvard Divinity School's founding professor had invited Elizabeth to borrow any book in his extensive personal library when she first moved to Boston, offered now to publish her six early essays on the "Spirit of the Hebrew Scriptures" if she polished them to his satisfaction. Elizabeth was ready to take them out of her desk drawer. And her one-time partner William Russell welcomed her contributions to his *American Journal of Education.* But her situation remained precarious. Elizabeth wrote Mary that soon after her move to the Rice household, in April 1834, Henry Rice announced at dinner that he'd lost $60,000 in the past six months. This setback wasn't enough to bring Henry Rice down, or to cost Elizabeth her job—boarding a governess was cheaper than sending the Rice children to private schools—but, she added, Henry Rice was "not in the sweetest humour imaginable." Much of her role at the Rices' became mediating between the short-tempered Henry Rice and his wife and children.

Although she had no idea that Horace Mann, too, was financially pressed—according to his own journals, Mann subsisted on just one meal a day for long stretches from 1834 to 1837, while saving to pay off his brother Stanley's debts—Elizabeth kept Mary informed of their mutual friend's spiritual welfare on an almost daily basis. With Mary at a safe distance, Elizabeth no longer held back any details of what had now become regular Sunday-evening meetings with Mann. There was the night, shortly after Mary's departure, when Mann's look of desperation as he sat next to Elizabeth on the sofa in Mrs. Clarke's parlor caused her "involuntarily" to move closer, take his "hand with my left hand and put my right over his shoulder," and assure him that his departed wife's spirit must still be close by. Mann responded by resting his head on Elizabeth's shoulder and pressing her hand as he whispered, "*I trust so.*"

A month later, on a cold March evening, after getting up to warm herself at the stove, Elizabeth returned to the couch, where Mann took both her hands in his and told her he feared he had "cast my shadows over you" and given her a chill. Elizabeth swiftly reassured him that "it was no pain to me to share the shadow with a friend." Then, as Mann continued to hold her hands, she told him the recent news of Walter Channing's wife's death, causing him to weep quietly as he murmured, "'Tis the survivor dies."

The following week, however, Elizabeth asked Mary to "reflect & rejoice" in the fact that Horace Mann had finally consented to hear the Reverend Channing preach on Easter Sunday. Elizabeth guessed correctly that Channing would address the occasion of his sister-in-law's tragic death—a scene that would surely evoke Mann's own loss of his wife and their unborn child. "The Future Life," with its depiction of a heaven where the souls of family members would be reunited, became one of Channing's most widely reprinted sermons, and Mann visited Elizabeth in a state of high emotion on the Sunday evening after its delivery. He took her hand in his, Elizabeth wrote to Mary, "as if he felt he needed support," and told her, with lips quivering, that "the veil had at last fallen, that the other world and his living wife had disclosed themselves to his imagination." To Elizabeth, a firm believer in the afterlife as a place of reunion rather than retribution, this confession was a victory.

Such intimate discussions had been difficult to carry on in the Clarke parlor. When the pair heard other boarders approach on the stairs, Mann slid to the far end of the sofa, then resumed his embrace once they were left alone again. After she moved in with the Rices, however, Elizabeth had her own sitting room—perhaps the best feature of her new living arrangement. Elizabeth wrote to Mary that she had told Mann he could still see her "privately, as if I were at board, perhaps more so." On his first visit to Elizabeth at the Rices', Mann "took hold of both my hands—and drew me for one moment absolutely in his arms" as he told Elizabeth how much he valued the letters of consolation she wrote to him at least once a week. Then he "held me very affectionately to him, with the most confiding brotherly manner, until he went," she wrote.

"It was a perfect comfort to me to think he could feel free to do this, without fear of misapprehension," she wrote to Mary in Cuba. Indeed, despite his often gloomy outlook, Elizabeth confided that "Mr. M. spreads sunshine round my heart by his brotherly tenderness, his stimulating approbation, and by expressing that I interest his mind and beguile his sorrows." The two had discussed Elizabeth's future employment, and Mann—who awarded his prolix friend the nickname "Miss Thesaura"—encouraged her to continue writing for publication, offering himself as her editor. He turned to Elizabeth for criticism of his own reports to the legislature as well. In these months when Elizabeth's economic future looked bleak and her sisters were far away, Horace Mann supplanted the Reverend Channing as "my chief comfort." What could Mary have felt, reading these words?

Whether out of tact, or because she persisted in viewing the friendship with Horace Mann as a three-way alliance, Elizabeth reported any thoughts about Mary that Mann revealed to her. After Mary's ship sailed for Cuba, Mann had suffered from a "mysterious sensation of uneasiness and insecurity," finding himself "starting with alarm only at the rattle of a window or the creaking of a sign," as he waited anxiously for news of Mary's safe arrival. Once Mary's letters began to arrive, Mann appeared to be visiting Elizabeth as much to hear her read the letters aloud—they "always put my nerves into beautiful tune"—as to receive her embraces. He offered to reimburse Elizabeth for the postage on letters from Mary that she read to him, and he coveted a pencil sketch of Mary that Sophia had drawn for their mother. Mann asked

Elizabeth to mention his Sunday visits in her letters to Mary, for "I love to know that she thinks of me."

Elizabeth participated happily in Mann's admiration for Mary; she was accustomed to applauding Mary's superior beauty. And if they marveled together at the "charm and grace" of her sister's writing, that took away nothing from Mann's encouragement of the serious work Elizabeth was now publishing in the *Christian Examiner,* the *Boston Observer,* Russell's *Journal of Education,* and the *Christian Register*—all important organs of the liberal vanguard. Elizabeth was most pleased with the series on the "Spirit of the Hebrew Scriptures," which she had written under the spell of Channing and Wordsworth in 1826. By the fall of 1834, three of the essays had appeared: her theory of "the social principle" was at last in print.

Emboldened by Elizabeth's reports of Horace Mann's interest, Mary began to write to him directly. Certainly she was pleased to learn of Elizabeth's frustration when Mann repeatedly forgot to bring along his own small store of letters from Mary for Elizabeth to read on Sunday evenings. Mary could imagine that Mann shared her desire to establish a private connection. Yet when he finally wrote back, Mann's declarations were ambiguous. He wrote of his "lively interest in your welfare" and his "desire for your happiness," and he begged Mary to send more letters. But Mann's praise for all the "goodness and sincerity and truth that are in you" and his gratitude for "the solaces which your gentleness can apply to a wounded bosom" were offset by his postscript telling of his pleasure in visiting Elizabeth, who "has a mansion in her heart for everybody who suffers and truths in her mind enough to heal them all." Horace Mann was not ready to admit a preference for Mary with Elizabeth's sympathy close at hand.

In any case, Mann's unshakable grief for Charlotte had by now settled into depression: he wrote to Mary that he did not "expect ever to have my activity again roused or this cold inertness of my mind quickened." Whenever Mann seemed to be approaching an outright statement of affection for Mary, Charlotte's memory intruded. One particularly warm letter from Horace Mann was written on the Fourth of July 1834; Mann had stayed away from the celebration on Boston Common to write to Mary, who he imagined was "thinking of your home & your country." He wanted her to know that "there was one at least here" who, in the hour of his nation's "deepest festivity," was "thinking only of you." Yet Mann's contemplation of Mary's absence instantly caused him to think of Charlotte, whose unalterable "*absence*" left him feeling "the pain but not the peace of death."

Mary's only possible long-distance strategy was to accuse Elizabeth of impropriety. Elizabeth insisted that her behavior was beyond reproach. The Rices knew all about Mann's visits to her parlor, she protested, and they approved.

She would never admit a man to her "bed-chamber," as Marianne Dwight had done. Nor would she allow a man to put his foot in her lap so she could mend his trousers, as Sophia had done with James Burroughs. And she had never "kissed Mr. Mann's forehead even when he wept upon [my] neck." She deferred to Mann's request that she not visit him in his room when he was sick, although she sent baskets of fruit, flowers, and medicinal herbs. Elizabeth proudly quoted Mann's letter turning down her offer to bring the gifts in person: "Oh, this generation! They never can appreciate the motives that make me desire to see you or you to see me. . . . On this we must withhold from them the opportunity to misconstrue."

Still, Mary's questions about whether Horace Mann's visits might be "misunderstood" ultimately prompted Elizabeth to take up the matter with Mann himself; and for once Mary must have been grateful for her sister's forthright nature. It had now been almost a year since Mary left for Cuba, a year of growing alarm over her sister's attachment to the man Mary privately thought of as "my husband." Mary could only have felt relief when she read the postscript Elizabeth scrawled across the closing lines of one of her journal letters in September 1834, telling of an evening spent discussing "the difference between love and friendship" with Horace Mann. The conversation had been "perfectly unembarrassed and pleasant," and by the end, Elizabeth wrote, she felt certain that "no misunderstanding can ever come between us, however affectionate we may be." While Mann had assured Elizabeth that "my friendship is a great comfort to him and he needs its constant ministrations," she was certain that "it is a brother's and sister's love on both sides and now I know he will never think otherwise."

Elizabeth had broached the subject, she explained to Mary, because she "wanted to be sure that he would never feel that I felt *more* than friendship for him," and he would feel no qualms about "receiving my kind offices." She did not want Horace Mann to think that their growing intimacy required him to steer the relationship toward marriage. "Not that it would not be possible for Mr. M. to make me love him exclusively," she wrote. "But I *could not* do it unless he *had* or *did* try for it. And his situation, his grey hairs and his sorrow, has ever *precluded from* my imagination that possibility." She recalled Lyman Buckminster's pursuit of her ten years before, saying, "I *know* what the feeling of *love* is, for I have been sought and all but *won.*" This early experience left Elizabeth convinced now, she assured Mary, that "strong as my friendship is, deep as my interest is in Mr. M., it is a totally different feeling."

Elizabeth concealed disappointment in these words. This conversation could well have prompted Horace Mann to "try for it"—if he had felt more than "a brother's love" for Elizabeth. There was a defensiveness in her list of Mann's flaws as a romantic prospect: his gray hair and his despondency. Just a month earlier, Elizabeth had written Mary that when she received a letter

"I *know* what the feeling of *love* is. . . .": Elizabeth's cross-written letter to Mary, recounting her conversation with Horace Mann

from Horace Mann apologizing for missing a Sunday-night visit because he was out of town, signed "Yours *very affectionately,* H. M.," she had "actually kissed those sweet words."

But as for Horace Mann, Elizabeth wrote, "I am quite sure he never felt more happy" about the friendship "than he did last night." And why not? Elizabeth had just invited him to carry on a relationship that offered more of the intimacies of marriage than any friendship he could have formed with a more conventional woman. Perhaps Elizabeth's embraces reminded Horace Mann of her younger sister Mary—a woman who surely would not have allowed such liberties without talk of an engagement. For her part, disappointed as she may have been, Elizabeth had won Mann's commitment to a more comradely relationship than any marriage she had yet to observe or to envision for herself. If marriage was not to be the result, perhaps that was the best for all concerned. Certainly it was the best possible news for Mary—unless, of course, from a distance of a thousand miles, she worried that the weekly solace of Elizabeth's "sisterly" embraces might cause Horace Mann to change his mind and "try for it" before Mary returned to Boston.

If anything reassured Mary that Elizabeth had given up hope of an exclusive connection with Horace Mann, it was her awareness that Elizabeth was making room in her heart for a new intellectual infatuation—this one with

Bronson Alcott

Bronson Alcott. The sisters had known Alcott and his wife, Abigail May, as early as 1830, when Sophia had unexpectedly found herself in attendance at their wedding following a Sunday-morning service at King's Chapel. Sophia wrote afterward in her journal that she was "very much struck by" the couple —Abby May, the high-spirited twenty-nine-year-old daughter of an old Massachusetts family, and Bronson Alcott, at thirty, a reform-minded teacher and "mystic visionary" who'd grown up in rural poverty in the Connecticut backwoods. After a failed attempt at establishing a children's "School of Human Culture" in Philadelphia, the Alcotts and their two young daughters, Anna and Louisa May, were back in Boston, "the most favorable place for action of any in our country," according to Bronson, where men and women "are born to think and to feel—and the patronage for action given."

Alcott's first school had failed, but the zealous, sharp-featured philosopher was not about to give up. He brought to Boston the journals he had required his young students to keep and showed them to Elizabeth Peabody, who was instantly "*amazed* beyond measure at the composition," she wrote to Mary in Cuba. As she listened to Alcott describe his "conversational" method of teaching—a wide-ranging use of the Socratic style Elizabeth already employed in the grammar lessons she called "examinations of words"—she decided to help Alcott gather a school in Boston. When she learned from Abby Alcott that Bronson was unqualified to teach Latin, arithmetic, and geography—subjects that Boston families naturally expected their children to master in school—Elizabeth volunteered her services "two hours and a half a day for a year for such compensation he could afford to pay." Abby was "in *rapture*—and Mr. A. too when he came in" and heard the news, Elizabeth wrote to Mary. As Elizabeth called on more than a dozen families and successfully enrolled eighteen pupils for the opening day of classes in September 1834, she gave no thought to the fact that she might have started a school of her own with the same children, or that "Mr. A." had not yet specified the amount of compensation he could afford. Foremost in her mind, she wrote to Mary, was her impression that "Alcott is a man destined ... to make an era in society, *and I believe he will.*"

Alcott was equally generous in his praise of Elizabeth, whom he considered to possess "the most magnificent philosophic imagination of any person he ever knew." Almost certainly Alcott had read Elizabeth's recent essays on the Hebrew scriptures in the *Christian Examiner*, which offered a theoretical basis for the work he had come to intuitively. Theirs was a partnership of like minds in which practicality and idealism seemed, for the moment, in perfect balance. Together they searched for the ideal schoolroom, and they found it on the second floor of the new Masonic Temple facing the Common from the corner of Tremont Street and Temple Place, a Gothic Revival structure made of stone and lauded since its completion in 1832 as "one of the chief architectural ornaments of the city." The sixty-foot-long classroom had such high ceilings that it proved difficult to heat in winter, but an immense cathedral window illuminated the space with a warm, otherworldly glow throughout the day. Alcott proceeded to furnish the room with a ten-foot-long teacher's desk, custom-made in the shape of a crescent, and seats for his students, which he arranged in a semicircle to foster open discussion—a startlingly novel idea at the time. Elizabeth supplied a green velvet couch for visitors and a portrait of the Reverend Channing, which was soon joined by busts of Plato, Shakespeare, Socrates, and Scott, acquired by Alcott with consultation from Elizabeth and set on pedestals in the four corners of the room. A bas-relief head of Christ was propped on a tall bookcase behind the teacher's desk "so as to appear to the scholars to be just over Mr. Alcott's head."

Early on, Alcott began to refer to his students at the Temple School as his "disciples." They were a receptive band of boys and girls, aged five to fifteen, whose parents were solid members of Boston's liberal elite. The Reverend Channing sent his daughter, Mary. Caroline Sturgis, the middle of the maritime tycoon William Sturgis's five daughters, joined the class along with Lemuel Shaw, son of the chief justice of the Massachusetts Supreme Court. The youngest pupil was the precocious five-year-old Josiah Phillips Quincy, whose grandfather was the president of Harvard and the former mayor of Boston. Alcott managed to hold them all spellbound as he discoursed on moral fables or scenes from *The Pilgrim's Progress* and engaged them in discussions designed to elicit their own opinions on everything from classroom discipline to the foundations of language.

Alcott urged complete openness among his students and required them to stand and speak their minds freely when answering questions. Their reward was the teacher's promise never to criticize their thoughts; Alcott's persuasive powers were enough to steer the conversation in any direction he chose. For children accustomed to schools where rote learning, recitation, and raps on the knuckles were the order of the day, the task was difficult at first. But soon there were comments such as one child's: "I never knew I had a mind till I came to this school." Elizabeth summarized one morning's classroom dialogue for Mary and concluded: "This is the way our children talk; *they create.*" The dialogues provided the foundation for the remarkable journals Alcott's Temple School students produced as well, the result of their teacher's success in "leading children to think vividly and consecutively, which leads of itself to expression," Elizabeth wrote. In response to their compositions, Alcott promised no "petty criticism" of spelling, grammar, or punctuation, which he believed caused young children to "suppress their own thoughts." Instead he prompted them to think more deeply by asking ever more probing questions.

Alcott's morning dialogues and journal-writing sessions flowed easily into Elizabeth's afternoon lessons on more conventional academic subjects in which, she wrote, "you never saw a deeper interest" from students. To Mary this report must have seemed a welcome burst of enthusiasm from Elizabeth, who had written just two months earlier, when her life seemed to have shrunk to a predictable routine of tutoring the Rice children and writing alone in her room, punctuated by lugubrious Sunday visits from Horace Mann, that "I am quite *starved* of soul's food." Now, in addition to days spent in a classroom that regularly "speaks the thoughts of Genius," there were long evenings of "delightful and harmonious talk" with Bronson Alcott on "Fate free will &c," the topics Elizabeth loved best.

In the spring of 1835, Elizabeth left the Rice household and moved into the Alcotts' boarding house, taking two tiny rooms for $8 a week; she was still re-

Masonic Temple, Boston (center)

lying on her historical classes and reading parties for support, having twice refused payment from Bronson Alcott, whose own shaky finances were painfully
apparent. But as the Temple School doubled in size over the winter and
Alcott's magic held sway over a class of thirty pupils, with the green velvet visitors' couch frequently occupied, Elizabeth began to record Alcott's dialogues
with his students and made plans to publish them as a book. She showed an
early draft to Waldo Emerson—she now took tea with him and his fiancée,
Lydia Jackson, "a real *Universal*," with whom Elizabeth was "as much in
love . . . as Mr. Emerson is," when both were in town. Emerson confirmed her
optimism about the project; he wrote that he had read the manuscript "with
greatest pleasure" and hoped that "it may be printed speedily" so that its usefulness could be tested.

Elizabeth was, by now, a full convert to Alcott's doctrine of open communication, which she began to apply, with mixed results, to other close relation-

ships. A year before, when her sisters left for Cuba, Elizabeth had been grateful to have "a chamber to myself" after sharing rooms with Mary for nearly a decade, and for the opportunity to "command my spirits" and resolve "[my] inward discords and disproportions" in solitude. She had begun to look on her urge to "communicate wherever there is a human being presented to my senses" as a compulsion, leading to "irritable nerves, and [an] overstrained mental, moral and physical system." Yet the free dialogue she had established with Alcott and seen him nurture in his students was causing her to think better of this propensity.

The winter and early spring of 1835, one of the coldest in memory, brought new intellectual heat to Boston. In January, Waldo Emerson began his first series of thematically linked lectures, on the uses of biography, sponsored by Boston's Society for the Diffusion of Useful Knowledge and delivered to full audiences in the main hall of the Masonic Temple. After resigning the ministry in 1832 and traveling in Europe during much of 1833, Emerson was remaking himself, at thirty-one, as a secular prophet. A tall man, ruggedly handsome with a shock of dark brown hair, Emerson read each lecture from a carefully honed forty-page manuscript, his hands folded across the lectern except when he turned a page, looking up at intervals to fix his intense blue eyes on a listener at the back of the hall to be sure he was heard. This glance, however, could be electrifying—one listener compared it to "the reveille of a trumpet." In a voice another early auditor described as "the sweetest, the most winning and penetrating of any I ever heard," Emerson spoke now of Milton, Michelangelo, and Martin Luther. But the lives he chose didn't matter so much as his line of argument. Emerson's lectures were not "original," Elizabeth wrote to Mary. Yet they brought together "most felicitously ... all the most important ideas—which we value—as this age's *spirit*." She could not remember when she had last been "so *excited* by a production of the human mind." In March 1835, as the series drew to a close, she wrote to Horace Mann, "I do not know when I have had such a *thinking time* as the last few weeks."

In Emerson's view, all men possessed the elements of greatness and, as Elizabeth summarized one early lecture for Mary, "the *individuality of a man*" required the recognition in himself of "some one element of the spiritual nature we all share." Emerson's message resonated with the philosophy of Peabody and Alcott's Temple School, where, Elizabeth wrote, dropping the masculine pronoun, "all minds are to be cherished ... [for] we never know but we have genius to deal with among our pupils." As she listened to Emerson lecture on "the absolute boundlessness of our capacity," Elizabeth no longer felt so inclined to apologize for her impulsive nature. Instead she realized that self-doubt had been the chief source of "so many dark times" in her life. Now she felt "*inspired*" by Emerson's lectures to "think better of myself than I have ever done before." With this realization came another: that "thoughts and processes of feeling are *events* with me," as she wrote to Horace Mann. "I do not have a conversation with you ... and come out of it just as I was before. I am a very different person from what I was one year ago. I am a different person from what I was six weeks ago." It was a revelation to Elizabeth of the value of social intercourse—an expansion of what she now called "my principle of the social sympathy"—every bit as powerful as the intuitions of nature's unity that Sophia was experiencing in the Cuban moonlight.

Elizabeth recounted one of these life-altering conversations in her Cuba Journal. This one was with Horace Mann, who had seemed more cheerful since, as the leader of an anti-Jackson landslide, he'd won a seat as a Whig in the Massachusetts Senate in November 1834. Elizabeth was pleased, too: Mann's belated decision to run had been in large part thanks to her persuading him to take seriously the offers of support from several wealthy backers. In her newly expansive mood, Elizabeth now asked Mann to give blunt answers to "any questions I ask him about myself." Mann admitted that he had heard Elizabeth criticized for "neglect of some outward matters." But when she pressed Mann to tell her whether "*he personally* ... thought that thro' earnestness—enthusiasm—or any other innocent cause even—I was ever betrayed into an overbearing—intrusive—masculine manner," his answer was "*No—indeed.*" There was a distinct note of triumph in her report to Mary that Mann had told her "it was remarkably the other way—and that I gave every mind a chance—and [was] remarkably free from taking advantage of my superior gifts of mind!"

During the remaining months of Mary and Sophia's stay in Cuba, Elizabeth turned her attention to establishing an open communication with Mary. Elizabeth envisioned a new era of harmony for the sisters. She urged Mary to recruit a half-dozen Spanish children in Cuba and bring them home with her to form the nucleus of a boarding school; Sophia could add art lessons to the academics Mary and Elizabeth would provide. She believed, Elizabeth wrote to Mary, that "there was that in each of us which might fully satisfy the wants of the other." Despite occasional tensions, "there were few sisters who had so much union as we—so much sympathy—& so much affection & respect for each other."

Yet Elizabeth was also aware of an undercurrent of disapproval in Mary's letters: the insinuations that Elizabeth would lose her reputation in a week in Cuba or that her meetings with Horace Mann might be "misunderstood," along with references to "those little things which were a constant eyesore" in Elizabeth's housekeeping and personal appearance. Worse still was Elizabeth's growing suspicion, based on chance remarks from Horace Mann, that Mary had confided in Mann her belief that Elizabeth was domineering and intrusive—even "*outré*." Mann had let slip his impression that Mary appeared "fearful of contradicting" Elizabeth, and "he had observed you always withdrew an opinion or forebore to express it when it was different from mine," Elizabeth wrote.

For a time, Elizabeth defended herself on the lesser charges, reporting a compliment she received from Aunt Sophia Pickman on "the tasteful way in which my hair was done up" and describing the dress with "plaited lace round the neck" and the silver combs borrowed from Maria Rice "quite neatly and prettily" arranged in her hair for the wedding of Susan Howe and George Hillard, their old friend from Somerset Court. After the Hillards' wedding, Elizabeth wrote to Mary, "a great many people say I was dressed beautifully!!!" But with her newfound self-confidence, Elizabeth quickly dropped even this means of conciliation. "I do not feel able to promise that you will ever see me more than barely tidy," Elizabeth wrote in a letter, which she closed with the challenge: "I am perfectly willing that you should know all about me."

Now Elizabeth began to recall just how annoyed she had always been by what she called Mary's "palpable forbearance": the way that, without once uttering "a word of censure," Mary still managed to convey a "*lurking doubt*" about Elizabeth's character, as if she were surveying "the ruins of a mind— even if all the fragments were diamonds." Elizabeth began a campaign to get Mary to drop her "habit of *brooding*" in silence over Elizabeth's faults, and commit to a relationship in which there would be absolute honesty on both sides: a "transparent intercourse" rather than a false "notion of keeping peace by *concealing* whatever would jar." Elizabeth claimed to be ready to hear Mary's criticisms, if only she would bring them out in the open.

In letter after letter, Elizabeth defended what she now called her "principles of communication." She touted Bronson Alcott as "the only person I have ever seen" who practiced free communication and insisted that, if Mary were to observe Alcott's teaching, she would soon "admit from his lips the very views on this subject which you have always rejected from mine." As Mary continued to ignore Elizabeth's salvos, refusing to "dwell upon the past," Elizabeth began to hint that it might be better if Mary and Sophia both settled in Salem, Mary to start a school of her own and Sophia to teach drawing, while Elizabeth remained in Boston assisting Alcott. "If you care to live with me enough to take your chance of my vicissitudes," she wrote Mary, "of course I shall be glad. But what will make you happiest will best please me." Elizabeth had decided that "I could not at the same time be true to myself & please you."

At last Mary had to respond or give up hope of living near Horace Mann in Boston. Mary admitted that she had "withheld my confidence at times," but, she wrote obliquely, "it was because I could not give it." Attempting appeasement, she confessed to having a "proud heart" that kept her from speaking openly, and allowed that "perhaps I have had [a] proud feeling more toward you than anyone else." Mary guessed that her habit of living "more in an inner world than in the outer one" had made her seem aloof. Then, coming as close as she dared to revealing her love for Horace Mann, she acknowledged that she too longed for a deeper connection. "I [have] ever had in my mind," Mary wrote, "an ideal image of one to whom I should open every avenue of my heart for the asking—and with that image have been connected all my visions of happiness in this world. Time must prove whether that ideal ever takes a human form."

Mary's apparent apology set Elizabeth revising her plans once again. "You shall certainly *live with me* if we both live on brown crusts," she wrote back immediately. Isolated at La Recompensa, Mary had not been able to attract any young Spaniards to a boarding school in Boston, and Elizabeth had handed over any Boston children she might have claimed to Alcott. But Elizabeth still hoped to gather a school of a half-dozen older girls. Sophia could stay in Salem with their parents, supporting herself "very handsomely" with afternoon drawing classes. Then "we will manage as well as we can till we are old and grey, keeping old maids hall and school."

This vision of the future must have struck Mary as alarming. Even as Elizabeth and Horace Mann were indulging in a self-congratulatory Sunday-evening chat—in which "*we agreed* that *you* were a rare specimen of perfection for this world, and that I was very much improved," Elizabeth wrote—Mary was composing a long letter on what she called the "endless topic" of open communication. Mary now gave Elizabeth what she had been asking for all along: she openly charged Elizabeth with being indiscreet, and she refused to confide in her. She knew that Elizabeth had spoken to Horace Mann of their disagreements, and she asked her to stop. Further, Mary did not believe that Elizabeth really wanted to hear criticism, nor would Elizabeth change her ways if she did hear it. All Elizabeth wanted, in Mary's view, was to make herself the center of attention. Mary would live with Elizabeth only if she promised to curb her "egotism" and limit conversation to topics on which they both agreed.

Elizabeth was irate. "I would rather be without a friend in the world," she wrote Mary, than go through the "fiddle-faddle" of guarding each other's feelings. And Mary's letter, she argued, simply amounted to her saying "I will be frank with you if you will never oppose me"—although Elizabeth herself countered with virtually the same directive. She demanded that both sisters "speak plain English" to each other, and "where I am mistaken shall expect you will explain yourself so that I can understand." Then Mary must "*listen* to what I have to say and be willing to believe you may be mistaken." She advised Mary to "reflect on my conditions—not as evils to be endured, but as principles to be adopted."

In an effort to show a measure of sympathy, Elizabeth guessed that the "different moral atmosphere" in Cuba had exaggerated in Mary her already characteristic reserve. Yet "if you think that on account of my temper or prejudices, reservations will always be necessary towards me," she advised Mary, "do not put yourself into daily intercourse with me." It was far better to "*live alone* unless you can live with somebody *frankly* and unreservedly." Elizabeth still hoped Mary would agree to her conditions. It would then be "my greatest happiness," Elizabeth wrote, to "use all my faculties and resources to obtain the means for our living together."

In fairness, Elizabeth was reeling from an encounter with another resentful younger sibling—Nat, who had suddenly announced that he'd set a wedding date, before even beginning to pay back his debts to his father. The ceremony would take place in May 1835, timed to coincide with Mary and Sophia's expected return from Cuba. Elizabeth's letter to Mary relaying the news showed her in a rare mood of defeat. She already took a dim view of the match: Nat was "*tyrannical* and overbearing" with the sweet-natured hat maker's daughter Elizabeth Hibbard, when he "ought to study what would make her happy." But worse still was Nat's failure to assume any responsibility for his future. He had even gone so far as to ridicule Elizabeth for "having given up my youth to *free* our family from debt. He thought it was 'not virtue but folly.'" Elizabeth despaired that Nat seemed to have "no more sensibility to the rights of property in other people *than a swindler*." Now, she feared, "the result will be that he will never be out of debt and as long as he can live on Pa he will." At sixty, Dr. Peabody was "getting old very fast," the result of his anxiety about his sons, and Elizabeth foresaw a day when he would be unable to provide Nat with a home. Then Nat would "sink in hopeless poverty, and you and I will have to work when we are grey to take care of his children, besides never having the satisfaction of seeing Pa out of debt," she wrote to Mary.

Sophia, at least, seemed to have profited from the Cuban sojourn. Her weight gain was a promising sign, and the sisters had stayed at La Recompensa well into the spring in hopes that "a second change of air may complete Sophia's cure." Yet Elizabeth marveled at Sophia's curious ability to have "preserved the child's mind through so many years of her life." To most of those who read her Cuba Journal, Sophia was "an embodiment of enthusiasm & genius." But her sisters knew that Sophia's unchecked enthusiasm could produce unintended consequences. Elizabeth, who prided herself on the character analyses she produced in her own Cuba Journal, had come to realize, in light of the James Burroughs affair, that the "paradisiacal people" who filled Sophia's Cuban landscape were "all made up." When Sophia wrote excitedly that she had invited the Morrell family to visit Salem and stay with the Peabodys, Elizabeth warned her to curb her generosity. Sophia should remember that her own home was merely "the humble dwelling of a New England physician, who has outlived his profession."

Although Elizabeth found herself unable to retract her demands on Mary, she reported a conversation with Horace Mann in one of her last journal letters which must have acted as a balm. Mann had pressed Elizabeth for details of Mary's return. "I do long to have her come back," he told Elizabeth. Then, "with one of those tones which thrill the soul," he had murmured, "she *can* come back"—and had fallen into a mournful silence that, Elizabeth wrote, "I did not know would ever break."

Mary sailed for Boston with Elizabeth's blistering letters packed away in her trunk. There had been no resolution to the questions of where she would work or live, beyond Elizabeth's suggestion that Mary take her place as assistant in Alcott's school for a promised $400 a year. Mary knew, however, that Alcott had yet to pay Elizabeth a cent. To Horace Mann, Mary wrote wryly that she had abandoned any plans of "setting up [as] a Spanish lady on my return." Instead he "must only expect to see a plain American woman with a knowing look" when he met her again in Boston. She confessed to feeling "behind the age . . . in regard to philosophy and all those great matters that interest the public mind" in New England. After the flurry of letters from Elizabeth, with their pleas for a "transparent intercourse" and their impassioned accounts of Alcott's school of infant geniuses and Emerson's oracular sayings, it was little wonder that Mary, her mind imprinted with brutal scenes of slave life in Cuba, felt compelled to admit, "I am not quite clear about the *transcendental* yet."

PART VII

"Before the Age in Salem"
1836–1839

❧ 25 ❧

Temple School Revisited

ON MAY 17, 1835, MARY AND SOPHIA'S SHIP, THE *WILLIAM HENRY*, reached port in Boston, and the sisters crammed themselves and their trunks into Elizabeth's rooms in the Alcott boarding house for a long-awaited reunion. Abby Alcott, eight months into her third pregnancy, looked in now and then to "nurse up" the travel-weary Sophia, whose exhaustion after the voyage was the first in a series of setbacks that would gradually erase the benefits of her Cuban rest cure. In an attempt to bring an end to their feud, Mary remarked pointedly on Elizabeth's "beauty"; clearly Elizabeth, too, was making an effort to please. Of the three sisters, it was Mary who was noticeably thin and pale now, after more than a year of the kind of work she least enjoyed in a family that did not even share her enthusiasm for reform.

Horace Mann was among the many friends who crowded in to greet the sisters, but Elizabeth's "monopolizing spirit" prevented the private conversation Mary wished for, she wrote to Mann two weeks later from Salem. She continued to feel that "the march of mind" had passed her by, she told him, but she intended to catch up. "I think I was meant for a statesman," Mary confided, so interested had she become in politics. Meanwhile, she had "turned violent housekeeper" — in part to help her mother, who had been without daughters in the house for so long, but primarily to "counteract the effect of being so long served by the poor slave."

It was not just "the march of mind" that had left the two sisters behind. While Mary and Sophia were in Cuba, the Boston goldsmith Louis Lauriat had begun experimenting with balloon travel. Soon after their return, his ascensions from the Common attracted crowds of several thousand curiosity seekers eager to watch M. Lauriat risk losing himself in the clouds. A more profound advance in transportation had come with the opening of three sepa-

307

The Peabody family, silhouettes, 1835: (*top row, left to right*) Mrs. Peabody, Dr. Peabody, Elizabeth, Nat; (*bottom row*) George, Sophia, Mary, Wellington

rate railway lines leading north, south, and west from the city. Mary became one of the first passengers on the latest of these to accept riders—the Boston-to-Lowell line—just a month after her return home, when she paid a visit to Lydia Haven, now critically ill with the tuberculosis she had suffered from as long as the sisters had known her. Mary had "some fears of that rapid mode of proceeding," which, astonishingly, made a day trip to Lowell, thirty miles distant, an attractive and affordable possibility. She took her brother George along so she wouldn't be alone in case of an accident. Exploding boilers and derailments were all too common in the early days of passenger trains. Still, Mary admired the speedy railroad "in the abstract": the steam-powered engines seemed to augur a day when technology would succeed in "bringing all space together." Along with Sophia, Mary dreaded another "vile separation" of the sisterhood after their return from Cuba.

Yet when Elizabeth announced that she would spend the summer with

Lydia in Lowell, where she planned to comfort the dying woman and her young son with an education in spiritual philosophy, leaving Mary to take her place in Alcott's school for the summer term, Mary was relieved. She was at last "perfectly happy" just to walk the streets of Boston, indulging in "the feeling of liberty and security" after so many months under posted sentinels at La Recompensa, and glad of the chance to relearn "the 'old familiar faces' and places." Mary arranged to board with George—who was still making good money as an importer's clerk—at Mrs. Vinton's on Pearl Street, where she would not feel pressured to keep up an Elizabeth-style open communication with the Alcotts, and the rent was lower than the sisters had ever managed in Boston.

Another event the two sisters had missed was their brother Nat's wedding. He'd rushed through the ceremony four days before their return to Boston and expected to bring his young wife Elizabeth Hibbard—"E. Nat," now, to a family with a surfeit of Elizabeths—into the Peabody household in Salem. The Peabodys would have to move from the "cubby house" on Church Street. The choice of a much larger, if shabbier, house on Charter Street proved fortunate, for at one time or another over the next five years, all six Peabody children would live at home again. Sophia was the first of the sisters to return; there simply had been no other choice.

Sophia's first look at the Charter Street house dismayed her. Just on the edge of a fashionable section of town, the blockish three-story clapboard building bordered one end of Salem's oldest cemetery and was "in the most ruinous condition," she wrote Mary in Boston, "antique and ugly—but full of rooms." Its fine points were "a nice portion of garden land" for the Peabodys' kitchen crops, "a *magnificent* stretch of kitchen & pantry," and six bedrooms with plenty of adjoining closets large enough to fit beds if needed. The graveyard, she wrote, was "close under the parlor windows—(Ugh!)," but the family had already endured a similar fate in Boston several years earlier. "I love the notion of living near the dead" was Sophia's doleful attempt at making the best of things. More troubling was her sense that no amount of fresh paint or wallpaper would ever make the parlors "even approach to looking handsome." The sole ornamental feature of the house was a pedimented entryway supported by columns that jutted awkwardly into the street.

By the time of the move at the end of June, however, Sophia's spirits had lifted. "After living in a swallow's nest so long," she wrote to Mary, "we feel as if we were in a palace." Sophia was able to make light of her parents' bickering when her mother insisted on transplanting the entire Church Street garden, even the blush roses then in full bloom: "Father was sure every thing would die—& Mother equally sure every thing w'd live," she wrote to Mary. While Mrs. Peabody and Wellington dug and weeded in the flower beds, seeing to it that "all the sweet company held up their heads," Dr. Peabody fussed over the planting of potatoes and beans. Sophia watched the proceedings from her second-story bedroom window, where she could look out past the gravestones, through the branches of a venerable elm, to the Pickman garden, once Mary's favorite childhood retreat.

Wellington had recently returned to favor in the family. Now eighteen, Welly considered himself to have "arrived at the turning point of my destiny," as he wrote to a friend, and he had determined to enter a profession. Law and the ministry were out, along with his botched Harvard career. But after reading a book celebrating the achievements of the heroic young Dr. James Jackson, Jr.—who'd left Boston for Paris at twenty-two to study a cholera epidemic, only to die of tuberculosis a year after publishing his pioneering results—Wellington had decided to become a doctor and signed on as apprentice to one of his father's former rivals, Dr. A. L. Peirson of Salem. Welly saw to it that first Elizabeth and then his parents also read the Jackson account, and soon the entire family was in "extacies" with the plan. Wellington hoped to duplicate Jackson's efforts, down to the trip to Paris, but intended to come out of it alive. His sisters would teach him French, his mother would teach him botany, and Dr. Peirson would take care of the rest. For the moment, everyone seemed to have forgotten the trouble Dr. Peabody once had establishing himself in the field. "In Medicine," Welly wrote to his friend, "how easy it is to be eminent, provided one is actuated by the right spirit & gives one's soul to it." He expected to be prepared for the trip to Paris in two years' time. If his family had known, as Welly confided in his friend, that it was the idea of living in Paris that excited him most, they might not have supported the plan so enthusiastically.

In August, Sophia reported from Salem that Wellington was studying anatomy and chemistry with an "earnest purpose" and that "everything seems coming into lovely order in his mind and heart." Sophia had organized her own efforts with uncharacteristic efficiency as well. In her room at Charter Street, she set up a circular worktable with a glass of her mother's flowers at the center, and she arranged her plaster casts of Hercules and Apollo on the mantel. A large adjoining closet would do for her "paint chattels." Elizabeth had borrowed another Allston painting for Sophia to copy.

Jessica and Lorenzo, completed in 1832, pictured a scene from the final act of *The Merchant of Venice* with the eloped lovers seated, their arms intertwined, in the foreground of a moonlit Italian landscape. The painting was one of Allston's smaller works and easily portable, but the painter also considered it "one of his most highly finished." The combination of idealized couple and romantic landscape inspired in Sophia a "state of profound reverence." Allston had told Elizabeth he spent more time on *Jessica and Lorenzo* than on one four

The Peabody house, Charter Street, Salem

times its size; the fact that he delayed sale of the painting—for which he planned to ask $500—so that Sophia could copy it was a sign of his belief that Sophia's was a talent worth fostering.

Sophia began work on the painting in her usual "furor." For several days she was so "thoroughly roused" that she found it difficult to take her customary naps or to sleep at night. Even when she was not painting, she busied herself washing dishes and clearing out closets in the new house, for "I could not get my mind down," she wrote in an exultant letter to Elizabeth. Before long, Sophia had finished the first coloring, satisfied that she had captured the "air of the figures very well."

Sophia also found that she had a "greater facility for painting" now than before she left for Cuba—"even without practicing"—although she was careful not to sound boastful. "Every new stroke was a surprise," she maintained, "for I do not feel that I possess power, excepting so far as faith and hope go." She had learned nothing more of "technacalities or secrets" and continued to paint, she claimed, in a state of "ignorance." Indeed, she professed to feel "a sort of impatience at dwelling upon rules." Instead, it was a "Presence" that could not be "put by," a feeling that "divine harmonies are in my ears—divine hues flit before my eyes, giving life to forms divine," which enabled her to

Jessica and Lorenzo, by Washington Allston, 1832

work again. The notion that she could be driven by an external, sacred force of inspiration was a safer explanation for Sophia of her artistic gifts than admitting she "possess[ed] power": this way she was protected from the risk of personal failure that came with taking responsibility for her own "genius."

Full of the optimism that accompanied such periods of high energy, Sophia wrote Elizabeth that she hoped soon to be painting original work—to "shadow my images forth"—for she would "never be satisfied till I *create* something." She envisioned a literary scene of her own, using her cousin Mary Toppan Pickman as a model, thereby guaranteeing a sale to Mary Top's aunt, Miss Rawlins Pickman. Yet despite the soundness of her plan, Sophia, as always, left herself an out. Acknowledging that she had "never produced anything" yet, and that she believed there was no "great capacity shown in copying—w'h is all I have done," Sophia assured Elizabeth, in a phrase adapted from her Cuba Journal, that "I create—not with hands" but "within."

Sophia did her skills a disservice here: with apparent ease, and with very little technical instruction, she had produced finely realized copies of more than a half-dozen complex paintings. Surely this achievement showed genuine "capacity." Yet the training Sophia did have, gained from close proximity to the signal artists of her day, only served to emphasize her position as novice or acolyte. Perhaps Sophia could not be blamed for trying to persuade herself that the images that now flooded her mind, adding to the works she had already committed to memory for her "inner gallery," might, in the end, be satisfaction enough. The habit of illness, which permitted Sophia to lead a passive, interior life—and to be admired for it—would be hard to break, as long as the alternative was to suffer the conflicts and uncertainty sure to result from admitting to, and then attempting to realize, her ambition to "create" as an artist. Creation—"not with hands" but "within"—would become a theme for Sophia as she looked for ways to justify her lack of output, not only to others, but to herself.

That same August, on what was now the third anniversary of Charlotte Mann's death, both Mary and Elizabeth sent long letters of sympathy to the "unconsoled mourner" Horace Mann—and both invited him to visit. Mary was on a school vacation in Salem—"this primitive town," she called it, in comparison to forward-thinking Boston—where she assured Mann that her mother, who was "never happier than when welcoming our friends," had "seconded" the invitation. Mary imagined walking with Horace Mann after tea on a "leisure" Sunday afternoon, she told him, through "the very grass and trees" that had been the scene of her youthful "aspirings and hopes." He might even stay over, spending the night in Sophia's room while the two sisters bunked in together in an attic bed, if he wished. Elizabeth was still in Lowell, where Lydia's doctor had asked her to perform the grim task of telling Sam Haven that his wife was going to die. The Sunday visit she invited Horace Mann to make was as much for her benefit as for his.

Mann refused both invitations. To Elizabeth, he sent a newsy letter citing "a hundred things to attend to" that prevented him from traveling. To Mary, Mann confessed to having sat down with her "sweetly mournful letter" for over an hour without being able to write a single word. He longed for her letters, he wrote, as "messengers from a happy land" and read them many times over. But, in a typically guarded phrase, Mann explained that he could not "individualize my feelings enough to express them" in reply. He begged Mary to continue sending letters and to understand that his inability to answer them was "the very reason I need to have you write to me most." He could not come to Salem, but he hoped Mary would return to Boston soon. He signed both letters, "Yours very affectionately, Horace Mann."

Both sisters were disappointed. Other women might have resented what was beginning to look like manipulation of their sincerely expressed affection —or at least a callous assumption of the right to receive comfort while giving little in return. But neither Mary nor Elizabeth would stop writing to Horace Mann. In equal measure, they believed in his capacity for greatness; both were willing to put aside feelings of disappointment to support him—and perhaps, in the end, to have a share in his glory. Elizabeth, who, along with other friends concerned about Mann's thin frame and his frequent illnesses, viewed the politician as "a *public treasure* . . . to be watched and guarded and taken care of," feared that excessive grief might kill him; she wanted to keep her friend alive for the sake of the good he might do, and for the gratification of knowing she had helped. For Mary, there was the private hope that one day Horace Mann would permit himself to "individualize" his feelings for her— and discover that love was among them.

Horace Mann's refusal did not leave so big a gap in Elizabeth's life as in Mary's. Energized by the new intellectual friendships she was making in Boston and the ideas she gained from teaching in Alcott's school, Elizabeth began to feel for the first time in many years that her talents might find a forum. She had still not been able to persuade Sophia to publish any of the "theosophy" from her Cuba Journal. Instead Elizabeth produced a Transcendentalist manifesto of her own during the summer of 1835. *Record of a School,* the book she published based on her transcripts of Alcott's dialogues with his students at the Temple School during 1834 and 1835, turned out to be the movement's opening salvo.

Elizabeth's *Record of a School* ushered in a year that would later be recognized as the Transcendentalists' "annus mirabilis," in which the first declarations in book form were issued by the movement's leaders, from George Ripley's *Discourses on the Philosophy of Religion* to Orestes Brownson's *New Views of Christianity, Society, and the Church,* and crowned with Emerson's *Nature,* which appeared in September 1836. Elizabeth's was not just the first, but also the most candid of these attempts to lay the groundwork of Transcendental spirituality: to prove, as Emerson succinctly phrased it, "we are born believing." This notion was radical, even dangerous, at a time when most New Englanders still accepted the Calvinist doctrine of innate depravity—"we are born sinners"—and looked to their church leaders to set the terms of belief.

If faith originated in the individual soul, as the Transcendentalists argued, was there a need for organized religion? Was Christianity itself under attack? In the background of these fundamentally spiritual questions, giving them urgency, lay frightening new political realities as well. In September 1834, as the Temple School opened its doors, an anti-Catholic mob burned down the Ursuline Convent across the river in Charlestown; a month later, the abolitionist William Lloyd Garrison was attacked, his clothes torn from his body, and dragged across Boston Common in a noose by another angry mob, nearly losing his life. Elizabeth Peabody and Bronson Alcott hoped to counter the ominous trend toward mobocracy—the Reverend Channing's subject in his first major antislavery sermon, delivered in response to these incidents—with their own benign experiment in educating young souls; yet their project would come to be interpreted by outsiders as another kind of attack on the social order.

Record of a School was no slight book of pedagogy; Elizabeth's aim was to diagram the unfolding of the human soul. In the Temple School, as described in Elizabeth's *Record*, children were viewed as possessing an intuition of God and goodness that their teachers helped them to recognize and cultivate. Under Alcott's guidance, the class discussed the "innocence" of childhood as a "positive condition," one that "comprehends all the instincts and feelings which naturally tend to good, such as humility, self-forgetfulness, love, trust, &c." They learned what must have seemed at first a topsy-turvy notion to many of the children, that the "true method of self-cultivation is to retain these feelings or return to the childish state and reproduce them." This was Wordsworth in prose: a more audacious version of the Saturday-morning classroom discussions that had caused Elizabeth so much trouble in Brookline ten years earlier.

In the Temple School, the imagination was "called into life." Readers of Elizabeth's *Record* could follow Alcott's discourse on "the inward truth" as "the first truth," as it led his students to consider the artist who crafted the bust of Shakespeare on display in the classroom. "Did that bust of Shakespeare exist really in a mind, before it existed out of a mind?" one child asked. The resulting conversation on artists and creativity brought about a group discovery of "the advantage of having an imagination." Even Mary, increasingly cool to her older sister's enthusiasms, found herself "extremely interested" in the Temple School, where she was teaching in July as Elizabeth's *Record* went to press. What Mary called the "steam-engine system" of cramming students' minds with facts and rules to be tested in daily recitations "is entirely laid aside in this school," she wrote to Miss Rawlins Pickman in Salem. Alcott's aim was instead to "cultivate the heart, and to bring out from the child's own mind the principles which are to govern his character." Judging from the well-behaved, thoughtfully engaged children she taught each day, Mary felt he had succeeded.

One of the best descriptions of the Temple School came from the English political observer Harriet Martineau, who had seen it in operation during its first winter. Martineau ultimately dismissed the school as faddish, but not before summarizing the progressive theory Alcott and Peabody espoused in *Record of a School*, along with the reasons it so appealed to the Transcendentalists. Bronson Alcott "presupposes his little pupils possessed of all truth, in philosophy and morals," Martineau wrote in her 1837 *Society in America*, "and that his business is to bring it out into expression; to help the outward life to conform to the inner light; and, especially, to learn of these enlightened babes, with all humility." She then took Alcott to task for the "mischief" he was doing the children by "pampering their imaginations" and "over-stimulating the[ir] consciences." That a writer as clear-eyed and prescient as Martineau— she also wrote of the "political non-existence of women" and the "apathy" of American voters—could not appreciate the Temple School experiment was a testament to its radical program.

To those ready to hear its message, however, *Record of a School* appeared as welcome evidence of spiritual truths. Waldo Emerson, who had already praised the book in manuscript, wrote Elizabeth of the "pleasure & hope the Rec. of a School has given me," when he read it in final form during August 1835, the month before his wedding to Lydia Jackson. He called it "the only book of facts I ever read" that was as "engaging" as a Maria Edgeworth novel—a line that Elizabeth grew fond of quoting in letters to family and friends. And he recommended it as a "beautiful book . . . certain true & pleasant" to his brother William and sister-in-law Susan, who had recently become parents, for use as a child-rearing manual.

How much of *Record of a School* was Elizabeth's and how much Alcott's? Undeniably, these dialogues were Alcott's—recorded, amplified, and explained by Elizabeth, who also occasionally offered points of disagreement. This mélange of reporting and analysis proved to be an ideal format for Elizabeth, who, like Sophia as a painter, struggled with internal obstacles when attempting to "create" on her own. Elizabeth was far more prolific than Sophia. Her early translations of La Motte-Fouqué and de Gérando had been rehearsals of the process, like Sophia's copies of Doughty, Harding, and Allston paintings. Since then she had written at every possible opportunity: essays for prize competitions, articles for newspapers and magazines when she found a sympathetic editor, books of her own. But Elizabeth's original work rarely achieved the ease of expression that flowed from what she called "my long-tongued pen" in her private letters and journals. When she wrote for publication, her style was labored, overly referential, and at times impenetrably abstract, as if she felt a need to bring all of her thinking and learning to bear at once. Elizabeth's essays on the Hebrew scriptures for the *Christian Examiner*, in which she had promoted "the social principle," suffered from this flaw as well. When, to Elizabeth's dismay, the editor Andrews Norton cut off the six-essay series after just three installments, preventing her publication of "the word *transcendentalism*," few readers had taken note of the radical ideas the articles contained and that had compelled the increasingly reactionary Norton to silence her. Elizabeth succeeded at last with *Record of a School* because she was performing a literary version of what she was beginning to recognize as her vocation in life: to nurture and promote the men she admired, helping them to achieve a greater range of action than she could ever hope to attain as a woman.

Elizabeth didn't receive the same recognition from *Record of a School* that she would have if it had been *her* school, *her* theory. But the men whose minds she hoped to capture would not have paid attention to a woman's book about a girls' school. And she might never have had the self-assurance to write such a book about a school of her own. Playing the role of facilitator—or "Recorder," as she referred to herself in later editions—freed Elizabeth first to produce and then to promote the book more vigorously than she ever had one of her own, without appearing unfeminine or immodest in character, an aspect of her reputation that she continued to care about even as she habitually disregarded the niceties of dress.

To his credit, Alcott, who had not written a single word of it, viewed *Record of a School* from the start as Elizabeth's book. He knew the Temple School would not have existed without Elizabeth; his growing reputation relied almost solely on her organizational powers, and it would spread further still as a result of the influence she wielded in bringing her book to press. The publisher Elizabeth found for *Record of a School* was James Munroe, the same one Emerson would later use for *Nature* and his groundbreaking "American Scholar" and "Divinity School" addresses.

In June 1835, as Alcott looked over the proofs of *Record of a School* while Elizabeth was away in Lowell nursing Lydia Haven, he wrote a letter expressing his gratitude for the fruits of their collaboration. "How much life you can breathe into me from your sympathy in my pursuits and purposes," he told Elizabeth. "I know not that I have another to whom I can truly apply the name of friend as yourself." Joining in the spirit of mutual admiration, Elizabeth wrote back commending Alcott's "genius for education" and admitting, "I am vain enough to say, that you are the only one I ever saw who, I soberly thought, surpassed my gift in . . . this divinest of all arts." She was "delighted" by Alcott's urgent request that she return to board at his house, where, he had written, "we quiet folk need your assistance to help us to some excitement and set us to talking." Elizabeth was committed to spending the summer in Lowell, but her presence was felt with the Alcotts in Boston nonetheless. Within a week, she learned, a third Alcott daughter was born, joining four-year-old Anna and two-year-old Louisa May. The girl who would one day become famous as "Beth" in her older sister's novel *Little Women* started life with the name her father gave her to honor his friend: Elizabeth Peabody Alcott.

At the end of the summer, the first full year of the Temple School's operation, the pupils staged a festival to thank their teachers. There were "flowers & fruits—as well as conversations—& wreaths of flowers as crowns"; Mary and Elizabeth received gold pencil cases, with their names inscribed on them; Bronson Alcott a handsome edition of Milton's poetry. Buoyed by the school's evident success, along with Emerson's high opinion of her book, Elizabeth sent a copy of *Record of a School* to Wordsworth in early September, with a letter drawing his attention to a dialogue sparked by six-year-old Josiah Quincy's response to a classroom reading of the poet's "Intimations of Immortality." "I wish you could have seen," Elizabeth wrote of the assembled children, how "the very sound of wakening nature seemed to breathe from their lit-up faces."

This letter was the third that Elizabeth had sent to Wordsworth. The last had been more than six years ago, in 1829: a confessional one in which she had been forced to decline the poet's invitation to visit Dove Cottage. Elizabeth had written then of the "young men come down from our back woods . . . having conversed alone with the powers of nature . . . to fill our first rank of society." By way of introduction now, she recalled that young "American girl, to whom you were kind enough once to write." Much had changed for Elizabeth since then. Now, in September 1835, she was writing as a thirty-one-year-old woman who could employ "a reputable bookseller of our city" to deliver to the poet her own account of a backwoods genius—one she had helped to create. Wordsworth was one of four European literary celebrities to whom Elizabeth requested delivery of *Record of a School*. The other copies were directed to Maria Edgeworth in England, and in France to Baron de Gérando and Madame Necker de Saussure, the biographer and cousin of Elizabeth's girlhood heroine, Madame de Staël.

The Temple School had become the showplace of liberal Boston in little over a year, its green velvet visitors' couch regularly occupied by the likes of the Reverend William Ellery Channing, Harriet Martineau, and Waldo Emerson. Just as quickly, it all unraveled—and with it the "spiritual intellectual sympathy" between Elizabeth Peabody and Bronson Alcott.

Elizabeth moved back to Boston in the fall of 1835 to share rooms with Mary at Mrs. Vinton's, where she hoped to gather a school of their own. The two women simply could not afford to continue volunteering their time at Temple School. Mary would give the plan six months, during which the sisters would share duties as Alcott's assistant. To make ends meet, Mary would offer private lessons in German and Spanish, and Elizabeth would continue her historical classes. If no school materialized, Mary would retreat to Salem. Almost immediately, the sisters' hopes of subsisting on the proceeds from *Record of a School* were dashed when a warehouse fire destroyed the six hundred remaining copies of the first printing of one thousand in October, along with the remaining stock of Elizabeth's earlier translation of de Gérando's *Visitor of the Poor*. Elizabeth quickly readied another edition for the printer, with a new, comprehensive "Explanatory Preface," but it would not be out until January 1836.

At the same time, Elizabeth began to entertain serious doubts about Alcott

The Temple School, interior, drawing by Francis Graeter

and some of his more extreme classroom methods. As *Record of a School* caught on with the reading public, Alcott let the favorable publicity go to his head, even as Elizabeth became concerned that the children might suffer from "being talked about by the whole city." While Elizabeth was still hoping to sell out her new edition of *Record*, Alcott started planning a second book of dialogues—*Conversations with Children on the Gospels*, he would call it—in which he insisted on printing the pupils' names. Elizabeth worried that Alcott was manipulating the children for his own ends at a vulnerable time in their lives; she didn't like the way he spoke to them of their "superiority to others" in a self-serving fashion, taking credit for the progress that she believed, in accordance with the school's stated principles, was their own achievement. More fundamentally, she began to view the self-control the children exhibited in class at Alcott's urging as unnatural, his method of achieving it suspect.

One of Alcott's favorite devices was to actively invite disobedience in his pupils. While few children had the nerve to accept his offers to sled on Boston Common in winter or to leave their seats for a glass of water in summer, rather than stay in the classroom circle to hear his stories and engage in discussion—some did. Those few were swiftly punished in a uniquely Alcottian manner that had always disturbed Elizabeth. They were excluded, sometimes sent out of the room or required to sit silently with their backs turned to Alcott and their classmates even if they changed their minds before misbehaving. Alcott believed his style of discipline gave children a visceral experience of what it meant to lose God's love and would teach them not to turn away from spiritual sustenance in the future. Elizabeth argued the opposite: that "all cultivation should be directed to give positiveness . . . to all kinds of good." Tempting students to stray and then shaming them for falling into the trap was simply wrong. Elizabeth had hoped Alcott would manage to persuade her otherwise, she wrote to him during the fall term of 1835, but "a year's observation of your practice has not convinced me, and my own opinion and feeling have only grown more strong."

Alcott had never liked it when Elizabeth disagreed with him. On one such occasion, he had recorded with some pique in his diary his perception that Elizabeth was "becoming offensively assertive." When Bronson Alcott wasn't directly benefiting from the sympathy of his one true friend, he was inclined to find "too much of the man and too little of the woman in her familiarity and freedom." Still, in the fall of 1835, he managed to ignore her dissent; Alcott was enjoying his first stay in Concord with Waldo Emerson, the direct result of Elizabeth's efforts on his behalf. In March 1836, when Mary finally moved back to Salem, where a small class of girls awaited her, Alcott pressed Elizabeth to join his family again in a new, larger boarding house on Front Street (now Harrison Avenue), in a semirural neighborhood south of the Common. Alcott had rented the "mansion," as he called it, on the assumption that the Temple School would flourish economically now that its philosophical underpinnings had been secured through the publication of *Record of a School.* He offered Elizabeth her own room as compensation for the many hours she had given voluntarily to the school and to codifying his philosophy.

Elizabeth accepted with some trepidation. During the months with Mary at Mrs. Vinton's, she had begun to realize that Bronson's intransigence was more than matched by his wife's emotional "impetuosity." After a scene in which Abby Alcott had crossed town to pay Elizabeth a visit, burst into Mrs. Vinton's parlor interrupting conversation to inveigh against Harriet Martineau, and left again "still speaking" to herself, Elizabeth had written to Mary, "I think it will be more comfortable to live on the top of a whirlwind than to live with her." The spacious quarters at 26 Front Street would prove too small to contain the coming storm.

The month of April started off well enough. The Alcotts awarded Elizabeth a large upstairs room with a view through trees and across the mudflats of Boston Harbor's South Cove (rapidly being filled in to become a railway terminus) to the low hills of Dorchester Heights. She furnished it with rugs, vases, and oil paintings that the Parks had been unable to sell at Goodrich's, a desk and bookcase belonging to the Alcotts, a writing table and couch of her own, and a pretty stove at the fireplace with brasses "kept in the most exemplary brightness." Best of all were two "very large deep closets" into which Elizabeth had disposed "all my goods & chattels . . . in an order that would surprise you," she wrote to her brother George. "You cannot think what luxury my life now is," she gloated. Once the Alcott family had settled in, with their own old Franklin stove and borrowed silver and crockery, Elizabeth thought it "really delightful to find ourselves in a small family by ourselves." She spent an entire afternoon playing happily with her ten-month-old "namesake."

In a journal purchased especially to mark the change, Elizabeth recorded her vow to start a "new era of things." An encouraging review of *Record of a School* by the novelist Catharine Maria Sedgwick, which appeared as the lead article in the February issue of the popular New York City magazine *The Knickerbocker,* had singled out "Miss Peabody" for praise as "evidently a woman of genius." Elizabeth was determined now to make better use of her own talents. She cut back her hours at the Temple School to afternoon Latin classes and one morning of recording each week: she planned to "ply the pen for bread and butter" and to commit herself "to a more regular prosecution of study" than she had managed since beginning to teach school in Lancaster as a teenager. On behalf of her new friend Margaret Fuller and herself, Elizabeth approached Park Benjamin, editor of the *American Monthly,* who "seems really desirous to help . . . in making our thoughts known," Elizabeth reported to Mary. She consulted Waldo Emerson on her "style of writing" and accepted his criticism that her "faults . . . chiefly arose from undisrupted exuberance," resulting in a "hurry of ideas & images." Emerson's advice to pursue "quiet study—& all calm influences" echoed her own resolve, and he recommended that she adopt his own method of setting down ideas in notebooks just as they came to her, in no particular order. Afterward she could "run a heading of subjects over the top" so that later, "when I wanted to make up an article— *there* were all my thoughts *ready.*"

Still, Elizabeth had trouble restraining herself. Now that her new room in the Alcott mansion allowed her "complete power to withdraw . . . at any time into absolute solitude," she found that "I do not get tired with ever so much labor." Although she worried that her increasing fondness for being "alone— absolutely alone" contradicted "my principle of the social sympathy," she was pleased with the results. By May, she had already completed a lengthy panegyric to Washington Allston and published it in the *American Monthly,* winning Allston's gratitude in the bargain.

But increasingly Elizabeth used her new journal to register her frustration with Bronson Alcott. After less than a week they had argued at dinner over Sylvester Graham's dietary lectures. Alcott considered Graham to have proved that the medical profession—indeed, "every profession"—was "a greater evil than good," and he declared Graham's advocacy of a vegetarian diet with whole-wheat "Graham" flour as its staple, of equal merit with the cause of abolition. When Elizabeth objected, Alcott only grew more vehement, unable as always, she wrote afterward in her journal, "to take *tit* for *tat.*" Elizabeth trudged upstairs to her room, wondering how she would manage in the future to "sit silent under this wholesale abuse of whatever has become the order of society." She considered herself "very little of a conservative—& exceedingly trustful of the Future." But she believed that in Alcott's case, "envy & misanthropy have crept into his heart—under the guise of ardour to reform." Three days later, Elizabeth asked herself whether, in an effort to avoid becoming "old maidish—inflexible—& hard," she had too frequently sacrificed her own interests to others'. She planned to "sit down & think out where I ought to have drawn the line."

For a time, in the aftermath of each spat, the two would arrive at a "treaty of peace," or at least agree to engage in "amicable combat." Alcott's own journals make no mention of the quarrels—only of "Miss Peabody" taking him to discuss Coleridge with Washington Allston in Cambridge, or to hear Waldo Emerson preach one of his last sermons in Lexington. Elizabeth, however, recorded her own determination to "put a smiling countenance upon any kind of a heart," and for a while her efforts paid off. At the end of May, when Alcott celebrated the arrival of spring weather with a ceremonial baptism of his three daughters in the parlor at Front Street, Elizabeth was the only friend in attendance to be honored with a namesake. When she told Horace Mann of the event and he "made himself merry with the rite of baptism," Elizabeth defended Alcott. He had been in his element that day, invoking the "Divine Unity" and discoursing on "the significant imagery of Names"; Elizabeth herself approved the ceremony as a means of "awakening sentiments in Parents." In the coming weeks, she even considered enrolling Lydia Haven's young son, Foster, in the Temple School and bringing him to board with the Alcotts as her special ward; five-year-old Foster was now a half-orphan, after his mother's death in early spring.

The trouble really started in midsummer when Elizabeth and Bronson began to tussle over the new volume, *Conversations with Children on the Gospels*. This time Alcott wanted more control. Elizabeth stayed up till 1:00 some nights copying over the rough transcript she had scribbled during class that morning—only to have Alcott take up her pages the next day and alter the dialogues to suit his own purposes. He told Elizabeth he wanted to "have the book a perfect one"; Elizabeth was appalled that "the truth might be sacrificed" to Alcott's ego. Elizabeth confided her increasing distress in a series of letters to Mary, who now freely offered her own critique. Mary had seen Alcott "lead the minds of his scholars" and "heard them questioned out of their opinions" by their teacher "more than once." She believed that "these faults of Mr. A's have grown upon him very much," affecting his "whole manner." In Mary's opinion, no doubt influenced by her veneration of the excessively self-abnegating Horace Mann, there was "*one* essential element of true greatness" that

Alcott lacked: "and that is modesty." Elizabeth had gone on far too long "sacrificing your own comfort for his convenience"—teaching for no pay, recording his dialogues for posterity, and now putting up with a "perfectly harrowing" daily life for the sake of keeping the whole quixotic enterprise afloat.

Mary advised Elizabeth to refuse to have anything to do with the new volume "unless it can be a true record." But Elizabeth found it difficult to extricate herself. Mary proposed trading places with Elizabeth again, offering to "adopt any measures" that would "succeed in getting you out of Mr. A's school." With her own school blossoming, however, Mary couldn't leave Salem, and in early July she sent Sophia instead, on the pretext of sketching illustrations for Alcott's *Conversations*. Mary might have expected that Sophia would fall under Alcott's spell. Sophia began to attend school every morning, keeping the record in Elizabeth's place and working on line drawings of the classroom in the style of Flaxman. She even joined the pupils in some of their assignments, composing an allegory, which Alcott declared "a beautiful thing." Now it was Sophia he favored with remarks on their "similarity of temperament and of taste" and their essential "sympathy of spirits."

Elizabeth was too exasperated to care. But when she read over the dialogues Sophia had recorded and discovered that one of them was a frank conversation about conception—in which young Josiah Quincy had volunteered that "the formation of the body" was the result of "the naughtiness of other people"—she was aghast. While Elizabeth privately believed it was "impossible to keep children ignorant" of the facts of life, and it was better for teachers and parents to "lead their imaginations" than to "leave them to be directed by idle" fancy, she felt it was crucial to delete these passages from the published volume. No reader could be expected to understand the innocent spirit in which the questions were raised. For days she argued with Alcott, who now took up the banner of veracity, and with Sophia, who defended Alcott's benign intentions. Making quiet inquiries, Elizabeth learned that several of the Temple School families—those with daughters in the class—were considering withdrawing their children after hearing of the classroom talk. How much worse would it be when the book was in print? The whole project—book, school, reform of the human soul—would be ruined. But Alcott would not heed her warnings.

By the end of July, instead of "commencing a life of study," as she had planned back in April, Elizabeth found herself scrambling to salvage her own reputation by inserting notes in Alcott's text that Mary warned her he would very likely leave out. Everyone knew Elizabeth was the recorder, and unless she indicated otherwise, she would be assumed to "agree in all his measures." Elizabeth hoped that by dropping in comments such as "the Recorder omitted Josiah's answer in this place," the passages Alcott insisted on including would be "entirely disconnected from *me*." Yet after all Elizabeth had told her, Mary did not trust Alcott to let the book "be honestly printed." Mary advised Elizabeth to take a more dramatic step and quit copying Alcott's dialogues for the printer, in order to "free yourself from any participation in the course or the consequences of Mr. A's mistaken views." Blocking publication of the *Conversations* in this way might be the best possible thing for Bronson Alcott as well, Mary argued. Then he could turn his attention to making a success of his school on its own merits, and to paying his bills. At the very least, the scandal would be limited to the small amount of damage already done. In an effort to underline the importance of making this decision, Mary told Elizabeth she was sure that if she consulted Horace Mann, he would counsel her to do the same.

Mary begged Elizabeth to "come away from the Alcotts." She could move back home to Salem—although Mary doubted she would be happy there. No one could dispute their mother's early assessment that Elizabeth, with her questing intelligence and reformer's zeal, was "before the age in Salem." Elizabeth had, in fact, been relieved to cede Salem to Mary, where she imagined her younger sister finally "unfolding your faculties and applying your talents —unshadowed by" herself, "the queen of *Mal-apros-pos*." Mary offered to pay Elizabeth's board in Concord near the Emersons, or in Groton, near Margaret Fuller, where Elizabeth might "take a class of country young ladies" and "write your thoughts . . . and give yourself a chance to have a little tranquillity— there you will see the grass grow, and the brooks run & hear the wind in the trees." By now, both sisters had come to suspect Alcott's honesty. But neither could have predicted the next disaster.

"Don't you think that Mrs. Alcott came into my room & looked over my letters from you & found your last letter to me," an astonished Elizabeth wrote to Mary in late July, "& carried it to Mr Alcott—& *they have read them*." Elizabeth had been out of the house when the deed was done. The Alcotts were waiting to blast her when she returned. Abby Alcott prophesied "'eternal' damnation for what she calls the 'greatest crime' she ever knew of"—that of writing and receiving letters critical of her husband. Both Bronson and Abby Alcott considered the evidence of subversion they had turned up in the letters to have trumped any crime they committed in opening and reading Elizabeth's private mail. Mary's reference to Horace Mann had convinced them that Elizabeth had "talked to Mr M about them," along with "all the rest of my acquaintances." Neither Abby nor Bronson could be persuaded otherwise —even when Elizabeth protested that these were *Mary's* letters, not Elizabeth's, *Mary's* thoughts, not hers. "Words cannot describe just how tremendous it all is," Elizabeth wrote in despair. Worse, to Elizabeth's amazement, Sophia took the Alcotts' side, volunteering the information that *she* had received letters from Elizabeth critical of Bronson Alcott as well.

At last Elizabeth was forced to recognize the impossibility of living in a house with "people who would do such things." The next morning she composed a letter to Bronson Alcott stating that "our relations were at an end" and started packing her belongings. She would move back to Salem after all. To Mary, she admitted that the decision left her feeling more calm than she had for many months. But Sophia had still not come around. Elizabeth concluded, morosely, that at least "Sophia is compensated for any pain of thinking ill of me—by being able to keep up her adoration of Mr. Alcott."

As for Bronson Alcott, he noted simply in his journal on August 1, 1836: "Miss Peabody left me today for Salem. She will not resume her connections with the school after the holidays." He continued to solicit illustrations from Sophia, who—after a period of illness provoked by the "fatigues and excitements of her visit"—continued to provide them. In late fall, Margaret Fuller arrived to replace Elizabeth as assistant and recorder. Quite likely Alcott never paid Fuller either; she stayed only four months, content to have gained "many valuable thoughts." Meanwhile, Abby Alcott crossed out her youngest daughter's middle name in the family register, substituting one drawn from her own ancestry. Despite the jubilant baptism of May 1836, at which Bronson Alcott had celebrated "the larger synthesis of spirits," one-year-old Elizabeth Peabody Alcott would henceforth be known as Elizabeth Sewall Alcott.

Elizabeth never told anyone but Mary the facts of the "late sudden rupture" with Alcott. In her view, the sin of opening other people's mail was far more damning than talking about sex with children; the incident was too ugly to mention. When *Conversations with Children on the Gospels* finally appeared, running to two volumes in Alcott's unexpurgated version, and scandal broke out as Elizabeth had predicted, people assumed the once loyal partners had separated over the disputed passages, and she let them. Within weeks of the publication of the first volume of *Conversations* in December 1836, Alcott was assailed in the Boston press as "an ignorant and presuming charlatan," either "insane or half-witted," and his book condemned as "one third absurd, one third blasphemous, and one third obscene." The last of these slurs came from none other than Harvard's professor emeritus of divinity Andrews Norton, who was fast earning himself the nickname "Pope Andrews." Elizabeth could not have been surprised after Norton's censorship of her 1834 essay series interpreting the Hebrew scriptures. The man who over a decade ago had offered Elizabeth the run of his Cambridge library was now an old-guard Unitarian whose reputation as an entrenched reactionary would be secured when he attacked Ralph Waldo Emerson's "Divinity School Address" with equal gusto the following year.

And all because of the "physiological" passages Alcott had refused to delete. For the most part, the critique of Alcott's *Conversations* did not even take up the fundamentals of his "spiritual philosophy." Perhaps Alcott's critics hoped to quickly rid Boston of this "modern infidelity"—the phrase increasingly adopted by orthodox Trinitarians and conservative Unitarians alike to denounce the Transcendentalists—by branding his ideas "indecent and obscene." It would not be so easy: there were larger and less yielding targets than Bronson Alcott already on the horizon.

By the spring of 1837, the Temple School had all but dissolved. Alcott continued to teach a handful of pupils for one more year in a basement room of the Masonic Temple, selling his precious library of schoolbooks to cover the rent. After that, Alcott never taught school again; for the next five years, he was unable to find work of any kind in New England. Eventually his few loyal supporters, Waldo Emerson chief among them, took up a collection and sent him to England for a year of study. Inexplicably to almost everyone, Elizabeth remained one of Alcott's most faithful public champions. In a letter to the *Christian Register,* written at the height of the controversy, when linking herself with Alcott could only do her own reputation further harm, Elizabeth nonetheless spoke up on behalf of both "Mr. Alcott's Book and School." At the heart of Alcott's reform impulse, she wrote, was the laudable urge to reject "tyrannical custom, and an arbitrary imposition of the adult mind upon the young mind" and instead to create an environment for learning in which "the imagination leads the understanding." Although she would later admit privately that "there [was] a great deal of nonsense about Mr Alcott all along," Elizabeth would always insist, as she wrote to Horace Mann a year after the blowup, that there was "a current of the true method—an infusion of Truth" in Alcott's teachings, which "neutralizes the error."

Of course she was right: Peabody and Alcott had founded and run—if only for three years—America's first open school. Their notion that good teaching was a matter of cultivating each student's innate gifts would become the hallmark of progressive education in America for the next two centuries. At the time, however, Elizabeth Peabody simply refused to accept the possibility that she had backed the wrong genius.

⮕ 26 ⮔

Little Waldo, Jones Very,
and the "Divinity School Address"

ELIZABETH WAS SORELY TEMPTED TO CATALOGUE HER TRIALS WITH
Bronson Alcott one afternoon, while visiting the Emersons in Concord during
November 1836. Waldo was having some fun at Alcott's expense—laughing
over a report of Bronson's most recent birthday fete, for which the teacher had
composed a celebratory ode for his students to recite. Elizabeth wrote afterward in her journal that Waldo had "seemed infinitely entertained" with the
notion of a man who "gets up a festival in his own honor & writes the glori-
fication himself." But she bit her tongue and simply enjoyed hearing her erst-
while hero—whom Emerson continued to regard as "a good and guileless
man"—taken down a peg.

As Elizabeth listened to Emerson poke gentle fun at Alcott—"a man of
genius but with very few talents"—she was reminded of the reason she so enjoyed being in Waldo Emerson's company: his surprising mix of keen attentiveness and sympathetic toleration for idiosyncrasy. She had discovered as
early as her first overnight visit to Concord, in the company of Harriet Martineau the previous January, that talking to Waldo Emerson "makes me feel
free." His indisputably powerful influence somehow never left her feeling
"constrained." Instead, she wrote in her journal, "he responds with entire fulness to what ever truth I utter" and "feels my infinite capacity just as I do
myself." Quite likely Alcott felt the same benign acceptance from Waldo Emerson when they were together, the reassuring certainty that, in Elizabeth's description, "he will not withdraw the light of his mind & the genial warmth of
his kindness . . . because I make mistakes, occasionally offend his taste, or jar
with his opinions." After all, despite his awareness of Alcott's shortcomings,

Emerson had made sure that Bronson joined the newly formed Transcendental Club, whose all-male membership at the outset was otherwise exclusively drawn from the dissenting Unitarian clergy.

No place else but at the large white Emerson house on the Cambridge Turnpike did Elizabeth feel so sure of achieving an "inspiring communion"— a phrase full of meaning for a woman who had actually preceded her host in rejecting the ritual of communion in church. So Elizabeth had come to Concord in November 1836 to lick her wounds. Back home in Salem after the break with Alcott, she had thrown her energies into editing a new magazine, *The Family School.* In the first issue, published on September 1, she announced her hope that the journal would become "a weekly visitor to the domestic fireside, as a friend to the mother in her duties; an intelligent counsellor to her elder daughters in their moral and intellectual self-culture . . . and a not unwelcome play-fellow to boys and girls." This publication was the first to which she had signed her full name, "Elizabeth Palmer Peabody," and she did the same in advertisements for what was at the time a remarkably ambitious venture for a woman. Perhaps she had rushed into the project too soon, however, or possibly a family magazine with a Transcendental flavor was doomed to fail when launched from "primitive" Salem. Whatever the reason, by November, after two issues filled chiefly with compositions by her mother, sisters, and herself, and an occasional poem by Washington Allston or James Freeman Clarke, Elizabeth had to acknowledge that there were not enough subscribers to continue.

Despite the united front the women of the Peabody family presented in *The Family School*, there had been strains once Elizabeth returned home, as Mary had foreseen. Even though Mary had supported Elizabeth through the summer of her struggle with Alcott, Mary had simultaneously accused Elizabeth of "punish[ing] me" by withholding details of her ongoing Sunday visits with Horace Mann. Mary had counted on Elizabeth's letters as "the only way in which I expected to be at all compensated for never seeing him"; missing out on Mann's weekly visits felt to Mary like "an entire loss—an utter *blank.*" But when Elizabeth obliged by letting Mary know that Mann had allowed her to soothe his nerves by combing his hair while he talked for much of the evening, Mary may have regretted pressing for details. Now, in the aftermath of the Front Street fiasco, into which the Alcotts had insisted on dragging Horace Mann's name, Mary worried intensely that Elizabeth would mention the episode to Mann, who might then stop writing to her altogether. "I cannot but hope you will say nothing to cut off entirely the only remnant of communication I have with him," she warned Elizabeth.

For her part, once the sisters were living together again, Elizabeth was irritated to discover the extent to which Mary was carrying on a "confidential

The Emerson House, Concord

correspondence" with Horace Mann and would not share her private letters to or from their mutual friend. Elizabeth had always maintained that "I do not wish to be preferred," as she had once written to Mary, and indeed "I am rather better pleased that you should be preferred, as you are certainly preferable." But that did not stop her from longing for the days at Somerset Court and "that happy union which for a time I enjoyed with you & him." Elizabeth wanted to be privy to any news from Horace Mann in Boston, who was now contemplating a move from the Massachusetts Senate to the secretaryship of the state board of education, an institution that his own lobbying efforts on behalf of public education was soon to create. She claimed not to mind that "I do not receive the same free communication that you do," because "I think it is so essential to him to have freedom, and unbounded confidence with some[one]." But Elizabeth still wanted to know "*why* I should be excluded from confidence of the same nature he bestows upon you." And she threatened to ask him directly. Mary knew the answer, or at least one answer: Elizabeth could not be trusted to keep Mann's, or anyone's, confidences secret for long. Although, as in the case of the Alcott debacle, Elizabeth was capable of suppressing her own feelings of hurt and anger, her instinct to help along her friends' private ambitions, or to solve their personal problems, too often led to disclosure.

Elizabeth also continued to clash with Sophia over Alcott. Sophia, she knew, was in regular contact with both Abby and Bronson. As the scandal over *Conversations with Children on the Gospels* raged, Sophia wrote to Abby that "I could not have imagined that those conversations about Birth would not be received with reverence and thanks. I felt my own mind elevated by them." Sophia deplored "the public stupidity" and offered the comforting thought that "new ideas are always received with consternation." Perhaps it was no surprise that Sophia would want to defend the volume, in which several of her own illustrations saw print for the first time—albeit without attribution. More fundamentally, however, the two sisters had never quite recovered from an old quarrel over Sophia's illness.

Elizabeth wanted to believe that Sophia had achieved a cure in Cuba. The frenetic activity Sophia had boasted of a year earlier, during her early work on *Jessica and Lorenzo,* seemed proof enough that she had. Noticing that Sophia had managed to clean closets when she wasn't painting, Elizabeth suggested she spend a few hours each day tutoring a young Salem girl, in order to secure "a *certain* stipend" of her own. Sophia bristled—and took to her bed for the next several weeks with the migraine that her furious energy had presaged, arguing to Elizabeth that she needed to "reserve all my strength for painting." Working on *Jessica and Lorenzo* "swallows me up completely," she wrote, for "I cannot do any thing with half a heart." Elizabeth responded by flatly accusing her invalid sister of being a "hypochondriac."

"I am not & never was self-indulgent," Sophia shot back. If she were, she would never be out of bed. "My nerves have no shelter now," she wrote in her own defense, and "violent palpitations & syncope whirling of my brain" were her constant enemies when upright. For many years, Sophia explained, she had become accustomed to forcing herself to paint or to socialize, despite the pain that virtually any activity brought her. Even while in Cuba she could have rested far more. "Hours & hours I sat in the hall when I would have given the world to have been on the bed," she wrote, but "I was a guest, & I had no option." Mary's continual urging her to paint had also "haunted the hours of repose I could sneak, & made them uneasy." "The simple truth is," she wrote her oldest sister, "that my physics have laws wh[ich] if transgressed inevitably & always produce suffering"—whether she was doing something she enjoyed, such as painting or engaging in "interesting conversation," or whether she was "set[ting] a chair straight or dust[ing] a table." In short, "*every* emotion whether pleasurable or painful, produces actual & immediate pain."

Elizabeth relented, accepting Sophia's version of her illness, even offering to return home to care for her sister if her case was so serious. But that was not what Sophia wanted. Even if she hadn't rested enough at La Recompensa, Sophia had gained some valuable distance from Elizabeth, the sister who had taken over her spiritual education in childhood, who had provided her with master teachers and masterworks to copy, and to whom Sophia had written on the eve of her departure for Cuba: "There has been nothing to me in the whole range of *human causes* that has [had] so intense and powerful an effect upon me as your mind." Elizabeth, even more than their mother who cared for her daily, had prodded Sophia to live a life beyond what she considered to be her own capabilities—a life different from the one Sophia envisioned for herself.

Sophia took some satisfaction now in telling Elizabeth, "you must take my nature as it is." She would paint or teach or not do either of these in her own time, for "whatever I am about my whole being is in it." Perhaps more than either sister was willing to acknowledge, Elizabeth and Sophia shared a passionate impetuosity. Yet unlike the headlong Elizabeth, Sophia was determined not to give in to it, "not to force the creative power, but wait till it mastered *me*." She insisted, "I cannot drive my muse." Illness was the bar that kept her emotions—and ambitions—in check, making even the practice of art an "intolerable joy." After all, what did she see that Elizabeth had gained from forcing her way into the world? Plenty of dashed hopes, the ambivalent regard of a half-dozen men of promise, and, finally, a retreat to a family that was inclined to resent her interference. Sophia held her ground.

If Elizabeth continued to doubt the genuine nature of Sophia's illness, she didn't say so. But she was being forced to recognize the seriousness of her brother George's condition. During the winter, when Elizabeth was still in Boston, the Peabody household in Salem had been turned into a "hospital," by Sophia's account. Added to Sophia's recurrent sick "turns" was Nat's alarming fever, lasting more than three weeks, which Wellington, the budding physician, took to be typhus; for a month afterward, Nat had been too weak to come downstairs. Then George, long plagued with digestive ailments, was stricken with the "numb palsy"—an inexplicable weakness in his legs—and had to be installed on a cot in the front parlor. Nat recovered, but George's symptoms persisted, although by spring he was able to walk. He was now in New Orleans, again seeking work in a warmer climate, but Elizabeth despaired that George, "the only hope of the family in a pecuniary point of view," might never fully recover if he could not keep to a strict diet. "I am *sorry* to hear of that exquisite dinner at Henshaws," she wrote sternly to her brother in New Orleans, "you speak of 'fowls—roast beef—ices—madeira—champaign—' not one of which ought to go into your stomach." The Peabody family had yet to discover that George was suffering from an advancing case of tuberculosis that had already attacked his gut and now was lodged in his spine—both common sites of infection, along with the lungs, for what was then New England's most deadly disease.

At least there had been some signs of self-sufficiency in her other brothers, Elizabeth tried hard to believe. Nat's first child—a daughter named Ellen Elizabeth—was born in the spring of 1836, and the new small family had settled into the Peabody house. But Nat, whose faltering South Salem store had failed during his illness, was in the process of transferring his stock to a shop in South Boston, where he promised to move his wife and daughter soon. Wellington had already left Salem for Boston, shifting his apprenticeship to a Dr. Putnam; the reason for the change turned out to be his secret engagement to an orphaned heiress with a $20,000 legacy in neighboring Charlestown.

Only Elizabeth knew the full facts of that case: Wellington had coaxed her into visiting his sweetheart's legal guardian to attest to her brother's sound character. Even though Elizabeth was "a little afraid" that Mary Boardman's inheritance had "helped the matter along" with Wellington, she obliged; Elizabeth convinced herself that her brother was "really in love" with the "little short modest looking girl," as she wrote to George in New Orleans. When Mary Boardman's guardian allowed Wellington's suit, cautioning him, to Elizabeth's delight, that he "was not to have Mary" until his medical training was complete and "unless he continues to behave well," Elizabeth felt relieved to know that the substantial dowry would permit Wellington to "choose a pleasant place to live & pursue his profession—without going through an initiation of desperate poverty" as their father had. It seemed now that at least one of the Peabody children would marry well.

In August 1836, when she'd quit the Temple School, Elizabeth had instantly received an invitation from Waldo Emerson to spend several weeks in Concord. Lidian Emerson conveyed the message—"he asks me if you would not like to visit us before you decide upon any new arrangement—and in the quiet of our Lethean town—clear your ideas of what you wish to do, or shall be able to undertake." But Elizabeth had put her off, having already made the decision to return to Salem and start her own magazine. It wasn't until November, when she saw *The Family School* failing, that Elizabeth finally accepted the Emersons' offer "to collect and refresh your spirit" as their houseguest. By then, Lidian had given birth to a son, "Little Waldo," and Elizabeth was welcomed as both intellectual companion to Waldo Sr. and nurse to Lidian.

The Emersons themselves had had a difficult year, in which Waldo's favorite younger brother, Charles, died of tuberculosis, the second of the five Emerson brothers to succumb to the disease. As newlyweds, Waldo and Lidian (her first name altered from the more prosaic "Lydia" by her husband) had planned to share their new Concord house with Charles, a lawyer engaged to marry Elizabeth Hoar, the daughter of his mentor, Concord's "Squire" Samuel Rockwood Hoar. After Charles's sudden death in the spring of 1836, the Emersons agreed instead to open their house to friends as often as possible for long visits, to provide the intellectual stimulation that Waldo, at least, craved. Elizabeth,

Ralph Waldo Emerson

as friend to both Lidian and Waldo, had received one of the first invitations.

The left-hand front parlor across the hall from Waldo's study was converted to a guest room, and there Elizabeth settled in for the first of what would be three long vacations with the Emersons over the next three years, each at critical junctures for visitor and hosts as the Transcendentalist controversy, inadvertently touched off in Boston with the Temple School uproar, escalated. From her corner room, Elizabeth looked out toward the passing coaches and heavily laden wagons that traveled the broad turnpike linking Concord to its county seat fifteen miles distant in Cambridge. Behind the house, a brook ran through pastureland over which an easy tramp led to Walden Pond and its woods, placing the house and its ambitious thirty-three-year-old owner in equipoise between the worlds of commerce and nature.

Little wonder that Elizabeth felt, when staying with the Emersons, that "here I am . . . in the center of all things, on ideal ground, around which all actualities revolve."

In 1836, Elizabeth herself was, for a brief moment, on nearly equal footing with her host—a man just one year older than she, who had once declared her his match in the study of Greek. Four years earlier, Emerson had removed himself from a prestigious Boston pulpit to embark on an uncertain career as lecturer and essayist—a move he might never have made without the tragic dashing of his hopes for a family life with his first wife, Ellen, dead of tuberculosis in 1831 after little more than a year of marriage. The legacy he inherited from Ellen had enabled the purchase of his Concord home. Although he'd been to Europe, become friendly with Carlyle and paid his respects to Wordsworth, by the fall of 1836, both Waldo Emerson and Elizabeth Peabody had published just one important book, each with some hesitation. Emerson's *Nature* had come out in September and was an instant success in the Transcendentalist circle. But he had not put his name on the slim volume; in two months he had sold fewer copies than Elizabeth's *Record* in its first months on the market.

Elizabeth might revere Waldo Emerson as an oracle of truth, but Waldo held Elizabeth in high esteem too. Her 1830 translation of de Gérando's *Self-Education* inspired him, and her manuscript translation of the French mystic Guillaume Oegger's *True Messiah* had provided "good things" as well. At this formative time in his life, Waldo Emerson found in Elizabeth Peabody both a woman who knew the ins and outs of the publishing world—she would advise him on dealings with their mutual publisher, James Munroe—and a raconteur with the "authority of a learned professor or high literary celebrity in her talk." For the most part, as Elizabeth had intuited, Waldo was able to disregard the less compelling aspects of her personality that, to a man whose feminine ideal was still the nineteen-year-old invalid bride he had lost to tuberculosis, were inclined to "offend," and accept her as a fellow being of "infinite capacity."

In September 1835, Waldo had married the *"very refined"* Lydia Jackson, another woman of personal wealth, a year older than Waldo, whom many considered to be his intellectual equal. During the year before the Emersons' wedding, Elizabeth had sought out Lydia Jackson for conversation almost as avidly as she'd sought out Lydia's fiancé, finding her to possess "the rare characteristic of genius—inexhaustible originality." Lydia Jackson was also taken with Elizabeth Peabody, writing a month before her wedding that "no two women extant could [talk] more easily than you and myself." But when Elizabeth visited the couple a year later in November 1836, she quickly saw that marriage had changed more than the spelling of her friend's first name. Waldo Emerson may have been a prize catch—"mine own *angel*-man," Lidian called him in an early letter to her sister. Yet becoming the wife of the free-lance philosopher also required "the giving up of an existence she thoroughly enjoyed," as one of the Emerson children later wrote, describing their mother's transformation from self-sufficient intellectual to *genius domi*. The birth of "Little Waldo" on October 30 changed Lidian even more.

When Elizabeth arrived in Concord, Waldo Sr. was holding the three-week-old baby in his arms, marveling at "what a wonderful being a child is. Every part so finished!"—while noting that "I do not feel myself in it as Mr Alcott told me I should." Little Waldo was still an "it" to his father, who might show him off to visitors and speculate on the lessons of parenthood, but would never have to feed the baby or change his infant dresses. Lidian was upstairs in bed, unable to sit up, daunted by the prospect, at thirty-four, of caring for a second very real "him" along with a large household always open to her husband's friends. If Waldo had the ability to make his intellectual companions "feel free," he seemed to have the opposite effect on his new wife. She would recover from this birth and bear three more children in the next eight years, but increasingly Lidian sought refuge in illness and, when well, in an obsessive attention to the details of housekeeping, as her husband's heart remained with his first wife, Ellen, after whom their first daughter, born in 1839, would be named.

For now, Elizabeth traveled easily between Waldo's and Lidian's worlds. The weeks following the birth of a child were commonly ones in which a wife gave herself over to the care and counsel of female friends and family members. Perhaps the distance Elizabeth observed between "Mr. Emerson," as Lidian persisted in calling her husband despite his urging her to use his first name, and "Queenie," the nickname Waldo favored for the increasingly remote woman he had married, was only natural. Elizabeth could not have known, for example, that Lidian had dressed the couple's bedstead in white dimity curtains in anxious anticipation of Little Waldo's birth, only to have her husband demand that she take them down as too ostentatious. Yet Elizabeth did hear, in conversation "over the coals" that first night with Waldo and his mother, Ruth Emerson, who also lived at the house, about the family's continuing sorrow over the lost brother Charles, six months dead. The talk of Charles inspired Mrs. Emerson's disquisition on the virtues of another absent family member, "my dear Ellen," Waldo's first wife, dead now five years: "She was beautiful and as good as [she was] beautiful. Every body loved her." Unlike Horace Mann, who lost his own child bride to consumption just a year after Ellen Emerson died, Waldo had determined to move forward in his personal life; but he had also installed his very different second wife in a household of ghosts.

Elizabeth ate breakfast in the mornings with Ruth Emerson and then took

Lidian Emerson

"my turn" minding the baby while Waldo wrote in his study. Within a few days she was also sleeping with Lidian in her curtainless bed at night, helping care for both mother and child through the midnight hours in ways her husband, apparently, could not. But even though Elizabeth readily fulfilled the duties expected of a female guest and professed continued admiration for the Emersons' marriage—the "reverent husband" and the "Theosophist wife"—she pulled away from Lidian, favoring Waldo's company. It was the late-autumn afternoons and evenings spent in conversation with Waldo Emerson that she had really come for. Lidian showed no signs of jealousy and, indeed, seemed to welcome the diversion for her husband, particularly as Elizabeth's much-needed assistance came along with it. Waldo may have sought the company of his visitors all the more as his wife adopted an increasingly formal reserve.

On walks in the woods, "which are his studio," Elizabeth wrote in her journal, the thirty-three-year-old author of *Nature* found signs of a guiding aesthetic power all around them. "We looked for the Gothic architecture, or rather it showed itself to us," Elizabeth wrote, "the low Saxon Arch, and the painted Gothic window, formed by the naked branches against the sunset sky." They toured the ponds of Concord, ending at Walden, where a breeze ruffled the pond's surface, "losing thereby its own peculiar and transparent beauty," the disappointed Waldo commented, and instead "mimicking the ocean in tiny wavelets." But "I saw how clear the water was," Elizabeth wrote.

On the way back they talked of Margaret Fuller, the younger friend Elizabeth had introduced to Waldo and who had made her first visit to Concord in midsummer. Waldo remarked that Fuller had told him "all the marriages she knew were a mutual degradation." Had she meant to include the Emersons' marriage in that list? Almost certainly, like Elizabeth, Fuller revered both Emersons in these early years and merely sought to engage her newly remarried host in a general discussion. Yet did Waldo's quotation of her comment, made four months before, reveal the direction of his own thoughts? In her midtwenties, and eager for a grand passion of her own, Fuller was closely examining the relations between the men and women of their circle, ready to test their limits, and beginning to form the ideas that would shape her feminist critique, *Woman in the Nineteenth Century*, within a decade.

Salem seemed brighter to Elizabeth on her return from Concord—or perhaps it was the energy she had gained from the opportunity to "catch and rebound . . . Emersonian life" that allowed her to face the winter of 1836 to 1837 with optimism, despite the failure of *The Family School*. Teaching a Sunday school class of teenage girls absorbed her, as she introduced them to concepts like "intuitive reason," which she had discussed with Waldo on their walks in the woods. In turn, Elizabeth became intrigued by the poems of Jones Very, the older brother of one of her students, now a Greek tutor at Harvard studying part-time at the Divinity School. Very had written a somewhat perfunctory hymn for the dedication of the Unitarian North Church's new stone building in Salem the summer before: "O God; On this, our temple, rest thy smile, Till bent with days its tower shall nod." But he also composed Wordsworthian lyrical ballads with titles like "The Boy's Dream" or "The Torn Flower," which spoke of "my heart's mad passion," and he had begun to show an uncanny facility with sonnets—to "Nature" and "The Winter Bird"—several of which had appeared in the *Salem Observer*.

Just twenty-three years old, Jones Very had read Emerson's *Nature* and heard his call: "There are new lands, new men, new thoughts. Let us demand our own works and laws and worship." He had even experienced an epiphany when riding in a train—a "Commodity" of the modern era that Emerson had celebrated, in which "man . . . darts through the country from town to town, like an eagle or a swallow through the air." In August 1837, while traveling north from Boston on the new line to Andover, Very was suddenly overwhelmed by the rapid movement of the train through the rural landscape, and by a "sense of man's power and gifts," he wrote afterward in his journal. A feeling of terror yielded to the conviction that he was being "borne along by a divine engine and undertaking his life-journey." Jones Very returned to Harvard that fall with a new sense of mission—one that would eventually come to alarm the staid Unitarian faculty that supervised his studies and teaching.

That same month, Elizabeth received another invitation to visit the Emersons. The entire household, Lidian wrote, was bustling with preparations for the last day of August when Waldo would give the Phi Beta Kappa oration at Harvard's commencement, an annual event that attracted New England intellectuals from well beyond the circle of Harvard's faculty and students. Horace Mann, now the actively proselytizing secretary of the state board of education, would be there in Cambridge's First Parish Church to hear him, along with Oliver Wendell Holmes, James Russell Lowell, Richard Henry Dana, and U.S. Supreme Court justice Joseph Story. The invitation to speak was a sign of the respect Emerson still retained in the Unitarian establishment, despite his controversial resignation from Boston's Second Church. Since moving to Concord, Emerson had continued to preach on a supply basis when needed in nearby Lexington, and he readily accepted the opportunity to deliver what was expected to be a pious hymn to the virtues of a Harvard education the day after graduation. But his friends and family knew enough to expect something different.

It had been almost a year since Elizabeth's last visit when Lidian wrote in early August inviting her to come to Concord "on the Monday after PBK and remaining with us till duty draws you homeward." Later in the month, however, Lidian revised her invitation, asking Elizabeth instead to come "in the course of a fortnight after Commencement; when I hope to be free to have some good talks with you—and to hear you hold many more with my good lord." The day after Waldo was to be the featured speaker at Harvard, Lidian explained, *she* was "to be honoured with the opportunity of ministering to the earthly comfort of the whole transcendental coterie," who would descend on Concord for a picnic. At Waldo's instigation, Margaret Fuller and several friends planned to crash the party, bringing women into the Transcendental Club's fold for the first time; Fuller had elected the following week for her own Concord vacation, pushing back Elizabeth's till later in the month. Lidian worried, she wrote Elizabeth, that by September she would have fallen so far behind in her "female exercises" that she would never catch up. Between Fuller's visit and Elizabeth's, she planned to scour the house "and peep in at every nook—and order every thing to know its place." Lidian apologized for her scrawl; she was dandling the eight-month-old baby Waldo on her left arm as she wrote.

Elizabeth may have minded being jilted in favor of Margaret Fuller; she may have been sorry to miss the first meeting of the Transcendental Club that included women: the picnic in Concord the day after Emerson's speech turned into an "all-day party," with eighteen at the Emersons' dinner table. She even skipped Waldo's performance at commencement, possibly out of pique—more likely because she couldn't afford to leave Salem twice in the same month. But she heard about it afterward from Horace Mann. Emerson had used the occasion to deliver a speech that simultaneously affronted New England's intellectual establishment and galvanized his freethinking comrades. "The American Scholar," as Emerson titled the speech for a press run of five hundred copies that swiftly sold out, pointedly omitted any acknowledgment of Harvard's role in educating the rising generation. Rather it was an impassioned appeal to the individual man—any man—to "plant himself indomitably on his instincts, and there abide." The speech was a hymn to self-education, to the scholar as a man of action, and an implicit denunciation of life within the academy. Oliver Wendell Holmes would later call it "our intellectual Declaration of Independence."

"I embrace the common, I explore and sit at the feet of the familiar, the low," Waldo announced to a stunned audience gathered to celebrate one of the nation's most exclusive initiation rites. Horace Mann, previously distrustful of Emerson's "ultra idealism," was won over by this down-to-earth, populist Emerson and enjoyed seeing *le tout* Harvard snubbed in this way. Yet he worried afterward that the speech had been "very good—for any body else—but hardly so" for Emerson. According to one history of Transcendentalism, Mann judged the audience correctly: the majority of Emerson's listeners were "seriously offended." But Mann misread the speaker. The ensuing contention seemed to buoy Emerson's spirits. When, three weeks after his Phi Beta Kappa oration, Emerson received an invitation to lecture in Salem, "provided no allusions are made to religious controversy, or other exciting topics," he relished the opportunity to refuse.

On her way to Concord on the weekend following Emerson's address, Elizabeth made sure that she was not left out of the second coed meeting of the Transcendental Club at James Freeman Clarke's house in Newton on September 6. The Transcendental Club, which Emerson had pronounced "dead" the year before after just four gatherings—"People do not receive revelations from their genius, except when alone—never in company," Waldo had told Elizabeth—was thriving now in the days following his "American Scholar" address.

"The congregation of bright youths from all parts," as Elizabeth called it, was swiftly becoming the Transcendentalists' "true forum."

At the Newton meeting, Elizabeth did more listening than talking; yet hers remains the only record of the conversation that day, which ran from "the progress of society" to the "most effective" means of reaching "the minds of people." The group had, almost overnight, transmuted from a collection of disaffected ministers preoccupied with Alcottian abstractions—genius, religion versus morality—to a mixed band of reformers, male and female, ready to preach a cause. There were nine men present—Emerson, Alcott, and George Ripley among them—and three women—Elizabeth Peabody, Margaret Fuller, and Sarah Clarke. Elizabeth managed a friendly conversation with Alcott, and guessed that "he had learned something of people, by the last year's experience ... whatever may be said of his want of sense about some things." Most of all, she was more ready than ever, afterward, to spend time with Waldo Emerson—the man at the forefront of "the newness" whom she considered "not only the most live man I know, but the completest." Elizabeth was even willing now to "yield up my Dr. Channing as second" and admit "Mr. Emerson is a more various oracle."

In Concord on her second long visit, in mid-September 1837, Elizabeth felt impelled to record Emerson's "daily walk and conversation," and she imagined "what a heavenly dream" it would be to write his biography. She rode with Emerson to Lexington on a Sunday, where he delivered a sermon, and they discussed Goethe's *Ganymede* all the way there and back again. She listened to him discourse, with Little Waldo in his arms, on the "beautiful provision" that allows "every man ... his little angel." Watching a son grow up, Emerson theorized, reveals "a part of his own life a man never sees. It is the unconscious projected upon a diagram" for man's understanding. At this assertion, the boy began to clap his hands and crow, and the philosopher mocked himself, "Much you care for being father's diagram!"

Elizabeth made time for a long talk with Lidian, who outlined "the theosophy of her marriage and of marriage in general"—a theory by which "each human soul has its own relation to the universe" through ever widening social circles that make up one "harmonious whole"—which Elizabeth considered fodder for an article she planned to write on "the institution of the Family." Lidian's "theosophy" held echoes of Waldo's plea in *Nature*—"Why should not we also enjoy an original relation to the universe?"—but with an emphasis on social cohesion, not individuality. Elizabeth could not have been surprised to hear this version of her own "principle of the social sympathy" from Lidian— a woman even more enmeshed than Elizabeth in family relationships.

Lidian had written to Elizabeth during the winter that she and Waldo had been "learning to get along very comfortably" with the baby at night and that "we get *used* to the care of him." Still, Elizabeth could not help but notice that her host's "ultra idealism" was matched in his wife by what Waldo himself appreciatively called "ultra benevolence," a domesticity that effectively eliminated Lidian from the "transcendental coterie," except as ministering angel. When, on a later occasion, Emerson tried "all ways" to persuade his wife to join him and Elizabeth on an afternoon's walk in Concord's Sleepy Hollow, Lidian maintained that "she did not want to go—that is 'felt' she could not," because of duties at home. Elizabeth was determined not to be left out in this way, even as she continued to help Lidian on this vacation by minding Little Waldo and taking on some of the family sewing.

Before spending so much time in close proximity with the Emersons, Elizabeth had believed that "there is but one relation that is perfect in this world," and that was marriage. She was still inclined to view the Emersons' marriage as approaching perfection, but what that "one relation" required of a woman, and whether Elizabeth herself might ever want to meet those requirements, were troubling matters. She had also once considered, when sharing rooms with Mary at Somerset Court, that "sisters might imitate" that "perfect" relation, but, as differences had mounted with Mary, Elizabeth had become "convinced that they cannot . . . if I am one of the sisters." Would the same be true of marriage for Elizabeth? In her circle, Elizabeth was certainly not too old to marry, as Lidian Emerson's example made plain. But would marriage be a wise choice for any woman who had contented herself with a single life well into her thirties? Much as she might have felt for her friend—the woman of once seemingly "inexhaustible originality," now so clearly worn down by family life—Elizabeth may have found, in observing Lidian's plight, some consolation for the feelings of disappointment and rejection she had so swiftly suppressed in the wake of Horace Mann's declaration, two years earlier, that his love for her was brotherly, and nothing more.

Elizabeth, who desired as much to be an intellectual sparring partner to the great thinkers of her time as to be their sisterly friend and aide—or wife —may have taken the Emersons' model of marriage as an omen. Perhaps Elizabeth herself was not meant to marry—even though she vigorously promoted the family as the "only divine institution on earth," as she had written in *The Family School,* and claimed to find Lidian's "theosophy of marriage" just as inspiring as Emerson's call to self-reliance. In Concord in 1837, she was as happy to have Waldo Emerson hand her a sheaf of his manuscript lectures to organize as she would have been to receive an engagement ring—probably more so: clearly even a man ready to do battle with the Unitarian establishment would not permit the woman he married to serve as both intellectual comrade and light of the home.

Elizabeth set to work supplying the synopsis Waldo asked for; he had always admired her "methodising faculty" and "wonderful literary head," he wrote in his journal. Emerson also knew his own tendency to proceed rapidly from one perception to another—in Elizabeth's terms, to "create . . . a constant series of surprises" for his listeners. The lectures "astonish, satisfy, delight me," Elizabeth wrote in her own journal as she read them through in Concord, and "prove Mr E. to be a far greater man than I thought him." But he was "not logical." Elizabeth puzzled over whether Waldo ought to "discipline himself to integrate his thoughts," but she welcomed this opportunity to help focus the lectures and thereby increase his "carrying power with the masses." She acknowledged that Emerson's lectures "can not be understood fully at the time," which permitted his critics to "rail at them or to laugh" and dismiss them. Elizabeth believed, however, that if Emerson "starts a thousand trains" of thought, "but pursues few," the resulting lack of coherence was "the fault only of a man of genius" blessed with an "encumbrance of ideas." Along with her synopsis of the lectures, which outlined subjects he had covered and those he had given short shrift, Elizabeth left Waldo with a "written exhortation to print them."

Elizabeth left Concord in late September 1837 exhorting herself in Emersonian style to "be simple, be true, be as little in a hurry" as possible—and with a list of projects she planned to accomplish in the coming year in Salem, along with teaching a class of older girls and lecturing on Greek myth to her women's reading party. She planned to write odes to Emerson, Channing, and Washington Allston, essays on American history and on the family, and to edit an anthology in which she expected to publish one of Emerson's lectures. But life took a new direction that December when she heard Jones Very give a lecture on epic poetry. Elizabeth immediately thought of signing him for her anthology, and invited Very home afterward—he was an "uncertain, shy" man who "grasped my outstretched hand like a drowning man a straw"—where they discussed "transcendental topics." Very admitted to being "an enthusiastic listener to Mr. Emerson." Elizabeth promptly wrote to Emerson suggesting that he invite Very to give his lecture in Concord. Emerson followed Elizabeth's recommendation and asked Very to stay with him as well. The encounter would prove fateful.

After hearing Very's Concord lecture in April 1838, Emerson praised Elizabeth's "sagacity" in discovering "such wise men as Mr. Very." Waldo felt "anew" in Very's company, he wrote Elizabeth, and, after discussing an essay the young poet planned to write on Shakespeare, judged him to possess "all the air & effect of genius." Emerson invited him to join the Transcendental Club, and Very became one of the group's more faithful members—except for one notable period of absence.

Perhaps encouraged by Elizabeth's and Waldo Emerson's enthusiasm for

Jones Very

his "genius," Very began to shift the focus of his Greek tutorials at Harvard away from the dead language and toward what he considered to be more urgently needed spiritual instruction. Then, six months after his meeting with Emerson, and three weeks into the fall term of 1838, Very felt "a new will" stir within him, the fulfillment of the vision he had experienced a year before on the speeding train to Andover. Very's Transcendentalism gave way to ecstatic revelation: "I was moved entirely by the Spirit within me to declare to all that the coming of Christ was at hand," he wrote in a confessional letter to a college friend. Very gathered his Greek students in Cambridge and warned them to "flee to the mountains, for the end of all things is at hand." Later that same day, Very barged into a meeting of a debate society, took the podium, and, in "tremulous tones," declared that "the Holy Spirit was speaking through him." On learning of Very's erratic behavior, Harvard president Josiah Quincy—the grandfather of Elizabeth's Temple School protégé Josiah Phillips Quincy—fired the once promising Greek tutor and ordered him home to Salem.

Back in Salem, Jones Very made his way to the Peabody house on Charter

Street, where Elizabeth answered the door. The young man on her front steps was scarcely recognizable. Very appeared "much flushed and his eyes very brilliant, and unwinking," Elizabeth would later recall. It was clear at once that "there was something unnatural—and dangerous in his air." Finding herself alone with a madman on the first floor of the house, Elizabeth determined "not to antagonize" Very, and she let him in. Once inside the door, Very ceremonially laid his hand on Elizabeth's head and declared, "I come to baptize you with the Holy Ghost & with fire." He began to pray. Elizabeth found his words "thrilling—and as I stood under his hand, I trembled to the centre." But when Very had finished his prayer and asked Elizabeth expectantly, "How do you feel?" she replied honestly, "I feel no change." Very insisted, "But you will . . . I am the Second Coming."

Throughout the encounter Elizabeth had remained "silent but respectful even tenderly so," hoping "this was perhaps a passing frenzy caused by overtaxing his brain." But others in Salem were not so tolerant. Elizabeth learned that Very had stopped at the houses of several Salem ministers to "baptize *them*" on his way to the Peabodys', and "two had resisted him *bodily*." A third, the Reverend Upham of the Unitarian First Parish Church, threatened to send him "to the Insane Asylum." Elizabeth herself was unsure of the proper treatment for Very—particularly after he returned to the Peabody house later the same day in a quieter mood and presented Elizabeth with "a monstrous folio sheet of paper, on which were four double columns of sonnets" that Very told her "the Spirit had enabled" him to write. Should such a flow of creativity be stopped? But it was too late: Upham, backed by the Harvard authorities, would have his way. Within seventy-two hours of his doomsday prophecies at Harvard, Jones Very was delivered to the McLean Asylum at Charlestown, "contrary to my will," he wrote to his college friend.

When Emerson heard the news, he was astonished. Very had completed his essay on Shakespeare in the days before his dismissal from Harvard and sent it to Emerson, who declared it "a noble paper," without a trace of Very's alleged madness. To Margaret Fuller, Emerson wrote, recalling conversations with Very that had been as inspiring to the philosopher as to the young poet: "Such a mind cannot be lost." Indeed, Emerson would feel compelled to defend Very's sanity in the coming months in the face of palpable evidence to the contrary; he would even take it upon himself to publish a volume of Very's essays (a move that coincidentally put a stop to Elizabeth's planned anthology), along with a selection of the brilliant poetry Very continued writing at a white heat while at McLean.

Why would Emerson go to such lengths for a deranged Harvard tutor? During the summer of 1838, as Very's "new will" was gestating, Emerson had delivered a revelation of his own at Harvard in the form of an address to the graduating class of the Divinity School, a speech that was far more incendiary than "The American Scholar" and eminently more persuasive than his young disciple's messianic ravings. This one so angered the Harvard authorities that Emerson was barred from the college for almost thirty years. In the furor that followed Emerson's delivery of his "Divinity School Address," the descent into madness of a once promising Harvard divinity student like Very, a known follower of Emerson, was more than just another strike against the renegade minister. It completed the portrait of Ralph Waldo Emerson, at least in the eyes of the old guard, as a dangerous man—an infidel capable of spreading false religion. And it compelled Emerson to defend his protégé, the madman Elizabeth Peabody had delivered to his doorstep.

Elizabeth had been visiting the Emersons at Concord again in the days following the "Divinity School Address." The mood, unlike the previous summer, was somber. Emerson was as talkative as ever, but "deepened, rendered more earnestly serious by this late opposition," Elizabeth recorded in her journal. The step away from conventional Unitarianism that Emerson had taken with "The American Scholar" the year before had opened up a path that carried him beyond the limits of organized religion. Emerson was now preaching a religion so large—so "universal"—that he refused any longer to name it Christianity. In his "Divinity School Address," Emerson told the small band of would-be ministers that gathered to hear him speak—the best and brightest Harvard had to offer the pulpits of the young nation—to "go alone" and "dare to love God without mediator or veil." In Emerson's view, worship of Christ had become a "fetish," the sign of "a decaying church and a wasting belief." Emerson admonished the fledgling ministers to "cast behind you all conformity" and listen to their congregations—for "all men have sublime thoughts." Including both preacher and parishioner in his rallying cry, Emerson proclaimed, "Wherever a man comes, there comes revolution."

It was ironic, of course, that Jones Very, whose insanity quite explicitly involved a Christian revelation, would be tarred with the same brush, his visions put down to "nothing but *transcendentalism*." But Transcendentalism *was* the problem, Emerson's increasingly vociferous critics argued in the weeks and months following his 1838 address. If "all men have sublime thoughts," as Emerson claimed, what was to stop any man from declaring himself the Messiah? Harvard Divinity School's founding professor, Andrews Norton, the man who had labeled Alcott's *Conversations on the Gospels* blasphemous and censored Elizabeth's essays on the Hebrew scriptures, branded Emerson's speech an "incoherent rhapsody" and an "insult to religion." Others accused him of "foulest atheism." But at the heart of the controversy, which raged in the press into the following year, was the conviction on the part of Emerson's opponents that "we must have Christianity through . . . the church and its authorities, or not at all." The old guard was determined to hold the line against Emerson's revolution.

Elizabeth herself did not go so far as Waldo Emerson. She would not drop "Christ" from Christianity after so many years spent arguing his importance as a fully human exemplar. But she knew Emerson's purpose: he had identified "the evils of the church" in order to inspire the young ministers to "rekindle the smouldering, nigh quenched fire on the altar." Having missed Emerson's Phi Beta Kappa oration the year before, Elizabeth had found her way to Divinity Hall to hear "this truly prophetic discourse," which became "the apocalypse of our Transcendental era in Boston." She felt the importance of the moment along with the transformative power of Emerson's testimony. As she wrote in her journal, the fact that "this last lecture excited opposition, is only another proof of how much the community needed it."

Elizabeth was also acutely aware of the risk Emerson took—perhaps more so than Emerson himself. Earlier that summer, another Boston freethinker, the avowed atheist Abner Kneeland, had been imprisoned for blasphemy after publishing his views in a newspaper he called the *Boston Investigator*. Were Emerson's ties to the Boston establishment as the scion of a long line of prominent ministers strong enough to save him from such a fate if, as his opponents insisted, Emerson could be convicted of spreading "the latest form of infidelity"? Already Harvard had banished him from campus. Late in 1838, after Jones Very was released from McLean still claiming divine inspiration, Elizabeth, who continued to sympathize with Very privately, nevertheless warned Waldo against him, writing that the poet was "as crazy as ever." She explained that Salem's Unitarian clergy were trying to prevent Very from seeing Emerson, who was himself "now universally acknowledged to be & denounced as an atheist." She alerted him that "measures are taking!! To prevent you from having any more audience to corrupt."

But Emerson would hear none of it. Instead he welcomed a visit from Very, who stayed with the Emersons in Concord for five days soon after leaving McLean. "Talk with him a few hours and you will think all insane but he," Emerson wrote afterward to Margaret Fuller, describing his "memorable conversations" with Jones Very. Acknowledging that his guest was "not in a natural and probably not in a permanent state," Emerson nevertheless concluded that Very was "a treasure of a companion." To Elizabeth, whose attempts to manage this friendship he may have begun to resent, Emerson stated unequivocally, "he is profoundly sane."

In August 1838, however, while Elizabeth was on vacation at the Emersons' in Concord, the debate over Very's mental state—"Monomania, or mono*sania*," in Emerson's terms—lay in the future. Now, riding back to Concord from Lexington after delivering what would be one of the last sermons of his career,

Little Waldo Emerson

Emerson confided to Elizabeth that he had decided "the lyceum chair must be my pulpit" in the future. He was determined to reach a wider audience of young people like those in the back pews of the church that morning who had restlessly turned the pages of their hymnals during his sermon. To be heard, he would need the fresh air of the secular stage and a new mode of address. "Whoever would preach Christ in these times must say nothing about him!" he told her.

At home, Waldo tinkered with the proof sheets of his "Divinity School Address" and consulted with Elizabeth and Lidian, as they sat together "at our needlework," on whether he should insert a paragraph he had omitted on the day of the speech for the sake of brevity. The paragraph would have explained some of the disputed points, Elizabeth observed, and she argued for its inclusion. In the end, however, Emerson decided to print the speech as he'd delivered it, keeping the battle fair for his critics. "Apology, and even explanation," he told Elizabeth, are "the blunders of egotism."

In Concord's late-summer heat, Elizabeth talked with Waldo in his study as his son played on the floor beside them. She noted that death seemed as much on his mind as the young life of Little Waldo. For two years Emerson had toyed with the idea of writing a book about his dead brother Charles, or at least collecting his letters and essays into a volume. He told Elizabeth now that he had decided against it; the prospect was too dispiriting. "One writes what one can, not what one ought," Emerson defended his choice. Standing to gaze out the window, he spoke regretfully: "We cannot understand" death, he mused; "our vision" does not reach far enough. Then he bent down to Little Waldo and lifted him up off the floor and onto his shoulder. "Waldo! Why do people die?" he asked, as if playfully probing the two-year-old boy's mind for an intuition of divine reason. "Will you die Waldo? Say 'no papa, I will not die —nothing is farther from my thoughts than dying!'"

In this darker mood, Emerson seemed more than usually attuned to his guest. The two walked in Sleepy Hollow, coming back "over the hills," where "we talked of many things," Elizabeth wrote in her journal. Emerson spoke of a dilemma he would take up in much of his future writing, one he seems never to have resolved—and one he shared, perhaps without knowing, with his "Theosophist" wife. "He said we had not learned yet how to live so that what was best for ourselves should be combined with duty to others," Elizabeth recorded, comforted by the thought that Waldo might sympathize with her own quandary.

Then Waldo turned to Elizabeth and, to her surprise, addressed her directly, expressing concern for the "difficult position" that bearing the financial burden for her family had placed her in for so many years. Waldo advised her not to "blame yourself . . . if overpowered by your relations to others." Elizabeth, who had so far avoided confiding anything beyond her intellectual concerns in the philosopher, and "never . . . talked of my personal relations to him," was deeply affected by Waldo's effort at consolation, especially at a time when he was under public attack. "Give me the friend who divines my needs," Elizabeth wrote that night in her journal. "This is the true heart."

❦ 27 ❧

The Sister Years

WHAT EMERSON COULD HAVE ONLY DIMLY DIVINED WAS THAT ELIZA-
beth's "difficult position" had become a nearly intolerable one, finally driving
her from home for the several months preceding her visit to Concord in the
summer of 1838. She was indeed feeling "overpowered" by relations to others,
but she could confide in no one. Now, perhaps more than ever, Elizabeth
lacked a "true" friend, despite the closeness she longed to achieve with her sisters or with the several men whose intimate acquaintance she had cultivated
in recent years.

Elizabeth's predicament had its roots in the dismal autumn of 1837, when
the family in Salem—now reduced to the three sisters and their parents—received word from George in New Orleans that Wellington had died suddenly,
the victim of a yellow fever epidemic that he had traveled south to study. Despite his engagement to the Charlestown heiress Mary Boardman, Wellington
had gone ahead with his ambitious plans to find the cure to a virulent disease.
He had dropped the idea of moving to Paris and seized on a nearer pestilence,
taking a job as medical resident at a yellow fever hospital in New Orleans.

Wellington reached New Orleans in August, the peak of yellow fever
season, in the middle of the worst outbreak in fifteen years. The "tropical
scourge" was claiming more than fifty lives a day, and the hospital run by Dr.
MacFarlane was the only one in the city devoted to the disease. George wrote
afterward that Wellington had quickly become "the greatest possible favorite"
with Dr. MacFarlane and his patients: with MacFarlane because Wellington
happily worked long days at the hospital that his superior considered too dangerous to visit; with the patients because he seemed to be curing them. It
would be more than half a century before yellow fever's true means of transmission—the female *Aedes aegypti* mosquito—was discovered. Unlike MacFar-

lane, who suspected patient-to-patient transmission and maintained his hospital chiefly as a means of quarantining the sick, Wellington believed that yellow fever was caused by "miasmatic" air in low-lying tropical cities. He had no fear of contagion on the hospital ward. Welly threw himself into his work with an energy and dedication that his family had not known he possessed. He lanced, dosed with calomel, and by the end of his first month, had lost only one of the twenty patients he treated.

Yellow fever takes its victims quickly. Most patients well enough to reach the hospital would have survived anyway, but Wellington didn't know that. It was a thrill, "raising from the brink of the grave, the suffering patient," he wrote to Elizabeth, still his mediator with Mary Boardman's guardian. He asked Elizabeth to pass along the news that he expected to return to Boston in a year's time, "a well developed physician, ready for action." This new work, the twenty-year-old Wellington boasted, "will make a man of me." And he might have been right. At least chances had been good that he would survive. By shutting the hospital windows against the night air from dusk till dawn, Wellington took little risk of infection while at work. And when he walked home in the evening, he wore a heavy coat and puffed on a cigar to counteract the evil effects of the "miasmatic" air, doubtless shooing away infected mosquitoes as well.

On September 27, one of Wellington's patients died—only the sixth, now, out of 120 treated in two months. Feeling invincible, Wellington insisted on performing an autopsy himself, probing the dead man's intestines with his bare hands as he searched for new evidence to include in the thesis with which he planned to "astonish" the Massachusetts Medical Society. By Dr. MacFarlane's lights, Wellington had "exposed himself considerably." Within hours, he was sick. After four days of fever, culminating in delirium and "the black vomit," he was dead. Dr. MacFarlane was right, this time, about the route of infection. The live virus must have penetrated Welly's skin, entering his bloodstream, as he zealously handled the infected organs without gloves. The need to protect against microscopic germs was also unknown through most of the nineteenth century.

It became George's "melancholy duty" to deliver the sad news to his family. He would have liked to come home to tell them in person, he wrote, but he had no money. For the past year George had been forced to give up every job he took within a matter of weeks because of his own chronic illness. Moreover, George had discovered that, along with burial expenses, Wellington left a debt of close to $100 for boots, cigars, and a pair of gold eyeglasses that he had almost instantly lost.

Each of the surviving siblings found a different lesson in Wellington's death. "His ardor of character made him very impetuous," Mary wrote to a

friend. Yet in one month Wellington had "found his place," and "all the resources of his nature had been drawn forth." Now that Wellington had at last
made his family proud, Mary could feel "willing" to have him go. And she delivered this version of Wellington's final days to "poor little Mary Boardman,"
for whom Wellington's death would be "the greatest misfortune." Nat, now a
married man with a family, sermonized on the importance of caution. "We
can rush into danger & perish," he wrote to George, urging him to come
home, or "we can choose the path of moderate and patient desire in safer
places, and may live to bless ourselves and mankind."

Sophia took to her bed, where she cried most of every day for a week, managing to shift the focus of her family's anxiety back home. But her anguish
was genuine, if extreme. Wellington, the youngest in the family, had been her
special "care & pet" in childhood, and during recent years in Salem, Sophia
had come to depend on her brother's "tender affection" in return, Mary wrote
to their mutual friend Sally Gardner. The "bitterness of parting" hit her especially hard. Wellington was not the one who was supposed to die. Once
Sophia was well enough to write, she also begged George to come back to
Salem, for "home is the place for the sick."

Elizabeth was more hardheaded. As she saw it, there were "no elements" in
Wellington's character to promise "a steady strong conduct of life." He had
been meant to live just twenty years. But George was another matter. She ordered George to leave New Orleans before he contracted the disease. He was
needed at home, the only brother who might one day take over the support of
their invalid sister from their aging parents, she persisted in believing, despite
the obvious signs that George's own condition was worsening. Still, Elizabeth
remained emotionally fragile through the fall—crying easily over Carlyle's
French Revolution; or newspaper accounts of bank closings, which came thick
and fast in the "panic" year of 1837; or the congressional debates over the abolition of slavery in the District of Columbia.

But unlike her brothers and sisters, Elizabeth had a knack for making
things happen, which, at the very least, could distract her from present trouble. She would never forget the evening of November 11, 1837, when "a great
ring came at the front door," and a little-known writer of short stories,
Nathaniel Hawthorne, entered her life "in all the splendor of his young
beauty": a man just her own age, whose palpable shyness only slightly diminished the magnetic power of his dark-haired good looks. It was a meeting that
Elizabeth had worked to bring about for most of the year since her return to
Salem, when she'd learned that the anonymous author of tales she'd admired
in *The Token* and *The New-England Magazine* lived just a few streets away—
indeed was the same neighbor boy she'd seen almost thirty years ago playing
in the yard behind the Peabodys' Union Street house, now grown.

Falling under the spell of stories like "The Gentle Boy," in which a young Quaker child in Puritan times dies a martyr's death, and "Little Annie's Ramble," which she thought showed that "ideal beauty may be seen clearest and felt most profoundly in the common incidents of actual life," Elizabeth had sought out Nathaniel Hawthorne at his own house to no avail. She had waited for a return invitation promised by his younger sister, but it never came. Finally—after receiving a presentation copy of his first book, the recently published *Twice-told Tales*, inscribed to "Miss Elizabeth Peabody, with the respects of the Author"—she sensed a willingness on Hawthorne's part to make her acquaintance. She had engineered this meeting, she would later recall, "on the pretext" of asking Hawthorne's advice about publishing an essay of her own in the new *Democratic Review*, to which Hawthorne had begun to contribute. Or had Hawthorne himself decided the time was right and made sure the meeting would take place for his own reasons?

Nathaniel Hawthorne did not come alone that Saturday night, but with "a hooded figure hanging on each arm": his two sisters, the older, bookish Elizabeth (known as Ebe) who, as a girl, had been called upon to help a four-year-old Elizabeth Peabody with her studies; and the younger Louisa, now the most sociable member of the reclusive Hawthorne family. The image of the strikingly handsome author in black cape and silks—he made a point of dressing well in public, Hawthorne later confided, in an effort to conquer his reserve—flanked by two women would become an indelible one in Elizabeth's mind. In retrospect it seemed to forecast the contest for Nathaniel Hawthorne's favor that she would soon be waging with her own sister Sophia.

On November 11, Elizabeth welcomed the three Hawthornes into the parlor, where they sat stiffly in a row. It was dark, or her guests might have peered out the parlor windows at the neighboring cemetery, where they could easily have seen the gravestone of their ancestor John Hathorne, the "hanging judge" of Salem's long-ago witchcraft frenzy, a few yards off. Instead, by the light of an astral lamp, Elizabeth tried easing their shyness by showing off a volume of Flaxman drawings she had borrowed from the Harvard professor Cornelius Felton. Succeeding in engaging her guests' attention with illustrations of the *Iliad*, she left them turning the pages to run upstairs to Sophia in her sickroom. "Mr. Hawthorne and his sisters have come," she burst out, "and you never saw anything so splendid—he is handsomer than Lord Byron!" As Elizabeth told the story years later, she urged Sophia to dress and come down to meet the writer, but Sophia refused. "I think it would be rather ridiculous to get up," Sophia tweaked Elizabeth, impatient at being pressed by her older sister to share in yet another of her enthusiasms. "If he has come once he will come again," she predicted.

For Sophia, this scenario was all too familiar—the ring of the doorbell, the

Nathaniel Hawthorne, by Charles Osgood

greetings and chatter below, the sound of Elizabeth's voice rising to command the flow of conversation, the rush to judgment that a "genius" had arrived in the house. Minutes after Elizabeth ducked out of her room and returned to her guests, Sophia heard Mary's voice join the hubbub as she came home from her own round of evening calls. Why would Sophia want to enter this fray, certain to be outdone in high literary talk by one or even both of her older sisters? It was Mary who described Hawthorne's visit afterward in a letter to their brother George in New Orleans, reporting that the writer had "lived the life of a perfect recluse till very lately" and was "so diffident he suffers inexpressibly in the presence of his fellow-mortals." Yet Mary also noted Hawthorne's "temple of a head" and "eye full of sparkle glisten & intelligence," along with his promise to come again. Hawthorne, at five feet ten, wasn't as tall as Emerson or Mann was—but he was perfectly proportioned, with "beauty" in the "outline of all his features," as Elizabeth would later say. "If we can get fairly acquainted," Mary wrote, she and Elizabeth expected to "find much pleasure in him."

But Sophia held back. Whether in reaction to Wellington's frightening death, or simply, as Sophia herself theorized, the result of progressive weakening from recurrent migraine attacks over so many years, she had lately become, in her own description, "to all appearances *a bed case*—a poor, miserable, maimed—nerve twisted—trembling, wearied concern." She had finished painting *Jessica and Lorenzo* over a year ago and sold it to her friend Mary Benjamin, the editor Park Benjamin's sister, for $125, earning "great fame—& *golden* opinions" in Boston besides. But, despite numerous requests for more copies, and a plea from Dr. Walter Channing, who had seen *Jessica and Lorenzo* in Boston, to "work from your own mind," Sophia had scarcely lifted her brush since. According to her close friend Sarah Clarke, who visited the Peabodys in late 1837, Sophia was now "more susceptible and requiring more careful nursing and seclusion than ever." In desperation, Sophia had submitted to the care of a mesmerist, her father's associate Dr. Fiske, who was experimenting with hypnosis as a pain reliever in dentistry. She found his sessions soothing, although he had not yet succeeded in guiding her into a trance. Sophia would not come downstairs that Saturday night to meet Nathaniel Hawthorne. She would not come downstairs for meals or to see anyone until the early spring of 1838. For now, Nathaniel Hawthorne was Elizabeth's property.

And for a time, the man Elizabeth called in a letter to his older sister "one of Nature's ordained priests" willingly accepted her proprietary interest. In a series of intense confessional meetings over the next weeks, the thirty-three-year-old Nathaniel Hawthorne revealed the facts of his family life to Elizabeth—ones that made him particularly susceptible to Elizabeth's yearning to manage an undiscovered genius. Even in insular Salem, where eccentrics like Jones Very were hardly unusual, the Hawthorne household was exceptional. Nathaniel Hawthorne explained to Elizabeth that he had come by "my cursed habit of solitude" during a childhood lived in the houses of his maternal grandparents and uncles in Salem and rural Maine after his sea captain father died in Surinam, a victim of yellow fever when Nathaniel was three years old. He had been raised by a mother who, Elizabeth herself observed, had adopted an "all but Hindoo self-devotion to the manes of her husband" in widowhood, rarely venturing out into public and keeping her children close around her. The children found it just as hard to leave their mother. As a young woman, the older daughter, Ebe, held to her mother's example most closely, retreating to her room after a rumored disappointment in love to spend most of her time reading. Nathaniel wished he could follow suit, writing to his mother at age sixteen, on the eve of his departure for college at Bowdoin, "Why was I not a girl that I might have been pinned all my life to my Mother's apron?"

Hawthorne told Elizabeth that, after graduating from Bowdoin, he could not bring himself to enter any of "the three professions" customary for college men—the law, medicine, or the ministry—and had instead vowed to cultivate "the literary part of his life." He returned home to Salem, rejoining his mother and sisters, who had by then retired from the world "so completely that they do not know its customs." A modest inheritance allowed him to delay employment, and for the next ten years he wrote stories at a desk in his upstairs bedroom, burning the pages he didn't like, slowly developing the brooding, revelatory style of the *Twice-told Tales*. In a large house once filled with his maternal relatives—grandparents, uncles and aunts, most now dead—the Hawthornes ate their meals alone in their rooms. Nathaniel saw his younger sister, Louisa, each day at tea and his mother, occasionally, after tea. But he had gone as long as three months without encountering the "very witty and original" Ebe, he told Elizabeth, to whom he was nonetheless devoted.

When Elizabeth asked her new friend if he considered it "healthy to live so separated," Nathaniel readily admitted, "It is the misfortune of my life. It has produced a morbid consciousness that paralyzes my powers." Although Elizabeth would eventually discover that Hawthorne hadn't mentioned the regular walks his sister Ebe took to the Salem Athenaeum to select books for him, the long summer rambles away from home he took each year in the company of a male relative or college friend, a fruitless half year spent in Boston trying to establish himself as a writer for magazines, and even a brief romantic entanglement with a Salem heiress, there was no disputing the emotional truth of Hawthorne's lament: "We do not live at our house."

There was also no disputing the fact that the years spent writing alone in his room—the "morbid consciousness" Hawthorne developed there—had produced the haunting *Twice-told Tales*, a volume that, while it sold few copies, marked the debut of a significant American literary voice. Several months after meeting Nathaniel Hawthorne, Elizabeth wrote a review of this "little book of caged melodies" for Horace Greeley's *New-Yorker*. It would be hard now to fault Elizabeth for her superlatives. She predicted that Nathaniel Hawthorne would "take his place amongst his contemporaries, as the greatest artist of his line; for not one of our writers indicates so great a variety of the elements of genius." In her review, Elizabeth also used what Hawthorne had told her of his home life to trace the sources of his genius, helping to establish a myth of the writer's origins to complement his *Tales*. "We have heard that the author of these tales has lived the life of a recluse," she wrote, "that the inhabitants of his native town have never been able to catch a glimpse of his person; that he is not seen at any time in the walks of men." Elizabeth saw Hawthorne as a Wordsworthian self-inspired genius, nurtured in near solitude, who wrote with "the wisdom which comes from knowing some few hearts well." He had "communed with the earnest spirits of the past," but his brilliance came chiefly from having followed the injunction "know thyself." Elizabeth had carried Hawthorne's own version of his life several steps further—he could only be grateful.

Was Hawthorne using his new friendship with Elizabeth Peabody to promote his career? Nearly a year before Elizabeth's review appeared, when *Twice-told Tales* was first published, Hawthorne sent a copy of the book to his Bowdoin classmate, the Harvard professor and poet Henry Wadsworth Longfellow, along with a letter making a case similar to the one he had made with Elizabeth. "For the last ten years, I have not lived, but only dreamed about living," Hawthorne had written, describing his days devoted to writing, adding, "I seldom venture abroad till after dusk." Striking a plaintive note, he elaborated: "By some witchcraft or other I have been carried apart from the main current of life, and find it impossible to get back again." The result was a glowing review by Longfellow in the *North American*, judging Hawthorne "a new star ris[ing] in the heavens" and declaring that this "sweet, sweet book ... comes from the hand of a man of genius." Since then, however, there had been a long silence from reviewers and diminishing sales. It is not hard to imagine that Hawthorne, whose decade sequestered in his attic workroom revealed as much ambition as diffidence, might have sought out Elizabeth Peabody with a similar gambit.

Elizabeth proved a far better target. In truth, although Hawthorne never knew it, Longfellow had initially been put off by his fellow writer, who had squandered his college years at Bowdoin in drinking and cardplaying while Longfellow studied hard and landed the part of lead commencement speaker. A year after he reviewed *Twice-told Tales*, Longfellow wrote to a friend describing Hawthorne as "a strange owl; a very peculiar individual, with a dash of originality about him"—although, admittedly, "very pleasant to behold." But Elizabeth Peabody, for whom Hawthorne's good looks may have counted for more, found Nathaniel Hawthorne's tale of solitary apprenticeship irresistibly romantic; when it became clear that he was willing to accept her help, she proceeded to try every means at her disposal. She sent *Twice-told Tales* to Horace Mann in hopes he would hire Hawthorne to write stories for schoolchildren. Even before she'd written her *New-Yorker* review, in February 1838 she sent *Twice-told Tales* along with Emerson's *Nature*—first books for both writers—to Wordsworth in England. In an accompanying letter, Elizabeth concentrated her promotional efforts on Hawthorne's book, expressing the view that America's "popular story tellers are the ballad makers of the nation." Hawthorne's tales were the "best in this line," she asserted, because "he dares to write for Beauty's sake."

Henry Wadsworth Longfellow, sketch by Maria Rohl

Although she would later deny it vehemently at almost every opportunity, during the winter of 1837 and 1838 Elizabeth allowed Nathaniel Hawthorne to become more than just another genius to promote. She fell in love—with the man, with his stories, even with the eccentric family that had nurtured him. And, unlike Horace Mann, Nathaniel Hawthorne let Elizabeth believe— may have himself believed—that he loved her back. Just a week before Hawthorne paid his first visit to the Peabody household, Elizabeth had received another dreary letter from Mann. While he went about his work for the state board of education with a firm will, Mann wrote, "I doubt I have much feeling left,—none for pleasure & little for pain"; he was sure he would never "pass thro' the human again."

How much more vividly alive was this stirringly handsome teller of tales with "the pure complexion" and "the wonderful eyes, like mountain lakes seeming to reflect the heavens," who ardently confessed his loneliness in terms that could not have been more different from Horace Mann's lawyerly calibrations of sentiment. "There is no fate in this world so horrible as to have no share in either its joys or sorrows," Hawthorne had written in his letter to Longfellow half a year before he met Elizabeth Peabody. He was ready to enter the world, to "pass thro' the human," and Elizabeth was poised to serve as his guide. That winter, Hawthorne told Elizabeth outright that he wished she had written to him years before, in the days when she had first begun to admire his stories. It would have made "an epoch" in his life, he said, for he had felt, then, "like a man talking to himself in a dark place." Hawthorne invited her now to visit his house, ostensibly to see his sisters. But his urgent— "I will come for you whenever you say I may, and wait on you home"—conveyed more. And he let slip: "I wish you would come for my sake."

The two traded visits during the winter months, meeting most often in the Peabody parlor, which Hawthorne entered cautiously, checking first to see that no other guests preceded him. The attachment became deeper, and a private "understanding" was reached: they would marry.

Elizabeth Peabody was an unconventional woman—not unattractive, shiny-haired, slim, and small—a woman who talked easily and could coax a shy man to speak freely as well. She was also messy, headlong and headstrong. But Nathaniel Hawthorne was accustomed to unconventional women, both independent-minded and willful ones, like his older sister, Ebe, and passive, retiring ones, like his widowed mother. For much of his life, Hawthorne had found the pull of these women—who had refused to learn the "customs" of the world—undeniable. Elizabeth Peabody was like them, but perhaps not quite enough. The same qualities that allowed her to help him professionally—her enterprising, almost meddlesome nature—may have begun to put him off.

And Nathaniel Hawthorne had not yet met her youngest sister, the twenty-eight-year-old Sophia, although Elizabeth spoke of her often. Why wouldn't she? Sophia had always been Elizabeth's own "care & pet." When Hawthorne learned of Sophia's illnesses, her beatific suffering, her refined artistic sensibility, he declared her—still without having laid eyes on her—"a flower to be worn in no man's bosom, but let down from heaven to show the human soul's possibilities." Elizabeth was satisfied that he understood the situation.

Yet Hawthorne could not have helped but recognize in Elizabeth's description of Sophia a woman both willful *and* retiring, one who harmonized the traits of the Hawthorne women and set them in a major key. Was she really to be possessed by no man? Elizabeth had relayed to him Sophia's own publicly stated view on the subject, perhaps issued defensively, that she was "never to be married." Elizabeth herself did not know of Sophia's secret wish, expressed in the long-ago poem, to find her "Unknown yet known" lover, the poet or artist who was meant to be her life mate. Elizabeth knew nothing, either, of a dream that Sophia had confided to Mary over a year earlier, following a chance visit from Horace Mann when Sophia had been the only sister at home to receive the politician. That night after he left, Sophia dreamed that a warmly solicitous Horace Mann reappeared to sit beside her every day as she drew in her portfolio. "At those times," Sophia told Mary, she experienced "perfect repose & cessation from pain." Sophia had her own notion of what was needed to cure her illness and motivate her as an artist.

During the early months of 1838, Sophia remained upstairs in her room, waging her inner battle with pain. In January, George Peabody made an arduous trip home from New Orleans to Salem. Just twenty-four years old, his legs were now completely paralyzed; Elizabeth wrote to Horace Mann of the family's shock on discovering that George had become "a hopeless cripple." Worse, the tuberculosis that was slowly consuming his spinal marrow left him in almost constant pain. George was installed in the room across the hall from Sophia on a "hydrostatic" bed—a six-inch-deep trough filled with water and sealed with a waterproof India rubber sheet—supported by two sawhorses, meant to promote healing and keep him from contracting bedsores. The two invalids kept close tabs on each other through the day, calling out on occasion to ease their loneliness. When Sophia felt well enough to cross the hall—and to withstand the shock to her "hyper-sympathetic" nervous system that was the inevitable result of visiting a fellow sufferer—she sat in George's room offering bits of advice gleaned from her long years combating pain. She recommended that he take his daily doses of morphine in the morning, as she did, to avoid opium nightmares. And she described the benefits of the hammock she slept in at night—the "dear little couch" that delivered a pleasant sensation of weightlessness, reviving memories of the sea voyage to Cuba.

But Sophia was a tiny woman, and not nearly as sick as her brother. George was struggling with a terminal illness. Indeed, George's condition seemed to confound all Sophia had come to believe about invalidism. "It is the lot of woman to be ill," she wrote her friend Mary Wilder White Foote in early March, after two months of mutual confinement to the second floor. She could hardly bear "to see such an energetic, action-loving creature" as George, "a man whose sphere is abroad, and in the very glory of his youth, shut up in one room and fastened to one chair." She sketched him in pencil, reclining on that chair: a bear of a man at twenty-four, in mustache and sideburns, obviously unable to find comfort even in repose. As Sophia began to consider the possibility that she might lose a second brother to disease, and to reckon with the evident truth that George's suffering was of an unyielding and far less

George Peabody, sketch by Sophia Peabody

metaphysical nature than her own, the boundaries she had set at the walls of her room began to mock her.

By March, Sophia was feeling "better than for a month" and ready to contemplate the journey downstairs. She warned the friends she had not seen since the previous fall to be prepared for "my sword face and white hue" and to "see me shrink at the sound of my own voice." But she knew that soon the clematis vine climbing toward her window would bloom, and she wanted to gather the blossoms herself. Downstairs, too, she would find the strikingly handsome writer—"handsomer than Lord Byron"—that her sister had been urging her to meet all winter long.

We cannot know on which of the first voyages beyond her room during the spring of 1838 Sophia Peabody finally met Nathaniel Hawthorne face-to-face. But on that day Sophia dressed herself in a "simple white wrapper" and summoned just enough strength to reach the parlor, where she sank onto the couch reserved for her use, interrupting a conversation between Elizabeth and Nathaniel Hawthorne. "He rose and looked at her—he did not realize how intently," Elizabeth later recalled. The startled older sister watched as each of Sophia's infrequent remarks, delivered "in her low sweet voice," was met with that "same intentness of interest." With horror, Elizabeth began to wonder, "What if he should fall in love with her?" Could the very weakness that had disqualified Sophia for romance in Elizabeth's eyes make her that much more appealing to this shy writer, a man who may have needed a woman to care for in order to feel strong? And what if Sophia should return that love? "I was struck with it, and painfully," she later wrote. Elizabeth, who had once accused her little sister of being a hypochondriac, had always suspected Sophia of retaining the power to cure herself when she felt like it.

What did Sophia Peabody see in Nathaniel Hawthorne on that first meeting? A man so handsome that women were known to stop and stare when he passed them on the other side of the street? A man whose accomplishments might one day trump even Horace Mann's? Whose worth was validated by the fact that Sophia's older sister, with her unerring eye for genius, already loved him? Surely Sophia had sensed all along that Elizabeth's passion for Hawthorne was more than intellectual, although neither had spoken of it. This first encounter did not last long. Soon Sophia was back in her room, listening from behind her open door to Elizabeth's conversation, overhearing her make plans to walk in the countryside beyond Salem on the next fine spring day with the writer Sophia had instantly recognized as her soul mate—no longer "Unknown." What was Sophia to do? As she pondered the situation over the next several days, she began to paint again: not yet in oils, but quick watercolor sketches of butterflies and birds, creatures of flight.

Elizabeth had seen what transpired between her sister and the man she hoped to marry. In one late account, Elizabeth claimed to have written to Hawthorne immediately, breaking off their engagement, telling him "I was leaving home for some time—that it was best to look upon the chapter of our pleasant companionship as closed. That I felt convinced it had been a mistake on both our parts to regard it other than mere friendship. Certainly I knew it was best for me so to consider it, and that I believed he would later on come to the same conclusion. I bade him farewell and then I went away." In fact, shortly after Sophia made her springtime descent from her sickroom, Elizabeth announced her startling decision to leave Salem for the Boston suburb of Newton Corner. Loudly professing concern that she might appear to be deserting the family invalids, Elizabeth nevertheless made plans to move in with her brother Nat, whose barely concealed dislike for his oldest sister must have made the option particularly unattractive. Unaware of Elizabeth's present romantic distress, Nat had chosen this moment to berate her by letter for not marrying Lyman Buckminster almost two decades before "when you had the opportunity," for then "the fortunes of your own and our family would have been different, perhaps prosperous." Elizabeth moved to Newton all the same. Starting in late April 1838, she would devote herself to helping her luckless brother open and run a school for boys.

But had Elizabeth broken off relations with Hawthorne? In truth, the situation was considerably murkier. Hawthorne himself wrote half-jokingly to friends in Boston at the time, "I have heard recently the interesting intelligence that I am engaged to two ladies in this city"—and it was little wonder. The once reclusive author was now seen squiring around town one or more of the Peabody sisters, whether on walks in the countryside or to the Saturday-evening salons held by the wealthy Miss Susan Burley—the most literary-minded hostess in backward-looking Salem. First he had taken Elizabeth, and sometimes Mary. Now that Elizabeth was away, Sophia was finding herself well enough to walk out with Hawthorne and even to attend an occasional Saturday-night "Hurley-Burley."

As a parting shot, Elizabeth had loaned Hawthorne the hand-stitched volumes of Sophia's Cuba Journal before leaving for Newton. There he could read just how debilitating her little sister's illness was and, presumably, recognize the burden of care that would fall to any man who tried to love her. But instead, Elizabeth soon learned, Hawthorne was entranced by the record of Sophia's *innere*. He kept the volumes for more than a month, copying numerous passages into his own notebooks. Here was material he could draw on for years to come in his fiction: the uncensored thoughts of a woman writing to other women. When he returned them, he told Sophia—who told Elizabeth—that she was "the Queen of Journalizers." By then the two were carrying on an advanced flirtation, as Elizabeth easily read between the lines of the journal letters Sophia sent to Newton.

Elizabeth pressed Sophia to supply all "the little items about Hawthorne" that she could manage in her daily record, and the picture that emerged confirmed her worst fears. Although Sophia's recovery, once she had Hawthorne to herself, was by no means immediate, a pattern developed, familiar from the days when Dr. Walter Channing was Sophia's chief passion and comfort. If

Sophia expected a visit from Hawthorne, she would be up and dressed. If he failed to appear, she took to her bed and then punished him at his next visit by refusing to see him.

But unlike Channing, whose motives in seeing Sophia were more purely medical, Hawthorne persisted. Under the pretext of entertaining George, Hawthorne would mount the stairs all the same, where he could be sure that Sophia would overhear him chatting with her invalid brother across the hall. Perhaps the keenly observant Hawthorne even caught a glimpse of Sophia on his way past her door, stretched out on her hammock, where she had "pulled all the combs out of my hair, and sent it streaming like a comet over my shoulders, and untied all my dress, supposing that I should have no occasion to appear." Indeed, she may have wished him to. On such days Sophia deliberately left her door open in order to eavesdrop, as she reported to Elizabeth, being "sorely disappointed" that "it was absolutely impossible for me to see him, unless he had come into my room." The fact that Sophia never invited Hawthorne to her room—even when she was fully dressed—signaled to Elizabeth just how differently her sister regarded the new gentleman caller. In times of relative good health, Sophia frequently entertained men in her bedroom-studio, anyone from local ministers to the likes of Ralph Waldo Emerson when he was in town for a lecture series. But these men were potential patrons or fellow artists to whom she displayed her works in progress—not romantic prospects.

Sophia began to have a sixth sense for when Nathaniel Hawthorne rang the bell, feeling "just as sure it was Mr. Hawthorne as if I had seen him." Then she could dress hurriedly and descend, "armed with a blue odorous violet," as she did one day, determined to prove to the doubting Hawthorne that certain violets were capable of emitting strong perfumes. She gave him a nosegay of English sweet violets, a rarity in New England, where native violets have no scent. He kept the flowers in water for a week before taking one to Boston to be set under black crystal, "enshrined from every possible harm," on a gold brooch he intended to wear himself. Yet, still unready for that step—to wear Sophia's flower in his bosom—Hawthorne declared the brooch "too fine" for himself when he returned to Salem and left it behind at the Peabody house, pinned to Sophia's bodice. By now the violet had become, in the language of the novice sweethearts, a "Forget-me-not": their first token of mutual affection.

Elizabeth did not take this news easily. She complained that Sophia was "cutting" her out of the friendship by accepting so many visits from Hawthorne while she was away. Sophia insisted the opposite was true, that "Mr. H's coming here is one sure way of keeping you in mind." She was certain, Sophia wrote, that Hawthorne found her own companionship "excessively tame" compared with Elizabeth's "society and conversation so that I think you will shine more by contrast." Elizabeth was not convinced.

But worse still was Hawthorne's apparent inability to clarify his feelings for her. Before leaving Salem, Elizabeth had exacted a promise from him to carry on a correspondence—although Hawthorne had made her pledge, in return, to burn his letters after reading them. So far, in response to her several letters, Elizabeth had received nothing. Tantalizingly, Sophia wrote in late April that Hawthorne had drafted a letter to Elizabeth and "it was a great thing for him" to have completed it. Could Sophia have known the letter's contents? Sophia reported next that Hawthorne was carrying a packet of letters with him to Boston in hopes of a meeting with Elizabeth. He might even take the fifteen-minute train ride out to Newton to find her. Not trusting a promise delivered by proxy, Elizabeth took the train into Boston and waylaid Hawthorne in the lobby of his hotel only to discover that the letters he had were all from Sophia. Later she learned that it was on this trip that Hawthorne had set the violet under crystal for Sophia.

At what point did Elizabeth begin to tire of hearing from Sophia about Hawthorne's "celestial expression," how "brilliant" he looked, or that Sophia had dreamed all night about him? Of their meetings in the parlor perfumed by a "host" of blue and white violets *oderata*, which Hawthorne now declared "too overpowering," while Sophia delighted in their fragrance—"I soar and sing with it"? Was it when Sophia reported, after reading a book about Persia, that she hoped to travel there someday, like retired Harvard president John Kirkland and his wife—then caught herself, "Oh! I forget. I never intend to have a husband"? Perhaps it was when Sophia mentioned that Hawthorne planned to write a story based on an incident from Sophia's stay in Cuba. Sophia had told him how, while visiting friends in Havana, she had cleaned a sooty religious painting, using her fingers dipped in aromatic oils, and uncovered an astonishingly beautiful Mary Magdalene, which she took to be the work of the great seventeenth-century Spanish painter Murillo. Hawthorne set to work transposing the scene to colonial New England. "To be the means in any way of calling forth one of his divine creations, is no small happiness, is it?" Sophia asked Elizabeth.

The resulting story was "Edward Randolph's Portrait," with its heroine, Alice Vane, a woman "clad entirely in white, a pale, ethereal creature . . . almost a being from another world," who "exhibited no inferior genius" as an artist. Yet this same woman, "so child-like, so wayward . . . so apart from ordinary rules," was able to disrupt a colonial war council and nearly persuade the bellicose Governor Hutchinson to resist battle by cleaning an earlier governor's grimy portrait hanging in the council chamber, revealing a dark omen. The invalid artist Sophia Peabody had given Nathaniel Hawthorne his first substantial heroine. More than that, Alice Vane was a character imbued with Hawthorne's own ambitions as a creative artist. The outraged Hutchinson rebukes Alice Vane: how dare she bring into his offices "your painter's art—your Italian spirit of intrigue—your tricks of stage-effect—and think to influence the councils of rulers and the affairs of nations, by such shallow contrivances?" What more could Hawthorne have wished from the success of his own "shallow contrivances"—his stories—than to influence high councils and affairs of state?

Nathaniel Hawthorne had willingly accepted Elizabeth's consolations and her efforts to promote his career—but he had never written a story inspired by her. She was not his muse; Sophia was. Elizabeth responded to this last news by chiding Sophia for her excessive use of superlatives and directing her, as the suddenly petulant Sophia understood it, to leave off the accounts of "my visitations of truth" and stick to "what I see and do." Elizabeth wanted to hear no more of her little sister's soaring and singing—the Transcendental ramblings that revealed all too explicitly her surging emotions. "My whole being chords with nature," Sophia had written in early May. "There is one Life within me and abroad today."

In mid-June, Elizabeth at last received a single letter from Hawthorne with a cryptic message. She must have burned the letter according to Hawthorne's request, for it does not survive. But it was "queer and written in some sort of excitement when he was fighting with some unhappiness," Elizabeth wrote to Sophia, perhaps hoping to reestablish her authority on the writer's emotional life. Frustratingly, Elizabeth complained to Sophia, Hawthorne had also let her know that he had written another one, "quite a different sort of letter that he had concluded not to send." Elizabeth implored him to mail it anyway, but the letter—one that he told her he had written "out of his heart"—never arrived.

Could a man—particularly a shy one, who had spent more time imagining life than living it—be faulted for savoring the feeling of being loved by two women, two equally passionate sisters, at least for a time? Yet it proved too much. Shortly after writing his "queer" letter to Elizabeth, Hawthorne left Salem to travel. Sophia gave this terse account of his parting visit in a letter to her oldest sister: "He said he was not going to tell anyone where he was to be the next three months—that he thought he should change his name so that if he died no one would be able to find his grave stone. He should not tell even his Mother where he could be found—that he neither intended to write to any one nor be written to." Sophia added, "Perhaps he desired us to tell you this last resolve. He said he hardly thought he should go to Newton. He seems determined to be let alone."

Now Sophia was angry at Elizabeth for pestering Hawthorne, perhaps even driving him from Salem. Could Elizabeth have thought the same? This abrupt leave-taking was eerily reminiscent of Horace Mann's sudden departure from Somerset Court just five years before, dissolving the "happy union" that Mary and Elizabeth had enjoyed with the politician. Elizabeth was the one sister who could be implicated in both losses.

As soon as Nathaniel Hawthorne left Salem, Elizabeth began to hint that she'd like to come home. She complained to Sophia that in spite of all she had done for their brother Nat—finding him a house with an ample schoolroom, supplying him with pupils, teaching part of every day—he appeared "utterly indifferent" to her efforts. He seemed to believe, Elizabeth wrote in exasperation, that she had "come merely to gratify my own wilfulness," rather than to "set him up in life." On Elizabeth's single visit home in early July, Mrs. Peabody noticed that her oldest daughter looked unhappy and ominously thin. She encouraged her to move back home. But Elizabeth was undecided. She had no real work to do in Salem, and she was intellectually out of step there. She had begun to feel, she confided in her mother, as if she was of no use and had no place to go.

Much of Elizabeth's uncertainty had to do with her increasingly tense relations with Sophia. She was no longer certain she was welcome at home. To test the waters, Elizabeth wrote Sophia that she had entered a period of self-examination. After three months of Nat's silent treatment, she had concluded that "integrity" was more important than "charity": she hoped to find a way to live in more honest communication with others.

But Sophia misunderstood. Like Mary, Sophia tended to see Elizabeth as overbearing, inclined to push her younger siblings into ambitious and ill-conceived projects. Just that spring, Elizabeth had written from Newton Corner asking Sophia to produce more of her watercolors to decorate Nat's house and schoolroom, to which Sophia, fully occupied with the romance unfolding in her parlor, had responded with horror: "It makes one faint to think of it. Do not suggest any plans to me . . . I do not want anything expected of me." What's more, Sophia often squirmed inwardly when Elizabeth dominated conversations with guests—especially, of course, *important* guests, like Nathaniel Hawthorne. She was tired of listening to Elizabeth overdramatize or stretch the truth to suit her own ends. Sophia thought Elizabeth was admitting, now, to a lack of personal honesty, to the tendency to exaggerate and overwhelm that, Sophia wrote back, had long ago "destroyed your influence over me." Sophia welcomed Elizabeth "home to our very heart of hearts," now that she was willing to admit her faults and attempt to correct them. "I shall never be satisfied without you at my side," Sophia wrote, but she asked Elizabeth to promise not even to "mention my drawing" and to allow her to "follow the dictates of my mind."

Elizabeth was livid. She blasted Sophia as she had Mary in the past. "I do not tell lies—*but the truth* . . . as it appears to me," she defended herself. "An exaggeration in words sometimes conveys an idea much more completely than literal exactness." She despaired over Sophia's lack of "confidence" in her but stubbornly refused to change, assuring her sister that "you will find *me* going on just the same as ever." And she railed, "Conversation is hacked down to concentrated mediocrity" when polite speech matters more than full self-expression. Sophia's letter only pushed Elizabeth to make a more passionate statement of her views. "I feel as I never felt before that to be true to one's self is the first thing," she wrote, "that to sacrifice the perfect culture of my mind to social duties is not the thing . . . that one's inward instinct is one's best guide." The argument about whose sense of "veracity" was most genuine— about Sophia's need to "follow the dictates of my mind" and Elizabeth's desire to let her own "inward instinct" serve as her guide—was as close as either sister would come to acknowledging the summer-long tussle over Nathaniel Hawthorne.

Struggling to accommodate herself to the almost certain loss of the future that she had let herself imagine with Hawthorne, Elizabeth told Sophia, as she had written to Mary in Cuba, that she had made a mistake in not insisting on "a room to myself" when the whole family had lived together in Boston ten years earlier. She might then have been able to devote more time to her own interests, keep her volatile emotions in check, and in the end make a success of the venture. "It is better," she concluded now in sharp contrast to her choice to play conciliator with Bronson Alcott just two years earlier, "to be called selfish and oldmaidish than to lose one's own soul." Or to lose one's heart, she might also have said, if being truly honest with Sophia. Even in her journal, in which she now had "little heart to write," Elizabeth could speak only obliquely of the hurt she felt over Nathaniel Hawthorne's withdrawal of affection: "Dissolution is painful" when "attraction of cohesion ceases."

In the end Elizabeth took her August vacation with the Emersons in Concord on the way home to Salem, immersing herself in the controversy touched off by Waldo's "Divinity School Address"—and hoping to receive a friendlier letter from Sophia before her return. After all, it was Sophia who was winning this particular battle.

In Concord, Elizabeth was instantly comforted by the sense that Emerson "talks to me . . . with more freedom than ever." Back for her third stay at "the center of all things," Elizabeth was able, as on previous visits, to shake off much of her mournfulness and feel that "here I am myself in the highest sense," she wrote in her journal. In a long letter to her brother George, she explained the philosophy that she had gleaned from Emerson's "Cambridge sermon," as she called his "Divinity School Address." She paraphrased, "The central Idea is, there is something within the individual *me* which is *One* with the Father," and "above all things [one must] discriminate the traditional God from the real God that is within our own deepest *me*." It was no surprise that, jilted by the first man she had really let herself love, Elizabeth gravitated toward Emerson's philosophy of self-reliance.

"I begin to grow independent," she wrote to George; she was discovering that "wherever I can be myself and *act* if not speak my own soul, is my home." She was looking forward to returning to Salem because "I not only am coming to the *place* home, but to the *being* home. Such a combination of *homes* cannot but succeed." As the feeling of independence grew, Elizabeth became entranced with another idea of Emerson's, that "*Power* is the eternal life we find ourselves to have." The notion gave her a way of understanding her attraction to the three men she now described in a lengthy journal entry as "the three greatest actual powers" with whom "I am in direct relation": Waldo Emerson, Horace Mann, and Nathaniel Hawthorne. Elizabeth had long struggled to make sense of the strong emotions that drew her to such men and then caused her to feel that she was "losing my feet" when in their presence. In the case of Hawthorne, most recently, she had thought it was love. But now she told herself that it was "the divine in them" that "clutches my imagination and melts away my understanding." Inevitably, these men "master me."

Long ago in Brookline, in her early twenties, Elizabeth had dreamed of what she might do with "power, when, in the course of providence it may be, I gain it myself." Now she was thirty-four years old, with nearly two decades of experience in trying to attain and wield influence. It had never been simple: treading a path between personal ambition, something denied to well-mannered women, and the more acceptable choice to commit her formidable energy and intellect to serving the men of promise she seemed almost mystically able to recognize and draw out.

Finally, for a few short months, she had envisioned herself the wife of one such man—only to be turned away, she guessed, for the very qualities that had first attracted him to her. What long-term role, Elizabeth asked herself now, could she play with any of these men, if not wife? Could she still even count all three of them as friends? She feared that both Hawthorne and Mann were drifting away from her as confidants. Did they mistake her devotion to them for unrequited love—or, perhaps worse still, *flattery*, when she meant only to help them realize their own genius and bring it forward? In fact, she viewed all three men as "imperfect & undeveloped," even as she revered them. "Does the becoming interest the human heart," she asked herself, "more than the arrived?" Certainly the "becoming" of these particular men interested Elizabeth Peabody.

She considered the three: two of them unmarried, the third, Waldo Emerson, "just as beautiful"—spiritually, she meant—at thirty-five and married to his second wife, Lidian, as when Elizabeth had known him as her Greek tutor in his late teens. Nathaniel Hawthorne was "beautiful unmarried, because true to himself in being so," although he had "tenderness enough to make a hundred husbands." But she suspected that "at this very moment Hawthorne may be passing out of the state of celibacy," emotionally, at least, as he ceded his heart to Sophia. She vowed not to risk further hurt by writing to him, since he still had not sent the second letter, the one he had told her was written "out of his heart." As for Horace Mann, Elizabeth worried that, although he now seemed certain of "his duty," the reformer's grasp on life was tenuous. This same August, Mann had observed that after six years, the "anniversary" of his wife, Charlotte's, death fell on the same day of the week that she had died, a Wednesday. Alone in his office he "lived the events of the scene, successively over again," feeling an even "stronger semblance of reality." Charlotte's suffering came back to him, along with his anguish that she had died so suddenly, without saying "farewell." "Oh, my love!" he wrote in his journal, "let me still and forever love you."

Dallying in Concord, Elizabeth finally received the conciliatory letter she'd hoped for from Sophia, one that was "true, truer than usual." The letter does not survive, but from it Elizabeth concluded that both Sophia and Nathaniel Hawthorne were "coming to understand that wholeness of communication is truth of intercourse" and to share her impatience with "limited communications." For "this wholeness from these I have pined," Elizabeth wrote in her journal, and she brushed away Sophia's earlier outburst: "She is too delicate in health to endure full communication reciprocally—in this world of inevitable mistakes." Elizabeth had always managed to overcome her anger at her youngest sister by reminding herself of Sophia's physical weakness. This time, the hardest time of all—the one that put her in such visible torment that even Waldo Emerson had "divine[d]" she was in a "difficult position"—would be no different. Elizabeth would make sure it was so. Otherwise, she knew, she would lose her connection with Nathaniel Hawthorne entirely.

The fall of 1838 found all three sisters in Salem rallying around their invalid brother, George. The usual guests passed through the parlor on Charter Street. Jones Very anointed Elizabeth there in September and returned for her solace in October after his stay in McLean Asylum. Very appeared again on a cold autumn night when Nathaniel Hawthorne was already visiting. The inspired poet "delivered his mission to Mr. Hawthorne," Elizabeth wrote to Emerson late in the year, and Hawthorne "received it in the loveliest manner," commenting afterward that he thought Very "better remain as he is ... as long as he can write such good sonnets." But rather than dwell on Very's case in her letter, Elizabeth took the occasion to "castigate" Emerson for his "obstinate blindness" to Hawthorne, the "real *Poet.*" Elizabeth had sent Hawthorne's story "Foot-prints on the Sea-shore" to Emerson the previous summer only to have the philosopher complain "there was no inside to it." To Elizabeth's chagrin, Emerson had quipped, "Alcott & he together would make a man."

Neither Emerson's dismissal nor Hawthorne's apparent rejection lessened the vigor with which Elizabeth worked to promote the storyteller's career through that fall. Since graduating from college, Hawthorne had been living frugally on his share of the income from his mother's family stagecoach line; but business had declined sharply as railroads spread across New England and was near collapse by the summer of 1838 when train service finally connected Salem to Boston. Elizabeth knew Hawthorne would soon have to go to work to support himself and any woman he took for a bride. She continued to press his case as a children's book author with Horace Mann, even arranging for the two to meet in the Peabody parlor in Salem, where, Elizabeth later wrote to Mann, she hoped that "the frigidity" of Hawthorne's "diffidence" did not "quite destroy the brilliancy of his beauty." It was hard for Mann to "see him to advantage," she admitted, but "no stranger can." She maintained, "I expect great things of him for his country, notwithstanding he works in Fancy's stuff. . . . He is an embodiment of Genius."

Elizabeth was more successful in badgering her friends in high places to find Hawthorne a political appointment "requiring very little time & work— & having abundant leisure and liberty" for writing. By November, she had wangled him the offer of a post as customs inspector at the Port of Boston, for which he would receive $1,100 a year—not a large sum, but he could expect to supplement it with the sale of his stories. The offer came from the prominent Democratic lawyer and politician George Bancroft as a result of pressure that Elizabeth applied through Bancroft's wife, Elizabeth Bliss Bancroft, a former student, and another mutual friend, Orestes Brownson. Although it would mean leaving Salem at the start of the new year, Hawthorne was sorely tempted.

Sophia had done no less in her own way. Without telling Hawthorne of her plan, she began work on an illustration of her favorite story from *Twice-told Tales*, "The Gentle Boy." Sophia chose the opening scene, in which the young boy Ilbrahim is found weeping beneath the gallows tree in a colonial New England village, where his father has been put to death for Quaker heresies. "My home is here," declares the child to the Puritan townsman who offers him shelter, pointing to his father's grave. When Sophia's drawing was done, she showed it to Hawthorne, asking, "I want to know if this looks like your Ilbrahim?" Hawthorne—himself a fatherless son—studied the sketch for a moment and replied, "He will never look otherwise to me!"

Sophia Peabody's illustration for *The Gentle Boy*

Word of the successful drawing traveled fast in Salem and even to Boston. Soon there were plans to publish the story and illustration in a special edition, subsidized by Salem's Susan Burley. A well-known engraver, Joseph Andrews, would do the job of transferring Sophia's sketch to a lithographic stone. *The Gentle Boy: A Thrice Told Tale* wasn't a new work, but it would be the first volume Hawthorne had sent to the printer since *Twice-told Tales* nearly two years before. Its appearance would remind reviewers and the reading public of Nathaniel Hawthorne's existence as a writer. Moreover, the project accomplished Sophia's scheme to establish Hawthorne as an author worthy of illustration—an American Shakespeare, Homer, or Goethe. It was after such volumes by Flaxman and Moritz Retzsch that Sophia had modeled her stylized sketch. And it was for qualities her drawing shared with the work of these European masters—its "simple severe lines"—that the illustration won the approval of Washington Allston, who allowed his "warm recommendation" to be quoted in Hawthorne's preface to the edition.

But, finally, it was the praise Nathaniel Hawthorne himself lavished on the drawing that meant the most to Sophia. Hawthorne trumpeted his dedication of the book to its illustrator in capital letters on the book's title page:

To Miss Sophia A. Peabody
THIS LITTLE TALE,
TO WHICH HER KINDRED ART HAS GIVEN VALUE,
IS RESPECTFULLY INSCRIBED
BY THE AUTHOR

He expanded his praise in a brief preface, describing the drawing as "a creation of deep and pure beauty" that had "caught and embodied" in its "few and simple lines" all that the author himself had failed to "shadow forth in language." It was Sophia's drawing that made *The Gentle Boy* a "thrice told tale."

In reviews afterward, Park Benjamin, writing in *The New-Yorker*, judged Sophia's drawing "a display of the most exquisite genius." The frontispiece was "softly and delicately drawn," he wrote, the expressions on both faces "angelic," and the entire composition "highly poetic." Washington Allston weighed in again in print, devoting nearly half of his review in the *Christian Register and Boston Observer* to Sophia's drawing, praising the "pathetic and beautiful" face of the boy and urging "the young artist" to illustrate more of "Mr. Hawthorne's exquisite fancies." Might they go on to practice their "kindred" arts together?

But even as *The Gentle Boy* went to press, Sophia was making another drawing that would prove even more valuable, securing Nathaniel Hawthorne to her in a lasting way. This one was not meant for public viewing. Hawthorne was visiting the Peabody household on an evening in early December 1838 when Sophia took up a pencil to make a "sketch of your countenance." She studied her subject intently before starting to draw. "I had never beheld your face before I tried to reproduce it," Sophia would write to Hawthorne. She was searching his features and expression to locate the "ideal perfection" of his character, the inner spirit that is "truer than what passes before our careless glance." Finding it difficult to sit still under Sophia's steady gaze, Hawthorne teased that in years to come "such changes would come over my face" that she "would not know me when we met again in Heaven." Sophia retorted, pencil in hand and smiling to undercut her challenge, "See if I don't!"

Later that night, at home in his study, Hawthorne confided in his journal that there had seemed "the most peculiar and beautiful humor" in Sophia's reply, "in the point itself, and in her manner, that can be imagined." Sophia picked up the thread in a letter she sent to Hawthorne two days later, written with the sketch propped on her desk and wishing "you would look round, my dear friend," and speak. Now, she insisted she would "recognize" Nathaniel Hawthorne's face "through all eternity."

Did all this talk of meeting in heaven, of knowing each other through all eternity, mean that Sophia Peabody and Nathaniel Hawthorne had formed a

Nathaniel Hawthorne, sketch by Sophia Peabody

romantic bond? With the promise of work ahead of him—Elizabeth had gotten Bancroft to raise the salary to $1,500 and upgrade the author's title from "inspector" to "measurer"—and with Sophia's devotion and drawing skill available to support him as well, Nathaniel Hawthorne was finally in a position to propose marriage to Sophia Peabody. As for Sophia, her love for Nathaniel Hawthorne was revealed in her sketch: a face that was more a boy's than a thirty-four-year-old man's, round, smiling, with curls and long lashes, cherubic, yet still recognizably Hawthorne. It was the face the writer wanted her to see—guileless, guiltless—and the one she would commit to "eternal" memory.

By New Year's Day 1839, the two were secretly engaged. There still remained too many unknowns—Sophia's health, Hawthorne's finances—to make their plan public. But Sophia's gift of a handsome volume of Wordsworth's poetry sealed the pact. On its title page, along with her inscription to "Nathaniel Hawthorne, Esq. from his very true and affectionate friend S. A. Peabody, January 1st 1839," Sophia wrote out a portion of one of Wordsworth's lyrics with the pronouns altered to suit their new state:

> For we have waking empire, wide as dreams;
> An ample sovereignty of eye & ear,
> Rich *are our walks* with supernatural cheer;
> The region of our inner spirit teems
> With vital sounds and monitory gleams
> Of high astonishment & pleasing fear.

Sophia's *innere* had expanded to become "our inner spirit," enfolding Nathaniel Hawthorne. The only step that remained was for Hawthorne to make his intentions plain to Elizabeth. Speaking his mind on difficult personal subjects was close to impossible for the man. But he could write—and write he did, a New Year's message addressed both to the city of Salem, where rumors of his romantic life continued to circulate, and to the two sisters he had loved during the previous year. If he had known they would read it sitting next to each other on a train bound from Salem to Boston, would he have reconsidered?

Sophia was traveling to Boston to oversee corrections to the engraving of *The Gentle Boy* (she felt that Andrews had gotten the nose all wrong) and to visit the studio of the sculptor Shobal Clevenger, celebrated for his marble bust of Daniel Webster, to ask his advice on beginning to work in clay. Elizabeth rode along only to be sure that Sophia made the trip safely; she would return the same day with news for Hawthorne on his position at Boston's Custom House. Sophia wrote to their father that she and Elizabeth had "passed the time" on the train reading aloud Hawthorne's "The Sister Years," his New Year's "address" printed in the January 1 edition of the *Salem Gazette*, and finding it "full of wisdom" and "illuminated with wit." But what were their innermost thoughts? The allegory was all too obvious.

In "The Sister Years"—a story Hawthorne liked so well that he included it in later editions of *Twice-told Tales*—the writer pictured the New Year as a young maiden full of "smiling cheerfulness," dressed in light clothing and carrying a basketful of roses, arriving in Salem on the first morning train of January 1839. The young New Year has come to replace her "disconsolate" older sister who waits for her at the station, burdened with an enormous folio volume, her "Book of Chronicles." Spilling from the arms of the Old Year are more remnants of the difficult months of 1838: "several bundles of love-letters, eloquently breathing an eternity of burning passion, which grew cold and perished, almost before the ink was dry," as well as "an assortment of many thousand broken promises" and "a large parcel of disappointed hopes." The New Year listens uncomprehendingly to her older sister's catalogue of woes and dire predictions of future trouble, then offers up as consolation the "fine lot of hopes here in my basket" before starting up the street, "a wonderfully pleasant looking figure," handing out sweet-smelling roses to everyone she meets.

Sophia had already given Nathaniel Hawthorne the ethereal free-spirited artist Alice Vane of "Edward Randolph's Portrait." Now she appeared again, unmistakably, as the younger of the two "Sister Years," a woman full of "so much promise and such an indescribable hopefulness in her aspect, that hardly anybody could meet her without anticipating some very desirable thing—the consummation of some long sought good."

Both Sophia and Elizabeth knew the meaning of Hawthorne's allegory—read his love for Sophia in these words. That Elizabeth had, at last, found her way into one of Hawthorne's stories as the disappointed and disheveled Old Year was small consolation for the rejection that she now understood was final. For Sophia, however, the tale was confirmation of the happy secret she carried with her on the train to Boston: her engagement to Nathaniel Hawthorne. How curious that the same railroad line on which she was now riding had put Hawthorne's family, with whom he had so long sequestered himself, out of business. But in his story, the railroad delivered "the consummation of some long sought good" to Salem. And so it did to the author as well—making a man of Nathaniel Hawthorne, transporting him into the world of work and love, and bringing him, along with his blossoming fiancée, the promise of a new life in the New Year.

PART VIII

13 West Street, Boston

1840–1842

❧ 28 ❧

Conversation

MARY COULDN'T STAND IT ANYMORE. THREE YEARS' EXILE IN SALEM was long enough. Yet she guarded the reason for her move to Boston in January 1839 as closely as Sophia did her secret engagement to Nathaniel Hawthorne—more so. Mary's love for Horace Mann was her secret alone. She let her friends and family believe she was leaving Salem to seek higher wages as a teacher in Boston. With three invalid dependents at home now—Sophia, George, and Dr. Peabody, who was ill all winter—Mary seemed "the only one to obtain what they need." But the truth was, Mary was moving to Boston to live closer to Horace Mann, and he was helping her do it. Mann had enlisted his friend Mary Jane Quincy—wife of the influential politician Josiah Quincy and daughter-in-law of Harvard's president of the same name—to gather a school for Mary to teach with her three children as its core.

Not that Mann had given Mary indications that his affections were turning toward her in any more than a brotherly fashion. But she sensed a lessening of mournfulness in his letters and an intensifying of interest and concern directed her way. Although Mann was careful to use the same salutation—"My dear Miss Peabody"—when writing to both Elizabeth and Mary, his tone with Mary was more playful and gallant, less apt to stray into admonition. In one recent letter, Mann had ordered Elizabeth to delete "anything of ... 'the absolute' & 'the infinite'" in a prize essay that she was drafting on common school reform and to "keep to Saxon language *mainly* & to Saxon sense *wholly*," if she had any hope of winning the cash award. When writing to Mary of the Boston school plan he was helping her implement, however, Mann spoke only in positives—of the children who would soon be "nestling under your wing."

If, as Mary wrote to her friend Sally Gardner at the end of December 1838, "my cheeks have got into a habit of flushing" whenever the subject of Emerson's recent Boston lectures on "Human Life" came up, it was because she had been attending them with Horace Mann. The new train to Boston, along with the complimentary tickets Waldo had sent to the Peabodys in Salem, made it all possible. But it was Mann who found lodging for Mary with the Quincys at 4 Park Street, across the Common from the Masonic Temple, for the nights following the lectures, and "arrogate[d] to myself the honor of escorting you there" and back again. The last lecture of the year had been on "Love." In closing, Emerson, who like Mann had lost a young wife to tuberculosis, left his audience with words that Mary must have hoped her beloved would take to heart. "Though slowly and with pain, the objects of the affections change," Emerson told the crowd. "That which is so beautiful and attractive as these relations must be succeeded and supplanted only by what is more beautiful."

Still, Mary didn't expect a marriage proposal any time soon, if ever. In making her move to Boston, she was operating on a theory—one she would set down decades later in an essay on "single blessedness"—that "it is far better for the soul to live in an ideal union with a possible twin-soul than to enter marriage upon a low plane of thought or feeling." What she meant was that she preferred her unrequited love for Horace Mann to the marriage she might have made with Benjamin Lindsay of New Bedford five years earlier. As she had written then, "I would never accept a heart unless I *knew* I could give full measure." Mary was willing to become one of the "noble army of unmarried women" who remain single because "their ideal of the marriage state is far beyond that of the average woman." And she would make the best of the situation by living as close as she could to that "possible twin-soul," helping him by reading proofs of his annual reports from the board of education to the state legislature or by contributing anonymously to his *Common School Journal.* She would pour the rest of her energy into her own work.

For although Elizabeth had gained more recognition as an educator, Mary had been teaching longer—every year, without interruption, since the summer before her eighteenth birthday. She was now thirty-two. Gone were the days when her mother had to urge her to put her daydreams aside and concentrate on schoolroom tasks. Once she stopped working as Elizabeth's partner in schools for adolescent girls and turned to teaching mixed classes of very young children, Mary discovered that she, too, was an instinctive teacher—bred for it, like Elizabeth, in the Peabody "family school." Like her older sister and their mother before them, Mary had her own ideas and was quick to claim them as such. "I will tell you . . . how I found out methods," she once wrote a young teacher just starting out, "because they were *not* practiced upon me."

Once settled in her Boston school, Mary took the children out on the Common twice a day to coast on its snowbanks in winter and, when spring arrived, to observe flowers and butterflies and learn their names and growth cycles. As her small pupils grew to know and love the open park, in which all paths seemed to lead to the elegant brick State House at the top of the hill, she gave them their first lessons in history and civil government by describing the town fathers' efforts to establish and then preserve the communal land over the two centuries since the founding of the city. Mary made a story of it, just as in the classroom she relied on telling stories and fables or reading aloud to cultivate a love of literature. She taught her young pupils to read individually and only when she decided each one was ready, starting with single words for objects they had learned to care about—"bird, nest, tree"—then helping the child recognize those words in printed versions of the tales she had already recited. Mary would never "force helpless little ones" to memorize the alphabet, she wrote, before "every letter is interesting to them from the position it holds in some symbolic word." The six-year-old boy on whom she had first tried this experiment years earlier in Salem had learned to read fluently within six weeks.

Above all, Mary talked with the children "about every thing that interested them," she later recalled. She became the "repository of all their joys and sorrows" and even of their "home trials" with "careless or exacting fathers" or "pleasure-hunting and selfish mothers." For "I do not feel satisfied till the most timid and reserved are confiding to me, smile when they meet my eye, and come to me in the hour of trouble; nor till the most perverse and reckless take my reproofs in sorrow and not in anger, and return to me for sympathy when they are good." She approached teaching with what she called a "spirit of adoption." And in another letter of advice to the same young teacher, she wrote, "When my little scholars call me 'mother,' which they often do from inadvertence, I feel most that I am in the true relation to them." Like Elizabeth, but without the burden of philosophical schematics, Mary considered her vocation to be one of training the whole child, not just the child's intellect. She aimed to "seize every opportunity to unfold thought in a natural way, to consider duty, and keep alive conscience" in her students. But she would also see to it that "the flow of happy spirits should be unchecked." The conscience might be awakened and kept alive, but it would never be manipulated—as it had been, in Mary's view, by Bronson Alcott at the Temple School with his leading questions and temptations to misbehave.

Indeed the Temple School scandal nearly threatened the success of Mary's new class, even three years after Elizabeth's break with Alcott. Mary wrote to Sophia early in 1839 that she was questioned "at every turn" as to whether she had recorded any part of *Conversations with Children on the Gospels* or had taken Alcott's side in the controversy. One mother told her that "if I did sympathise with Mr A. she could not think of putting [her] Willy under my charge!" Mary mounted a campaign to ensure that "my real views upon this subject" were known. Elizabeth testified that Mary had not recorded any of the *Conversations*, carefully omitting the truth—that Sophia had. Mary counseled Sophia to keep silent about her own involvement in the matter, if asked, as "very likely" she would be when in Boston, and to emphasize that Mary herself "did not approve of the book." Horace Mann's good word took care of the rest.

As Mary's school expanded and she moved from the Quincys' house to a rented room of her own on Chauncey Place, her residence became a Boston foothold for her sisters. In May and June 1839, Elizabeth, who had taken over Mary's Salem school, spent her spring recess in the city attending a retrospective exhibition of Washington Allston's work and writing regular dispatches for the *Salem Gazette*. Nearly fifty paintings, virtually all of the artist's work available in America, were mounted in Chester Harding's portrait gallery on School Street. Allston was still Boston's most widely known cultural celebrity —perhaps the only one with an international reputation. The New York banker Samuel Ward sent his daughters Julia (later Julia Ward Howe) and Louisa (who would marry the sculptor Thomas Crawford) to stay in Boston with their tutor and take in the exhibition, with its enormous biblical scenes, lavish Italian landscapes, and representations of characters from Dante, Spenser, and Shakespeare. Twenty-nine-year-old Margaret Fuller, who spent so much time at the exhibition that she began referring to the gallery as her "home," was rumored to have fainted while looking intently at one of Allston's paintings. If she did, it was little wonder, as thousands of admirers crowded into the small gallery rooms during the show's two-and-a-half-month run.

Fuller took extensive notes, which she turned into an article on the Allston exhibit a year later. But Elizabeth's series for the *Salem Gazette* was the most thorough analysis of the show at the time, and some of the best writing on Allston for decades to come. She treated more than a dozen works in detail, provided a chronology (that she noted was lacking from the exhibition itself), and ventured some Transcendentally inclined aesthetic theory derived from Allston's landscapes: "It is precisely the proof of the highest artist that he suggests more than he expresses; that he touches the imagination. The highest art does more than give us a *fac-simile* of a piece of Nature; it selects and combines natural objects under the inspiration of a sentiment or idea, so that the whole is suggested by the miniature." Later in the year, the fledgling publisher William D. Ticknor printed the series as a pamphlet, *Remarks on Allston's Paintings*.

Sophia, too, stayed with Mary when she came down from Salem to meet with the wunderkind Shobal Clevenger and discuss her new work in clay. (It was a mark of Sophia's increasing self-confidence that she had ventured into the medium: sculpture was valued even more highly by the New England avant-garde than landscape painting for its capability of expressing the ideal in form.) Sophia spread her visits among a network of Boston friends in order to conceal the frequency of her other meetings—with Nathaniel Hawthorne, now officially a measurer at the Custom House. Sophia's first effort in clay, which she planned to cast in plaster, was a bas-relief profile of her brother George, whose health was deteriorating rapidly. When Clevenger finally saw the finished "medallion," as Sophia called it—a classically inspired oval in which George appeared heroically full-scale as "Georgius Imperador"—he approved of all but "the whiskers," and found fault with these only because Sophia's careful rendition of George's beard was "too fine work to look well in plaster."

Sophia had the piece cast all the same and made corrections in the plaster with a penknife. She feared that George might not live long enough for her to make another trip to Boston, and she wanted to be sure he saw the finished piece. Sophia's Boston friends all expressed "great admiration" and exclaimed over the medallion's likeness to George; even the Italian artisans who set the piece in plaster declared it "very good for the first." But Sophia took the most pride in a parting offer from Clevenger, who would settle in Rome as soon as he finished the commissioned portrait bust of Washington Allston that had brought him to Boston. Clevenger promised personally to oversee the production of any pieces Sophia might send to him in Italy, where he would have them "put into marble . . . and add the finishing touches" himself.

While Sophia allowed her friend Sarah Clarke, who had recently assumed the enviable position of Washington Allston's sole Boston pupil, to address her now as "thou sculptor," Sophia had not put aside painting entirely. She was at work on two Italian landscapes derived from scenes in a prized book of Lake Como etchings. She planned to present them to her fiancé—the man she now addressed in her private letters as "my husband," just as he called her "my wife." Both knew it would be some time before "our union is to be revealed to the world," as Nathaniel wrote to Sophia, but took comfort in the notion that "we *are* married . . . God knows we are," during the long weeks of separation. The couple's intuitive grasp of each other's *innere* had only been confirmed by the passing of time. Hawthorne, with his own secretive writing habits, even seemed to understand the freedom from expectation that Sophia needed in order to work. When Elizabeth ran into him at the Allston exhibition one evening and told him that Sophia had "several things a-going, but did not like to tell of her plans," the writer responded that he supposed then Sophia "would be more likely to execute them." He added, "It was a good thing to have several paintings at once" because Sophia could then "rest" herself "by change."

Hawthorne seemed "transported with delight" to hear that Sophia was well enough to paint, Elizabeth reported to her younger sister. He knew that meant his "wife" was also well enough to travel to Boston, where she too now spent full weeks at a time. Her visits to the city were as much to see Nathaniel as to take instruction from Clevenger, which may have provided a convenient cover. By early April 1839, just three months into their engagement, Sophia had already found a number of opportunities to "nestle upon my heart" and exchange kisses and embraces, as Nathaniel wrote longingly to "my Dove," the nickname he favored in his increasingly frequent letters to Sophia in Salem. Neither one wanted to see an end to such stolen moments.

Nathaniel may have missed Sophia more, for he was living alone in the city and struggling to adapt to the "pester and plague" of his mind-numbing duties — actually measuring out salt and coal in the holds and on the decks of ships. But he wrote to Sophia, the woman he hoped to impress and one day support with his labors, that "I need such training, and ought to have undergone it long ago. It will give my character a healthy hardness as regards the world; while it will leave my heart as soft—as fit for a Dove to rest upon—as it is now, or ever was." For her part, Sophia was thriving—wearing her hair in a "Grecian braid," sleeping "soundly" on the nights after she'd seen Nathaniel, and hearing from more than one Boston friend that "I never looked so well before" — a comment she was not inclined, as in previous years, to refute with recitations of dire symptoms.

Not all of the couple's Boston encounters were private. In late October 1839, both Nathaniel and Sophia met Elizabeth's friend Margaret Fuller for the first time at a party in Connie Park's rented rooms. (Connie was still waiting for her husband, Tom, to send for her from California.) More Transcendental company was on hand, including the Reverend George Ripley, to partake in an Elysian feast of preserved Greek roses and oranges. But it was Fuller who held the floor, entertaining the guests with "another species of fare," in Sophia's account, discoursing on music and sculpture "like a sybil on her tripod"—the mythic priestess at Delphi, an oracular maiden perched on a tripod spanning a cleft in the Sibylline Rock and uttering prophesies in song. Afflicted with curvature of the spine, Fuller may have appeared awkward in form—like the sibyl on her roost—yet her conversation, Waldo Emerson could attest, was the "most entertaining" in America. With a "muscular and well-developed frame . . . gray eye, rich brown hair and light complexion," by one male friend's report, Fuller was nevertheless considered no "beauty"; perhaps her barbed wit, and the freedom with which she used it, disqualified her, in men's eyes. But she exerted a "commanding charm" on all who met her, "a haughty assurance,—queen-like," in Emerson's estimation. Oliver Wendell Holmes compared her to a swan. While Sophia found Fuller "not so graceful as I imagined a Greek sybil to be," she felt the meeting to be significant—"my first interview," she recorded afterward.

Like the Peabody sisters, Margaret Fuller was a woman thrown on her own resources, although Fuller's reversal of fortune dated back only as far as 1835,

Margaret Fuller

the year of her lawyer father's sudden death. In 1839 she had moved her
family to Jamaica Plain, five miles outside Boston, ending several years as an
itinerant schoolteacher. She was determined to break into print with ideas
that she had been forming in a long intellectual apprenticeship, beginning at
age six with a rigorous education in classical and modern languages under
her father's supervision. Fuller now lived near enough to attend Transcenden-

tal Club meetings on a regular basis, and after the most recent session, Emerson had named her editor of *The Dial*, the new magazine that would serve as the club's mouthpiece, circumventing the Unitarian journals now mostly closed to the radical band. The job promised modest financial support and may also have added to the air of authority that Fuller radiated at Connie Park's soiree. But confidence in social situations was something Fuller had never lacked. When given the chance to hold forth in public, "she smites and kindles, with all the force, irregularity, and matchless beauty of lightning," the young Reverend Theodore Parker, now also a regular at Transcendental Club meetings, rhapsodized to Elizabeth late in the summer of 1839.

Since August, Fuller had been contemplating another moneymaking scheme that would capitalize on this talent: a class for women in the art of conversation. Elizabeth had already been working to get Fuller assignments for the *Democratic Review*. (Fuller's single question had been whether the editor would "pay me *unasked* . . . or torture all my lady like feelings" by forcing her to request payment; Elizabeth was still awaiting payment for an article that had appeared in the fall of 1838.) Learning of Fuller's new plan, Elizabeth put aside any competitive feelings—it was Elizabeth, after all, who had conducted Boston's first intellectual discussion groups for women, starting with her historical courses in 1831—and turned her attention to helping her younger colleague. She volunteered Mary's room at 1 Chauncey Place as a space for daytime classes while Mary was out teaching, and she did her best to find Fuller students.

Gathering this class was not at first as easy as collecting pupils for Bronson Alcott had been. When Elizabeth tried Lydia Parker, Theodore Parker's wife and a former student, the minister wrote back declining Elizabeth's invitation on Lydia's behalf because of the "reluctance she feels at conversing at all." The feminine timidity Fuller hoped to overcome—the same distressing silence Elizabeth had noted decades earlier in the Reverend Channing's Bible study classes for women—was preventing potential students from joining. It seemed for a time that, aside from Peabody and Fuller, men were the prime supporters of the plan. Emerson, Channing, and Alcott were all active partisans, and Parker too expected Fuller "will *awaken* minds, to think, examine, doubt, and at last conclude," as he wrote to Elizabeth, lamenting that all too often the conversation of "ladies of the best circle even in Boston . . . turns on subjects of no consequence."

Yet by November, a dozen women had signed up. With few exceptions, they came from Elizabeth's circle of friends and former students: among them Sally Gardner; Connie Park; Elizabeth Bliss Bancroft; Caroline Sturgis and her two sisters Anna and Ellen, both now married to Hooper brothers, doubly uniting two important New England mercantile families; Mary's employer,

Mary Jane Quincy; and Sophia Dana Ripley, the Cambridge girl who had so impressed Elizabeth with her breadth of knowledge over a decade before, now George Ripley's wife. It was settled that the "Conversations," as Fuller began to call them, would be held on Wednesday mornings so that out-of-town members could stay into the evening for Waldo Emerson's lectures on "The Present Age" at the Masonic Hall. Fuller had borrowed the term from Alcott, for whom she had served as assistant in the few months after Elizabeth's departure, before the Temple School's demise; aside from his *Conversations with Children on the Gospels*, Alcott had begun holding Friday-evening "Conversations" for Boston schoolteachers in the fall of 1836. But such was the force of Fuller's personality that, as with anything else she appropriated from others, the term "Conversations" would afterward always be associated with her.

Elizabeth took the train down from Salem for both Fuller's classes and Emerson's lectures, spending the dinner hour and late evenings with the Reverend Channing, whose gender in the first case and declining health in the second prevented him from attending either one. At the first Conversation on November 6, 1839, Fuller laid out an ambitious agenda. In the coming weeks she hoped to raise and answer "the great questions" facing women: "What were we born to do? How shall we do it? which so few ever propose to themselves 'till their best years are gone by." Fuller herself intended to serve as the "nucleus of conversation," to be just "*one* to give her own best thoughts on any subject that was named, as a means of calling out the thoughts of others." But she could never entirely cede the reins to her students. By the second session, on November 13, the group had consented to Fuller's proposal that they discuss Greek mythology in future meetings; Fuller would expound on the tales and characters as representations of qualities in human nature and invite the response of class members. It was a subject, Fuller said, "on which we knew words—& had impressions, & vague irregular notions." Fuller's aim was to "compel ourselves to define those words, to turn these impressions into thoughts, & to systematise these thoughts."

Fuller deplored the scattershot education most schoolgirls received, taking up "superficially even *more* studies" than boys, so that when, as women, they "come to the business of life & the application of knowledge they find that they are *inferior*—& all their studies have not given them that practical good sense & mother wisdom & wit which grew up with our grandmothers at the spinning wheel," Elizabeth recorded in her notes on the meeting. The sessions were to carry through till the spring, twenty in all. Fuller expected that "we should probably have to go through some mortification in finding how much less we knew than we thought—& on the other hand we should probably find ourselves encouraged by seeing how much & how rapidly we should gain by making a simple & clear effort for expression." While Elizabeth almost certainly knew more Greek mythology than any woman present—her knowledge of the Greek language itself surpassed all others, Fuller's included—she willingly placed herself among the group, ready to learn what she could from Fuller about "simple & clear" communication. And, as with Channing's sermons and Alcott's classroom dialogues in past years, Elizabeth took up the role of recorder, sensing, once again, that she was about to witness a display of genius. Many years later, Elizabeth recalled, "I think no one attended that course . . . who did not pronounce [Fuller's] initial statements and occasional bursts of eloquence the most splendid exhibitions of conversational talent, not only that they ever heard, but that they ever heard of."

Elizabeth was in Boston attending Fuller's second Conversation when Sophia wrote to say that George had suffered "a dangerous bleeding," continuing for two days. Elizabeth returned to Salem immediately. There she found George still alert, despite intense pain and exhaustion, and asking to hear the doctor's prognosis—"he did not want to go without knowing it." The doctor expected George to live only a few more days. Desperately ill, George nevertheless found the strength to tell Sophia that her "medallion" had been "finished just at the point of time." Sophia marveled at her brother's "perfect serenity" and "composure" in the face of death. She had never seen "a more entire resigning of life . . . than his."

In less than a week, George was dead, buried with his brother Wellington in a single grave beside the infant Catharine's at Salem's Howard Street Cemetery, a bleak few acres behind the town prison on the banks of the North River. George's "entire" resignation, his bravery through the final months of affliction, made his family's discovery of six small packets of braided hair in his wallet, each marked with a different woman's initials, along with a poem clipped from a newspaper titled "Flirtation," all the more poignant. George had just passed his twenty-sixth birthday; he had spent the last two years of his life confined to his room, unable to rise from his bed or easy chair.

Elizabeth had been the one to sit with George, holding his hand and wiping his brow, during the last forty-eight hours of his "death struggle," when even their mother left the room, unable to bear the sight of her son's agony. George was by then "long past recognition," Elizabeth wrote to Horace Mann, and even longer past speaking. "I never saw death before," she wrote, "that final look of distress, that convulsion, and then that *sudden peace and sweetness*." Elizabeth was thankful on George's behalf that his suffering was over, but she felt that she had "lost what loved me best, with an infinite affection." Nine years younger, George had never joined his sisters and older brother in rivalry with Elizabeth. He had even welcomed her efforts to direct his future; in return,

Elizabeth had confided her own hopes in George as he grew older, sure of his admiration and love. Now this support was gone. Yet, as Wellington's death two years before had prompted Sophia to venture from her room, so did George's seem to release Elizabeth: first, literally, from the obligation to help care for him in Salem, and then from the ceaseless self-questioning that had so often stood in the way of her resolve to "be myself and *act*," as she had written to George the year before from Concord.

For years Elizabeth had tormented herself with the thought that, as she once wrote Horace Mann, "I never performed the promise of my childhood." What had become of the girl who sought out British Socinian texts all on her own, argued over Swedenborgian theology with adults three times her age, read the New Testament thirty times in one summer, and taught herself Hebrew so that she could make her own translation of the Old Testament? There had been many obstacles. Because of financial hardship, she had been "thrown too early" into the working world, teaching long hours when she might have studied and written more. And there was the fact of her sex. Without the option of college or a profession, Elizabeth had not known how or where to apply herself. She had looked to men of genius to confirm her talents and grown "dependent on the daily consolations of friendship." She could see now that she had "constantly craved . . . assurances" that should have "come from within."

Yet these same men often curbed her enthusiasm with comments on her dress, her manner, her aspirations. Even her beloved Reverend Channing had required her to limit her ambitions; she was haunted, now, by the recollection of his admonishment to "devote your powers to the service of your fellow creatures, and not use them to make yourself distinguished" which had immediately followed his praise of her "original thoughts" in her paraphrase of the Gospel according to Saint John. Would he have said the same to a young man whose writing and ideas he admired? The memory was all the more disturbing as Elizabeth recognized a similarity in the ideas in that early paper—one she had also shown Waldo Emerson when they met again in Boston in 1832, after his first wife's death—and the very ideas that now were creating such a stir in Emerson's "Divinity School Address." "It was my creed before I knew it was his," she wrote to a friend in defense of Emerson's speech, "this heresy does not belong to his mind alone."

On the whole, however, Elizabeth still agreed with Channing; she would not seek personal fame. Yet new thoughts gained from her recent talks with Emerson made her want to find a better way to be of service, one that would captivate her mind and capitalize on her talent for nurturing genius. Emerson's "sympathy and the development of these ideas has restored the youthful vigor of my spirit," she wrote to a friend in the weeks following her 1838 visit to Concord. During 1839, as Mary moved to Boston and Sophia found more frequent excuses to visit the city, Elizabeth remained rooted in Salem; she taught Mary's class, which earned enough to cover the rent on the family's Charter Street house, and continued teaching her own course for women. But it was a period of gathering strength.

One source was the women's class that Elizabeth was leading through a program of mutual self-analysis, inspired by her talks with Emerson. This year, the group's objective had been nothing less than to "learn the secret of Life." In a paper summing up the discussions the class had "set ourselves," Elizabeth wrote that the women had decided that achieving "constancy of character" should be the aim of all individuals. But what was "constancy of character," and how could one achieve it? "All agreed that we must live an *inward* life"; yet "experience" was important too. The women recognized the necessity of "*trying to do something ourselves.*" Elizabeth concluded, "We must act out our impulses," for in the end, "the measure of our Life is our Power." Living an "inward life" of study and reflection was not enough; effective action based on inward impulse—the assertion of one's personal "power"— counted most. Coming to this realization, first under Emerson's guidance and then with her class in Salem, strengthened Elizabeth's resolve to try to "*do something*" herself.

During the early months of 1839, Elizabeth wrote several articles defending Emerson's "Divinity School Address." "I am interested deeply in his having a chance to promulgate views so dear to my own soul," she wrote to a friend at the time. "I know he is not an atheist or Pantheist or unChristian just as ... I know I am not one myself." But even the liberal Unitarian *Christian Examiner* (no longer under Andrews Norton's editorship) refused to publish them. Elizabeth continued to copy and edit Channing's writing for the press when he sent his rough pages to her in Salem, and she struggled over the prize essay, refusing, in the end, to take Horace Mann's advice to cut its theoretical underpinnings. She did not win. Briefly, she entertained the hope that Mann might employ her in establishing Massachusetts's first normal school, a state-funded institute to train women as teachers for the common schools—the first such school in the nation. But the same theoretical differences that separated Elizabeth and Horace Mann in the matter of the prize essay doomed this prospect as well.

What Elizabeth really wanted to do was to imitate Emerson's model of inspiring his friends. "If I study his methods," Elizabeth wrote in her journal, she hoped that, "in a smaller circle," she too might "arrange all whom I know around me as my 'leaves & fruit.'" As she attended Fuller's Conversations into the early months of 1840, Elizabeth was increasingly drawn to Boston as a potential center for action, just as she was compelled by Fuller's discourse to seek her own answers to her initial questions—"What were we born to do? How shall we do it?"—questions that seemed to follow directly from the work Elizabeth had done with her own class the previous winter. Elizabeth had once described herself to Mary as "the only practical transcendentalist there is," and she was determined now to prove it.

By April 1840, she had conceived a plan. She would open a bookstore and circulating library specializing in books and journals imported from Europe: the texts that had brought Transcendentalism into being, that fed it still, and yet were so expensive and hard to find. All her life, Elizabeth had depended on the generosity of men with fine libraries—from the Reverend Abbot and Nathaniel Bowditch in the Salem of her childhood, to Andrews Norton, John Kirkland, and Jared Sparks in Cambridge and Boston. For one brief season in 1833, she had been allowed to borrow books from Boston's only lending library, the privately owned Boston Athenaeum, a privilege that required a special vote of the trustees; in just one month she'd taken out twenty-one titles, ranging from Barthold Niebuhr's *History of Rome* to J. G. Spurzheim's phrenological treatise *Observations on the Deranged Manifestations of the Mind*, all of them published first outside the United States. Norton's library was locked away to Elizabeth now that they stood on opposite sides of the line that Emerson had drawn for himself and the rest of the Transcendentalists with his "Divinity School Address." But it was not her own selfish interest in books that Elizabeth hoped to serve.

She envisioned her book room as a gathering place for her intellectual companions, a locus of conversation both organized and informal, and she began to enlist the support of Emerson, Channing, and others for the project. Emerson asked Margaret Fuller to advertise the shop in the first issue of *The Dial*, scheduled for publication in July 1840. Theodore Parker, one of the most avid and wide-ranging readers of the group (he was known to have checked out more than four hundred books, a quarter of them in foreign languages, from the Harvard College library during his two years as a divinity student in the mid-1830s), wrote Elizabeth assuring her that such a plan would "fill a vacancy, and supply a want that has long been felt in Boston." Channing donated a small sum toward her expenses. George Bancroft lent Elizabeth the Italian books he'd collected in Europe to help form the basis of the circulating library, and Emerson followed suit with books in German and English. Elizabeth took out a $500 loan to cover the rest of her initial costs, guaranteed by Judge Charles Jackson, whose daughters had attended her Boston school earlier in the decade. Soon she would be selling books and gathering subscribers for the library at $5 each. The plan had to work.

By August 1, 1840, Elizabeth was ready to make her "debut in the mercantile world," as she wrote to Channing. She had rented a brick townhouse at 13

West Street, Boston, seen from the Common

West Street, a short half block from the Common, with rooms for the family
and Mary's school upstairs; she filled its front parlor with a large stock of
books in English, French, German, Italian, Greek, and Latin, selling at prices
from 50 cents for pocket editions of Shakespeare's plays to $65 for a hand-
somely illustrated forty-eight-volume set of Scott's Waverley novels. The neighborhood was more commercial than residential; a stable was in noisy operation across the way, and Washington Street—known as "publishers' row"—was
just around the corner. But establishing a thriving business was what Elizabeth had in mind.

An eighteen-year-old Caroline Healey ventured into the store during its first
week of operation and wrote afterward in her diary of hungering for a "magnificent" illustrated edition of the *Arabian Nights*, priced at $16, and yearning
"to have money at my own command" to purchase "those splendid English

Editions of the Classics—how my eyes longed to read them! And Dante Petrarca—& Ariosto—in the finest of Paris print & paper." The bulk of Elizabeth's selections, however, were moderately priced volumes of Wordsworth, Shelley, and Coleridge; Jean-Paul Richter and Schiller in German; Tasso and Manzoni in Italian; Montaigne, Racine, and de Staël in French; and dictionaries to aid readers in each of these languages. There were also "Boston editions" of Shakespeare and Milton, Horace Mann's School Library volumes, Mrs. Peabody's retelling of Spenser's *Legend of St. George* for schoolchildren, and Hawthorne's *The Gentle Boy* with Sophia's illustration. In addition, Elizabeth promised to fill individual orders for books from abroad, relying on Cunard's Steamer Line—which had only recently chosen Boston over New York as its American terminus—to deliver within six weeks.

Elizabeth imagined that she would someday travel to France and Germany to make her own contacts with European booksellers, but to start out she had contracted with an agent in New York, John Wiley, to advance her the stock, an arrangement that cleared her of financial risk. Even if it took some months to realize a profit, Mary's school would pay the rent on the West Street townhouse in the meantime, and Mary would save herself the cost of boarding away from home. Bringing the rest of the family down to Boston "so that all branches go on under one roof," as Dr. Peabody described the plan in a letter to his brother, was actually an economy move. Now nearly seventy, Dr. Peabody had been unable to compete successfully for patients with the handful of younger dentists in Salem since his winter-long illness the year before. "My circumstances are more strait than they have been for many years," he wrote his brother in May 1840, "I am beginning to be considered an old man." For some time he had relied first on Mary's Salem school and then Elizabeth's to pay the rent on the Charter Street house. In Boston there would be only one rent for the two sisters to cover, and he could help with the running of the shop, as would Mrs. Peabody, who had literary projects of her own: she was teaching herself German and translating tales for children.

What concerned Elizabeth was not so much financing the operation—she taught herself bookkeeping in a week, and the arrangement with Wiley seemed safe enough. But was bookselling an appropriate line of work for a woman? There were no other female booksellers in Boston and none that she knew of beyond New England. Indeed, as Elizabeth would later write, managing a store specializing in foreign books was "a thing not then attempted by anyone." She confided her worry in the Reverend Channing, who guardedly assured her that, in his view, there was "nothing in the business inconsistent with your sex." Channing expected that Elizabeth's bookstore might even serve as a "favored resort of your sex. The ladies want a literary lounge, and good might come from the literary intercourse that would spring out of such a place of meeting." Yet he could not be absolutely certain that "in this age of proprieties, difficulties" might not arise. There had been "misunderstandings and ugly things said" about Margaret Fuller's Conversations. Might they not be said of Elizabeth and her bookstore as well, if it were to become a gathering place for women who were already asking themselves, "What were we born to do?" Elizabeth's clientele would not be limited to women, either. She expected Emerson, Parker, Ripley, and the men of the Transcendentalist circle to visit the book room as often as Fuller and her protégées, perhaps more.

Yet Elizabeth's question may only have been *pro forma*, raised in order to have it acknowledged and then dismissed by her mentor. In the end, Elizabeth decided that as long as the men and women of the Transcendentalist circle deemed her business plan "ladylike"—and they did—she would proceed. Still, Channing had been right to call the mid-nineteenth century an "age of proprieties." More accurately, it was an age of contested proprieties. Elizabeth had already shown herself ready to cast her lot with the defiant: she had acted on her impulse to support Alcott in print when the whole city shunned him, to open her family's house to the messianic poet Jones Very when Salem's Unitarian clergy wanted him institutionalized as a madman, and to pen articles in defense of Emerson when the authorities at his own school of divinity turned him away, branding him an atheist. Opening the West Street bookstore put Elizabeth at the center of the movement, and she welcomed it. Indeed, she may have foreseen that all the Transcendentalists needed was a Boston meeting place to set their radical agenda in motion.

In August 1840, a parade of young rebel clergy—"the seekers," Elizabeth called them—passed through the doors of her book room. There was William Henry Channing, the Reverend William Ellery Channing's nephew, in town with a commission to purchase books for the library in Cincinnati, where he was posted; he spent every penny in Elizabeth's store, accounting for a sizable portion of the $100 worth of books she sold that first month. Henry Hedge, a founding member of the Transcendental Club's dissenting clergy, came down from Maine, possessed of "an intellectual thirst for activity" and brimming with ideas for the lecture series he planned to give in Boston that winter, arguing the possibility of forming "a real tangible church militant." Theodore Parker appeared as well, "fervent in spirit . . . eloquent & evidently effective," and recently installed as preacher to a small congregation in West Roxbury on the outskirts of Boston. "I long to see him in a large sphere," Elizabeth wrote to the Reverend Channing in a "newspaper" letter recounting the highlights of her first month in business. The Reverend James Walker, a charismatic Unitarian of an earlier generation, now teaching at Harvard, had dropped in as well to buy a membership in Elizabeth's circulating library. Walker brought the disturbing news that a rich Bostonian had just donated a large sum to the

Harvard Divinity School, where the old-guard conservative Andrews Norton still held sway, to boost the school's standing as "an antidote" to Harvard College. It was rumored that professors like Walker himself were "teaching Atheism." Walker, who would become president of the college a decade later, called it "pitiful" to see "what a state of panic the community" was in. There was almost no point in talking ideas with the "conservative part," he fumed, for "ideas could not be awakened in people so armed."

Yet the Transcendentalists were already sending more ideas into the fray. Elizabeth's bookstore carried the first issue of *The Dial* with Emerson's introductory essay describing the Transcendentalists' new journal as "one cheerful rational voice amidst the din of mourners and polemics." Emerson had cut the whole of Fuller's original introduction, calling it too defensive and counseling her, "Don't cry before you are hurt." But he had seen fit to publish his own elegantly polemical protest poem, "The Problem," which rehearsed, in no uncertain terms, his rejection of the pulpit:

> I like a church; I like a cowl;
> I love a prophet of the soul ...
> Yet not for all his faith can see
> Would I that cowled churchman be.

In September, when the Reverend Channing returned from his summer in Newport, he too bought a subscription to Elizabeth's library and took to spending his mornings in the book room reading foreign periodicals — Elizabeth had invested $150 of her $500 loan in subscriptions, knowing how much her clientele valued being *au courant*. Channing was sixty years old now, but the small man seemed older. In July he had resigned his pulpit, for reasons of health rather than conscience, although the outspoken preacher had often jousted with the monied "conservative part" of his congregation, who condoned the antiabolitionist violence in Boston in recent years; some of these parishioners even refused to speak to him when they met on the street. Channing would not enter a silent retirement, however. He had written Elizabeth earlier in the summer that not only did he provisionally support her becoming a bookseller — "if [women] may sell anything, why not books?" — he also wished "to see a variety of employments thrown open to women." Now he handed Elizabeth another one, offering her the proceeds of an antislavery pamphlet he was writing if she would act as his publisher.

By December, Elizabeth had seen a thousand copies of *Emancipation*, which had expanded to a 111-page book, through the press with the pleasing lines "Boston: Published by E. P. Peabody, 13 West Street, 1840" beneath her mentor's name on its title page. On the strength of Channing's faith in her,

Elizabeth had by then also persuaded Nathaniel Hawthorne to let her publish his first book of historical tales for children, *Grandfather's Chair*, which appeared in December as well. Two more Hawthorne volumes—*Famous Old People* and *The Liberty Tree*—would follow, along with a half-dozen other books that Elizabeth selected for publication under her imprint in 1841. There could hardly have been a more diverse first list for a novice publisher, with Channing's tract applauding the recent abolition of slavery in the West Indies sharing space on the shelf with Hawthorne's graceful tales of Puritan New England, meant to inspire a nostalgic patriotism in the young. Elizabeth had gathered two of the nation's greatest talents into her small stable of authors.

Elizabeth's real coup in September 1840, however, was in luring the Transcendental Club to 13 West Street for what turned out to be its final meeting. Three years before, she had been passed over in favor of Margaret Fuller for the first meeting to which women had been invited. Now Elizabeth had made herself the first woman to host a Transcendental Club gathering. Passions ran high as members took opposing sides of a fundamental question: could the church be reformed? George Ripley brought the matter to a head, arguing that the church was "vicious in its foundations." No church could accomplish the radical reform of society that he envisioned: a wholesale transformation of everything from daily labor to modes of worship. Ripley, who had been studying the writings of utopian "Associationists," argued in favor of forming "a new organization" of like-minded people to purchase and run a communal farm, with members sharing equally in labor and profits. His idea was to start over from scratch, creating an ideal society on a small scale as a model for the rest of the world to imitate. Henry Hedge took the opposite view, defending the church as having succeeded in "educating the Reason" and giving "a true culture to the Imagination" in music, art, and architecture—even as he allowed the truth of Ripley's statement that "the church of Humanity [had] yet to grow." Still, he thought such growth must be "as another branch from the same trunk—& not on the ruins" of a church destroyed from the inside by its own ministers. Elizabeth must have been particularly grateful to hear her theory of "the social principle" taken up by Hedge as he conceded that society had "yet to be educated" toward benevolent cooperation.

William Henry Channing turned aside the whole question of institutions as irrelevant, asserting that the private relation—"the union of man with God"—was the "true church." Margaret Fuller discoursed on Jesus Christ as "a true man." Theodore Parker's "organ-like voice" rang out in support of each view as he attempted to moderate the discussion, biding his time. But Waldo Emerson, feeling pressure from Ripley to throw his weight behind the Associationist plan, had stayed home. Indeed, his decision not to attend, and the reason for it—the mounting dissension within the group in response to demands for collective action—may have spelled the end of the club meetings. At a session in Parker's house the week before, he'd pronounced his own ambiguous verdict on the question. Emerson would commit to neither side, yet he declared it was "the essence of atheism" to despair of the "Divine Soul" finding "its own organs." He preferred a passive optimism: we must "let what would die" alone, and go on "ourselves [to] *live* & trust."

There would be no consensus; the Transcendental Club could hold together no longer. The imperative that Elizabeth had reached—"to be myself and *act*"—was felt now by all the Transcendentalists. Bronson Alcott had decamped with his family to a small house in working-class Concord, nicknamed "Dove Cottage" after Wordsworth's Lake District home, to make his own plans for a "New Eden"—eventually to materialize as the Fruitlands commune in the western hills near Lancaster, where Elizabeth had taught her first school two decades before. Emerson was establishing a far more loosely organized community in his own Concord neighborhood. With two small children at home now, he and Lidian were tired of constant entertaining; Waldo had taken to urging his favorite companions to rent, buy, or build houses nearby. Both the Emersons were cultivating the friendship of a young eccentric, Henry David Thoreau: poet, surveyor, naturalist, and already a resident of Concord. Four years earlier, Emerson had predicted a swift end to the Transcendental Club because "people do not receive revelations from their genius, except when alone—never in company." It had been a curious statement for a man who liked to test out his ideas in conversation; in fact the Transcendental Club had thrived, and Emerson with it. Yet perhaps now, as the younger ministers prepared to act, Emerson needed both his solitude and a different company, one he could select and control.

For those who remained in and around Boston—and there were many—Elizabeth Peabody's bookstore now served as meeting place and mail drop, a clubhouse open to a widening circle of reformers even as the club itself disbanded. By opening her bookstore, Elizabeth would one day recall, "I came into contact with the world as never before." The 1840s were, for Elizabeth and her comrades, "very living years." The six months following the dissolution of the Transcendental Club would see the establishment of the first of two new Boston churches, the Church of the Disciples, organized by Sarah Clarke's older brother, James, and a band of Unitarian dissenters, all West Street regulars, who continued to believe in reforming the church from within. At the same time, Theodore Parker would finally speak his mind in a brilliant sermon refuting fundamentalist interpretations of the Bible: it so angered Boston's orthodox clergy and even most liberal Unitarians that Parker eventually found himself without a church. He landed first in Boston's Melodeon Theater, then the more spacious Music Hall, on Sunday mornings, where by midcentury thousands turned out each week to hear his impassioned sermons on religion, politics, and anything else that mattered to this inspired "son of Thunder," as Elizabeth dubbed him. Parker would achieve the "large sphere" Elizabeth envisioned for him.

George Ripley, too, used the West Street shop as a base of operations. When "too large a party" met to discuss "*community* ideas" in his own small parlor on Bedford Place, he led them all around the corner to continue their planning session in Elizabeth's book room. Ripley had assembled a motley cast drawn from the "Abolitionist and the Non-resistant Societies," along with the "Mendon Associationists": "a most picturesque assembly of all the bats and owls that hoot in the night-times of our civilization," Elizabeth later wrote, "together with the inspired prophets of the new Protestantism." Ripley's "new organization"—the Brook Farm Association—would prove the most ambitious and most unwieldy experiment of them all. And it would bring Sophia Peabody and Nathaniel Hawthorne tantalizingly close to setting a wedding date.

"Mr. Ripley's Utopia"

MARY HAD BEEN RIGHT IN THINKING THAT MOVING TO BOSTON WOULD improve her chances with Horace Mann. Although he never wrote about her in his daily journal, Mann wrote less about Charlotte during 1839 than in any other year since her death. In April, after Mary had been living in Boston for almost four months, he registered a first sign that his frozen emotions were beginning to thaw. "I want some inward life," he admitted, at last, to himself. "I have no bosom friend, with whom to sympathize, or who can sympathize with me." That summer on the seventh anniversary of Charlotte's death, his journal entry marking the occasion was perfunctory; a few days later Mann noted that he felt "less of acute suffering than heretofore"—and chastised himself for it. In September, he let his wedding anniversary pass without comment.

Mann was conscious only of a greater absorption in his work—the reform of the Massachusetts public schools. "My whole life is now one continued effort to bring something to pass for the improvement of the great body of people," he wrote in his journal on the same day he acknowledged his need of "some inward life." Although Massachusetts had been the first state—indeed, the first colony—to guarantee a schoolteacher to every town, the "common schools," as they were known, offered no consistent curriculum and lacked a well-trained faculty. Mann was now following a grueling schedule of travel across the state to inspect schools and drum up support for the reforms he was working to enact as secretary of the state board of education—among them the establishment of a normal school for teacher training and a Common School Library of texts he hoped would elevate standards for learning.

"Labors and anxieties accumulate upon me," Mann wrote in late summer, after several days spent in the Berkshires speaking to small, unreceptive audiences; he slept little, ate less, and was frequently sick. Yet playing martyr to the cause of education reform was a role he seemed to relish as it began to take the place of his longing for Charlotte. "I may perish in the cause," he wrote in his journal in August, a month in which Mann normally found himself overcome with anguish as another anniversary of Charlotte's death passed, "but I will not abandon it, and will only increase my efforts as it needs them more." Several weeks later he was mourning not Charlotte, but the cause. Education, "the greatest of all interests," he wrote, is "the least attended to." Again he speculated that "I may perish in the effort," but "defeat in this is better than triumph in any other."

"Shall I shrink when called to the post of higher duty?" Mann exhorted himself as he continued his travels during the fall, and when, at the end of the year, he received an offer to become president of a new college in Missouri, with an annual salary of $3,000, "a splendid house, gardens, etc.," he refused it. "I would rather remain here and work for mere bread, than to go there for the great wealth of the Valley of the Mississippi," he wrote on Christmas Day 1839. "Oh, let me prosper in this. I ask no other reward for all my labors. This is my only object of ambition, and if this is lost, what link will bind me to earth?" One link binding him to earth—and to Boston—was Mary. When she left the city briefly in late November, ill herself and mourning her brother George's death, Mann wrote anxiously to Elizabeth, "I have not heard from Mary. . . . Have I done any thing to forfeit my right to know how she is? Even if I have, still let me know & punish me some other way." Mary was back in Boston almost as soon as the letter arrived.

In January 1840, a new and unreceptive governor and his crew of supporters in the state legislature—"bigots and vandals," in Mann's view—threatened to cut the state board of education's budget and eliminate Mann's job entirely. Mann thought back over the previous year of hard work and his sufferings "from ill health, from opposition in the sacred cause." It had been "the most painful year save *the year,* that I have ever suffered." Feelings of "homelessness, uselessness, friendlessness—the very elements out of which suicide is born, press upon me with almost overwhelming intensity," he wrote. Yet at least he was associating these dark feelings with a new, living "cause." In March, as he waited anxiously to discover whether his efforts to persuade the state legislature to retain his post and endorse his reforms would be successful, Mann took time out to visit Mary, addressing her in a letter with the familiar "thee," as the secretly engaged Sophia and Nathaniel Hawthorne now also did: "If it pleaseth thee, I shall be happy to call . . . & enquire after your health &c."

It was the kind of easy social call—one of frank interest and concern— Mann had never made to Elizabeth when she lived in town. In the early years of his overpowering grief, Elizabeth's intensity had been a welcome distraction, her fascination with him a boon, her willingness to stretch the limits of propriety a godsend when he needed physical comfort. They had seen each other often—more often than Mann now saw Mary. But that was a phase in his life that Mann was ready to forget. Now the ritual of a proper social call was itself a form of comfort, one that might lead to a future in which, as Emerson had proposed in his lecture on love, "the objects of the affections change" and are "succeeded and supplanted" by something "more beautiful." And Mary *was* the more beautiful of the sisters.

Emerging victorious from his State House battle at the end of March, Mann left Boston for nearly two months on an educational tour of the nation's capital and the western states with a new friend, the Scottish phrenologist George Combe. Mann was appalled by Washington, D.C.—his arrival there was "the first day I have set my foot on soil polluted by slavery" —and by its politicians: "How much good might these men do, if they would forget the interests of party & attend to the welfare of mankind!" But he was astounded by the west as he traveled by railway, river, canal, and even "macadamized" road through Pennsylvania and into Ohio: "No imagination can give a realization of its vastness." By the time he'd returned to Boston, Mann himself was in an expansive mood and quite eager to see Mary. "I meant to have treated my eyes with the sight of you for a few minutes last evening," he wrote to her in early June 1840, but Mary had not been home, and so Mann "was obliged to send my heart to bed supperless." He asked Mary instead to "transcribe your heart and send it to me, & I will do the same to you."

Was Elizabeth making sure she would not be left out of the new alliances her sisters were forming with two of the "three greatest actual powers" with whom she had once been "in direct relation," by renting the West Street house and moving the entire family down to Boston? Nathaniel Hawthorne looked forward to Sophia's permanent residence in the city. "My heart throbs mightily," he wrote to Sophia when he learned in late June 1840 that the Peabody family would be installed at West Street, just across the Common from his Beacon Hill rooms, within a month. "Oh what joy to think that henceforth there shall be no long separations for us." But, he added, the change had also "taken me so by surprise that I know not what to say upon the subject." The presence in Boston of Elizabeth, the older sister he had courted briefly and then spurned, and of Sophia's parents, must surely put a damper on the freedom the couple had enjoyed on Sophia's previous visits—as long as the engagement was to remain a secret. And Nathaniel wanted it kept that way, until he could find an adequate means of support.

Neither Horace Mann nor Nathaniel Hawthorne seemed eager to attend the Wednesday-evening open houses that Elizabeth instituted at West Street in the early 1840s to take the place of Wednesday-night Transcendental Club meetings—even though "the chosen, whom you gather about you," in Theodore Parker's phrase, inclined more to "prophets" like Parker, Ripley, and Clarke, than to "bats and owls." Both men instinctively mistrusted the Transcendental philosophers. Mann sometimes took a "wicked" pleasure in the opportunity to "snub your idols," he once wrote to Elizabeth, and bristled when she "seemed to think me a wanderer, & houseless & homeless in a spiritual sense, until I get with the Emersons." Hawthorne steadfastly refused any invitations to hear Emerson lecture once he moved to Boston—"that everlasting rejecter of all that is, and seeker for he knows not what," Hawthorne once described the rebel philosopher. But more fundamentally, relations with Elizabeth became increasingly strained as the two men's feelings for her sisters intensified. And neither man much liked the other. Indeed Elizabeth may have been the only woman in Boston capable of maintaining a circle of acquaintance that included "prophets" of such diverse persuasions—for despite their resistance to Emerson and the Transcendentalists, Mann and Hawthorne, in their separate arenas, were also heralds of a new era.

Two more different suitors than the stern, silver-haired Horace Mann, with the occasional glint in his violet eyes, and the cagey Nathaniel Hawthorne, with his Byronic good looks, could hardly be imagined. While Mann spent many of his days giving speeches in town meetinghouses and legislative chambers, Hawthorne continued to dread almost any public gathering. In December 1839, Nathaniel wrote to Sophia of his relief that pressing business had obliged him to miss a dinner at George Bancroft's house, where Margaret Fuller was also expected. In the future, when Sophia became his wife and could attend such parties with him, he would "not be afraid to accept invitations to meet literary lions and lionesses." He would put the more sociable Sophia "in the front of the battle." Friends were pressing him to make a "caucus-speech" as well, to show his support for the Democratic party, which had provided him with his job. But "I give up all notion of speechifying at a Caucus," he wrote Sophia, "I would not do it, even if thou thyself besought it of me."

Mann had already expressed to Elizabeth his dislike of Hawthorne's tales, his preference for something "nearer home to duty and business," and his outright incomprehension of the darker stories, such as "The Wedding Knell": "wherefore is it and to what does it tend?" As far as literature itself was concerned, Mann considered the whole enterprise a slight one, writing once to his friend Samuel Gridley Howe, "I should rather have built up the Blind Asylum than to have written *Hamlet*." Hawthorne and Mann were united only in their distaste for Transcendentalists and politicians. Mann despised the double-dealing legislators who threatened his cause, and Hawthorne both loathed and feared the spoils system on which his job and hopes for a future with Sophia depended. "I want nothing to do with politicians—they are not men," Nathaniel wrote to Sophia in mid-March 1840, the same day that Mann reported in his journal another "atrocious attack" from Governor Morton's cronies.

Almost as soon as he'd taken up his post in Boston, Nathaniel had been led to believe that, as the result of "the omission of Congress to pass a certain regulation," his work at the Custom House might actually net him twice the salary he expected—as much as $3,000, the same spectacular sum that Mann had been offered for a college presidency in the west. By the spring of 1840, he began to hint to Sophia that in another year he might have saved enough to make wedding plans. Yet, "cramped by a sense that I am no longer master of my own time and motions," he also found it impossible to write. To his editor at the *Democratic Review*, John O'Sullivan, Hawthorne declared himself "no longer a literary man." Nathaniel's correspondence with Sophia grew in length and significance partly as a means of shoring up his literary aspirations against the "grievous thraldom" of his employment—both by the act of writing and in receiving Sophia's assurances of her belief in his talent—and he began to yearn for a means of "escaping from this unblest Custom House." And then, whether he wished for it or not, Hawthorne's dilemma was resolved for him—by politicians. In November 1840, Hawthorne learned that Democratic president Martin Van Buren was expected to lose the upcoming election. He resigned his job immediately, rather than be fired by the incoming Whigs, and retreated to Salem to consider his prospects. It had been less than six months since Sophia moved to Boston, supposedly bringing the era of "long separations" to an end.

"What a year has this been to us!" Sophia had written to Nathaniel on New Year's Eve 1839, as the first anniversary of their engagement was about to dawn. "It has proved the year of our nativity. Has not the old earth passed away from us?—are not all things new?" She had walked that morning in the cold all the way from Salem to Danvers and back, "full of the glory of the day"—an outing that would have been inconceivable the winter before she met Nathaniel Hawthorne. The year had also been an extraordinarily prolific one. Aside from the bas-relief profile of George, begun in the spring and completed in the fall, Sophia had set to work in midsummer, possessed by a "Demon" that "demanded" her to draw illustrations for her mother's retelling of Spenser's *Legend of St. George*. The knight, Una, and a horse had all "leaped out of my mind," Sophia wrote to Elizabeth. "You cannot imagine with what ease I draw; I feel as if I could and might do anything now." After a hiatus of nearly two years, Sophia announced that she was ready to paint in oils again and began work on the two Como landscapes that she would finish by the end of the year. To Elizabeth, who could take whatever meaning she wished from the comment, Sophia supplied the reason: "*Now* I am indeed made deeply conscious of what it is to be loved."

In Nathaniel Hawthorne, Sophia had found the soul mate, the "artist & a poet too," who would return her love in the ways she wished for, who shared her vision of a marriage of creative partners whose passion would consecrate their work and themselves to each other. Later that summer, Nathaniel wrote Sophia of his eagerness to share "a cottage, somewhere": "Then how happy I would be ... when I should rest nightly in your arms. And you should draw, and paint, and sculpture, and make music, and poetry, too, and your husband would admire and criticize; and I, being pervaded with your spirit, would write beautifully, and make myself famous for your sake." Sophia's admiration and criticism would be required too: "I shall always read my manuscripts to you, in the summer afternoons or winter evenings; and if they please you I shall expect a smile and kiss as my reward—and if they do not please, I must have a smile and kiss to comfort me." In late November, when George died and Sophia grieved, Nathaniel encouraged her "not to muse too much upon your brother" and to "resume all your usual occupations as soon as possible— your sculpture, your painting," as well as walks and rides in the open air, in hopes that "mine own wife ... should come quite safe through the trial." Sophia went back to work on the landscapes, and when she told Nathaniel late in the year that they were intended for him as anniversary gifts, he was stunned. "I never owned a picture in my life," Nathaniel wrote Sophia, although they were "among the earthly possessions" he "most coveted." Her landscapes would be "incomparably more precious" to him "than all the productions of all the painters since Apelles," the most celebrated painter of Greece's golden age. Again he evoked a time "when we live together in our own home, belovedest": then "we will paint pictures together."

By the time Sophia's paintings reached Nathaniel in Boston, in January 1840, he was living in a new set of rooms at 54 Pinckney Street on Beacon Hill, rented from the lawyer-editor George Hillard and his wife, Susan. The Hillards were longtime Peabody family friends and sure to look the other way if Nathaniel arranged to "meet his own wife within his own premises," as he wrote Sophia when he first considered the move. But, he asked, would Sophia "deem it a sin against decorum to pay a visit to her husband?" No, Hawthorne answered his own question, at the same time reassuring Sophia that nothing untoward would happen when the two were alone in his suite: "your out-gushing frankness, is one of the loveliest results of your purity, and innocence, and holiness." Although Hawthorne closed most of his letters now by conjuring an image of Sophia "nestled into my very heart, and there [to] sleep a sweet sleep with your own husband," their "conjugal embrace," as he sometimes referred to the way they spent many of their precious moments alone together, was still limited to kisses and hugs stolen on walks in the countryside, in the parlors or boudoirs of close friends, and now, less guardedly, in the privacy of Hawthorne's own rooms. And both were satisfied to keep it that way.

Sophia Peabody was thirty, Nathaniel Hawthorne thirty-five; both were so accustomed to single life that neither, at first, strained too hard against the terms of a long engagement. To Hawthorne's way of thinking, he had discovered Sophia "in the shadow of a seclusion as deep as my own had been." Despite their relatively advanced ages, both were used to playing the role of pampered child within their own families and being given a wide berth for their eccentricities. It would not be easy for this pair to make any kind of move toward parenthood, the virtually inevitable result of a fully conjugal embrace. Both seemed content with the merging of spirits that their exchange of letters enabled—a sense of being "mutually within one another," in Nathaniel's phrase, sharing one "*innere*," in Sophia's—as they negotiated the terms, financial and psychological, of an actual marriage in the future.

Their first steps toward domestic life together were small: Sophia chose a carpet for Nathaniel's new parlor and sent a bundle of allumettes at Christmastime, paper spirals she'd twisted by hand for him to use in lighting his reading lamp from the hearth fire; Nathaniel asked Sophia to provide a list of books she would like to own so that "whenever the cash and the opportunity occur together . . . to fill up our new bookcase," he could feel that "I am buying them for both of us." His first purchase was a three-book set of Coleridge's poems to join the Wordsworth volume that Sophia had given him the year before as an engagement present. These were lovers for whom the life of the mind and spirit was as vivid, sometimes more so, than physical life itself. For them, an idealized life together was—almost—enough.

Nathaniel was the first to render their prenuptial "marriage" in words—recalling, in a letter of September 1839, one significant walk on which the two had imagined they were watching "our souls" drift "far away among the sunset clouds, and wherever there was ethereal beauty, there were we, our true selves; and . . . there we grew into each other, and became a married pair." The paintings Sophia sent Nathaniel four months later in January 1840 gave this walk and their "marriage" visual form. She chose two scenes of Italy's Lake Como: images that had been part of her "inner gallery" since 1830, when she had studied them intently in a borrowed book of etchings during the months when she was first learning to paint. That year she had carried the heavy book to friends' parlors all over Boston, slowly turning the pages and discussing the images with Dr. Walter Channing, the Reverend Francis Greenwood, and her teachers Graeter and Doughty. One friend, Mrs. Reed, had been "affected to tears" by their beauty; George Hillard had been so captivated by the views of Italian villas set in a sylvan landscape that he'd declared, "the men who lived round that lake must have genius," and proposed impulsively to Sophia, "Oh let us go and live there!" It was a time when few besides extremely wealthy Bostonians could visit Italy, but virtually all of the "literary class" longed to see the treasures of art and architecture that they read about in de Staël's *Corinne* and Samuel Rogers's *Italy*. Sophia could not even afford to buy a copy of this treasured book of etchings. That year she copied at least one of the black-and-white scenes in pencil; when she painted them in miniature on the basket she sold at the Salem Blind Fair in 1833, she was already working from memory and adding color. By the time she painted them in oils for Nathaniel, she had made them her own.

Working with a newfound steadiness of purpose, Sophia produced two landscapes of "superlative" beauty—one she titled *Villa Menaggio, Lago di Como*, the other *Isola San Giovanni*—and into both of them she painted herself and Nathaniel Hawthorne as small figures in the foreground. Distant craggy mountains and the calm, reflective lake provided the dramatic contrast of sublime and pastoral she had learned from copying Allston's landscapes; tall trees painted in the feathery style Doughty taught her framed the compositions. All was bathed in a golden light. The two figures—a black-suited Nathaniel Hawthorne and his "Dove" dressed in white, strolling arm in arm in one painting, embracing on the shore of the other—were Sophia's own invention. Perhaps they were an anachronism: Nathaniel and Sophia had not been to Italy any more than they had lived among the "sunset clouds" of Hawthorne's word picture. But the figures carried Sophia's message to Nathaniel. The two scenes brought together everything Sophia envisioned for their future: a setting where "men of genius" lived in harmony with nature, and where Sophia could thrive as both creator and muse.

The message took. Nathaniel wrote afterward to Sophia that his fingers had "trembled" as he undid the package in which the paintings arrived. He addressed her in improvised Italian as "Dearissima" and told her "there never was anything so lovely and precious in this world" as these two "perfect" paintings. He set them on the mantelpiece and "sat a long time before them with clasped hands, gazing, and gazing, and gazing, and painting a facsimile of them in my heart." It was all he could do to prevent himself from kissing "Sophie Hawthorne" in the picture, but he restrained himself for fear she might have "vanished beneath my kiss." And "what a misfortune would that have been to her poor lover!—to find that he kissed away his mistress." Nathaniel professed, at first, not to believe that the "very noble-looking cavalier with whom Sophie is standing" was himself. Yet "it must be my very self . . . not my picture, but the very I," for "my inner self belongs to you," he affirmed. "There we are, unchangeable," he wrote Sophia, his "blessedest and blessingest"—"wife." "Years cannot alter us, nor our relation to each other."

He hid the paintings away in his closet, where no one else could see them; and when he finally hung them on his walls, he rigged up a curtain to cover them when he was out of the room. It was too soon to expose their love to public view.

The spring of 1841 was a time for maturing of plans: reform for the Transcendentalists and a wedding for the already "married" Hawthornes. James Freeman Clarke's new Church of the Disciples was now meeting regularly in Boston, and Theodore Parker readied his heretical sermon on the Christian miracles for its May delivery, writing to Elizabeth that he was looking forward to "helping to turn the world upside-down." When Clarke's sister Sarah wrote to him that winter, "It is astonishing what a wide-spread desire there is for a new mode of life," she was referring to George Ripley's project located on the two hundred "undulating acres" of Brook Farm in West Roxbury, nine miles from Boston, where the first hopeful utopians took up residence in an old, rambling farmhouse in early April.

It may have been Sophia's painted visions as much as anything else that inspired Nathaniel Hawthorne to join that band of hardy idealists and eventually to buy two shares in "Mr. Ripley's Utopia," as he called it, at $500 each—one for Sophia and one for himself—after leaving his post at the Custom House in January 1841. Certainly his decision was not made out of any fondness for the Transcendentalists who were initiating the experiment, although for a time—perhaps for Sophia's sake—he was able to convince himself that he was "engaged in a righteous and heaven-blessed way of life." In truth, Hawthorne had found his work at the Custom House so dreary that the opportunity to live in the countryside, even if it meant becoming a "laboring man," seemed attractive to the increasingly desperate author. To his friend and editor John O'Sullivan, Hawthorne confessed he had come to feel "a most galling weight upon me—an intolerable sense of being hampered and degraded" by his working conditions; he regretted most of all his confinement to "one filthy dock or other" during "every golden day" of summer. He hated even more, he wrote to Sophia, the thought of returning to the "lonely chamber" in his family's house in Salem, which only reminded him "how dark my life would be, without the light that thou shedst upon it," and he could not afford to continue renting at Pinckney Street indefinitely without a steady income. *Grandfather's Chair* was not selling well in Elizabeth's edition, and a project of starting a Boston evening newspaper, sharing the editorship with Longfellow, fizzled.

George Ripley's plan might have seduced any man in Nathaniel Hawthorne's position. At Brook Farm, which was to be established as a democratically run joint-stock company, Ripley aimed "to insure a more natural union between intellectual and manual labor than now exists; to combine the thinker and the worker, as far as possible, in the same individual," and in the end to "prepare a society of liberal, intelligent and cultivated persons, whose relations with each other would permit a more wholesome and simple life than can be led amidst the pressures of our competitive institutions." There were to be few rules and no religious observances required. Residents who worked on the farm three hundred days out of the year would receive bed and board; shareholders would earn a fixed 5 percent interest on their investment and could expect to build their own houses on the property once the farm was established. It was this last point—the prospect, finally, of inhabiting "a cottage, somewhere" with Sophia—that most attracted Nathaniel Hawthorne, along with Ripley's promise that at Brook Farm daily labor would consist of "industry without drudgery." Taking Ripley at his word, and counting on the rejuvenating effects of work in the open air, Hawthorne hoped to be able to write in the evenings after putting in the requisite hours in the field. Winters would be free for long days at his desk.

Sophia, too, worried about finances. During that first "year of our nativity," 1839, she had learned from friends of the stark poverty suffered by the writer Thomas Carlyle and his wife, Jane, in England. Sophia trusted in her future husband's genius but knew all too well how little that might count for in the marketplace. She kept her worries from Nathaniel, but they may have been among the thoughts that had set her back to work. In the early months of 1840, as Nathaniel delighted privately in her Como landscapes, Sophia undertook a second portrait medallion in clay, this one of Waldo Emerson's beloved brother Charles. She did the work unpaid—except for a vacation in Concord, and the gift of a set of etchings Emerson procured for her from Italy—but news of the Emerson family's enthusiasm for her work spread. Waldo judged the piece a "striking likeness," all the more remarkable because Sophia had seen Charles just once before his death in 1836 and was working only from that memory and a silhouette no one thought much good. He extolled Sophia's "genius" in a letter to his brother William, and had eight medallions cast in plaster for family members and Charles's still grieving fiancée, Elizabeth Hoar. Hawthorne, too, was impressed: "Thou hast called up a face which was hidden in the grave," he wrote Sophia. "Thou art a miracle thyself, and workest miracles." A year later, in June 1841, Sophia was in Milton completing a third such piece for the family of China trade baron John Murray Forbes. By the end of that summer she had received a commission from Samuel Gridley Howe's blind asylum to sculpt a bust of his star pupil, the twelve-year-old blind and deaf Laura Bridgman.

In late May, Sophia had visited Hawthorne at Brook Farm to judge for herself the prospects of setting up housekeeping there. Until then she had learned of Brook Farm life only by letter from Nathaniel. Initially the couple had hoped to marry as early as March and enter the commune together. But when Nathaniel discovered that even George Ripley's wife planned to stay in Boston until May, while a mostly male crew broke the fields for farming, the wedding was put off. Sophia was to "think that I am gone before, to prepare a home for my Dove," Nathaniel instructed, "and will return for her, all in good time."

Nathaniel had arrived at Brook Farm alone, in the midst of an April snow squall. But the weather soon cleared, and he wrote jauntily to Sophia of his first days spent learning to milk cows—and subsequent ones, many more of them, spent shoveling in the manure pile, or "gold mine," as the Brook Farmers preferred to call it, intended to enrich the unexpectedly rocky soil on which their livelihood depended. Nathaniel boasted of "what a great, broad-shouldered, elephantine personage I shall become by and by!" He appeared to enjoy the company of "the brethren," a handful of variously disgruntled or dreamy ministers and misfits who had "thrown aside all the fopperies and flummeries, which have their origin in a false state of society," Nathaniel wrote, to join Ripley's community. Through his first month as a "husband-man," Nathaniel counted on Sophia to join him at "our home" by summer, and imagined warm evenings when the two would lie awake and listen to the ripple of the brook that ran by the house; he marveled at having found "such seclusion, at so short a distance from a great city. . . . If we were to travel a thousand miles, we could not escape the world more completely than we can here." Nathaniel hung the two Comos on the walls of his room in the communal farmhouse, still expecting vision to become reality.

Postponing the wedding had been a disappointment to Sophia. She suffered more colds and fevers that spring than she had during any other season since her engagement, and when she arrived at Brook Farm in late May to inspect the setting of her future home, she was still coughing, "pale and languid," in Nathaniel's anxious judgment. But Sophia could see for herself that life in the community was all wrong for her "husband," let alone for starting married life together. Although "I wish far more than ever to be with thee continuedly," she wrote to Nathaniel once she was back in Boston, "I want a home for thee to come to, after associating with man all day, where thou shouldst rest from toil under my own ministration, & where but one thing should be going on, instead of twenty." She was determined that their home should be "a sacred retreat" from "all men." Sophia had watched her fiancé nod and smile his way through "the various transactions & witticisms of the excellent fraternity," yet she could tell that his was "the expression of a witness & hearer rather than of comrade-ship." Perhaps no one could understand Nathaniel's need for solitude quite so well as Sophia, who had long required—and had relied on her illness to guar-antee—a private retreat in a bustling household. As for Brook Farm itself, the

Brook Farm, by Josiah Wolcott

countryside had "far surpassed my expectations . . . for its own beauty," and Sophia could not "conceive of a greater felicity than living in a cottage, built on one of those lovely sites, with thee." But until that was possible, she would defer.

Yet deferring was getting to be no easy matter for either of the lovers. Nathaniel Hawthorne was finally becoming impatient with writing letters. Increasingly, it seemed "as if a sheet of paper could only be a veil betwixt us." He wrote to Sophia, "I used to think that I could imagine all passions, all feelings, all states of the heart and mind; but how little did I know what it is to be mingled with another's being! Thou only hast taught me that I have a heart." For Sophia, Nathaniel had become "a necessity of my nature," she wrote after her May visit to Brook Farm. "Words cannot tell how immensely my spirit demands thee. Sometimes I almost lose my breath in a vast heaving towards thy heart. It is plain enough that for me there is no life without a response of life from thee." If Brook Farm did not provide the location, then "our Heaven is wherever we will make it," Sophia prodded Nathaniel.

Elizabeth caught wind of her youngest sister's plans—how could she not have? Elizabeth had seen Sophia painting the landscapes; these were the "several things a-going" she had reported to Nathaniel Hawthorne when Sophia began work on them during the summer of 1839. Precisely how much the entire Peabody family—and even the "brethren" at Brook Farm—knew of the romance is impossible to say, but Hawthorne sent his letters to Sophia care of her father, and often received hers hand-delivered by Mary or the Ripleys. Their regular "private" correspondence was an open secret. In the spring of 1841, Hawthorne's departure for Brook Farm and the seeming inevitability of the marriage reawakened Elizabeth's pain at the loss of Hawthorne's affectionate friendship and pushed her to confide her sorrow for the first time in a new friend, Theodore Parker.

Since the summer of 1840, the thirty-year-old Parker had moved into a spot previously occupied by Horace Mann and then Nathaniel Hawthorne—that of intellectual companion and emotional support. When Elizabeth sought reassurance before opening her bookshop, she turned to Parker, whose enthusiasm for the project and for Elizabeth had been instrumental in giving her the confidence to act. "My dear Elizabeth," Parker had begun his letter, quickly dispensing with the formal "Miss Peabody" that most other men she knew employed, explaining, "You are the only *Elizabeth* of my correspondents, and the *onlyness* by no means consists in the name."

More than any other man Elizabeth had been close to, Parker's intellect matched hers. Like Elizabeth, Parker had been capable of prodigious intellectual feats as a child, such as memorizing a hundred-line poem after reading it through just once. At twenty he'd passed the entrance exam for Harvard, but could not afford the tuition; instead he completed the course of study on his own, teaching by day and saving up to attend Harvard Divinity School. There he earned his degree in two years instead of the usual three, while reading his way through the college library's extensive holdings in philosophy and theology in a half-dozen foreign languages. Although Parker's first church was the small parish in West Roxbury, at least he had earned a posting near Boston, unlike so many other newly minted Unitarian preachers who were forced to leave the hub of their intellectual universe to find work. In 1840, Parker became the first man without an undergraduate degree to be awarded an honorary master's degree from Harvard.

Parker was married, but unhappily so, and childless—ripe for the kind of platonic intimacy Elizabeth also hungered for. A man of strong-featured good looks, Parker was pleased to hear friends tell him he resembled Boston's best-known woman of letters, Elizabeth Peabody. The resemblance wasn't only physical. Parker was equally energetic, idealistic, and impulsive—and, to Elizabeth's pleasure, more of a believer than Emerson. Parker would never leave the Unitarian Church, although he defied the Church to follow him on his rebel path. Six years older, Elizabeth may have served as a maternal figure for the man who had lost his own mother at age eleven; as his wife, Lydia's, former teacher, Elizabeth could also sympathize with Parker's disappointment in Lydia's limited intellectual and emotional range, even as she presented no threat to the marriage; and Elizabeth provided Parker with intellectual stimulation equal to that of any member of Boston's rebel clergy, while inspiring no competitive feelings.

Parker admired Elizabeth for the qualities she most valued in herself, dubbing her "the all-sympathizer" and praising her efforts to help her family and friends. "How wise must that heart be which can contain so many in its hold," he once wrote to her, "and how deep its spiritual springs whence they can all drink, and be satisfied." He refused to hear Elizabeth "speak of your own limitations and infirmities and the like ... *extensive* and *rich* as you are." When they were together in the bookstore, Parker enjoyed her talk, dubbing her the "Boswell" of Transcendentalism and the "narrative Miss Peabody." Parker welcomed her suggestions for his Sunday sermons, writing once, "I shall get *several sermons* out of the hints the letters contain, as I have often done before now," and he rehearsed ideas for his notorious "Discourse of the Transient and Permanent in Christianity" with her as well. He often sent Elizabeth his sermons for criticism after delivering them, telling her, "I think I can bear any severity which *you* would be apt to display." Parker even praised Elizabeth's poetry, especially three sonnets she had sent him, which "cheer and bless me," along with the "force and beauty" of her letters, which "have given me much comfort." And Parker was one of Elizabeth's best customers, buying whole sets of books at West Street and placing large orders for delivery from overseas.

This flood of affectionate praise from Parker must have induced Elizabeth to confide her troubled love affair in the spring of 1841 when she was—perhaps for the first time—feeling "cruelly wronged" by Hawthorne. What had come to disturb her even more than the initial forsaken "understanding" was Hawthorne's treatment of her since his engagement to Sophia. For a time, as Elizabeth had hoped, the writer had continued to rely on her as a business contact, even turning to her as publisher for his historical tales for children. Whatever guilt Hawthorne may have felt over jilting his fiancée's older sister had converted to a desire to smooth over hard feelings; just a few months after his engagement to Sophia, Hawthorne had commended Elizabeth to John O'Sullivan as "a good old soul [who] would give away her only petticoat, I do believe, to anybody that she thought needed it more than herself." But as the unsold copies of *Grandfather's Chair* remained stacked in Elizabeth's publishing headquarters on Washington Street—eventually to be sold as trunk linings for less than the price of the paper they were printed on—and Elizabeth managed to bungle, in Hawthorne's opinion, a deal with James Munroe for a second edition, he took an increasingly dim view of her benefactions and turned a cold shoulder to the woman who had long been among his most enthusiastic supporters—and, for a brief while, his most intimate confessor.

Theodore Parker

As Elizabeth told the story to Theodore Parker, what once was "Love" had "changed to a different feeling,—to one almost *opposite*." She recognized that by now there was little she could do besides "bear it," although Parker wrote in response to her startling confession, "I can't think the person you speak of will always remain in the dark on this point. Sometime the light must fall on his veiled lids—and he will see the deep of affection he has disturbed." Elizabeth was not so sure and almost instantly regretted having painted Hawthorne as a rogue. She wished to maintain Parker's good opinion of the writer even more than she longed for sympathy, which came as no surprise to Parker. "I said to myself, as I went to bed, Sunday night," he wrote in a succeeding letter to Elizabeth, "'Now after all this Miss Peabody will find *some excuse* for the offending party ... to justify him in my eyes.'"

Parker also expressed frank amazement that, in spite of "*bearing* sorrow ... the doors of your good heart, are still wide open as before, and filled with welcome guests." Parker's affectionate salutations alone—"My ever dear Elizabeth," "Most Patient and long-suffering Eliz," "My dear and very dear Elizabeth"—would have been enough to ease Elizabeth's sadness and coax her onward. But he went further in his proffered consolations. "If my heart were big enough," he wrote Elizabeth, "I would put you to bed in it, and sing you to sleep—as mothers do with children that have aches." He was sorry that "this goes only with children."

In return for Parker's own large-hearted sympathy, and perhaps as a means of distracting herself from private woes, Elizabeth became one of Parker's most vocal champions in the controversy that erupted over the delivery of his May 19, 1841, sermon, "Discourse of the Transient and Permanent in Christianity." In the most widely attended preaching performance of his career to date, the ordination sermon for a young minister in South Boston, Parker daringly asserted that belief in the literal truth of Christ's miracles—raising Lazarus from the dead, turning water to wine and stones into loaves of bread—was irrelevant to Christian faith. No one, not even Emerson in his "Divinity School Address," had ventured so far from orthodoxy in a public venue, and Parker was roundly condemned, not just by Boston's fundamentalist clergy, but by most Unitarian ministers as well.

Perhaps better than anyone, Elizabeth could appreciate the intensive scholarship that led Parker to conclude that "the stories of impossible miracles" were simply "refractions" of the light of Christ's influence on primitive minds. She defended Parker in letters and in person to Boston's Unitarian ministers, from James Freeman Clarke to William Ellery Channing. She wrote a long article in support of the sermon, maintaining that "if the Unitarian sect had known what it was about ... if it had not forgotten entirely the Ideas in which it originated, it would have embraced Mr. Parker as its last hope, and supported him in his statements." It was one of her most plainly written and passionately argued pieces—and no one would print it. (In the end, the article appeared as "Mr. Parker and the Unitarians," in Orestes Brownson's radical *Boston Quarterly Review* a full year later; by then the controversy had died down, but Elizabeth still wished to show "what views are rejected by the present Unitarian leaders, as fatal to their own.")

Meanwhile, as Elizabeth reported excitedly to a friend in late June 1841, the printed version of Parker's sermon had "gone off like wildfire" in Boston. "The first edition is almost all sold—He has his audience—enthusiastic—satisfied." Elizabeth herself published a third edition of the sermon to keep up with the demand. Although Parker had been denounced by nearly every minister in Boston, she wrote to her friend, "this has made the people so wrothy—that they say to one another—why not do the thing ourselves." Soon, by popular request, Parker was lecturing in Boston on weeknights and was well on his way to the free-lance pulpit he eventually established at Boston's Music Hall, where he drew overflow crowds on Sunday mornings on into the 1850s in a career that came close to eclipsing Waldo Emerson's in contemporary influence.

Buoyed by Parker's praise for her "great-heartedness," Elizabeth next turned her attention to boosting George Ripley's experiment at Brook Farm—perhaps hoping to regain a place in Hawthorne's affections at the same time. In the end, of all the Transcendentalists not actually living on the commune, Elizabeth worked the hardest to ensure the success of the project. She opened her bookshop for a meeting in May 1841, at which Ripley hoped to interest investors to raise the $10,000 necessary to purchase the property and farmhouse, and again when the fledgling association's sixteen "Articles of Agreement" were proposed. She also worked at recruiting members, such as the recently ordained Reverend John Sullivan Dwight, whose preference for music over the ministry caused him to seek a haven outside the church. As Dwight was wavering, Elizabeth informed him that "Hawthorne has taken hold with the greatest spirit—& proves a fine workman," and that, while the community's numbers were few and the work hard, "their health & courage rises to meet the case." Once Dwight had officially vacated his Northampton pulpit, she assured him that it was better to "minister in a truly transcendental way to a true church of friends without aid of surplice—pulpit—sermon—or ordinance—without money & without price—. . . without sanctimonious form." Joining the community at Brook Farm would be just the thing to counteract "the evils arising out of the present corrupt—or petrified—organization." Dwight signed on, "well rid of the mournful obligation of earning a living through a calling from which the zest was gone," according to one account of his Brook Farm years. He became one of the community's most dedicated members, a teacher of Latin and music in its school and an assistant editor of the *Harbinger*, Brook Farm's newspaper, in which he began a career as music critic.

Still, Elizabeth remained concerned that "the community" at Brook Farm would never "step out of its swaddling clothes" if something of a "magnetic character" were not done soon to attract more members and investors. She drafted two articles for publication in *The Dial* advertising Brook Farm's purposes and organizing principles. In the first, "A Glimpse of Christ's Idea of Society," published in October 1841 as the group met to make its plans final, she praised the association's aim to permit members to cultivate the "infinite worth and depth in the individual soul" while "doing fuller justice to the social principle" by entering into a pact to "love and assist each other." The

Brook Farmers would "live purely and beautifully now" rather than in the hereafter. In the second, "Plan of the West Roxbury Community," published in January 1842, Elizabeth wrote more specifically of the "little company in the midst of us" intent on "being wholly true to their natures as men and women," and who "feel it is necessary to come out in some degree from the world, and to form themselves into a community." Agriculture would be "the basis of their life," she explained, "it being the most direct and simple in relation to nature," but "none will be engaged merely in bodily labor." Farm work would be limited to a reasonable number of hours, and "means will be given to all for intellectual improvement and for social intercourse, calculated to refine and expand," for "this community aims to be rich, not in the metallic representative of wealth, but in ... leisure to live in all the faculties of the soul." By the spring of 1842, construction had begun on the first of several new buildings, a school was established for children living on the farm and in the village nearby, and the "little company" at Brook Farm had expanded from the half dozen of the previous April to nearly fifty.

But Sophia Peabody and Nathaniel Hawthorne were not to be among their number. By midsummer, Nathaniel had found it impossible, once again, to write in combination with day labor. "My mind is bothered with a sort of dull excitement, which makes it impossible to think continuously of any subject," he wrote to George Hillard, letting him know he could not provide a story he had promised for the 1842 *Token*, which Hillard was editing. "My former stories all sprung up of their own accord, out of a quiet life," he explained. "Now, I have no quiet at all." Worse still, the thought of the unwritten story had "tormented me ever since I came here, and has deprived me of all the comfort I might otherwise have had, in my few moments of leisure." With Hillard, he had no need to present himself as a new Adam in a latter-day Eden, as he did sometimes to Sophia. Now Nathaniel admitted he was having trouble even writing a letter: his hands were covered "with a new crop of blisters—the effect of raking hay." A few days later he wrote to an acquaintance, "The summer is passing with so little enjoyment of nature and my own thoughts" that he might as well have been measuring salt and coal on the docks in Boston.

Hawthorne had begun to see that Ripley's "zeal" for reform clouded his judgment, and while the writer still planned to "give his experiment a full and fair trial," he feared that "from external circumstances—from the improbability that adequate funds will be raised, or that any feasible plan can be suggested, for proceeding without a very considerable capital," the whole quixotic enterprise would fail. He decided to withdraw from active membership in the community at the end of August. He would quit working in the fields and instead pay $4 a week for room and board in the farmhouse, now known to the communards as the "Hive." Then he could "begin to write," he informed his sister Louisa in Salem, who had worried all along that, despite the Brook Farmers' plans to implement "the most liberal and scientific principles of English husbandry," thereby causing the earth "to yield her increase in a style hitherto unknown in New England," they had planted their crops too late to realize any profit.

When Nathaniel wrote to Sophia a week later telling her of the new arrangement, he covered over any qualms he felt about their future at Brook Farm, asking her instead to share the "joyful thought" that "thy husband will be free from his bondage—free to think of his Dove—free to enjoy nature—free to think and feel!" He admitted to Sophia now that "even my Custom House experience was not such a thraldom and weariness; my mind and heart were freer. . . . Thank God, my soul is not utterly buried under a dung-heap." Or perhaps he stated the case in such extremes to defend, both to his "Dove" and to himself, a decision he felt forced to make in order to obtain the "quiet" he needed to write—despite what he imagined to be Sophia's eagerness to marry and settle in whatever "Heaven" they could find.

Just ten days later, however, he wrote Sophia outright of his concern that "thou and I must form other plans for ourselves." He was becoming "more and more convinced, that we must not lean upon the community. What ever is to be done, must be done by thy husband's own individual strength." Still, he acknowledged that "whatever may be thy husband's gifts, he has not hitherto shown a single one that may avail to gather gold." He would try, once again, to make a living from his books: a reissued *Grandfather's Chair* that he asked Sophia to illustrate in hopes that a more handsome volume would sell better and an expanded edition of *Twice-told Tales*. "How much depends on those little books!" He would not spend the winter at Brook Farm, he promised Sophia, "unless with an absolute certainty that there will be a home ready for us in the spring." Perhaps all Hawthorne knew for certain, as he wrote to his "most dear wife," was that "I love thee with infinite intensity, and think of thee continually, and desire thee as never before." Even the quiet he sought would be an empty stillness, now, without Sophia.

But Hawthorne quailed under the pressure to produce—"external pressure always disturbs, instead of assisting me." The flood of suggestions for illustrations he sent to Sophia, each one more elaborate than the next, seemed to have the same effect on her; Sophia had always insisted, "I do not want anything expected of me." In the end she produced only a handful of designs, not the dozen or more Nathaniel envisioned, before turning her efforts to the sculpture of Samuel Gridley Howe's star pupil, Laura Bridgman, the first deaf-blind child ever to be formally educated. For this work, at least, she was guaranteed a commission.

The piece Sophia produced was a remarkable likeness, as her three portrait medallions had been, and a handsome sculpture on its own merits, conferring a quiet dignity on the girl who was just months away from becoming "the most celebrated child in America," according to one biographer, and, "with the exception only of Queen Victoria . . . the most famous female in the entire world." Sophia's bust captured Bridgman in a pensive mood on the verge of fame, her unseeing eyes masked with the cloth band she always wore, her youth and vulnerability poignantly expressed in delicate, bare shoulders and loose, lanky hair. By early 1842, Laura Bridgman's achievements had been so well advertised by the entrepreneurial Howe that when Charles Dickens visited America, he made a special trip to Howe's Perkins Institution for the Blind, to see her read and recite her lessons. In his *American Notes,* Dickens devoted most of a chapter to the "sightless, earless, voiceless" girl, thereby securing her international celebrity and elevating Howe's school to the status of major tourist attraction. In some ways, Sophia's sculpture was no less prodigious than her subject: the first three-dimensional work in clay she had produced from a live model would one day be cast into copies for blind schools across America, themselves brought into being because of Howe's widely broadcast success with Laura Bridgman.

In September, while Sophia made regular visits to the Perkins School to fashion young Laura's likeness out of "cold clay," Nathaniel stayed on at Brook Farm as a boarder, still hoping to "see these people and their enterprise under a new point of view, and perhaps be able to determine whether thou and I have any call to cast in our lot among them." He was suffering, he wrote, a "famished yearning" for Sophia and indulged in a fantasy, inspired by the discovery of wild grapes growing in a distant meadow—"white and purple grapes, in great abundance, ripe, and gushing with rich juice when the hand pressed their clusters." Nathaniel imagined, "If we dwell here, we will make our own wine," and Sophia—"my Dove"—"will want a great quantity," he was sure. Four days later he allowed himself to be elected a trustee of Brook Farm and chairman of the newly formed finance committee.

But his new status did nothing to lessen his growing certainty that life at Brook Farm "was an unnatural and unsuitable, and therefore an unreal one," as he confided in Sophia that fall. "The real Me was never an associate of the community." As Sophia had noticed, Nathaniel remained a detached witness, able to play "horn-sounder, cow-milker, potato-hoer, and hay-raker" if necessary, he wrote—but any of "the brethren" who took him as such "do not know a reality from a shadow." Less than a week after assuming his trusteeship, he wrote longingly to Sophia, "Thou art my only reality," and he packed his bags and moved out of Brook Farm's Hive. He had given this "righteous and heaven blessed way of life" a "full and fair trial" of just six months.

Grandfather's Chair, frontispiece by Sophia Peabody

There are no letters surviving to reveal Sophia's feelings as her fiancé vacillated over the Brook Farm plan. But in the past year she had cut her thumb with a penknife, sprained her ankle, suffered headaches, and lost almost two months to a cough and cold. Hawthorne wrote that he wished he could hold her in his arms perpetually, for "thou wouldst be much better—perhaps quite well!" there. "I am given thee to repose upon, that so my most tender and sensitivest little Dove may be able to do great works." Yet he had so far failed to make good on his promises, even as he turned to Sophia increasingly for reassurance about his talents, for illustrations, and even for business advice. When Nathaniel sent her several stories he was considering for the new collection, she did not hold back her opinion—giving one her "severest reprehension." He promptly dropped it from the volume. Did Sophia's stern critique

Laura Bridgman, by Sophia Peabody

betray some impatience with her fiancé? Or were her illnesses, her resistance to Nathaniel's suggestions for illustrations, signs that she too was faltering under the pressure to produce and, like her "husband," confronting the disturbing certainty that married life would bring an end to the seclusion and quiet, the lack of expectation, she needed in order to paint and sculpt? Poverty would only exacerbate both harsh realities.

Nathaniel was tormented by such thoughts. At times he felt more helpless than supported by his love for Sophia. "Thou art a mighty enchantress, my little Dove, and hast quite subdued a strong man, who deemed himself independent of all the world," he wrote only half in jest as the third anniversary of their engagement approached. "I am a captive under thy little foot, and look to thee for life. Stoop down and kiss me—or I die!" To a pair of editors soliciting new stories, he confessed his deepest fear: "I do not believe that I shall ever write any more—at least, not like my past productions; for they grew out of the quietude and seclusion of my former life." He explained, "During the last three or four years, the world has sucked me within its vortex; and I could not get back to my solitude again, even if I would." Was the "reality" Sophia had drawn him to swirling vortex or soaring heaven?

Ironically, Hawthorne made his own $1,000 investment in Brook Farm just a month before quitting the "queer community" for good. In the end, he never saw a penny of the promised 5 percent interest and would have to sue George Ripley to get even a small portion of the sum back. Although the Brook Farm experiment would last another five years—thriving for a time, in Emerson's words, as "a perpetual picnic, a French Revolution in small, an Age of Reason in a pattypan"—it had already become for Sophia Peabody and Nathaniel Hawthorne an "exploded scheme for beginning the life of Paradise anew." Out $1,000 and with only the slightest of prospects for a future income, Nathaniel Hawthorne didn't even have a wall to hang Sophia's pictures on.

❧ 30 ❧

Two Funerals and a Wedding

LIVING IN BOSTON NEAR HORACE MANN WAS ONE THING. BEARING HER feelings of longing for him was another. It was now almost ten years since Mary met the grieving reformer and fell in love with him. There had been occasions that allowed her to maintain a "prophetic hope" that someday "I should be one with him & he would be one with me": when Mann had greeted her with "deeply expressed joy" on her return from Cuba, when he'd encouraged her to move down from Salem to teach school in Boston. At those times, Mary had almost been tempted to break down the walls of "caution & reserve" she had "erected for my defense & his" and let him know how she felt. But she feared losing Mann's confidence entirely; instead she became his friend, letting him "share his griefs, his cares, & his returning interest in life" in conversation with her. In this way she began to understand all too well Mann's reservations about marrying again—his "pecuniary misfortunes" and his "forebodings of shortened life" through overwork and a constitution weakened by grief.

Mary did her best to keep her yearning a secret from her family—particularly from Sophia, whose not-so-secret passion for Nathaniel Hawthorne increasingly dominated the Peabody household as her hopes for a wedding waxed and waned. "How nicely I dusted thy little eyes," Mary once congratulated herself. "I would not have had you know that the large joy of knowing & loving him stood so near the large sorrow of apprehension that I should never dwell wholly by his side." Mary did not want anyone, particularly the obviously enraptured Sophia, feeling sorry for her. As delicate as she was, Sophia at least had daily visits from her beau when he was in town and dispensation to let him "fold his arms around her" in whatever private quarters the two could find. Sophia and Nathaniel were, after all, engaged. By now, everyone in the Peabody family knew it.

Mary was thirty-five years old during the winter that Sophia and Nathaniel faced the collapse of their Brook Farm plans. She had no way of knowing— for he maintained so steadfast a silence in regard to his private feelings—that Horace Mann was developing a "secret affection" for her; that she had "long since won" his "admiration and love," as he would one day confide in his journal, and was only reckoning with his awareness that "it is impossible that the ardour of a first love should ever be again kindled within me." Could that "intense, burning, glowing, excitation of mind" be satisfactorily replaced by feelings for Mary that were more "calm, serene," and, he hoped, "prophetic of endurance"? Nor did Mary know that Mann's friend George Combe had been urging him, ever since their trip out west in the spring of 1840, to "rise above fate & admit the idea of another partner of your affections." For Mary there were no love letters, no brooches or books, no premarital "conjugal embrace" —nothing. Only her "sore heart," which she managed to conceal as long as "it was my own sorrow," guarded as fiercely as her pride.

Mary made the objects of her second-floor schoolroom—the purple carpet, the maps and worktables—the furniture of her world; the young Quincy children and their fellows were her well-tended population. With her students in mind, she worked late into the night devising textbooks that would serve her own teaching methods: a geography text and a primer, to be published by Elizabeth in the cottage industry that was bringing them closer together than they had been in years. Mary was most proud of *The Flower People*, a children's guide to seasonal plants that took the form of dialogues between a little girl and the magically talking flowers growing in her mother's garden. She had begun writing the book five years before in installments for Elizabeth's magazine *The Family School*. Now Elizabeth arranged for an illustrated edition, with the plates to be hand-colored by the sisters and their mother at West Street. Early on, Elizabeth had expanded her stock to include imported art supplies, selected by Washington Allston—"beautiful colours" that had caught the eye of even the resolutely logocentric Waldo Emerson.

Yet as Emerson also noticed, although the paints Elizabeth offered for sale at West Street might serve the needs of artists like "Mr Allston and Mr Cheney," the engraver, "her shop has no attraction for house builders & merchants." Too much of the stock in Elizabeth's store appealed only to a select group, the most forward-thinking of Boston's none too prosperous "literary class." Her friends applauded her decision to carry "only that in my shop which I *chose*—& could in a measure recommend"; there were to be "*no worthless* books—shadows of shadows—and nothing of any kind of a secondary quality." But would anyone buy? Even Waldo Emerson, who could afford to, prided himself on "seldom" purchasing a book, preferring to borrow from friends or the Harvard library when possible—although he generously offered to "be a buyer in the last resort for books of a good name." After several months of slim sales, Elizabeth's agent John Wiley altered the terms of their agreement, limiting Elizabeth's credit on books to ten days, forcing her to do most of her business through special orders; for the same reason, her subscription library was faltering as Wiley demanded payment on books before they could circulate often enough to cover the purchase price.

In June 1841, less than a year after opening the shop, Elizabeth wrote to the Reverend Channing of her "disappointments" not just in business, but in "finding rules of the trade so bad morally, and the whole concern so rotten." She had discovered "here and there a man who cares more for his conscience than for money." But each of these was, like Elizabeth, a "poor—small dealer." Her hopes of earning enough to subsidize buying trips to Europe had long since faded as she discovered the shop "only paid itself and a very little over." The bookstore, she believed, "ought at least to fill the requisitions of a life asking so little as mine," but it was Mary's school that paid the rent at 13 West Street.

Elizabeth's bookshop, like most of the Transcendentalists' ventures, survived more on enthusiasm than on cash. Brook Farm would never turn a profit, but as many as a hundred idealists made it their home during its peak years in the early 1840s, so that even Hawthorne came to regret his lost opportunity "to see the unfolding & issue of so much bold life." Elizabeth's bookstore and subscription library succeeded most of all as a meeting place—a "Transcendental Exchange," in the words of one memoirist. Margaret Fuller moved her Conversations there for yearly sessions through the spring of 1844; the sisters' Wednesday-night open houses continued; and in early 1842, West Street became the headquarters for another floundering Transcendentalist enterprise, *The Dial.*

No one ever expected *The Dial* to be a commercial success—its founders' mission was to spread ideas. But when Margaret Fuller agreed to serve as editor in the fall of 1839, she counted on being paid for her work. It was not to be; Boston simply did not have enough readers to support such a publication. At its peak, *The Dial* had just three hundred subscribers, whose $750 in yearly fees barely covered production costs. It mattered little to anyone outside the Transcendental coterie that Bronson Alcott had finally written something publishable—his "Orphic Sayings"—for the opening issue; or that an unemployed schoolteacher named Henry David Thoreau had his first piece published in its pages. While most of Boston was still reeling from Theodore Parker's heretical interpretation of the Christian gospels, *The Dial* began to feature in each quarterly issue a column titled "Ethnical Scriptures": "selections from the oldest ethical and religious writings of men, exclusive of the Hebrew and Greek scriptures." Acknowledging the foundational writings of eastern religion to be as valuable as the Christian scriptures was truly heretical in nineteenth-century Boston—if anyone cared to notice. "Each nation has its bible more or less pure," Emerson wrote by way of introducing the first column, an excerpt from Vishnu Sarma's *Hitopadesa* in the summer of 1842. Succeeding issues brought glimpses of the wisdom of Confucius, various Persian prophets, and the first English translation of a key Buddhist text, the *Lotus Sutra*, to appear in print on either side of the Atlantic—this last completed by Elizabeth Peabody in early 1844. All these were brave new utterances; but there did not yet exist in America an audience eager, or even particularly willing, to hear them.

The Dial's first blow came when its publisher, Weeks, Jordan and Company, went bankrupt in the fall of 1841. Fuller and Emerson decided to transfer the work to "a friendly publisher": Elizabeth Peabody. Even though Emerson had been less than friendly himself to Elizabeth's initial efforts to publish in *The Dial*—in the fall of 1840 he had turned away the three unpublished installments on the "Spirit of the Hebrew Scriptures," the ones Andrews Norton had suppressed in 1834, preventing her early use of "the word *transcendentalism*" as possessing now "a certain air of unseasonableness"—Elizabeth accepted the post, glad of the opportunity to take an active part in the project. Emerson may not have been won over by Elizabeth's elucidation of "the social principle," but he was eager to harness her goodwill to his own cause. In Emerson's view, the new "arrangement . . . promises to be greatly more satisfactory to Miss F. & so to all of us," as he wrote to one of *The Dial*'s contributors, the poet Christopher Pearse Cranch. Emerson thought Elizabeth would be able to manage the journal so as to "at least, pay the Editor, which it never has yet a penny." No consideration was given to Elizabeth's finances.

Nevertheless, Elizabeth went to work attracting subscribers from outside New England and even overseas. Through the bookshop, she arranged an exchange of *The Dial* with Horace Greeley, now the editor of the *New York Tribune*—a publication that, Greeley kindly wrote, was "a less deserving & therefore more popular paper," already reaching some 20,000 readers. Greeley promised to print advertisements and extracts in the *Tribune* in hopes that "I may be able to win friends and readers for *The Dial* in time." He confessed to delighting in the magazine's "luxuries" himself, on those rare occasions when he could afford to "escape into the Ideal"; based on Elizabeth's account of Brook Farm, he considered sending his invalid wife to board there for the summer. But Greeley also warned that "my own experience in publishing leads me to feel many doubts" that Elizabeth and her friends would be able to "sustain" the journal for long.

When, after another two issues, there was still not enough revenue for Fuller to be paid, she resigned. Editorial duties were enormously time-consuming, and being second-guessed by Emerson, who had jettisoned her lead editorial for the inaugural issue, replacing it with one of his own, was simply not worth it. Not that Fuller hadn't enjoyed the excuse to remain in close contact with the philosopher. Through most of 1841, their intimate working relationship may have been the root cause of Emerson's increasingly dark thoughts on the subject of marriage. "Plainly marriage should be a temporary relation," he wrote in his journal that year. "When each of two souls ha[s] exhausted the other of the good which each held for the other, they should part . . . [when] drawn to new society. The new love is the balm to prevent a wound from forming where the old love detached."

Aside from the attractions of other women, Waldo was troubled by a domestic life that distracted him from his work. "I guard my moods as anxiously as a miser his money," he wrote: "household-chores untune and disqualify me for writing." Ideally, a writer "ought not to be married, ought not to have a family." If married, a writer should have a wife with the "sense that her philosopher is best in his study" and who lets him stay there as long as he likes while she manages the household on her own. Lidian, apparently, did not always manage so well. At the end of the summer, anticipating yet another extended September visit from Margaret Fuller, and with Lidian unwell and entering the final months of a third pregnancy, Emerson wrote more bleakly still of what he termed the "Mezentian marriage," a concept derived from the tale of the depraved King Mezentius, who tied men together with corpses and left them to die. Perhaps any marriage was deadly to the soul: "It is not in the plan or prospect of the soul, this fast union of one to one," Emerson wrote. "The soul is alone." He urged himself to cultivate self-sufficiency, drawing on "the resources of the all-creating, all-obliterating spirit." In such a frame of mind, "the griefs incident to every earthly marriage are the less." For the self-reliant man, Emerson justified his feelings of increased alienation from his wife, "the Universe is his bride."

The third Emerson child, a second daughter, Edith, was born in November, just as Elizabeth Peabody took over as publisher of *The Dial*. Then, in January, the Emersons' precious Little Waldo, now five years old, caught scarlet fever and died after an illness of just three days. The parents were devastated. Waldo retreated, ashen, to his study. "Shall I ever dare to love anything again?" he wrote to Margaret Fuller. His railings against family life and the petty "griefs" of "every earthly marriage" seemed inconsequential, even shameful now. Lidian entered a depression that would last so long she later believed she had "lost" her oldest daughter, Ellen's, childhood. Elizabeth Peabody was one of the first outside Concord to learn the news. Emerson wrote the day after Little Waldo's death, declining to attend a gathering Elizabeth had arranged for "a few persons to meet Charles Dickens," then in Boston on his American tour. "Thanks for your kind invitation, my friend," he explained, "but the most severe of all afflictions has befallen me, in the death of my boy ... & with him has departed all that is glad & festal & almost all that is social even, for me, from this world." Emerson never did meet Dickens on this visit, and it is not certain that Elizabeth did either.

When Margaret Fuller resigned as editor of *The Dial* less than two months later, in March 1842, it came almost as a relief to Emerson to take over the position. Now well established as a free-lance lecturer, he didn't need a salary, but he welcomed the extra work as a distraction. "Let there be rotation in martyrdom," he wrote to Fuller, in an effort to shake off his gloom. Now it was Elizabeth Peabody with whom he would be working most closely on this "bold bible for the Young America," in which he invested much effort and all the hope he could muster. Over the next two years, Emerson would write fifty-three pieces for *The Dial*, along with soliciting and supervising the publication of nearly every other contribution to the magazine. He estimated that as much as a third of his working hours were devoted to *The Dial*—an act, he wrote in his journal, of "petty literary patriotism." At the same time, in early 1842, Elizabeth stepped up her own production, adding to the quarterly "grinding out of *Dials*" several new books from the offices of "E. P. Peabody, Publisher": Margaret Fuller's translation from the German of Bettine von Arnim's novel *Günderode;* and Elizabeth's own editions of St. Augustine's *Confessions*, the first to be issued by an American publisher, and Guillaume Oegger's *True Messiah*, the work that, in her earlier manuscript translation from the French, had inspired Emerson while he was writing *Nature*.

Like Waldo Emerson, Elizabeth was keeping busy, guarding against loss. During the spring of 1842, her youngest sister, the one everyone in the Peabody family had expected to remain at home all her life, had at last found that "cottage, somewhere" to share with her future husband, the only man Elizabeth had ever wanted to marry. Come summer, thirty-two-year-old Sophia would finally break up "the sisterhood," leaving West Street without its resident artist and invalid, its precious "hot-house plant."

It was Elizabeth Hoar's doing; Sophia would afterward call her an "agent of Heaven" for arranging the plan. But Elizabeth Hoar wasn't just looking for a way to thank her friend Sophia Peabody for producing the uncannily evocative medallion of her own lost fiancé, Charles Emerson. She also wanted to do something for Charles's surviving brother Waldo, who had made her a "sister" in his household in the years since Charles's death. Now, in the difficult months after the death of his oldest child and only son, Emerson diverted himself with thoughts of forming "a good neighborhood" in Concord, consisting of his closest Transcendental comrades. If he could lure Nathaniel Hawthorne and Sophia Peabody, Henry Hedge, Margaret Fuller, and several others, he wrote in his journal, "these if added to our present kings & queens would make a rare, an unrivalled company," providing "a solid social satisfaction" and putting an end to what he saw now as the "disgust and depression of visitation" that had proved so disruptive to family life. "Those of us who do not believe in Communities," Emerson wrote to Charles Newcomb, a young Brown University graduate and friend of Fuller's who had spent a season at Brook Farm, "believe in neighborhoods & that the kingdom of heaven may consist of such."

In March 1842, the Old Manse, the house overlooking the Concord River by the Revolutionary battle site—weathered bridge, shining granite monument, and all—became available for rent. Since the war, the Manse had served as parsonage for Waldo Emerson's grandfather William and then for his step-grandfather, the Reverend Ezra Ripley, Concord's First Parish minister for more than sixty years until his death at age ninety. Waldo himself had begun work on *Nature* in the house before his marriage to Lidian, before Charles's death; he would serve as rental agent.

New paint in the downstairs rooms and a yearly rent of just $75 had not been enough to attract the first couple Emerson showed the house to that spring—Elizabeth and George Bancroft, historian and, as collector of the Port of Boston, Nathaniel Hawthorne's one-time patron—who considered taking it as a summer house and then declined. Then Elizabeth Hoar mentioned the place to Sophia Peabody. Emerson already knew Sophia, but he had not yet met her fiancé, whose work he had so far given only grudging respect. While showing the couple the house in early May, warming to his new role as Concord booster, Emerson decided now that "I like him well," as he wrote to Hoar, thanking her for sending Hawthorne his way. Margaret Fuller, too, advertised Hawthorne's merits: "You will find him more *mellow* than most fruits at your board, and of distinct flavor too." Dark as his thoughts were about his own marriage and writers' marriages generally, Emerson was hopeful on Sophia and Nathaniel's behalf, and above all "pleased with the colony he is collecting," Sarah Clarke reported to Margaret Fuller when she heard about the visit. Most important to all concerned, Nathaniel and Sophia liked the Old Manse. Sophia saw at once that the house and grounds could serve as "that profound retreat" both of them longed for. To Nathaniel, the "antique" house seemed "created by Providence expressly for our use, and at the precise time when we wanted it."

A ten-minute walk from Concord's town green, the large gray house stood alone on a rise above a bend in the Concord River where the water flowed so peacefully that Hawthorne claimed it was impossible to tell which way the current ran. A long grassy drive lined with black ash trees led down to the road into town. Vegetable gardens and a spreading lawn lay in front of the house, an orchard of fruit trees on the hillside; the river, full of fish—"savory"

The Old Manse, Concord

bream in great abundance—was no more than fifty paces from the back door. The rent was high for Concord, but reasonable compared to Boston rates, and included the garden produce and orchard fruit—apples, pears, peaches, and cherries. The couple believed they might even afford a cook. Hawthorne was determined "to remove everything that may impede" his future wife's "full growth and development," and as much as possible to allow her "freedom from household drudgery": for "she has many visions of great deeds to be wrought on canvass and in marble."

For the first time, Sophia could envision her married life, "with such a world of happiness lying round me ... the blue, fresh river, the long, quiet lawn—the woods near by—the innumerable riches of earth & sky." The house itself was large enough to afford Nathaniel "a study & I a studio, one over the other." The two had already planned their days. "While he is in the hands of his Muse in the morning, I shall be subject to mine," Sophia explained in a letter to her Salem friend Mary Foote. "In our several vocations we shall joyfully exert our faculties during the first hours—then after noon we shall meet to interchange the thoughts that have visited us from the Unknown deep." She imagined the "felicity" of hearing Nathaniel read his stories out loud, "and also of telling him all I have discovered & shewing him my inscriptions with pencil & sculpting tool—and he so just & severe & true a critic!" Never mind that the two were practitioners in different fields: "the artistic mind & eye are identical in all."

Sophia was "penetrated with joy" over the new plans, she wrote to Margaret Fuller, whose frequent appearances at West Street had made her a close friend during the past year—for they had materialized none too soon. In early February, a frustrated Sophia, tired of keeping a secret that had not been her idea in the first place, issued an "injunction" to Nathaniel to tell his mother and sisters about their engagement. She had gone along with Nathaniel's request for secrecy in large measure because of the initial awkwardness with Elizabeth. But after three years, Sophia may at last have wondered how serious her fiancé could be about a romance that he would not confess to his closest relatives. She may also have expected that after making the announcement, Nathaniel would feel obliged to set a wedding date. At any rate, she no longer felt comfortable dissembling.

But the writer pleaded with her. Nathaniel had recently visited Salem, staying in his old bedroom, where, he joked bleakly, "doubtless, in all succeeding ages, pilgrims will come to pay their tribute of reverence." He imagined his latter-day admirers pointing and exclaiming: "There is the pine table—there the old flag-bottomed chair—in which he sat, and at which he scribbled, during his agonies of inspiration! There is the old chest of drawers, in which he kept what shirts a poor author may be supposed to have possessed! There is the closet, in which was reposited his threadbare suit of black!" Even stated ironically, Hawthorne's ambitions were immense—as outsized as his fears that he would never realize them. Only Sophia knew just how much he yearned for fame. How could he tell his mother and sisters that he wanted to marry when he had no income and little reputation? They, too, counted on his eventual celebrity as a writer and considered marriage an absolute impediment.

And there was more. Nathaniel confided to Sophia the "strange reserve, in regard to matters of feeling" among his family members. "There seems to be a tacit law, that our deepest heart-concernments are not to be spoken of," he wrote. "I cannot take my heart in my hand, and show it to them." It was the same tale of estrangement—"we do not live at our house"—that he had first confided in Elizabeth and that had impelled him toward intimacy with both of the sisters. Nathaniel speculated that "something wrong in our early intercourse"—something as profoundly disruptive as the original shock to the family of his father's death—was the cause of "this incapacity of free communion, in the hour of especial need" that so constrained his family relationships. Whatever the source, Nathaniel felt powerless to break the spell—or, just yet, to announce his plans to break the family circle.

Indeed, Nathaniel wrote Sophia, he found it "hard to speak of thee—*really* of thee—to any body!" From the earliest days of their engagement he had enjoyed the thought of their love as private. "Nothing like our story was ever written—or ever will be—for we shall not feel inclined to make the public our confidant," he had declared to Sophia more than two years earlier. He asked Sophia now to understand "what a cloudy veil stretches over the abyss of my nature," and he urged her to "find [her] way there," for the "involuntary reserve" he felt with almost anyone besides Sophia was something he could not, and perhaps would not, wish to change. That reserve "has given the objectivity to my writings," he believed, even when "people think that I am pouring myself out in a tale or essay." Rather, he told her, "I sympathize with them—not they with me." It was a separateness he both prized and cursed, and that he allowed only Sophia to intrude upon. And so his longing for her increased, even as he insisted on keeping their love a secret, thereby postponing the "external pledge of our eternal and infinite union": the earthly consecration of the marriage he liked to believe had already been made in a heaven absent the mother and sisters whose emotional sustenance depended on his exclusive devotion to them.

By now Nathaniel had become a master of the distant lover's avowal of passion. "It is a happiness to need thee, to sigh for thee, to feel the nothingness of all things without thee," he wrote Sophia in the same letter in which he had refused to comply with her "injunction." How could Sophia stay angry with so eloquent a suitor, even if he dallied? "This yearning that disturbs my very breath—this earnest stretching out of my soul towards thee—this voice of my heart, calling for thee out of its depths, and complaining that thou art not instantly given to it—all these are a joy; for they make me know how entirely our beings have blended into one another," Nathaniel wrote. "Absence, as well as presence, gives me this knowledge—and as long as I have it, I live." Perhaps Sophia, at home in her room, felt lodged in a similar limbo of contrary emotions.

And just when Sophia may have feared her "husband" was content to dwell in a world of theoretical love, he would deliver a paean to the actual. "We have left expression—at least, such expression as can be achieved with pen and ink—far behind us," he wrote her in January 1842 from Salem, where the lack of "free communion" with his family always preyed on him, causing him to miss Sophia most acutely. "Even the spoken word has long been inadequate. Looks—pressures of the lips and hands, and the touch of bosom to bosom—these are a better language." In early spring he wrote, "My breast is full of thee; thou art throbbing throughout all my veins." He felt "as if nothing had ever existed before—as if, at this very *now*, the physical and spiritual world were but just discovered, and by ourselves only."

In the end, despite Sophia's desire to make their plans public, she let him off the hook. But somehow, in March, word of the engagement spread around Boston. "Some person betrayed my secret," Sophia wrote in April to her Salem friend Mary Foote, who had heard the news, "and this is why it is now so universally talked of. But it has never been officially announced." An official announcement might have helped prevent what would become a persistent rumor—that Hawthorne was engaged to Elizabeth Peabody, not Sophia. The rumor seemed to take hold in Salem, where Elizabeth and Nathaniel's intense early friendship might have attracted notice. One purveyor of the tale, Benjamin Merrill, wrote to the Salem lawyer and politician Leverett Saltonstall, "I heard a rumor that N. Hawthorne and Miss E. P. Peabody or some of the Sisters are betrothed—so the world may be blessed with transcendental literary productions—hope they will preserve their Copy-Right." When an announcement was finally printed, it didn't help matters that Sophia was listed in one paper simply as "the accomplished Miss Peabody."

By then it was mid-May. The Old Manse had been rented, a wedding date set for six weeks hence—Monday, June 27. Only now did Nathaniel Hawthorne pay a visit to Salem to tell the Hawthorne women his news. Could his mother and sisters have missed the rumors flying around Salem, along with what must have been clear signs of an alliance forming between Nathaniel and Sophia going back as far as the joint publication of *The Gentle Boy*? They pretended to. That allowed them to harden their opposition—or distaste, for the whole "affair."

No account survives of what must have been a painful encounter. Nathaniel's older sister, Ebe Hawthorne, was the one to write Sophia a note of congratulations afterward, although the word *congratulations* never entered into it. "Your approaching union with my brother makes it proper for me to offer you my assurances of a sincere desire for your mutual happiness," Ebe began her letter icily. "I hope nothing will ever occur to render our future intercourse other than agreeable, particularly as it need not be so frequent or so close as to require more than reciprocal good will, if we do not happen to suit each other in our new relationship." The news had been "especially due to my mother," Ebe chafed; it was not easy for Mrs. Hawthorne to understand how "her only son" could have left her with just a few weeks "to prepare her feelings for his marriage." The greater portion of Ebe's anger was reserved for Nathaniel, however. "I speak thus plainly," Ebe wrote, "because my brother desired me to say only what was true: though I do not recognise his right to speak of *truth*, after concealing this affair from us so long." All three Hawthorne women found excuses to refuse invitations to the wedding.

Sophia could not have been terribly surprised. After all, Ebe was the one who had sent acorn caps, moss, and seaweed to the house on Charter Street— "hideous," George had called them—in return for bouquets of spring flowers from the Peabody sisters. All her life Ebe had been known for her unconventional habits and strong opinions, strongly stated. "Consult your own comforts and forswear self-sacrifice" would become one of her mottoes in later years—

a view almost unthinkable for a woman of her era. Perhaps because she was a confirmed recluse herself, Ebe was, she wrote, "hard hearted towards confirmed invalids." They gave the life she had chosen a bad name. Ebe didn't need to be sick to exercise "the power to withdraw." But she may have worried that Sophia, the woman her adored younger brother had chosen to marry, did, and would continue to. Perhaps most important, Ebe, as articulate and well-read as Nathaniel, had long enjoyed the role of her brother's "severest critic." Now Sophia—with her Transcendental optimism, and an accomplished artist in her own right—had taken that from her.

Sophia managed a "most beautiful—sweet, gentle, and magnanimous" letter in reply, in Nathaniel's view, delivered the next day. "If they do not love thee, it must be because they have no hearts to love with," her fiancé consoled her. It took Ebe more than two weeks to respond, but when she did it was with an apology for seeming "very cold and even apathetic to you," for having "said any thing in my note to give you pain." She described her mother now as being "prepared to receive and love you as a daughter." Ebe herself hoped Sophia could "forget the past" and "look forward to the future," which "seems to promise much of happiness to you." She assured Sophia that "certainly I think your disposition and my brother's well suited to each other." Now Ebe puzzled, instead, over Sophia's decision. "Have you no dread of the cares and vexations inevitable in married life?" As if reading Sophia's mind, Ebe wrote of her own reservations about marriage—or "any responsibility not forced upon me by circumstances beyond my control": "I should not like to feel as if much depended upon me." It was a sentence Sophia herself had spoken and written many times over.

Indeed, once the wedding plans were set and "the world found out," and presents—silver fruit knives, flowered plates, books of poetry, an alabaster vase—started to arrive at West Street, Sophia began to suffer mysterious fevers. She consulted a homeopath and a mesmerist—her friend Connie Park, who had turned to the occupation in some desperation once she realized her absentee husband, Tom, was never going to send for her from California. What Sophia most needed, however, was to test her future husband's willingness to care for her. Nathaniel had already assured Sophia, when she had suffered headaches and fatigue the previous fall while working simultaneously on Laura Bridgman's sculpture and the illustrations for *Grandfather's Chair*, that "it is not what thou dost, but what thou art, that I concern myself about." Now, as she fell sick in mid-June, and the wedding was postponed for one week, then another, Sophia felt grateful for "this arrest," she wrote to Mary Foote. "I congratulate myself upon this illness, for it has created another divine phasis of Mr. Hawthorne. To be so watched over—so nursed—who would not gladly have a nervous fever?"

As June turned to July, and the new wedding date—July 9—approached, Sophia felt "like a rising Phoenix" thanks to the ministrations of her fiancé, "so powerful & gentle—so tender & noble." Nathaniel had proved himself eminently capable of "lingering here," as he wrote to Sophia, "visiting thy couch every evening, and hearing thee say thou art better than the night before." Because of Sophia's illness, Mary had gone out to Concord to arrange the house, overseeing the placement of the maple bedroom furniture that Sophia had painted with details from the Roman frescoes of Guido Reni, the carpet Sophia had selected two years earlier, and the *Comos*, destined for Hawthorne's study. The late Reverend Ripley's heirs had seen to it that more coats of paint were applied and new wallpaper hung, until the house was "all new & bright again as a toy," Waldo Emerson judged. Henry Thoreau, now living in the Emerson house and serving as handyman in exchange for room and board, had planted the vegetable garden with several varieties of squash, peas, currants, cucumbers, corn, and string beans—all of them beginning to ripen.

The morning of July 9 arrived. At 11:30, under the Reverend James Freeman Clarke's direction, the "execution" took place—the only term Nathaniel Hawthorne could bring himself to use when referring to the wedding in letters home to Salem. None of his family attended. In the back parlor at West Street, dressed in white, lilies braided into her hair, and with her closest friends —Sarah Clarke and Connie Park—as well as her mother and sisters gathered around, Sophia felt as if "in a trance," too dazed to notice whether her father congratulated her after the short ceremony. Soon the newlyweds were riding by carriage to Concord in the summer heat, interrupted first by a light "diamond" shower, then by the drenching rain of an afternoon thunderstorm, before continuing on through a green landscape that "shone like polished emerald," and reaching the Old Manse before sunset. Sophia and Nathaniel had missed the conventionally matrimonial roses and honeysuckle of June, but Elizabeth Hoar had filled every vase she could find in the house with coreopsis, meadowsweet, and water lilies, the wildflowers of July. She was making good on the promise she had written in verse to Sophia the week before:

> ... These and more July shall ope'
> Their blossoms wait for thee,
> And what in June was only hope
> Shall bright fulfilment be.

Sophia and Nathaniel Hawthorne swiftly found fulfillment as "Adam and Eve" in their "perfect Eden," the bride wrote home to her family a day later. In another week, Sophia boasted of "my wonderful cure" and of a husband who "blooms into more consummate perfection every day." Meanwhile, her parents and sisters continued "toasting in West Street"—not with wine, but with Boston's unremitting summer heat—and rattled about the suddenly empty house. "We seem to have no centre here," Mary wrote to Sophia two days after the wedding.

Sophia's room—her "chamber, studio & boudoir (all in one)"—at 13 West Street was soon rented out to Seth Cheney, the engraver. Now that there was no longer any need to help Sophia with her trousseau, Mary busied herself in after-school hours dispensing Elizabeth's library books to the workmen in the stable across the street in hopes that "they will read & get civilized," and translating German articles on drawing instruction for Horace Mann's *Common School Journal.* Mann himself had been elated since winning a $6,000 yearly commitment from the state legislature in March to support his common school reforms—"the great work is done!" he'd written in his journal. Eighteen thousand copies of the report he'd issued to garner the financing had been rushed into print in New York State alone, where like-minded reformers hoped to repeat his triumph. "We will make something better than the present out of this infernal world," Mann wrote to his friend Samuel Gridley Howe, flush now, too, with the success of his work with Laura Bridgman at the Perkins Institution for the Blind. "Never give up" was the lesson Mann drew from his victory; "Massachusetts may yet be a spectacle for men & angels." Of course Mann was soon torturing himself about the next challenge—the invitation to deliver Boston's July 4 oration, when he would "submit" his plans, once again, "to the terrible ordeal of public opinion."

In May, "on the Eve" of Nathaniel Hawthorne's "marriage with my youngest sister," Elizabeth had written again to Wordsworth. She sent her letter, along with a copy of Hawthorne's new edition of *Twice-told Tales,* by the hand of the still unemployed Bronson Alcott, whose friends had passed the hat to send him to England for a year, where a country boarding school named Alcott House had been founded on the principles outlined in *Record of a School.* Elizabeth, along with Emerson and the others, hoped that "perhaps English good sense will assist him to make the compromise—with the finite —which *men must come to,*" as she wrote in her letter to Wordsworth.

Elizabeth believed she had come a long way toward achieving that necessary compromise herself, since first writing to Wordsworth at twenty-one, with "a heart troubled too deeply by the meeting of sensibility & reflection— amid heavy responsibilities of life." Now, rather than pour out her soul as she had in earlier letters to the poet, she put forward Hawthorne's volume as "the only American production, which shows our capability . . . of the romance of History." And she wrote of Wordsworth's old friend Washington Allston—"I see him frequently, and we *always* talk of you and Mr. Coleridge." At sixty-three, Allston was working with some desperation on the enormous canvas of his long unfinished masterwork, *Belshazzar's Feast,* exhausting himself in climbing a ladder to adjust features in the upper portions of the canvas, then climbing back down again to judge the changed effects from a distance. But his conversation was brilliant as always, revealing an "Immortal youth" fired "by the life of his genius," Elizabeth wrote.

Elizabeth was trying to keep the old guard together by recalling Allston to his English friend. But now, too, in other ways she was leaving the old guard behind. "In looking round among Unitarians, I see, on the faces of all the best, a sadness, and, in their tones, I hear a note of sorrow," she had written that same spring in her article defending Theodore Parker. "The Unitarian Church has proved herself, in my inward experience, for years, no real mother to me." She visited the Reverend Channing in June, as he packed for a summer in the Berkshires, and confessed that her religious views were taking a "new turn." She doubted that he would approve. In the coming months she would even consider having herself baptized as a Trinitarian; yet she also threw herself into annotating tales from Vishnu Sarma's *Hitopadesa* for *The Dial.* Channing asked Elizabeth to write him during the summer and "make me partner of your new thoughts." He asked, "Don't you think *I* have the *first* right?" But for the only time in her life, Elizabeth declined a request from her mentor. She did not write.

How much this quest for a new "philosophy of religion that unlocked and explained mysteries of my own experience," as Elizabeth stated it afterward, had to do with Sophia's marriage is hard to know. Elizabeth struggled with the fact of her singleness. Even with Mary for a companion, she had to reckon with the knowledge that most women—nine out of ten, by U.S. Census statistics—married. Elizabeth had taken notes on one of Margaret Fuller's Conversations, in which the participants grappled with the question of why women failed to produce works of artistic genius. Was it because "at the period of life when men gave themselves" to such pursuits, "most women became mothers"? Then what of the women who didn't marry? Why weren't they more productive? The two most accomplished single women present— Peabody and Fuller—sparred over the question. Elizabeth offered the opinion that single women "too often spent the rest of their lives in mourning" over lost opportunities to marry: "society spoke so uniformly of woman as more respectable for being married—that it was long before she entirely despaired." Fuller snapped back that "there came a time however when every one *must give up.*" Elizabeth responded that "then it was but too common for youth to be past—& the mind to have wedded itself to that mediocrity, which is too commonly the result of disappointed hope."

No one could ever say that Elizabeth Peabody had wed herself to mediocrity. But had she now reached a point when she *"must give up"*? She was thirty-eight. Several years earlier, when the pain of Hawthorne's rejection was still fresh, she had written in her journal, "Ah woman is still the same nature whether she is in love or not. All the suffering of disappointed hopeless love, or the joy of happy answered affection, she must experience whether or not there is an embodied hero to the romance. I have loved excellence. . . . Who knows whether the ideal may not yet shadow forth his glory into human mortal?" But that was four years ago, before West Street, before Wednesday evenings, Brook Farm, *The Dial.* Before Elizabeth had made herself the "friendly publisher" to the Transcendentalists. Before Theodore Parker had thought to praise her "onlyness."

Elizabeth may have quested for a new "philosophy of religion" during the summer after her little sister's wedding. But she knew herself well enough to stay the course that she had set since leaving Salem for Boston—to "be myself and *act.*" She shrugged off Channing's efforts to monitor her spiritual development and kept busy at the bookshop and with her work on *The Dial.* When Samuel Soden, publisher of the *Boston Miscellany,* a magazine with eight thousand subscribers, stopped in at West Street one afternoon in late July to ask Elizabeth's advice on finding a new editor, she immediately proposed her brother-in-law; Hawthorne's marriage to her sister would not put an end to her efforts to help along his career.

Mary, too, had ideas for Hawthorne. The life of Peter Schmid, the German drawing master whose biography she was translating, seemed an ideal subject; Hawthorne could "take the facts & make the most beautiful story of them." And she dropped another broad hint to Sophia: "Dr. Howe will offer up any documents he has about Laura [Bridgman] for the sake of having Mr. Hawthorne write a memoir of her." Couldn't Hawthorne spare an evening in Boston to meet Howe and his pupil? Likely Sophia never even passed along that proposal, although she did let Mary know that her husband's "abomination of visiting . . . still holds strong, be it to see no matter what angel."

In any case, the Hawthornes were determined to spend the summer doing nothing but "enjoy each other," as Sophia wrote firmly to her mother. Caroline Sturgis had paid a visit to the Old Manse, bringing a bust of Apollo as a wedding gift, and left expressing to Sophia the expectation that "many pictures will come from these long quiet summer hours." But Sophia responded, "Were you in my place, dear Caroline, you would recognize the impossibility of making pictures yet. The attempt at expression in any way seems absurd & useless. These summer months . . . I am entirely occupied with being supremely happy & in traversing the vast nature of my husband." To a letter from her mother—who worried about her former invalid, and may have been troubled by a vestigial memory of Royall Tyler, that "polished man of literary eminence" who had ruined her own early family life—expressing the concern that "I shall be too subject to my Adam," Sophia responded, "His will is strong, *but not to govern others.* Our love is so wide and deep and equal."

The mornings of work in study and studio that Sophia had envisioned were put off in favor of gathering wildflowers, boating on the river in a canoe purchased from their most prized new friend, Henry Thoreau—the man was "ugly as sin," Hawthorne thought, but "with much of wild original nature still remaining in him"—or roaming the woods, allowing themselves time to lie "down upon the carpet of dried pine leaves" and rest "a few moments on the bosom of dear Mother Earth," as Sophia wrote, recounting one morning's walk in the journal she and Nathaniel now kept jointly. "Then I clasped him in my arms in the lovely shade ... Oh how sweet it was! ... There seemed no movement in the world but that of our pulses." On another day, the couple set out in search of "the Cliffs," a picnic spot recommended by Emerson, but found instead a "lovely sapphire little sea" and "concluded we had discovered it." Nathaniel swam while Sophia "paddled over my ankles in the pure water"; they named the pond "Hawthorne."

Writing in the same common journal, Nathaniel admitted that "it might be a sin and shame, in such a world as ours, to spend a lifetime in this manner." But, he concluded, "for a few summer-weeks, it is good to live as if this world were Heaven." In the evening, by the light of an astral lamp, Nathaniel cranked the handsome music box they'd received as a wedding gift—"our domestic harmony," the couple called it—and Sophia danced for her husband, "the Cachucha, Cracovienne or whatever jig." It was the first dancing she had done since Cuba. Nathaniel told her she danced so well that "I deserve John the Baptist's head."

In late September, Nathaniel spent a night away from Sophia, trekking with Waldo Emerson to visit the Shaker community in the nearby town of Harvard, Massachusetts. Hawthorne enjoyed the outing, and even the philosopher's company, although since moving to the Old Manse he had become less certain of the other "originals" Waldo was hoping to attract to Concord: "after one has seen a few of them, [they] become more dull and common-place than even those who keep the ordinary pathway of life." Gone for just two days and one night, Nathaniel missed his wife—that "beloved woman" who "gets into the remotest recesses of my heart, and shines all through me." When he returned, Nathaniel wrote in their journal, it was "the first time that I ever came home in my life; for I never had a home before."

Early frosts killed the squash and bean vines in the vegetable garden at the Old Manse, but a succession of "mild, sweet, perfect days" followed in which "the warm sunshine seemed to embrace the earth, and all earth's children, with love and tenderness," Nathaniel wrote. On these same days a migrant band of Penobscot Indians camped on the banks of the Concord River, near the bridge. Henry Thoreau had already shown Sophia and Nathaniel where they could find arrowheads in the field behind their house. The Penobscots returned to the same bend in the river each year to sell handmade baskets in town. Sophia walked among them late one afternoon, listening to them speak a "gurgling purling" language, mixed with English. She watched them spread their tents, admired the "beautiful workmanship" on the canvas, and gazed at the women, their long hair tied in cloth bags behind their heads, as a "heavenly sunset gilded them." In the gathering dusk, the women began cooking at their fires, and Sophia returned to the gray house on the hillside where she "made some bread myself, and succeeded very well," she wrote to her mother.

It was on one of those same mild sweet October days that Elizabeth received word in Boston that the Reverend Channing had died on his travels, in Bennington, Vermont. "I still held the letter in my hand," she later recalled, her cheeks "wet with tears," when Washington Allston walked in—"the only visit I ever had from him" at the bookshop. Elizabeth told Allston the news; the artist turned pale, stepped back as if struck, and sank into the nearest chair. Channing—his brother-in-law by his first marriage and a lifelong friend—had been ill so often, Allston explained when he could finally speak, that "I had ceased to think of his dying." The two men were nearly the same age; Channing, at sixty-two, was just a year younger than Allston. Unable to remember the errand that had brought him to Elizabeth's store, Allston left, still visibly shaken.

The minister's body was returned to Boston by train for the funeral at the Federal Street Church, where he'd presided for thirty-nine years, and interment at Mount Auburn Cemetery. Elizabeth learned that Channing had preached his last sermon two months earlier in Lenox, Massachusetts, a stirring antislavery address delivered with an "inspired expression" to a congregation whose rapt attention he held for over an hour. The effort had exhausted him, leaving him susceptible to the typhoid fever that carried him off, although not before his brother Walter had arrived to attend him in his final days. By then the fever was bringing him "crowds of images . . . visions of immensity, and rushing thoughts," but Channing asked family members to help direct his attention toward "common things," for, in a phrase Elizabeth, even in her "new turn," would have approved, he insisted: "We need to feel the *reality*, the REALITY of the spiritual life."

In the end, Channing died "so gently that they did not know surely for fifteen minutes whether he lived or not," his daughter, Mary, told Elizabeth. Mary, the girl who had once tormented Mary Peabody as governess, and had proved to her father Elizabeth's skills as a Latin teacher, was now grown and married to a Unitarian ministerial candidate, Frederic Eustis. Elizabeth visited Mary

Eustis now at the Channing house, where her mentor's body lay in state, the soft hair, still dark, framing the always pale face. Mary Eustis told Elizabeth that she had been missed at Channing's deathbed. But along with his family, Elizabeth stayed home from the Federal Street funeral service, not wishing "to be tortured by poor" Ezra Stiles Gannett, Channing's lackluster successor.

Elizabeth had been undone by significant deaths in the past—most notably J. G. Spurzheim's a decade before. But now, despite their break during the summer, Elizabeth felt only that Channing had "come nearer to me" and that "the difficulty of expression was now gone." They had always shared "an identical love and desire for the truth." Even if "his intellect lingered" in the "formulas of Unitarianism," she believed that "his faith had always transcended" them.

"That there is a better world you believe as well as I," Elizabeth had once written to Mary in the midst of a quarrel over Horace Mann. "I believe it is nearer than you do—even *at hand*—& *within*." Elizabeth may not have achieved the "clear new life" in an earthly "Paradise" that Sophia found with Nathaniel Hawthorne in Concord; and she may have envied her youngest sister the experience of becoming "absorbed into another being." But in her own way, Elizabeth succeeded in living every day "as if this world were Heaven": a heaven made up of causes to support, geniuses to foster, ideas to claim and be claimed by.

It was Mary both sisters now worried about: Mary who, Sophia wrote, seemed to be living a "*half life* . . . year after year toiling for all but herself, & growing thin & pale with too much effort"; Mary, the middle sister who, Elizabeth had charged in that long-ago argument, believed in a heaven "above the region of Circumstance," and so might "never find it till beyond the grave."

℞ EPILOGUE: MAY 1, 1843 ℞

ON THE MORNING OF THIS WEDDING DAY, RAIN FELL STEADILY. ONE BY one the messages arrived at West Street—Miss Rawlins Pickman would not ride the train down from Salem, Sophia Hawthorne was stranded at the Old Manse in a sea of mud. The minister, James Freeman Clarke, delayed the ceremony as long as possible, waiting for the groom's two nieces, both schoolteachers, who never did appear; they were marooned south of the city in New Bedford. But time was of the essence. Indeed time had been a precious commodity ever since March 26, the day five weeks before when Horace Mann had suddenly proposed marriage to Mary Peabody and invited her to travel with him to Europe on a six-month tour of schools, prisons, and asylums with Samuel Gridley Howe and his own bride-to-be, the New York society girl Julia Ward. Mann had already booked passage for himself on the Cunard steamship *Britannia* for May 1; the decision to travel forced his realization that "it would be too painful to go and leave so lovely a being and one in whom I had such an interest, behind me." When Mary said yes, he bought a second ticket. "It cannot be otherwise, now," Horace Mann wrote in his journal on the last night of April, contemplating his wedding the next day. "Oh Mary, I think you will bless me, I trust I shall bless you."

The ship was set to sail at 2:00 that afternoon. Only Dr. and Mrs. Peabody, Elizabeth, Nat and his wife and two daughters—Mary and Ellen Elizabeth, ages five and seven—were on hand at 11:30 when James Freeman Clarke finally pronounced "the sacred words" and Mary and Horace Mann were married. It was the same hour that the Hawthornes' "execution" had taken place, "the hour of *ratification*," Mary called it. The bride wore a plain white grasscloth dress with lace-trimmed embroidery at the neck—the collar the gift of her former student Sarah Hathaway, now married to the China trade baron John Murray Forbes. Horace Mann had given Mary a gold chain that she wore around her head, a gleaming band across her pale brow and against her smooth dark hair. Mary had already packed away in her traveling case the gems she'd received as wedding presents—a large amethyst from her students Annie and Willie Hooper, and a pearl pin from her friend Sarah Shaw. Today she wished to be adorned only by her husband's gift. And, as her older sister wrote, "the greatest adornment of the wedding" was Horace Mann's face, "in which once the expression of pain was so fixed & so heartrending to see." Now "the illuminated countenance of Mr. Mann, so full of joy & tenderness was the ornament you would have most enjoyed," Elizabeth wrote to the absent Miss Rawlins Pickman, "as I did."

By noon the skies had cleared, and after a hastily consumed wedding lunch at a table decorated with pungent geranium leaves—there were no flowers to be had so early in spring—the Manns made their way to the Cunard wharf in East Boston. The day had turned into as "beautiful" an afternoon "as ever shone," Horace Mann observed from the deck of the *Britannia*, the first steam-powered sailing ship to cross the Atlantic from Liverpool, three years earlier. "A floating palace," the vessel had been called on that glorious occasion. Nearly a third again the size of a conventional transatlantic packet, the ship housed twelve coal-burning furnaces fueling four enormous boilers and two giant paddle wheels at midships, along with opulent men's and ladies' lounges, a dining "saloon," and cabins for a hundred passengers. Cunard's choice of Boston over New York for its western terminus had been considered a major coup for the city, and indeed the newlywed Howes had traveled from New York to Boston to catch the boat, which cut the usual Atlantic crossing time from six weeks to twelve days.

Elizabeth followed along for a tour of the Manns' stateroom. It looked small to her, roughly six feet by twelve, with narrow bunks along one wall and an even narrower couch opposite, a washstand with tumblers "all in fixtures" at one end, hooks for coats, and two drawers tucked beneath the lower bunk. Mary, "being rather short," set her traveling basket at the foot of the top bunk and left the drawers for her husband, who would need the full length of his berth to stretch out his six-foot frame. A skylight made the tiny cabin sunny, and the door could be left open for fresh air and a view of the open sea. Given the still considerable risk of a boiler explosion on any steam-powered conveyance, Elizabeth was relieved to note that two life preservers were "in *the room*."

Soon she was back on shore with the "crowd of spectators & friends," who sent up three cheers at seven minutes past two, when the ship pulled away from the dock. The passengers gathered on deck returned each cheer, "but the third stuck in my throat," Horace Mann said later, as he considered the perils of a sea voyage in this still novel means of transportation. He would turn forty-seven while crossing the Atlantic: was he tempting fate to marry at this late age, a woman ten years his junior? Mann calmed himself with the notion that both he and Mary were "full of courage for the work" ahead of them. "We hope to prepare ourselves for doing more good when we return, & this is an all-sustaining motive." Marriage would change little in his exhortatory rhetoric but the pronouns.

Indeed, for several days aboard ship, their partners on this double honeymoon, Samuel and Julia Ward Howe, repeatedly exclaimed that they could not believe the Manns were married. Mary felt the same for a time. "When I was being married I realised that I could not grasp the felicity that was mine," she wrote Elizabeth, "but, soon after it seemed all natural, like the stars, & the ocean & the course of the sun." What mattered nearly as much to her was how Elizabeth—bereft now of sisters—was taking the sudden turn of events. "You looked perfectly satisfied that day we went down to the steamer, deary," Mary wrote, "and I think of you with that look very often. A spectator would have said we all took the matter very quietly."

But how did Elizabeth really feel? Elizabeth claimed to be "so rejoiced" for Mary and her new husband, she wrote in a letter describing their departure to Mann's sister Rebecca, "that I have not even a tear for myself—& yet it would be difficult to describe the infinite loss of such a creature as she—out of *our house*." To Miss Rawlins Pickman, the old family friend from Salem, Elizabeth hinted at the ambivalence she felt that day on the Cunard dock: "We parted with smiles—not tears—& when I saw the great monster creep away with her there was no discord in my heart."

Now it was Sophia and Mary who could "nod our heads grandly at each other in saucy defiance, & say I am as happy as you! (Secretly believing *happier than*)," as Sophia wrote in the Hawthornes' conjoint journal, and who were allied in a wish to see Elizabeth "take up the wondrous tale & echo 'And I as you!'" Sophia's honeymoon had scarcely ended with the past summer's warm weather, although she and Nathaniel began to devote mornings and even afternoons to work—Sophia to a clay bust of her husband, Nathaniel to tales that he easily sold to magazine editors, who then never seemed to pay. By the time of Mary's wedding, money was a pressing concern, along with Sophia's health. She had become pregnant in early winter and miscarried in late February, after a bad fall while walking with Nathaniel on the iced-over Concord River. The accident came just as the couple were beginning to count on the "promised child" as a blessed eventuality that "time will bring to light." Both Sophia and Nathaniel rallied. "The longer we live together—the deeper we penetrate into one another, and become mutually interfused—the happier we are," Nathaniel wrote in the Old Manse journal. "God will surely crown our union with children, because it fulfils the highest conditions of marriage."

Mary and Horace Mann as newlyweds, silhouette by Auguste Edouart

In March, Elizabeth produced a triumph of her own: the lead article for the third issue of James Russell Lowell's new magazine, *The Pioneer*. Called "A Vision," the article related an experience Elizabeth had while reading: a moment of inspiration in which all of world history, literature, and religion had come together in her mind at once. She roamed in her imagination through Asia—"the gorgeous and magnificent, but melancholy East"—witnessing Vishnu and Brahma "undergoing their transformations in cycles, and millions of sages following," then on to Egypt and Greece, where "not only the real personages of history, but the fictitious beings of poetry and romance—equally palpable—were present, and all the creations of the masters of art." She spoke with Socrates, Clio, and Plato: "It was all, and more than all, than is told in the mythologies of the nations."

The message Elizabeth received and delivered to her readers was: "Leave behind . . . the gloomy precincts of being which thou callest matter, and become wholly the living soul thou art," a soul that comprehends "the land of Thought" and "Beauty," but knows it to be limited and transitory. "My soul seemed to rush, with an immeasurable longing, from the Elysium of Art, even from the Paradise of Nature," she wrote, "crying for the Secret of Life." Her cry was answered by a thrilling silence in which she found herself in the company of "a Personal Presence, tender as Love, beautiful as Thought, terrible as Power": the unitary God she had known since her childhood intuitions, not Unitarian, she understood now, not Trinitarian, Hindu, or Buddhist, but her own.

The vision, and the writing of it, in some ways resolved the spiritual crisis Elizabeth had experienced the previous summer. Yet, as Mary would one day comment admiringly of her older sister: "The world is always a new world to her." For Elizabeth, the movement from crisis to resolution, chaos to revelation, was a way of life—was life itself. As Elizabeth would write to Waldo Emerson's prodigiously learned aunt Mary Moody Emerson later in the year, she had come to recognize that life "is a becoming." If Sophia and Mary wished her to be married, perhaps they were hoping for the wrong kind of consummation for their oldest sister—a woman whose energy and intellect had already made her one of Transcendentalism's most influential "mystagogues." Perhaps they were wrong in hoping for any sort of consummation, when Elizabeth so reveled in the search itself. Although she sorrowed over lost love, Elizabeth may have chosen, in the end, to make herself a woman men were drawn to but ultimately rejected, as a means of protecting the driving passions she could best realize as a single woman, with the freedom to pursue her own thoughts and visions, to engage with many different men and women, to teach children but not to rear them. Nearly two decades later, this restless searching brought her to a cause that both Elizabeth and the nation could commit to: the establishment of kindergartens, by the end of the century, in every state of the union.

So Elizabeth was content to learn in late May 1843, along with the rest of the Peabody family, that Mary had survived the ocean voyage—indeed had been the "only live lady" on deck, free of seasickness, as the *Britannia* began to "roll and pitch" on the open water beyond Boston Harbor. Mary's first letters home told of a whirlwind of school and factory visits on the way from Liverpool to London, and a stop at Eaton Hall, where Horace Mann complained that the "wealth and accomplishments" of the Marquis's daughters should have been "turned to charity work." After a daylong train ride through the English countryside, Mann declared the "fields so monotonously green that at last I began to long for a piece of Cape Cod for variety."

Mary, on the other hand, was no more homesick than she had been seasick. "I have not felt myself in a strange land," she wrote Sophia, "for my home is essentially here ... by the side of this blessed one," her new husband, Horace Mann. Yet Mary's attention was caught by signs of human misery— the "wretched" villages the train passed through near the industrial city of Birmingham. "Every thing bears the marks of neglected, degraded, crushed human beings here." The green countryside seemed oppressive to Mary as well: "These splendid parks, miles & miles in extent, are robbed of half their glories by the thought that they take up room & consume money that might make so many comfortable." Once in London, she was disturbed by the street cries that "assail my ears all the time." Too many of them, Mary thought, were cries of the hungry for bread.

But after a few days in London, the Old World sights began to impress. There were mansions and royal palaces the size of "the whole of West Street," and St. Paul's Cathedral: a space so vast "you could stow away" as many as seventy or eighty New England meetinghouses in its sanctuary. Stowed away in St. Paul's on the day the Manns visited were 10,000 children from London's charity schools rehearsing for a choir concert; their music "rose like an incense" to the three-hundred-foot ceiling when they sang. Still, most days were spent pursuing the good "work" the Manns had come to do. They toured the Hanford Lunatic Asylum, and Westminster Bridewell prison, meant to be a model of order and discipline run on the silence system, in the company of Charles Dickens, who refused to commend any prison that housed children. Mary overheard Dickens exclaim "with an earnest oath" that a mother who knew her child was born to such a fate "was justified in infanticide."

A few weeks later, riding on top of a coach to Scotland, Mary caught glimpses of her beloved Sir Walter Scott's Abbotsford estate and wondered at "his strange ambition to possess these broad lands which indeed were beautiful enough to enchant any one, *but why* need they be *one's own*?" She nearly gave up describing the schools and prisons the couple visited in Edinburgh and Glasgow in favor of the several castles where Mary Queen of Scots was born, lived, and was imprisoned. Scotland's craggy shores left her breathless— "Nahant rocks are pebbles in comparison," she informed Elizabeth—and she thrilled to the sight of Rob Roy's cave on the banks of Loch Lomond.

Mary's taste for romance was heightened now that she felt herself at last to be the heroine of her own tale. She looked back with pride on the "ten holy years" when it was "all I could do [to] keep my heart still and let no one suspect its agonies," and she had not "betrayed" her secret passion for Horace Mann. "Never be afraid to love" was the lesson she had learned in the end. "Surrender yourself to its sway, & even if it tears your earthly fibres to tatters, it will strengthen the heavenly ones. Such love is the only *proof* of Immortality." Mary would continue to be proved right in her dedication to this love: her marriage to Horace Mann brought each their most productive years, as Mann went on to a brilliant career in Congress, and the couple moved west to Ohio to found Antioch College, the first coeducational institution of higher learning. After Mann's early death in 1859, Mary finally became a writer, publishing first a celebratory biography of her late husband, another on the Paiute Indian activist Sarah Winnemucca Hopkins, and finally, posthumously under Elizabeth's direction, *Juanita,* her novel of slave life in Cuba.

New England had its own share of spectacles during the summer of 1843. Finally, the 221-foot-tall Bunker Hill Monument, the most ambitious war memorial erected anywhere in the nation, was completed in Charlestown. Elizabeth could still recall the cornerstone-laying ceremony in 1825, when she had walked in from Brookline to hear Daniel Webster speak, his cloak flying in the breeze. She had turned teary at the sight of the aged battle veterans and had shaken hands with a somber Lafayette. She still had the glove she wore that day. Back then no one had guessed the project would take almost two decades to complete. The monument required the construction of America's first railroad line to transport the enormous blocks of granite from quarries south of the city to barges that floated them across the bay to Charlestown; funds repeatedly ran dry and work was halted while ladies' benefit fairs and other fundraising campaigns were waged. In the end, the Bunker Hill Monument Association was forced to sell off most of the ten-acre battle site as house lots to pay for the imposing spire.

Now on June 17, 1843, the sixty-eighth anniversary of the first pitched battle of the Revolution, a procession three miles long headed by President John Tyler, riding in a barouche drawn by six horses, and made up of federal, state, and local dignitaries, marching bands, and sixty companies of citizen soldiers from across New York and New England numbering four thousand men, wound its way through the streets of Boston and across Warren Bridge—named for the battle's martyr, General Joseph Warren—into Charlestown and up the broad green hillside to the granite obelisk. One hundred eight Revolutionary War veterans, many of them lame and all of them "bowed down with years," arrived by carriage and took seats at the monument's base, where crowds cheered them vigorously. Twelve had fought in the battle itself. All were "representatives of an army," the *Boston Post* editorialized, "which did more with the sword for the cause of rational political liberty and public virtue than had been accomplished in all preceding time by all the heroes and orators of the old world."

The population of Boston doubled that day—reaching 200,000—with as many "strangers" on hand as residents, lining the parade route and flocking to Monument Square to hear Daniel Webster speak once again at the battle site. Eighteen years before, Webster had conjured up this very scene, commanding: "Let it rise, till it meet the sun in his coming; let the earliest light of the morning gild it, and parting day linger and play on its summit." Now in the bright sunshine of another summer afternoon, with 100,000 citizens and "strangers" gathered on the hilltop to hear him, Webster declared the towering structure a "monument to the past, a monument of the present, and a monument to all succeeding generations" that was "itself the great orator of the occasion"—and went on to deliver an address that lasted more than an hour.

While Dr. Peabody had stood on a street corner in Boston to watch the parade pass, no one in the family attended Webster's speech. A small but growing minority of antislavery advocates in New England had been angered by what they perceived as Webster's "defection," his unwillingness to serve "the cause of abolition of Slavery, in Congress," as Waldo Emerson wrote in his journal during the coming year. If Elizabeth or any of her Transcendentalist colleagues had been on hand, they would certainly have found Webster hypocritical in his depiction of the monument as a visible reproach to any man who threatened "disunion."

The Transcendentalists had their attention focused, instead, on what would prove to be one of the last issues of *The Dial*, the July 1843 number in which Margaret Fuller had published her far-ranging analysis of contemporary gender politics, "The Great Lawsuit. Man *versus* Men. Woman *versus* Women." Two years later, Fuller would publish an expanded version in book form as *Woman in the Nineteenth Century*. But for now, it was *The Dial*'s select audience of three hundred subscribers and their friends who pondered Fuller's charge that man is "vain, and wishes to be more important to woman than by right he should be," along with her assertions that women were more than "beings of affection and habit alone" and that the emerging "self-dependence" of single women was one of the most positive developments in modern history. Fuller devoted one long passage to the problems of marriage, writing that "civilized" society is "still in a transition state about marriage, not only in practice, but in thought," and describing four types in ascending order based on their ability to sustain both "partners in work and in life, sharing together, on equal terms, public and private interests."

Henry Thoreau, who "never likes anything," Emerson reported to Fuller, called the essay "a noble piece, rich extempore writing, talking with pen in hand." And Emerson allowed that its publication was "quite an important fact in the history of Woman," while praising Fuller's "wit" and "character," rather than her ideas. But Sophia Hawthorne, who must have read the article around the time of her first wedding anniversary, considered it a crack in the armor of her one-time heroine. "What do you think of the speech which queen Margaret Fuller has made from the throne?" she asked her mother. "It seems to me that if she were married truly, she would no longer be puzzled about the rights of woman."

In reply, Eliza Peabody, whose long marriage made her more qualified to judge, wondered, "How is it that one who talks so admirably should write so obscurely?" Yet the faults Mrs. Peabody found with the piece were not the same ones her daughter identified. While Mrs. Peabody did not comment directly on Fuller's analysis, which she may have approved, she offered her own even darker one: "I believe that woman must wait till the lion shall lie down with the lamb, before she can hope to be the friend and companion of man. He has the physical power, as well as conventional, to treat her like a plaything or a slave, and will exercise that power till his own soul is elevated to the standard set up by Him who spake as never man spoke."

The irony of it all was that Fuller had the Hawthornes' marriage in mind as she wrote the laudatory passages on unions derived from "intellectual companionship," in which "literary men, and artists have . . . found in their wives companions and confidants in thought no less than in feeling." She too believed the Hawthornes' marriage fulfilled what Nathaniel had called "the highest conditions." In a letter written the previous winter, Fuller told Nathaniel that he was the "serenest and most resolute man" and revealed a dash of envy for what she called the couple's "happy duet" as they went about their days "writing, or drawing or modelling" in clay. Perhaps Sophia could be forgiven for misconstruing Fuller's discursive essay, if she sensed the powerfully charismatic woman's jealousy directed her way.

As the day of her first wedding anniversary dawned—"a sweet return of that happy hour," with "the loveliest weather & the moon . . . about full"— Sophia could think of little but her own happiness, claimed in spite of straitened circumstances and the calamity of an early miscarriage. The couple had survived a winter with little heat in their old house, living primarily on the stored produce of their orchard and garden. "Our state now is one of far deeper felicity than last 9th of July," Sophia wrote in the Old Manse journal. "Then we had visions & dreamed of Paradise. Now Paradise is here & our fairest visions stand realized before us." Sophia was pregnant again, and although she had "not felt very well for two weeks" she "rejoice[d] at every smallest proof" of her condition, and delighted in her husband, "so tender &

indulgent to all my whims & moans." To Sophia, Nathaniel had always been a man of "peerless beauty." Now she made a wish: "may our little lovelet look like thee!"

Sophia looked forward to the day when the Hawthornes would become "triune," she wrote to the friend whose babies she had sketched for anatomy practice in the years before she ever expected to have a family of her own. Some days Sophia could scarcely believe the transformation. "My duty seems plainly . . . to become a saint through rejoicing instead of through suffering," wrote the woman who had nearly consigned herself to a life of illness under the dominion of a "silent ministry of pain."

Far away in Germany, Mary too was pregnant, and the Manns sped through their school visits, intending to cut their European tour short. The two sisters would deliver their first children a week apart in late February and early March of the following year; within the decade, each would be the mother of three. Now, in Concord, as Sophia walked in the grassy former battleground just beyond her front door, gathering Elizabeth's favorite flowers— columbines—to send to her sister at West Street, she "hate[d] to think of you two prisoners in the bookroom this lovely time," she wrote to her mother. But Sophia doubted that Elizabeth would ever be happy living in the country, "because men & women are her flowers & they do not grow on hills & slopes."

Both Elizabeth and her mother had become concerned, recently, with the next generation. Nat's girls were getting older, and he refused to teach them anything but the most rudimentary skills—no foreign languages, dead or living; no drawing or music lessons; no readings from Madame de Staël or *The Memoirs of Madame Roland*. "The faults of fashionable girls . . . he ascribes to the accomplishments taught to them," Mrs. Peabody would write of her only surviving son. She claimed not to care whether her granddaughters ended up as "mantuamakers"—seamstresses, like her own mother and aunts and "the whole W[atertown] concern" that Eliza had been so eager to leave behind. But she wished Nat would "cultivate their minds," as she had her own daughters': "as if they were to be Queens."

In fact, Nat's critique of his mother and sisters' views of educating girls was far more sweeping than Mrs. Peabody realized. Nat disputed the value of learning anything that smacked of "*aesthetic* culture"—indeed he found fault with the whole "aesthetic portion of our community." To Elizabeth he wrote some years later, "I have very little sympathy with those who admire and worship brilliant men, and the enthusiasm which many persons feel for art." Too many such "individuals . . . are remarkable only for saying brilliant things, uttering striking thoughts or broaching profound views, but . . . are detestable in respect to personal character." Whom did he have in mind? His sisters and their husbands? Elizabeth and her friends—Emerson, Alcott, Fuller, Thoreau, Allston?

Allston was dead now too. On July 9, as Sophia and Nathaniel marked their first wedding anniversary, a blissful day in which they became "acquainted with every hour of it and every phase," the painter had died of heart failure, resting in his chair after another day spent toiling over *Belshazzar's Feast*. "Is it not beautiful that he should have gone to meet Raphael & Michelangelo on that superb moonlight night?" Sophia wrote to Elizabeth when she heard the news—that "his last day on earth" was "one of the most perfect days the earth ever saw?"

Elizabeth had visited Allston just three weeks earlier, beginning a conversation that both looked forward to continuing at another meeting "very soon." When she heard that Allston had died, Elizabeth walked across the bridge from Boston to his Cambridgeport studio, intent on seeing the painter one last time. There she was permitted some moments alone with Allston's "majestic" body, dressed in a long white robe. One arm was bent across his chest, and his hand "had fallen into the attitude of holding a pencil" as if starting to draw, Elizabeth thought. She was struck painfully with the wish to carry on that earlier conversation and found herself forming questions: "What was he thinking now? Is he here? Does he know my thoughts?" If Allston could have spoken, what would he have told her?

The burial service took place on another July night several days later, when "the moon and dark clouds contended strongly for the sky," Elizabeth wrote afterward, "in wonderful consonance to the tone of our feelings, which were now rising on the triumphant wings of faith, now bowing under the load of sorrow." As she stood in the Cambridge churchyard, in a company that included most of Harvard College, and watched Allston's closest male relatives lower his coffin into the grave and begin to cover it with earth, Elizabeth thought of what she had learned of Allston's last night. He had been deeply engaged in talk about the "perfecting of the character" with a small group of friends and family, all of whom seemed aware that this might be a final encounter. Allston had spoken his parting words to his niece—words that, in Elizabeth's troubled state of mind, now seemed meant for her: "God bless you!" he had said, placing his hands on her head and stooping to kiss her. "Go on to perfection, my child!"

❧

The three Peabody sisters' lives spanned most of the nineteenth century. As might have been expected, Sophia died the youngest, at age sixty-one, in London, after twenty-two years of marriage and seven years as a widow. She had lived a life "bound up in that of her husband," a sorrowing friend wrote in eulogy. Her last painting was *Endymion,* a seated male nude completed at the Old Manse in 1844, just before her first child, Una, was born.

Mary lived till age eighty, when she died in an apartment she shared with Elizabeth in Jamaica Plain, Massachusetts. She had at least one manuscript novel in her desk, and a short story in which two women vied for the love of "an ideal being"—a charismatic widower.

When Elizabeth died in 1894, at almost ninety, she was widely celebrated as the founder of kindergartens in America. A settlement house was established in her memory—the Elizabeth Peabody House—which still operates in Somerville, Massachusetts. The honors more than counterbalanced the gently satirical portrait painted of her as Miss Birdseye by Henry James in his novel *The Bostonians.* Elizabeth had outlived her fellow Transcendentalists; her "practical" Transcendentalism would survive them all.

Acknowledgments
Notes
Index

ℛ ACKNOWLEDGMENTS ℘

THE WORK OF A BIOGRAPHER MAY SEEM A LONELY TASK, WITH SO MUCH time spent sorting through notes and reference texts at one's desk in the effort to establish the facts of past lives. Yet every venture to an archive brought me new colleagues whose advice improved the book immeasurably and whose friendship provided an energizing sense of collaboration. From the beginning, Justin Kaplan, Jean Strouse, and Joel Porte helped me believe that I could write this book. Along the way I benefited greatly from conversations and correspondence with fellow scholars Margaret Neussendorfer Billias, Paula Blanchard, Marie Cleary, Helen R. Deese, Robert Derry, Elisabeth Gitter, Rita Gollin, Gary Sue Goodman, Joan Goodwin, Dean Grodzins, Robert A. Gross, Robert N. Hudspeth, Buford Jones, Amalie Kass, Mary Kelley, Louise Knight, Diana Korzenik, Leah Lipton, Sharon O'Brien, Stephen D. Pratt, Robert D. Richardson, Sarah Sherman, Nancy Simmons, Diana Strazdes, Jurij Striedter, Amanda Vaill, and Dr. Carol Zuckerman. Deborah Pickman Clifford, T. Walter Herbert, Susan Quinn, Phyllis Cole, and Joan Deming Ensor generously read the book in manuscript at various stages and offered valuable criticism while cheering me on.

Staying the course would have been impossible without the monthly meetings of a Boston-area group of women biographers whose membership has varied only slightly over the past twenty years. These mentors—Phyllis Cole, Susan Quinn, Ruth Butler, Lois Palken Rudnick, Judith Tick, Joyce Antler, Frances Malino, and the late Barbara Miller Solomon—helped me grow up as a writer.

During early years of intense research, the Massachusetts Historical Society became a second home to me: Peter Drummey, Celeste Walker, Katherine H. Griffin, Brenda Lawson, Anne E. Bentley, Richard A. Ryerson, Conrad E. Wright, and Louis Leonard Tucker provided the education in archival research I sorely needed. Other librarians and archivists were equally generous in sharing their knowledge: Deborah Kelly Milburn of Harvard's Widener Library; Nina Myatt, curator of the Antiochiana Collection at the Olive Kettering Library, Antioch College; John and Kate Mustain of the Stanford University Libraries Special Collections; Sally Pierce, curator of Prints and Photographs at the Boston Athenaeum; Christine Nelson of the Pierpont Morgan Library; Kenneth Stuckey of the Perkins School for the Blind; Alan Seaburg of the Andover-Harvard Theological Library; Teresa A. Thomas of the Lancaster Historical Commission; Jonathan Fairbanks and Rebecca Reynolds, curators in American Decorative Arts at Boston's Museum of Fine Arts; Eleanor M. Lewis of the Sophia Smith Collection, Smith College; Paula Richter, Richard Fyfe, Ellen Steeves, Eugenia Fountain, Christine Michelini, and Irene Axelrod of the Peabody Essex Museum; Leslie Perrin Wilson, curator extraordinaire of Special Collections at the Concord Free Public Library; and the late Lola Szladits of the New York Public Library's Henry W. and Albert A. Berg Collection.

On research trips beyond Massachusetts, I received generous hospitality from Lee and Vicki Morgan in Yellow Springs, Ohio; Tod and Kate Sedgwick in Washington, D.C.; Eleanor and Sam Osborne in Hanover, New Hampshire; Amy Marshall and Tim Zenker in New York City; the George W. Gibson family in Hallowell, Maine; Woody Marshall and Polly Covell in Oakland, California; and Sally and Arthur Zarnowitz in San Jose, California. These research missions could not have been successful without on-site babysitting help from Amy Hassinger, Tracy Howard, and Marya Maddox Hughes. Caroline Preston and Christopher Tilghman also provided a needed retreat for writing in Dorset, Vermont, where I began the final draft.

A number of Peabody descendants have been so remarkably generous in sharing family artifacts and lore that I can never adequately thank them. These include Hawthorne descendants Joan Deming Ensor, Olcott Deming, Imogen Hawthorne Howe, Rosamond Mikkelsen, and Alison Hawthorne Deming, as well as descendants of Nathaniel Cranch Peabody, Jean Johnston Holmes, Margaret Johnston Kinsler, and Bradford G. Johnston. Stephen and Linda Weld generously shared their store of information on the Hathaway twins, one-time students of the Peabody sisters. Mr. and Mrs. Berkley Peabody kindly showed me through their house, once the Peabody sisters' home on Charter Street in Salem, while being careful to point out that they are not descendants, only relations of the sisters.

Many friends, most of them writers, helped shore up my belief in the project at times when my spirits flagged: Anne Bernays, Sally Brady, Gail Caldwell, James Carroll, Christopher Jane Corkery, Susan Cory, Elizabeth Cox, Mark Edmundson, Helen Epstein, Stephen Fox, Erica Funkhouser, Bonnie Lee Grad, Scott Harney, Emily Hiestand, Alice Hoffman, Joseph P. Kahn, Tony Kahn, Perri Klass, Rosemary Mahoney, Fred Marchant, Alexandra Marshall, Gail Mazur,

Allyssa McCabe, Jill McCorkle, Diane McWhorter, Sue Miller, Pamela Painter, Caroline Preston, Harriet Reisen, Lloyd Schwartz, and Susan Twarog. The Cabot House Senior Common Room, Harvard University, provided challenging intellectual companionship as well as indispensable access to the Harvard Libraries. My agent, Katinka Matson, has been a true supporter of the project from the very beginning, as has my publisher, Houghton Mifflin. Robie Macauley was my first editor, and I like to think he would be proud of the ultimate result. John Sterling, Katrina Kenison, Janet Silver, and Deanne Urmy each had a hand in the production of this book, with Deanne Urmy taking up the burden at the last and giving the project her all. Jayne Yaffe Kemp's expert manuscript editing has made the book shine.

My work on *The Peabody Sisters* has been supported by fellowships from the National Endowment for the Humanities (enabling a year's assistance from the indefatigable researcher Tamara Harvey, now a scholar in her own right), the John Simon Guggenheim Foundation, and the Massachusetts Artists Foundation. Through all these years, my husband, John Sedgwick, has been my foundation in so many ways; *The Peabody Sisters* could not have been completed without his support and the affectionate forbearance and clever insights of my daughters, Sara and Josie Sedgwick.

❧ NOTES ❧

The following abbreviations are used for frequently cited names:
ABA: Amos Bronson Alcott
WC: Dr. Walter Channing
WEC: Rev. William Ellery Channing
RWE: Ralph Waldo Emerson
MF: Margaret Fuller
NH: Nathaniel Hawthorne
HM: Horace Mann
TP: Theodore Parker
EPP: Elizabeth Palmer Peabody
Mrs. EPP: Mrs. Elizabeth Palmer Peabody ("Eliza")
GFP: George Francis Peabody
MTP: Mary Tyler Peabody (MTM after her marriage to Horace Mann)
Dr. NP: Dr. Nathaniel Peabody
NCP: Nathaniel Cranch Peabody ("Nat")
SAP: Sophia Amelia Peabody (SAH after her marriage to Nathaniel Hawthorne)
WP: Wellington Peabody

For frequently cited libraries or manuscript depositories, the following abbreviations are used. Many collections included numerous undated letters. In cases in which I was able to date the letters based on internal evidence or comparison with dated letters from other collections, I have supplied my own date after first giving dates conjectured by the archive. In the case of diaries or journals in which dates of entries were recorded only sporadically or partially by the writer, I have supplied dates when I could determine them. These dates are preceded by the notation "entry of" as an indication that the full date that follows may not be found in the text of the journal itself but still could be useful in locating a specific passage within the journal. I would like to thank all these institutions for granting me permission to quote material from their collections.

A-HTL: Andover-Harvard Theological Library, Harvard Divinity School, Harvard University, Cambridge, Massachusetts
Antiochiana: Robert L. Straker Collections of Mann and Peabody Letters, Antiochiana, Antioch College, Yellow Springs, Ohio. Most citations refer to the several thousand pages of typescripts made by Robert Lincoln Straker from letters and journals in private collections or acquired by Straker and donated to Antioch College. These I have called "Straker typescripts," giving his page numbers as well.

459

Bancroft: Hawthorne Family Papers, Bancroft Library, University of California at Berkeley

Berg: Berg Collection of English and American Literature, The New York Public Library, Astor, Lenox and Tilden Foundations. In the case of several undated letters that could not otherwise be clearly identified, I have used an accession code number assigned to these letters but not listed in the Berg's catalogue. In some cases, the code number is stamped on the letter itself; in others it is written on the folder in which the letter has been stored.

Brown: Brown University Library, Providence, Rhode Island

Countway: Boston Medical Library in the Francis A. Countway Library of Medicine, Boston, Massachusetts

Dartmouth: Dr. Nathaniel Peabody Papers, Dartmouth College Library, Hanover, New Hampshire

Houghton: Houghton Library, Harvard University, Cambridge, Massachusetts

HUA: Harvard University Archives, Cambridge, Massachusetts

Huntington: The Huntington Library, San Marino, California

LH: National Park Service, Longfellow National Historic Site, Cambridge, Massachusetts

LHC: Lancaster Historical Commission, Lancaster, Massachusetts

LOC: Library of Congress, Washington, D.C.

MHS: Massachusetts Historical Society, Boston. The collections I have cited include the Adams Papers; Caroline Wells Healey Dall Papers ("Dall Papers"); Dana Family Papers; Horace Mann Papers ("HM Papers"); Horace Mann II Papers ("HMII Papers"); Horace Mann IV Papers ("HMIV Papers"); Theodore Parker Papers ("TP Papers"); Peabody Family Papers, 1790–1880; Mary Tyler Peabody Correspondence ("MTP Correspondence"); Saltonstall Family Papers; Catharine Maria Sedgwick Papers; Biography of Elizabeth Palmer Peabody, manuscript draft by Mary Van Wyck Church ("MVWC").

Morgan: The Pierpont Morgan Library, New York

PEM: Phillips Library (formerly Essex Institute), Peabody Essex Museum, Salem, Massachusetts

Schlesinger: Schlesinger Library, Radcliffe Institute, Harvard University, Cambridge, Massachusetts

SLU: The Ulysses Sumner Milburn Collection, Mss. Coll. #3. Special Collections, Owen D. Young Library, St. Lawrence University, Canton, New York

Smith: Sophia Smith Collection, Smith College, Northampton, Massachusetts

Stanford: Department of Special Collections, Stanford University Libraries, Stanford, California

UVA: Clifton Waller Barrett Library, Special Collections, University of Virginia Library, Charlottesville

VtHS: Royall Tyler Collection, gift of Helen Tyler Brown, Vermont Historical Society, Montpelier

Wherever possible I have referred to the works of Nathaniel Hawthorne and Ralph Waldo Emerson in the Library of America editions, which are easily available to the general reader. The following abbreviations are used for frequently cited books and manuscripts:

AN: *American Notebooks, Centenary Edition of the Works of Nathaniel Hawthorne*, vol. VIII, Claude Simpson, ed. (Columbus: Ohio State University Press, 1972).

JMN: *The Journals and Miscellaneous Notebooks of Ralph Waldo Emerson*, William H. Gilman et al., eds. (Cambridge, Mass.: Harvard University Press, 1960–1982), 16 vols.

The Letters, 1813–1843: Centenary Edition of the Works of Nathaniel Hawthorne, vol. XV, Thomas L. Woodson, Neal Smith, and Norman Holmes Pearson, eds. (Columbus: Ohio State University Press, 1984). Commonly referred to as "CXV" in scholarly works on Hawthorne.

Letters of EPP: The *Letters of Elizabeth Palmer Peabody, American Renaissance Woman,* Bruce Ronda, ed. (Middletown, Conn.: Wesleyan University Press, 1984).

Letters of MF: The *Letters of Margaret Fuller,* Robert Hudspeth, ed. (Ithaca, N.Y.: Cornell University Press, 1983), 5 vols.

Letters of RWE: The *Letters of Ralph Waldo Emerson,* vols. 1-6, Ralph L. Rusk, ed.; vols. 7-8, Eleanor Tilton, ed. (New York: Columbia University Press, 1939-).

MVWC: Biography of Elizabeth Palmer Peabody, manuscript draft by Mary Van Wyck Church, Massachusetts Historical Society. This six-hundred-page manuscript contains numerous letters and lengthy extracts from journals that are not available in manuscript originals. In the few cases in which originals are available for checking, or published versions of the same letters exist, it is clear that Church's copies are highly accurate. Elizabeth's nephew and executor, Benjamin Pickman Mann, loaned Church many of Elizabeth's letters and journals for the purpose of work on this biography, which was never published. Letters exchanged by Mann and Church, also deposited at MHS, reveal that the two came to an impasse about what material should be included in the biography. Mann recalled his aunt's manuscripts from Church and forbade her to publish the work. The location of most of these letters and journals is not now known; possibly Mann destroyed them.

[Mrs. EPP] ms. novel: incomplete unsigned manuscript novel written by Mrs. Elizabeth Palmer Peabody, catalogued by the Massachusetts Historical Society, where it is held, as "Story of the Palmer Family during the American Revolution." This fictional rendering of Palmer family lore is written in Mrs. Peabody's hand, and she refers to it in correspondence with her daughters. The family name used in the manuscript is Lawson, not Palmer. Peabody Family Papers, 1790-1880, MHS.

NCP Genealogies: typescripts made by Robert Lincoln Straker from Nathaniel Cranch Peabody's extensive notes on the genealogies of the Cranch, Palmer, and Peabody families. Some of the original manuscripts are held at the Massachusetts Historical Society, but the entire set is available only in Straker's typescripts covering sixty pages, 5425/1-61, in the Robert L. Straker Collections of Mann and Peabody Letters, Antiochiana.

Rem of WEC: Elizabeth Palmer Peabody, *Reminiscences of Rev. William Ellery Channing, D.D.* (Boston: Roberts Brothers, 1880).

SAP *CJ:* The *Cuba Journal, 1833-35, by Sophia Peabody Hawthorne,* Claire Badaracco, ed. (Ann Arbor, Mich.: University Microfilms International, 1985).

PAGE   *Preface*

xv   American Renaissance: The literary critic F. O. Matthiessen coined the phrase in his 1941 *American Renaissance: Art and Expression in the Age of Emerson and Whitman* (New York: Oxford), the first comprehensive study to link Emerson, Thoreau, Hawthorne, Melville, and Whitman as collaborators, if unconscious ones, in creating an American literature. Since then the term has gained wide use, most notably in the twenty-volume series *Studies in the American Renaissance* (Charlottesville [etc.]: University Press of Virginia [etc.]), published annually from 1977 to 1996 under the editorship of Joel Myerson, which greatly expanded the list of American Renaissance writers and thinkers. Jane Tompkins treated women writers of the era in her chapter "The Other American Renaissance," *Sensational Designs: The Cultural Work of American Fiction, 1790-1860* (New York: Oxford University Press, 1985). Finally, Charlene Avallone questioned the validity of the term in the article "What American Renaissance? The Gendered

Genealogy of a Critical Discourse," *PMLA* 112 (October 1997). Avallone sensibly asks whether there could have been a "renaissance" in American literary culture when there was no American literary culture to begin with. Yet the term has been so widely accepted, and now so expansively redefined, that it continues to be a useful one.

xv   "more interior revolution": EPP to William Wordsworth, March 27, 1829, Margaret Neussendorfer, ed., "Elizabeth Palmer Peabody to William Wordsworth: Eight Letters, 1825–1845," *Studies in the American Renaissance 1984* (Charlottesville: University Press of Virginia), p. 190.

xvi   "knowledge," "love," and "activity": John White Chadwick, *William Ellery Channing: Minister of Religion* (Boston and New York: Houghton Mifflin, 1903), p. 82.
"a decent independence": Eliza Palmer quoted in Elizabeth Hunt Palmer to Mary Smith Cranch, May 9, 1798, Peabody Family Papers, 1790–1880, MHS.
"without wealth . . . fashionable world": HM to George Combe, April 19, 1843, HM Papers, MHS
"come down from our back . . . first rank of society": EPP to William Wordsworth, March 27, 1829, quoted in Neussendorfer, ed., "Elizabeth Palmer Peabody to William Wordsworth: Eight Letters, 1825–1845," p. 187.

xvii   "Caravanserai": NH to SAH, December 2, 1844, *The Letters, 1843–1853, Centenary Edition of the Works of Nathaniel Hawthorne*, vol. XVI, Thomas L. Woodson, Neal Smith, and Norman Holmes Pearson, eds. (Columbus: Ohio State University Press, 1985), p. 67.
"Transcendental Exchange": George Bradford quoted in Bruce Ronda, *Elizabeth Peabody: A Reformer on Her Own Terms* (Cambridge, Mass.: Harvard University Press, 1999), p. 182.
"principle desire . . . one long wearisome burden": MTP to Miss Rawlins Pickman, January 4, 1834, HMII Papers, MHS.
"woman in our society": Ralph Waldo Emerson, William Henry Channing, and James Freeman Clarke, eds., *Memoirs of Margaret Fuller Ossoli* (Boston: Phillips, Sampson, 1852), pp. 321–22.
"shine by borrowed light": SAP to EPP, June 1822, Berg. "I am rather a planet that shines by borrowed light" is the direct quotation.
"be myself and *act*": EPP to GFP, Monday, August [6, 1838], Straker typescripts, pp. 1297–98, Antiochiana. (Bruce Ronda dates the letter August 8 in his *Letters of EPP*, p. 229, but that is based on the postmark. August 8, 1838, was a Wednesday.)

xix   "whenever within her circle . . . true objects of life": HM to George Combe, April 19, 1843, HM Papers, MHS.

xx   "the newness": RWE, "Experience," *Essays and Lectures* (New York: Library of America, 1983), p. 483.

PAGE   *Prologue: July 9, 1842*

2   "independant & useful": Mrs. EPP to EPP and MTP, October 4, 1824, Straker typescripts, p. 250, Antiochiana.
"destination for a sphere": Mrs. EPP to EPP, October 12, 1823, Straker typescripts, p. 187, Antiochiana. Mrs. Peabody had more literally named her daughters after herself and her own sisters, but she thought of Queen Elizabeth I as "your great name sake," as she wrote to Elizabeth in the same letter. When Mary Peabody grew up, she liked to think of Mary Queen of Scots as her namesake.
"so linked in heart": Mrs. EPP to MTP, March 1, 1834, Berg.

"atom of a shop": Thomas Wentworth Higginson, *Cheerful Yesterdays* (Cambridge, Mass.: Riverside Press, 1898), p. 86.

"the newness": RWE, "Experience," *Essays and Lectures* (New York: Library of America, 1983), p. 483.

"who have dared to say": EPP, "A Glimpse of Christ's Idea of Society," *The Dial*, vol. II, no. 2, October 1841, p. 222.

3 perhaps, one day, marble: American wunderkind sculptor Shobal Clevenger offered to oversee the rendering of Sophia's work in marble when he moved to Rome in 1842, if she would ship pieces to him there. SAP to GFP, October 27, 1839, Berg.

4 "dearest mother in the world": Dr. NP and SAP to EPP, June 14, [1835], Berg.

"exquisite light figures": George Frisbie Hoar, *Autobiography of Seventy Years* (New York: Charles Scribner's Sons, 1903), p. 69. The young Transcendentalist Caroline Healey, protégée of both Elizabeth Peabody and Margaret Fuller, also had an opportunity to view Sophia's hand-painted furniture, which does not survive. Healey wrote in her journal on June 13, 1842, "I did my few errands and hurried home—staying longest at Elizabeth Peabody's, to look at Sophia's furniture. She showed it to me herself—explaining the beautiful designs upon her chairs taken from the life of Penelope—the return of Eneas & so on—Her toilet table—is ornamented with a Venus—attired by the Graces—& Persuasion—. On one part of her washstand—was Neptune—on the other the effect of purification—Venus—rising from the waves. On her bedstead—was Guido's Night—and his day break—Aurora—lighting up the East with her torch the morning star—above—and Apollo with his coursers—and retinue." Dall Papers, MHS. I am grateful to Helen R. Deese, editor of the voluminous Caroline Healey Dall journals, for directing me to this passage.

"handsomer than Lord Byron": Norman Holmes Pearson, "Elizabeth Peabody on Hawthorne," *Essex Institute Historical Collections*, July 1958, p. 264.

"the very king": SAP to Mary Wilder White Foote, June 19, 1842, Berg.

"pour out light": HM, *An Oration Delivered before the Authorities of the City of Boston, July 4, 1842* (Boston, 1842).

5 20,000 copies: HM journal, vol. I, entry of August 21, 1842, HM Papers, MHS.

"sisterhood": Mrs. EPP to MTP and SAP, May 1834, Berg 371406B.

"You know, dear": MTP to SAH, [September 1842], Berg.

"great occasions . . . it is Mr. Hawthorne": MF to SAP, June 4, 1842, *Letters of MF*, vol. 3, p. 65.

"to prepare [their] feelings": Elizabeth Manning Hawthorne to SAP, May 23, 1842, Berg.

"have you no dread . . . depended upon me": Elizabeth Manning Hawthorne to SAP, June 15, 1842, Berg.

6 "little Dove": NH to SAP, June 20, 1842, *The Letters, 1813–1843*, p. 630.

"species of communion . . . part us now": NH to SAP, June 20, 1842, *The Letters, 1813–1843*, p. 630.

"all perfectly rigged . . . than the reality would": *AN*, pp. 233–34. During his term as measurer for the Custom House in Boston, 1839–1841, Hawthorne frequently boarded ships to inspect cargo, but he did not sail on them in this capacity.

"idle nature": NH to SAP, June 11, 1840, *The Letters, 1813–1843*, p. 472.

Six months after his wedding, Hawthorne was to write from Concord, where he was pleased to discover that married life had "brought back many of my school-day enjoyments": "How few people in this world know how to be idle!—it is a much higher faculty than any sort of usefulness or ability." NH to MF, February 1, 1843, *The Letters, 1813–1843*, pp. 671–72.

6   "the most splendid": *Boston Evening Transcript,* July 5, 1842.

leading port city: An article in the *Boston Evening Transcript,* July 9, 1842, reported that the *New York Evening Post* "states as a fact that Boston enjoys a far greater proportion of trade than any other city of its size in the Union, and is at a loss whether to refer it to the superior management of her banks, the great Western Railroad, or both."

7   "Magnificent Temple ... assembled multitudes": "Order of the Fireworks," *Boston Morning Post,* July 2, 1842.

"The ceremony is nothing": SAP to Mary Wilder White Foote, June 19, 1842, Berg.

"thrust himself between us": NH to SAP, June 20, 1842, *The Letters, 1813-1843,* p. 630.

"many visions": NH to MF, August 25, 1842, *The Letters, 1813-1843,* p. 647.

"blessedest": NH to SAP, June 11, 1840, *The Letters, 1813-1843,* p. 472.

"brawling slang-whangers": NH to SAP, March 30, 1840, *The Letters, 1813-1843,* p. 430.

"sacred": NH to SAP, January 24, 1840, *The Letters, 1813-1843,* p. 401.

8   "utterly destitute of imagination": SAP to NH, June 12, 1841, Berg.

just one volume of stories: Hawthorne succeeded so well in suppressing his first novel, *Fanshawe,* published anonymously in 1828, that Sophia would not learn of its existence until after his death. In December 1841, he had published an expanded edition of *Twice-told Tales,* with twenty-one additional stories selected in consultation with Sophia.

"the world's admiration ... reverence": SAP to NH, May 30, 1841, Berg.

"Being pervaded": NH to SAP, August 21, 1839, *The Letters, 1813-1843,* p. 339.

"gets into the remotest": *AN,* p. 349.

"Words cannot tell": SAP to NH, May 30, 1841, Berg.

"kingly looks ... agitate": MTP to SAH, Monday evening [early July? 1842], Berg. My date: [July 11, 1842].

"execution ... straight to Paradise": NH to Louisa Hawthorne, July 10, 1842, *The Letters, 1813-1843,* p. 639.

9   "low thunder ... clear new life": SAH to Mrs. EPP, July 10, 1842, Berg.

10   "how sweet would be": NH to SAP, August 26, 1839, *The Letters, 1813-1843,* p. 341.

"as if this world were Heaven": *AN,* p. 334.

"Very different": Mrs. EPP to EPP, April 9-12, 1824, Straker typescripts, p. 212, Antiochiana.

PAGE   *1. Matriarch*

13   "The love which settles down": Mrs. EPP to SAP, [Salem, 1838 or 1839?], Berg 231776B.

15   "I could see in you": SAH to Mrs. EPP, August [5], 1842, Berg.

"in memory I always see": WC to MTM, March 2, 1853, Straker typescripts, p. 1741, Antiochiana.

"Republican Motherhood": For more on the ideology of "Republican Motherhood," see Linda Kerber, *Women of the Republic* (Chapel Hill: University of North Carolina Press, 1980), pp. 269-93, and Mary P. Ryan, *Womanhood in America* (Irvine: University of California Press, 1983), p. 102 ff. The following writers have expanded on the work of Kerber and Ryan: Lisa Wilson, *Life After Death: Widows in Pennsylvania, 1750-1850* (Philadelphia: Temple University Press,

1992); Anya Jabour, *Marriage in the Early Republic: Elizabeth and William Wirt and the Companionate Ideal* (Baltimore: Johns Hopkins University Press, 1998); Elizabeth R. Varon, *We Mean to Be Counted: White Women and Politics in Antebellum Virginia* (Chapel Hill: University of North Carolina Press, 1998); Joyce Appleby, *Inheriting the Revolution: The First Generation in America* (Cambridge, Mass.: Belknap Press of Harvard University Press, 2000). An article by Sarah Robbins gives a comprehensive summary of writings on the concept: "'The Future Good and Great of Our Land': Republican Mothers, Female Authors, and Domesticated Literacy in Antebellum New England," *New England Quarterly*, vol. 75, no. 4, December 2002, pp. 562–91.

"I long for means": Mrs. EPP to EPP and MTM, January 12, 1851, Straker typescripts, p. 1540, Antiochiana.

16   "patriotic mother . . . age of the country's history": from the editor's biography of EPP that accompanies EPP's "Childhood" in Raymond L. Bridgman, ed., *Concord Lectures on Philosophy* (Cambridge, Mass.: Moses King, 1883), p. 119.

PAGE   ## 2. Legacies

17   The novel was never published: [Mrs. EPP] ms. novel, MHS, catalogued as "Story of the Palmer Family during the American Revolution." The Palmer family is never mentioned by name in the manuscript, however, which is a fictional rendering of Palmer family history, written in Mrs. Peabody's hand. The family name used is "Lawson."

"more like an old fashioned": [Mrs. EPP], "Biographical Sketch of Gen. Joseph Palmer," *The New Englander*, vol. IX, January 1845, p. 2. Mrs. Peabody's son Nathaniel Cranch Peabody attributes this article to his mother (see "Bibliography of Elizabeth Palmer Peabody, 1778–1853," Straker typescripts, Antiochiana). Other scholars have assumed it is the work of Charles S. Palmer, a great-grandson of General Palmer, who is credited in a footnote with gathering "a large part of the materials" upon which the "memoir" is based. But this footnote itself suggests that Charles Palmer was not the author, if he is acknowledged merely for assembling documents. General Palmer did not live long enough to know any of his great-grandchildren, so the term *memoir* also suggests a writer of Mrs. Peabody's generation.

1776, 1777, or 1778: Mrs. Peabody's children agree that she was born in Watertown, Massachusetts, although town records give no evidence. Her descendants agree, as well, that her birthday was in February, yet they contradict one another, and themselves, on the day and year of birth. Mary Mann's family Bible records in separate entries that her mother died at "nearly 76" on January 11, 1853, which would place her birth in February 1777, *and* that she died "11th of January 1853–aged 76," which would put her birth year in 1776 (MHS). In his genealogical notes on the Palmer family, Mrs. Peabody's son Nathaniel Cranch Peabody also contradicts himself: first he gives her birth date as February 2, 1777, but later gives her life span as 1778 to 1853 (NCP Genealogies, Straker typescripts, pp. 5425/6 and 5425/16, Antiochiana). Her grandson Benjamin Pickman Mann, also a family genealogist, gives her birth date as February 28, 1778 (NCP Genealogies, Straker typescripts, p. 5425/53, Antiochiana).

The printed record is also contradictory. An obituary notice in the *Boston Transcript* of January 12, 1853, gives Mrs. Peabody's age as seventy-six, again suggesting the birth year of 1776. The first of two articles devoted to the history of female education in Andover, Massachusetts (the second of which is devoted entirely to a short biography of Mrs. Peabody, who once taught there), gives her birth year as 1777; see S.L.B. [Sarah Loring Bailey], "Young Ladies at Andover," January 30, 1879, and "Mrs. Elizabeth Palmer Peabody," February 5, 1879, *Boston Daily Advertiser.* Much of the biographical information in these two articles seems to have been acquired from her daughter Elizabeth. J. H. Temple uses Benjamin Mann's date of February 28, 1778, in his entry on the Palmer family in his *History of Framingham, Massachusetts, 1640–1880* ([Framingham]: Town of Framingham, 1887), p. 657. In her *Peabody Sisters of Salem* (Boston: Little, Brown, 1950), p. 12, Louise Hall Tharp gives Mrs. Peabody's birthday as February 25, 1778, borrowing the date given in Eliza's older sister, Mary's, memoir: Frederick Tupper and Helen Tyler Brown, eds., *Grandmother Tyler's Book: The Recollections of Mary Palmer Tyler (Mrs. Royall Tyler) 1775–1886* (New York and London: G. P. Putnam's Sons, 1925), p. 47. In his introduction to the *Letters of EPP*, p. 9, Bruce Ronda gives the unlikely birth year of 1781; by then, according to Mary Palmer Tyler, a fourth child had been born to Joseph Pearse Palmer and Elizabeth Hunt Palmer, and a fifth conceived.

Throughout this book, I have calculated Mrs. Peabody's age based on the birth year 1777 because Mrs. Peabody herself seems to have used that date. A letter from Mrs. Peabody to her daughter Mary, dated February 28, 1847, mentions having "lived the allotted years of man," that is, the biblical three score and ten (Straker typescripts, p. 1415, Antiochiana).

18   "a settlement of free": [Mrs. EPP], "Biographical Sketch of Gen. Joseph Palmer," p. 1.

northernmost corner of Braintree: The portion of Braintree where Germantown was located, as well as the Adams family property, became part of the new town of Quincy in 1792.

19   "city upon a hill": John Winthrop, "A Model of Christian Charity," a sermon delivered aboard the *Arbella*, [1630].

"Grandpapa Palmer": Mrs. EPP to EPP, January 16, 1824, Straker typescripts, p. 196, Antiochiana.

"sitting rocking the baby . . . salt water tea": Tupper and Brown, eds., *Grandmother Tyler's Book*, pp. 32–33.

20   captured by the British: A letter from SAP to EPP, September 23, 1825, describes a visit by the sisters' aunt Amelia Curtis to Friendship Hall and recounts some tales of Revolutionary times, including the capture of the ship *Ballesarious*. Louise Deming typescripts, private collection.

5,000 pounds sterling: [Mrs. EPP], "Biographical Sketch of Gen. Joseph Palmer," p. 20.

"Burlesque": Nathaniel N. Shipton, "General Joseph Palmer: Scapegoat for the Rhode Island Fiasco of October, 1777," *New England Quarterly*, vol. 39, no. 4, December 1966, p. 506.

"boats and everything ready": Shipton, "General Joseph Palmer," p. 499.

"artificers": Shipton, "General Joseph Palmer," p. 504.

"Neglect and Disobedience": Shipton, "General Joseph Palmer," p. 511.

21   "The sun rose on a scene": [Mrs. EPP] ms. novel, p. 67, MHS.

"the spring time of existence": Mrs. EPP's commonplace book 1829–1832, entry of July 4, 1830, Peabody Family Papers, 1790–1880, MHS.

"pink frocks and red morocco": Tupper and Brown, eds., *Grandmother Tyler's Book*, p. 65.

22 "We were the happiest group": Mrs. EPP to EPP, January 16, 1824, Straker typescripts, p. 196, Antiochiana.

"Sisterhood . . . preserve their independance": [Mrs. EPP] ms. novel, pp. 79-80, MHS.

23 "Watertown beauties": Tupper and Brown, eds., *Grandmother Tyler's Book*, p. 18.

"exposed shoes, stockings": John Langdon Sibley et al., "John Hunt," *Biographical Sketches of Graduates of Harvard University* (Cambridge and Boston, 1873-), vol. 9, p. 414. This story originates in Tupper and Brown, eds., *Grandmother Tyler's Book*, pp. 5-6.

"quite enough if they": Tupper and Brown, eds., *Grandmother Tyler's Book*, p. 9.

"What books have you read? . . . quite pleased with him": Tupper and Brown, eds., *Grandmother Tyler's Book*, p. 16.

24 celebrating her marriage: Mary Palmer Tyler paints this rosy picture of her parents' courtship and marriage in her memoir, published in Tupper and Brown, eds., *Grandmother Tyler's Book*, p. 19. But some evidence suggests that the romance may not have taken so neat a course, and there may have been early signs of trouble in the marriage. One letter surviving from the months before the wedding shows Betsey Hunt worrying over Joseph Pearse Palmer's health and expressing "little hope for happiness" with him "in this life." Elizabeth Hunt Palmer to Joseph Pearse Palmer, March 25, 1772, James R. Cameron, *Calendar of the Papers of General Joseph Palmer 1716-1788* (Quincy, Mass.: Quincy Historical Society, 1978), p. 25. It is also possible that Betsey Palmer's in-laws still did not approve of the match by the time of the wedding. On November 2, 1772, the couple took a party of friends along to a tavern in Hampton, New Hampshire, for a wedding ceremony that was attended by no near relations from either the Hunt or Palmer families. And in a letter dated three weeks after the wedding, Betsey writes to her husband of her concern that his father has so far refused to meet hers. Elizabeth Hunt Palmer to Joseph Pearse Palmer, November 24, 1772, Cameron, *Calendar*, p. 25. It is not surprising, however, that in the stressful years just preceding the Revolution, an alliance of two such differently educated young people would show signs of strain.

25 "trembling and feeble . . . timid infant": [Mrs. EPP] ms. novel, pp. 88-89, MHS.

"literary genius": Tupper and Brown, eds., *Grandmother Tyler's Book*, p. 23.

"reclining on the grass . . . wondrous strength of nerve": Tupper and Brown, eds., *Grandmother Tyler's Book*, pp. 23-25.

"fell as if shot by a cannon-ball": [Mrs. EPP] ms. novel, p. 85, MHS.

"fits . . . she bore no malice": Tupper and Brown, eds., *Grandmother Tyler's Book*, pp. 23-25, 50. Evidently Polly Palmer's infirmity came and went, to a certain extent, by her choice. In 1776 she was still able to assist her father at times. During a period of several months when Abigail Adams was ill with smallpox, General Palmer asked Polly to write in Abigail's place. She sent dispatches containing war news to John Adams, who appreciated Polly's "good description" and sent her a copy of the Declaration of Independence on July 5, 1776, to deliver to her "Papa," General Palmer. Cameron, *Calendar*, pp. 44-47.

"provoked . . . mangled": Tupper and Brown, eds., *Grandmother Tyler's Book*, p. 55. A somewhat less tragic account of Nathaniel Cranch's death appears in NCP's genealogical notes: "He was found fallen off a wharf or abutment, with his head broken, upon some rocks. It was supposed he fell off in endeavoring to recover his hat blown off by the wind. It was snowing at the time." But Nat, too, connects the death with a misunderstanding between Nathaniel Cranch and Elizabeth Palmer, forcing Cranch to "travel home in a driving snow storm." NCP Genealogies, Straker typescripts, p. 5425/3, Antiochiana.

26   "a long and severe fever . . . subdued": [Mrs. EPP] ms. novel, pp. 63–64, MHS.
"has scarcely ceased": Alexis de Tocqueville, *Democracy in America*, Henry Reeve, tr. (New York: Alfred A. Knopf, 1963), vol. II, pp. 198, 201.

27   "my greatest fault": Elizabeth Palmer to Nathaniel Peabody, March 1, 1800, Peabody Family Papers, 1790–1880, MHS.

PAGE   *3. Seductions*

28   "a man of almost feminine": [Nathaniel Cranch Peabody], "Joseph Pearse Palmer," *Standard*, Woodstock, Vt., April 28, 1870, Straker typescripts, p. 3034, Antiochiana.
keeping house for other families: Perhaps not surprisingly in the close-knit world of post-Revolutionary Boston, the Palmers' boarders included a Mrs. Clarke, whose future daughter-in-law would one day rent rooms to the Peabody sisters in Boston in the 1830s. Other boarders included several members of the family of the painter Washington Allston, who would also become one of the Peabody sisters' close associates.
"being caged": Tupper and Brown, eds., *Grandmother Tyler's Book*, p. 142.
never to return: Joseph Palmer (b. 1773) appears to have died of unknown causes in his mid-twenties. After two sea voyages, Palmer suffered a breakdown, became "deranged," and was "confined" for an unspecified period beginning in October 1798. In his last known letter to his family, written previous to his confinement, Joseph writes that he "had suffered everything but death." He was thought to have moved to the south during the spring of 1799, but could not be located; one family tradition holds that he was taken captive on a French war vessel and died in La Rochelle prison, France. NCP Genealogies, Straker typescripts, p. 5425/14, Antiochiana.

29   her father traveled to Maine: NCP Genealogies, Straker typescripts, p. 5425/12, Antiochiana.
"first tragedy in the family history": NCP Genealogies, Straker typescripts, p. 5425/16, Antiochiana.

30   "polished man of literary eminence . . . basest purposes": [Mrs. EPP], "Seduction," *Christian Examiner*, no. LIX, New Series no. XXX, November 1833, p. 163. In his genealogical notes on the Palmer family, Nathaniel Cranch Peabody writes of his mother: "I can learn nothing about her in her younger days, beyond the relation of her childish experiences, as given in the article on Seduction, written by her for the Christian Examiner of the year 1833. The tenor of the concluding portion of that article long ago excited in my mind a desire to know what it meant. She refers to that which she witnessed. It has been found impossible to obtain from anyone informed as to the mystery, anything like a clear and plain statement in regard to it . . . it is nevertheless of a nature that repels speech." NCP Genealogies, Straker typescripts, p. 5425/16, Antiochiana. The essay "Seduction" is signed with the cryptic pseudonym "U-A," probably a reference to Una, the chaste heroine of Eliza Palmer's beloved *Faerie Queene*, and later the name of Sophia Peabody Hawthorne's first child.
        Nat also writes that his great-aunt Mary Smith Cranch and his mother's youngest sister, Catherine, knew the full story, explaining that his mother was "of this more communicative to her elder daughters than to her sons." Nat reveals

that his sister Mary Peabody once gave him "a long account of events connected with Tyler's desire for secrecy [in his marriage to Mary Palmer], which bordered closely upon the tragically romantic." Using this account and other bits of family lore, Nat drew his own conclusions about Royall Tyler's connection to the Palmer family. Throughout his notes on the Palmer family, Nat places broad hints that Royall Tyler was the biological father of his mother's younger sister Sophia. Conceived and born during Royall Tyler's stay in the Palmer household, Sophia is described by Nat as a "peculiar but interesting child, differing in features and character from the other children. Her resemblance to Mr. Tyler was striking." And he notes that Sophia Palmer [Pickman] eventually died of the same lingering cancer of the eyes that killed Royall Tyler. NCP Genealogies, Straker typescripts, pp. 5425/16, 5425/23, 5425/25, Antiochiana.

The most conclusive evidence of the liaison between Royall Tyler and Betsey Hunt Palmer comes in the series of letters written by Mary Smith Cranch to her sister Abigail Adams around the time of Sophia Palmer's birth in September 1786, quoted here in my text.

"seduced the woman": [Mrs. EPP], "Seduction," p. 163.

"cheerful, musical voice . . . anything so beautiful": Tupper and Brown, eds., *Grandmother Tyler's Book*, p. 74.

"polluted wretch . . . prey to his designs": [Mrs. EPP], "Seduction," p. 162.

31   "so much Speculatin . . . not possible": Mary Smith Cranch to Abigail Adams, September 24, 1786, Adams Papers, reel 368, MHS.

"should be continu'd": Mary Smith Cranch to Abigail Adams, October 8, 1786, Adams Papers, reel 369, MHS.

"suffer the enemy": Mary Smith Cranch to Abigail Adams, October 9, 1786, Adams Papers, reel 369, MHS.

32   "they have made a bargain": Mary Smith Cranch to Abigail Adams, October 8, 1786, Adams Papers, reel 369, MHS.

"the disgrace": Mary Smith Cranch to Abigail Adams, October 9, 1786, Adams Papers, reel 369, MHS. Increasingly convoluted versions of the tale were still being circulated by Cranch descendants as late as the 1840s; see Caroline Healey Dall's journal, entry of October 6, 1842, Dall Papers, MHS. I would like to thank Helen R. Deese, editor of the Dall journals, for bringing this passage to my attention.

"deep-seated agony . . . betrayed, insulted": [Mrs. EPP], "Seduction," p. 168.

"distress and privations . . . never knew why": Tupper and Brown, eds., *Grandmother Tyler's Book*, p. 139.

"martyr": [Mrs. EPP], "Seduction," p. 168.

33   "Salem End": William Barry, *History of Framingham, Massachusetts* (Boston: James Munroe, 1847), p. 32.

mail came only once: Tupper and Brown, eds., *Grandmother Tyler's Book*, p. 144.

Hunts kept a tavern: J. H. Temple, *History of Framingham, Massachusetts, 1640–1880* ([Framingham]: Town of Framingham, 1887), p. 360.

share the profits: NCP Genealogies, Straker typescripts, p. 5425/13, Antiochiana.

"change work": Tupper and Brown, eds., *Grandmother Tyler's Book*, p. 140.

"she shone conspicuous": Tupper and Brown, eds., *Grandmother Tyler's Book*, p. 145.

"knew nothing of the art . . . literary improvement": S.L.B. [Sarah Loring Bailey], "Young Ladies at Andover," *Boston Daily Advertiser*, January 30, 1879.

"an irripressible desire": Mrs. EPP to GFP, October 30, 1836, Straker typescripts, p. 1118, Antiochiana.

34   "to a wood lot": S.L.B. [Sarah Loring Bailey], "Young Ladies at Andover," *Boston Daily Advertiser*, January 30, 1879.

34   "whipt, shut up . . . every feeling of tenderness": Mrs. EPP's commonplace book 1829–1832, entry of July 18, 1830, Peabody Family Papers, 1790–1880, MHS.

Palmer's refined manners: John Langdon Sibley et al., "Joseph Pearse Palmer," *Biographical Sketches of Graduates of Harvard University* (Cambridge and Boston, 1873–), vol. 17, p. 589.

Palmer heated a cup: Tupper and Brown, eds., *Grandmother Tyler's Book*, p. 142. There is some evidence that Betsey Hunt Palmer's last child, Catherine, born in Framingham in 1791, was not Joseph Pearse Palmer's child, although "she was always so considered" by the immediate family. See NCP Genealogies, Straker typescripts, p. 5425/26, Antiochiana.

"had a vocabulary": Tupper and Brown, eds., *Grandmother Tyler's Book*, p. 157.

"some very pretty girls": Royall Tyler to Joseph Pearse Palmer, Pittsfield, February 11, 1787, VtHS.

"my little wife": Royall Tyler to Joseph Pearse Palmer, Bennington, February 17, 1787, VtHS.

35   "with a fine span of black horses": Tupper and Brown, eds., *Grandmother Tyler's Book*, p. 177.

"little less rejoiced than myself": Tupper and Brown, eds., *Grandmother Tyler's Book*, p. 179.

"he was about to put . . . baggage being impossible": Tupper and Brown, eds., *Grandmother Tyler's Book*, p. 204.

"go to housekeeping": Laurel Thatcher Ulrich, *A Midwife's Tale: The Life of Martha Ballard, Based on Her Diary, 1785–1812* (New York: Alfred A. Knopf, 1990), p. 141. Common-law marriages also had their start in the years following the Revolution. Adam Haslett writes, "In the early days of the American Republic, with a population scattered across the continent, there were simply too few ministers and justices of the peace to go around. . . . If you said you were married and the neighbors tended to believe you, then in the eyes of the law you were." "Love Supreme," *The New Yorker*, May 31, 2004, p. 78. A lack of town officials was an unlikely factor in the Tylers' "secret" marriage in eastern Massachusetts, where ministers and justices of the peace were plentiful. Still, the practice may have aided Mary Palmer in her efforts to persuade her neighbors that she was married and her son legitimate.

"intense": Tupper and Brown, eds., *Grandmother Tyler's Book*, p. 205.

36   "reputation as an author": Tupper and Brown, eds., *Grandmother Tyler's Book*, p. 207.

"my mother would not understand me . . . sinful nature": Tupper and Brown, eds., *Grandmother Tyler's Book*, p. 212. In his genealogical notes on the Palmer family, Eliza's son Nat paraphrases a 1798 letter in which she lists her miseries of the Framingham years, including "her sister's relations to Mr. Tyler as his betrothed wife (although she makes no mention of the married life of her sister)." Nat must also have had the impression that the secret marriage between Mary Palmer and Royall Tyler never took place. NCP Genealogies, Straker typescripts, p. 5425/17, Antiochiana.

"betrayer of innocence": [Mrs. EPP], "Seduction," p. 162.

"personally independent": EPP, "Letter from Miss Elizabeth Peabody," printed as part of S.L.B. [Sarah Loring Bailey], "Mrs. Elizabeth Palmer Peabody," *Boston Daily Advertiser*, February 5, 1879.

She launched her experiment: NCP Genealogies, Straker typescripts, p. 5425/13–24, Antiochiana.

37   "I can see no good . . . first acquainted": Joseph Pearse Palmer to Mary Palmer, August 7, 1794, Tupper and Brown, eds., *Grandmother Tyler's Book*, p. 191. Eliza's

younger brother Edward drowned a few days after his father, near Brattleboro, Vermont, at age fifteen. He was working in the printing office of the *Federal Galaxy*, a position arranged for him by Royall Tyler. NCP Genealogies, Straker typescripts, p. 5425/24, Antiochiana.

loosening of sexual mores: Daniel Scott Smith and Michael S. Hindus, "Premarital Pregnancy in America, 1640–1971: An Overview and Interpretation," *Journal of Interdisciplinary History*, vol. V, no 4, Spring 1975, p. 537.

only to her two oldest daughters: NCP Genealogies, Straker typescripts, p. 5425/16, Antiochiana.

"suffered much": MTM to HM, January 23, 1853, HM Papers, MHS.

38   "of a nature that repels": NCP Genealogies, Straker typescripts, p. 5425/16, Antiochiana.

PAGE   *4. "Belinda"*

39   "whole W[atertown] concern": Mrs. EPP to [MTM or EPP], May 6, 1852, Straker typescripts, p. 1693, Antiochiana.

"very much disgusted": EPP, "Letter from Miss Elizabeth Peabody," printed as part of S.L.B. [Sarah Loring Bailey], "Mrs. Elizabeth Palmer Peabody," *Boston Daily Advertiser*, February 5, 1879.

"I have known her frequently . . . pen and books": Elizabeth Hunt Palmer to Mary Smith Cranch, August 13, 1799, Peabody Family Papers, 1790–1880, MHS.

"*this* of all families": Elizabeth Hunt Palmer to Mary Smith Cranch, April 20, 1799, Peabody Family Papers, 1970–1880, MHS.

40   "a good girl . . . future subsistance": Elizabeth Hunt Palmer to Mary Smith Cranch, May 9, 1798, Peabody Family Papers, 1790–1880, MHS.

"My heart glows with delight . . . every necessary caution": Elizabeth Hunt Palmer to Mary Smith Cranch, July 6, 1798, Peabody Family Papers, 1790–1880, MHS.

41   "Parson" Peabody: S.L.B. [Sarah Loring Bailey], "Mrs. Elizabeth Palmer Peabody," *Boston Daily Advertiser*, February 5, 1879. For more on the household and school run jointly by the Reverend Stephen Peabody and his wife, see William C. Todd, *Biographical and Other Articles* (Boston: Lee and Shepard, 1901), pp. 63–82.

42   "Miss Palmer . . . large Family": Abigail Adams to Elizabeth Smith Shaw Peabody, December 30, 1798, Shaw Family Papers, LOC.

"a most amiable person": Elizabeth Smith Shaw Peabody to Mary Smith Cranch, January 1, 1799, Shaw Family Papers, LOC.

"all the mental acquisitions": Mrs. EPP to EPP, [April 25], 1819, Straker typescripts, p. 105, Antiochiana.

"will not be contented . . . yonder cold sod": Elizabeth Smith Shaw Peabody to Mary Smith Cranch, January 1, 1799, Shaw Family Papers, LOC. In this collection of letters, as well as in her sister Mary Palmer Tyler's memoir, Eliza is referred to as Betsy Palmer. But in her own letters she signs herself Eliza, and so I have used this name to refer to her throughout this chapter as a means of distinguishing her from several other Elizabeths.

"maid of all work": S.L.B. [Sarah Loring Bailey], "Mrs. Elizabeth Palmer Peabody," *Boston Daily Advertiser*, February 5, 1879.

"assist in preparing": S.L.B. [Sarah Loring Bailey], "Mrs. Elizabeth Palmer Peabody," *Boston Daily Advertiser*, February 5, 1879.

472 NOTES

42   frequently torn clothing: Elizabeth Smith Shaw Peabody to William Smith Shaw, March 20, 1799, Shaw Family Papers, LOC.

43   "walking dictionary": EPP, "Letter from Miss Elizabeth Peabody," printed as part of S.L.B. [Sarah Loring Bailey], "Mrs. Elizabeth Palmer Peabody," *Boston Daily Advertiser,* February 5, 1879.

"In the midst ... will think me unkind": S.L.B. [Sarah Loring Bailey], "Mrs. Elizabeth Palmer Peabody," *Boston Daily Advertiser,* February 5, 1879.

the pseudonym "Belinda": Eliza Palmer's "Belinda" poems appeared in the *Haverhill Federal Gazette* on February 15, March 15, April 5, May 10 and 31, June 14, and August 15, 1799. The confirmation of her authorship comes in two letters that she wrote the following year to her future husband, Nathaniel Peabody, dated February 17 and March 1, 1800. In the first, she writes that she has enclosed a *"very poor poem"* of her own composition; in the second she refers again to that poem and quotes from it. The poem was Belinda's March 15 "A True Lady." Peabody Family Papers, 1790–1880, MHS.

Eliza's children knew of these poems and may have read them. Her son Nathaniel mentions them in his genealogical notes on the Palmer family (NCP Genealogies, Straker typescripts, p. 5425/16, Antiochiana). He may also have known of two prose compositions that appeared in the same newspaper and express themes so close to his mother's heart that she may have been their author. When Sarah Loring Bailey wrote her biographical sketch of Mrs. Elizabeth Palmer Peabody for the *Boston Daily Advertiser,* based largely on Nathaniel's testimony, she noted that Eliza contributed both "prose and poetry" to the *Gazette* (February 5, 1879).

One of these pieces was a short paragraph titled "Seduction." Published anonymously, it read in part: "How abandoned is that heart which ... is the cause, the fatal cause, of overwhelming the spotless soul, and plunging the yet untainted mind into a sea of sorrow and repentance! Though born to protect the fair, does not man act the part of a demon?—first alluring by his temptations, and then triumphing in his victory.... *Ye fair! beware of such a character!*" (April 12, 1799). The language of this short passage is very close to the longer 1833 essay "Seduction," in which Eliza refers to her mother's and sister's seductions.

In May 1799, a short story appeared in the *Haverhill Federal Gazette* titled "Sorrows of Amelia, or Deluded Innocence: An Historiette Founded in Fact." The fate of Amelia (also the name of one of Eliza Palmer's sisters) is unmistakably similar to that of her older sister, Mary Palmer. This Amelia was "unrivalled in sweetness and tender sensibility." She had a "lovely countenance," and "in her infantile years, she was deprived of the tender care of parental affection, and her blooming beauty was exposed to all the fascinating snares of artful dissimulation." When Amelia was scarcely sixteen, "the perfidious Alonzo by his persuasive flattery, and external charms, ensnared her susceptible heart, and under the most sacred promises of matrimony, betrayed her female innocence" (May 10, 1799).

Eliza Palmer may not have written either of these pieces, but she certainly read them along with countless others like them. Tales of seduction were frequently printed—as fact or fiction—in newspapers of the time and elaborated on for their moral significance in popular novels. Cathy N. Davidson has written on the emergence of the "novel of seduction" just at this time, when the moral codes of Puritanism had eroded, leaving America's youth to discover for themselves Victorian prudishness. *Revolution and the Word: The Rise of the Novel in America* (New York: Oxford University Press, 1986). See also Jane Tompkins, *Sensational Designs: The Cultural Work of American Fiction, 1790–1860* (New York: Oxford

University Press, 1985), and Donna R. Bontatibus, *The Seduction Novel of the Early Nation: A Call for Socio-Political Reform* (East Lansing: Michigan State University Press, 1999).

". . . First I ask . . . sad degen'racy of *man*": Belinda [Eliza Palmer], "Some Thoughts Occasioned by the Present Juncture," *Haverhill Federal Gazette*, March 15, 1799.

44   "This is the language . . . 'unflattering praise'": Belinda [Eliza Palmer], "A True Lady," *Haverhill Federal Gazette*, April 5, 1799.

45   favorite poet: Paul C. Nagel, *The Adams Women: Abigail and Louisa Adams, Their Sisters and Daughters* (New York and Oxford: Oxford University Press, 1987), pp. 55, 62.

"Did you hear . . . present Juncture of Affairs": Elizabeth Smith Shaw Peabody to William Smith Shaw, March 20, 1799, Shaw Family Papers, LOC. In his biography *John Adams* (New York: Simon and Schuster, 2001), David McCullough argues that Adams's successful effort to maintain peace with France, despite popular sentiment in favor of war, was the signal achievement of his presidency.

"Remember the Ladies": Abigail Adams to John Adams, March 31, 1776, L. H. Butterfield et al., eds., *Adams Family Correspondence* (Cambridge, Mass.: Belknap Press of Harvard University Press, 1963), vol. I, p. 370.

"the effusions of Miss Palmers pen": Elizabeth Smith Shaw Peabody to William Smith Shaw, November 20, 1799, Shaw Family Papers, LOC.

"feels hurt and dissatisfied": S.L.B. [Sarah Loring Baily], "Mrs. Elizabeth Palmer Peabody," *Boston Daily Advertiser*, February 5, 1879.

46   "'Tis then sweet friendship": Belinda [Eliza Palmer], "A True Lady," *Haverhill Federal Gazette*, April 5, 1799.

"It is a received opinion": S.L.B. [Sarah Loring Bailey], "Mrs. Elizabeth Palmer Peabody," *Boston Daily Advertiser*, February 5, 1879.

"Sister Peabody . . . frozen Age": Abigail Adams to Mary Smith Cranch, March 15, 1800, printed in Abigail Adams, *New Letters of Abigail Adams*, Stewart Mitchell, ed. (Boston: Houghton Mifflin, 1947), pp. 238–42.

"round of duties . . . repose of others": Elizabeth Smith Shaw Peabody to Abigail Adams, March 30, 1800, Adams Papers, reel 397, MHS.

47   "O! she has sufferd . . . her circumstances": Elizabeth Hunt Palmer to Mary Smith Cranch, August 13, 1799, Peabody Family Papers, 1790–1880, MHS.

"I mean to do . . . work of some kind": S.L.B. [Sarah Loring Bailey], "Mrs. Elizabeth Palmer Peabody," *Boston Daily Advertiser*, February 5, 1879.

PAGE   *5. Flight into Union*

48   "placed every stone": Dr. NP to Francis Peabody, April 22, 1835, Dartmouth.

Peabodys born in America: In *Nathaniel Hawthorne and His Wife*, Julian Hawthorne writes that Francis Peabody arrived in America in 1640 and raised ten children: "For nearly a hundred years there were ten children in each generation in the line of direct descent, not to mention the offspring of the collateral sons and daughters, which accounts for the large number of persons now bearing the name of Peabody in New England" (Hamden, Conn.: Archon Books, 1968, reprint of 1884 edition), vol. I, p. 44.

As a result of this expansion, there were many other Peabodys living in Salem and Boston in the early nineteenth century not closely enough related to

the family of Nathaniel and Elizabeth Palmer Peabody to be recognized as relatives. A more thorough and accurate listing of the branches of the Peabody
family in the United States can be found in Selim Hobart Peabody, LL.D.,
Peabody Genealogy (Boston: Charles H. Pope, 1909).

48   "all the letters of your own name": Dr. NP to Isaac Peabody, April 5, 1819, Dartmouth.

49   "I was launching": Dr. NP to Francis Peabody, Boston, April 15, 1846, Dartmouth.
"virtue": Eliza Palmer to Nathaniel Peabody, March 16, 1800, Peabody Family
Papers, 1790–1880, MHS.
"merit, good sense ... something original in his genius": Elizabeth Smith Shaw
Peabody to Abigail Adams, March 30, 1800, Adams Papers, reel 397, MHS.
"I beheld you ... suddenly formed": Eliza Palmer to Nathaniel Peabody, February 17, 1800, Peabody Family Papers, 1790–1880, MHS.
"I flattered myself": Eliza Palmer to Nathaniel Peabody, March 1, 1800, Peabody
Family Papers, 1790–1880, MHS.
"raking up objections": Mrs. EPP to EPP and MTP, [1827], Straker typescripts, p.
431, Antiochiana.

50   "Instructor ... favourites of fortune": Eliza Palmer to Nathaniel Peabody, March
16, 1800, Peabody Family Papers, 1790–1880, MHS.
"*very poor poem*": Eliza Palmer to Nathaniel Peabody, February 17, 1800, Peabody
Family Papers, 1790–1880, MHS.
"to endeavor to persuade": Eliza Palmer to Nathaniel Peabody, March 1, 1800,
Peabody Family Papers, 1790–1880, MHS.
"Mr. R ... lighted at the same taper": Eliza Palmer to Nathaniel Peabody, March
16, 1800, Peabody Family Papers, 1790–1880, MHS.
"fair defects in Nature ... greatness of mind": Eliza Palmer to Nathaniel
Peabody, March 1, 1800, Peabody Family Papers, 1790–1880, MHS.
"The necessity of cultivating ... better acquainted than I am": Eliza Palmer to
Nathaniel Peabody, February 17, 1800, Peabody Family Papers, 1790–1880, MHS.

51   "ornament ... flourish near us": Eliza Palmer to Nathaniel Peabody, March 16,
1800, Peabody Family Papers, 1790–1880, MHS.
"I think she has been a little too premature": Elizabeth Smith Shaw Peabody to
Mary Smith Cranch, May 1, 1800, Shaw Family Papers, LOC.
"in the infancy of his education": Elizabeth Smith Shaw Peabody to Abigail
Adams, March 30, 1800, Adams Papers, reel 397, MHS.
"not wholly determined ... genteel maintenance": Elizabeth Smith Shaw
Peabody to Mary Smith Cranch (and Betsey Palmer quoted in), May 1, 1800,
Shaw Family Papers, LOC.

52   "my heart is unreservedly yours": Eliza Palmer to Nathaniel Peabody, March 16,
1800, Peabody Family Papers, 1790–1880, MHS. Of courtship and marriage in
the period 1770 to 1840, Ellen K. Rothman writes, "The timing of marriage generated far more conflict than did the choice of a mate." Anxiety about practical
matters commonly led to lengthy engagements of two years or more, with men
concerned about finding means to support a wife and children, women reluctant
to leave the relative security of home. According to Rothman, however, "women
consistently sought longer, and men shorter, engagements." Perhaps Elizabeth
Smith Peabody was right to point out Eliza Palmer's deviation from standard
courtship etiquette. Ellen K. Rothman, *Hands and Hearts: A History of Courtship in
America* (New York: Basic Books, 1984), pp. 56, 72.
"accusing spirit ... school of adversity": Eliza Palmer to Nathaniel Peabody,
March 16, 1800, Peabody Family Papers, 1790–1880, MHS.

first incorporated academy: Sarah Loring Bailey, *Historical Sketches of Andover Massachusetts* (Boston: Houghton Mifflin, 1880), p. 543.

coeducational academy drew: S.L.B. [Sarah Loring Bailey], "Young Ladies at Andover," *Boston Daily Advertiser,* January 30, 1879.

"remarkably social town": Bailey, *Historical Sketches of Andover Massachusetts*, p. 552.

53   "needlework, grammar, geography . . . with pleasure": S.L.B. [Sarah Loring Bailey], "Young Ladies at Andover," *Boston Daily Advertiser,* January 30, 1879.

"content to begin . . . embarrassing situation": Eliza Palmer to Nathaniel Peabody, January 30, 1802, Peabody Family Papers, 1790–1880, MHS.

"no friend of yours . . . sacrifice of your repose": Eliza Palmer to Nathaniel Peabody, February 16, 1802, Peabody Family Papers, 1790–1880, MHS.

54   "Some place happiness . . . must sail with them": Eliza Palmer to Nathaniel Peabody, April 11, 1802, Straker typescripts, pp. 26–27, Antiochiana.

"determination of going": Elizabeth Hunt Palmer to Mary Smith Cranch, October 5, 1802, Peabody Family Papers, 1790–1880, MHS.

55   "You must not expect . . . never could remove": Mrs. EPP to [EPP], [1834], Straker typescripts, p. 722, Antiochiana.

"would match any lovers . . . early associations": Mrs. EPP to EPP, Salem, October 2, [1827], Straker typescripts, p. 426, Antiochiana.

"strong prejudices against": Mrs. EPP to EPP and MTP, [1827], Straker typescripts, p. 431, Antiochiana.

"jealousy of my assuming power": Mrs. EPP to [EPP], [1834], Straker typescripts, p. 722, Antiochiana.

6. *"My Hopes* All *of Happiness"*

59   "born and nursed . . . firmest constitution": Mrs. EPP to SAP, n.d., Julian Hawthorne, *Nathaniel Hawthorne and His Wife* (Hamden, Conn.: Archon Books, 1968, reprint of 1884 edition), vol. I, pp. 70–71. The original manuscript is in the Berg Collection; it is slightly longer, and Julian Hawthorne altered some of the passages, but not those quoted here. The manuscript is catalogued with the tentative date "[Salem, 1828?]," but internal evidence sets the date several years later.

"first-born child": Maria S. Porter, "Elizabeth Palmer Peabody," *The Bostonian*, vol. 3, no. 4, pp. 340–50.

60   "family school": term used in reference to such schools of the time by EPP in "Schools for Girls at Hingham," *Barnard's Journal of Education*, vol. 5, July 1880, p. 588. She would also take the term for the title of a family magazine she published briefly from Salem in 1836.

entered in the church records: *Vital Records to 1850, Billerica, Massachusetts* (Boston: New England Historic Genealogical Society, 1908), p. 148.

almost 1,200 to nearly 1,400: *Vital Records to 1850, Billerica, Massachusetts*, [p. 4].

61   earn an M.D. at Harvard: See Philip Cash, "The Professionalization of Boston Medicine, 1760–1803," and Whitfield J. Bell, Jr., "Medicine in Boston and Philadelphia: Comparisons and Contrasts, 1750–1820," *Medicine in Colonial Massachusetts: 1620–1820* (Boston: Colonial Society of Massachusetts), vol. 57, 1980.

62   "in a pleasant but retired spot": Mrs. EPP to Sally, August 29, 1806, Straker typescripts, p. 81, Antiochiana.

location midway between: Harvard moved its medical school across the river to Boston in 1810.

62   Cambridgeport was nothing like: For information on the early history of Cambridgeport I have relied on Samuel Atkins Eliot, *A History of Cambridge, Massachusetts, 1630–1913* (Cambridge, Mass.: *Cambridge Tribune*, 1913).

63   "our number of pupils": Mrs. EPP to Sally, August 29, 1806, Straker typescripts, p. 81, Antiochiana.

PAGE   *7. Salem Girlhoods*

64   Captain Nathaniel Hathorne: William H. Manning, *The Manning Families of New England* (Salem, Mass.: Salem Press, 1902), pp. 713–15. The Hawthorne name was spelled without a "w" until Captain Hathorne's son, Nathaniel, began experimenting with a new spelling around the time of his graduation from Bowdoin College in 1825, perhaps to ensure proper pronunciation when he might become famous as a writer. By February 1827, he had adopted the new spelling for good. Nathaniel's sisters eventually changed the spelling of their names too. "We were in those days . . . absurdly obedient to him," his oldest sister, Ebe, later recalled. But Captain Hathorne had died in 1808, long before his son would institute the change. Brenda Wineapple, *Hawthorne: A Life* (New York: Alfred A. Knopf, 2003), p. 64.
      "there was a decidedly": Caroline Howard King, *When I Lived in Salem, 1822–1866* (Brattleboro, Vt.: Stephen Daye Press, 1937), p. 22.

65   Thomas Jefferson's Embargo Act: For information on the town of Salem during Jefferson's embargo and the War of 1812, I have drawn on James Duncan Phillips, *Salem and the Indies: The Story of the Great Commercial Era of the City* (Boston: Houghton Mifflin, 1947), pp. 262–81, 308–28, 340–59; Charles S. Osgood and H. M. Batchelder, *Historical Sketch of Salem, 1626–1879* (Salem, Mass.: Essex Institute, 1879), pp. 220–27; and Margaret B. Moore, *The Salem World of Nathaniel Hawthorne* (Columbia: University of Missouri Press, 1998), pp. 81–87.
      "the harbors were filled": Alonzo Lewis and James R. Newhall, *History of Lynn, Essex County, Massachusetts* (Boston: John L. Shorey, 1865), p. 369.
      Union Street: Nathaniel Hawthorne was born in a house on Union Street in July 1804. By the time the Peabodys had moved to Union Street, however, Hawthorne's father had died and his family had joined the Manning household in a building around the block on Herbert Street; its back yard adjoined the Peabodys' on the corner of Union and Essex streets.

66   "so very young . . . independent action": EPP, *Lectures in the Training Schools for Kindergartners* (Boston: D. C. Heath, 1897), pp. 102–103. Although the Peabody sisters may never have known it, they were descendants of the *Mayflower* Pilgrims John Alden and Priscilla Mullins. Gary Boyd Roberts, "Nineteenth-Century Heroines, Part One: Literature and Feminism," *NEXUS: The Bimonthly Newsletter of the New England Historic Genealogical Society*, vol. VII, no. 5, October–November 1990, p. 156.

67   establish a new school: Indeed Elizabeth was to see two of her mother's younger sisters, Catherine and Amelia, open schools for girls in Salem.

68   "My sister Mary . . . keep it looking nice": EPP journal [1815–1822], MVWC, pp. 11–12, MHS.
      "nearly all the advantages . . . tenderness & encouragement": Mrs. EPP to MTP, 1824, from SAP copybook "letters from home," Berg.
      "Any other mother": EPP to Mrs. EPP, February 8, 1847, MVWC, p. 6, MHS.

"a dull little girl ... youthful admiration": EPP to Francis Henry Lee, [1885], *Letters of EPP*, p. 419.

69   "head of clustering locks": Norman Holmes Pearson, "Elizabeth Peabody on Hawthorne," *Essex Institute Historical Collections*, July 1958, p. 263.

"caressing me ... punish offenders": EPP, *Lectures in the Training Schools for Kindergartners*, pp. 70-72.

"young people": Elizabeth Peabody [Mrs. Elizabeth Palmer Peabody], *Sabbath Lessons, or an abstract of Sacred History* (Salem, Mass.: Thomas C. Cushing, 1810), p. 5.

"confidence": EPP journal [1815-1822], MVWC, p. 14, MHS.

70   Sophia baptized: *Salem Vital Records to 1850* (Salem, Mass.: Essex Institute, 1918), vol. II, p. 146; Osgood and Batchelder, *Historical Sketch of Salem*, p. 93.

"It takes genius ... face to face": *Rem of WEC*, p. 13. Channing preached in Salem's North Church on August 18, 1811.

72   "perfection ... and in *activity*": John White Chadwick, *William Ellery Channing: Minister of Religion* (Boston and New York: Houghton Mifflin, 1903), p. 82.

"rebellious spirit": Mrs. EPP to SAH, n.d. [December 1850], Straker typescripts, p. 1529, Antiochiana.

"very wilful, obstinate child": MTM, "Reminiscences," Straker typescripts, p. 103, Antiochiana.

"I firmly resisted": Mrs. EPP to SAH, n.d. [December 1850], Straker typescripts, p. 1529, Antiochiana.

"my love ... any other person": SAH to Mrs. EPP, Lenox, February 12, 1851, Berg.

"my soul is knit to hers": SAH to MTM, [1853], HM Papers, MHS.

"delicacy ... bad temper": Mrs. EPP to SAH, n.d. [December 1850], Straker typescripts, p. 1529, Antiochiana.

"ever since I saw": SAH to [EPP?], incomplete, [1852 or 1853?], Berg.

73   teething or its complications: Sylvia D. Hoffert, *Private Matters: American Attitudes Towards Childbearing and Infant Nurture in the Urban North, 1800-1860* (Urbana and Chicago: University of Illinois Press, 1989), pp. 143, 149, 161.

Massachusetts Medical Society: The Massachusetts Medical Society, chartered in 1781 by the Commonwealth of Massachusetts, a year before the founding of the Harvard Medical Institution, did not license physicians but awarded "certificates of approval" as a means of identifying doctors it considered most qualified to practice. Membership in the Massachusetts Medical Society may have carried greater weight than a medical degree from Harvard; Harvard's B.M. was not judged the equivalent of a certificate of approval by the state legislature until 1803. The Medical Society was founded chiefly by Boston doctors trained in Europe (Dr. Jeffries, who trained in London and received an M.D. in Aberdeen, was an early and active member), whereas only one of the three founding professors of Harvard's Medical Institution held academic degrees. See Philip Cash, "The Professionalization of Boston Medicine, 1760-1803," *Medicine in Colonial Massachusetts: 1620-1820* (Boston: Colonial Society of Massachusetts), vol. 57, 1980.

popular child-rearing manuals: [Mary Palmer Tyler], *The Maternal Physician: A Treatise on the Nurture and Management of Infants, From the Birth Until Two years old* (New York: Isaac Riley, 1811). See Chapter 2, Section 1: "On Teething and the Management of Infants during the often painful and critical Period of Dentition."

74   "trembling, anxiety, weakness": Martha Saxton, *Louisa May* (Boston: Houghton Mifflin, 1977), p. 246.

74   ill effects were linked to mercury: Dr. Peabody recognized sooner than most the harmful effects of mercury dosing on the teeth themselves, although he continued for at least another decade to recommend other purgatives. In an 1824 pamphlet he published in order to attract customers to his Salem dental practice, Dr. Peabody wrote, in a section devoted to "Infantile or Temporary Teeth": "Some experienced Dentists, who have written on the subject, are of opinion, that *mercurial medicines*, taken during the formation and growth of teeth, are injurious to the constitution of them. Observation certainly does not contradict it. If this be the case, great caution should be observed in the use of it, and other cathartical remedies resorted to." By 1824, however, Sophia was fifteen years old, and the damage had been done—presumably her teeth were among those Dr. Peabody had observed to be weakened by early dosing with mercury. *The Art of Preserving Teeth* (Salem, Mass.: Joshua and John D. Cushing, 1824), p. 25.

"severe disciplinarian . . . innocent dove": The Watertown stories are contained in a manuscript at the Berg Collection, catalogued as "Remembrances of a visit to her grandmother," dated 1859, and titled "Extract of stories Sophia Hawthorne wrote for her children, some of which were based upon experiences of her childhood with her Grandmother Betsy Hunt Palmer and Aunt Alice Palmer." Probably Great-Aunt Kate Hunt was the model for "Aunt Alice": there was no Aunt Alice Palmer, although Sophia gives her aunt the name Alice in the story. Julian Hawthorne printed portions of these stories in *Nathaniel Hawthorne and His Wife* (Hamden, Conn.: Archon Books, 1968, reprint of 1884 edition), vol. I, p. 55 ff, but altered the text in some details.

75   "My sensitiveness": Julian Hawthorne, *Nathaniel Hawthorne and His Wife*, vol. I, p. 55.

"gobbling like so many fiends": SAH, "Remembrances of a visit to her grandmother," Berg.

"mantuamakers": Mrs. EPP to MTM, n.d., Monday morning, [January 1845?], HM Papers, MHS. My date: [April 1845].

extended stay away from home: As a very young child, Sophia was also occasionally deposited at her father's family farm during the summer for "rustications," as she later called them. These visits were likely intended to produce health benefits, as well as to ease Eliza's household burdens. There, too, Sophia experienced conflict. On one occasion she failed in her efforts to milk a cow, spilling a precious pail in the process. Her Grandmother Peabody's solemn rebuke "doubled my remorse of conscience," Sophia wrote many years later—and also brought a welcome end to Sophia's barnyard chores. SAP *CJ*, p. 406.

"first independent stroll . . . maul": SAH, "Remembrances of a visit to her grandmother," Berg. It is interesting that Sophia chose the word *maul* for this threatening incident. Not many years earlier her husband had published a novel in which a humble Salem villager, Matthew Maule, had been hanged for witchcraft, dying with a curse on his lips for the judge who condemned him to death.

76   "controlled her without": Julian Hawthorne, *Nathaniel Hawthorne and His Wife*, vol. I, p. 48.

"hot-house plant": Mrs. EPP to EPP, n.d. [February 1827], Straker typescripts, p. 397, Antiochiana.

"delicate nerves": Mrs EPP to MTP, Friday morning, n.d. [1832?], HM Papers, MHS.

"in and out": MTM, "Reminiscences of School Life and Teaching," *Female Educa-*

tion in Massachusetts, republished from *Barnard's American Journal of Education* (Hartford, Conn.: 1884), p. 312.

"dwell more in trees and skies": MTM, "Reminiscences," Straker typescripts, p. 103, Antiochiana.

77   "in a state of salivation": MTM, "Reminiscences of School Life and Teaching," p. 313.

Essex and Cambridge streets: This corner house had long been occupied by a branch of the Hathorne family; EPP to Francis Henry Lee, [1885], *Letters of EPP,* p. 419. The connections between the Hawthorne and Peabody families via Salem real estate are numerous. The Union Street house in which Nathaniel Hawthorne was born in 1804 had been built before 1685 by an early member of the Pickman family, to which Mary Peabody was to become so attached after the move to the corner of Cambridge and Essex.

78   inferior education: Mrs. EPP to MTP, March 1, 1834, Berg.

avoid the company: Mrs. EPP to SAP and MTP, December 8, 1833, Berg.

"little Mary P": MTP to Miss Rawlins Pickman, January 13, 1828, HMII Papers, MHS.

"almost every day": MTM, "Reminiscences of School Life and Teaching," p. 312.

frequent visitor: George Francis Dow, ed., *The Diary and Letters of Benjamin Pickman* (Newport, R.I.: 1928), p. 191 ff.

"kind and partial": MTP to Miss Rawlins Pickman, April 16, 1826, HMII Papers, MHS.

"the most beautiful chapter": MTP to Miss Rawlins Pickman, n.d. [1833?], HMII Papers, MHS.

"with its forty cows ... swallows' nests": MTM, "Reminiscences of School Life and Teaching," pp. 312–13.

79   "learned to read ... when no one knew it": MTM, "Reminiscences of School Life and Teaching," pp. 311–12.

"satellite ... studious child": MTM, "Reminiscences of School Life and Teaching," p. 312.

"My existence ... way I feel about it": MTP to Miss Rawlins Pickman, October 1, 1834, HMII Papers, MHS.

80   "I used to think ... calm exterior": MTP to EPP, May 11, 1834, Berg.

"imagined ... wife of the best of men": MTM, "Estimate of Horace Mann," ms. journal, entry of August 13, 1860, Journal X, HM Papers, MHS.

"baby passion": MTM to SAH, October 17, 1859, HMII Papers, MHS.

"the noblest, the purest": MTM, "Estimate of Horace Mann," ms. journal, entry of August 13, 1860, Journal X, HM Papers, MHS.

"reverence ... fair haired ideal": MTM to SAH, October 17, 1859, HMII Papers, MHS.

getting himself expelled: Faculty Records, vol. X, p. 28, UAIII 5.5.2, HUA.

"earthly object": [MTM], "An Experience," n.d., HM Papers, MHS; also published as "Mary Peabody Mann's Short Story, 'An Experience,'" Megan Marshall, ed., *Proceedings of the Massachusetts Historical Society,* vol. 98 (1986), pp. 76–89.

"ideal perfection": MTM to SAH, October 17, 1859, HMII Papers, MHS.

81   "a taste and enthusiasm for genius": EPP journal [1815–1822], MVWC, p. 18, MHS.

"education, the cultivation": EPP journal [1815–1822], MVWC, p. 92, MHS.

"bare and rocky height ... spirit-stirring": MTP to HM, August 2, 1835, HM Papers, MHS.

PAGE   *8. The Doctor and His Wife*

82   "clouded with sorrows and cares": EPP to HM, September 4, 1836, Straker type-
        scripts, p. 1094, Antiochiana.
        "shrink from the sound of his own voice": Mrs. EPP to EPP and MTP, [1827],
        Straker typescripts, p. 431, Antiochiana.
        "find out the language . . . motherly instinct": EPP, "My Experience as a Teacher,"
        Female Education in Massachusetts, republished from *Barnard's American Journal of
        Education* (Hartford, Conn.: 1884), p. 19.
        "make [her] Pupils happy": Mrs. EPP to EPP, April 9–12, 1824, Straker type-
        scripts, p. 211, Antiochiana.
        "did not *talk down*": EPP, *Lectures in the Training Schools for Kindergartners* (Boston:
        D. C. Heath, 1897), p. 102.

83   "the idea that women": EPP, "Mrs. Elizabeth Palmer Peabody," *Female Education
        in Massachusetts,* republished from *Barnard's American Journal of Education* (Hart-
        ford, Conn.: 1884), p. 309.
        "nothing venture nothing have": John Peabody to Dr. NP, Salem, May 7, 1803,
        Straker typescripts, p. 41, Antiochiana.
        contemplate his errors: Dr. NP to Francis Peabody, February 9, 1816, Dartmouth.
        lower cost of bail . . . "getting along well": Dr. NP to Francis Peabody, March 6,
        1817, Dartmouth.
        "Deliberate well before": Dr. NP to Francis Peabody, March 29, 1816, Dartmouth.

84   "it may be for my good . . . support of any country": Dr. NP to Francis Peabody,
        August 27, 1815, Dartmouth.
        singing school: Dr. NP to Francis Peabody, March 6, 1817, Dartmouth.
        "I wonder!": Dr. NP to Francis Peabody, January 1, 1819, Dartmouth.
        "half Physician": William Bentley, D.D., entry of July 23, 1815, *The Diary of
        William Bentley, D.D.* (Gloucester, Mass.: Peter Smith, 1962), vol. 4, p. 342.
        third to be consulted: James R. Mellow, *Nathaniel Hawthorne in His Times* (Boston:
        Houghton Mifflin, 1980), p. 18.
        "sickly": Dr. NP to Francis Peabody, June 1, 1815, Dartmouth.
        flour cost $15 a month: Dr. NP to Francis Peabody, August 27, 1815; March 6,
        1817; July 15, 1817, Dartmouth.
        "I never was more put to it": Dr. NP to Francis Peabody, March 6, 1817, Dartmouth.
        Wellington in 1815: Wellington was born on December 16, 1815. His birth year
        is given erroneously as 1816 in many archives, probably due to the record of his
        baptism in January 1816 in *Salem Vital Records* (Salem, Mass.: Essex Institute,
        1918), vol. 2, p. 146.
        copyrights for the textbooks: Aside from *Sabbath Lessons* (1810), Mrs. Peabody
        also published a loose "translation" and study guide to Spenser's *The Faerie
        Queene,* titled *Holiness: or the Legend of St. George: A Tale From Spenser's Faerie Queene*
        (Boston: E. R. Broaders, 1836).
        "a day of quiet": EPP, *Lectures in the Training Schools for Kindergartners,* p. 101.

85   "to refuse to eat sugar": EPP to Theodore Dwight Weld, November 11, 1886, Au-
        tograph file, Houghton.
        "never fully perceived": NCP Genealogies, Straker typescripts, p. 5425/23, Anti-
        ochiana.
        "watchful tenderness . . . telling him of wants": Mrs. EPP to EPP, Salem, October
        2, [1827], Straker typescripts, p. 426, Antiochiana.
        "family malady . . . effort is vain": Mrs. EPP to EPP, n.d., Straker typescripts, p.
        1071, Antiochiana.

"the most agonized period": Mrs. EPP to SAP, [Salem? 1828?], Berg.

"stupyfying": Mrs. EPP to SAH, January 8, 1844, Berg 229919B. My date: [February 8, 1847].

"suspicion": Mrs. EPP to MTM and EPP, April 13, [1852], Straker typescripts, p. 1676, Antiochiana.

86   "This is almost always ... wounded than have his": "Mrs. EPP to EPP and MTP, [1827], Straker typescripts, p. 431, Antiochiana.

"averse to contention": NCP Genealogies, Straker typescripts, p. 5425/23, Antiochiana.

"dread of violent emotions": MTM to HM, Monday Morning, January 1853, HM Papers, MHS.

"excessive violence ... where there is a child": SAH to MTM, May 2, [1852], Berg.

87   "raised platform in one corner": NCP Genealogies, Straker typescripts, p. 5425/19, Antiochiana.

PAGE   *9. "Heretical Tendencies"*

89   "remarkable little girl ... arbitrary gift": *Rem of WEC*, pp. 30-31.

Noah Worcester's *Bible:* Noah Worcester, *Bible News of the Father, Son, and the Holy Ghost* (Concord, N.H.: 1810).

"it gave me relief": EPP journal [1815-1822], MVWC, p. 18, MHS.

never to preach again: Moved by Worcester's plight, the Reverend Channing brought him down to Boston in 1813 to serve as editor of the publication he used as his own forum, *The Christian Disciple*. Later Worcester became editor of *The Friend of Peace*, a journal in which Mrs. Peabody published at least one poem, according to her son: "The Indian," vol. III, no. XII, April 1824, pp. 378-79.

"plunged into": EPP journal [1815-1822], MVWC, p. 29, MHS.

90   "disgusted": EPP journal [1815-1822], MVWC, p. 28, MHS.

"in vain ... entirely dropped between us": EPP journal [1815-1822], MVWC, p. 30, MHS.

"unreasonable religion ... and to the *heart*": William Ellery Channing, *A Sermon, delivered at the ordination of the Rev. John Emery Abbot to the pastoral care of the North Church of Christ in Salem; April 20, 1815* (Salem, Mass.: Thomas C. Cushing, 1815), pp. 15, 18.

"one friend to whom": EPP journal [1815-1822], MVWC, p. 28, MHS.

"had no pilot": EPP journal [1815-1822], MVWC, p. 29, MHS.

"revolted ... judge for myself": EPP journal [1815-1822], MVWC, p. 25, MHS.

91   "and find out the *truth* ... commentary on every verse": EPP journal [1815-1822], MVWC, p. 32, MHS.

Christ was human, not divine: Elizabeth's introduction to Socinianism came through Nathaniel Lardner's "Letter on the Logos," as she and others referred to it: Nathaniel Lardner, D.D., "A letter written in the year 1730, concerning the question, whether the logos supplied the place of an human soul in the person of Jesus Christ," (London: 1793). She recalled beginning to read Lardner "with deep prejudice ... but before I got to the end I was deeply & entirely engaged in it. I read it through and through ... [and] it destroyed forever all fear of socinianism." EPP journal [1815-1822], MVWC, pp. 32-33, MHS. She wrote of being inspired, as well, by Lant Carpenter's *Unitarianism the Doctrine of the Gospel: A View of the Scriptural Grounds of Unitarianism* (London: 1811).

91   "like taking hold of hot coals": EPP journal [1815-1822], MVWC, p. 32, MHS.
"with horror . . . clearness in my ideas": EPP journal [1815-1822], MVWC, p. 33, MHS.
"pageant": EPP journal [1815-1822], MVWC, p. 29, MHS.
"the literal humanity of Christ": EPP journal [1815-1822], MVWC, p. 49, MHS.
"my relations were . . . 'degraded' in my ideas": EPP journal [1815-1822], MVWC, p. 45, MHS.
"painful": EPP journal [1815-1822], MVWC, p. 32, MHS.
"alone and unhappy . . . with desperate feeling": EPP journal [1815-1820], MVWC, p. 30, MHS.
"fly into a passion": EPP journal [1815-1822], MVWC, p. 32, MHS.
"much alarmed": EPP journal [1815-1822], MVWC, p. 33, MHS.
"At the end of the time . . . distinctive doctrines of orthodoxy": EPP journal [1815-1822], MVWC, p. 34, MHS.
"corruptions": EPP journal [1815-1822], MVWC, p. 29, MHS.
"the more deeply": EPP journal [1815-1822], MVWC, p. 36, MHS.
"as if I had": EPP journal [1815-1822], MVWC, p. 35, MHS.
"heretical": EPP journal [1815-1822], MVWC, p. 37, MHS.
"had talents . . . worth something": EPP journal [1815-1822], MVWC, p. 31, MHS.

92   "weakened and narrowed": EPP to Maria Chase, April 1820, Peabody Family Papers, Smith.
"take the position": Rem of WEC, p. 34.
"the silence was appalling . . . hardly thirteen years old": Rem of WEC, p. 32.

93   "When word was brought . . . stretched out to take mine": Rem of WEC, pp. 36-37.
"I need not say . . . utter confidence of my sympathy": Rem of WEC, p. 38.
students in divinity at Harvard: Channing's recommended course of study is outlined in Robert D. Richardson, Emerson: The Mind on Fire (Berkeley: University of California Press, 1995), p. 57.
"nothing had been said . . . to the carpet again": EPP journal [1815-1822], MVWC, p. 37, MHS.
"my father & mother found": EPP journal [1815-1822], MVWC, p. 38, MHS. The precise chronology of events in Elizabeth's spiritual quest, covering ages ten to fifteen, is difficult to determine. I have drawn on accounts she gave at various stages of life, each of which contradict the others in certain specifics, but which concur on the general outline of her progress. I have then tried to match these reminiscences (written in her twenties, thirties, sixties, and seventies) with documented events, such as Channing's sermons in Salem and Baltimore, to provide what seems to me the most accurate account. The memoirs I have used include: EPP's journals excerpted in MVWC, Rem of WEC, Lectures in the Training Schools for Kindergartners, and several letters she contributed to William B. Sprague, D.D., Annals of the American Pulpit; or Commemorative Notices of Distinguished American Clergymen of the Various Denominations (New York: Robert Carter and Brothers, 1865), vol. VIII.

PAGE   10. "Beginning to Live"

94   widely published piece of literature: Jack Mendelsohn, Channing: The Reluctant Radical (Boston: Unitarian Universalist Association, 1979), p. 160.
"before the age in Salem": Mrs. EPP to MTP and SAP, July 25, 1834, Berg.

"never should hear . . . instruction for the future": Norman Holmes Pearson, "Elizabeth Peabody on Hawthorne," *Essex Institute Historical Collections,* July 1958, p. 270. Although in this memoir, written for her nephew Julian Hawthorne in the 1880s, Elizabeth writes that she was given the "religious guardianship" of Sophia "when I was ten years old, and very precocious," it seems likely, given the more contemporary evidence of Elizabeth's struggle with her mother through her early teens, that Sophia was the one who was ten years old when Elizabeth was given responsibility for her spiritual education. By then, the family was in agreement with Elizabeth's views.

95   "doubtful": Mrs. EPP to EPP, April 1819, Straker typescripts, p. 105, Antiochiana. Catharine: Although her name has been spelled "Catherine" in several published accounts, it is spelled "Catharine" on her gravestone, Howard Street Cemetery, Salem.

"a tall little girl": MTM, "Reminiscences," Straker typescripts, p. 103, Antiochiana. opium . . . morphine: David T. Courtwright, *Dark Paradise: Opiate Addiction in America Before 1940* (Cambridge, Mass.: Harvard University Press, 1982), p. 45.

"in my young girlhood": SAH to Mrs. EPP, [1852], Julian Hawthorne, *Nathaniel Hawthorne and His Wife* (Hamden, Conn.: Archon Books, 1968, reprint of 1884 edition), vol. I, p. 483.

using it daily: SAP to EPP, April 24, [1838], BANC MSS 72/236Z, Bancroft.

nineteenth-century opium addiction: Alethea Hayter, *Opium and the Romantic Imagination* (Berkeley and Los Angeles: University of California Press, 1968), p. 57.

96   most widely prescribed drug: Courtwright, *Dark Paradise,* p. 45.

"change of character": EPP to MTP, [August 26–30?, 1834], Berg.

"a shadow fell": SAH to MTM, February 3, 1851, Berg.

"pleasant . . . much sorrow": MTP, "Reminiscences," Straker typescripts, p. 103, Antiochiana.

97   "the indulgence of unbridled . . . rankour and malignity": Mrs. EPP to EPP, n.d. ["Sept 1819" in EPP's hand], Straker typescripts, p. 107, Antiochiana.

"excited state": *Rem of WEC,* p. 19.

"self-created mythology": EPP, *Lectures in Training Schools for Kindergartners* (Boston: D. C. Heath, 1897), p. 102.

"suffering from want of clear ideas": EPP journal [1815–1822], MVWC, p. 44, MHS.

"bring forward the minds of the young": EPP journal [1815–1822], MVWC, p. 45, MHS.

"vast deal of *impudence* . . . without much pleasure": EPP to Maria Chase, April 1820, Peabody Family Papers, Smith.

98   "a common calamity . . . first drawn together": EPP to MTP, [August 26–30?, 1834], Berg.

"All the members": MTM to HM Jr., March 27, 1864, Straker typescripts, p. 2416, Antiochiana.

"because they have heard . . . opportunity to search": EPP to Maria Chase, June 14, 1821, Peabody Family Papers, Smith.

99   "the time has gone by . . . whistle for their dues": Dr. NP to Francis Peabody, December 28, 1820, Dartmouth.

brought suit: *Salem Town Records,* minutes of May 14, 1821, meeting, p. 106, reel 1818–1831, Graphic Microfilms of New England, PEM.

100   "We hope we are now": Dr. NP to Francis Peabody, May 17, 1821, Dartmouth.

"LANCASTER BOARDING SCHOOL": *Massachusetts Spy,* May 23, 1821 (Worcester, Mass.).

103   "the brightest spot on the globe": SAP to Maria Chase, April 15, 1825, Peabody Family Papers, Smith.

"the meeting of the waters": Joseph Willard, *Topographical and Historical Sketches of the Town of Lancaster* (Worcester, Mass.: Charles Griffin, 1826), p. 9.

twelve bridges: MTP, "Reminiscences," Straker typescripts, p. 104, Antiochiana. According to Willard, there were more than ten bridges at this time, pp. 5–6.

Nashua River: The information on the town of Lancaster not gleaned from the sisters' own letters comes from the Reverend Abijah P. Marvin, *History of the Town of Lancaster, Massachusetts* (Lancaster, Mass.: Town of Lancaster, 1879), and Willard, *Topographical and Historical Sketches of the Town of Lancaster.*

"mansion": SAP to Maria Chase, April 15, 1825, Peabody Family Papers, Smith.

104   "for exercise": SAP to EPP, May 1822, Berg.

105   "social enjoyments ... fashionable life": Mrs. EPP to EPP, May 5, 1821, Straker typescripts, p. 116, Antiochiana.

by way of Boston: EPP journal [1815–1822], MVWC, p. 49, MHS.

"my eyes ... enchanting valley": EPP journal [1815–1822], MVWC, p. 50, MHS.

"Highly cultivated": EPP to Maria Chase, June 14, 1821, Peabody Family Papers, Smith.

106   "symposia": EPP to Abijah P. Marvin, April 1, [1870s], LHC.

"without her knowing it": EPP to Maria Chase, June 14, 1821, Peabody Family Papers, Smith.

"It was a bright": Octavius Brooks Frothingham, *Memoir of William Henry Channing* (Boston: Houghton Mifflin, 1886), pp. 396–97.

107   "neatness is a duty ... purity in dress": Mrs. EPP to EPP, September 13, 1819, Straker typescripts, p. 110, Antiochiana.

"on the eve of entering ... intellectually from the first": *Rem of WEC*, p. 40.

Amelia Tyler ... earned just $24: Marilyn S. Blackwell, "The Republican Vision of Mary Palmer Tyler," *Journal of the Early Republic*, vol. 12, no. 1, Spring 1992, p. 30.

108   "intensely interested ... heroic deeds": Norman Holmes Pearson, "Elizabeth Peabody on Hawthorne," *Essex Institute Historical Collections*, July 1958, p. 270.

"arithmetic is the exercise": EPP, "My Experience as a Teacher," *Female Education in Massachusetts*, republished from *Barnard's American Journal of Education* (Hartford, Conn.: 1884), p. 295.

"discover and make the rules": EPP to Abijah P. Marvin, April 1, [1870s], LHC.

"touches into life ... recitation of it": EPP, "My Experience as a Teacher," pp. 291–93, 297.

109   "a thorn in her flesh": MTP, "Reminiscences," Straker typescripts, p. 104, Antiochiana.

"many of the most": Sally Schwager, "Educating Women in America," *SIGNS*, vol. 12, no. 2, Winter 1987, p. 345. Schwager references Barbara Miller Solomon's *In the Company of Educated Women: A History of Women and Higher Education in America* (New Haven, Conn.: Yale University Press, 1985) and Anne Firor Scott's "The Ever Widening Circle: The Diffusion of Feminist Values from the Troy Female Seminary, 1822–1872," *History of Education Quarterly*, vol. 19, no. 1, Spring 1979, pp. 3–25.

Paley's ... Sparks's: EPP journal [1815–1822], MVWC, p. 50, MHS.

"catechumen": EPP journal [1815–1822], MVWC, p. 50, MHS.

"women could take": EPP, "Mrs. Elizabeth Palmer Peabody," *Female Education in Massachusetts*, republished from *Barnard's American Journal of Education* (Hartford, Conn.: 1884), p. 309.

110   notoriously rowdy class of 1823: Samuel Eliot Morison, *Three Centuries of Harvard* (Cambridge, Mass.: Harvard University Press, 1936), p. 231.

      "combination against . . . Professor Downing": Pickering Dodge, "Pickering Dodge's Brief Account of the Class of 1823," entry of November 2, 1820, HUD 223.703, HUA.

111   "beautiful": SAP to EPP, May 1822, Berg.

      "consigned for negligence": Faculty Records, vol. IX, entries of December 10, 1821, and March 18, 1822, pp. 283, 292, UAIII 5.5.2, HUA. The Tolman Catalogue of Harvard students identifies the "Brown" referred to in these entries as John F. Brown of Charleston, S.C.

      "the worst crime": EPP to Maria Chase, July 11, 1821, Peabody Family Papers, Smith.

      "the Knight of the fiery spirit": SAP to EPP, July 20, 1823, Berg.

      impromptu dances: MTP, "Reminiscences," Straker typescripts, p. 104, Antiochiana.

      "affair": EPP to [Mrs. EPP], May, 1822, Mrs. EPP copybook, letter 24, Peabody Family Papers, 1790–1880, MHS.

      "L.B.": EPP to MTP, [July] 15, [1834], Berg. Previous biographers believed "L.B." might have been John F. Brown, to whom the Peabodys referred in their letters only as "Brown," or a man named Levi Bridge, whom Elizabeth may have met several years later on a boat to Maine. Robert Lincoln Straker, a biographer of Horace Mann and scholar of the Peabody family, proposed Brown (see his unpublished manuscript "A Gloss Upon Glosses," p. 12, Antiochiana). In *The Peabody Sisters of Salem* (Boston: Little, Brown, 1950), Louise Hall Tharp offers Levi Bridge as "L.B.," a name she discovered by tracing genealogies in Maine. But even she recognized that Levi Bridge, thirty years older than Elizabeth, was not a likely candidate. Tharp adds in an unconventional footnote: "It is my hope that someone reading this book will be moved to look through old letters and records and solve this mystery," p. 343.

      "paid a liberal salary": EPP to Abijah P. Marvin, April 1, [1870s], LHC. This letter, a memoir of Elizabeth's Lancaster days solicited by Marvin in his research for his *History of the Town of Lancaster* (1879), at last offered a full name—Lyman Buckminster—to match the initals "L.B." My research into Buckminster's records at Harvard University Archives combined with occasional remarks in Elizabeth's letters from the spring of 1822 confirm that he was the mystery suitor.

112   Boston Association of Ministers: Boston Association of Ministers, Records, 1755–1960, bMS 71, Record Book 2, entries of May 7, 1821, and June 18, 1821, A-HTL.

      "delight and wonder": *Sermons by the Late Rev. Joseph Stevens Buckminster, with a Memoir of his Life and Character* (Boston: John Eliot, 1814), p. xxi.

      "ever-lamented": EPP to Maria Chase, May 1821, Peabody Family Papers, Smith.

      "with a passion fond": Eliza Buckminster Lee, *Memoirs of Rev. Joseph Buckminster, D.D., and of his son, Rev. Joseph Stevens Buckminster* (Boston: Wm. Crosby and H. P. Nichols, 1849), p. 460.

      "strong and tender": Reverend George M. Adams, *An Historical Discourse on the North Church, Portsmouth, New Hampshire* (Portsmouth, N.H.: Frank W. Robinson, 1871), p. 62.

      "a nameless depression": Lee, *Memoirs of Rev. Joseph Buckminster, D.D., and of his son, Rev. Joseph Stevens Buckminster*, p. 463.

      "was beginning to gather . . . had ever been connected": Lee, *Memoirs of Rev. Joseph Buckminster, D.D., and of his son, Rev. Joseph Stevens Buckminster*, pp. 463–64, 62.

486 NOTES

113   "followed": Adams, *An Historical Discourse on the North Church, Portsmouth, New Hampshire*, p. 63.

His text was Timothy 1:15: Boston Association of Ministers, Records, 1755–1960, bMS 71, Record Book 2, entry of June 18, 1821, A-HTL.

"*our* friend Lyman": EPP to Mrs. EPP, [February 1824], Mrs. EPP copybook, letter 23, Peabody Family Papers, 1790–1880, MHS.

small volume of Virgil: SAP to EPP, April 10, [1829? 1833?], Berg. My date: April 10, [1833].

"came to the point": EPP to [Mrs. EPP], May 1822, Mrs. EPP copybook, letter 24, Peabody Family Papers, 1790–1880, MHS.

"sought and all but *won*": EPP to MTP, [September 20–October 6, 1834], Berg.

"When did you see Alonzo?": EPP to Maria Chase, January 18, 1822, Peabody Family Papers, Smith. This "Alonzo" may have been the poet and town historian Alonzo Lewis (1794–1861) of Lynn, Massachusetts, who published two volumes of poetry in 1823 and 1831, and a *History of Lynn* (Boston: J. H. Eastburn) in 1829, which was reprinted several times throughout the century. During the summer of 1821, Elizabeth had also mentioned Alonzo in a letter to Maria Chase, written from Lancaster on June 14, closing: "Give my love to Anna [Chase?] and to our friend *Alonzo*." Peabody Family Papers, Smith.

married a Frenchwoman: EPP to Maria Chase, April 28, 1822, Peabody Family Papers, Smith.

"go into the world": EPP to Maria Chase, July 11, 1821, Peabody Family Papers, Smith.

114   *Coelebs in Search of a Wife:* Hannah More's novel was first published in England in 1808. For my citations I have used an 1857 edition (New York: Derby and Jackson).

"a directress for his family": More, *Coelebs in Search of a Wife*, p. 48

"You will want . . . you may hire": More, *Coelebs in Search of a Wife*, p. 21

"may rather be said": More, *Coelebs in Search of a Wife*, p. 106.

"modesty and diffidence . . . very much overstrained": EPP to Maria Chase, July 11, 1821, Peabody Family Papers, Smith.

"remarkably healthy": Dr. NP to Isaac and Mary Potter Peabody, January 20, 1822, Dartmouth.

115   "the feast of reason": from Samuel Johnson's *Imitations of Horace*, More, *Coelebs in Search of a Wife*, p. 31.

"high wrought romance . . . published until revised": EPP to Maria Chase, January 18, 1822, Peabody Family Papers, Smith.

116   "would be good for nothing": Mrs. Dorcas Cleveland quoted in Mrs. EPP to EPP, June 1822, Straker typescripts, p. 145, Antiochiana.

"this little Paradise": EPP to Maria Chase, September 22, 1822, Peabody Family Papers, Smith.

Encouraged by Russell Sturgis's father: EPP Brookline journal, entry of May 25, 1826, MVWC, p. 157, MHS. The house was on Mt. Vernon Street.

"in a high heroic mood": Pearson, "Elizabeth Peabody on Hawthorne," p. 271.

"a great man": SAP to EPP, [Lancaster, 1822], Berg 228102B.

consented to marry Lyman Buckminster: "I can have no better example of entire disinterestedness and self-sacrifice for imitation than your own life, for I have not forgotten your story told me of your early trials in school keeping in Boston. Whether such self-denial is *proper* among those who should be as brothers and sisters, I mean the whole human race, helping one another, is a question. Perhaps if you had been married when you had the opportunity, the fortunes of your own and our family would have been different, perhaps prosperous, and I believe it was as much your duty to have been married when you could, as to have toiled for your own and other's subsistence by your personal labors in a single state, unless indeed you preferred a single state." NCP to EPP, April 13, 1838, Straker typescripts, p. 1251, Antiochiana.

117   "mental feasts . . . child of my hopes & prayers": Mrs. EPP to EPP, n.d. [August 1822], Straker typescripts, p. 152, Antiochiana. My date: [May 1822].

PAGE   *12. Boston*

118   "towered . . . islands and vessels": EPP to Maria Chase, May 20, 1822, Peabody Family Papers, Smith.

119   "long and intently": EPP to [Mrs. EPP], May 1822, Mrs. EPP copybook, letter 24, Peabody Family Papers, 1790–1880, MHS.

120   "preparing for mercantile": *Warren Colburn's School for Boys* (broadside, 1820), MHS.

In 1822: *Stimpson's Boston Directory, 1822* (Boston: Charles Stimpson Book-binder, 1822).

"the gentlemen": Dr. NP to Joseph Willard, May 1, 1823, Nathaniel Peabody Papers, PEM.

121   "the focus of all": EPP to Maria Chase, May 20, 1822, Peabody Family Papers, Smith.

"there is a constant stimulus . . . dress and visiting": EPP to Maria Chase, May 1821, Peabody Family Papers, Smith.

"has ever been the resort": EPP to Maria Chase, April 28, 1822, Peabody Family Papers, Smith.

"perfectly graceful and elegant": EPP to [Mrs. EPP], May 1822, Mrs. EPP copybook, letter 24, Peabody Family Papers, 1790–1880, MHS. Martha Dana, Washington Allston's fiancée, was also the first cousin of his first wife, Ann Channing, the older sister of the Reverend William Ellery Channing.

"a man more generally beloved": EPP to Maria Chase, May 1821, Peabody Family Papers, Smith.

"history and characteristics . . . activity among them": EPP letter, June 3, 1854, William B. Sprague, D.D., *Annals of the American Pulpit; or Commemorative Notices of Distinguished American Clergymen of the Various Denominations* (New York: Robert Carter and Brothers, 1865), vol. 8, p. 279.

"paid not a little . . . Cambridge society": EPP to Maria Chase, April 28, 1822, Peabody Family Papers, Smith.

122   "*talking statues* . . . restrained": EPP to Maria Chase, December 30, 1822, Peabody Family Papers, Smith.

danced with George Emerson: EPP to Mrs. EPP, May 1822, Mrs. EPP copybook, letter 35, Peabody Family Papers, 1790–1880, MHS.

"We looked over the library . . . very melancholy": EPP to [Mrs. EPP], May 1822, Mrs. EPP copybook, letter 24, Peabody Family Papers, 1790–1880, MHS.

123   "green carpet . . . like the shadow of a shade": EPP to Maria Chase, May 20, 1822, Peabody Family Papers, Smith.

"painful to look": EPP to [Mrs. EPP], May 1822, Mrs. EPP copybook, letter 24, Peabody Family Papers, 1790–1880, MHS.

debilitating eyestrain: It is possible that Elizabeth's blindness was the result of an untreated infection, such as conjunctivitis, in this era before antibiotics. Yet she mentions no symptoms besides temporary blindness. In recent years, writers attempting to diagnose eye ailments in nineteenth-century literary figures have explored a variety of possibilities, including uveitis, at one time thought to be the result of tuberculosis lodging in the eye. See Robert D. Richardson, *Emerson: The Mind on Fire* (Berkeley: University of California Press, 1995), p. 63. But this diagnosis is considered unlikely by the medical historian C. Michael Samson, M.D., who has found that the incidence of ocular tuberculosis was extremely rare ("Ocular Tuberculosis," article published by the Massachusetts Eye and Ear Infirmary, Ocular Immunology and Uveitis Service, 1998). In the absence of any symptoms of infection, the combination of eyestrain (Elizabeth's own explanation) and psychological stress seems the best explanation for a condition that disappeared as quickly and mysteriously as it arrived. I am grateful to Dr. Carol Zuckerman for directing me to Samson's work.

124   "nothing but the success": Elizabeth Hunt Palmer and Sophia Palmer Pickman to Mary Palmer Tyler, June 27, 1822, VtHS.

"breaking the tenderest . . . may be my trials": EPP to Mrs. EPP, May 1822, Mrs. EPP copybook, letter 35, Peabody Family Papers, 1790–1880, MHS.

"not so varied . . . fresh wind": [EPP] to Mrs. EPP, Boston, 1824, Mrs. EPP copybook, letter 17, Peabody Family Papers, 1790–1880, MHS. My date: [ca. June 1822].

125   "opposite each other . . . any other conversation: EPP, "Emerson as Preacher," F. B. Sanborn, ed., *The Genius and Character of Emerson* (Port Washington, N.Y.: Kennikat Press, 1971, reprint of 1885 edition), p. 150.

126   "very ugly": EPP to Maria Chase, May 1821, Peabody Family Papers, Smith.

"most popular . . . immense fortune": EPP to Maria Chase, June 12, 1822, Peabody Family Papers, Smith.

Andrews Norton had married: EPP to Maria Chase, May 1821, Peabody Family Papers, Smith.

127   "literally *ruining*": MTP to EPP, June 6, 1822, Berg.

unfortunate habit: NCP Genealogies, Straker typescripts, p. 5425/35, Antiochiana.

glasses from Mrs. Cleveland: SAP to EPP, June 1822, Berg.

"spectacles shone . . . sick at heart": SAP to EPP, July 23, 1822, Berg.

"future usefulness . . . retard her progress": Mrs. EPP to EPP, June 1822, Straker typescripts, p. 145, Antiochiana.

"when he came on": SAP to EPP, June 11, 1822, Berg.

"every smooth tree": SAP to EPP, May 1822, Berg.

128   "If we do not . . . *Frank Dana?*": SAP to EPP, June 11, 1822, Berg.

"delicacy of your situation . . . on the watch": Mrs. EPP to EPP, June 1822, Straker typescripts, p. 145, Antiochiana.

"not as a *child* . . . a serious thing": EPP to SAP, June 23, 1822, in series "60 a.l. EPP to SAP," Berg.

"Miss Elizabeth P. Peabody, D.D.": SAP to EPP, May 11, [1824?], Berg.

"lot . . . minds of *girls*": EPP to SAP, June 23, 1822, in series "60 a.l. EPP to SAP," Berg.

"fondness for dwelling . . . authors upon this subject": EPP to Maria Chase, October 6, 1822, Peabody Family Papers, Smith.

129   "mind has no sex . . . mathematical reasoning": EPP to SAP, June 23, 1822, in series "60 a.l. EPP to SAP," Berg.

"horse & chaise": John S. Tyler to Joseph Willard, Esq., September 15, 1822, Nathaniel Peabody Papers, PEM.

"we knew nothing . . . more experienced than yourself": Sophia Dana quoted in May Elizabeth [Dana] to EPP and MTP, September 1822, HMII Papers, MHS.

130   "one of my old tricks": Dr. NP to Joseph Willard, May 11, 1823, Nathaniel
           Peabody Papers, PEM.
           "very industrious . . . worthy": Dr. NP to Francis Peabody, April 23, 1822, Dartmouth.
           "honestly straining": Dr. NP to Joseph Willard, May 1, 1823, Nathaniel Peabody
           Papers, PEM.
           "dead weight": Dr. NP to Joseph Willard, December 22, 1822, Nathaniel Peabody
           Papers, PEM.
           "pacify Lancaster folks . . . *suing mania*": Dr. NP to Joseph Willard, November 20,
           1822, Nathaniel Peabody Papers, PEM.
           "get along": Dr. NP in letter by various Peabody family members to GFP, Octo-
           ber 14, [1837], Straker typescripts, p. 1218, Antiochiana.
           "firmness of constitution . . . destructive of usefulness": Mrs. EPP to EPP, Thurs-
           day, November 1822, Straker typescripts, p. 159, Antiochiana.
131   "Your countenance . . . reinstate it": Dr. NP to EPP, April 17, 1823, Straker type-
           scripts, p. 166, Antiochiana.
           In March 1823, Elizabeth strained: Dr. NP to Francis Peabody, March 6, 1823,
           Dartmouth.
           Dr. Peabody told his lawyer: Dr. NP to Joseph Willard, March 27, 1823, Nathaniel
           Peabody Papers, PEM.
           hinted to Elizabeth: Dr. NP quoted in Mrs. EPP to EPP, n.d., "Fast Day," Straker
           typescripts, p. 165, Antiochiana.
           "It is a little more necessary . . . carelessness in your person": Dr. NP to EPP,
           April 17, 1823, Straker typescripts, p. 166, Antiochiana.
           "turban . . . expect to make my fortune": Elizabeth Hunt Palmer to EPP, April 23,
           1823, Straker typescripts, p. 167, Antiochiana.
           "few young men": Louisa Davis Minot to Mrs. R[obert] H[allowell] Gardiner,
           May 11, 1823, Education Collection, Smith.
132   "in spite of fate": "Sarah" quoted in MTP to Lydia Haven, June 20, 1833, MTP
           Correspondence, MHS.
           "I sent for his bill . . . stream of eloquence": EPP, "Emerson as Preacher," p. 150.
           "If any [woman] is raised": John T. Kirkland to EPP, May 17, 1823, MVWC, p. 60,
           MHS.

PAGE   *13. Maine*

133   Plymouth Company: Robert H. Gardiner, "History of the Kennebec Purchase,"
           Collections of the Maine Historical Society (Portland: Published for the Society, 1847),
           vol. II, p. 269 ff, and Gordon E. Kershaw, *The Kennebeck Proprietors, 1749–1775*
           (Portland: Maine Historical Society, 1975).
           Lydia Maria Child: See Deborah Pickman Clifford, *Crusader for Freedom: A Life of
           Lydia Maria Child* (Boston: Beacon Press, 1992), pp. 20–33.
           Joseph Priestley . . . William Enfield: MVWC, pp. 38–40, MHS.
134   Suffering religious prejudice . . . Kennebec properties in 1797: Mary Vaughan
           Marvin, *Benjamin Vaughan, 1751–1835* (Hallowell, Me.: Hallowell Printing, 1979).
           "An English family . . . comfort and plenty": Marvin, *Benjamin Vaughan*, p. 60.
135   "metaphysical class": EPP to SAP, December 24, 1823, in series "60 a.l. EPP to
           SAP," Berg.
           education of his own daughters: MTP to Mary Tyler, January 1824, VtHS.
           Town House: H. K. Baker, ed., *The Hallowell Book* (Hallowell, Me.: Hallowell Reg-
           ister Press, 1902), p. 19.

135   wrote home advising her protégée: EPP to Mrs. EPP, [before July 20, 1823], Mrs.
EPP copybook, letter 25, Peabody Family Papers, 1790–1880, MHS. In his *Letters of EPP*, Bruce Ronda incorrectly dates this letter September 1823, p. 65.
"little white lyceum": SAP to EPP, September 21–27, 1823, Berg.
take in $600: Dr. NP to Francis Peabody, August 16, 1823, Dartmouth.

136   several young collegians: EPP's beaus on packet and steamboat from Portland to
Boston were Moses Whittier and a Mr. Bridge: EPP to SAP, December 24, 1823,
in series "60 a.l. EPP to SAP," Berg.
"Blues . . . talk loud": EPP to Maria Chase, October 4, 1823, Peabody Family
Papers, Smith. The original Bluestocking Club, from which American clubs bor-
rowed the name, was a group of British writers—Elizabeth Montague, Elizabeth
Vesey, Hester Thrale, Hannah More, and Fanny Burney—who met regularly for
intellectual discussion in the late eighteenth century. The club was given its
name by derisive outsiders who took note of the unusual blue worsted stockings
worn by Benjamin Stillingfleet, one of the few men in the group. See Susan
Branson's account of American literary salons, *These Fiery Frenchified Dames:
Women and Political Culture in Early National Philadelphia* (Philadelphia: University
of Pennsylvania Press, 2001), p. 127. Mary Kelley's "'A More Glorious Revolution': Women's Antebellum Reading Circles and the Pursuit of Public Influence,"
New England Quarterly, vol. 76, no. 2, June 2003, pp. 163–96, gives a fuller account of groups such as the Hallowell Blues. Within a few years of these meetings in Hallowell, the term "bluestocking" became associated with women agitating for rights, so that by 1826 Mary Peabody commented, on meeting the
novelist Catharine Maria Sedgwick, "She is perfectly unassuming, and perfectly
charming—without a tinge of blue." MTP to Maria Chase, November 10, 1826,
Peabody Family Papers, Smith.
"Haggard students": [EPP], "Blue-Stocking Club," Baker, ed., *The Hallowell Book*,
p. 19.
"bright, penetrating . . . Methodist enthusiast of Bath": EPP to Maria Chase, October 4, 1823, Peabody Family Papers, Smith.
"particular friend": EPP to Maria Chase, May 31, 1824, Peabody Family Papers,
Smith.
"accused of indifference . . . under a little restraint": EPP to SAP, December 24,
1823, in series "60 a.l. EPP to SAP," Berg. Although Elizabeth referred to the
book as Professor Frisbie's *Fragments*, she was probably reading from Andrews
Norton, ed., *A Collection of the Miscellaneous Writings of Professor Frisbie: with Some
Notices of His Life and Character* (Boston: Cummings, Hilliard, 1823).

137   "reinstated . . . *un*favorable ones": Dr. NP postscript to Mrs. EPP to EPP, December 14, 1823, Straker typescripts, p. 191, Antiochiana.
"the decencies of dress": Mrs. EPP to EPP, August 1823, Straker typescripts, p.
176, Antiochiana.
abruptly resigned: EPP to SAP, December 24, 1823, in series "60 a.l. EPP to SAP,"
Berg.
"precious apparatus": EPP to Maria Chase, May 31, 1824, Peabody Family Papers,
Smith.

138   "Let me urge . . . storms from without": Mrs. EPP to EPP, [May? June?] 1823,
Straker typescripts, p. 174, Antiochiana.
"wants to go *very* . . . *I* come to teach": SAP to EPP, [October 9, 1823], in series
"20 a.l.s. SAP to EPP," Berg 228172B.
"The demon in my head . . . grows *worse*": SAP to EPP, October [1823?], Berg.

"real blue . . . beat me out and out": EPP to Maria Chase, May 31, 1824, Peabody Family Papers, Smith.

139   "we never did such a thing": MTP to Mrs. EPP, June [1824], Mrs. EPP copybook, letter 18, Peabody Family Papers, 1790–1880, MHS.

first poem in almost twenty-five: [Mrs. EPP], "The Indian," *The Friend of Peace* (Cambridge, Mass.: Hilliard and Metcalf), vol. III, no. XII, April 1824, pp. 378–79. The poem strongly condemned the U.S. government's treatment of American Indians. Coincidentally, this journal was edited by the same Noah Worcester whose controversial *Bible News* had set in motion the Peabody family's religious inquiries over a decade earlier. NCP identifies "The Indian" as Mrs. EPP's work, although it was published anonymously. NCP Genealogies, Straker typescripts, p. 5425/16, Antiochiana.

Dr. Peabody had also published during 1824. *The Art of Preserving Teeth* (Salem, Mass.: Joshua and John D. Cushing) was a pamphlet meant primarily to establish his expertise as a dentist. Its thirty-two pages were full of useful and detailed advice on everything from brushing teeth to extractions. Typically, however, he began with an introductory statement so self-deprecatory and cranky that readers, let alone prospective patients, may have been put off. "The Author," he wrote, "has stated nothing, but what is grounded upon the result of a number of years' experience and critical observations, and has been careful not to raise expectations, which cannot be satisfied." He warned those who already knew the importance of cleaning teeth that they might find much of the pamphlet "minute and tedious," and added that there would be nothing "to assist the professional Dentist" either. And finally, "There is another class of people which the following work is not expected to benefit. I mean those, who are either so ignorant, or so skeptical, that they cannot or will not be informed, or who think, that every one, who pretends to benefit teeth, by operating upon them, does it, as a mere trade to get money by, without any principle of honesty, and as a juggler or mountebank."

"Rise Genius of Freedom!": Mrs. EPP copied her "Ode Sung on the Fourth of July" into a journal she began keeping later in the decade. The poem appears after an entry dated June 18, 1830, the day after another patriotic holiday nearly as significant in Massachusetts at the time as July 4: Bunker Hill Day. Peabody Family Papers, 1790–1880, MHS.

140   "Gardiner": Robert Hallowell Gardiner, *Early Recollections of Robert Hallowell Gardiner* (Hallowell, Me.: White and Horne, 1936).

"most elegant . . . very cold": EPP to Mrs. EPP, June 20, [1824], Mrs. EPP copybook, letter 20, Peabody Family Papers, 1790–1880, MHS.

"wind . . . windings": MTM, "Reminiscences of School Life and Teaching," *Female Education in Massachusetts,* republished from *Barnard's American Journal of Education* (Hartford, Conn.: 1884), pp. 311, 314.

141   "an injury to the public . . . flow of soul": EPP to Maria Chase, September 3, 1824, Peabody Family Papers, Smith.

"more acquainted . . . better than I do": MTP to Mrs. EPP, n.d., Mrs. EPP copybook, letter 22, Peabody Family Papers, 1790–1880, MHS. My date: [ca. September 14, 1824].

"learn French . . . into everything": SAP to EPP, August 4, 1824, Berg.

Unitarian controversy struck Maine: The arrival of the Reverend Dantworth in Hallowell had this effect. *Rem of WEC,* pp. 42–50.

"missionaries": *Rem of WEC,* p. 50.

142   lecture on sulphur: EPP to NCP or GFP, February 1, [1825], Mrs. EPP copybook

letter 7, Peabody Family Papers, 1790–1880, MHS. Mrs. Peabody had been pleased to hear that Elizabeth would be learning chemistry from a college professor, which she assumed would help Elizabeth to teach the subject herself. The occasion prompted one of her many astute pedagogical observations: "Nothing is a surer death-blow to the promotion of a love of science, in the mind of a child, than long and confused explanations." Mrs. EPP to EPP and MTP, October 4, 1824, Straker typescripts, p. 252, Antiochiana.

The winter of 1824 to 1825 may have been the period during which, Elizabeth wrote "I once studied chemistry with a great enthusiasm in Dr. Thompson's large work in which experiments are described—and I went over these in my imagination & enjoyed it infinitely. For years after I knew the proportions of everything to the very decimal expression of the facts": EPP to Horace Mann, Jr., January 1, 1862, Straker typescripts, p. 2291, Antiochiana.

142   "death-like stillness . . . almost in a whisper": MTP to Maria Chase, September 14, [1824], Peabody Family Papers, Smith.

"dejected and melancholly . . . equal to those of his brother": "Records of the Class of 1815," HUD 215.777, HUA.

"horrid feelings . . . agonize": EPP to MTP, [July] 15, [1834], Berg.

"neglect of externals . . . purity of the heart": EPP quoted in Mrs. Susan Channing to EPP, June 20, 1824, MVWC, p. 70, MHS.

"tedious toils": EPP quoted in Mrs. Susan Channing to EPP, June 20, 1824, MVWC, p. 71, MHS.

other accusations: EPP quoted in Mrs. Susan Channing to EPP, April 4, 1825, MVWC, p. 73, MHS.

"paralysing effect": EPP quoted in Mrs. Susan Channing to EPP, June 20, 1824, MVWC, p. 70, MHS.

143   "ridiculed . . . in perfect taste": EPP Brookline journal, entry of June 23, 1826, MVWC, pp. 172–73, MHS.

On January 22, the desperately depressed: "Records of the Class of 1815," HUD 215.777, HUA.

Vital Records: The account of Lyman Buckminster's death on January 22, 1825, reads: "by discharging a gun the contents of which went into his mouth and out at the back of his head." Vital Records of Norton, Massachusetts, to the Year 1850 (Boston: New England Historic Genealogical Society, 1906), p. 360.

"poor LB . . . dead weight on my heart": EPP to MTP, [July] 15, [1834], Berg.

"steamboat beaux": EPP to SAP, December 24, 1823, in series "60 a.l. EPP to SAP," Berg.

"blasts . . . how to torment me": EPP Brookline journal, "Friday," 1826, MVWC, p. 80, MHS.

144   "power over my mind": EPP Brookline journal, entry of July [June] 10, 1826, MVWC, p. 163, MHS.

"never experienced a calamity": EPP Brookline journal, entry of October 20, 1825, MVWC, p. 136, MHS.

"infinite indolence": EPP Brookline journal, "Friday," 1826, MVWC, p. 80, MHS.

"There are some things the prosperous": EPP Brookline journal, entry of June 23, 1826, MVWC, p. 173, MHS.

"I wish I had the blessed faculty . . . dash into the middle": EPP Brookline journal, ca. 1825, MVWC, p. 114, MHS.

"gives my voice a tone": EPP Brookline journal, ca. 1825, MVWC, p. 115, MHS.

"misery": EPP Brookline journal, entry of July [June] 10, 1826, MVWC, p. 163, MHS.

"steeped in a fountain": EPP Brookline journal, entry of June 22, 1826, MVWC, p. 171, MHS.

"Had I lived two years more": EPP to MTP, May 18, [1824], Peabody Family Papers, Smith.

"an era in my life": *Rem of WEC*, pp. 73–74.

PAGE
14. "I Am Always My Own Heroine"

147 "weakened by light reading": Mrs. EPP to EPP, June 1822, Straker typescripts, p. 146, Antiochiana.

"contended with obstacles": MTM ms. novel, "The Traffords," HM Papers, MHS.

"What is life": MTP to Miss Rawlins Pickman, January 19, 1829, HMII Papers, MHS.

"delicious . . . reverie": MTP to Miss Rawlins Pickman, October 3, 1827, HMII Papers, MHS.

"imaginary world": MTP to HM, n.d. [September 1834], HM Papers, MHS.

"all things present": MTP to Miss Rawlins Pickman, October 3, 1827, HMII Papers, MHS.

"I am always my own heroine": MTP to Lydia Sears Haven, June 20, 1833, MTP Correspondence, MHS.

"plainness . . . curved mouth": SAH to MTM, February 3, 1851, Berg.

148 "called beautiful": [MTM], "An Experience," n.d., HM Papers, MHS. The strictures against vanity were so severe that it was only in this thinly fictionalized autobiographical fragment that Mary could admit to her beauty. See Megan Marshall, ed., "Mary Peabody Mann's Short Story, 'An Experience,'" *Massachusetts Historical Society Proceedings*, vol. 98 (1986), pp. 78–89.

"think I came to see him": MTP to EPP, June 6, 1822, Berg.

"careless, kindly, improvident . . . her heart clung": Mrs. Alexander [pseudonym for Annie French Hector], *The Wooing o't* (New York: A. L. Burt, [18——]), p. 32.

North Church choir: *The First Centenary of the North Church and Society, in Salem, Massachusetts, Commemorated July 19, 1872, Salem* (Salem, Mass.: Printed for the Society, 1873), p. 149. According to the same publication, MTP joined the North Church in 1823, SAP in 1827.

"the highest moments": MTM to HM, January 12, 1850, HM Papers, MHS.

149 "one half of a large": NCP Genealogies, Straker typescripts, p. 5425/20, Antiochiana.

"we had no fearful associations": MTM, "Reminiscences of School Life and Teaching," *Female Education in Massachusetts*, republished from *Barnard's American Journal of Education* (Hartford, Conn.: 1884), p. 313.

sole heir to her father's share: Joan M. Maloney, "Mary Toppan Pickman: The Education of a Salem Gentlewoman, 1820–1850," *Essex Institute Historical Collections*, vol. 123, no. 1, January 1987, p. 5.

150 "merciless . . . love the very act of study": MTM, "Reminiscences of School Life and Teaching," pp. 315–16.

"literary paper": MTP to Mary Tyler, January 1824, VtHS.

Salem Recorder: SAP to EPP, July 4–7, [1823], Berg.

"the Spinster's Review": EPP to Maria Chase, March 18, 1824, Peabody Family Papers, Smith.

"poetry, essays . . . the North American": MTP to Mary Tyler, January 1824, VtHS. Three years earlier, in 1821, the seventeen-year-old Nathaniel Hawthorne had

produced several issues of a similar handwritten newspaper he called *The Spectator*, in imitation of Addison and Steele's celebrated publication of the same
name. Hawthorne wrote all the articles and poetry himself and seems to have
distributed the paper only to family and friends in Salem.

150 Sophia wrote poetry: MTP to Mary Tyler, January 1824, VtHS.
analysis of Thomas Brown's philosophy: EPP to MTP, March 18, 1824, Peabody
Family Papers, Smith.
"the equality of the female . . . darn stockings!": MTP to Mary Tyler, January
1824, VtHS.

151 "all the heart-rending": MTP to Mrs. EPP, n.d. [ca. September 14, 1824], Mrs. EPP
copybook, letter 22, Peabody Family Papers, 1790–1880, MHS.
"the hard duty": Mrs. EPP to EPP, April 9, 1824, Straker typescripts, p. 210, Antiochiana.
"novels more than . . . purity of character": Mrs. EPP to EPP, February [1824],
Straker typescripts, pp. 198–99, Antiochiana.
"so much of the wickedness": Mrs. EPP to EPP, April 9, 1824, Straker typescripts,
p. 210, Antiochiana.
"safty I mean": Mrs. EPP to EPP, [June] 1823, Straker typescripts, p. 174, Antiochiana.
"take a chamber": EPP to MTP, March 18, [1824], Peabody Family Papers, Smith.
"riding along in a stage coach . . . I forgot the gal": Horatio Bridge quoted in *The
Letters, 1813–1843*, p. 689, n. 2. By chance, Horatio Bridge, a friend of Nathaniel
Hawthorne's on his way to Bowdoin College, was riding in the same coach, and
was able to tell the story many years later. He was the one to remember Mary as
"a young and extremely pretty girl of 18 or 19," who sat so quietly that the two
men on her right and a third to her left forgot she was there. By modern standards, this episode is hardly alarming. But in 1824 it was shocking enough for
Mary's traveling companion to remember for half a century and then recite in
detail when he heard once again of Mary Peabody, who had been marked indeli-
bly in his mind as "the gal of the stage coach story."
    By contrast, Elizabeth had "a delightful journey" later the same year in the
company of a Mr. Longfellow, "whom she admired extremely," probably Stephen
Longfellow, a Bowdoin trustee and the father of Henry Wadsworth Longfellow,
then a student at Bowdoin College. The man was "a most *delightsome* character &
he was very- very- very kind and attentive & fatherly in his attentions to me the
two days I rode with him," Elizabeth wrote to Mary. Perhaps Elizabeth's gregarious nature was the chief difference between her delightful ride and Mary's
dreadful one. SAP and EPP to MTP, Salem, [late November or early December
1824], SAP copybook "letters from home," Berg.
"the horrors . . . How she screamed!": MTP to Mrs. EPP, April 10, [1824], Mrs.
EPP copybook, Peabody Family Papers, 1790–1880, MHS.

152 "over-refined and unapproachable": MTP to SAP, July 7, 1825, Peabody Family
Papers, Smith.
"villainy of man": Mrs. EPP to EPP, April 9–12, 1824, Straker typescripts, p. 210,
Antiochiana.
"You must forego . . . your scholars by gentleness": Mrs. EPP to MTP, April 18,
1824, SAP copybook "letters from home," Berg.
"walls were oppressive to me": MTM and EPP, *Moral Culture of Infancy, and
Kindergarten Guide* (Boston: T.O.H.P. Burnham; New York: O. S. Felt, 1863), p. 114.
A large portion of this book is made up of a series of letters that Mary wrote,

probably in the late 1830s, to a former student who was beginning her teaching career.

"all the people are prepared": MTP to Mrs. EPP, May 1825, Mrs. EPP copybook, letter 19, Peabody Family Papers, 1790–1880, MHS.

15. *"There Is No Scandal in Brookline"*

153   "serpentine paths": MTP to Maria Chase, n.d. [summer 1825], Peabody Family Papers, Smith.

"there is no scandal in Brookline": MTP to Mrs. EPP, May 1825, Mrs. EPP copybook, letter 19, Peabody Family Papers, 1790–1880, MHS.

$4 a week: Susan Channing to EPP, April 4, 1825, MVWC, p. 72, MHS.

$500 a year: MTP to Miss Rawlins Pickman, Brookline, March 22, [1826], HMII Papers, MHS.

boarded with a shoemaker's family: The Tolman house is one of just a few modest residences of the era still standing in Brookline: Harriet F. Woods, *Historical Sketches of Brookline, Massachusetts* (Boston: R. S. Davis, 1874), pp. 149–50.

154   "proposed being a horse ... *feelings* again": MTP to Maria Chase, n.d., "Sunday eve 10 o'clock," [June? 1825], Peabody Family Papers, Smith.

155   "his arms flung ... not time to take off": EPP to ?, [June 1825], Mrs. EPP copybook 16, Peabody Family Papers, 1790–1880, MHS; Elizabeth's annotated program is held by the Morristown National Historical Park, Morristown, N.J.

"nobody but gentlemen ... 'kicked up the row'": EPP to ?, [June 1825], Mrs. EPP copybook, letter 15, Peabody Family Papers, 1790–1880, MHS.

"the ineffable light": EPP to Mrs. EPP, [June 1825], Mrs. EPP copybook, letter 30, Peabody Family Papers, 1790–1880, MHS.

"If I could put in a letter": MTP to Maria Chase, n.d. [summer 1825], Peabody Family Papers, Smith.

"gracious time ... spiritual communion": EPP to MTM, August 14, 1882, Straker typescripts, p. 3319, Antiochiana.

"intimate ... playmate only": SAH to MTM, February 3, 1851, Berg.

156   "roaring": MTP to SAP, July 7, 1825, Peabody Family Papers, Smith.

"a little chaos": MTP to Mrs. EPP, May 1825, Mrs. EPP copybook, letter 19, Peabody Family Papers, 1790–1880, MHS.

"quite crazed ... dancing jigs": MTP to Maria Chase, October 28, 1826, Peabody Family Papers, Smith.

usually woke slowly: EPP Brookline journal, entry dated July 9, 1825, by MVWC, p. 78, MHS. My date: July 9, [1826].

"E[lizabeth] has spirit enough": MTP to Lydia Sears, November 15, 1826, Berg.

"that favorite of fortune": SAP to MTP, Salem, [late November or early December], 1824, SAP copybook "letters from home," Berg.

"A mind like yours": Mrs. EPP to MTP, 1824, SAP copybook "letters from home," Berg.

"a source of daily ... marked out for you": Mrs. EPP to EPP and MTP, June 5, 1824, Straker typescripts, p. 237, Antiochiana.

Elizabeth-inspired regimen: MTP to Mrs. EPP, ca. October 1824, Mrs. EPP copybook, letter 21, Peabody Family Papers, 1790–1880, MHS.

157   "her sentiments": MTP to Miss Rawlins Pickman, July 21, 1826, HMII Papers, MHS.

157 "no woman of sensibility ... redeem": MTP to Miss Rawlins Pickman, January 27, 1825, HMII Papers, MHS. My date: January 27, [1826].
"dry French and Latin verbs": MTP to SAP, July 7, 1825, Peabody Family Papers, Smith.
"time seem[ed] to droop": MTP to Miss Rawlins Pickman, July 21, 1826, HMII Papers, MHS.
"fearful experiment ... reaction of dullness": EPP to SAP, August 23, 1825, in series "60 a.l. EPP to SAP," Berg.

158 "may I be preserved": EPP Brookline journal, ca. August 25, 1825, MVWC, p. 91, MHS.
"in itself a summer": MTP to Miss Rawlins Pickman, October 15, 1825, HMII Papers, MHS.
"laziness": MTP to Maria Chase, September 14, [1824], Peabody Family Papers, Smith.

159 "I take my [needle]work": MTP to Lydia Sears Haven, May 26, 1832, Straker typescripts, p. 598, Antiochiana. Mary's recollection begins: "It is like Brookline days when we lived in the schoolroom and slept under the roof."
"an era in my life": Rem of WEC, pp. 73–74.
"His voice so unexpectedly ... Of course I went": EPP Brookline journal, entry of October 12, 1825, MVWC, pp. 121–22, MHS.
short walk to Channing's ... early age: EPP gives further accounts of her first visit to WEC's house as an adult in her Rem of WEC, pp. 52, 60 ff. The passages from EPP's Brookline journal transcribed in MVWC, pp. 121–22, MHS, confirm that this meeting took place as described in Rem of WEC.

160 "Each of us felt ... demonstration of principles": Rem of WEC, p. 251.
"religion, manners, dress ... for a whole hour": MTP to Miss Rawlins Pickman, October 30, 1825, HMII Papers, MHS.

161 "beauty ... mere neatness": Rem of WEC, pp. 105–106.
"her very beautifullest": MTP to Mrs. EPP, March 1826, Mrs. EPP copybook, letter 34, Peabody Family Papers, 1790–1880, MHS.
"long apprenticeship": Rem of WEC, p. 367.
"spoke of me affectionately": EPP Brookline journal, entry of October 12, 1825, MVWC, p. 133, MHS.
"expressed a wish": EPP Brookline journal, entry of October 20, 1825, MVWC, p. 136, MHS.
"persons ... of a timid disposition ... common creed": William B. Sprague, D.D., Annals of the American Pulpit; or Commemorative Notices of Distinguished American Clergymen of the Various Denominations (New York: Robert Carter and Brothers, 1865), vol. 8, p. 380.
"talked to him as none else": MTP to Mrs. EPP, January 8, 1826, Mrs. EPP copybook, letter 32, Peabody Family Papers, 1790–1880, MHS.
"my peculiarity to sound": EPP Brookline journal, entry of May 13, 1826, MVWC, p. 148, MHS.
"so filled with painful ... naked will": Rem of WEC, pp. 73–74.

162 "forget this bitter": Rem of WEC, p. 130.
"bring the mind ... more hopeful": Rem of WEC, p. 244.
transcendental ... "Divinity": Rem of WEC, p. 364.
"gazing on me ... impression on me": Rem of WEC, p. 127.

163 "one would prefer": EPP Brookline journal, entry of December 20, 1825, MVWC, p. 139, MHS.

"She has been living": MTP to Maria Chase, March 8, 1826, Peabody Family Papers, Smith.

"She sits with a ream": MTP to Maria Chase, [December 1825?], Peabody Family Papers, Smith.

"the first year of my intellectual life": EPP to Orestes Brownson, [ca. 1840], *Letters of EPP*, p. 248. Here Elizabeth explains that her "articles on the Hebrew Scriptures" were "published in the Christian Examiner in 1834—but *written* in 1826."

164   "free paraphrase . . . moral truth-speaking": EPP, "Emerson as Preacher," F. B. Sanborn, ed., *The Genius and Character of Emerson: Lectures at the Concord School of Philosophy* (Port Washington, N.Y.: Kennikat Press, 1971, reprint of 1885 edition), p. 151.

"original thoughts . . . mingled terror & delight": EPP to Mrs. Benjamin Guild, [1838], MVWC, p. 341, MHS.

"in the poetical vein . . . see himself *good*": EPP, "Spirit of the Hebrew Scriptures —No. I. The Creation," *Christian Examiner* no. LXII (New Series no. XXXII), May 1834, p. 199.

165   "every one of us . . . inward revelation": EPP, "The Creation," pp. 190–91; "*inalienable, absolute being*," p. 201; "moral equality of woman and man," p. 195; "the social principle . . . rooted": pp. 188–89; "It is the consciousness": pp. 189–90; "recognition of personal identity . . . power of choosing": p. 200. I am grateful to Phyllis Cole, Emerson scholar and biographer of Mary Moody Emerson, for conversations that greatly enhanced my understanding of these texts.

"*transcendentalism* . . . being an author": EPP to Orestes Brownson, [ca. 1840], *Letters of EPP*, p. 248. In this letter, which Elizabeth wrote to accompany the unpublished fourth essay of the series that she hoped Brownson would consider for his *Boston Quarterly Review*—sixteen years after it was written, six years after the first three essays appeared in the *Christian Examiner* in 1834 (only to be censored by the editor, Andrews Norton)—Elizabeth explained: "even then [1834] the questions that have since been so warmly discussed as to inspiration miracles &c had not been brought up in our community—& the word *transcendentalism* I never had seen except in Coleridge's [F]riend. Had not Mr Norton cut off untimely my little series which consisted of six numbers, it would have [been] recorded quite a little historical fact, [that] there in the bosom of Unitarianism, an unlearned girl, with only the help of those principles of philosophizing she gathered from the perusal of Coleridge's [F]riend, & . . . relying simply on her own poetical apprehension, as a principle of exegesis, should have seen just what is here expressed."

"thoughts of my own": EPP journal, n.d., MVWC, p. 213, MHS.

"what is in my heart . . . dare not ask advice": EPP to William Wordsworth, December 9, 1825. Margaret Neussendorfer, ed., "Elizabeth Palmer Peabody to William Wordsworth: Eight Letters, 1825–1845," *Studies in the American Renaissance 1984* (Charlottesville: University Press of Virginia), pp. 183–84. On June 17, 1827, Elizabeth added a postscript before mailing her letter: "I have kept the above letter since its first date—endeavouring to get courage to send it."

166   "older young ladies . . . principle of life": *Rem of WEC*, p. 148.

"the Development . . . as he actually was": EPP Brookline journal, entry of November 11, 1825, MVWC, pp. 137–38, MHS.

"taking children out of": *Rem of WEC*, p. 266.

"In every instance . . . grow with his": *Rem of WEC*, pp. 148–49.

167   "we were studying together": *Rem of WEC*, p. 279.

"the view of the mind . . . foundation of Religion": EPP Brookline journal, entry of November 11, 1825, MVWC, pp. 137–38, MHS.

"Domestic affections . . . of the muses": EPP Brookline journal, entry of December 23, 1825, MVWC, p. 142, MHS. In another instance in which a disgruntled Brookline father questioned her methods, however, Elizabeth held her ground. This man "came to me, very seriously to remonstrate with me for 'not teaching English grammar,'" Elizabeth wrote. She invited him to study the passage from Thomson's *Seasons* that the class was to discuss the following day and to observe the class pursue an "examination of words" under Elizabeth's guidance. "After the lesson was over, the gentleman said I had conquered his doubts and fears; that he had never passed a more intellectual hour, or received a more thorough lesson in grammatical analysis." EPP, "My Experience as a Teacher," *Female Education in Massachusetts,* republished from *Barnard's American Journal of Education* (Hartford, Conn.: 1884), p. 292.

168   "I heard from them . . . unkind and ungenerous": EPP Brookline journal, entry of May 12, 1826, MVWC, pp. 146–47, MHS.

"coming to me with . . . shrink from": EPP Brookline journal, entry of May 17, 1826, MVWC, p. 154, MHS.

"with tenfold force . . . unprotected by home": EPP Brookline journal, entry of May 12, 1826, MVWC, pp. 147–48, MHS.

"injured in that reputation": EPP Brookline journal, entry of May 27, 1826, MVWC, p. 162, MHS.

"unaccountably depressed": EPP Brookline journal, entry of May 27, 1826, MVWC, p. 161, MHS.

"atrocious and contemptible . . . large letters on my forehead": EPP Brookline journal, entry of May 17, 1826, MVWC, pp. 149–50, MHS.

169   "poet-prophet": EPP to Maria Chase, March 16, 1826, Peabody Family Papers, Smith.

"my own friends": EPP journal, entry of September 22, 1826, [Salem], MVWC, p. 197, MHS.

"I don't think you ever . . . all the delightfuls": MTP to Miss Rawlins Pickman, June 7, 1826, HMII Papers, MHS.

"fierce . . . tiger": MTP to Miss Rawlins Pickman, April 16, 1826, HMII Papers, MHS.

"never was in love": MTP to Miss Rawlins Pickman, January 27, 1825, HMII Papers, MHS. My date: January 27, [1826]. Evidently Francis had modeled one of her characters in *The Rebels* on the Reverend Mather Byles (1707–1788) of Boston, who had been imprisoned for his loyalty to England during the Revolution. Her portrayal angered Byles's two surviving daughters; they claimed that Francis had questioned them extensively about their father without telling them that she intended to use the material in her book. When Francis sent a written apology and asked to meet with them, the Byles sisters responded with "a very dry note, refusing to see her . . . & saying that they hoped to meet her in another world." EPP journal, entry following September 22, 1826, MVWC, p. 198, MHS.

Further information on Lydia Maria Francis [Child] (1802–1880) can be found in Deborah Pickman Clifford's excellent biography, *Crusader for Freedom: A Life of Lydia Maria Child* (Boston: Beacon Press, 1992), and Carolyn Karcher's *The First Woman in the Republic: A Cultural Biography of Lydia Maria Child* (Durham, N.C.: Duke University Press, 1994).

"we have been trying to procure": MTP to Miss Rawlins Pickman, July 21, 1826, HMII Papers, MHS.

170   "a seal with a heart . . . You merit it": EPP to SAP, August 14, 1825, Peabody Family Papers, Smith.

"one of the pleasantest . . . close contact with it": EPP Brookline journal, entry of August 12, 1826, MVWC, p. 180, MHS.

"making a good deal . . . of my plans": EPP journal, entry of September 20, 1826, [Salem], MVWC, p. 194, MHS.

"perhaps all the suffering": EPP Brookline journal, entry of June 23, 1826, MVWC, p. 173, MHS.

PAGE   *16. "Life Is Too Interesting to Me Now"*

171   "flashed upon the world": MTP to Miss Rawlins Pickman, January 27, 1825, HMII Papers, MHS. My date: Janaury 27, [1826].

"a bird of passage . . . permanency": MTP to Miss Rawlins Pickman, September 22, 1827, HMII Papers, MHS.

"new pleasure": EPP to Sarah Russell Sullivan, September 4, 1829, Straker typescripts, p. 528, Antiochiana.

"those on the verge": EPP, "Postscript to Prospectus," *The Family School*, no. 2, November 1, 1836.

172   "it was as much . . . enough to be *charitable*": EPP to Sarah Russell Sullivan, September 4, 1829, Straker typescripts, p. 528, Antiochiana.

"never to find fault": EPP to Dorothea Dix, July 8, 1827, *Letters of EPP*, p. 75.

"extended full length": MTP to Maria Chase, n.d. [October 1827], Peabody Family Papers, Smith.

173   "beloved & revered": EPP to Dorothea Dix, July 8, 1827, *Letters of EPP*, p. 75.

"The minutiae of the tenses": *Rem of WEC*, p. 262.

"mind has no sex": EPP to SAP, June 23, 1822, in series "60 a.l. EPP to SAP," Berg.

"was self-imposed . . . You have triumphed": *Rem of WEC*, p. 263.

"All great acquisitions . . . rather than profound": *Rem of WEC*, p. 261.

One student who was not initially responsive to Elizabeth's methods was Fanny Appleton, daughter of the Lowell Mills founder Nathan Appleton and the future wife of Henry Wadsworth Longfellow. Elizabeth had no qualms about writing of the problem to Fanny's father in a letter in which she described the young girl as "exceedingly careless and rather indolent." Although possessing "natural talent in abundance," Fanny was "too willing to be assisted, and often when *we* would throw her upon her own resources, she obtains assistance from her schoolfellows." In this impressively forthright letter to an industrial magnate, the twenty-three-year-old Elizabeth outlined her curriculum and methods and laid the blame squarely on the Appletons. She urged Mr. Appleton to permit Fanny to make up her lessons at home, the "one punishment in our school . . . when there is neglect and carelessness in schoolhouse." Evidently he allowed his daughter "the privilege" of "never studying at home," a policy Elizabeth could scarcely imagine and considered detrimental "to the health of [Fanny's] mind." Elizabeth left it to Appleton to accept or reject her plan; in the end, Fanny stayed on at "Miss Peabody's school," writing to her brother, "I like her very well." EPP to [Nathan Appleton], [1827], *Letters of EPP*, pp. 78–82.

173   "I have ... more feeling ... *my craft*": EPP to Sarah Russell Sullivan, September 4, 1829, Straker typescripts, p. 528, Antiochiana.

William Russell: Margaret Neussendorfer, ed., "Elizabeth Palmer Peabody to William Wordsworth: Eight Letters, 1825–1845," p. 187, n. 22.

174   "courage ... odd": MTP to Maria Chase, November 10, 1826, Peabody Family Papers, Smith.

"not been able to feel ... the public": EPP to Sarah Russell Sullivan, September 4, 1829, Straker typescripts, p. 527, Antiochiana.

only for teenagers or young adults: Elizabeth herself opposed Channing's view of small children as too young for religious instruction, and may have persuaded him to see the matter differently in the course of the Sunday school teachers' meetings. In a letter to a Brookline friend, Sarah Russell Sullivan, written in September 1826 (Straker typescripts, p. 340, Antiochiana), she wrote:

"I wish I could have been present when Dr. Channing said he did not believe any religious impressions could be made upon children. I should like to hear what he has to say in defence of a position contradicted by so much experience —I should like to know exactly what he meant—for my part I see no reason why a child when he first is told that what he feels as restraining him from some actions is conscience—something which he must obey—I surely see no reason why he cannot be taught that this conscience is the breath of the Almighty—a stream from an inexhaustible fountain,—with which communion is ever to be held. A child certainly may be made to act from a regard to the sentiments of justice, honour, &c—And if these abstractions are referred to the presence of God by his education (and surely they can be), what is this but a religious impression?"

175   "education party": EPP to Dorothea Dix, January 24, 1828, *Letters of EPP*, p. 82.

"less favored": *Rem of WEC*, p. 268.

"No book ever gave ... interesting to me now": EPP to Dorothea Dix, January 24, 1828, *Letters of EPP*, pp. 83–84.

"listening to an interesting ... severe test": *Rem of WEC*, p. 9.

176   "the literary sermon": Van Wyck Brooks, *The Flowering of New England* (Boston: Houghton Mifflin, 1981, reprint of 1936 edition), p. 12.

if Channing was unwell: Channing was only the most celebrated of Boston's invalid ministers. There was also Francis Greenwood of King's Chapel, whose loyal congregation agreed to let him read his old sermons—widely considered "gem[s] of literary art"—every Sunday rather than risk the exhaustion that came with writing and delivering new ones; and Joseph Tuckerman, who took on a freelance position overseeing Boston's Ministry of the Poor after ill health forced him to resign his pastorate in Chelsea. Elizabeth would frequently overhear Channing and Tuckerman dispute the best means of using the "small bodily strength" allotted to them: whether in composing and delivering sermons or in making pastoral visits. Illness seemed a badge of dedication to the spiritual life. William B. Sprague, D.D., *Annals of the American Pulpit; or Commemorative Notices of Distinguished American Clergymen of the Various Denominations* (New York: Robert Carter and Brothers, 1865), vol. 8, pp. 491, 356.

"the habit of spending": Sprague, *Annals of the American Pulpit*, vol. 8, p. 354.

"extremely intimate": Sprague, *Annals of the American Pulpit*, vol. 8, p. 379.

"transcendent ... find heaven there": EPP and MTP to Mrs. EPP, February 1826, Mrs. EPP copybook, letter 31, Peabody Family Papers, 1790–1880, MHS.

178   "inquiring into the aspect": *Rem of WEC*, p. 16.

"contraction of the stomach ... support a man's body": *Rem of WEC*, p. 327.

"bathing bombasets . . . exhilarating to Dr. Channing": *Rem of WEC*, p. 328.

"perfectly blissified": MTP to Maria Chase, n.d. [summer 1829], Peabody Family Papers, Smith. My date: [August 1828].

"passed through the furnace . . . fellow-being": WEC to EPP, August 11, 1828, *Rem of WEC*, pp. 302–303.

PAGE | *17. An Interior Revolution*

179 "I injured you by attention": WEC to EPP, August 11, 1828, *Rem of WEC*, p. 302.

"calumnious . . . impecunious young friend": *Rem of WEC*, p. 10.

"knowledge . . . enthusiastic youth": *Rem of WEC*, p. 11.

"Miss Peabody . . . Thucydides": Catharine Maria Sedgwick to Catharine Watson, January 6, 1827, Catharine Maria Sedgwick Papers, MHS. I am grateful to Mary Kelley for bringing this letter to my attention.

180 "taken with a library of books": Mrs. EPP to EPP, n.d. [ca. January 8, 1828], Straker typescripts, p. 472, Antiochiana.

"Elizabeth! . . . mistaken": Mrs. EPP to MTP, [January 8, 1828], Straker typescripts, p. 461, Antiochiana.

New York City warehouse fire: By then the Harding portrait was the property of Elizabeth's niece, Rose Hawthorne Lathrop. Benjamin Pickman Mann to Mary Van Wyck Church, March 1, 1904, correspondence accompanying MVWC, MHS.

181 "judge of herself": Mrs. EPP to MTP, [November 1827], Straker typescripts, p. 437, Antiochiana.

182 "doing hurt . . . wish for more": Mrs. EPP to EPP and MTP, n.d. [ca. January 8, 1828], Straker typescripts, p. 472, Antiochiana.

"active life": EPP Brookline journal, entry of July 9, 1826, MVWC, p. 78, MHS.

"take to farming business": Mrs. EPP to Lydia [Peabody], n.d., after May 1826, Dartmouth.

"I am sure the mind of a Boy": Mrs. EPP to EPP and MTP, June 5, 1824, Straker typescripts, p. 237, Antiochiana.

"very uncommon talent": EPP journal, ca. September 22, 1826, MVWC, p. 197, MHS.

183 "talk": Only a fragment of Wordsworth's answer to Elizabeth's first letter has survived. In this he declines her suggestion that he write poetry for children with the observation, "If I am to serve the very young by my writings, it must be by benefiting at the same time, those who are old enough to be their parents." Alan G. Hill, ed., *The Letters of William and Dorothy Wordsworth, Part I, 1821–1828* (Oxford: Clarendon Press, 1978), p. 565. The respectful tone of Wordsworth's full response is evident in Elizabeth's reply of March 27, 1829. The correspondence continued at lengthy intervals until 1845, five years before the poet's death.

"I fear I shall never see . . . first rank of society": EPP to William Wordsworth, March 27, 1829, reprinted in Margaret Neussendorfer, ed., "Elizabeth Palmer Peabody to William Wordsworth: Eight Letters, 1825–1845," p. 187 ff.

"a pale midget with a trembling voice": Jack Mendelsohn, *Channing: The Reluctant Radical* (Boston: Unitarian Universalist Association, 1979), p. 56.

"political ambition . . . every woman": EPP to William Wordsworth, March 27, 1829, Neussendorfer, ed., "Elizabeth Palmer Peabody to William Wordsworth: Eight Letters, 1825–1845," p. 187 ff.

184 *The Casket:* The anthology was subtitled *A Christmas and New Year's Present for Children and Young Persons 1829* (Boston: Bowles and Dearborn, 1828). It is not

known whether this collection was Elizabeth's own project or one she was hired to complete; her name appears nowhere in the volume. "The Water-Spirit" was widely acknowledged to be her work, and the editor's preface is written in her style. The selections that can be identified are largely the work of Elizabeth and her friends and family. Mrs. Peabody contributed a historical tale: "The Two Portraits," pp. 160–81.

184   "whip syllabubs of literature": SAP to Maria Chase, January 6, 1829, Peabody Family Papers, Smith.

fellow Sunday school teacher Eliza Cabot: Eliza Lee Cabot had a long and productive career as a writer in various genres. Aside from her translation, *Selections from the Writings of Fenelon* (1829), she wrote numerous books of stories and verse for children ("The Three Little Kittens" is her best-remembered nursery rhyme), two novels, antislavery tracts, and a memoir of her husband Charles Follen, most of them published under her married name, Eliza Cabot Follen. Perhaps because Cabot had already published a volume of children's stories, *The Well-Spent Hour* (1827), her entries in *The Casket* received the attribution "E.L.C.," whereas Elizabeth's and her mother's entries were published anonymously.

"the author of Undine": EPP to MTP, June 23–26, [1834], Berg. In a note included in a later edition of the tale, Elizabeth wrote, "the story . . . would probably have borrowed more from the original, had not the latter been but dimly remembered, through an interval of several years, which had elapsed since its perusal." [EPP], *The Water-Spirit* (Boston: Stimpson and Clapp, 1833).

"faery race": EPP to Marian, ca. 1825, MVWC, p. 125, MHS.

"frolicsome . . . to attend and remember": EPP, "The Water-Spirit," *The Casket*, p. 36.

185   "vivacity, wit, brilliancy": EPP to Marian, ca. 1825, MVWC, p. 221, MHS.

"care for nothing but herself": EPP, "The Water-Spirit," *The Casket*, pp. 11–12.

"maidenly timidity": EPP, "The Water-Spirit," *The Casket*, p. 20.

"real women never do . . . strangeness": EPP, "The Water-Spirit," *The Casket*, p. 23.

"changed from a child . . . tender": EPP, "The Water-Spirit," *The Casket*, p. 31.

"which prefers the things": EPP, "The Water-Spirit," *The Casket*, p. 46.

"a living, spiritual": EPP, "The Water-Spirit," *The Casket*, p. 36.

"employing himself": EPP, "The Water-Spirit," *The Casket*, p. 60.

"little fountain . . . worship God together in Heaven": EPP, "The Water-Spirit," *The Casket*, pp. 62–63.

"love without shadow": EPP, "The Water-Spirit," *The Casket*, p. 36.

186   "the golden toils": Mrs. EPP to EPP and MTP, "Thursday morn. June—1827," Straker typescripts, p. 415, Antiochiana.

"What alone is divine . . . *destiny* of the human soul": EPP to Sarah Russell Sullivan, [November 1827], *Letters of EPP*, p. 78.

PAGE   *18. Dr. Walter*

189   "profitable": Dr. NP to Francis Peabody, June 6, 1828, Dartmouth.

"beautiful prospect": MTP to Miss Rawlins Pickman, September 25, 1829, HMII Papers, MHS. Paul Revere, Samuel Adams, and Thomas Paine are buried in what is now known as the Old Granary Burial Ground.

"my *snuggerie* . . . without seeing the sun": SAP to Maria Chase, October 16, [1829?], Peabody Family Papers, Smith.

"never entirely free": NCP to MTP, n.d. [June 1827], Peabody Family Papers, 1790–1880, MHS.

190   "excruciating torture": Dr. NP to Francis Peabody, June 6, 1828, Dartmouth.
"confusion": The earliest usage may have been Mrs. Peabody's comment, "Sophia has been tolerably easy at times; but can not yet bear any application. Her mind has, however, been far less confused than some time past." Mrs. EPP to EPP and MTP, n.d. [1827], Straker typescripts, p. 402, Antiochiana.
"a floating off of my senses": SAP to Mrs EPP, August 11, 1834, SAP *CJ*, p. 253.
"syncope of the brain": SAP to EPP, [1835?], Berg 52B2464. My date: [late September or early October 1835].
"the Faculty": SAP to the Misses Chase, [January 1830], Peabody Family Papers, Smith.
"a life-long invalid": Norman Holmes Pearson, "Elizabeth Peabody on Hawthorne," *Essex Institute Historical Collections*, July 1958, p. 262.
Dr. Peabody favored: "Her Father intends to blister her repeatedly and for some length of time, when the weather moderates a little." Mrs. EPP to MTP, postscript to letter from SAP to MTP, January 26, 1827, Straker typescripts, pp. 368–69, Antiochiana.

In *Migraine: Understanding a Common Disorder* (Berkeley and Los Angeles: University of California Press, 1985), Oliver Sacks quotes the sixth-century Greek physician Alexander Trallianus's elucidation of this theory, which remained one of two primary and competing views of the sources and treatment of migraine at the end of the eighteenth century: "If therefore headache frequently arises on account of a superfluity of bilious humor, the cure of it must be affected by means of remedies which purge and draw away the bilious humor," p. 3.

191   "I have not the least doubt . . . exciting": MTP to SAP, [September 19, 1823], Berg. My date: [September 19, 1832].
"abstinence from animal food": Mrs. EPP to EPP, [1835], Straker typescripts, p. 1009, Antiochiana. My date: [fall 1826].
"my rebellious head": SAP to MTP, July 2, 1826, Berg.
"generous, fine, disinterested": SAP to EPP and MTP, June 17, 1826, Berg.
"the very quietest": SAP to "Cousin Harriet" [Merrick], May 28, 1826, Berg.
"so essentially better": SAP to EPP and MTP, June 17, 1826, Berg.
"little vile imps of darkness": SAP journal April 1–August 8, 1829, entry of May 12, Berg.
"cannonaders in my temples and forehead": SAP to Maria Chase, January 31, 1828, Peabody Family Papers, Smith.
"this capital of my world": SAP to Mary Wilder White, January 3, Berg. My date: January 3, [1828].
"Sophia took to her chamber . . . bear the least noise": Dr. NP to Francis Peabody, June 6, 1828, Dartmouth.

192   "terrific visions": Sophia frequently referred to such visions, generally without specific descriptions of the images perceived. Probably akin to night terrors, they seem to have been a common feature of her disturbed sleep. In Cuba for a rest cure during 1834 and 1835, Sophia wrote to her mother: "I must not omit telling you that my *nights* are better than they ever were—I am not so [disturbed] with terrific visions & seldom wake after I am once asleep. . . . Nature is beginning to rest herself after such a desperate action & wakefulness of years." SAP *CJ*, p. 25.
"no 'sweet restorer' ": MTP to Maria Chase, [late March 1831], Peabody Family Papers, Smith. Mary wrote that she had reached this judgment after her 1828 reunion with Sophia.
"a speedy termination": Dr. NP quoted in EPP to Sarah Russell Sullivan, [April 1828], Straker typescripts, p. 479 ff, Antiochiana.

192   "bright . . . submissive to pain": EPP to Sarah Russell Sullivan, [April 1828], Straker typescripts, p. 479 ff, Antiochiana.
"very great blessing of sickness": SAP to Mrs. EPP, August 11, 1834, SAP *CJ*, p. 250.
"inner temple": SAP journal April 1–August 8, 1829, entry of March 30, 1831, Berg. [This journal also contains entries from 1831.]
　　In a letter to Sarah Russell Sullivan describing Sophia's crisis of April 1828, Elizabeth wrote that although Sophia was "still very ill" and their father expected her to die, "it is almost impossible to realize that any emotion but happiness can be connected with the thought of her. . . . Sophia seems to have no apprehensions or hopes but tranquilly *enjoys* or *endures* the present as the momentary condition may be. 'How wonderful is *happiness* (she said to me a day or two since)—it comes without any apparent cause—the more I suffer—the more I feel it is in my heart of hearts.' Every feature radiates with this sentiment whenever she opens her eyes." [April 1828], Straker typescripts, p. 479 ff, Antiochiana.
"How fortunate": MTP to Miss Rawlins Pickman, February 28, 1827, HMII Papers, MHS.
"felt a perfect exhilaration": SAP to EPP, [Salem, 1827?], Berg.
"Blessed be . . . how my headache did": SAP to MTP, [Salem, 1827?], Berg.

193   "sympathetic nerves": Sacks, *Migraine*, p. 5. See also Amalie M. Kass, *Midwifery and Medicine in Boston: Walter Channing, M.D. 1786-1876* (Boston: Northeastern University Press, 2002), pp. 26–40.
"a romantic flair": Kass, *Midwifery and Medicine in Boston*, p. 12.

194   "intellectual forcing": Kass, *Midwifery and Medicine in Boston*, p. 57.
one-quarter of all deaths: Karen Robert, ed., *New Year in Cuba: Mary Gardner Lowell's Travel Diary, 1831-1832* (Boston: Massachusetts Historical Society, Northeastern University Press, 2003), p. 13.
"It must be expected . . . prepare my mind": Mrs. EPP to MTP, [1827?], Straker typescripts, p. 403, Antiochiana.
"bed case . . . morbidly acute": WC, *Bed Case: Its History and Treatment* (Boston: Ticknor and Fields, 1860), p. 8.
"troubles . . . threaten life": WC, *Bed Case*, p. 6.
neurasthenia: For an excellent discussion of neurasthenia and the history of its diagnosis and treatment, see Jean Strouse, *Alice James: A Biography* (Boston: Houghton Mifflin, 1980), pp. 103–106, 222–24. See also F. G. Gosling, *Before Freud: Neurasthenia and the American Medical Community, 1870-1910* (Urbana and Chicago: University of Illinois Press, 1987).

195   "the great object . . . its increase": WC, *Bed Case*, p. 35.
"by means so gentle": WC, *Bed Case*, p. 52.
"entire absorption": WC, *Bed Case*, p. 13.
"a refuge from a thousand annoyances": WC, *Bed Case*, p. 26.
"with its promises . . . home of the sick": WC, *Bed Case*, p. 27.
"abandonment of these cases": WC, *Bed Case*, p. 43.
"cure is to be regarded": WC, *Bed Case*, p. 52.
"a new physician . . . almost as miraculous": WC, *Bed Case*, p. 43.
"habit alone has kept": WC, *Bed Case*, p. 51.

196   "habitual . . . unremitting migraines": Sacks, *Migraine*, p. 178.
"trusting relationship": Sacks, *Migraine*, p. 213.
"deeply incapacitated . . . left open to them": Sacks, *Migraine*, p. 218.

"Get all health": WC to SAP, May 30, [1829], Berg.

Channing's prescriptions: WC to SAP, August 12, 1828, Berg.

"always leaves me in a glow": SAP journal April 1–August 8, 1829, entry of April 18, Berg.

197   *United States Literary Gazette:* SAP journal April 11-[July] 31, [1830], entry of June 19, Berg. Channing's biographer Amalie Kass notes one article by Channing that appeared in the *United States Review and Literary Gazette:* "The Book of Nature, by John Mason Good," vol. 1, 1827, pp. 407-17.

"his productions": SAP journal April 11-[July] 31, [1830], entry of July 24, Berg.

"wakes the sweetest echoes": SAP to Mrs. EPP, June 12, [1831], Berg.

"It is one of the privileges": WC to SAP, August 12, 1828, Berg.

"another proof to me . . . esteemed friend and patient": WC to SAP, November 17, 1828, Berg.

"perfect submission . . . martyrdom in my friends": WC to SAP, October 11, [1829], Berg.

"in your case . . . you must do well": WC to SAP, November 17, 1828, Berg.

"primary object in every man's mind": SAP journal January–February 1832, entry of February 15, Berg.

"*dear* Dr. Walter": a much-used phrase by SAP. For example, SAP journal April 11-[July] 31, [1830], entry of May 11, Berg.

198   "looked so *beaming* bright . . . weary dizzy body": SAP journal April 1–August 8, 1829, entry dated July 30, 1831, Berg. [This journal also contains entries from 1831.]

"felt shockingly all day": SAP journal April 11-[July] 31, [1830], entry of April 23, Berg.

"chaise came up . . . well on such a day": SAP journal April 11-[July] 31, [1830], entry of April 20, Berg.

"utterly banished": SAP to MTP, July 4, 1833, Berg.

"without any disease": MTP to Maria Chase, January 17, 1830, Peabody Family Papers, Smith.

"she so loves Dr. C. . . . she could not endure": Mrs. EPP to MTP, n.d. [1828], Straker typescripts, p. 470, Antiochiana. My date: [after September 19, 1832].

199   "*kind Dr. Walter* . . . rescued me": SAP journal April 11-[July] 31, [1830], entry of June 13, Berg.

"knock with the greatest animation . . . a word could I say": SAP journal April 1–August 8, 1829, entry of March 24, 1831, Berg. [This journal also contains entries from 1831.]

200   "one of her sickest turns": Dr. NP to Francis Peabody, May 8, 1831, Dartmouth.

"I awoke with fierce pain": SAP journal April 1–August 8, 1829, entry of April 21, 1831, Berg. [This journal also contains entries from 1831.]

"inexpressible agonies . . . obliged": SAP journal April 1–August 8, 1829, entry of May 7, 1831, Berg. [This journal also contains entries from 1831.]

"unwearied solicitude . . . cure at last?": SAP journal April 1–August 8, 1829, entry of May 8, 1831, Berg. [This journal also contains entries from 1831.]

"my kind potion": SAP journal April 1–August 8, 1829, entry of May 10, 1831, Berg. [This journal also contains entries from 1831.]

"as usual invaluable": SAP journal April 1–August 8, 1829, entry of May 7, 1831, Berg. [This journal also contains entries from 1831.]

"refreshing": SAP journal January–February, 1832, entry of February 15, Berg.

"one must be sick": SAP to MTP, July 4, 1833, Berg.

19. "My Soul Steps Forth upon the Paper"

201   "lay aside": SAP Boston journal, entry of September 3, 1829, Berg 228144B.

"Whatever is living ... up to nature": [Francis Graeter], *Mary's Journey; A German Tale* (Boston: S. G. Goodrich and Co., 1829), p. 126. Before coming to Boston, Graeter taught both German and drawing at the progressive Round Hill School in Northampton, Massachusetts, for a short time, overlapping with George Peabody's brief term there.

"Have you no word ... envy you": Norman Holmes Pearson, "Elizabeth Peabody on Hawthorne," *Essex Institute Historical Collections,* July 1958, p. 273.

202   "genius": Numerous references, including EPP to MTP, [August 27–August 30?, 1834], Berg: "[Miss Rawlins Pickman] spoke of Sophia too & so did Mr. William —as an embodiment of enthusiasm & genius." Also EPP to GFP, May 15, 1836, Straker typescripts, p. 1052, Antiochiana: "You are the only hope of the family in a pecuniary point of view.—The only hope we have of our dear Sophia's genius having the atmosphere it ought to have—is from you."

"much too difficult": SAP to MTP, June 19, 1826, Berg.

"so perfect": Pearson, "Elizabeth Peabody on Hawthorne," p. 272.

"I could not possibly ... wither away": SAP to EPP and MTP, December 3, 1826, Berg.

203   copied long passages: SAP commonplace book, January–June 18, 1826, Berg. Sophia probably read the play *Correggio—A Tragedy* by the Danish poet Adam Oehlenschlaeger in *Blackwood's Edinburgh Magazine,* where it was published under the heading "Horae Danicae No. II," vol. VIII, no. XLV, December 1820, pp. 290–305.

"all the fine paintings": MTP to Maria Chase, in a joint letter from EPP and MTP to Maria Chase, May 2, [1825], Peabody Family Papers, Smith. My date: May 2, [1827].

204   In 1827, the Athenaeum: For this description of the founding of the Boston Athenaeum Gallery I have drawn from two sources: Mabel Munson Swan, *The Athenaeum Gallery, 1827-1873* (Boston: Boston Athenaeum, 1940), pp. 3–34; and *A Climate for Art: The History of the Boston Athenaeum Gallery, 1827-1874,* an exhibition catalogue dated October 3–29, 1980, published by the Boston Athenaeum.

"her darling art": Eliza White Dwight to MTP, December 27, 1830, HMIV Papers, MHS.

206   "excellent copies ... great prices": Rembrandt Peale to Thomas Wren Ward, February 15, 1831, *A Climate for Art: The History of the Boston Athenaeum Gallery, 1827-1873,* p. 22.

"from nature": SAP to Maria Chase, December 15, 1829, Peabody Family Papers, Smith.

207   *"because Raphael ... every advantage":* SAP journal April 11–[July] 31, [1830], entry of April 26, Berg.

208   "Mr. Dowdy": SAP journal April 11–[July] 31, [1830], entry of June 4, Berg.

"my whole organization ... any such thing before": SAP journal April 11–[July] 31, [1830], entry of June 8, Berg.

"keep my eyes upon ... suffocating": SAP journal April 11–[July] 31, [1830], entry of June 12, Berg.

209   "attacked the board": SAP journal April 11–[July] 31, [1830], entry of June 15, Berg.

"rather too purple": SAP journal April 11–[July] 31, [1830], entry of June 23, Berg.

"I cannot possibly . . . as well as Mr. Doughty's": SAP journal April 11-[July] 31, [1830], entry of July 19, Berg.

"What an intense delight": SAP journal April 11-[July] 31, [1830], entry of June 12, Berg.

"which he would not suffer": SAP journal April 11-[July] 31, [1830], entry of July 12, Berg.

"the most capital portrait": Leah Lipton, *A Truthful Likeness: Chester Harding and His Portraits* (Washington, D.C.: National Portrait Gallery, 1985), p. 98.

"so quick—so masterly": SAP journal April 11-[July] 31, [1830], entry of July 22, Berg.

chose to copy Harding's 1827 portrait: Although Louise Hall Tharp conjectures that the unsigned copy of Harding's *Washington Allston* owned by the Massachusetts Historical Society was done by Sophia Peabody, it is simply a guess, based on Harding's offer to permit Sophia to make a copy (*Peabody Sisters of Salem*, p. 345). There is no evidence that she ever made such a copy, and much to suggest that she did not.

Unfortunately, Leah Lipton accepts Tharp's judgment in her otherwise authoritative biographical catalogue of Harding's work, *A Truthful Likeness: Chester Harding and His Portraits*, p. 156. Lipton quotes as evidence a journal passage of July 14, 1830, in which Sophia describes Harding's *Allston* in glowing terms. But this entry is dated several weeks before Sophia began to visit Harding's studio regularly, first to sit for her own portrait and, later, to copy Harding's *Margaret*. Patricia Valenti perpetuates this misattribution in her biography *Sophia Peabody Hawthorne: A Life, Volume One, 1809-1847* (Columbia: University of Missouri Press, 2004). Similarly, Valenti mistakenly describes a *Flight into Egypt*, owned by the House of Seven Gables in Salem, as an "original canvas" of Sophia's; if Sophia ever completed a *Flight into Egypt*, about which there is some doubt, it was not an original but a copy of a painting owned by the Rice family of Boston and thought to be the work of the French landscape artist Claude Lorrain. See Valenti, pp. 127, 88.

Sophia must have found *Margaret* better suited to her own interests and capabilities. She had a fondness for drawings and paintings of children and had made several attempts at copying in pen and ink a widely printed etching made from Thomas Lawrence's famous *Master Charles William Lambton* ("The Red Boy"), which she called "The Boy on the Rock," before she began to work in oils. Elizabeth had used the *Master Lambton* etching as an illustration for her mother's story "The Two Portraits" in her 1828 anthology, *The Casket*.

Sophia mentioned her completed copy of *Margaret* several times in the spring and summer of 1832. In an 1834 letter she wrote that she had so far painted just two portraits, the first one a copy (i.e., *Margaret*), the second one of a friend, which must have been the portrait of Thomas Park that she painted in August and September 1832. SAP to Isabel, September 1834, Berg.

"dear little chamber": SAP to EPP, October 22, 1832, in series "20 a.l.s. SAP to EPP," Berg. It is interesting to consider what effect the art supplies Sophia stored and used in her room might have had on her continued ill health. Sophia's headaches predate her use of oil paints and lead-based glazes, yet paint fumes and lead dust may have exacerbated them or further weakened a "constitution" already compromised by the ingestion of mercury at a young age.

211   "such a studio": SAP journal April 11-[July] 31, [1830], entry of June 19, Berg.

"dangerously narrows . . . agreeable to her": Ralph Waldo Emerson, William Henry Channing, and James Freeman Clarke, eds., *Memoirs of Margaret Fuller Ossoli* (Boston: Phillips, Sampson, 1852), pp. 321-22.

211   "To the Unknown yet known": SAP ms. poem, n.d., SAH Papers, box 1, folder 14, Stanford.

    It is interesting to contrast Sophia's unequivocal desire to marry a poet or visual artist with the sentiments expressed by her sisters' student Fanny Appleton, a girl just eight years younger than Sophia, who would grow up to marry the poet Henry Wadsworth Longfellow, Nathaniel Hawthorne's college classmate. In 1827 at age ten, Fanny wrote to her older brother Thomas Gold Appleton, then attending the Round Hill School in Northampton, that her dancing mistress had instructed her to tell him "that you must not be a poet, because if you were, you would be poor." Fanny was one of the wealthiest women in Boston when she married Longfellow, however, thanks to the generosity of her father, the textile magnate Nathan Appleton. Fanny Appleton to Thomas Gold Appleton, February 20, 1827, Frances Elizabeth Appleton Longfellow (1817–1861) Papers, 1825–1861, LH. I am grateful to Diana Korzenik for bringing this letter to my attention.

    Sophia herself wrote poetry on more than this occasion, although she never took the art as seriously as painting. During the summer of 1830, she was so intrigued by Coleridge's unfinished poem "Christabel" (1816) that she completed it with her own "Continuation" in nine competent stanzas, which she entered in her journal on July 21. See Patricia Valenti, "Sophia Peabody Hawthorne's Continuation to 'Christabel,'" *Nathaniel Hawthorne Review*, vol. XIII, no. 1, Spring 1987, pp. 14–16. Although the date of "To the Unknown yet known" cannot be ascertained, it is certain that Sophia was writing poetry at least as early as 1830.

PAGE   *20. "First Retreat into Solitude"*

213   "I was a divine ... divine truth": SAP to EPP, August 2, 1822, Berg.

    "president of Uncle Sam!!! ... the Sons of the Forest": SAP to EPP, March 6, [1824], Berg.

    "like an Adonis ... come asunder": SAP to EPP, March 13, 1825, Berg. The Reverend Charles Wentworth Upham was ordained associate pastor of Salem's First Church in December 1824, almost as soon as he had completed his Harvard Divinity School course. He was twenty-two years old.

214   "mind on fire": I am grateful to Robert D. Richardson, Jr., author of *Emerson: The Mind on Fire* (Berkeley: University of California Press, 1995), for countless useful suggestions during the research phase of my work on the Peabody sisters.

    "with a fire in my brain": SAP journal April 11–[July] 31, [1830], entry of May 16, Berg.

    "inner temple": SAP journal April 1–August 8, 1829, entry of March 30, 1831. [This journal also contains entries from 1831.]

    "sanctuary": SAP to Mrs. EPP, October 14, 1830, Berg. The longer passage reads: "... at length I began to enter the inner sanctuary that I might find the peace that was no where without. 'God is here,' said the voice of my spirit.... My whole frame had been wrought up to the highest pitch of excitement, and my pulses were beating madly; but then I sank from the painful height, and all was still, and I actually smiled!"

    "ministered to ... a minister of good and plenty": WC to SAP, May 30, [1829], Berg.

    "I do believe th[at] Sickness": SAP journal, Boston, 1829, entry of September 3, Berg 228144B.

"My heart never moves": SAP to EPP, [1835], Berg 52B2464. My date: [late September or early October 1835].

"silent ministry of pain ... Providence of GOD": SAH to EPP, May 14, 1865, MA 3400 (SH 39), Morgan.

215   "fussation": EPP to MTP, February 24–25, 1834, Berg.

"contention": NCP Genealogies, Straker typescripts, p. 5425/23, Antiochiana.

"craze": EPP to MTP, February 24–25, 1834, Berg.

"I never knew any human": Norman Holmes Pearson, "Elizabeth Peabody on Hawthorne," *Essex Institute Historical Collections*, July 1958, p. 273.

"tame": Pearson, "Elizabeth Peabody on Hawthorne," p. 273.

"trials rarely endured": Mrs. EPP to GFP, n.d., Straker typescripts, p. 1046, Antiochiana. My date: [spring 1836].

"nature ... devised than pain": Julian Hawthorne, *Nathaniel Hawthorne and His Wife* (Hamden, Conn.: Archon Books, 1968, reprint of 1884 edition), vol. I, p. 47.

"years of pain ... obstinacy": Mrs. EPP to SAP and MTP, September 9, 1834, Berg.

"I have repeatedly felt ... to myself": SAP to EPP, October 15?, 1835?, Berg.

"what partially destroyed": MTM, "Reminiscences," Straker typescripts, p. 103, Antiochiana.

"reading party ... fellow being": SAP to Lydia Sears Haven, December? 1830, Straker typescripts, p. 580, Antiochiana. My date: [December 10, 1830].

innovative grammar textbook: Mentioned in a letter from MTP to Maria Chase, January 17, 1830, Peabody Family Papers, Smith, the book was probably *First Lessons in Grammar on the Plan of Pestalozzi* (Boston: Carter and Hendee, 1830). Elizabeth's nephew Benjamin Pickman Mann lists the book in a bibliography of her work, although it was published anonymously "By a Teacher in Boston."

worked tirelessly on translations: Baron Joseph-Marie de Gérando, *Self-Education; or The Means and Art of Moral Progress* (Boston: Carter and Hendee, 1830) and *The Visitor of the Poor* (Boston: Hilliard, Gray, Little, and Wilkins, 1832).

216   "the life of man": Richardson, *Emerson: The Mind on Fire*, p. 102.

thirty-page defense: George Ripley's review appeared in the *Christian Examiner*, vol. IX, New Series vol. IV, no. 1, September 1830, pp. 70–107.

"vague and misty ... scientific method": "Degerando," *Massachusetts Journal and Tribune*, September 4, 1830, p. 2. The article was signed "A Lover of Literature" and had much worse to say about Elizabeth's translation, and, along with a second negative review appearing on September 25, was found to be so excessive in its criticisms that the *Massachusetts Journal* editors published on October 2, 1830, an excerpt from Ripley's *Christian Examiner* defense, with this apology: "Degerando's History of Philosophy is a glorious work—and we know that some of the finest and best minds among us are enthusiastic admirers of his work on Self-Education; with regard to the translation, we have never heard but one opinion—and that was an expression of praise."

"Religion is one thing": MTM to Dora, eldest daughter of the Reverend Edward T. Taylor, in Reverend Gilbert Haven and the Honorable Thomas Russell, *Father Taylor, the Sailor Preacher* (Boston: B. B. Russell; San Francisco: A. L. Bancroft, 1872), p. 331.

217   "hatches ... brothers": Dumas Malone, ed., *Dictionary of American Biography*, (New York: Scribner's, 1935, 1936), vol. IX, p. 321.

"what a true and noble ... lightened every thing": MTM to Dora, in Haven and Russell, *Father Taylor, the Sailor Preacher*, pp. 328–29.

217   "ridiculous . . . my own chemise": MTP to Miss Rawlins Pickman, October 15, 1825, HMII Papers, MHS.

218   *I* would marry": MTP to Mary Wilder White, [n.p., n.d], Berg. My date: ca. November 15, 1827.

first in his class to leave: Charles Horatio Gates, *Memorials of the Class of 1835, Harvard University* (Boston: D. Clapp and Sons, 1886), p. 95.

"a steady strong conduct": EPP to GFP, October 14, [1837], Straker typescripts, p. 1214, Antiochiana.

A family legend among the Peabody descendants tells that Wellington "went off to sea" after quarreling with his father; documents of the time, however, suggest that the plan was one approved of by the entire family. The tale says more about the strength of Dr. Peabody's reputation as "a strict disciplinarian" and a man easily angered, which seems to have carried across the generations. For this information I am grateful to Olcott Deming, who allowed me to read his late wife, Louise Deming's, manuscript introduction to her typescripts of Sophia's letters.

"could not say . . . managed excellingly": SAP journal April 1–August 8, 1829, entry of April 14, 1831, Berg. [This journal also contains entries from 1831.]

"aid her husband": Mrs. EPP to GFP, June 12, 1836, Straker typescripts, p. 1061, Antiochiana.

"girls in that class": Mrs. EPP to EPP, n.d. [1836?], Straker typescripts, p. 1069, Antiochiana.

"very neat . . . capable of being improved": Mrs. EPP to GFP, June 12, 1836, Straker typescripts, p. 1061, Antiochiana.

219   "the social powers": Mrs. EPP commonplace book 1829–1832, entry ca. July 3, 1830, Peabody Family Papers, 1790–1880, MHS.

"it is *forgotten*": Mrs. EPP commonplace book 1829–1832, entry ca. June 29, 1830, Peabody Family Papers, 1790–1880, MHS.

"Not a joy lives": Mrs. EPP commonplace book 1829–1832, entry ca. July 3, 1830, Peabody Family Papers, 1790–1880, MHS.

"voluntary rustication": WC to SAP, September 9, 1830, Berg.

"my first retreat into solitude": SAP Dedham journal, entry of August 26, 1830, Berg.

"a sweep of sky": SAP Dedham journal, entry of August 30, 1830, Berg.

220   "Here I am . . . raging head": SAP Dedham journal, entry of August 26, 1830, Berg.

"clishmaclavering among the cows": SAP Dedham journal, entry of August 30, 1830, Berg.

"cannot believe": SAP Dedham journal, entry of August 31, 1830, Berg.

"cool and fresh . . . feeling more alive": SAP Dedham journal, entry of August 30, 1830, Berg.

"singular elation": SAP journal, Boston, 1829, entry of September 3, Berg 228144B.

"every inch of me": SAP journal April 1–August 8, 1829, entry of April 20, 1831, Berg. [This journal also contains entries from 1831.]

"supernatural force": SAP journal April 1–August 8, 1829, entry of March 28, 1831, Berg. [This journal also contains entries from 1831.]

"I could study Hebrew": SAP journal, Boston, 1829, entry of September 3, Berg 228144B.

"excessive agitation . . . utter prostration": SAP to EPP, July 1833, Berg.

"blinding and annihilating": SAP to EPP, n.d., Lowell, in series "20 a.l.s. SAP to EPP," Berg. My date: [ca. July 10, 1835].

"powerless": SAP journal April 1–August 8, 1829, entry of March 27, 1831, Berg. [This journal also contains entries from 1831.]

"bound": SAP to Dr. and Mrs. EPP, July 23, 1832, Berg 229844B.

"a coronet of thongs": SAP to MTP, July 28, 1832, Berg.

"as if a tempest": SAP journal April 1–August 8, 1829, entry of March 28, 1831, Berg. [This journal also contains entries from 1831.]

"a vacuum within": SAP journal January–February 1832, entry of January 12, Berg.

"I am always better than usual": SAP to MTP, [fall? 1835, Salem], Berg. My date: [fall, before October 14, 1835].

"incessant unremitting migraines . . . emotional 'bind'": Oliver Sacks, *Migraine: Understanding a Common Disorder* (Berkeley and Los Angeles: University of California Press, 1985), p. 178.

"fill a dramatic role": Sacks, *Migraine*, pp. 207–208.

"summoned to serve": Sacks, *Migraine*, p. 180.

221   "starts as a reflex": Sacks, *Migraine*, p. 209.

"is both a friend": Sacks, *Migraine*, p. 219.

"pain clinging to me": SAP Dedham journal, entry of September 20, 1830, Berg.

"rage": SAP journal April 1–August 8, 1829, entry of July 24, 1831, Berg. [This journal also contains entries from 1831.]

"insurrection": SAP journal beginning October 1832, entry of November 15, 1832, Stanford.

"How wonderful": SAP quoted in EPP to Sarah Russell Sullivan, [April 1828], Straker typescripts, p. 480, Antiochiana.

"inner sanctuary . . . nowhere without": SAP to Mrs. EPP, October 14, 1830, Berg.

222   women outnumbered men: "Males and Females," *Christian Register*, December 22, 1832.

"The Ladye's Brydalle": Just a few years later Nathaniel Hawthorne composed his own macabre version of such a scene in his story "The Wedding Knell." His later stories "The Lily's Quest" and "The Birthmark," composed after he met Sophia, also conclude with a young wife's death soon after marriage and with an expression of the view that the truest love is "immortal." Given the frequency of early deaths from tuberculosis at the time—Dr. Walter Channing, Horace Mann, Ralph Waldo Emerson, and Henry Wadsworth Longfellow were all widowed early—it may be no surprise that such a prospect was of concern to Hawthorne when he was becoming romantically involved with an invalid.

"too trembly": SAP Dedham journal, entry of September 7, 1830, Berg.

"I could not endure . . . such loveliness": SAP Dedham journal, entry of September 26, 1830, Berg.

"my whole inward being": SAP Dedham journal, entry of September 11, 1830, Berg.

223   "Man has a universe": SAP Dedham journal, entry of August 29, 1830, Berg.

"feed upon the air . . . sang a hymn": SAP Dedham journal, entry of September 11, 1830, Berg.

"draw, draw, draw": SAP to Mrs. EPP, [1830?}, Berg 229824B. My date: [October 24, 1830].

"the slightest cold . . . vast deal of strength": SAP to Mrs. EPP, September 20–25, [18]30, Berg.

"I held my breath": SAP Dedham journal, entry of October 5, 1830, Berg.

21. "Scatteration"

"under the mooney . . . pouring over": SAP to Lydia Sears Haven, December [1830], Straker typescripts, p. 580, Antiochiana.

225 "great & mighty rich . . . nothing to lose!": SAP to MTP, August 8, 1829, in series "22. a.l.s. SAP to MTP," Berg.

"a perfect jewel": EPP to Ruth Gibbs Channing, Boston, August 31, [1829], bMS Am 1428 (150), Houghton.

"People feel poor": EPP to Sarah Russell Sullivan, October 11, 1830, Straker typescripts, p. 579, Antiochiana.

"The Great Rotch Scandal": For the details of this affair, I have drawn on John M. Bullard, *The Rotches* (New Bedford, Mass.: 1947), pp. 159–65, and Marc Friedlaender and L. H. Butterfield, eds., *The Diary of Charles Francis Adams* (Cambridge, Mass.: Harvard University Press, 1974), vol. 6, pp. xi–xii, along with EPP's letters and deliberately oblique published accounts.

"deepest religious sympathy . . . reform of the criminal": *Rem of WEC*, p. 316.

"purifying furnace": *Rem of WEC*, p. 317.

"indiscretion": EPP to MTP, [May 15, 1836], Berg.

226 "that terrible winter": EPP to MTP, [week of May 16, 1836], Berg.

"shattered . . . mind and nerves": EPP to MTP, January 16–21 [20?, 1835], Berg.

"exertions . . . daily task": WEC to EPP, January 29, 1831, *Rem of WEC*, pp. 316–17.

"got tired of me": EPP to MTP, April 19[–20], 1834, Berg. Interestingly, Mary noted several years later that Channing "is like Elizabeth in the impetuosity of his nature—I have no doubt that he was once as uncontrolled in the use of it." Perhaps Channing's impatience with Elizabeth's involvement in the Rotch affair resulted from an essential sympathy. MTP to Lydia Sears Haven, June 20, 1833, MTP Correspondence, MHS.

"New Bedford affair": EPP to MTP, [week of May 16, 1836], Berg.

"parasite . . . but could not": EPP to MTP, February 25, [1835], Berg.

"had too great . . . would have her be": Mrs. EPP to MTP, 1824, SAP copybook, "letters from home," Berg.

"do my duty . . . too great responsibility": Norman Holmes Pearson, "Elizabeth Peabody on Hawthorne," *Essex Institute Historical Collections*, July 1958, p. 274.

"scatteration plan": MTP to EPP, July 11, 1832, HM Papers, MHS. The Peabodys were not alone in moving into and out of Boston during the decade of the 1830s. One demographer has estimated that as many as 35,775 households took the same course between 1830 and 1840, a decade that saw the total population of Boston increase from a little over 60,000 to nearly 100,000. Transience was the norm. Despite the overall growth in population, only two in every five residents of Boston in 1830 were likely to remain in the city for the next ten years.

The most stable portion of the population was the wealthy, the prospective clients for the sisters' school. New England was fast becoming a region of class disparity, particularly in its cities. In Boston in 1833, the richest 4 percent of the population controlled 59 percent of the wealth, as compared to the early 1770s when 5 percent of the population owned just 44 percent of all taxable property. Yet recurrent financial panics threatened even these families, as Elizabeth reported during the early 1830s. Downward mobility became increasingly common in the decades preceding the Civil War. See Howard P. Chudacoff, *The Evolution of American Urban Society* (Englewood Cliffs, N.J.: Prentice Hall, 1981), pp. 53, 51.

227 "spirit tones": MTP to Lydia Sears Haven, Friday Morn, [July? 1831?], Berg.

"to a family of sisters . . . comprehend the future": EPP, *First Steps to the Study of*

History. Being Part First of a Key to History (Boston: Hilliard, Gray, 1832), pp. 13, 1.
"For the first time . . . hopeless misery!": Pearson, "Elizabeth Peabody on Hawthorne," p. 274.

"soft and misty": SAP to Lydia Sears Haven, n.d. [ca. December 10, 1830], Straker typescripts, p. 581, Antiochiana.

two lake scenes: Sophia adapted *Loch Lomond* and *Lake of Shade* from etchings she'd seen in travel books. *Lake of Shade*, which she described as "a view of Mont Blanc" modeled on a "faded engraving" ([SAP] to [Mary T. Hathaway], November 16, 1831, private collection), is probably the painting she completed: "Mr Allston's picture has given me power to finish yours better—But I do not think it has much capability in itself—I mean the Lake of Shade." SAP to EPP, December 27, [1831?], Berg.

"no idea . . . perfect health": SAP journal April 1–August 8, 1829, entry of July 28, 1831, Berg. [This journal also contains entries from 1831.]

"revolution . . . vivid memory": SAP journal April 1–August 8, 1829, entry of March 28, 1831, Berg. [This journal also contains entries from 1831.]

borrow a landscape: The Allston original cannot be identified, but Sophia's untitled landscape, now the property of Salem's Peabody Essex Museum, is almost certainly the copy. Dated January 9, 1832, with lake, trees, and mountains executed in the high-romantic style of Allston's early work, the Peabody Essex landscape matches the painting Sophia tells of beginning in a journal entry of January 10, 1832, Berg. There is a strong resemblance between Sophia's copy and Allston's 1804 *Landscape with a Lake*, property of the Museum of Fine Arts, Boston.

228   "enjoyment . . . perfect rapture": SAP journal January–February 1832, entry of January 10, Berg.

Sophia may have been experiencing a symptom known as "migraine aura," when brightly lit visions appear to the sufferer, sometimes nightmarish ones, but often radiant designs that shift in rapid succession. Oliver Sacks writes of Hildegard of Bingen as an artist whose work was derived from migraine visions: *Migraine: Understanding a Common Disorder* (Berkeley and Los Angeles: University of California Press, 1985), pp. 106–108. Sophia herself described an occasion when she experienced something like classic migraine aura: "I was in that acute agony —it seemed as if my thoughts were like lightning & my feelings like thunder— Such pictures as I saw! they blinded me with their splendor & glory. Now I was in a sweet valley with a silver stream in twilight & cool shadows." SAP to MTP, [fall? 1835, Salem], Berg. My date: [fall, before October 14, 1835].

Sophia sometimes tried to paint these visions, but more often the following day found her "whirling like a top," too sick to get out of bed and scarcely able to "command my attention": SAP to MTP, November 20, 1832, Berg.

"the very first time": SAP to EPP, December 27, [1831?], Berg.

"bodying forth": SAP journal January–February 1832, entry of January 13, Berg.

"atmosphere of turpentine . . . tranquil mind": SAP to Mrs. EPP, May 4, 1832, Berg.

"the sad lady": SAP to Mrs. EPP, July 13, 1832, Berg.

"sketched the beautiful . . . satisfaction": SAP to Mrs. EPP, May 4, 1832, Berg.

229   "delicate and fragile": SAP to Mrs. EPP, May 23, [1832], Berg.

"perfectly correct": SAP to Mrs. EPP, June 10, [1832], Berg.

"ancient . . . sunflower yellow": SAP to Mrs. EPP, May 12–15, 1832, Berg. Eliza Townsend (1788–1854) was in her midforties at the time of this meeting, but she was clearly an eccentric. Considered at one time to be "the first native poet of her sex whose writings commanded the applause of judicious critics," Townsend published anonymously in New England periodicals during the first decades of the nineteenth century. Her poetry was collected for publication after her death by her surviving sister, Mary, with whom she was said to have "lived secluded ... in the old family mansion in Boston, the last of their blood." *American Authors: 1600–1900* (New York: H. W. Wilson, 1938), p. 755.

229   "the Tiger ... fagging": SAP to Mrs. EPP, May 12–15, 1832, Berg.

Four years later, Ralph Waldo Emerson praised Sophia's copy of Allston's 1832 *Jessica and Lorenzo* in almost the same terms: "I rejoiced in the genius of the young lady very much for I feared she had been overpraised to me." RWE to Lidian Emerson, April 22 and 23, 1836, *Letters of RWE*, vol. 2, pp. 12–13. While New England's prominent male artists and intellectuals seemed willing to recognize "genius" in women, they were initially inclined to doubt. The condescension implicit in such remarks—"I feared she had been overpraised to me" or "it is superior to what I expected, although I have heard it much spoken of"—contributed to the reluctance a woman artist could feel about showing her work beyond a domestic circle of admiring female friends. George Flagg's early efforts were not greeted with similar disbelief. Rather he was, in a different sense, overpraised by his uncle. In the end, despite several years of sponsorship by the New York collector Luman Reed, his talent burned out early.

231   Ladies' Life Class: Christine Jones Huber, *The Pennsylvania Academy and Its Women: 1850 to 1920* (Philadelphia: Pennsylvania Academy of the Fine Arts, 1974), pp. 12, 16–17.
"my fair poetess ... altered every part": SAP to Mrs. EPP, June 25, [1832], Berg.
"no *fist* ... into my shell": SAP journal January–February 1832, entry of February 15, Berg.

232   "without legs ... sense of beauty": Washington Allston "Colorbook," p. 56, Dana Family Papers, MHS.
"not paint a stroke ... nutshell": SAP to Mrs. EPP, July 13, 1832, Berg.
"arrearages": Dr. NP to WC, 1832, B MS C75.2, Countway.
"distribution ... again in this world": Dr. NP to Francis Peabody, June 27, 1832, Dartmouth.

233   "we will read": SAP to Mrs. EPP, July 13, 1832, Berg.
"finishing": SAP to Mrs. EPP, July 6, 1832, Berg. Sadly, many paintings were eventually ruined by the same substances that once made them glow, as the finishes collected dirt and turned to obscuring films, sometimes corroding the paint beneath.
"to receive her last touches": SAP to Mrs. EPP, July 13, 1832, Berg.
"to hang up in my inner gallery": SAP to Mrs. EPP and Dr. NP, July 23, 1832, Berg.

PAGE   ## 22. Chastity

237   "bad tricks at school": MTP to EPP, n.d. [late July 1832], HM Papers, MHS.
238   Dorothea Dix: MTP to EPP, August 27, [1832], HM Papers, MHS: "I do not think she [Mrs. Channing] is *ever* pleased—except with Miss Dix, and she I have no doubt did flatter as you say—I came to that conclusion without your help." Dorothea Dix, a fiercely ambitious, yet consumptive young teacher, was still a decade away from her major work as an advocate for the mentally ill.
"the worst of all slaveries": MTM and EPP, *Moral Culture of Infancy, and Kindergarten Guide* (Boston: T.O.H.P.; Burnham, N.Y.: O. S. Felt, 1863), p. 190.

"willing to be baffled": MTP to GFP, October 14, 1837, Straker typescripts, p. 1219, Antiochiana.

"my secret mind": MTP to EPP, August 15, [1832], HM Papers, MHS.

"they give one a taste . . . dissolving": MTP to Miss Rawlins Pickman, September 25, 1829, HMII Papers, MHS.

"evaporating . . . seasons of the year": MTP to Miss Rawlins Pickman, January 13, 1828, HMII Papers, MHS.

"physicating . . . *women doctors*": MTP to SAP, September 19, 1823, Berg. My date: [September 19, 1832].

"I have come to the end . . . proper hard": MTP to Maria Chase, [late March 1831], Peabody Family Papers, Smith.

239   "came down to the rocks . . . all by ourselves!": MTP to EPP, August 16, [1832], HM Papers, MHS.

"delicious . . . had been in sickness": MTP to EPP, September 4, 1832, HM Papers, MHS.

"fictions . . . to their race": MTP to Lydia Sears Haven, June 20, 1833, MTP Correspondence, MHS.

240   "so painful . . . little school": MTM, "Estimate of Horace Mann," entry of January 24, 1860, HM Papers, Journal X, MHS.

"so queer . . . pleasanter winter": Caroline Dall, "Studies towards the life of 'A business Woman' being Conversations with Mrs. R. P. Clarke in the winter of 1864-5," Caroline Wells Healey Dall Papers, Schlesinger. See also note on pp. 518-19 on the reliability of Mrs. Clarke's reminiscences as she speculates on Elizabeth's attachment to Horace Mann.

"seems to be unfortunate": Mrs. EPP to GFP, n.d., HM Papers, MHS.

"every mite": MTP to Sally Jackson Gardner, November 17, 1832, HM Papers, MHS.

$25 fees per term . . . "Miss E. P. Peabody's school" EPP to SAP, n.d., in series "60 a.l. EPP to SAP," Berg 135144B. My date: [ca. October 16, 1832].

"If we have . . . for that": MTP to Lydia Sears Haven, n.d. [November 8 and 11, 1832], Berg.

Elizabeth's credit: EPP to SAP, n.d., in series "60 a.l. EPP to SAP," Berg 135127B. My date: [October 24, 1832].

"apron full . . . Mrs. Clarke!": Caroline Dall, "Studies towards the life of 'A business Woman' being Conversations with Mrs. R. P. Clarke in the winter of 1864-5," Caroline Wells Healey Dall Papers, Schlesinger.

"our own personal poverty": MTP to Lydia Sears Haven, n.d. [November 8 and 11, 1832], Berg.

"interest in life itself": MTM, "Estimate of Horace Mann," entry of January 24, 1860, HM Papers, Journal X, MHS.

241   "set out to examine . . . finely developed": SAP journal April 11-[July] 31, [1830], entry of April 12, Berg.

Far from quackery: John D. Davies, *Phrenology, Fad and Science: A Nineteenth-Century American Crusade* (New Haven, Conn.: Yale University Press, 1955), pp. 12-29.

fascination and influence: Madeleine B. Stern, *A Phrenological Dictionary of Nineteenth-Century Americans* (Westport, Conn., and London: Greenwood Press, 1982).

thousands of mourners . . . landscaped hillside: Davies, *Phrenology*, pp. 17-18; also MTP to SAP, Tuesday, [November 20?, 1832], Berg.

242   "discovered a truth": MTP to SAP, Tuesday, [November 20?, 1832], Berg.

"absolutely necessary": MTP to Sally Jackson Gardner, November 17, 1832, HM Papers, MHS.

242   "we view the decease": "Remains of Dr. Spurzheim," *Boston Medical and Surgical Journal,* November 21, 1832.

"left unsaid ... totally irreparable": MTP to SAP, n.d. [November 12?, 1832], Berg.

"I want to die": MTP to Sally Jackson Gardner, November 17, 1832, HM Papers, MHS.

cities gained the advantage: Howard P. Chudacoff, *The Evolution of American Urban Society* (Englewood Cliffs, N.J.: Prentice Hall, 1981), pp. 62, 53.

five thousand single women: Joanne J. Meyerowitz, *Women Adrift: Independent Wage Earners in Chicago, 1880–1930* (Chicago and London: University of Chicago Press, 1988), p. 3.

one-third of the adult male: Howard P. Chudacoff, *The Age of the Bachelor: Creating an American Subculture* (Princeton, N.J.: Princeton University Press, 1999), p. 29.

243   Mrs. Clarke's household: By coincidence, Mrs. Rebecca Clarke's mother-in-law, an earlier Mrs. Clarke, was proprietress of the first boarding house near King's Chapel in Boston, where the Joseph Pearse Palmer family lived after the sale of Friendship Hall in the 1780s. At that time urban boarders were primarily families or married couples who could not afford their own homes—or single men, such as Royall Tyler. It is unlikely that either Rebecca Clarke or the Peabody sisters knew of this connection.

"immense & choice ... letters in manuscript": MTP to Lydia Sears Haven, May 26, 1832, Straker typescripts, p. 598, Antiochiana.

"the two intellectual Mr. Emersons": EPP to HM, n.d. [December 30, 1833], Straker typescripts, p. 693, Antiochiana.

The notion that Mary Moody Emerson pushed her nephew Ralph Waldo in Elizabeth Peabody's direction is likely a matter of legend; it was reported more than a half century afterward without substantiation in Franklin Sanborn's "A Concord Note-Book: The Women of Concord—III. Louisa Alcott and her Circle" (The Critic, vol. 48, no. 4, April 1906, p. 345), along with Sanborn's speculation that Miss Peabody was "probably too talented and amiable for the match." The case for Charles is stronger. Mary Moody Emerson wrote of Elizabeth to Charles on March 13, 1833: "You 'do not take' to a certain correspondent of mine. She does to you—hopes you will call. My devout wish is that you might take so strongly to some [illegible] character of the sex as will give your life new interest."

Charles wrote back his opinion of Elizabeth Peabody on April 11, 1833: "I think we are as well acquainted as we ever shall be—for a certain measure of fine taste & delicate manners ... I require in a woman in order to be attracted." In August 1833, Charles became engaged to Elizabeth Hoar, a Transcendentally inclined neighbor in Concord and daughter of a prominent judge. Mary Moody Emerson to Charles Chauncy Emerson and Charles Chauncy Emerson to Mary Moody Emerson, Emerson Family Papers, bMS Am 1280.226 (724) and (76), Houghton. I am grateful to Phyllis Cole, biographer of Mary Moody Emerson, for directing me to these letters.

"one of those conversations ... free paraphrase": EPP, "Emerson as Preacher," F. B. Sanborn, ed., *The Genius and Character of Emerson: Lectures at the Concord School of Philosophy* (Port Washington, N.Y.: Kennikat Press, 1971, reprint of 1885 edition), pp. 151–52. By Elizabeth's account, Emerson's aunt Mary was more interested in brokering an intellectual match than a romantic one.

first state-sponsored railroad: While the charter for the new railroad coincided with the opening of America's first commercial railroad in South Carolina, the nearly insurmountable problem of laying track through the rough granite of the Berkshires in western Massachusetts ultimately stalled the completion of a rail connection to the west until after the Civil War. This delay may have been the primary reason that Boston fell behind New York City as a commercial force by midcentury.

244   "a learned, pious": Jonathan Messerli, *Horace Mann* (New York: Alfred A. Knopf, 1972), p. 99.

"invasion . . . inquiries after truth": Messerli, *Horace Mann*, p. 100.

"I believe in the rugged": HM to MTM, May 25, 1850, Messerli, *Horace Mann*, p. 7.

245   "young men come down": EPP to William Wordsworth, March 27, 1829, Margaret Neussendorfer, ed., "Elizabeth Palmer Peabody to William Wordsworth: Eight Letters, 1825-1845," *Studies in the American Renaissance 1984* (Charlottesville: University Press of Virginia), p. 188.

246   "is elicited . . . his own": HM, "American Genius," n.d. [1816], HM Papers, MHS.

"a long series": HM, "Against Novels," October 1817, HM Papers, MHS.

"the imagination is . . . nor ideas enlargement": HM, "Against Fiction," November 22, 1817, HM Papers, MHS.

"there is by nature . . . philosopher": HM, "Self-Improvement," n.d. [1819], HM Papers, MHS.

"the common idea": HM, "Oration. Delivered at the final examination Dinner of the Senior Class, July 13, 1819," HM Papers, MHS.

"'Tis pleasant . . . consuming": HM to Rebecca Mann, June 7, 1819, HM Papers, MHS.

247   "in the character of an *avowed*": HM to Charlotte Messer, July 8, 1829, HM Family Papers, Brown.

Charlotte became pregnant: Charlotte Messer Mann to HM, March 17, 1832, HM Family Papers, Brown. The passage reads: "I intended to devote yesterday afternoon *exclusively* to you, to satisfy you that my health is really good and that— *something else.*"

"a scene of anxiety": Messerli, *Horace Mann*, p. 160. One scholar of Horace Mann's life theorizes that Charlotte died of "childbed fever or hemorrhage following a still-birth" rather than from tuberculosis: Robert Lincoln Straker to Orville Prescott, January 17, 1950, Antiochiana. Straker draws on his own interview ca. 1950 with an elderly "Miss H." in Dedham, who had known a former neighbor of the Manns in her childhood. The neighbor, Mrs. Abby Guild, herself quite old at the time of her acquaintance with a much younger "Miss H.," reportedly said that "Charlotte had died because of premature birth of a child or in childbed, and that the child also died." Straker ultimately concluded that "there was a miscarriage about two weeks before Charlotte's death, that she was thought to be recovering, that the suddenness of her death indicates hemorrhage though possibly childbed fever": Robert Lincoln Straker to Horace Mann III, n.d., Antiochiana. Mann himself, however, never referred to a child or a pregnancy, perhaps out of delicacy, or grief. In any case, Charlotte had long suffered from tuberculosis, and her poor health was at the very least a significant factor in her death, and in the doomed pregnancy.

turned Mann's dark hair: The story of Horace Mann's hair changing color virtually overnight was widely told and was quite likely true—although some accounts gave the color as white, and others as gray. In 1834, Elizabeth arranged a meeting between Horace Mann and a Dedham friend, Catherine Haven Hilliard, who had not seen Mann since just before Charlotte's death in 1832. "She said he looked better than she expected," Elizabeth wrote in a letter to Mary, "except that his hair was grey. I asked her if she did not know *that* before, and she said *no*. I told her it was so when I first saw him. She said yes, it was probably an immediate effect": EPP to MTP, [August 26–30(?), 1834], Berg.

248   "He came into my sphere ... would have marred it": [MTM], "An Experience," n.d., HM papers, MHS; also published as "Mary Peabody Mann's Short Story, 'An Experience,'" Megan Marshall, ed., *Proceedings of the Massachusetts Historical Society*, vol. 98 (1986), pp. 76–89.

    "corruscations ... back to us": MTP to SAP, February 17–[18], 1833, Berg.

249   "People's ideas get": MTP to SAP, n.d., Berg 371465B. My date: [March or April 1833].

    "he poured out his grief": MTM, "Journal of Remembrance," entry of January 24, 1860, from "Estimate of Horace Mann," HM Papers, Journal X, MHS.

    "I regret exceedingly ... strangers": HM to MTP, n.d. [April 1833], HM Papers, MHS.

    "I have felt ... countenance": MTP to SAP, n.d., Straker typescripts, p. 642, Antiochiana. My date: [April 1833].

250   "never imagined": SAH to MTM, February 6, [1844], Berg.

    "comfort": SAP to EPP, "Friday eve.," March 1, [n.y.], in series "20 a.l.s. SAP to EPP," Berg. My date: March 1, [1833].

    "thought me perfection ... not satisfied": [MTM], "An Experience," n.d., HM Papers, MHS.

    "radiant mood": SAP to MTP, July 11, [1833], Berg.

    "sublime face ... glorious": MTP to SAP, n.d. [early July 1833], Straker typescripts, pp. 647 and 649, Antiochiana.

    "a sort of little ecstacy ... electrifying part": MTP to SAP, n.d. [early July 1833], Straker typescripts, pp. 647–48, Antiochiana.

    "The Little Dove": Frederic Adolphus Krummacher's collection of fables *Parabelin* was first published in 1805. "The Little Dove" was not translated into English until 1839 (Boston: Weeks, Jordan); this translation was reviewed by Margaret Fuller in the January 1841 *Dial*. Mary had not written out a translation of "The Little Dove," but, now more adept at German than Elizabeth, she had retold the story in her own words to Horace Mann.

    "*he* was the man ... con amore": MTP to SAP, n.d. [early July 1833], Straker typescripts, pp. 647–48, Antiochiana. Although I have been unable to find the article, Mary seems to have been certain that it would see print: "I have been writing an account of it for the Christian Register which you will see." Her chief concern was that Sophia and her parents "not tell a mortal that I wrote it." She closed her letter with a reminder to Sophia to "tell Father not to tell any one that I wrote that account for the paper."

251   "talk, talk, talk, ad infinitum": MTP to Lydia Sears Haven, March 31, 1833, Straker typescripts, p. 638, Antiochiana.

    "hold metaphysical arguments ... taking in the subject": MTP to SAP, n.d., Berg 371486B. My date: [ca. July 2, 1833].

    other boarders speculating: In a much-quoted passage from Caroline Dall's interview with Mrs. Clarke in the winter of 1864–1865, Clarke states:

    "Everybody thought Miss Elizabeth was dead set on Horace Mann. He wouldn't come out of his chamber for a week after his first wife died, & I had to send his dinner up. One day Elizabeth Peabody wanted to take it. 'No' said I 'it isn't proper Miss Peabody. I don't want you to.' 'Oh but I must' said she 'I've got something to say to Mr. Mann.' Then they all began to talk about Mr. Mann's marrying again. Elizabeth declared indignantly that he'd never be married again. 'In your presence' said Mr. Fairbanks, laying his hand on his heart, 'In *your* presence Miss Elizabeth I think he will!' Great fool! He really seemed to think he'd said just the right thing."

There is much in the passage, such as Mrs. Clarke's placing the date of Horace Mann's wife's death during his residence in her household, as well as in the rest of the interview, to cast doubt on the accuracy of her recollections. Mrs. Clarke may not have particularly liked Elizabeth as a renter, but more likely she was thinking of Elizabeth's much more public and eccentric persona at the time of this interview. Further, the younger fiery-tempered Dall had recently had a falling-out with Elizabeth, once her mentor, and seems here to have transferred her adoration to Mrs. Clarke. Dall was ready to hear nasty gossip, and Mrs. Clarke was happy to provide it. Caroline Dall, "Studies towards the life of 'A business Woman' being Conversations with Mrs. R. P. Clarke in the winter of 1864-5," Caroline Wells Healey Dall Papers, Schlesinger.

"She wanted to excel ... strength of her nature": [MTM], "An Experience," n.d., HM Papers, MHS.

"I can get food": EPP to Sarah Russell Sullivan, November 1827, Straker typescripts, p. 454, Antiochiana.

252 "deep gloom ... tears flow": EPP to SAP, n.d., in series "60 a.l. EPP to SAP," Berg 135152B. My date: [after March 18, 1833].

"he laid his head ... feelings": EPP to MTP, January 16-21 [20?, 1835], Berg.

"I do not know": EPP to MTP, [week of May 16, 1836], Berg.

"one of the few": EPP to SAP, February 24, [1833], in series "60 a.l. EPP to SAP," Berg 135137B. In *Letters of EPP*, pp. 154-56, Bruce Ronda misdates this letters as [February 21, 1836].

"Jupiter brow": EPP to SAP, n.d., in series "60 a.l. EPP to SAP," Berg 135151B. My date: [ca. April 10, 1833].

"one of Nature's noblemen": EPP to SAP, February 24, [1833], in series "60 a.l. EPP to SAP," Berg 135137B. In *Letters of EPP*, pp. 154-56, Bruce Ronda misdates this letter as [February 21, 1836].

"Love-in-the-Eternal-Reason ... I rise!": EPP, "Chastity," 1833, Autograph file, Houghton. Elizabeth wrote the poem after seeing her friend Mary Ann Dwight's drawing of the Gorgon Medusa, perhaps the most powerful female figure in Greek mythology and one of three sisters. Dwight's drawings can be seen in her illustrated volume *Greek and Roman Mythology* (New York: Putnam, 1849), facing page 283.

Chastity was a concept that had powerful meaning for men of this proto-Transcendentalist era as well. Two years later, Elizabeth wrote to Mary summarizing an early lecture by Ralph Waldo Emerson: "Did I tell you of W.E.'s lecture on Milton? It was beautiful. He called him the poet of Chastity. He said every now and then a being was born who might be called *an Adam*, so entirely was he himself alone—uncontaminated humanity. Homer, Milton, George Washington, and I forget who else was among these *Adams*." EPP to MTP, February 25, [1835], Berg.

253 "I did feel ... we both could drink": EPP to MTP, [week of May 16, 1836], Berg.
"It is the supreme delight": EPP to MTP, January 16-21 [20?, 1835], Berg.
"happy union ... circumstances": EPP to MTP, [week of May 16, 1836], Berg.
"to take out his heart": [MTM], "An Experience," n.d., HM Papers, MHS.
"my dear friend ... composed of affection": HM to MTP, August 26, 1833, HM Papers, MHS.

254 "had I not given him": MTM, "Journal of Remembrance" from "Estimate of Horace Mann," entry of January 24, 1860, HM Papers, Journal X, MHS.
"Our school has about": MTP to Lydia Sears Haven, March 15, 1833, Straker typescripts, p. 637, Antiochiana.
"I intend to live in Boston": MTP to Lydia Sears Haven, June 20, 1833, MTP Correspondence, MHS.
"feebler & more easily tired": EPP to SAP, n.d., in series "60 a.l. EPP to SAP," Berg 135126B. My date: [ca. July 11, 1833].

255 "If I can get E. . . . *out of the country* first": MTP to Lydia Sears Haven, March 15, 1833, Straker typescripts, p. 637, Antiochiana.
"dwelling too intently": MTP to HM, August 24, 1833, Straker typescripts, pp. 663-64, Antiochiana.
"the impressions our manner": EPP to MTP, January 16-21 [20?, 1835], Berg.
"tyrannize . . . distrust": EPP to MTP, January 5 [6?]-7, [1835], Berg.
"I found every female . . . current of thought": HM to EPP, n.d. [late July or August 1833], HM Papers, MHS.
"you will then truly": HM to MTP, August 26, 1833, HM Papers, MHS.
wanted to economize: Messerli, *Horace Mann*, p. 168. Messerli writes that Mann moved into his law offices, where he lived "sleeping on a horsehair couch" for the next three years. However, Mary Peabody reports that Mann had "commenced his solitary life at the French lady's rooms where he is to take his breakfast and tea alone, and dine at the Tremont": MTP to SAP, n.d., Berg 52B2457. My date: [August 1833?]. The Straker collection includes receipts for lodging paid to a Madame Coiffard. Perhaps his office was in his rooms at Mme. Coiffard's.
"frolic . . . gayest hearted creature": MTP to SAP, n.d. [early July 1833], Straker typescripts, p. 648, Antiochiana.

256 "time will do . . . *anguish*": EPP to SAP, Thursday p.m. [August 1833], in series "60 a.l. EPP to SAP," Berg 227451B.
"the sound of his voice . . . remark about him": [MTM], "An Experience," n.d., HM Papers, MHS.
"abomination of desolation": MTP to SAP, n.d. [late July 1833], Straker typescripts, p. 658, Antiochiana.

PAGE   *23. Blind Fair*

257 "hypersympathetic": SAP to EPP, May 26, 1838, Berg.
"perpetual torture": SAP to MTP, July 28, 1832, Berg.
"such a passion": MTP to Mrs. EPP, September 6, 1832, MTP Correspondence, MHS.
"retreat of the Arts and Graces": SAP to William Russell, December 8, 1832, Autograph file, Houghton.
"spicy flowers . . . rude sound": SAP to MTP, July 28, 1832, Berg.

258 "we enjoy him imprisoned": SAP to MTP, August 5, 1832, Berg.
"absconded to the attic . . . overfatigue": SAP to William Russell, December 8, 1832, Autograph file, Houghton.
favorite books: Samuel Rogers, *Italy, A Poem* (London: T. Cadell and E. Moxon, 1830), p. 207. The *Temple of Paestum* and *Galileo's Villa* (p. 115) became standard subjects for Sophia, used on the hand-painted baskets and cigar cases she began to sell in 1833.

"natural ... treasures of Boston": SAP to William Russell, December 8, 1832, Autograph file, Houghton.

"let your pen be my eyes": SAP to MTP, [January 8]–9 [1832?], Berg. My date: [January 8, 1833].

"minimum of a house ... want of room": SAP to unknown correspondent, October 22, 1832, Rose Hawthorne Lathrop, *Memories of Hawthorne* (Boston and New York: Houghton Mifflin, 1897), p. 8. Sophia repeated the phrase "minimum of a house" as well as several other comments on her arrival in Salem in her retrospective letter to William Russell, December 8, 1832, Autograph file, Houghton.

"peculiar bond ... invalid state": SAH to MTM, Thursday, [1853], HM Papers, MHS.

259   "my soul is knit": SAH to MTM, n.d. [1853], HM Papers, MHS.

"demon in my head": SAP to EPP, October [1823?], Berg.

"There is no person living": SAP to EPP, n.d. [after September 29, 1835], Stanford.

"We live for ... their comfort": Mrs. EPP to SAP, [Salem?, 1828?], Berg 229967B.

"specimens of genius ... valued for her sake": [Mrs. EPP] ms. novel, MHS. Like Eliza Peabody and Sophia, Polly Palmer used the spelling "headach" in her letters and journals.

"future usefulness": Mrs. EPP to EPP, June 1822, Straker typescripts, p. 145, Antiochiana.

"to be independant": Mrs. EPP to SAP, July 3, 1827, Berg.

"independant & useful ... girls as well as boys": Mrs. EPP to EPP and MTP, October 4, 1824, Straker typescripts, p. 250 ff, Antiochiana.

"fussation": EPP to MTP, February 24–25, 1834, Berg.

"frequent and severe headachs": Mrs. EPP to EPP, June 1822, Straker typescripts, p. 145, Antiochiana.

"avoidance of circumstances": Oliver Sacks, *Migraine: Understanding a Common Disorder* (Berkeley and Los Angeles: University of California Press, 1985), p. 215.

previous biographers: Both Louise Hall Tharp, in *Peabody Sisters of Salem* (Boston: Little, Brown, 1950), and James Mellow, in *Nathaniel Hawthorne in His Times* (Boston: Houghton Mifflin, 1980), promoted the theory that Mrs. Peabody was an overprotective mother whose desire to control and confine her youngest daughter was the chief source of Sophia's invalidism. This view of Mrs. Peabody has spread through most published accounts of the sisters in books on the Hawthorne family and the Transcendentalist era published since then. A thorough reading of Mrs. Peabody's letters to her daughters, however, yields little evidence to support this theory. Indeed, Mrs. Peabody seems to have been primarily an inspiration and a support to her independent-minded daughters.

260   "look upon herself": Norman Holmes Pearson, "Elizabeth Peabody on Hawthorne," *Essex Institute Historical Collections*, July 1958, p. 267.

"Unknown yet known": SAP ms. poem, n.d., SAH Papers, box 1, folder 14, Stanford.

"love & loveliness ... and headach": SAP to William Russell, December 8, 1832, Autograph file, Houghton.

"sweet little chamber ... is to me now": SAP journal beginning October 1832, Salem, entry of October 22, Stanford. Mary Newhall's benefactor Mary Rotch of New Bedford had been among the first to purchase one of Sophia's copies.

261   "What think you ... *create*": SAP to MTP, November 20, 1832, Berg.

"added a castle ... first creation": SAP journal beginning October 1832, Salem, entry of November 19, Stanford.

"Do you wonder": SAP to MTP, November 20, 1832, Berg.

261 "Landscape after landscape ... my senses": SAP journal beginning October 1832, Salem, entry of November 19, Stanford.

medieval mystic: Oliver Sacks writes about Hildegard of Bingen in *Migraine*, pp. 106–109. The neurologist Alice Flaherty, author of *The Midnight Disease* (Boston: Houghton Mifflin, 2004), lists among the well-known writers influenced by migraine: Virginia Woolf, Henry James, Dostoevsky, and Lewis Carroll, for whom "Alice-in-Wonderland" auras, "in which visual objects shrink or enlarge," are named. I am grateful to Dr. Flaherty of Boston's Massachusetts General Hospital for providing me with this information.

"whirling like a top ... command my attention": SAP to MTP, November 20, 1832, Berg.

Salvator Rosa ... Mount Vesuvius: Mary Newhall may have been working from an engraving based on Angelica Kauffman's 1785 painting, which pictures Pliny the Younger studying with his mother as they observe the eruption of Vesuvius from a safe distance. Sophia appears not to have known of Angelica Kauffman, nor of any of the several successful female painters in Europe whose accomplishments might have inspired her. But Kauffman's work was frequently engraved and could have crossed the Atlantic unattributed in this manner.

The Salvator Rosa landscape that Sophia copied was probably a copy itself, although the owners, Maria and Henry Rice, viewed it as an original; "sacred" and "so old": SAP to MTP, January 17, 1833, Berg. Rosa was at the start of a long line of artistic influence that reached Sophia Peabody through Washington Allston. One of Allston's early works, *Saul and the Witch of Endor* (1820), was painted "after" Benjamin West's version of the same subject, which in turn was inspired by Salvator Rosa's. See Richard W. Wallace, *Salvator Rosa in America: Catalogue* (Wellesley, Mass.: Wellesley College Museum, Jewett Art Center, 1979).

"profound quiet ... possession of soul": SAP to William Russell, December 8, 1832, Autograph file, Houghton.

262 "I assure you ... benevolence and excellence": EPP to SAP, February 24, [1833], in series "60 a.l. EPP to SAP," Berg 135177B. In *Letters of EPP*, pp. 154–56, Bruce Ronda misdates this letter as [February 21, 1836].

"benign & sweet": SAP to EPP, June 28, 1833, in series "20 a.l.s. SAP to EPP," Berg.

"half-dozen first pupils ... highways and byways": Franklin B. Sanborn, *Dr. S. G. Howe: The Philanthropist* (New York: Funk and Wagnalls, 1891), p. 118.

"one of the most romantic": Elisabeth Gitter, *The Imprisoned Guest: Samuel Howe and Laura Bridgman, the Original Deaf-Blind Girl* (New York: Picador, 2001), p. 28.

"invented and laboriously executed ... self-denial": Sanborn, *Dr. S. G. Howe*, p. 118.

264 "a great advantage ... of contributing all": EPP to SAP, n.d., Saturday night, February 24, [1833], in series "60 a.l. EPP to SAP," Berg 135137B. In *Letters of EPP*, pp. 154–56, Bruce Ronda misdates this letter as [1836].

"bazaar": Deborah Pickman Clifford, *Crusader for Freedom: A Life of Lydia Maria Child* (Boston: Beacon Press, 1992), p. 109.

"Boston and Salem seemed": Samuel Gridley Howe, *Second Annual Report of the Trustees of the Perkins Institution and Massachusetts Asylum for the Blind*, quoted in Gitter, *The Imprisoned Guest*, p. 43.

special benefit edition: This second edition of *The Water-Spirit* (Boston: Stimson and Clapp, 1833) joined a distinguished list that included Samuel Knapp's *Life of Daniel Webster* and the multivolume *American Library of Useful Knowledge*, published under the auspices of the Boston Society for the Diffusion of Useful Knowledge, then New England's preeminent lecture society and soon to be sponsor of Ralph Waldo Emerson's early career as a public speaker.

Elizabeth's free translation of La Motte-Fouqué's *Undine* had first appeared without attribution in her anonymously edited 1828 anthology, *The Casket*. Now she added an introductory "Advertisement," announcing the purpose of the new edition: "reprinted for the benefit of the School of the Blind, to which the proceeds of the edition are dedicated." She signed this preface "E.P.P.," among the first instances of her use of her initials as her signature in print. Copies were sold at both the Salem and Boston Blind Fairs.

"I may as well suffer . . . rational philosophy": SAP to EPP, April 10, [1833? 1829?], Berg. My date: April 10, [1833].

265 "when I [may] come": SAP to MTP, January 17, 1833, Berg.

"Four of them . . . too beautiful for the fair": SAP to MTP, no. 12 in series "22 a.l.s. SAP to MTP," Berg. My date: [April 7, 8, 9, 1833].

"2 splendid Paintings": *Catalogue of Articles to be offered for Sale at The Ladies' Fair* (Salem, April 10, 1833), Houghton. The other item listed by name was a story called "Blind Miriam Restored to Sight" by Sarah Savage, who operated a girls' academy in Salem.

Scene near Bristol, England (illustration on p. 266), owned by the Peabody Essex Museum, is likely one of the two paintings Sophia offered for sale at the fair.

gift of an estate: Perkins had promised to donate the mansion house and grounds if $50,000 were raised from other sources (Gitter, *The Imprisoned Guest*, p. 43). After the second fair in Boston, Mary wrote to Sophia, "It is supposed they took ten or twelve thousand dollars—and with this all but 15,000 of the 50,000 is subscribed!" MTP to SAP, n.d., Berg 371364B.

"nutshell": SAP to MTP, in series "22 a.l.s. SAP to MTP," Berg. My date: April 13, [1833].

266 "for the first time": SAP to EPP, n.d., "Monday eve. 15th 6 oclk," in series "20 a.l.s. SAP to EPP," Berg. My date: [April 15, 1833].

"pleasant . . . ought to be framed": SAP to EPP, November 2, 1833, Berg.

267 "Everybody who sees": SAP to MTP, "Monday eve. 15th 6 oclk," in series "22 a.l.s. SAP to MTP," Berg. My date: [April 15, 1833].

$68 ("I found that edition of Flaxman sold for *68 dollars—today!* My illustrations will not cost a third as much") . . . "gems": EPP to Sarah Hale, [May 15, 1833], *Letters of EPP*, p. 110.

"enchanting": SAP to EPP, May 21–22, [1833], Berg.

268 "the idea of being": SAP to EPP, May 21–22, [1833], Berg. Sophia added extra steps to the procedure because she was reluctant to draw freehand on the lithographic stones; it was a medium that did not allow for correction of mistakes. Sophia first drew the outlines on tissue paper and then followed a method she described several years later in a letter to Elizabeth: "My process was to rub in the red powder upon the back of the tissue paper—after tracing the picture with the steel point upon one side—& then I laid the powdered side upon the stone very carefully—sealing each corner to prevent its stirring—& then with the point went over every line again so as to impress them in red upon the stone—Then with the peculiar brushes & ink I went over the lines—& it is necessary to make the line black & distinct at the *first stroke* or it will look badly—. . . My soul aches to think of it." SAP to EPP, May 19, [1836?], Berg. The "red powder" Sophia refers to was red ocher. EPP to MTP, [May 15, 1836], Berg.

"deepest despair": SAP to MTP, June 17, 1833, Berg.

268   "violent headach": SAP to MTP, n.d., in series "22 a.l.s. SAP to MTP," Berg. My date: June 27, [1833].

"a tide of disappointment": SAP to MTP, June 17, 1833, Berg.

"a great and noble undertaking": WEC quoted in MTP to SAP, June 19, 1833, Lathrop, *Memories of Hawthorne*, p. 12.

Inman, Allston, Morse, Sully: WEC to EPP, n.d., Records of New England Hospital for Women and Children, box 22, no. 698, Smith. My date: [after August 21, 1833].

"taken to whirling": SAP to MTP, August 7, [1833], Berg.

"more feeble . . . last summer": SAP to EPP, [August] 1833, Berg 227451B.

"the lowest ebb of declension": MTP to Lydia Sears Haven, March 15, 1833, Straker typescripts, p. 637, Antiochiana.

below eighty pounds: In June, Sophia wrote to Elizabeth from Salem that she had stepped "out of bed, all stuffed up with a cold in my head, with seventy six pounds upon every muscle." SAP to EPP, June 28, 1833, in series "20 a.l.s. SAP to EPP," Berg.

269   "You and I would be . . . little boys to teach": MTP to SAP, Wednesday evening, [September? 1833?], Berg 52B2456.

"abomination of desolation": MTP to SAP, n.d. [late July 1833], Straker typescripts, p. 658, Antiochiana.

"nothing but *muslin* or *linen*": SAP to Misses Chase, n.d., Peabody Family Papers, Smith. My date: [1833 before departure to Cuba].

"a dread vacuum of waiting": SAP to Lydia Sears Haven, October 25–November 1, 1833, Berg.

"a tossing condition of mind": MTP to Miss Rawlins Pickman, Tuesday Eve., n.d., Straker typescripts, p. 653, Antiochiana. My date: [1833].

"*delicious* sympathy": MTP to SAP, Wednesday evening, [September? 1833?], Berg 52B2456.

"engaged to any body . . . decided your mind": EPP to MTP, July 15, [1834], Berg.

"When the ocean rolled . . . outside of creation": [MTM], "An Experience," n.d., HM Papers, MHS.

270   Athenaeum's 1834 exhibition: There were several other women whose work was shown in the Athenaeum's 1834 Eighth Exhibition. One was Sarah Clarke, the daughter of Mary and Elizabeth's landlady Rebecca Clarke, whose *Moonlight* was her first Athenaeum entry of several during the next two decades. Another, Mrs. S. C. Richardson, entered her *Portrait of S. B. Knox, U.S. Navy* in the miniatures category. There was a portrait of Bishop Griswold with "head by Stuart, drapery by his daughter," and a copy of Leonardo's *John the Baptist* by Sarah W. Lippett of Providence, which may have been the first work by a woman to join the Athenaeum's permanent collection, probably as a donation from the artist. There were 225 paintings in the show and 9 miniatures. *Catalogue of the Eighth Exhibition of Paintings in the Athenaeum Gallery* (Boston: J. H. Eastburn, 1834).

PAGE   *24. Cuba Journals*

271   "squalling . . . night till morning": SAP to Mrs. EPP, January 13, 1834, in Claire Badaracco, ed., *The Cuba Journal, 1833–35, by Sophia Peabody Hawthorne* (Ann Arbor, Mich.: University Microfilms International, 1985), p. 12. This annotated version of Sophia Peabody's three-volume manuscript journal (SAP *CJ* in these notes) was completed as a dissertation in 1981. All of Sophia's letters in this journal

were addressed to her mother; several of Mary's letters home, addressed either to her mother or her father, were bound with Sophia's volumes and also appear in Badaracco's edition. When I quote from Mary's letters, I identify both Mary and her correspondent.

"gross immorality and vice": Dorcas Hiller Cleveland to SAP, February 18, 1830, HM 25370, Huntington.

"the ever-faithful isle": See Karen Robert's excellent introduction to *New Year in Cuba: Mary Gardner Lowell's Travel Diary, 1831-32* (Boston: Massachusetts Historical Society, Northeastern University Press, 2003), p. 16.

"any woman ... assignation": Dorcas Hiller Cleveland to SAP, February 18, 1830, HM 25370, Huntington.

"lose [her] reputation in a week": MTP quoted in EPP to MTP, [August 8-10, 1834], Berg.

272   "lofty and luxuriant ... full of birds": MTP to Mrs. EPP, January 8, 1834, SAP *CJ*, p. 183.

"vast garden of the island": Reverend Abiel Abbot, D.D., *Letters Written in the Interior of Cuba, Between the Mountains of Arcana, to the East, and of Cusco, to the West, in the Months of February, March, April, and May, 1828* (Boston: Bowles and Dearborn, 1829), p. xiii.

"with soft dark eyes": SAP to Maria Chase, January 12, 1834, Peabody Family Papers, Smith.

"has taken my case": letter of January 13, 1834, SAP *CJ*, p. 13.

"genial perspirations": letter of August 11, 1834, SAP *CJ*, p. 250.

"hard, red earth": letter of January 17, 1834, SAP *CJ*, p. 19.

"plains": SAP to Mary Wilder White [Foote], January 30, 1834, Berg 72B4936.

"just made": letter of March 16, 1834, SAP *CJ*, p. 58.

274   "vast colonnade ... white as marble": SAP to Mary Wilder White [Foote], January 30, 1834, Berg 72B4936.

"What are two or three": WC quoted in EPP to MTP, June 23-26, [1834], Berg.

Tuberculosis was the common element in the deaths of invalids who traveled to the Caribbean in hopes of recovery. Ralph Waldo Emerson's brother Edward died in Puerto Rico in 1834 at age twenty-nine, after suffering with the illness for most of his adult life. Yet the Reverend Channing, who had spent the winter of 1830 to 1831 in St. Croix, experienced some relief from his ailments, which did not include TB. Tuberculosis may have accounted for as many as one-quarter of the deaths of all New Englanders during the first half of the nineteenth century and was the single deadliest disease in North America at the time. For a tuberculosis patient, a voyage to the tropics was unlikely to provide anything more than a diversion from an inexorably downward course. See Robert, ed., *New Year in Cuba*, p. 13.

"My old tired ... blood grows thinner": letter of January 17, 1834, SAP *CJ*, p. 15.

275   "the incubus of slavery": MTP to EPP, May 13 or 14, [1834], Berg.

"enthusiastic, devoted ... she is near": SAP to Mary Wilder White [Foote], January 30, 1834, Berg 72B4936.

"get used to": On February 16, 1834, Mary wrote to Miss Rawlins Pickman, "I can not get used to this slavery, nor do I wish to" (HMII Papers, MHS. My date: February [10? 16?], 1834). Elizabeth, who must have read the February 16 letter, or received one of her own in which Mary expressed the same sentiment, had responded on April 19, 1834, "I am worried about you.... This slavery too oppresses you. If you cannot feel better you must let me change places with you." EPP to MTP, April 19[-20], 1834, Berg.

275   "transcendental company": EPP to MTP, [February 28–March 15, 1835], Berg.

In August 1833, as the sisters made plans to sail for Cuba, Lydia Maria Child, the novelist who had burst upon the Boston literary scene in the mid-1820s with *Hobomok* (1824) and *The Rebels* (1825), and then became the best-selling author of *The Frugal Housewife* (1829), published *An Appeal in Favor of that Class of People Called Africans*, a work eventually credited with "converting more men and women to abolitionism than any other publication." Child was instantly denounced in Boston, her reader's privileges in the library of the Boston Athenaeum revoked, and her editorship of the children's magazine *Juvenile Miscellany* withdrawn. Her fellow abolitionist John Greenleaf Whittier later recalled that after *An Appeal*, Child "found no market for her books and essays and her praises were suddenly silenced." Elizabeth Peabody may have been both too much *of* Boston and too dependent *on* Boston to take a similar stand in 1833.

The Reverend Channing, however, paid Child a visit to discuss her book. Channing was not won over to the cause of abolition; he remained a "gradualist," believing that southern slave owners would eventually be persuaded to release their slaves. Yet a year later, in the fall of 1834, after an antiabolitionist mob had attacked William Lloyd Garrison on Boston Common, Channing delivered an eloquent sermon on slavery, admonishing Bostonians to tolerate the work of its abolitionist few, and deploring the slave system, which made property of the human soul. It was enough to let loose a storm of dissent in the clergy and within his congregation; Channing expanded the sermon into a 150-page book, *Slavery* (1835), which became a national bestseller even as he found himself reviled by many of his parishioners. Still, Channing would never be a one-issue prophet. At the same time as he was reworking *Slavery* for the press, he shepherded his 1834 Easter sermon, *The Future Life* (1835), into print; his 1839 address on "Self-Culture," a topic he had frequently discussed with Elizabeth as she translated de Gérando's *Self-Education*, was to be reprinted many times as well. What angered Channing most about slavery was typical of this progressive-minded Unitarian: its consignment of an entire race "generation after generation, to a merely animal and unimproving existence." See Deborah Pickman Clifford, *Crusader for Freedom: A Life of Lydia Maria Child* (Boston: Beacon Press, 1992), pp. 99–107; Jack Mendelsohn, *Channing: The Reluctant Radical* (Boston: Unitarian Universalist Association, 1979), pp. 233, 245–60; and Anne C. Rose, *Transcendentalism as a Social Movement, 1830–1850* (New Haven, Conn.: Yale University Press, 1981), pp. 20–21.

island with a population: According to 1827 census figures, Cuba's population numbered 286,946 slaves, 106,494 free blacks, and 311,051 whites. Robert, ed., *New Year in Cuba*, p. 16.

276   "like brutes": MTP to Dr. NP, March 27, 1834, SAP *CJ*, p. 196.

"nothing but fear . . . no slavery": MTP to EPP, August 21, 1834, Berg.

277   "whipped in a savage manner . . . out of sight": MTP to EPP, May 13 or 14, [1834], Berg.

"perfectly sick . . . her gown": MTP to EPP, August 21, 1834, Berg.

efforts at reform: Sophia joined Mary in this project to the extent of admonishing the Morrell boys to treat the house slaves with greater respect. In a late memoir, Mary writes: "One day when the little boy of six years old gave way to his anger with one of the gente, or *the people*, as the slaves were called, my sister said, 'That is not the way to treat people.' He looked at her amazed, and exclaimed, 'Is Tecla a people?' Upon which she laid open the principle that all souls are white, whatever may be the color of the skin. The child understood her perfectly, and from that time comported himself accordingly": MTM, "Reminiscences of School Life and Teaching," p. 317. The view that "all souls are white," while sounding racist today, was common among white Americans who opposed slavery.

"there is as much religion": MTP to Miss Rawlins Pickman, February 16?, 1834, HMII Papers, MHS.

distant Spanish monarch: Ferdinand VII had died in 1833, provoking concern among plantation owners in Cuba that the new queen, Isabella II, might enforce laws against the slave trade and bring a swift end to slavery on the island. When Mary heard Dr. Morrell express this worry, she secretly hoped he would be proved correct. "The regular course of things seems to be bringing the dreadful traffic to a close even here," she wrote home early in 1834, "and heaven grant that it may be so in spite of the Dr.'s wishes to the contrary": MTP to Mrs. EPP, March 16, 1834, SAP *CJ*, p. 202. But it was not to be. Spain held Cuba as a colony until 1898; slavery was not abolished until 1886.

"majestic figure": letter of January 21, 1835, SAP *CJ*, p. 565.

"this land of bondage": MTP to Miss Rawlins Pickman, August 6, 1834, HMII Papers, MHS.

Mary's novel, *Juanita: A Romance of Real Life in Cuba Fifty Years Ago* (Boston: D. Lothrop Company), was published shortly after her death in 1887. Mary worked on the book sporadically over many years, first making an outline for the novel while in Cuba in 1834 and 1835, then completing much of a draft during the 1850s, and finally revising the draft for publication in the 1880s. According to Elizabeth's preface to the 1887 edition, Mary decided she could not publish the novel while members of the Morrell family were still alive. A new edition of *Juanita*, with a useful preface by Patricia M. Ard, has been published by the University Press of Virginia (2000).

It should be noted that Mary and her mother and sisters were "gradualists" on the issue of slavery—along with Horace Mann and the Reverend William Ellery Channing—during the 1830s. Although virtually all in their circle agreed that slavery was wrong, there was great debate about the best means of ending slavery, and the Peabodys favored the least violent. An 1829 journal entry shows Mrs. Peabody's views on a variety of reform issues and on slavery's place among them:

"It is an encouragement to virtue to trace with accuracy and candour, the actual progress of society. . . . The Bible is circulated, slavery is slowly, but surely receding from the civilized world, moral instruction finds its way into the abodes of guilt, food and clothing into the abodes of penury; the treasures of science and literature are placed within reach of every aspirant after knowledge. Women are rising to their proper place in the seat of being . . . peace societies are increasing. . . ." Mrs. EPP commonplace book 1829–1832, Peabody Family Papers, 1790–1880, MHS.

Elizabeth also took the long view. In 1836, she led one of her historical classes in a discussion of the Saxons and the "old histories of the emancipations of serfs —which would be valuable to show what should be avoided & what might be imitated by our states in the work of gradual emancipation." Elizabeth tread a cautious line between the interests of the wealthy Boston women who supported her and the more radical members of her own circle. When she discussed the issue over lunch that same day with Bronson Alcott, a fervent abolitionist and advocate of immediate emancipation, she made a point of "avoiding the word 'gradual' & there was no explosion." EPP to MTP, April 11?–12?, [1836], Berg.

For her part, Mary objected to Charles Follen's 1834 advocacy of "amalgamation": interracial marriage in order to break down the divisions of the races. Follen, once an instructor of German languages at Harvard and a would-be Unitarian minister, lost his Harvard post and was refused a pulpit because of his views. Mary argued that Follen, along with the more extreme Quakers who favored amalgamation as well as abolition, had done harm to the cause, permitting slave owners like Dr. Morrell to dismiss all their antislavery efforts "because they *love a black skin.*" Eventually Follen established his own church in Lexington, Massachusetts; it was Unitarian in theology but independent of church authority.

Mary wrote to Elizabeth that she hoped Horace Mann "will not join that party" (MTP to EPP, August 20–23, [1834], Berg), but she need not have feared. Mann, who later made a valiant attempt to have slavery ruled unconstitutional in the District of Columbia by arguing the famous 1848 *Pearl* case, remained a gradualist through the 1830s. Mann's sympathies were with the American Colonization Society, founded in 1817, which promoted voluntary emancipation and proposed resettling black Americans in Liberia, rather than with William Lloyd Garrison's New England Anti-Slavery Society, founded in Boston in 1832, which took immediate emancipation as its goal.

278   "pour everything": Mrs. EPP to SAP, [Salem, August? 1834], Berg 231774B.

ninety-eight pounds: After barely a month in Cuba, Sophia, who had weighed only about eighty pounds the previous summer, wrote home that "my cheeks are rounder" due to an increased appetite (letter of February 3, 1834, SAP *CJ*, p. 25), and three weeks later mentioned again the "roses and plumpness" that Cuba's "beneficent heavens" had bestowed on her cheeks (letter of February 28, 1834, SAP *CJ*, p. 41). Almost two years later, toward the end of her stay in Cuba, Sophia wrote to Mary from a neighboring plantation that she had just weighed in at ninety-eight pounds (SAP to MTP, January 14 [15?], 1835, Berg).

freely gave away: Sophia also decorated several jewelry or keepsake boxes with classical scenes or Claude Lorrain landscapes recollected from paintings belonging to the Rice family. These, too, she presented to the women of the Morrell family as hospitality gifts. She described one such painting in detail: a version of Claude Lorrain's *Annunciation*, of which "one corner is mine entirely, & it is a dear little green, dewy nook where I should like to sit on a bank all my life, & look at two 'sweet cows' . . . that stand in a cool laguna chewing the cud of sweet & bitter fancy—I should like to be the herdsman that I have put upon that bank." Although the painting was not meant to be a Cuban landscape, Sophia was pleased with the "true Cuba glow" she achieved in the coloration. She affixed this scene to a box that she gave to Luisa Morrell, Eduardo and Carlito's sister (letter of December 1, 1834, SAP *CJ*, pp. 467, 472).

literary Transcendentalism: Writing about Emerson, Thoreau, and Theodore Parker, Lawrence Buell has cleverly defined the literary work of the Transcendentalists as "neither art nor argument but a compound of both." Their work shared the positive qualities of "suggestiveness, rhetorical power, and fineness of discernment," all of which Sophia aspired to in her journal, and often attained. Lawrence Buell, *Literary Transcendentalism: Style and Vision in the American Renaissance* (Ithaca, N.Y.: Cornell University Press, 1973), pp. 1–2.

Although little can be ascertained about Sophia's opium use, she wrote to Elizabeth in 1838 that it was her custom at that time to take opium each morning (SAP to EPP, April 24, [1838], BANC MSS 72/2367, Bancroft); it is interesting to consider the effects such use might have had on her morning rides in

Cuba, and on the journal passages she wrote each day on her return. Sophia was likely unaware of the extent of opium use by one of her English heroes, Samuel Taylor Coleridge, but opium may have been another of Sophia's links with the Romantic poets, who were guiding lights for all of the American Transcendentalists.

"How beautifully": letter of March 31, 1835, SAP *CJ*, p. 624.

"intuition . . . Unity": letter ca. January 13, 1835, SAP *CJ*, p. 585. Emerson's journals of this period contain similar responses to the natural world; these ideas were in the air that liberal-minded New Englanders breathed. His first published expression of his Transcendentalist views was a small book he called *Nature* (1836). Throughout his long career, this remained his most coherent statement of principles. As it did for Sophia, nature offered Emerson "a perfect exhilaration" and a feeling of "perpetual youth." But most importantly, his experience of the natural world revealed higher spiritual truths, as in this famous passage: "Standing on the bare ground,—my head bathed by the blithe air, and uplifted into infinite space, —all mean egotism vanishes. I become a transparent eye-ball; I am nothing; I see all; the currents of the Universal Being circulate through me; I am part or particle of God." RWE, *Essays and Lectures* (New York: Library of America, 1983), p. 10.

"consecrated by the breath": letter of March 11, 1835, SAP *CJ*, p. 617.

"optimism of nature": RWE, "Spiritual Laws," *Essays and Lectures*, p. 307.

"determination upward": letter of October 1, 1834, SAP *CJ*, p. 341.

"see more in a blade": letter of July 30, 1834, SAP *CJ*, p. 234.

"never should hear . . . for the future": Norman Holmes Pearson, "Elizabeth Peabody on Hawthorne," *Essex Institute Historical Collections*, July 1958, p. 270.

279   "to day is as yesterday": Mrs. EPP to SAP, [August? 1834], Berg 231774B.

"horrors of . . . fruits of sin": [Mrs. EPP], "Seduction," *Christian Examiner*, no. LIX, New Series no. XXX, November 1833, p. 163.

280   785 pages: The volumes, some portions of which are copies in Mrs. Peabody's hand, are now held by the Berg Collection of the New York Public Library.

"only a record of my uprisings": letter of March 9, 1834, SAP *CJ*, p. 46.

"ravished": EPP to MTP, October 24, [1834], Berg.

"all are in love": EPP to MTP, October 31, [1834], Berg.

"as if the nation": letter of December 1, 1834, SAP *CJ*, pp. 470–71.

"black art": MTP to Mrs. EPP, May 12, 1834, SAP *CJ*, p. 207.

"I doubt ever such . . . hoard it": EPP to MTP, [November] 18, [1834], Berg.

circulating highly prized women's journals: Abigail Adams's shipboard diary, written during the summer of 1784 when she traveled to England to meet her husband, John, is printed in John Adams's *Diary and Autobiography*, L. H. Butterfield et al., eds. (Cambridge, Mass.: Harvard University Press, 1961), vol. 3, pp. 154–66; and a similar account written in the form of a letter to her sister Mary Cranch, dated July 6–30, 1784, is printed in *Adams Family Correspondence*, L. H. Butterfield et al., eds. (Cambridge, Mass.: Harvard University Press, 1963-), vol. 5, pp. 358–83.

Eunice Paine: See EPP to Mrs. Richard Sullivan, November 1826 and November 1827, Straker typescripts, pp. 364, 454, Antiochiana.

"real picture of natural": Anna Jameson, *Diary of an Ennuyée* (Boston: Lilly, Wait, Colman, and Holden, 1833), p. 1. The heroine of *Corinne* also died, heartbroken, at the end of de Staël's novel, but the book did not deliver the same first-person verisimilitude as Jameson's *Diary*, in which invalidism was a theme throughout.

281   *Society in America:* An entertaining account of both Elizabeth Peabody's and Martineau's uncertainty about involving themselves with the fledgling antislavery

movement, just gathering momentum in Boston, can be found in Madelon Bedell's *The Alcotts: Biography of a Family* (New York: Clarkson N. Potter, 1980), pp. 107–109.

281   "gossipy pages": Frances Trollope, *Domestic Manners of the Americans* (New York: Alfred A. Knopf, 1949), p. xi.

Ironically, Sophia published a book of her travel letters, *Notes in England and Italy* (New York: G. P. Putnam, 1870), many years later when widowhood forced her to resort to publication of her own and her husband's private writings to support herself and her children. Like Mrs. Trollope, she published under her married name, "Mrs. Hawthorne." Sophia died a year after the book was published.

"devotedly attentive": letter of December 20, [1833], SAP *CJ*, p. 9.

"complete drenching": SAP, "Letter from the Sea," *The Family School*, vol. I, no. 2, November 1, 1836, p. 4.

"marry . . . match": EPP to MTP, [September 20–October 6, 1834], Berg.

282   *"la belle passion"*: EPP to MTP, [November] 18, [1834], Berg.

"sisterly": EPP to MTP, [September 20–October 6, 1834], Berg.

"execrable": EPP to MTP, April 19[–20], 1834, Berg.

"two traveling Ps": EPP to MTP, [July] 15, [1834], Berg.

"admired . . . convinced": EPP to MTP, August 18, [1834], Berg.

"infinity": EPP to MTP, July 25, changed to 26–[30, 1834], Berg.

"rascally dolt": EPP to MTP, August 18, [1834], Berg.

"ignorant, sensual . . . brute in his habits": EPP to MTP, August 18, [1834], Berg.

"a perfect Cain": EPP to MTP, [September 20–October 6, 1834], Berg.

283   "beguiled": EPP to MTP, August 18, [1834], Berg.

"the transient era . . . affectionate communication": EPP to MTP, [September 20–October 6, 1834], Berg.

"admit . . . bank in future": EPP to MTP, August 18, [1834], Berg.

"There is a kind of love . . . embarrassment": EPP to MTP, October 24, [1834], Berg.

"sadly bruised and commoted": SAP to Maria Chase, August 14, 1834, Peabody Family Papers, Smith.

"aristocracy of cultivation": SAP to Mary Wilder White [Foote], July 7, 1834, Berg 72B4939.

"really *in love* . . . any thing interesting": EPP to MTP, [September 20–October 6, 1834], Berg.

284   "Some things . . . intellectually weak": EPP to MTP, October 25–26 [27, 1834], Berg.

"all three of us": EPP to MTP, [July] 15, [1834], Berg.

"we may *all three*": EPP to MTP, February 24–25, 1834, Berg.

"the future is our own": EPP to MTP, [September 20–October 6, 1834], Berg.

"a *mother* before she was a wife": EPP to MTP, February 10, [1835], Berg.

George Hillard, the lawyer and editor who had boarded at Somerset Court, confessed to Elizabeth that he no longer loved Susan Howe, the schoolteacher to whom he was already engaged, and asked her advice. Elizabeth urged Hillard to honor his commitment. In the end, the couple married, and only Elizabeth—and Horace Mann, to whom she had confided the dilemma—were the wiser.

Another friend, Susan Minot, had been assembling her trousseau when her fiancé, a Mr. Humphrey, abruptly called off the wedding. Unlike Hillard, Humphrey was still in love, but his father had threatened to cut off his inheritance if he married the penniless Minot.

The unwed mother was Sarah Jackson, daughter of the prominent art patron

Patrick Jackson and older sister of one of Elizabeth's students at Bronson Alcott's Temple School, who came to class in tears the day after Sarah had given birth. Sarah Jackson had managed to hide her pregnancy for nine months but was forced by her parents to name the baby's father—William Russell—when she went into labor. Russell was summoned, and the two were married "in the midst of her labour," Elizabeth reported.

Elizabeth also wrote to Mary about another former student, the famously beautiful Mary Ann Marshall, who had inspired two men to a duel: one charged that Mary Ann had flirted with yet a third man; the other accused the first of slander. Both survived the gunfire, but were forced to leave town with their seconds to escape prison for dueling. When Elizabeth learned that Mary Ann was "not sorry" for her role in the matter, she sent her a reproving letter. Elizabeth reported that Mary Ann was now engaged to a fourth man, Samuel Gridley Howe—an alliance that was not to last. Samuel Gridley Howe married Julia Ward in 1843. EPP to MTP, February 12-[16, 1834], Berg.

slit her throat: In January 1835, Charles Barnard, one of Joseph Tuckerman's ministers to the poor, came home to dinner and found that his wife of three weeks, Adeline Russell, had slit her throat.

Gilbert Stuart Newton, whose paintings were among those in the Athenaeum's permanent collection, was married to Sarah Sullivan, the older sister of Eliza Sullivan, who had traveled to Cuba in a failed attempt to cure her tuberculosis. Both Sullivan sisters had been students of Elizabeth and Mary in Brookline. Sally Newton, as she was known, had left her husband behind in England and returned to Boston with their infant child in 1834. Gilbert Stuart Newton died a year later.

285   "He took away a beautiful boy": EPP to MTP, [March 22-24?, 1834], Berg.

"Father rips out . . . wild schemes": EPP to MTP, August 9-[17, 1834], Berg.

"public sentiment . . . public patronage": EPP to MTP, [February 19]-21, [1834], Berg.

"rub along": Dr. NP to MTP and SAP, March 27, 1834, Berg.

"honest, industrious . . . man of the world": Mrs. EPP to SAP and MTP, March 29, 1834, Berg.

"destitute of all kinds": EPP to MTP, [August 26-30?, 1834], Berg.

"mania for spending": EPP to MTP, June 2-[5], 1834, Berg.

"dandyish": EPP to MTP, November 29-[30, 1834], Berg.

"lowlived, blackguard . . . compelled to associate": WP quoted in EPP to MTP, January 8-[24, 1834], Berg.

"cegars": Mrs. EPP to MTP and SAP, July 25, 1834, Berg.

286   "dissipation, drinking . . . family was poor": EPP to MTP, November 29-[30, 1834], Berg.

"the evil genius": EPP to MTP, December 16, [1834], Berg.

"palaver": EPP to MTP, January 8-[24, 1834], Berg. Elizabeth also reported to Mary that their brother George *thinks all* Well's talk is *palaver.*" EPP to MTP, June 16-20, [1834], Berg.

"extravagant *sottise*": EPP to MTP, June 10-[13, 1834], Berg.

"mutual benifet": Mrs. EPP to MTP and SAP, November 8, 1834, Straker typescripts, p. 910, Antiochiana.

"supplying each others' deficiencies": Miss Rawlins Pickman quoted in EPP to MTP, November 29-[30, 1834], Berg.

"what can have made my boys": Mrs. EPP to SAP and MTP, [February or March? 1834], Berg.

286   "linked in heart": Mrs. EPP to MTP, March 1, 1834, Berg.
        "bored . . . 'masculine progeny'": Mrs. EPP to MTP and SAP, April 5, 1835, Berg.
        "those sweet sympathies . . . sisterly interest": Mrs. EPP to SAP and MTP, December 8, 1833, Berg.
        "my three beloved girls": Mrs. EPP to SAP and MTP, April 13, 1834, Berg.
        "villains in the world": Mrs. EPP to SAP and MTP, [December 22, 1833], Berg.

287   "having an improper intercourse": EPP to MTP, January 30, [1835], Berg.
        "all sorts of privileges": EPP to MTP, January 16–21 [20?, 1835], Berg.
        "occasionally exposes . . . purity of manners": Catharine Maria Sedgwick quoted in EPP to MTP, March 15–17, 1835, Berg.
        "blow up . . . hold in adoration": GFP to MTP, February 23, 1835, Berg.
        "quite slack . . . every fibre in the country": Dr. NP to Francis Peabody, May 15, 1834, Dartmouth.

288   "failed . . . dreadful times": EPP to MTP, February 8 [5?, 1834], Berg.
        reducing the $1,100 debt: NCP to MTP, February 8, 1835, Peabody Family Papers, 1790–1880, MHS.
        "Raising money here": EPP to MTP, March 5–[10, 1834], Berg.
        "Historical Conferences . . . historical reading": EPP, "My Experience as a Teacher," pp. 304–305. Elizabeth had begun these classes as historical reading parties in the winter of 1830 to 1831 (SAP to Lydia Sears Haven, [December 1830?], Straker typescripts, p. 580, Antiochiana). By 1833, they had become more ambitious in scope. In "My Experience as a Teacher," Elizabeth described several of her Historical Conferences in detail. For a series on "ancient history before the eighth century . . . [t]he text-books I used were Heeren's researches in Ancient India, Persia, Babylon, Egypt, Ethiopia, Phoenicia, and Ancient Greece; Layard's Nineveh, Landseer's Cylinders of Babylon, Karl Otfried Müller's History of the Dorians and his work on the Etruscans." The next year's "conference took up the eight centuries immediately before Christ. Our text-books were Herodotus, Thucydides, Xenophon, Livy, and Plutarch. . . . [W]e would converse, and I read to them K. O. Müller's history of Greek Literature, some of Augustus Schlegel's lectures on the Greek theatre, Mitchell's Introduction to Aristophanes, Xenophon's Memorabilia of Socrates, and Plato's Eutyphron, Apology of Socrates, Crito and Phaedo, and I think we took some extra sessions to read translations of the Greek tragedies."

289   "not in the sweetest humour": EPP to MTP, April 26, 1833 [1834], Berg.
        one meal a day: HM journal, vol. 1, entry of November 28, 1837, HM Papers, MHS.
        "involuntarily . . . *I trust so*": EPP to MTP, February 12–[16, 1834], Berg.
        "cast my shadows . . . survivor dies": EPP to MTP, [March 22–24?, 1834], Berg.
        "reflect & rejoice": EPP quoted in MTP to EPP, May 11, 1834, Berg.

290   "as if he felt . . . his imagination": EPP to MTP, April 6 [5–9], 1834, Berg.
        "privately . . . fear of misapprehension": EPP to MTP, May 4–[10, 1834], Berg.
        "Mr. M. spreads sunshine": EPP to MTP, February 8 [5?, 1834], Berg.
        "Miss Thesaura": HM to EPP, January 8, 1838, HM Papers, MHS.
        criticism of his own reports: HM to EPP, [March 2, 1835], HM Papers, MHS: "I send you a Report . . . it seems to me to contain matter for extended and destructive criticism. Please look over it, and send me a transcript of the reflections which the perusal of it will excite in your mind."
        "my chief comfort": EPP to MTP, June 16–20, [1834], Berg.
        "mysterious sensation . . . creaking of a sign": HM to EPP, copied by EPP into her letter to MTP, dated January 8–[24, 1834], Berg.

"always put my nerves": HM quoted in EPP to MTP, February 12-[16, 1834], Berg.

291   "I love to know": HM quoted in EPP to MTP, December 16, [1834], Berg.

"charm and grace": EPP to MTP, [March 22-24?, 1834], Berg. Most of the articles Elizabeth published during the interval of her sisters' absence in Cuba were theoretical in nature. But she also published a poem, "A Birth-day Blessing," a Wordsworthian hymn to childhood, in the *Boston Observer and Religious Intelligencer* (January 8, 1835, p. 16), a Unitarian weekly edited by the Reverend George Ripley, who would later found Brook Farm. In a letter to Mary dated January 30, [1835], Elizabeth wrote, "My poetry is very much liked and especially 'the birthday blessing.' He wants me to write all sorts of things" (Berg).

"Spirit of the Hebrew Scriptures": Three of Elizabeth's original six articles were published in the *Christian Examiner* during 1834: "The Creation," LXII (New Series no. XXXII), May 1834, pp. 174-202; "Temptation, Sin, and Punishment," LXIII (New Series no. XXXIII), July 1834, pp. 305-20; "Public Worship: Social Crime and its Retribution," LXIV (New Series no. XXXIV), September 1834, pp. 78-92.

"lively interest . . . my mind quickened": HM to MTP, March 26, 1834, HM Papers, MHS.

"thinking of your home . . . peace of death": HM to MTP, July 4, 1834, HM Papers, MHS.

"bed-chamber . . . upon [my] neck": EPP to MTP, August 18, [1834], Berg.

292   "Oh, this generation! . . . misconstrue": HM quoted in EPP to MTP, [September 2?-7, 1834], Berg.

"misunderstood": MTP quoted in EPP to MTP, [July] 15, [1834], Berg.

"the difference between . . . totally different feeling": EPP to MTP, Saturday night [September 20]-Monday [October 6, 1834], Berg.

293   "Yours *very affectionately* . . . sweet words": EPP to MTP, August 9-[17], 1834, Berg.

"I am quite sure . . . last night": EPP to MTP, [September 20-October 6, 1834], Berg.

294   "very much struck by": SAP journal April 11-[July] 31, [1830], entry of May 23, 1830, Berg.

"mystic visionary": Madelon Bedell, *The Alcotts: Biography of a Family* (New York: Clarkson N. Potter, 1980), p. 41.

"the most favorable place . . . action given": Bedell, *The Alcotts*, p. 38.

295   "*amazed* beyond measure": Josephine Roberts, "Elizabeth Peabody and the Temple School," *New England Quarterly*, vol. XV, no. 3, September 1942, p. 498.

"conversational": Bedell, *The Alcotts*, p. 90. Elizabeth learned from Alcott, but many of his methods were amplifications of her own experiments begun in Lancaster and Brookline. As Mrs. Peabody learned more about Alcott and his successes from Elizabeth, she too became more fully aware of the progressive nature of her early ideas and practice as a teacher. In April 1835, she wrote to Mary and Sophia: "I mark with deep satisfaction the gradual developement of notions about education, that I, had I been rich and influential, would have sounded throughout our land thirty years ago. . . . I might believe this mere imagination—had I not some written memorials of what I thought so long ago." April 5, 1835, Berg.

"two hours and a half . . . he came in": Bedell, *The Alcotts*, p. 92.

"Alcott is a man": EPP to MTP, [July] 15, [1834], Berg.

"the most magnificent": ABA quoted in SAH to EPP, December 11, 1853, Berg.

295   "one of the chief architectural": Robert Campbell and Peter Vanderwarker, "Temple Place," *Boston Globe Magazine*, March 4, 2001, p. 16.
"so as to appear": Bedell, *The Alcotts*, p. 93.

296   "disciples": Bedell, *The Alcotts*, p. 99.
"I never knew": Bedell, *The Alcotts*, p. 96.
"This is the way": Roberts, "Elizabeth Peabody and the Temple School," p. 504.
"leading children . . . suppress their own thoughts": Bedell, *The Alcotts*, p. 95.
"you never saw": Roberts, "Elizabeth Peabody and the Temple School," p. 502.
"I am quite *starved*": EPP to MTP, July 17-[22, 1834], Berg.
"speaks the thoughts of Genius": Bedell, *The Alcotts*, p. 93.
"delightful and harmonious talk": EPP to MTP, February 20-22, [1835], Berg.
"Fate free will &c": EPP to MTP, [September 20-October 6, 1834], Berg.

297   "a real *Universal*": EPP to MTP, February 25, [1835], Berg.
"as much in love": EPP to MTP, [February 28-March 13, 1835], Berg. On the night of March 5, at a party celebrating the concluding lecture in Emerson's series "The Uses of Biography," Emerson had offered to loan Elizabeth his manuscript lectures for her to read to the Reverend Channing, clearly a sign of his trust in the growing friendship. The next day, at a tea arranged expressly for Elizabeth and the engaged couple in the home of Mrs. Elizabeth Davis Bliss, a widow who was to marry the historian George Bancroft in 1838, Elizabeth "*had a beautiful time.*" On this occasion Elizabeth also learned that "Miss Jackson told Mrs. Bliss that she loves me dearly, and she is glad to find that Waldo feels just as she does."
"with greatest pleasure . . . printed speedily." Bruce A. Ronda, *Elizabeth Palmer Peabody: A Reformer on Her Own Terms* (Cambridge, Mass.: Harvard University Press, 1999), p. 122.

298   "a chamber to myself . . . physical system": EPP to MTP, February 8 [5?, 1834], Berg.
"the reveille of a trumpet": Robert D. Richardson, Jr., *Emerson: The Mind on Fire* (Berkeley: University of California Press, 1995), p. 195. Richardson gives a vivid portrait of Emerson's style as a lecturer from which I have drawn many of these details. I have also relied on Helen R. Deese and Guy R. Woodall, "A Calendar of Lectures Presented by the Boston Society for the Diffusion of Useful Knowledge (1829-1847)," *Studies in the American Renaissance 1986* (Charlottesville: University Press of Virginia), p. 42.
"the sweetest": R. Jackson Wilson, "Emerson as Lecturer: Man Thinking, Man Saying," Joel Porte and Saundra Morris, eds., *The Cambridge Companion to Ralph Waldo Emerson* (Cambridge: Cambridge University Press, 1999), p. 76. The listener heard Emerson preach in Scotland in 1833.
"original . . . human mind": EPP to MTP, [January 31, 1835], Berg.
"I do not know": EPP to HM, March 2, 1835, Straker typescripts, p. 981, Antiochiana.
"the *individuality of a man* . . . we all share": EPP to MTP, [January 31, 1835], Berg.
"all minds are to be cherished": EPP, *Record of a School, Exemplifying the General Principles of Spiritual Culture* (Boston: James Munroe, 1835), p. 27.
"the absolute boundlessness": Richardson, *Emerson: The Mind on Fire*, p. 190.
"so many dark times . . . six weeks ago": EPP to HM, March 2, 1835, Straker typescripts, p. 981, Antiochiana.

299   "my principle of the social sympathy": EPP to MTP, [June 18-21, 1836], Berg.

"any questions ... gifts of mind!": EPP to MTP, January 6–7, 1835, *Letters of EPP*, pp. 138–39.

"there was that in each": EPP to MTP, February 28–[March 5, 1834], Berg.

"there were few sisters": EPP to MTP, April 26, 1833 [1834], Berg.

"those little things": EPP to MTP, February 28–[March 5, 1834], Berg.

300   "*outré* ... different from mine": EPP to MTP, January 5 [6?]–7 [1835], Berg.

"the tasteful way": EPP to MTP, April 26, 1833 [1834], Berg.

"plaited lace ... prettily": EPP to MTP, October 24, [1834], Berg.

"a great many people": EPP to MTP, October 25–26 [27, 1834], Berg.

"I do not feel ... all about me": EPP to MTP, [September 20–October 6, 1834], Berg.

"palpable forbearance": EPP to MTP, January 5 [6?]–7, [1835], Berg.

"a word of censure ... diamonds": EPP to MTP, February 28–[March 5, 1834], Berg.

"habit of *brooding*": EPP to MTP, May 4–[May 10, 1834], Berg.

"transparent intercourse": EPP to MTP, January 16–21 [20?, 1835], Berg.

"notion of keeping peace": EPP to MTP, March 5–[March 10, 1834], Berg.

"principles of communication": EPP to MTP, April 19[–20], 1834, Berg.

"the only person ... rejected from mine": EPP to MTP, March 15–[17, 1835], Berg.

"dwell upon the past": EPP to MTP: "I think you are very wise not to dwell upon the past which you say you do not comprehend": [February 19]–21, [1834], Berg.

"If you care to live": EPP to MTP, [September 14–19, 1834], Berg.

"I could not at the same time": EPP to MTP, February 28–[March 5, 1834], Berg.

"withheld my confidence ... human form": MTP to EPP, May 11, 1834, Berg.

301   "You shall certainly *live*": EPP to MTP, [November] 18, [1834], Berg.

"very handsomely ... old maids hall and school": EPP to MTP, February 25, [1835], Berg.

"*we agreed*": EPP to MTP, January 16–21 [20?, 1835], Berg.

"endless topic ... egotism": MTP quoted in EPP to MTP, March 15–[17, 1835], Berg.

"I would rather be without ... our living together": EPP to MTP, March 15–[17, 1835], Berg.

302   "*tyrannical* and overbearing ... make her happy": EPP to MTP, January 8–[24, 1834], Berg.

"having given up ... *swindler*": EPP to MTP, January 30, [1835], Berg.

"getting old very fast": EPP to MTP, November 29–[30, 1834], Berg.

"sink in hopeless poverty": EPP to MTP, [September 20–October 6, 1834], Berg.

"a second change of air": EPP to MTP, February 20–22, [1835], Berg.

"preserved the child's mind": EPP to MTP, [September 20–October 6, 1834], Berg.

"an embodiment of enthusiasm ... all made up": EPP to MTP, [August 26–30?, 1834], Berg.

303   "the humble dwelling": EPP to MTP, [July] 25, changed to 26–[30, 1834], Berg.

"I do long to have her": HM quoted in EPP to MTP, March 15–[17, 1835], Berg.

"with one of those tones": EPP to MTP, March 15–[17, 1835], Berg.

"she *can* come back": HM quoted in EPP to MTP, March 15–[17, 1835], Berg.

"I did not know": EPP to MTP, March 15–[17, 1835], Berg.

"setting up ... knowing look": MTP to HM, July 29, 1834, HM Papers, MHS.

"behind the age ... *transcendental* yet": MTP to HM, May 30, 1835, HM Papers, MHS.

25. Temple School Revisited

307   "nurse up": SAP to MTP, June 7, 1835, Berg.

"beauty": MTP to HM, May 30, 1835, HM Papers, MHS.

"monopolizing spirit . . . march of mind": MTP to HM, May 30, 1835, HM Papers, MHS.

"I think I was meant": MTP to HM, January 18, 1835, HM Papers, MHS.

"turned violent housekeeper . . . poor slave": MTP to HM, May 30, 1835, HM Papers, MHS.

Boston goldsmith Louis Lauriat: EPP to MTP, [late May or early June? 1836], Berg. Mrs. Peabody had also written of a "balloon mania raging" in Salem: "Mr. Durant and his splendid vehicle settled down in the bay between this and Marblehead, and was barely saved from drowning." Mrs. EPP to MTP and SAP, September 23, 1834, Berg.

308   "some fears of that rapid mode of proceeding . . . all space together": MTP to Miss Rawlins Pickman, Thursday evening, [July 1835], HMII Papers, MHS.

"vile separation": SAP to MTP, June 21, 1835, Berg.

309   spiritual philosophy: It was Mary who used the phrase "the spiritual philosophy" in a letter to Horace Mann referring to her feeling of being "behind the age . . . in regard to philosophy and all those great matters that interest the public mind here." MTP to HM, May 30, 1835, HM Papers, MHS.

"perfectly happy . . . 'old familiar faces' and places": MTP to Miss Rawlins Pickman, Thursday evening, [July 1835], HMII Papers, MHS.

"cubby house": SAP to EPP, June 30, [1835], in series "20 a.l. SAP to EPP," Berg 227486B.

"in the most ruinous . . . looking handsome": SAP to "Querida mia" [MTP], June 12, 1835, Peabody Sisters Collection (no. 6952), UVA.

pedimented entryway: The doorway was purchased in the 1920s by Salem's Essex Institute, where it was installed at the rear of the Phillips Library, now a property of the Peabody Essex Museum. More recently, the doorway was shortened to make room for a handicapped ramp.

"After living in a swallow's . . . up their heads": SAP to MTP, July 3, [1835], Berg.

310   "arrived at the turning point": WP to William [B. Richards], July 22, 1835, WP copybook of letters, Peabody Family Papers, 1790–1880, MHS.

Dr. James Jackson, Jr.: James Jackson, M.D., *A Memoir of James Jackson, Jr., M.D.: with extracts from his letters to his father; and medical cases, collected by him* (Boston: I. R. Butts, 1835).

Dr. A. L. Peirson: Wellington began his apprenticeship with Dr. Peirson of Salem on July 12, 1835, according to a letter of recommendation written by Peirson and dated May 20, 1837. Straker typescripts, p. 1172, Antiochiana.

"extacies . . . soul to it": WP to William [B. Richards], July 22, 1835, WP copybook of letters, Peabody Family Papers, 1790–1880, MHS.

"earnest purpose . . . mind and heart": SAP to EPP, August 12–13, [1835], Berg.

"paint chattels": SAP to "Querida mia" [MTP], June 12, 1835, Peabody Sisters Collection (no. 6952), UVA.

Jessica and Lorenzo: The painting has since come to be known as *Lorenzo and Jessica,* although Allston himself inscribed on the back the same title Sophia used, along with this line from *The Merchant of Venice,* act V, scene 1: "How sweet the moonlight sleeps upon this bank!" Edgar Preston Richardson, *Washington Allston: A Study of the Romantic Artist in America* (Chicago: University of Chicago Press, 1948), p. 211. The painting is number 138 in Richardson's catalogue. In the letters

I have read concerning the painting at the time that it was in Sophia's possession for copying, men tended to call it "Lorenzo and Jessica," whereas women
called it "Jessica and Lorenzo," as Sophia always did. Allston had already painted
the famous "Casket Scene" while living in Europe in 1807.

"one of his most highly finished": SAP to Mrs. EPP, May 12-15, 1832, Berg.

"state of profound reverence": SAP to EPP, August 12-13, [1835], Berg.

311   he delayed sale: For this interpretation of Allston's decision to allow Sophia to
copy his painting, I am grateful to Diana Strazdes and her letter to me of October 5, 1994.

"furor . . . within": SAP to EPP, August 12-13, [1835], Berg.

313   "unconsoled mourner": EPP to HM, [August 1, 1835], Straker typescripts, p. 1073,
Antiochiana; both Straker and Bruce Ronda incorrectly date this letter as being
from 1836, *Letters of EPP*, p. 176.

"this primitive town . . . aspirings and hopes": MTP to HM, August 2, 1835, IIM
Papers, MHS.

"a hundred things to attend to": HM to EPP, August 5, 1835, HM Papers, MHS.

"sweetly mournful . . . write to me most": HM to MTP, August 6, 1835, HM
Papers, MHS.

314   "a *public treasure*": EPP to HM, n.d. [fall? 1834], Straker typescripts, p. 876, Antiochiana. In this letter, Elizabeth urged Horace Mann to accept an invitation
from wealthy friends to dine regularly in their house, and even to stay for a
winter: "Let your friends have the comfort of feeling that you are a little better
off for their friendship."

"theosophy": Elizabeth began to use this word in her letters in the mid-1830s,
particularly in correspondence with Lidian (Lydia Jackson) Emerson. She may
have acquired the term from reading Jakob Boehme, a Prussian mystic and follower of Luther now generally considered to be the father of modern Theosophy
—although *Theosophy* was not a term used by Boehme. Boehme's perceptions that
"God's love is in men even before they search for him" and that "the visible
world is a manifestation of the interior spiritual world" were early and powerful
influences on the Transcendentalists (Robert D. Richardson, *Emerson: The Mind on
Fire* [Berkeley: University of California Press, 1995], p. 204). But in Elizabeth's
own vocabulary, the term, which can be literally defined as "wisdom from God,"
seems also to have included her "social principle"—the innate sympathy for
others that she would later call "the *socialism* of true Religion" (EPP to Orestes
Brownson, [ca. 1840], *Letters of EPP*, p. 248). The term was taken up—or reimag-
ined—by the Russian émigré and guru Madame Helena Blavatsky, founder in
1875 of the Theosophical Society, which promoted a philosophical system incor-
porating Eastern mysticism and Boehme's doctrines, with a dash of Emersonian
Transcendentalism.

"annus mirabilis": Perry Miller was the first to describe 1836 as the "annus
mirabilis" for the Transcendentalists in *The Transcendentalists* (Cambridge, Mass.:
Harvard University Press, 1950). A more recent and expanded description of the
events of that year, emphasizing Peabody and Alcott's role, appears in Barbara
Packer's entries on "The Transcendentalists" in *The Cambridge History of American
Literature* (Cambridge and New York: Cambridge University Press, 1994). The
year 1836 also saw the first meetings of the Transcendental Club, whose membership consisted solely of Unitarian ministers, with the exception of Bronson
Alcott, until women were allowed to attend the famous picnic held at the Emersons' house in Concord in September 1837, the day after Emerson delivered his
Phi Beta Kappa address, later known as "The American Scholar."

314   "we are born believing": RWE, *Essays and Lectures* (New York: Library of America, 1983), p. 1056.

315   "innocence ... reproduce them": EPP, *Record of a School, Exemplifying the General Principles of Spiritual Culture* (Boston: James Munroe, 1835), p. 105.

"called into life": EPP, *Record of a School*, p. 16.

"the inward truth ... the first truth": EPP, *Record of a School*, p. 60.

"Did that bust of Shakespeare": EPP, *Record of a School*, p. 61.

"the advantage of having": EPP, *Record of a School*, pp. 62–63.

"steam-engine system ... govern his character": MTP to Miss Rawlins Pickman, Thursday evening, [July 1835], HMII Papers, MHS.

"presupposes his little pupils ... consciences": Harriet Martineau, *Society in America* (New York: AMS Press, 1966), vol. 2, p. 175.

316   "political non-existence ... apathy": Martineau, *Society in America*, vol. 1, pp. 199, 154.

"pleasure & hope ... engaging": RWE to EPP, August 3, 1835, *Letters of RWE*, vol. 7, p. 245.

"beautiful book": RWE to William Emerson, July 27, 1835, *Letters of RWE*, vol. 1, p. 447.

"my long-tongued pen": EPP to HM, [fall? 1834?], Straker typescripts, p. 888, Antiochiana. Horace Mann told Elizabeth the same thing: "in my letters to him was '*incomparably* better' *composition* than in any thing I had ever *printed*." Still, to Elizabeth's relief, he "praised much that I had printed," especially portions of her preface to the second edition of *Record of a School*. EPP to MTP, [late May or early June? 1836], Berg.

"the word *transcendentalism*": EPP to Orestes Brownson, [ca. 1840], *Letters of EPP*, p. 248. Here Elizabeth explained that she had written the *Christian Examiner* essays on the "Spirit of the Hebrew Scriptures" in 1826. Had they been published then, "it would have [been] quite a little historical fact, [that] there in the bosom of Unitarianism, an unlearned girl, with only the help of those principles of philosophizing she gathered from the perusal of Coleridge's *Friend*," should have discussed "the word *transcendentalism*." Had Norton permitted the publication of all six essays in 1834, it would have been "quite a little historical fact" *then* as well. The first three essays were published in May, July, and September 1834; the unpublished essays have not been located, although Elizabeth circulated them again in an attempt at publication in 1840, as the letter to Brownson documents.

317   self-assurance to write: During 1836 and 1837, Elizabeth made some efforts toward compiling a "manual of Education" that was to be "general in its character, but leaning towards the subject of female education." The first essay was to be "from my own pen, upon the Idea ... of the Family, & the effect of its various relations in unfolding & cultivating the human being.—I wish to show that as it is the only Universal Institution, so it is the most effective." As the project evolved, however, it began to take the form of a literary anthology, and she solicited articles from a diverse group of writers, including John Sullivan Dwight, Jones Very, Robert C. Waterston, Francis Graeter, and Ralph Waldo Emerson, who appears to have promised one or more of his lectures on the "Aims & Uses of Biography." The book was never completed, although a decade later Elizabeth published a similar anthology, which she hoped to turn into a periodical: *Aesthetic Papers* (1849). In this volume she printed articles by Dwight ("Music"), Emerson ("War"), Hawthorne ("Main Street"), and Thoreau ("Resistance to Civil Government," the first publication of the essay later retitled "Civil Disobedi-

ence"). EPP to John Sullivan Dwight, n.d. [1836], *Letters of EPP,* p. 188; Robert C. Waterston to EPP, January 24, 1837, MVWC, p. 340, MHS.

To his credit, Alcott: Shortly after *Record of a School* came out, Alcott pasted the title page into his journal, alongside a favorable review from the *Western Messenger,* and inscribed "by E. P. Peabody" on it. See ABA's "Diary for 1834," MS Am 130.12 item 7, Houghton. In a letter to Wordsworth dated September 5, 1835, written to accompany a copy of *Record,* Elizabeth described it as "a book of my own writing which will make known to you something of a very interesting mind engaged in bringing the children of the English language under the fostering influences of the true English literature"—that is, Wordsworth's own poetry. Alcott had made the "Immortality Ode" the basis of significant conversations with his pupils. Margaret Neussendorfer, ed., "Elizabeth Palmer Peabody to William Wordsworth: Eight Letters, 1825–1845," *Studies in the American Renaissance 1984* (Charlottesville: University Press of Virginia), p. 193.

"How much life . . . friend as yourself": ABA to EPP, June 19, 1835, MVWC, p. 259, MHS.

"genius for education . . . delighted": EPP to ABA, copied into ABA's "Diary for 1834," MS Am 130.12 item 7, Houghton (the letter is misdated "Lowell 1834").

"we quiet folk": ABA to EPP, June 19, 1835, MVWC, p. 259, MHS.

"flowers & fruits": EPP to MTP, [summer? 1835], Berg.

318   "I wish you could have seen . . . bookseller of our city": EPP to William Wordsworth, September 7, 1835, Neussendorfer, ed., "Elizabeth Palmer Peabody to William Wordsworth: Eight Letters, 1825–1845," p. 193.

Wordsworth was one of four: Elizabeth had given five copies of *Record of a School* to the Boston publisher and bookseller Nahum Capen, who brought out a third edition of *Self-Education* and the second and third volumes of her *Key to History* series in 1833, when he traveled to Europe during the fall of 1835. Elizabeth hoped that Capen would use the fifth to persuade publishers in England or on the Continent to produce the book for European readers.

When Wordsworth responded to Elizabeth's letter and gift on April 7 of the following year, he apologized for the delay: "You may have perhaps heard that my eyes are subject to inflammations, which so curtail the little time I have for reading, that I have none almost for writing." It is not clear from his reply whether he actually read the book, although he thanked Elizabeth for the "interesting Contents of your Volume" and expressed "my good wishes that your efforts for the benefit of the rising generation may be crowned with the success they so amply deserve." He also enclosed a flower from his garden at Dove Cottage. Alan G. Hill, ed., *The Letters of William and Dorothy Wordsworth,* second edition, vol. VI, *The Later Years: Part III, 1835–1839* (Oxford: Clarendon Press, 1982), p. 194; MTP to EPP, n.d. [May 1836], MHS: "That flower from Wordsworth's garden was a lovely little act of his."

"spiritual intellectual sympathy": ABA to EPP, June 19, 1835, MVWC, p. 259, MHS.

first printing of one thousand: These sales figures were good for the time. By comparison, six years into his career as a lecturer, it took Emerson four years to sell out a printing of 1,500 copies of his first collection of essays. Sales of his first book, *Nature,* were even slower.

It was common practice for authors at this time—from Peabody to Emerson to Hawthorne—to front the publication costs of their books and receive the bulk of the profits themselves. Mary and Elizabeth's hope of relying on income from the sale of *Record* was not a misguided one. Although figures are not available for this venture, a project Elizabeth contemplated two years later involved printing costs of 12½ cents per copy and a retail price of 97½ cents for a print run of 2,500 copies, which would have allowed Elizabeth to clear 85 cents per copy, or more than $2,000 by the time the edition sold out—if it did. The problem was finding the money or a backer to cover the costs up front and then finding ways to sell the book and collect the proceeds. See Helen R. Deese, "The Peabody Family and the Jones Very 'Insanity,'" *Harvard Library Bulletin*, vol. 35, no. 2, p. 226.

If, however, an author wished the publisher to bear the risk of printing and selling the book, a contract could be remarkably similar to today's standards. In 1841, Nathaniel Hawthorne signed a contract for the publication of *Twice-told Tales* which allowed him 10 percent of the cover price once enough copies were sold "to defray the cost of publication." See C. E. Frazer Clark, Jr., "The Susan 'Affair,'" *Nathaniel Hawthorne Journal* (Dayton, Oh.: NCR Microcard Editions, 1971), p. 14.

319   "being talked about . . . grown more strong": EPP to ABA, October 8, 1835, *Letters of EPP*, p. 152.

320   "becoming offensively . . . familiarity and freedom": Odell Shepard, *Pedlar's Progress: The Life of Bronson Alcott* (Boston: Little, Brown, 1937), p. 128.

"mansion": Madelon Bedell, *The Alcotts: Biography of a Family* (New York: Clarkson N. Potter, 1980), p. 120.

"impetuosity . . . live with her": EPP to MTP, [summer? 1835], Berg.

"kept in the most . . . my life now is": EPP to GFP, June 18, [1836], Straker typescripts, p. 1062, Antiochiana.

321   "really delightful": EPP to MTP, [March 25, 1836], Berg.

"namesake . . . new era of things": EPP journal April 11–15, 1836, entry of April 11, Berg.

"Miss Peabody . . . woman of genius": [Catharine Maria Sedgwick], review of "Record of a School," *The Knickerbocker*, vol. 7, no. 2, February 1836, p. 129. Bronson Alcott identifies the review as the work of "Mrs. Sedgwick" in his 1836 journal, Joel Myerson, ed., "Bronson Alcott's 'Journal for 1836,'" *Studies in the American Renaissance 1978* (Boston: Twayne Publishers), p. 44. Catharine Sedgwick was not married but is certainly the writer Alcott had in mind.

"ply the pen": MTP to GFP, April 10, 1836, Straker typescripts, p. 1038, Antiochiana.

"to a more regular": EPP journal April 11–15, 1836, entry of April 11, Berg.

"seems really desirous": EPP to MTP, May 15, 1836, *Letters of EPP*, p. 166. Margaret Fuller, on the other hand, seems to have disdained Elizabeth's efforts to get her assignments for the *American Monthly*. In an undated letter from early in their acquaintance, Fuller wrote: "With regard to what you say about the American Monthly, my answer is, I would gladly sell some part of my mind for lucre, to get the command of time; but I will not sell my soul." Fuller explained that, instead, "I hope a periodical may arise, by and by, which may think me worthy to furnish a series of articles on German literature, giving room enough and perfect freedom to say what I please" (*Letters of MF*, vol. 6, p. 274). Unfortunately, Fuller's bold admission turned out to be a case of "pride goeth before a fall." Within a year she was writing an obsequious letter to Elizabeth accompanying her translation of "the little German tale 'Tasso Lasso.' . . . I feel a shame in looking it over that I could ever have thought it fit for publication in its present state. . . . Please let its perusal be confined to yourself and your sister, if indeed she has any desire to see it." MF to EPP, February 3, 1836, MVWC, p. 297, MHS.

"faults ... my thoughts *ready*": EPP to GFP, June 18, [1836], Straker typescripts, p. 1062, Antiochiana.

"complete power ... so much labor": EPP to MTP, [late May or early June? 1836], Berg. My date: [June 1836].

"alone ... social sympathy": EPP to MTP, [June 18–21, 1836], Berg.

lengthy panegyric: EPP, "Allston the Painter," *American Monthly Magazine*, New Series 1, May 1836, pp. 435–46.

"every profession ... ardour to reform": EPP journal April 11–15, 1836, entry of April 11, Berg.

322 "old maidish ... drawn the line": EPP journal April 11–15, 1836, entry of April 15, Berg.

"treaty of peace": MTP to EPP, n.d. [1836]. The letter begins: "I wish you would sit ..."; HM Papers, MHS.

"amicable combat": MTP to EPP, "Tuesday eve—," n.d. [1836], HM Papers, MHS.

"put a smiling countenance": EPP to MTP, [end of week of April 11?, 1836], Berg.

"made himself merry": EPP to MTP, [late May? 1836], Berg. My date: [after May 22, 1836].

"Divine Unity ... imagery of Names": Myerson, ed., "Bronson Alcott's 'Journal for 1836,'" p. 59.

"awakening sentiments in Parents": EPP to MTP, [late May? 1836], Berg. My date: [after May 22, 1836].

"have the book a perfect ... sacrificed": MTP to EPP, n.d. [1836]. The letter begins: "I wish you would sit ..."; HM Papers, MHS.

"lead the minds ... modesty": MTP to EPP, n.d. [1836]. The letter begins: "I did not get ..."; HM Papers, MHS.

323 "sacrificing your own comfort": MTP to EPP, n.d. [1836]. The letter begins: "I wish you would sit ..."; HM Papers, MHS.

"perfectly harrowing": MTP to EPP, n.d. [1836]. The letter begins: "The letter to Mr. Alcott ..."; HM Papers, MHS.

"unless it can be a true": MTP to EPP, n.d. [1836]. The letter begins: "I wish you would sit ..."; HM Papers, MHS.

"adopt any measures ... Mr. A's school": MTP to EPP, n.d. [1836]. The letter begins: "George has sent ..."; HM Papers, MHS.

"a beautiful thing ... sympathy of spirits": ABA to SAP, August 23, 1836, Richard L. Herrnstadt, ed., *The Letters of A. Bronson Alcott* (Ames: Iowa State University Press, 1969), pp. 28–29.

"the formation of the body ... directed by idle": EPP to ABA, August 7, 1836, *Letters of EPP*, pp. 180–81.

Elizabeth herself was not immune to criticism for stretching the bounds of proper taste in her own published work. When, later in 1836, she announced plans to publish her own magazine, *The Family School*, Horace Mann wrote her a letter in which he asked her to "let me warn you against touching one class of topics with which impure associations are connected, in the common mind. Angels may discuss all processes of nature & all parts of anatomy but that cannot be done upon earth—at least not yet. You will understand perfectly what I mean when I say that there is a passage in one part of your *Key to History* taken I believe from the *Iliad* where a disrobing scene is described, such as usually have curtains drawn between them & the public eye ... & there is a passage in your *Record of a School* Preface, pp. 11 & 12, which is partially, tho' less so. I know to be able to write them as you do, without certain associations, argues real purity, but there is not purity enough in the public mind *to bear them*, & a few passages of that sort would exclude any book or publication from most families, & you would not know why, for that is the last reason any body but an older brother would tell you of." HM to EPP, September 6, [1836], HM Papers, MHS.

323   "commencing a life of study": EPP to MTP, [week of May 16, 1836], Berg.

"agree in all his measures": MTP to EPP, n.d. [1836]. The letter begins: "I wish you would sit . . ."; HM Papers, MHS.

"the Recorder omitted . . . disconnected from *me*": EPP to ABA, August 7, 1836, *Letters of EPP*, pp. 180–81.

324   "be honestly printed . . . mistaken views": MTP to EPP, n.d. [1836]. The letter begins: "I wish you would sit . . ."; HM Papers, MHS. In the end, Alcott printed the dialogues Elizabeth found objectionable in an appendix, thereby drawing even more attention to the questionable passages.

"come away from the Alcotts": MTP to EPP, n.d. [1836]. The letter begins: "The letter to Mr. Alcott . . ."; HM Papers, MHS.

"before the age in Salem": Mrs. EPP to MTP and SAP, July 25, 1834, Berg.

"unfolding your faculties . . . *Mal-apros-pos*": EPP to MTP, [end of week of April 11?, 1836], Berg.

"take a class . . . wind in the trees": MTP to EPP, n.d. [1836]. The letter begins: "The letter to Mr. Alcott . . ."; HM Papers, MHS.

"Don't you think . . . adoration of Mr. Alcott": EPP to MTP, n.d., *Letters of EPP*, p. 157 ff. My date: [July 1836]. Bruce Ronda misdates this letter as [April 1836]. Internal evidence shows that the letter was written during Sophia's visit of July 1836. See Myerson, ed., "Bronson Alcott's 'Journal for 1836,'" p. 63, entry of July 9: "Miss Sophia Peabody is staying with us at this time."

325   "Miss Peabody left me": Myerson, ed., "Bronson Alcott's 'Journal for 1836,'" p. 64.

"fatigues and excitements": MTP to HM, August 4, 1836, HM Papers, MHS.

"many valuable thoughts": Charles Capper, *Margaret Fuller: An American Romantic Life, The Private Years* (New York and Oxford: Oxford University Press, 1992), pp. 196–97. According to Capper, Fuller began teaching in the Temple School in early December 1836 and resigned in mid-April 1837; the Temple School was Fuller's first exposure to "concentrated doses of Boston Transcendentalist philosophy."

"the larger synthesis": Myerson, ed., "Bronson Alcott's 'Journal for 1836,'" p. 59.

"late sudden rupture": MTP to HM, August 4, 1836, HM Papers, MHS. Sarah Clarke also knew about the episode—she had stopped in to visit Elizabeth at the Alcotts' on the afternoon of the blowup and spent the night in Elizabeth's room to comfort her.

In a letter to Wordsworth written almost two years after her resignation from the Temple School, Elizabeth reported her departure in terms that showed just how much she valued Alcott's enterprise and her role in it. She wrote of Alcott's "unwise" publication of *Conversations with Children on the Gospels* over her objections: "[I]n giving me up as his counsellor he made a mistake somewhat like that of Pestalozzi when he gave up his Niederer." She was referring to the great Swiss educator Johann Heinrich Pestalozzi (1746–1827), whose progressive theories can be said to have laid the foundation for modern elementary education. Johannes Niederer was his partner, "the less creative member, but the one who could articulate Pestalozzi's ideas and communicate them to others. Pestalozzi also valued Niederer's superior education and his willingness to defend the school in time of controversy." Neussendorfer, ed., "Elizabeth Palmer Peabody to William Wordsworth: Eight Letters, 1825–1845," p. 200.

"an ignorant . . . half-witted": Bedell, *The Alcotts*, p. 131.

"one third absurd": Capper, *Margaret Fuller*, pp. 198–99.

"Pope Andrews": TP quoted in Wesley T. Mott, ed., *Biographical Dictionary of Transcendentalism* (Westport, Conn.: Greenwood Press, 1996), p. 186.

"physiological . . . spiritual philosophy": Capper, *Margaret Fuller,* pp. 198–99.

326 "modern infidelity": In an undated letter to Elizabeth, likely written during July 1836, Mary wrote of an article in the *Christian Examiner* on "modern infidelity," HM Papers, MHS. Three years later, Andrews Norton titled his attack on Emerson and Transcendentalism *A Discourse on the Latest Form of Infidelity* (Cambridge, Mass.: John Owen, 1839).

"indecent and obscene": Capper, *Margaret Fuller,* p. 198.

"Mr. Alcott's book . . . leads the understanding": [EPP], "Mr. Alcott's Book and School," *Christian Register and Boston Observer* 16 (April 29, 1837), p. 65. Elizabeth's views on Abby Alcott also softened with time. After Abby's death in 1877, she wrote to Louisa May Alcott: "I lived with your mother in perhaps the most intense period of her suffering experience of life—and feel as if I knew the heights & depths of her great heart as perhaps only you & Anna can do. For a few months we were separated by stress of feeling in most tragic circumstances —and she doubted my friendship—. . . But God gave me an opportunity to withdraw the veil & I have under her own hand her written expression of her conviction that I was *true to her* & her deepest worth *at that very time.* I have never known a great, more devoted, more tender, more selfsacrificing human being; & it was all pure moral force & *character* for she owed nothing to the *Imagination.* . . . There was no froth on the cup of life for her—It was all reality down to its very dregs." EPP to Louisa May Alcott, [December? 1877], *Letters of EPP,* p. 382.

"there [was] a great deal . . . neutralizes the error": EPP to HM, April 2, 1837, MVWC, pp. 299–304, MHS.

PAGE ## 26. Little Waldo, Jones Very, and the "Divinity School Address"

327 "seemed infinitely . . . guileless man": EPP journal, entry of November 25, 1836, MVWC, p. 281, MHS.

"a man of genius": EPP journal, entry of November 15, 1836, MVWC, pp. 280–81, MHS.

"makes me feel free . . . inspiring communion": EPP journal, entry of August 5, 1838, MVWC, p. 360, MHS.

328 "a weekly visitor . . . boys and girls": EPP, "Prospectus," *The Family School,* vol. 1, no. 1, September 1, 1836, p. 1.

advertisements: *The Boston Reformer,* September 13, 1836, vol. 3, no. 71, p. 1.

not enough subscribers: Always ready to experiment with novel means of enlarging her income, Elizabeth had sent the magazine to a wide circle of associates with the advisory that she would assume they wished to subscribe unless the publication was returned to her by mail. Some, like Charles P. Curtis, who wrote "an impudent paragraph" about the magazine in *The Atlas,* found this system presumptuous, and refused to return the issue or to pay for a subscription: EPP journal, entry of November 30, 1836, MVWC, p. 286, MHS.

"punish[ing] me . . . utter *blank*": MTP to EPP, n.d., Sunday evening, [1836], HM Papers, MHS.

"I cannot but hope": MTP to EPP, n.d. [1836]. The letter begins: "I find if . . ."; HM Papers, MHS.

"confidential correspondence": EPP to MTP, [April 11?–12?, 1836], Berg.

329 "I do not wish . . . preferable": EPP to MTP, January 16–21 [20?, 1835], Berg.

329   "that happy union": EPP to MTP, [week of May 16, 1836], Berg.

"I do not receive . . . bestows upon you": EPP to MTP, [April 11?–12?, 1836], Berg.

330   "I could not have imagined . . . consternation": Sandford Salyer, *Marmee: The Mother of Little Women* (Norman: University of Oklahoma Press, 1949), p. 60.

several of her own illustrations: *Conversations on the Gospels* ultimately appeared in two volumes, the first published in 1836, the second in 1837, both illustrated with the same two drawings by Sophia, a schematic rendering of the Temple School classroom and a Bible scene depicting "Jesus conversing with the doctors."

"a *certain* stipend": EPP quoted in SAP to EPP, September 29, 1835, Berg.

"reserve all . . . half a heart": SAP to EPP, September 29, 1835, Berg.

"hypochondriac . . . self-indulgent": SAP to EPP, n.d., in series "20 a.l.s. SAP to EPP," Berg 52B2461. My date: [late September or early October 1835]. Full quotation: "Heaven forbid that I should ever have supposed you believed me a genuine hypochondriac."

"My nerves have no shelter now": SAP to EPP, September 29, 1835, Berg.

"violent palpitations . . . immediate pain": SAP to EPP, n.d., in series "20 a.l.s. SAP to EPP," Berg 52B2461. My date: [late September or early October 1835].

331   "There has been nothing": SAP to EPP, July 1833, Berg.

"you must take my nature . . . whole being is in it": SAP to EPP, September 29, 1835, Berg.

In the end, once her point had been made, Sophia did agree to give reading lessons to young Clara Peabody, the daughter of wealthy but distant relations in Salem. But Sophia put off the lessons until November, and then abandoned them for weeks at a time when she wasn't feeling well. Perhaps as a result of her efforts to combine assignments, Sophia's work on *Jessica and Lorenzo* stretched into the following spring. The painting was nearly complete in April 1836 when Waldo Emerson was in Salem giving a series of lectures and came to see it. In Mary's account of the visit, Emerson "enjoyed it to Sophia's entire satisfaction" and proceeded to look at "all Sophia's sketch books & portfolios—and we talked by the way, and his face was all light, and Sophia's was a gleam embodied." [MTP to EPP], April 18, 1836, HM Papers, MHS.

Emerson wrote of the visit to his wife, Lidian, "I saw Sophia Peabody's copy of Mr Allston's Lorenzo & Jessica, & the original side by side with it. The copy was admirable, & of Chinese exactness of imitation[.] I saw it late in the afternoon but by such light as I had, I tho't I could not have decided which was the original, had both pictures been framed alike." *Letters of RWE*, vol. 2, p. 12.

"not to force": SAP to MTP, November 20, 1832, Berg.

"I cannot drive my muse": SAP journal April 11–[July] 31, [1830], entry of June 5, Berg.

"intolerable joy": SAP to EPP, October 20, [1835], Berg.

"hospital . . . numb palsy": SAP to EPP, Wednesday, [November 11,] 1835, Berg.

"the only hope . . . your stomach": EPP to GFP, May 15, 1836, Straker typescripts, p. 1052, Antiochiana.

New England's most deadly disease: Fortunately for George's family, tuberculosis of the digestive tract was less contagious than pulmonary tuberculosis, and might have been contracted via contaminated milk. Karen Robert, ed., *New Year in Cuba: Mary Gardner Lowell's Travel Diary, 1831–1832* (Boston: Massachusetts Historical Society, Northeastern University Press, 2003).

332   "a little afraid . . . desperate poverty": EPP to GFP, n.d. [October 1836], Straker typescripts, pp. 1115–17, Antiochiana.

"he asks me . . . refresh your spirit": Lidian Emerson to EPP, [August 1836], Delores Bird Carpenter, ed., *The Selected Letters of Lidian Jackson Emerson* (Columbia: University of Missouri Press, 1987), p. 50. Elizabeth had delayed accepting the invitation, perhaps wishing to establish herself in Salem after resigning from the Temple School. By November, Waldo Emerson himself was pressing Elizabeth to visit "as soon as you can spare time," in order to help care for the new baby: "This kindness his mother particularly begs of you. . . ." RWE to EPP, November 15, 1836, *Letters of RWE*, vol. 2, p. 45.

second of five: A sixth Emerson brother had died in childhood, as had two sisters.

altered from the more prosaic: According to Emerson family lore, Waldo feared the introduction of an *r* at the end of "Lydia" in the common New England pronunciation when two vowels are elided. To avoid the otherwise inevitable "Lydiar Emerson," he inserted the more euphonious consonant *n*. Although he also altered the *y* to an *i*, he was certainly aware that he had renamed her for one of the twelve musical "modes," or scales, derived by Pythagoras—the plaintive yet predominantly major "Lydian" mode.

334   "here I am": EPP journal, entry of August 5, 1838, MVWC, p. 360, MHS.

"good things": RWE, July 24, 1835, *JMN*, vol. 5, pp. 60–61.

"authority of a learned professor . . . offend": RWE journal passages quoted in *Letters of RWE*, vol. I, pp. 445, 449.

"*very refined*": EPP quoted in Ronda, *Elizabeth Palmer Peabody: A Reformer on Her Own Terms* (Cambridge, Mass.: Harvard University Press, 1999), p. 123.

"the rare characteristic": EPP to MTP, February 25, 1835, *Letters of EPP*, p. 147n.

"no two women": Lydia Jackson to EPP, July 28, 1835, Carpenter, ed., *The Selected Letters of Lidian Jackson Emerson*, p. 27.

335   "mine own *angel*-man": Lidian Emerson quoted in Helen R. Deese, ed., *Jones Very: The Complete Poems* (Athens: University of Georgia Press, 1993), p. xiv.

"the giving up": Ellen Tucker Emerson quoted by Phyllis Cole in a joint review of *The Letters of Ellen Tucker Emerson*, Edith E. W. Gregg, ed. (1982), and Ellen Tucker Emerson, *The Life of Lidian Jackson Emerson*, Delores Bird Carpenter, ed. (1980), in *Studies in Romanticism* 24 (Fall 1985), p. 418. I am grateful to Phyllis Cole for many useful conversations about the women of the Emerson family, as well as for her article "'Men and Women Conversing': The Emersons in 1837," Wesley T. Mott and Robert E. Burkholder, eds., *Emersonian Circles: Essays in Honor of Joel Myerson* (Rochester, N.Y.: University of Rochester Press, 1997), pp. 127–59, and her indispensable biography and Emerson family portrait, *Mary Moody Emerson and the Origins of Transcendentalism: A Family History* (New York: Oxford University Press, 1998).

"what a wonderful being": EPP journal, entry of November 23, 1836, MVWC, p. 270, MHS.

"Queenie": EPP journal, entry beginning Friday, [August 10, 1838], MVWC, p. 380, MHS.

"over the coals": EPP journal, entry of November 24, 1836, MVWC, p. 272, MHS.

"my dear Ellen . . . loved her": EPP journal, entry of November 24, 1836, MVWC, p. 276, MHS.

336   "my turn": EPP journal, entry of November 29, 1836, MVWC, p. 283, MHS.

"reverent husband . . . his studio": EPP journal, [mid-September 1837], MVWC, p. 315, MHS.

337   "We looked . . . how clear the water was": EPP journal, entry of November 24, 1836, MVWC, p. 278, MHS.

"all the marriages": EPP journal, entry of November 25, 1836, MVWC, p. 280, MHS.

337 "catch and rebound": EPP journal, entry beginning Friday, [August 10, 1838], MVWC, p. 368, MHS.

"intuitive reason": EPP journal, late November 1836, MVWC, p. 294, MHS.

"O God": "Hymn, Sung At The Dedication of The New Stone Church of The North Society In Salem June 22d, 1836," Deese, ed., *Jones Very: The Complete Poems*, p. 42.

"my heart's mad passion": "The Torn Flower," Deese, ed., *Jones Very: The Complete Poems*, pp. 48–49.

338 "There are new lands": RWE, *Essays and Lectures* (New York: Library of America, 1983), p. 7.

"Commodity . . . through the air": RWE, *Essays and Lectures*, pp. 12–13.

"sense of . . . life-journey": Edwin Gittleman, *Jones Very: The Effective Years, 1833–1840* (New York: Columbia University Press, 1967), pp. 146–47.

"on the Monday": Lidian Emerson to EPP, [August 1837], Carpenter, ed., *The Selected Letters of Lidian Jackson Emerson*, p. 55.

"in the course . . . know its place": Lidian Emerson to EPP, August 22, 1837, Carpenter, ed., *The Selected Letters of Lidian Jackson Emerson*, p. 57.

339 "all-day party": Lidian Emerson to Lucy Jackson Brown, September 2, 1837, Carpenter, ed., *The Selected Letters of Lidian Jackson Emerson*, p. 59.

"plant himself indomitably": Robert D. Richardson, *Emerson: The Mind on Fire* (Berkeley: University of California Press), p. 265. My understanding of Emerson's "American Scholar" was helped immeasurably by Richardson's insightful commentary on the speech and on the occasion of its delivery.

"our intellectual Declaration": Richard Higgins, "Remembering the Emerson Who Sought God," *Harvard Divinity Bulletin*, vol. 31, no. 3, Summer 2003, p. 9.

"I embrace the common": Jonathan Messerli, *Horace Mann* (New York: Alfred A. Knopf, 1972), pp. 265–66.

"ultra idealism": EPP to HM, n.d. [1836], Straker typescripts, p. 1107, Antiochiana.

"very good": Messerli, *Horace Mann*, pp. 265–66.

"seriously offended": Joel Myerson, "A History of the Transcendental Club," Philip Gura and Joel Myerson, eds., *Critical Essays on American Transcendentalism* (Boston: G. K. Hall, 1982), p. 599.

"provided no allusions": RWE journal, entry of September 19, 1837, Joel Porte, ed., *Emerson in His Journals* (Cambridge, Mass.: Belknap Press of Harvard University Press, 1982), p. 168.

"dead . . . never in company": EPP journal, entry of November 25, 1836, MVWC, p. 281, MHS.

340 "The congregation of bright": EPP to WEC, [September 1837], MVWC, p. 329, MHS.

"true forum": Myerson, "A History of the Transcendental Club," p. 599.

"the progress of society . . . about some things": EPP to WEC, [September 1837], MVWC, p. 330, MHS.

"the newness": RWE, "Experience," *Essays and Lectures*, p. 483.

"not only the most . . . walk and conversation": EPP journal, before entry of September 21, 1837, MVWC, p. 314, MHS.

"what a heavenly dream": EPP journal, entry of September 21, 1837, MVWC, p. 319, MHS.

"beautiful provision . . . father's diagram!": EPP journal, before entry of September 21, 1837, MVWC, pp. 313–14, MHS.

"the theosophy of her marriage": EPP journal, before entry of September 21, 1837, MVWC, p. 316, MHS.

"each human soul . . . harmonious whole": Ronda, *Elizabeth Palmer Peabody,* p. 124.

"the institution of the Family": EPP to John Sullivan Dwight, n.d., *Letters of EPP,* p. 188. Bruce Ronda misdates this letter as being from the year 1836. Elizabeth's plans for this essay and the anthology project began to materialize in 1837.

"Why should not we": RWE, *Essays and Lectures,* p. 7.

341   "learning to get along . . . care of him": Lidian Emerson to EPP, January 8, 1837, Carpenter, ed., *The Letters of Lidian Jackson Emerson,* p. 53.

"ultra benevolence . . . transcendental coterie": Cole, " 'Men and Women Conversing,' " p. 133.

"all ways . . . 'felt' she could not": EPP journal, entry beginning Friday, [August 10, 1838], MVWC, p. 381, MHS.

"there is but one . . . of the sisters": EPP to SAP, n.d., in series "60 a.l. EPP to SAP," Berg 135140B. My date: [October–November 1835].

"only divine institution . . . theosophy of marriage": EPP, "Prospectus," *The Family School,* vol. I, no. I, September 1, 1836, p. 1.

342   "methodising faculty . . . literary head": *Letters of RWE,* vol. I, pp. 445, 449.

"create . . . a constant": EPP journal, entry beginning Friday, [August 10, 1838], MVWC, p. 398, MHS.

"astonish . . . not logical": EPP journal, before entry of September 21, 1837, MVWC, p. 314, MHS.

"discipline himself . . . encumbrance of ideas": EPP journal, entry beginning Friday, [August 10, 1838], MVWC, p. 397, MHS.

Around this time Mary recorded an amusing anecdote about attending several of Emerson's lectures with Elizabeth and their friend Sarah Clarke, probably the "Human Culture" series given in Boston in late 1837. After the lectures, Mary wrote, "Sarah and I try to tell what Mr. Emerson said, and first Sarah begins and then turns to me and says, 'what were the words Mary?' and I open my lips and think I am going to say them and then find that I cannot. In the mean time E[lizabeth] sits in an attitude of expectation, and then she tells us what she guesses that he said." MTP to Sally Jackson Gardner, December 29, 1837, HM Papers, MHS.

"written exhortation": EPP journal, "Sophia's birthday," [September 21, 1837], MVWC, p. 318, MHS.

"be simple": EPP journal, entry of September 22, 1837, MVWC, p. 321, MHS.

odes to Emerson: The "ode" to Emerson took shape as a long review of *Nature* and the Phi Beta Kappa oration, titled "Nature—A Prose Poem," published in *The United States Magazine and Democratic Review,* vol. I, no. 2, February 1838, pp. 319–29. Here, while extolling Emerson's genius and his book as "a divine Thought," Elizabeth also implicitly claimed a place for herself among critics, whom she described as "the priests of literature." She explained: "Criticism, in its worthiest meaning is not, as is too often supposed, fault-finding, but interpretation of the oracles of genius."

"uncertain, shy . . . to Mr. Emerson": Gittleman, *Jones Very,* p. 159.

"sagacity . . . effect of genius": Deese, ed., *Jones Very: The Complete Poems,* p. xiv. I am indebted to Helen Deese for her extensive scholarship on Jones Very, and especially for her astute biographical essay included in this volume.

343   "a new will . . . speaking through him": Deese, ed., *Jones Very: The Complete Poems,* p. xvi.

344   "much flushed . . . overtaxing his brain": Deese, ed., *Jones Very: The Complete Poems,* pp. xvii–xviii.

344   "baptize *them* . . . Spirit had enabled": EPP to William P. Andrews, November 12, 1880, *Letters of EPP,* pp. 406–407.
      "contrary to my will": Deese, ed., *Jones Very: The Complete Poems,* p. xvi.
      "a noble paper . . . cannot be lost": Deese, ed., *Jones Very: The Complete Poems,* p. xvii.

345   "deepened, rendered more earnestly": EPP journal, entry of August 6, 1838, MVWC, p. 366, MHS.
      "go alone . . . mediator or veil": RWE, *Essays and Lectures,* pp. 87–89.
      "fetish": RWE in conversation with EPP, EPP journal, entry of August 6, 1838, MVWC, p. 366, MHS.
      "a decaying church . . . comes revolution": RWE, *Essays and Lectures,* pp. 87–89.
      "nothing but *transcendentalism*": Helen R. Deese, "The Peabody Family and the Jones Very 'Insanity': Two Letters of Mary Peabody," *Harvard Library Bulletin,* vol. XXXV, no. 2, p. 220.
      "incoherent rhapsody . . . not at all": Richardson, *Emerson: The Mind on Fire,* p. 298. Emerson had been invited to speak by the Divinity School graduates themselves, however. At least one, Theodore Parker, who was not dissuaded from his calling and went on to establish his own church, responded differently. He found Emerson's address "the noblest most inspiring strain I ever listened to." See Parker's entry in Dumas Malone, ed., *Dictionary of American Biography* (New York: Scribner's, 1934), vol. VII, p. 239.

346   "the evils . . . fire on the altar": RWE, *Essays and Lectures,* p. 91.
      "this truly prophetic discourse . . . era in Boston": EPP, "Emerson as Preacher," F. B. Sanborn, ed., *The Genius and Character of Emerson: Lectures at the Concord School of Philosophy* (Port Washington, N.Y.: Kennikat Press, 1971, reprint of 1885 edition), p. 158.
      "this last lecture": EPP journal, entry of August 8, 1838, MVWC, p. 368, MHS.
      "the latest form of infidelity": "Pope Andrews" Norton made his objections to Emerson's speech public in an 1839 address to Harvard Divinity School alumni, published as *A Discourse on the Latest Form of Infidelity* (Cambridge, Mass.: John Owen, 1839). The extent of Emerson's risk is difficult to establish, but in a letter of November 24, 1838, Mary Peabody wrote to Elizabeth in Boston of action that was threatened from Salem: "they put Mr E. by the side of Abner Kneeland & if they could prove the charge of blasphemy against him they would deprive him of his liberty as they had done to A.K." This information came to Mary from Jones Very, so she was somewhat doubtful as to its accuracy, although it appeared that the Salem clergy had some hopes of using testimony from Very to convict Emerson: "[Very] said they thought Mr. Emerson had done him harm—that they had been questioning him about his visit" to Emerson in Concord the previous month. Deese, "The Peabody Family and the Jones Very 'Insanity,'" p. 223.
      "as crazy as ever": Deese, "The Peabody Family and the Jones Very 'Insanity,'" p. 221.
      "now universally acknowledged . . . corrupt": Deese, "The Peabody Family and the Jones Very 'Insanity,'" p. 220.
      "Talk with him . . . companion": Deese, "The Peabody Family and the Jones Very 'Insanity,'" p. 221.
      "he is profoundly sane": Deese, "The Peabody Family and the Jones Very 'Insanity,'" p. 222.
      "Monomania, or mono*sania*": Deese, "The Peabody Family and the Jones Very 'Insanity,'" p. 221.

347   "the lyceum chair": EPP, "Emerson as Preacher," p. 157.
      "Whoever would preach": EPP, "Emerson as Preacher," p. 161.

"at our needlework": EPP, "Emerson as Preacher," p. 159.

348   "Apology, and even explanation": EPP, "Emerson as Preacher," p. 161.
"One writes . . . true heart": EPP journal, entry beginning Friday, [August 10, 1838], MVWC, pp. 381–82, MHS.

PAGE   *27. The Sister Years*

349   "tropical scourge": WP to EPP, August 31, 1837, Straker typescripts, p. 1201, Antiochiana.
"the greatest possible favorite": GFP to Mrs. EPP, September 28, [1837], Straker typescripts, p. 1207, Antiochiana.

350   "miasmatic": WP to Mrs. EPP, September 22, 1837, Straker typescripts, p. 1204, Antiochiana.
"raising from the brink . . . man of me": WP to EPP, August 31, 1837, Straker typescripts, pp. 1202–1203, Antiochiana.
"astonish": WP to EPP, August 31, 1837, Straker typescripts, p. 1202, Antiochiana.
"exposed himself considerably": GFP to Mrs. EPP, September 28, 1837, Straker typescripts, p. 1207, Antiochiana.
"the black vomit . . . melancholy duty": GFP to EPP, September 30, 1837, Straker typescripts, p. 1208, Antiochiana.
"His ardor of character . . . willing": MTP to Sally Jackson Gardner, October 23, 1837, HM Papers, MHS.

351   "poor little Mary . . . greatest misfortune": MTP to NCP, October 13, 1837, Straker typescripts, p. 1211, Antiochiana.
"We can rush . . . ourselves and mankind": NCP to GFP, October 18, 1837, Straker typescripts, p. 1220, Antiochiana.
"care & pet . . . tender affection": MTP to Sally Jackson Gardner, October 23, 1837, HM Papers, MHS.
"bitterness of parting": MTP to NCP, October 13, 1837, Straker typescripts, p. 1211, Antiochiana.
"home is the place": SAP to GFP, in EPP, Mrs. EPP, SAP, Dr. NP, and MTP to GFP, October 14, [1837], Straker typescripts, p. 1214, Antiochiana.
"no elements . . . conduct of life": EPP to GFP, in EPP, Mrs. EPP, SAP, Dr. NP, and MTP to GFP, October 14, [1837], Straker typescripts, p. 1214, Antiochiana.
Elizabeth remained emotionally fragile: MTP to HM, n.d., Straker typescripts, p. 1224, Antiochiana.
"a great ring . . . young beauty": Norman Holmes Pearson, "Elizabeth Peabody on Hawthorne," *Essex Institute Historical Collections,* July 1958, p. 264.

352   "ideal beauty": EPP, "Review: *Twice-told Tales;* by Nathaniel Hawthorne," *The New-Yorker,* vol. 5, no. 1, March 24, 1838, p. 1.
"Miss Elizabeth Peabody . . . on the pretext": Pearson, "Elizabeth Peabody on Hawthorne," p. 263.
"a hooded figure": Pearson, "Elizabeth Peabody on Hawthorne," p. 264. Elizabeth remembered Ebe's intellectual prowess so vividly that she had at first assumed *The New-England Magazine* tales must have been written by Ebe, using her brother as an agent to guard her privacy.
"Mr. Hawthorne . . . he will come again": Pearson, "Elizabeth Peabody on Hawthorne," p. 264.

353   "lived the life . . . glisten & intelligence": MTP to GFP, November 16, 1837, Berg.

354   "beauty . . . all his features": Pearson, "Elizabeth Peabody on Hawthorne," p. 264.

354   "If we can get ... pleasure in him": MTP to GFP, November 16, 1837, Berg.

"to all appearances": SAP to EPP, September 29, 1835, Berg

"great fame": EPP to GFP, [October 1836], Straker typescripts, p. 1116, Antiochiana.

"work from your own mind": WC to SAP, August 9, 1836, Berg.

"more susceptible": Joel Myerson, "'A True & High Minded Person': Transcendentalist Sarah Clarke," *Southwest Review*, vol. 59, no. 2, Spring 1974, p. 164.

Sophia would not come downstairs: In a reminiscence for her nephew Julian Hawthorne during the 1880s, Elizabeth wrote that Sophia consented to meet Nathaniel Hawthorne on his next visit, "soon after" November 11 (Pearson, "Elizabeth Peabody on Hawthorne," p. 265). But it is clear from letters and journals of the time that Sophia kept to her bed that winter. Likely Elizabeth had become used to telling the tale of her sister's romance with Hawthorne in such a way as to conceal the period during which Elizabeth was Hawthorne's chief object of interest in the Peabody household. Nevertheless, she always noted the intimacy that grew up between herself and Hawthorne at this same time when she, not Sophia, was the writer's chief confidante.

"one of Nature's": EPP to Elizabeth M. Hawthorne, ca. March 21, 1838, *Letters of EPP*, p. 223. Elizabeth continued, acknowledging that Ebe might "think me rather enthusiastic; but I believe I say the truth when I say that I do not often overrate, and I feel sure that this brother of yours has been gifted and kept so choice in her secret places by Nature thus far, that he may do a great thing for his country."

"my cursed habit of solitude": Pearson, "Elizabeth Peabody on Hawthorne," p. 260.

"all but Hindoo": Pearson, "Elizabeth Peabody on Hawthorne," p. 267. In her biography *Hawthorne: A Life* (New York: Alfred A. Knopf, 2003), Brenda Wineapple points out that Hawthorne's mother kept up some activities outside the home during Nathaniel's childhood—leading a Bible discussion group and heading the household in rural Maine for several years. But Mrs. Hawthorne's seclusion in Salem had become confirmed by the time of Nathaniel's return from college.

355   "Why was I not a girl": NH to Elizabeth C. Hawthorne, March 7, 1820, *The Letters, 1813–1843*, p. 117.

"the literary part": EPP to HM, March 3, [1838], *Letters of EPP*, p. 199.

"so completely": Pearson, "Elizabeth Peabody on Hawthorne," p. 266.

Twice-told Tales: During this period Hawthorne also wrote and paid for the publication of a novel, *Fanshawe* (1828), set in a college town based loosely on Bowdoin's Brunswick, Maine. When the book was poorly received, Hawthorne ordered the printer to destroy all the remaining copies and never spoke of the novel again.

"very witty and original": Pearson, "Elizabeth Peabody on Hawthorne," p. 266.

"healthy to live ... not live at our house": Pearson, "Elizabeth Peabody on Hawthorne," pp. 266–67.

The heiress was Mary Crowninshield Silsbee, daughter of the retired U.S. senator and Salem merchant Nathaniel Silsbee. "A great coquette" and "mischief-maker," in Elizabeth Peabody's view, who "liked to create difficulties and intrigues," Mary Silsbee had even tempted Nathaniel Hawthorne to challenge his friend and editor John O'Sullivan to a duel in defense of her honor. Probably the romance had little chance of success from the outset—and less still once Silsbee let Hawthorne know that she expected him to raise $3,000 as a wedding purse. In the end, Silsbee married the Peabody sisters' fellow boarder at Somerset

Court, historian and future Harvard president Jared Sparks. See James R. Mellow, *Nathaniel Hawthorne in His Times* (Boston: Houghton Mifflin, 1980), pp. 102–107; Wineapple, *Hawthorne: A Life*, pp. 97–100.

"little book of caged melodies . . . know thyself": EPP, "Review: *Twice-told Tales*, pp. 1–2.

356   "For the last ten . . . get back again": NH to Henry W. Longfellow, June 4, 1837, *The Letters, 1813–1843*, pp. 251–52.

"a new star": Mellow, *Nathaniel Hawthorne in His Times*, p. 80.

"a strange owl . . . pleasant to behold": Henry W. Longfellow to George Washington Greene, October 22, 1838, *The Letters, 1813–1843*, p. 277.

Twice-told Tales to Horace Mann: Elizabeth wrote to Mann on March 3, 1838, describing Hawthorne as "a man of first rate genius" living "a life of extraordinary seclusion." But, she noted, "he has no genius for negotiation with booksellers" and hinted that Mann could put in a good word for him with Nahum Capen, the publisher who was to bring out a library of books for Massachusetts common school classrooms. *Letters of EPP*, pp. 199–200.

Mann, who had written essays "Against Fiction" while in college, found *Twice-told Tales* distasteful, writing to Elizabeth that "we want something nearer home to duty and business. I look upon the great mass of our popular literature as a popular curse. It is all outside of humanity." If, however, Hawthorne wished to turn himself to "something graver and sterner . . . a development of *duties* in all the relations of life," Mann wrote, and if Elizabeth considered him "competent" to do so, then "let him be *imported into this world* and set to work without delay": HM to EPP, March 10, 1838, HM Papers, MHS. Hawthorne's next published book was a collection of historical tales for children, *Grandfather's Chair*, which appeared in December 1840, but the stories were neither grave nor stern, and Elizabeth herself served as his publisher.

first books for both writers: Technically, Hawthorne's novel *Fanshawe*, published anonymously in 1828, was his first. But Hawthorne had succeeded so well in suppressing it that by 1838 few people knew of its existence.

"popular story tellers . . . Beauty's sake": EPP to William Wordsworth, February 1838, Margaret Neussendorfer, ed., "Elizabeth Palmer Peabody to William Wordsworth: Eight Letters, 1825–1845," *Studies in the American Renaissance 1984* (Charlottesville: University Press of Virginia), p. 198. Neussendorfer notes that this mailing was the first recorded instance of Wordsworth having been sent *Nature*, although Emerson himself sent his book across the Atlantic to his friend Thomas Carlyle in 1836. It is likely, however, that Wordsworth did not receive the books until the following spring. In April 1839, Elizabeth wrote Wordsworth that she would have been "tempted to send again by Miss [Catharine Maria] Sedgewick—did I not think you might yet receive them." In this letter she made it clear that she hoped the English poet might offer some words of praise for Hawthorne's tales which she might use in advancing her friend's career. Hawthorne is "so shy and so modest he does not realize his success at all with the public," she wrote. "How happy I should be if I could get for him a word of *Wordsworth's*—I would make it a text for a hundred homilies—and he would listen as to holy writ—for he would acknowledge this authority." EPP to William Wordsworth, April 20, 1839, in Neussendorfer, ed., p. 201.

357   "I doubt I have much . . . human again": HM to EPP, November 5, 1837, HM Papers, MHS.

358   "the pure complexion . . . reflect the heavens": Pearson, "Elizabeth Peabody on Hawthorne," pp. 264–65.

358   "There is no fate": NH to Henry W. Longfellow, June 4, 1837, *The Letters, 1813–1843*, p. 251.

"an epoch . . . a dark place": Pearson, "Elizabeth Peabody on Hawthorne," p. 261.

"I will come . . . for my sake": Pearson, "Elizabeth Peabody on Hawthorne," p. 266.

"understanding": Mary Van Wyck Church interview with EPP, MVWC, p. 344, MHS. Elizabeth confided the fact of this "understanding" to friends on several occasions throughout her life. In a March 21, 1872, journal entry, Caroline Dall, a friend of Elizabeth's since 1840, recorded that Elizabeth told her that Hawthorne always read any letters she sent to Sophia before passing them along. "Whether this was his usual practice with all correspondents," Dall wrote, "or whether it grew out of the fact that he had once been engaged to Elizabeth —& left her for her sister—a fact—Elizabeth asserted & which I think Sophia could not have forgiven, I cannot tell" (MHS). I am grateful to Helen R. Deese for bringing this passage to my attention. Elizabeth also confided the tale to Theodore Parker (see pp. 411–14). Sarah Sturgis Shaw, another of Elizabeth's close friends, was also known not to "think well of [Nathaniel Hawthorne] on account of his engagement to Miss E. P. his sister in law," according to a letter written to Annie Adams Fields by a neighbor and friend of Sarah Shaw. Laura Johnson to Annie Adams Fields, July 7, 1864, Rita Gollin, *Annie Adams Fields: Woman of Letters* (Amherst: University of Massachusetts Press, 2002), p. 153.

Mary Van Wyck Church gave the most extensive account of such a confession in her draft biography of Elizabeth Peabody, adding that "it has been difficult to bring into the light of day this very sacred confidence & only after careful consideration did I decide to give it as an incident of her life that tends to clear the atmosphere & put in right relation much that has seemed inexplicable and indeed must so remain until the whole truth were made known. Naturally it could never be during the lives of any who bore a part" (MVWC, p. 349, MHS). Indeed it proved more difficult to bring out the story than Church expected. When Elizabeth's nephew and literary executor, Benjamin Pickman Mann, discovered Church's intention to publish the story, he revoked permission to use extracts from journals and letters that he had provided to Church for the purpose of writing the biography, which was never published. It seems likely that Mann destroyed many of Elizabeth's journals at this time, for they are not part of the large collection of Peabody correspondence he later donated to the Massachusetts Historical Society.

Although in a memoir written for her nephew Julian, Elizabeth told the story that is used in most biographies since his was published in 1884—that Sophia and Nathaniel met "soon after" November 11, 1837, and Elizabeth saw their mutual attraction at that time—it is clear from contemporary documents that the meeting could not have taken place until early spring 1838. The weight of evidence supports instead the version in these confessions: that a period of intensely intimate friendship between Elizabeth and Nathaniel continued for several months before he met Sophia, and a relationship developed that was qualitatively different from any either had known before, leading to the "understanding" or engagement Elizabeth confided later to several close friends. During this time, however, Elizabeth's descriptions of her younger sister may have piqued the writer's fancy. Then, when Sophia and Nathaniel finally met, Elizabeth saw their mutual attraction and withdrew.

Even Elizabeth's well-known denials of the long-rumored engagement claim this early intimacy, which Elizabeth could not bring herself to suppress. In a letter of June 30, 1886, Elizabeth wrote to Amelia Boelte, "I must hasten to tell you that it is all a mistake.—It is true that for the first three years after Hawthorne became known to and a *visitor* in our family, it was *rumoured*, that there was *probably* an engagement between him and *me* for we were manifestly very intimate *friends* and Sophia was considered so much of an invalid as not to be marriageable by any of us, including *herself* and Hawthorne." But she adds that once Sophia and Nathaniel met she could see "that *he* was so much in love with Sophia—at first sight—that he would probably never marry any *other* woman." *Letters of EPP*, pp. 430–31.

Ten years after Nathaniel met Sophia, six years into their marriage, he was troubled by a dream that he described in a letter to Sophia: "that thou hadst now ceased to be my wife, and hadst taken another husband . . . hereupon, thy sister Elizabeth, who was likewise present, informed the company, that, in this state of affairs, having ceased to be thy husband, I of course became her's." *The Letters, 1843–1853*, p. 228.

"a flower to be worn . . . never to be married": Pearson, "Elizabeth Peabody on Hawthorne," p. 267.

359   "Unknown yet known": SAP ms. poem, n.d., SAH papers, box 1, folder 14, Stanford.

"At those times . . . cessation from pain": MTP to HM, [August? 1836?], HM Papers, MHS.

"a hopeless cripple": EPP to HM, March 3, [1838], *Letters of EPP*, p. 198.

"hydrostatic": SAP to EPP, May 2–3, 1838, Berg.

"hyper-sympathetic": SAP to EPP, May 26, 1838, Berg.

"dear little couch . . . my own voice": SAP to Mary Wilder White Foote, March 11, 1838, Louise Deming typescripts, private collection. (Sophia's friend Mary Wilder White had married Caleb Foote, editor of the *Salem Gazette*, in 1834.)

361   "simple white wrapper . . . painfully": Pearson, "Elizabeth Peabody on Hawthorne," p. 265.

"I was leaving home": EPP interview with Mary Van Wyck Church, MVWC, p. 347, MHS.

362   "when you had the opportunity": NCP to EPP, April 13, 1838, Straker typescripts, p. 1251, Antiochiana.

"I have heard recently": NH to Mrs. Lydia T. Fessenden and Catharine C. Ainsworth, April 12, 1838, *The Letters, 1813–1843*, p. 270.

"Hurley-Burley": NH to SAP, May 26, 1839, *The Letters, 1813–1843*, p. 316.

"the Queen of Journalizers": NH quoted in SAP to EPP, July 23, [1838], Berg.

"the little items": EPP to SAP, n.d., 1838, Rose Hawthorne Lathrop, *Memories of Hawthorne* (Boston and New York: Houghton Mifflin, 1897), p. 19.

363   "pulled all the combs": SAP to EPP, April 26–May 1, 1838, Berg.

"sorely disappointed . . . into my room": SAP to EPP, April 23–25, 1838, Berg.

"just as sure . . . odorous violet": SAP to EPP, April 26–May 1, 1838, Berg. In fact this argument would have been difficult for either Sophia or Nathaniel to win; the ionone in scented violets is known to dull the sense of smell after several inhalations of their fragrance. Yet when one turns away from the flower, the scent receptors in the nose recover, and the violet's perfume can again be detected for a few breaths until the process starts in again.

"enshrined . . . shine more by contrast": SAP to EPP, May 4–13, 1838, Berg.

364   "it was a great thing . . . sing with it": SAP to EPP, April 26–May 1, 1838, Berg.

"Oh! I forget": SAP to EPP, May 2–3, 1838, Berg.

"To be the means": SAP to EPP, April 26–May 1, 1838, Berg.

364   "clad entirely . . . inferior genius": NH, *Tales and Sketches* (New York: Literary Classics of the United States, 1982), p. 642.

365   "your painter's art": NH, *Tales and Sketches*, p. 650.

"my visitations of truth . . . see and do": SAP to EPP, July 23, [1838], Berg.

"My whole being . . . abroad today": SAP to EPP, May 4–13, 1838, Berg.

"queer . . . concluded not to send": EPP to SAP, Sunday–Monday, [1838?], Berg 52B2261. My date: [June 17, 1838].

"out of his heart": EPP journal, entry beginning Friday, [August 10, 1838], MVWC, p. 376, MHS.

"He said he . . . let alone": SAP to EPP, July 23, [1838], Berg.

366   "utterly indifferent": EPP quoted in SAP to EPP, Sunday, n.d. [ca. July 30, 1838], Peabody Sisters Collection (no. 6952), UVA.

"come merely to gratify . . . charity": EPP to SAP, July 31, 1838, Berg. Evidently the work itself was hard and scarcely rewarding as well. On May 18, Sarah Clarke, who was now a neighbor in Newton Corner, wrote to George, "I hope [Elizabeth] will not work herself to death in trying to develope the mental energies of our rustics—It seems to be a breaking up of the ground for the first time, with most of them—I, myself am one of her scholars and with a young friend of mine am studying German, or rather *receiving* it in a sort of railroad way which suits me well": Sarah Clarke to GFP, May 18, [1838], HM Papers, MHS.

"It makes one faint": SAP to EPP, May 2–3, 1838, Berg.

"destroyed your influence . . . dictates of my mind": SAP to EPP, Sunday, n.d. [ca. July 30, 1838], Peabody Sisters Collection (no. 6952), UVA.

367   "I do not tell lies . . . one's own soul": EPP to SAP, July 31, 1838, Berg.

"little heart to write . . . cohesion ceases": EPP journal, entries of [July 29] and June 29, [1838], MVWC, pp. 352, 354, MHS.

"talks to me": EPP to GFP, Monday, August [6, 1838], Straker typescripts, p. 1297, Antiochiana. In his *Letters of EPP*, p. 229, Bruce Ronda dates the letter August 8, based on the postmark, but August 8 was a Wednesday in 1838.

"here I am myself": EPP journal, entry of August 5, 1838, MVWC, p. 360, MHS.

"The central Idea . . . find ourselves to have": EPP to GFP, Monday, August [6, 1838], Straker typescripts, pp. 1297–98, Antiochiana.

368   "the three greatest actual powers . . . master me": EPP journal, entry beginning Friday, [August 10, 1838], MVWC, pp. 385–86, MHS.

"power, when, in the course": EPP Brookline journal, June 23, 1886, MVWC, p. 173, MHS.

"imperfect & undeveloped . . . the arrived?": EPP journal, entry beginning Friday, [August 10, 1838], MVWC, p. 385, MHS.

369   "just as beautiful . . . celibacy": EPP journal, entry beginning Friday, [August 10, 1838], MVWC, p. 375, MHS.

"his duty": EPP journal, entry beginning Friday, [August 10, 1838], MVWC, p. 386, MHS.

"anniversary . . . forever love you": HM journal, vol. I, entry of August 5, 1838, HM Papers, MHS.

"true, truer": EPP journal, entry beginning Friday, [August 10, 1838], MVWC, p. 376, MHS.

"coming to understand . . . limited communications": EPP journal, entry beginning Friday, [August 10, 1838], MVWC, pp. 376–77, MHS.

"this wholeness . . . inevitable mistakes": EPP journal, entry beginning Friday, [August 10, 1838], MVWC, p. 377, MHS.

"delivered his mission . . . real *Poet*": EPP to RWE, December 3, 1838, *Letters of EPP*, p. 221.

370 "there was no inside . . . would make a man": RWE journal, June 16?, 1838, Joel Porte, ed., *Emerson in His Journals* (Cambridge, Mass.: Belknap Press of Harvard University Press, 1982), p. 188.

"the frigidity . . . embodiment of Genius": EPP to HM, n.d., MVWC, p. 335, MHS.

"requiring very little": EPP to Elizabeth Manning Hawthorne, Friday, [October 19, 1838], *Letters of EPP*, p. 213. Here Elizabeth told Ebe that she had written to ask advice from Orestes Brownson, then working as a steward at the United States Marine Hospital, an appointment given by George Bancroft, collector of the Port of Boston, who in turn received his appointment from the newly elected Democratic president, Martin Van Buren. Brownson's post was meant to help subsidize his time spent editing the Democratically inclined *Boston Quarterly Review;* Elizabeth had asked for his help in finding "my townsman Hawthorne an office like his—requiring very little time."

"My home is here": NH, *Tales and Sketches* (New York: Library of America, 1982), p. 229.

"I want to know . . . otherwise to me!": Pearson, "Elizabeth Peabody on Hawthorne," p. 267.

371 "simple severe lines": A. [Washington Allston], "The Gentle Boy—with an Original Illustration," *Christian Register and Boston Observer*, vol. 18, no. 3, January 19, 1839, p. 1.

"warm recommendation": Arlin Turner, "Park Benjamin on the Author and the Illustrator of 'The Gentle Boy,'" *Nathaniel Hawthorne Journal*, 1974, p. 88. Sophia also borrowed design elements from the English portraitist Thomas Lawrence's *Master Charles William Lambton*, engravings of which were then enormously popular in the United States. Elizabeth had used the engraving to illustrate her mother's story, "The Two Portraits," in her early anthology *The Casket*, and Sophia had copied it many times since then in pencil and also posed young Eduardo Morrell for a pencil portrait in this manner in Cuba. *Master Lambton*, sometimes known as "The Red Boy," and always called "The Boy on the Rock" by Sophia, showed a handsome, soulful child dressed in a velvet suit, reclining on what seems to be an armchair of boulders overhung with branches and vines. The image merged two important themes of English Romanticism (and of American Transcendentalism): a reverence for nature and the notion that children have special access to nature's divine truths.

372 "TO MISS SOPHIA . . . in language": NH, *The Gentle Boy: A Thrice Told Tale* (Boston: Weeks, Jordan, 1839).

"a display . . . highly poetic": Park Benjamin, *The New-Yorker*, vol. VI, January 26, 1839, p. 301.

"pathetic and beautiful . . . exquisite fancies": A. [Washington Allston], "The Gentle Boy," p. 1.

"sketch of your countenance . . . careless glance": SAP to NH, December 6, 1838, Nathaniel Hawthorne Collection (no. 6249-A), UVA.

"such changes . . . See if I don't!": NH in Barbara S. Mouffe, ed., *Hawthorne's Lost Notebook* (University Park and London: Pennsylvania State University Press, 1978), [p. 80].

"the most peculiar . . . can be imagined": NH in Mouffe, ed., *Hawthorne's Lost Notebook*, [p. 80].

"you would look . . . all eternity": SAP to NH, December 6, 1838, Nathaniel Hawthorne Collection (no. 6249-A), UVA.

373    $1,500 . . . "measurer": Mellow, *Nathaniel Hawthorne in His Times*, p. 156.

374   "Nathaniel Hawthorne, Esq.": Inscription by SAP in Henry Reed, ed., *The Complete Poetical Works of William Wordsworth. Together with a description of the country of the lakes in the north of England* (Philadelphia: James Kay, Jr.; Boston: James Munroe; Pittsburgh: John J. Kay, 1837), volume in private collection. I am grateful to Imogen Howe and Joan Ensor for bringing this inscription to my attention. The passage from Wordsworth's poem "Though narrow be that Old Man's Cares" reads:

> For he hath waking empire, wide as dreams;
> An ample sovereignty of eye and ear.
> Rich are his walks with supernatural cheer;
> The region of his inner spirit teems
> With vital sounds and monitory gleams
> Of high astonishment and pleasing fear.

"address . . . illuminated with wit": SAP to Dr. NP, [Boston? 1839?], Berg 229909B. My date: [after January 1, before January 5, 1839].

"smiling cheerfulness . . . Book of Chronicles": NH, *Tales and Sketches*, p. 679.

"several bundles . . . here in my basket": NH, *Tales and Sketches*, p. 682.

375   "a wonderfully pleasant": NH, *Tales and Sketches*, p. 678.

"so much promise": NH, *Tales and Sketches*, pp. 678–79. Although Hawthorne had decided in favor of the younger Sophia, he could still be influenced by Elizabeth's opinions—even on love. At the start of 1839, he recorded these lines in his journal, attributing them to "E.P.P.": "The caress of affection is superfluous, and therefore seems a touch of the Divine. It is in human affection what the last touch of God is in Nature." Later on the same page, he quoted Sophia, or "S.A.P.": "There is no Measure for Measure in my affections. If the Earth fails me in love, I can die and go to GOD."

That Sophia had entered the writer's creative consciousness was evident in another passage in this same journal, which Hawthorne used primarily to record ideas for stories. Most such ideas were darkened by tragedy, regret, psychic danger, loss. But this one suggested by Sophia appeared as well, perhaps recorded at about the same time that Hawthorne was creating the optimistic young New Year of "The Sister Years": "A person to look back on a long life ill-spent, and to picture forth a beautiful life, which he would live, if he could be permitted to begin his life over again. Finally, to discover that he had only been dreaming of old age—that he was really young—and could live such a life as he had pictured. S. A. Peabody": Mouffe, ed., *Hawthorne's Lost Notebook*, [pp. 83, 82].

PAGE

28. Conversation

379   "the only one to obtain": [Sally Jackson Gardner] to MTP, January 10, [1839], HMII Papers, MHS. Dr. Peabody calculated that eventually Mary would take in $1,200 a year, once she had attracted the school of twenty children at the $15 a quarter that she expected. Dr. NP to Francis Peabody, January 14, 1839, Dartmouth. By mid-February, Mary had already sent an unspecified sum of money to her brother Nat, whose school in Newton was not prospering and who had

fallen deeper into debt. NCP to Mrs. EPP, February 17, 1839, Straker typescripts, p. 1285, Antiochiana.

"anything of . . . Saxon sense *wholly*": HM to EPP, December 9, 1838, HM Papers, MHS.

"nestling under your wing": HM to MTP, December 24, 1838, HM Papers, MHS.

380   "my cheeks have got into": MTP to Sally Jackson Gardner, December 10, 1838, HM Papers, MHS.

"arrogate[d] to myself": HM to MTP, December 24, 1838, HM Papers, MHS.

"Love": William Charvat, *Emerson's American Lecture Engagements: A Chronological List* (New York: New York Public Library, 1961), p. 17. Elizabeth may also have been in the audience—or perhaps she wasn't. It is not known when or why, but only that at some point Emerson gave her the manuscript of "Love," which she kept until after his death, when she returned it to his daughter Edith Emerson Forbes. *Letters of RWE*, vol. 7, p. 363.

"Though slowly . . . more beautiful": RWE, *Essays and Lectures* (New York: Library of America, 1983), p. 337.

"single blessedness . . . thought or feeling": MTM, essay in Julia Ward Howe, ed., *Sex and Education: A Reply to Dr. E. H. Clarke's "Sex in Education"* (Boston: Roberts Brothers, 1874), p. 53.

"I would never accept": MTP to Mary T. Hathaway Watson, September 7, 1834, private collection.

"noble army . . . average woman": MTM, essay in Howe, ed., *Sex and Education*, p. 52.

"I will tell you": MTM and EPP, *Moral Culture of Infancy, and Kindergarten Guide* (Boston: T.O.H.P. Burnham; New York: O. S. Felt, 1863), p. 115.

381   "bird, nest, tree . . . symbolic word": MTM and EPP, *Moral Culture of Infancy*, p. 128.

"about every thing . . . selfish mothers": MTM, "Reminiscences of School Life and Teaching," *Female Education in Massachusetts*, republished from *Barnard's American Journal of Education* (Hartford, Conn.: 1884), p. 318.

"I do not feel satisfied . . . be unchecked": MTM and EPP, *Moral Culture of Infancy*, pp. 117–19.

"at every turn . . . not approve of the book": MTP to SAP, February 5, 1839, Berg 371478B. My date: [January] 5, 1839.

382   regular dispatches: The articles were first published under the pseudonym "Philokosmos" in a series starting on May 9 and concluding on June 14, 1839, in the *Salem Gazette*.

"home": Charles Capper, *Margaret Fuller, An American Romantic Life: The Private Years* (New York and Oxford: Oxford University Press, 1992), p. 257.

Fuller took extensive notes: Margaret Fuller, "Exhibition of Allston's Paintings in Boston in 1839," *The Dial*, vol. I, no. 1, July 1840, pp. 73–82 (not to be confused with Elizabeth's article of the same title, the compilation of her *Salem Gazette* dispatches reprinted in *Last Evening with Allston, and Other Papers* [Boston: D. Lothrop, 1886]).

"It is precisely": EPP, "Exhibition of Allston's Paintings in Boston in 1839," p. 58.

383   "medallion . . . Georgius Imperador": SAP to GFP, October 29, [1839], Berg.

"the whiskers . . . look well in plaster": SAP to GFP, October 27, 1839, Berg.

"great admiration": SAP to GFP, November 1, 1839, Berg.

"very good for the first": SAP to GFP, November 3–5, [1839], Berg.

"put into marble . . . finishing touches": SAP to GFP, October 27, 1839, Berg. Clevenger was not yet thirty when Sophia met him in Boston, but he had already completed commissioned busts of Daniel Webster and President Martin Van Buren. He maintained a successful studio in New York City, despite his humble beginnings as a stonecutter in Cincinnati, where his carvings on gravestones brought him the attention of a sponsor. Clevenger did much of his work directly in freestone, skipping the steps Sophia was learning: first modeling in clay, then casting in plaster, before rendering in marble. Clevenger died in Europe at thirty-one of pulmonary phthisis as a result of inhaling stone dust, it was widely believed.

383   "thou sculptor": SAP to GFP, October 29, [1839], Berg.
"our union . . . God knows we are": NH to SAP, July 24, 1839, *The Letters, 1813–1843*, p. 329.
"several things a-going . . . transported with delight": EPP to SAP, June 23, 1839, *Letters of EPP*, p. 225.

384   "nestle . . . or ever was": NH to SAP, April 2, 1839, *The Letters, 1813–1843*, p. 296. Hawthorne succeeded in impressing not just Sophia with his labors. According to Elizabeth, by mid-June 1839, Hawthorne had earned a reputation as "the most efficient and best of the Custom House officers," in George Bancroft's words. EPP to SAP, June 23, 1839, *Letters of EPP*, p. 226.
"Grecian braid": SAP to Dr. NP, February 9, [1838], Berg. My date: February 9, [1839].
"soundly": SAP to GFP, May 21, 1839, Berg.
"I never looked so well": SAP to Dr. NP, February 9, [1838], Berg. My date: February 9, [1839].
"another species . . . tripod": SAP to GFP, October 27, 1839, Berg.
"muscular . . . commanding charm": William Henry Channing quoted in Capper, *Margaret Fuller*, p. 266.
"a haughty assurance": Capper, *Margaret Fuller*, p. 266.
"not so graceful . . . first interview": SAP to GFP, October 27, 1839, Berg.

386   "she smites and kindles": TP to EPP, August 30, 1839, letterbooks, vol. 7, p. 123, TP Papers, MHS.
"pay me *unasked*": MF to EPP, September 24, 1839, *Letters of MF*, vol. 2, p. 92. With Hawthorne's aid, Elizabeth had submitted "Claims of the Beautiful Arts" to Hawthorne's friend and the editor of the *Democratic Review*, John O'Sullivan. The piece was published in November 1838, pp. 253–68; in May 1839 Hawthorne wrote O'Sullivan that Elizabeth had asked him "to assure you that you need not trouble yourself about paying for her 'Beautiful Arts' . . . but I told her that I should do no such thing, nor that you would consent to such an arrangement. Nevertheless, it will make you easier to know that she is not in immediate want of the money." NH to John L. O'Sullivan, May 19, 1839, *The Letters, 1813–1843*, p. 313. Hawthorne's statement that Elizabeth was "not in immediate want of money" was probably not correct, and it was ironic as well, considering the thrust of her article, which advocated government subsidies for artists on behalf of struggling writers like Hawthorne.
volunteered Mary's room: Fuller wrote to Elizabeth, "I have not been able to look at Mary's room yet, but think I shall probably accept your kind offer." MF to EPP, September 24, 1839, *Letters of MF*, vol. 2, p. 92. There is no further evidence that the Conversations were actually held in Mary's room, but it is certain that this first series was not held in Elizabeth's bookstore at 13 West Street, as most accounts state (see Capper, *Margaret Fuller*, p. 293). There was no West Street bookshop until August 1840; the Peabody family lived in Salem until July

1840, and Elizabeth later recalled in *Rem of WEC* commuting from Salem to attend the first series of Conversations.

"reluctance she feels . . . no consequence": TP to EPP, August 30, 1839, letterbooks, vol. 7, p. 123, TP Papers, MHS.

387   "the great questions . . . gone by": MF to Sophia Dana Ripley, August 27, 1839, *Letters of MF*, vol. 2, p. 87. According to EPP's record of the November 6 Conversation, this letter was read and "enlarged upon." Nancy Simmons, "Margaret Fuller's Boston Conversations: The 1839–1840 Series," *Studies in the American Renaissance 1994* (Charlottesville: University Press of Virginia), p. 203.

"nucleus of conversation . . . effort for expression": Simmons, "Margaret Fuller's Boston Conversations," p. 203.

388   "I think no one": *Rem of WEC*, p. 404.

"a dangerous bleeding . . . without knowing it": SAP to EPP, November 14, [1839], Berg.

"medallion . . . than his": SAP to EPP, November 18, 1839, Straker typescripts, p. 1304, Antiochiana.

"Flirtation," and packets of braided hair: Peabody Letters, Antiochiana.

"death struggle . . . infinite affection": EPP to HM, December 1, [1839], Straker typescripts, p. 1306, Antiochiana.

389   "be myself and *act*": EPP to GFP, Monday, August [6, 1838], Straker typescripts, pp. 1297–98, Antiochiana. In his *Letters of EPP*, p. 229, Bruce Ronda dates the letter August 8, based on the postmark, but August 8 was a Wednesday in 1838.

"I never performed . . . come from within": EPP to HM, September 4, 1836, Straker typescripts, p. 1093, Antiochiana.

"devote your powers . . . his mind alone": EPP to Mrs. Benjamin Guild, [1838], MVWC, p. 341, MHS. Elizabeth's full explanation is worth quoting:

> As to [Emerson's] doctrine it was my creed before I knew it was his. It is a curious circumstance that in 1825 I made some paraphrases of St. John's Gospel in which I paraphrased 'the word' as moral truth and en[deavored] to state in some accompanying papers this very doctrine of God, which Mr Emerson labors to set forth and Mr Norton to call atheism. These papers I showed to Mrs. Sullivan who took great interest in them & copied some of them off, which were returned to me after her death. Dr. Channing also saw them & they were the foundation of our intimacy. . . .
>
> Well, as it happened those same papers which had been laid away seven years were brought out again to Miss Mary Emerson [Waldo Emerson's aunt]. She came to see me in 1832 and wanted to know what I thought and felt about God the theme of all her thoughts. I was intensely occupied and could not talk on general subjects so gave her these. She carried them down to Waldo Emerson's who had then just left his people and whom I had never seen or heard since he began to study Divinity scientifically, and I knew nothing of his views. He and Charles read them, and Charles immediately called on me to make my acquaintance, and Mr. Waldo Emerson wanted a copy of my paraphrases. It is pretty plain therefore that this heresy does not belong to his mind alone and it is not strange, is it, that I am interested deeply in his having a chance to promulgate views so dear to my own soul, being the theory of its life and resurrection from my long previous miseries of mind . . . I know he is not an atheist or Pantheist or unChristian just as well so I know I am not one myself.

Almost fifty years later, in a memorial to Emerson delivered at the Concord School of Philosophy the year after his 1883 death, Elizabeth made her point again, noting her first acquaintance with Emerson as her Greek tutor in 1822 (EPP, "Emerson as Preacher," F. B. Sanborn, ed., *The Genius and Character of Emerson: Lectures at the Concord School of Philosophy* [Port Washington, N.Y.: Kennikat Press, 1971, reprint of 1885 edition], pp. 151–52):

> After this our acquaintance lapsed for ten years, comprehending all the time Mr. Emerson was studying divinity and preaching at the Second Church in Boston. Then he resumed it (in 1833) on occasion of reading a little paper of mine which his aunt, Miss Mary Emerson—who was my great friend, and bent on bringing us into intimate acquaintance,—had found among some loose papers of a journal of thoughts I fitfully kept, on the same principle that Mr. Emerson kept a journal all his life. This paper was a very free paraphrase of the first chapter of the Gospel of Saint John, from the first verse to the fourteenth inclusive, in which I translated the word Logos into "moral truth-speaking," first by the things of Nature, then by the processes of conscious life and reason, Etc.
>
> He was on the eve of his first voyage to Europe, soon after the death of his first wife and relinquishment of his Boston pulpit. He was at the time too feeble in health to make visits, and sent to me to come to his house in Chardon Street, where I found him quite absorbed in Goethe and Carlyle; but he immediately turned his attention to Saint John's grand peroration, and we discussed every phrase of it. It was one of those conversations which 'make the soul,' to use a favorite expression of his aunt Mary's. It was, therefore, on the highest plane of human thought that we first met, our theme being the Eternal Relations of God, Nature, and Man; beginning an intercourse that continued there with more or less interval during his life-time.

It is interesting to note that by this late date, Elizabeth herself had reduced the significance of her paraphrase of St. John by referring to it as "a little paper of mine," even as she attempted to take credit as a co-originator of some of Transcendentalism's key precepts.

389   "sympathy and the development": EPP to Mrs. Benjamin Guild, [1838], MVWC, p. 341, MHS.

390   "learn the secret of Life . . . our Power": EPP, unpublished essay, "The measure of our Life is our Power," Straker typescripts, p. 1293, Antiochiana.

under Emerson's guidance: Emerson continued to work out this idea, which ultimately found its way into the conclusion of his 1844 essay "Experience": "The true romance which the world exists to realize, will be the transformation of genius into practical power." RWE, *Essays and Lectures*, p. 492.

"I am interested deeply": EPP to Mrs. Benjamin Guild, [1838], MVWC, p. 341, MHS.

Christian Examiner: TP to EPP, January 8, 1839, letterbooks, vol. 7, TP Papers, MHS.

first normal school: TP to EPP, October 3, 1839, letterbooks, vol. 7, p. 127, TP Papers, MHS.

"If I study . . . 'leaves & fruit'": EPP journal, entry beginning Friday, [August 10, 1838], MVWC, p. 388, MHS.

391   "the only practical transcendentalist": EPP quoted in MTP to HM, May 30, 1835,
HM Papers, MHS.
bookstore and circulating library: RWE to MF, April 21, 1840, *Letters of RWE*, vol.
2, p. 287.
It is possible that Elizabeth first planned to open the bookstore in Salem, for
as late as May 1, 1840, she wrote to her friend Rebecca Amory Lowell that she
did not expect to leave town again until the following winter. *Letters of EPP*, pp.
237–38. Salem's Susan Burley was also an early backer of the plan. On July 1,
1840, Theodore Parker wrote to Elizabeth that "the plan did not at first strike me
so favorably as it did you, and that *wise* Miss Burley." Letterbooks, vol. 7, p. 139,
TP Papers, MHS. By then, however, Elizabeth had already made plans to move
her family to West Street and open the bookshop there.
twenty-one titles: "Entry of Books Borrowed, vol. I, 1827–32," p. 337, Boston
Athenaeum.
first issue of *The Dial:* In the end, there were no such advertisements and no "Intelligence" column in the first issue of *The Dial*, which was given over entirely to
essays, poetry, and Bronson Alcott's "Orphic Sayings."
"fill a vacancy": TP to EPP, July 1, 1840, letterbooks, vol. 7, p. 139, TP Papers,
MHS. On Parker's reading while at Harvard Divinity School, see Dean Grodzins,
American Heretic: Theodore Parker and Transcendentalism (Chapel Hill and London:
University of North Carolina Press, 2002), p. 59. I am grateful to Dean Grodzins
for directing me to numerous manuscript sources on the relationship between
Elizabeth Peabody and Theodore Parker, as well as for this excellent account of
Parker's early life and work.
"debut in the mercantile world": EPP to WEC, July 10, 1840, MVWC, p. 402,
MHS.

392   "magnificent . . . print & paper": Caroline Healey Dall journals, entry of August
7, 1840, Dall Papers, MHS. I am grateful to Helen R. Deese, editor of the Dall
journals, for bringing this passage to my attention.

393   Elizabeth's selections: "New Bookstore and Foreign Library," Broadside, MHS.
John Wiley: Wiley was partner in publishing with Elizabeth's cousin George
Palmer Putnam, son of her mother's youngest sister Catherine Palmer Putnam, a
one-time schoolteacher in Salem. According to Dr. Peabody, it was "her cousin
George Putnam who has a house in New York & London" who "agreed to furnish her with books" (Dr. NP to Francis Peabody, October 25, [1840], Dartmouth). But it was Wiley's name that Elizabeth referred to in the few extant letters describing her business dealings.
"so that all branches": Dr. NP to Francis Peabody, October 25, [1840], Dartmouth.
"My circumstances . . . an old man": Dr. NP to Francis Peabody, May 25, 1840, Dartmouth. In a second letter to his brother Francis, Dr. Peabody explained the decline
in his business more specifically: "The nature of my business of Dentist has lately
changed considerably—Mineral teeth have become all the fashion & these I have
not got into the habit of making—True, I took a partner who understood it—But
this finally operated against me." After Dr. Peabody's long illness, his young partner was "doing most of the business, [and] his friends urged him to separate from
me . . . he made me some respectable consideration for relinquishing what hold I
had on the business." Dr. NP to Francis Peabody, October 25, [1840], Dartmouth.
translating tales for children: One of these was *The Christmas Eve* (Boston: E. P.
Peabody, 1842).

393   "a thing not then": George Willis Cooke, *An Historical and Biographical Introduction to Accompany "The Dial"* (New York: Russell and Russell, 1961, reprint of 1906 edition), vol. I, p. 148.

"nothing in the business": WEC to EPP, June 7, 1840, *Rem of WEC*, p. 408.

"favored resort": WEC to EPP, June 22, 1840, *Rem of WEC*, p. 409.

394   "in this age of proprieties": WEC to EPP, June 7, 1840, *Rem of WEC*, p. 408.

"misunderstandings and ugly things": *Rem of WEC*, p. 404.

"ladylike": "Every body assures me they think it perfectly *'ladylike.'*" EPP to WEC, July 10, 1840, MVWC, p. 402, MHS.

"the seekers . . . people so armed": EPP to WEC, August 1840, MVWC, p. 405 ff, MHS.

395   "one cheerful . . . cry before you are hurt": Joel Myerson, ed., *Transcendentalism: A Reader* (Oxford: Oxford University Press, 2000), pp. 291, 294.

"if [women] may sell . . . open to women": WEC to EPP, June 7, 1840, *Rem of WEC*, p. 408.

Emancipation . . . Grandfather's Chair . . . Famous Old People . . . The Liberty Tree: Grandfather's Chair was on sale as of December 1840, although the year 1841 is printed on its title page. Elizabeth's other publications in 1841 included Hawthorne's *Famous Old People* and *The Liberty Tree*, Anna Cabot Lowell's *The Theory of Teaching*, Mary Peabody's *Primer of Reading and Drawing*, Felix Paul Wierzbicki's *The Ideal Man*, a reprint (the third edition) of Theodore Parker's *A Discourse on the Transient and Permanent in Christianity*, and *A Method of Teaching Linear Drawing Adapted to the Public Schools*.

396   "vicious in its foundations": EPP to John Sullivan Dwight, September 20, 1840, *Letters of EPP*, p. 245. The meeting took place on September 9, 1840. See Grodzins, *American Heretic*, p. 537, n. 186.

"a new organization": EPP to John Sullivan Dwight, June 18, 1840, *Letters of EPP*, p. 243.

"educating the Reason . . . on the ruins": EPP to John Sullivan Dwight, September 20, 1840, *Letters of EPP*, p. 246.

"the social principle . . . to be educated": Carol Johnston, "The Journals of Theodore Parker: July–December 1840" (Ph.D. diss., University of South Carolina, 1980), p. 53.

"the union of man . . . *live* & trust": EPP to John Sullivan Dwight, September 20, 1840, *Letters of EPP*, p. 246.

There had been debate about how and whether to take action before as well. Hedge and others objected to the plan of establishing *The Dial* as a vehicle for publishing the group's views as early as September 1839. Emerson and Fuller proceeded with the plan anyway and may have found that dissension hard to live with after the first issue appeared in July 1840. Although Fuller was the nominal editor, Emerson retained considerable control: the first issue was an unstated homage to his dead family members, including poetry by his first wife, Ellen, and brother Edward, as well as an essay on Homer by his brother Charles. *The Dial* became Emerson's Transcendental experiment. See Joel Myerson, "A Calendar of Transcendental Club Meetings," *American Literature*, vol. XLIV, no. 2, May 1972, pp. 199–200.

397   "Dove Cottage . . . New Eden": Madelon Bedell, *The Alcotts: Biography of a Family* (New York: Clarkson N. Potter, 1980), pp. 195, 173.

"people do not receive": EPP journal, entry of November 25, 1836, MVWC, p. 281, MHS.

"I came into contact . . . very living years": Cooke, *An Historical and Biographical Introduction to Accompany "The Dial,"* p. 148.

brilliant sermon: TP, "A Discourse of the Transient and Permanent in Christianity; Preached at the Ordination of Mr. Charles C. Shackford, in the Hawes Place Church in Boston, May 19, 1841," Myerson, ed., *Transcendentalism: A Reader,* pp. 340–66. Initially Parker had difficulty finding a publisher for the sermon, but by the end of 1841 three separate editions had appeared. The third was published by E. P. Peabody.

398   "son of Thunder": EPP to John Sullivan Dwight, September 20, 1840, *Letters of EPP,* p. 247.

"too large a party . . . new Protestantism": *Rem of WEC,* pp. 413–14.

29. "Mr. Ripley's Utopia"

399   "I want some inward . . . sympathize with me": HM journal vol. 1, entry of April 21, 1839, MHS.

"less of acute suffering": HM journal vol. 1, entry of August 4, 1839, MHS.

"My whole life": HM journal vol. 1, entry of April 21, 1839, MHS.

"Labors and anxieties . . . needs them more": HM journal vol. 1, entry of August 19, 1839, MHS.

400   "the greatest of all . . . triumph in any other": HM journal vol. 1, entry of September 8, 1839, MHS.

"Shall I shrink": HM journal vol. 1, entry of November 17, 1839, MHS.

"a splendid house . . . bind me to earth?": HM journal vol. 1, entry of December 25, 1839, MHS.

"I have not heard": HM to EPP, November 28, 1839, HM Papers, MHS.

"bigots and vandals": HM journal vol. 1, entry of March 21, 1840, MHS.

"from ill health . . . ever suffered": HM journal vol. 1, entry of January 5, 1840, MHS.

"homelessness, uselessness": HM journal vol. 1, entry of December 29, 1830, MHS.

"If it pleaseth thee": HM to MTP, March 5, 1840, HM Papers, MHS.

401   "the objects . . . more beautiful": RWE, *Essays and Lectures* (New York: Library of America), p. 337.

"the first day I have set": HM journal vol. 1, entry of March 28, 1840, MHS.

"How much good might": HM journal vol. 1, entry of March 30, 1840, MHS.

"No imagination": HM journal vol. 1, entry of April 8, 1840, MHS.

"I meant to have treated . . . same to you": HM to MTP, June 1, 1840, HM Papers, MHS.

"My heart throbs . . . say upon the subject": NH to SAP, June 24, 1840, *The Letters, 1813–1843,* p. 479.

402   "the chosen . . . bats and owls": TP to EPP, Saturday Morning, [November 15, 1841], letterbooks, vol. 7, p. 136, TP Papers, MHS. My date: [May 15, 1841].

The young diarist Caroline Healey gives the flavor of one such gathering on the night of Wednesday, April 15, 1841: "Had a delightful evening at Miss Peabody's. Mr. Clarke—read to me from a letter from Dr Keates . . . Mr Wheeler showed me—an autograph letter from Tennyson—consenting to republish his Miscellanies[.] The author writes a marvelously plain hand" (Dall Papers, MHS). Clarke was the minister James Freeman Clarke, founder of the new Church of the Disciples; "Dr. Keates" was the English poet John Keats's brother George; Charles Stearns Wheeler produced an American edition of Tennyson's *Poems* in 1842. I am grateful to Helen R. Deese for bringing this passage to my attention and for these identifications.

402   "wicked ... get with the Emersons": HM to EPP, December 9, 1838, HM Papers, MHS.

"that everlasting rejecter": *AN*, p. 357.

"not be afraid ... besought it of me": NH to SAP, December 5, *The Letters, 1813–1843*, p. 382.

"nearer home to duty ... does it tend?": HM to EPP, March 10, 1838, HM Papers, MHS.

"I should rather have built": HM to Samuel Gridley Howe, May 20, 1841, HM Papers, MHS. Mann went further, in a conceit that may have drawn on what he'd learned from Elizabeth of Nathaniel Hawthorne's lonely apprenticeship. He hated, Mann wrote Howe, "to imagine you, like a shot eagle, caged in some old convent & pecking away at mildewed & dusty parchments."

"I want nothing to do": NH to SAP, March 15, 1840, *The Letters, 1813–1843*, p. 422.

403   "atrocious attack": HM journal vol. I, entry of March 15, 1840, MHS.

"the omission ... literary man": NH to John L. O'Sullivan, May 19, 1838, *The Letters, 1813–1843*, p. 313. Also NH to John L. O'Sullivan, April 20, 1840, *The Letters, 1813–1843*, p. 447.

"grievous thraldom ... unblest Custom House": NH to SAP, March 15, 1840, *The Letters, 1813–1843*, p. 422.

"What a year ... glory of the day": SAP to NH, December 31, 1839, Julian Hawthorne, *Nathaniel Hawthorne and His Wife* (Hamden, Conn.: Archon Books, 1968, reprint of 1884 edition), vol. I, p. 209.

This letter is one of the few of Sophia's from the courtship years which survive. In 1853, before the Hawthornes sailed for England, where Nathaniel was to serve as the American consul in Liverpool, he burned nearly all of Sophia's love letters, of which there were "hundreds," along with "great heaps of old letters and other papers" in a bonfire he set behind their house in Concord. *AN*, p. 552. One can only speculate on his reasons for doing so. Perhaps the simplest explanation is the best: the scrupulously private Nathaniel Hawthorne did not wish to carry his personal letters across the Atlantic, and he wanted to prevent their discovery by anyone else. Darker reasons have been proposed by biographers, including the possibility that Hawthorne wished to destroy evidence of his wife's early passion at a time in their marriage when, after the births of three children, the couple may have decided to practice celibacy as a means of birth control (common practice for married couples of their class at that time). Others have proposed that Hawthorne wished to quench any fledgling literary ambitions that Sophia retained.

Yet it is clear that at the time they were written Nathaniel treasured Sophia's "golden" letters. NH to SAP, September 18, 1840, *The Letters, 1813–1843*, p. 491. He considered her "an inspired little penwoman" (NH to SAP, August 9, [1840], p. 484), capable of demonstrating a high standard of epistolary art and often deferred to her superior powers of description: "[H]ow canst thou say that I have ever written anything beautiful, being thyself so potent to reproduce whatever is loveliest? ... Would that I had thy pen, and I would give thee pictures of beauty to match thine own." NH to SAP, June 22, 1840, pp. 475, 477. After almost three years of regular correspondence, Nathaniel was still complimenting her letters: "Thou ... dost express thy love in heavenly language." NH to SAP, September 3,

1841, p. 565. After burning them, Hawthorne wrote in his journal, "The world has no more such; and now they are all ashes." *AN*, p. 552.

"Demon . . . to be loved": SAP to EPP, July 5, [1839], Rose Hawthorne Lathrop, *Memories of Hawthorne* (Boston: Houghton Mifflin, 1897), p. 31. Mrs. Peabody's *Holiness: The Legend of St. George* was first published in 1836 (Boston: E. R. Broaders). Sophia's illustrations may have been intended for a later edition, which seems never to have been produced. The drawings do not survive.

404   "artist & a poet": SAP ms. poem, n.d., SAH Papers, box 1, folder 14, Stanford.

"a cottage . . . to comfort me": NH to SAP, August 21, 1839, *The Letters, 1813–1843*, p. 339.

"not to muse . . . through the trial": NH to SAP, November 29, 1839, *The Letters, 1813–1843*, p. 374.

"I never owned . . . paint pictures together": NH to SAP, January 3, 1840, *The Letters, 1813–1843*, pp. 397 98.

"meet his own wife . . . your own husband": NH to SAP, October 23, 1839, *The Letters, 1813–1843*, p. 357.

"conjugal embrace": NH to SAP, October 3, 1839, *The Letters, 1813–1843*, p. 350.

405   "in the shadow": NH to SAP, October 4, 1840, *The Letters, 1813–1843*, p. 494.

"mutually within one another": NH to SAP, November 25, 1839, *The Letters, 1813–1843*, p. 373.

"whenever the cash . . . both of us": NH to SAP, January 1, 1840, *The Letters, 1813–1843*, p. 395.

"our souls . . . married pair": NH to SAP, September 23, 1839, *The Letters, 1813–1843*, p. 347. See T. Walter Herbert's *Dearest Beloved: The Hawthornes and the Making of the Middle-Class Marriage* for a useful discussion of what he terms the Hawthornes' "premarital marriage" (Berkeley and Los Angeles: University of California Press, 1993), p. 115.

"inner gallery": SAP to Dr. NP and Mrs. EPP, July 23, 1832, Berg.

"affected to tears": SAP journal April 1–August 8, 1829, entry of July 27, 1831, Berg. (This journal also includes entries from 1831.)

"the men who lived . . . go and live there!": SAP journal April 11–[July] 31, [1830], entry of June 5, 1830, Berg.

406   "literary class": WEC to EPP, September 1840, *Rem of WEC*, p. 415. Channing seems to have meant something like the "educated class," made up of men working in professions for which a college education was necessary and women, like Elizabeth, who were teachers and writers.

Sophia produced two landscapes: The two Como paintings are now held by the Peabody Essex Museum, Salem, Massachusetts.

"superlative": NH to SAP, March 11, 1840, *The Letters, 1813–1843*, p. 415.

"trembled . . . our relation to each other": NH to SAP, January 24, 1840, *The Letters, 1813–1843*, pp. 401–403.

407   "helping to turn": TP to EPP, May [1841], letterbooks, vol. 7, p. 148, TP Papers, MHS.

"It is astonishing": Sarah Clarke to James Freeman Clarke, December 6, 1840, bMS Am 1569.3 (12), Houghton.

"undulating acres": Lindsay Swift, *Brook Farm: Its Members, Scholars, and Visitors* (Secaucus, N.J.: Citadel Press, 1973, reprint of 1900 edition), p. 26.

"Mr. Ripley's Utopia": NH to SAP, November 27, [1840], *The Letters, 1813–1843*, p. 505.

"engaged in a righteous": NH to SAP, May 4, 1841, *The Letters, 1813–1843*, p. 543.

"laboring man": NH to SAP, March 18, 1841, *The Letters, 1813–1843*, p. 522.

407   "a most galling weight": NH to John O'Sullivan, March 15, 1840, *The Letters, 1813–1843*, pp. 418–19.

"one filthy dock . . . every golden day": NH to John O'Sullivan, April 20, 1840, *The Letters, 1813–1843*, p. 448.

"lonely chamber": NH to SAP, October 4, 1840, *The Letters, 1813–1843*, p. 495.

"how dark my life": NH to SAP, January 27, 1841, *The Letters, 1813–1843*, p. 517.

"to insure . . . our competitive institutions": George Ripley to RWE, November 9, 1840, Swift, *Brook Farm*, pp. 15–16.

408   "industry without drudgery": George Ripley to RWE, November 9, 1840, Henry W. Sams, ed., *Autobiography of Brook Farm* (Englewood Cliffs, N.J: Prentice Hall, 1958), p. 6.

poverty suffered by the writer Thomas Carlyle: SAP to GFP, November 3–5, [1839], Berg.

"striking likeness": RWE to William Emerson, February 29, 1840, *Letters of RWE*, vol. 2, p. 257.

"genius": RWE to William Emerson, April 5, 1840, *Letters of RWE*, vol. 2, p. 274. Originally Emerson ordered six casts, as he wrote to Charles's surviving fiancée, Elizabeth Hoar, April 5, 1840, *Letters of RWE*, vol. 2, p. 274. On June 6, 1840, he wrote to his brother William saying he planned to have two additional casts made, *Letters of RWE*, vol. 2, p. 302.

This letter was not the first time Waldo Emerson had remarked on Sophia's artistic "genius." When he had visited the Peabody family in Salem while delivering a series of lectures there in April of 1836, he had been favorably impressed with Sophia's copy of Allston's *Jessica and Lorenzo* and wrote home to Lidian, "I rejoiced in the genius of the young lady very much." RWE to Lidian Emerson, April 22 and 23, 1836, *Letters of RWE*, vol. 2, p. 12.

Two years later, in January 1838, after Sophia had written Emerson a letter praising his *Nature* and recently published Phi Beta Kappa address, he responded acknowledging Sophia as "a true artist" with a "beauty making eye, which transfigures the landscape" and expressing concern for her health and the limitations her illness put on her ability to create original work, again citing her "genius": "I can never quarrel with your state of mind concerning original attempts in your own art. I admire it rather. And I am pained to think of the grievous resistance which your genius has been so long tasked to overcome, of bodily suffering." RWE to SAP, January 20, 1838, *Letters of RWE*, vol. 7, p. 294.

"Thou hast called up a face": NH to SAP, April 15, 1840, *The Letters, 1813–1843*, p. 442.

The full passage reads: "[T]hou hast achieved mighty things. Thou hast called up a face which was hidden in the grave—hast re-created it, after it was resolved to dust—and so hast snatched from Death his victory. I wonder at thee, my beloved. Thou art a miracle thyself, and workest miracles. I could not have believed it possible to do what thou hast done, to restore the lineaments of the dead so perfectly that even she who loved him so well can require nothing more;—and this, too, when thou hadst hardly known his living face. Thou couldst not have done it, unless God had helped thee. This surely was inspiration, and of the holiest kind, and for one of the holiest purposes."

Here Hawthorne adopts Sophia's tendency to attribute her artistic successes to external divine inspiration, not something he did in the matter of his own creative work. Perhaps he knew Sophia favored this explanation, or perhaps he was less able to attribute artistic agency to a woman than to a man. To all those concerned, however, there seemed something magical about the likeness Sophia achieved in the Charles Emerson medallion.

China trade baron John Murray Forbes: Forbes's brother-in-law William Hathaway, who died in 1841, was the likely subject of this medallion. Forbes's wife, Sarah Hathaway Forbes, had been a student of Elizabeth's in Boston, ca. 1830.

409 "think that I am gone": NH to SAP, April 13, 1841, *The Letters, 1813–1843*, p. 527.

"gold mine": NH to SAP, May 4, 1841, *The Letters, 1813–1843*, p. 542.

"what a great, broad-shouldered": NH to SAP, April 22, [1841], *The Letters, 1813–1843*, p. 533.

"the brethren": NH to Louisa Hawthorne, May 3, 1841, *The Letters, 1813–1843*, p. 539. In a letter to Sophia, Nathaniel also referred to "my brethren in affliction": NH to SAP, April 13, 1841, *The Letters, 1813–1843*, p. 527.

"thrown aside all the fopperies": NH to SAP, April 16, 1841, *The Letters, 1813–1843*, p. 531.

"husbandman": NH to SAP, April 13, 1841, *The Letters, 1813–1843*, p. 529.

"our home ... we can here": NH to SAP, April 28, 1841, *The Letters, 1813–1843*, p. 535.

"pale and languid": NH to SAP, June 1, 1841, *The Letters, 1813–1843*, p. 545.

"I wish far more ... lovely sites, with thee": SAP to NH, May 30, 1841, Berg.

410 "as if a sheet ... have a heart": NH to SAP, October 4, 1840, *The Letters, 1813–1843*, pp. 494–95.

"a neccessity of ... we will make it": SAP to NH: May 30, 1841, Berg.

Precisely how much: In his biography of his parents, Julian Hawthorne stated that "the lovers, aided by Miss E. P. Peabody, maintained a constant correspondence by letter." Julian Hawthorne, *Nathaniel Hawthorne and His Wife*, vol. I, p. 200. And in a letter written expressly to deny a rumored engagement between herself and Nathaniel (a rumor that had surfaced again after the publication of Julian's book in 1884), Elizabeth described herself as having been the "*confidante*" of Hawthorne's "determination" to marry her sister if she were to become well enough. EPP to Amelia Boelte, June 30, 1886, *Letters of EPP*, p. 431. There is, however, no contemporary evidence that Elizabeth played Pandarus in her sister's courtship—other than allowing her book room to serve as a mail drop, a service she provided to many frequent visitors to the shop.

In a letter of April 1842, Sophia wrote to her friend Mary Foote that when the Peabody family moved to Boston in 1840 and Nathaniel "wished to come every day, it was necessary to tell those who might meet him often, at least at the door," of the engagement. SAP to Mary Wilder White Foote, April 1842, Friday AM, postmarked April 22, 1842, Berg.

411 "My dear Elizabeth ... in the name": TP to EPP, July 1, 1840, letterbooks, vol. 7, p. 139, TP Papers, MHS.

Boston's best-known woman of letters: The chief rivals for this claim were now living outside Boston: Margaret Fuller, who lived in suburban Jamaica Plain, and Lydia Maria Child, who had moved away to Northampton. Fuller, in any case, was younger and still at the start of her career. Parker always considered Fuller less influential: her "rule is a yard long—nicely divided into 'feet and inches' ... and yours a forest, which may be measured by the rule," he wrote to Elizabeth, ca. 1841. TP to EPP, Wednesday morning, letterbooks, vol. 7, p. 147, TP Papers, MHS.

412 "the all-sympathizer": TP to EPP, December 18, 1840, letterbooks, vol. 7, p. 141, TP Papers, MHS.

412   "How wise ... *rich* as you are": TP to EPP, Wednesday morning, [1841?], letterbooks, vol. 7, p. 147, TP Papers, MHS.

"'Boswell' ... narrative Miss Peabody": F. B. Sanborn, *Recollections of Seventy Years*
(Boston: Richard G. Badger, 1909), vol. 2, p. 548.

"I shall get *several*": TP to EPP, Saturday morning, [1841?], letterbooks, vol. 7, p.
130, TP Papers, MHS.

rehearsed ideas for his notorious: TP to EPP, Saturday night, [1841], letterbooks,
vol. 7, p. 161, TP Papers, MHS.

"I think I can bear": TP to EPP, January 1841, letterbooks, vol. 7, p. 153, TP Papers,
MHS.

"cheer and bless me": TP to EPP, January 1841, letterbooks, vol. 7, p. 144, TP
Papers, MHS.

"force and beauty": TP to EPP, Friday Morning, [1841?], letterbooks, vol. 7, TP
Papers, p. 133.

"have given me much comfort": TP to EPP, January 1841, letterbooks, vol. 7, p.
144, TP Papers, MHS.

"cruelly wronged": TP to EPP, Saturday, [November 15, 1841], letterbooks, vol. 7,
p. 136, TP Papers, MHS. My date: [May 15, 1841].

Although Nathaniel Hawthorne is not mentioned by name in Parker's letters,
the wording of Elizabeth's complaint so precisely forecasts that of later confessions
to Caroline Healey Dall and Mary Van Wyck Church that it seems indisputable,
given the circumstances—Hawthorne's removal to Brook Farm, his anger over her
mishandling of *Grandfather's Chair*—that Hawthorne was the "offending party," the
source of "something exceedingly tragic in your history," that Elizabeth confided to
Parker. TP to EPP, Wednesday, letterbooks, vol. 7, p. 131, TP Papers, MHS.

Hawthorne was clearly troubled by his romantic entanglement with the sisters at this time, as is revealed in the novel he later wrote based on his Brook
Farm experience, *The Blithedale Romance*. Although there were indeed pairs of sisters in residence at Brook Farm, and various tales of seduction emerged from the
Brook Farm years, Hawthorne's plot, in which the protagonist, Hollingsworth,
becomes the object of the love of two women who consider themselves sisters,
had deep inner sources as well. "We are sisters," Priscilla implores, begging
Zenobia's forgiveness after Hollingsworth has chosen her, the less powerful,
more conventionally feminine of the two. "True, we are sisters!" Zenobia agrees,
suppressing any hostility she may have felt for her younger disciple. NH, *Collected
Novels* (New York: Library of America, 1983), p. 823. Nathaniel's attraction to
Sophia may have been all the more powerful because it derived from the rivalry
of the two sisters for his affection—he had won both, and it remained to him
only to choose; he may also have expected sisterly loyalty to cover over any
transgression on his part. In this, he was right.

"understanding": MVWC interview with EPP, MVWC, p. 344, MHS.

"a good old soul": NH to John O'Sullivan, May 19, 1839, *The Letters, 1813-1843*, p.
313. Of course Elizabeth was the same age as Nathaniel Hawthorne, no more an
"old" soul than he. Nathaniel seems here to have been continuing the conceit
begun in "The Sister Years," in which the Old Year, aged by just one year's experience of the world, gave up all her earthly possessions to her fresh-faced
younger sister, the incoming New Year.

413   "Love ... bear it": TP to EPP, Friday Morning, [1841?], letterbooks, vol. 7, p. 133,
TP Papers, MHS.

"I can't think ... in my eyes": TP to EPP, Wednesday, n.d., letterbooks, vol. 7, p.
131, TP Papers, MHS.

414   "*bearing* sorrow ... ever dear Elizabeth": TP to EPP, Friday Morning, [1841?], letterbooks, vol. 7, p. 133, TP Papers, MHS.

"Most Patient and long-suffering": TP to EPP, May 7, 1841, letterbooks, vol. 7, p. 151, TP Papers, MHS.

"My dear and very dear": TP to EPP, Wednesday morning, n.d., letterbooks, vol. 7, p. 147, TP Papers, MHS.

"If my heart ... only with children": TP to EPP, May 7, 1841, letterbooks, vol. 7, p. 151, TP Papers, MHS.

"the stories ... refractions": TP to EPP, Saturday Night, 1841, letterbooks, vol. 7, p. 161, TP Papers, MHS.

"if the Unitarian sect ... fatal to their own": EPP, "Mr. Parker and the Unitarians," *Boston Quarterly Review*, vol. V, no. XVIII, April 1842, p. 202.

"gone off like wildfire ... thing ourselves": EPP to John Sullivan Dwight, June 24, 1841, *Letters of EPP*, pp. 258–59.

415   "great-heartedness": TP to EPP, Wednesday, letterbooks, vol. 7, p. 131, TP Papers, MHS.

$10,000: EPP to John Sullivan Dwight, April 26, [1841], *Letters of EPP*, p. 251.

"Hawthorne has taken ... meet the case": EPP to John Sullivan Dwight, April 26, [1841], *Letters of EPP*, p. 250.

"minister in a truly ... petrified—organization": EPP to John Sullivan Dwight, June 24, 1841, *Letters of EPP*, pp. 258–59.

"well rid of the mournful": Swift, *Brook Farm*, p. 155.

"step out of ... magnetic character": EPP to John Sullivan Dwight, June 24, 1841, *Letters of EPP*, pp. 258–59.

"infinite worth ... beautifully now": EPP, "A Glimpse of Christ's Idea of Society," *The Dial*, vol. II, no. 2, October 1841, pp. 218–25.

416   "little company ... faculties of the soul": EPP, "Plan of the West Roxbury Community," *The Dial*, vol. II, no. 3, January 1842, pp. 361, 363–64. In *Brook Farm: The Dark Side of Utopia* (Cambridge, Mass.: Harvard University Press, 2004), p. 63, Sterling F. Delano conjectures that Elizabeth was also the author of the "first notice of Brook Farm that provides detailed information about its operations," the anonymous letter on "the Community at West Roxbury, Mass." that appeared in the August 1841 *Monthly Miscellany of Religion and Letters*.

"My mind is bothered ... raking hay": NH to George Hillard, July 16, 1841, *The Letters, 1813–1843*, p. 550.

"The summer is passing ... considerable capital": NH to David Mack, July 18, 1841, *The Letters, 1813–1843*, p. 553.

417   "begin to write": NH to Louisa Hawthorne, August 3, 1841, *The Letters, 1813–1843*, p. 555.

"the most liberal ... unknown in New England": Sarah Clarke to James Freeman Clarke, December 6, 1840, Brenda Wineapple, *Hawthorne: A Life* (New York: Alfred A. Knopf, 2003), p. 144.

"joyful thought ... dung-heap": NH to SAP, August 12, 1841, *The Letters, 1813–1843*, pp. 557–58.

"thou and I must ... in the spring": NH to SAP, August 22, 1841, *The Letters, 1813–1843*, p. 563.

"most dear wife": NH to SAP, August 22, 1841, *The Letters, 1813–1843*, p. 562.

"I love thee": NH to SAP, September 9, 1841, *The Letters, 1813–1843*, p. 568.

"external pressure": NH to SAP, August 22, 1841, *The Letters, 1813–1843*, p. 563.

produced only a handful: NH, *Grandfather's Chair* (Boston: Tappan and Dennett, 1842).

418   "the most celebrated ... entire world": Elisabeth Gitter, *The Imprisoned Guest: Samuel Howe and Laura Bridgman, the Original Deaf-Blind Girl* (New York: Picador, 2001), p. 4.

"sightless, earless, voiceless": Gitter, *The Imprisoned Guest,* p. 5.

cast into copies: In her editor's introduction to Sophia's *Cuba Journal,* p. xli, Claire Badaracco cites "an undated newsclip," ca. 1883, held by the Manuscript Division, New York Public Library, that states: "nearly every school for the blind and deaf mutes in this country which could afford the trifling cost ... procured one, and inquiries for copies came from England, France, Scotland and elsewhere abroad." The original plaster cast is still owned by the Perkins School, but it is in poor condition.

"cold clay": NH to SAP, January 1, [1842], *The Letters, 1813–1843,* p. 507. From Hawthorne's letters to Sophia, it appears that Laura sometimes came to sit for Sophia in her West Street studio. However, in her *Lectures in the Training Schools for Kindergartners* (Boston: D. C. Heath, 1897), p. 98, Elizabeth recalled Sophia making regular visits "to the asylum to model Laura's bust."

"see these people": NH to SAP, September 22, 1841, *The Letters, 1813–1843,* p. 576.

"famished yearning ... great quantity": NH to SAP, September 25, 1841, *The Letters, 1813–1843,* p. 579.

"was an unnatural ... reality from a shadow": NH to SAP, September 3, 1841, *The Letters, 1813–1843,* p. 566.

"Thou art my only reality": NH to SAP, October 4, 1841, *The Letters, 1813–1843,* p. 584.

419   "thou wouldst be much better": NH to SAP, September 16, 1841, *The Letters, 1813–1843,* p. 572.

"I am given thee to repose": NH to SAP, April 15, 1840, *The Letters, 1813–1843,* p. 442.

"severest reprehension": NH to SAP, September 16, 1841, *The Letters, 1813–1843,* p. 572.

420   "Thou art a mighty ... or I die!": NH to SAP, November 27, 1841, *The Letters, 1813–1843,* p. 596.

421   "I do not believe ... if I would": NH to Cornelius Mathews and Evert A. Duyckinck, December 22, 1841, *The Letters, 1813–1843,* p. 600.

"queer community": NH to SAP, September 22, 1841, *The Letters, 1813–1843,* p. 575.

"a perpetual picnic": RWE, "Historic Notes of Life and Letters in New England," Henry W. Sams, ed., *Autobiography of Brook Farm,* p. 224.

"exploded scheme": NH, *Collected Novels,* p. 639.

PAGE   *30. Two Funerals and a Wedding*

422   "prophetic hope ... shortened life": MTM journal, "Estimate of Horace Mann," January 24, 1860, HM Papers, MHS.

"How nicely ... wholly by his side": MTP to SAH, [early April 1843], Berg.

"fold his arms around her": NH to SAP, August 21, 1839, *The Letters, 1813–1843,* p. 337.

423   "secret affection ... admiration and love": HM journal, vol. 1, entry of March 26, 1843, HM Papers, MHS.

"it is impossible ... prophetic of endurance": HM journal, vol. 1, entry of April 2, 1843, HM Papers, MHS.

"rise above fate": George Combe to HM, March 31, 1841, HM Papers, MHS.

"sore heart": MTM journal, "Estimate of HM," entry of January 24, 1860, HM Papers, MHS.

"it was my own sorrow": MTP to SAH, [early April 1843], Berg.

children's guide to seasonal plants: [MTP], *The Flower People* (Hartford, Conn.: Tyler and Porter; Boston, E. P. Peabody, 1842).

"beautiful colours ... house builders & merchants": *JMN*, vol. VIII, p. 351.

"only that in my shop ... secondary quality": EPP to Samuel Gray Ward, September 13, 1841, Samuel Gray Ward and Anna Hazard Barker Ward Papers, bMS Am 1465 (955), Houghton.

"seldom ... of a good name": RWE to EPP, October 12, 1840, *Letters of RWE*, vol. 7, p. 419.

424   subscription library was faltering: Eventually it would be the Foreign Library—which finally exceeded a thousand items, shelved in brown paper wrappers to protect their bindings as they passed from hand to hand—that caught on most with Elizabeth's thrifty clientele.

A thorough account of Elizabeth Peabody's accomplishments as purveyor of books and ideas through her subscription library can be found in Leslie Perrin Wilson's excellent article "'No Worthless Books': Elizabeth Peabody's Foreign Library, 1840–1852," *The Papers of the Bibliographical Society of America*, vol. 99, no. 1, March 2005. Wilson has also made available a complete listing of the books still remaining from Elizabeth's Foreign Library stock: "Bibliography of the Remainder of a Gift of Books, Pamphlets, and Periodicals Presented by Elizabeth Palmer Peabody to the Concord Free Library," 2004, BibSite, The Bibliographical Society of America, http://www.bibsocamer.org/BibSite/bibsite.htm. I am grateful to Leslie Wilson for sharing information as we both completed our work on the Peabody family.

"disappointments ... so little as mine": EPP to WEC, June 1841, MVWC, p. 410, MHS.

"to see the unfolding": RWE to Charles Stearns Wheeler, April 30, 1843, *Letters of RWE*, vol. 7, p. 536.

"Transcendental Exchange": George Bradford, quoted in Bruce Ronda, *Elizabeth Palmer Peabody: Reformer on Her Own Terms* (Cambridge, Mass.: Harvard University Press, 1999), p. 185–86.

"selections from the oldest ... more or less pure": RWE, "Ethnical Scriptures," *The Dial*, vol. 3, no. 1, July 1842, p. 82.

425   did not yet exist in America: EPP's translation of the *Lotus Sutra* from the French of Eugène Burnouf (*La Revue Independante*, April and May 1843) appeared as "The Preaching of Buddha" in *The Dial*, January 1844. The translation has been variously attributed to Elizabeth Peabody and Thoreau, but Andy Nagashima documents Elizabeth's work on the translation in "*The Dial* and *The Lotus Sutra*," *Concord Saunterer*, vol. 12, 2004, p. 43.

A fair number of *Dial*s were dispatched to England each quarter, where British readers had a more favorable reaction; when Emerson traveled to England on a lecture tour in 1847, he found that *The Dial* was "absurdly well-known" by his audiences. The magazine had ceased publication three years earlier. Robert D. Richardson, *Emerson: The Mind on Fire* (Berkeley: University of California Press, 1995), p. 443.

"a friendly publisher": RWE to MF, November 14? 15?, [1841], *Letters of RWE*, vol. 2, p. 464.

"the word *transcendentalism*": EPP to Orestes Brownson, [ca. 1840], *Letters of EPP*, p. 248.

425   "a certain air of unseasonableness": RWE to EPP, October 1840, *Letters of RWE,* vol. 2, p. 346. Because only Emerson's letter survives, it cannot be established definitively that Elizabeth's purpose in sending him the remaining articles of the *Christian Examiner* series was for consideration for *The Dial.* However, she did at about the same time submit them to Orestes Brownson, editor of the *Boston Quarterly Review.* It is likely she had the same aim in mind when she sent them to Emerson as *The Dial* began to appear in the summer and fall of 1840. Although Emerson found Elizabeth's interpretations of the biblical prophets— "these old dead men," he called them—a bit like encountering "octogenarians at a young party," a young visitor to Elizabeth's book room to whom she also showed the articles at this time, Caroline Healey, read them with considerable interest: "how I envy—the knowledge of men & books—which enabled their author to compose them fourteen years since." Caroline Healey Dall journals, August 17, 1840, Dall Papers, MHS. Peabody must have told Healey, as she told Brownson in her letter, that she originally composed the articles in 1826. It is unfortunate that Emerson did not read the articles then, when he too was absorbed with biblical interpretation as a divinity student at Harvard: the radical nature of her thoughts at that time would have been readily apparent.

"the social principle": EPP, "Spirit of the Hebrew Scriptures—No. I. The Creation," *Christian Examiner* no. LXII (New Series no. XXXII), May 1834, p. 189.

"arrangement . . . to all of us": RWE to Chrisopher Pearse Cranch, October 1, 1841, *Letters of RWE,* vol. 7, p. 474. Cranch, who had served as a Unitarian minister in the late 1830s, went on to become better known as a painter in the style of the Hudson River school; his caricatures of fellow Transcendentalists, most famously of Emerson as a gangly figure supporting an enormous "transparent eyeball" for a head, are still well known. Cranch was also a distant relation of the Peabodys; his grandmother Mary Smith Cranch was Mrs. Peabody's great-aunt and one-time protector.

"at least, pay the Editor": RWE to William Emerson, *Letters of RWE,* vol. 2, p. 457.

"a less deserving & therefore . . . sustain": Horace Greeley to EPP, January 10, [1841—probably 1842], MVWC, p. 420a, MHS.

426   "Plainly marriage . . . old love detached": journal entry [1841], *JMN,* vol. 8, p. 95.

"I guard my moods . . . best in his study": journal entry following February 4, 1841, *JMN,* vol. 7, p. 420.

"Mezentian marriage . . . Universe is his bride": journal entry following August 27, 1841, *JMN,* vol. 8, p. 34. Lidian Emerson's jealousy of her husband's attentions to Margaret Fuller had surfaced on this visit in several tearful outbursts, and Waldo had confided in Fuller that he was "sorely troubled by imperfections in the tie." For an account of this episode, see Joan von Mehren, *Minerva and the Muse: A Life of Margaret Fuller* (Amherst: University of Massachusetts Press, 1994), pp. 156–58.

"Shall I ever dare to love": Richardson, *Emerson: The Mind on Fire,* p. 359.

"lost": Richardson, *Emerson: The Mind on Fire,* p. 360.

"a few persons to meet . . . from this world": RWE to EPP, January 28, 1842, *Letters of RWE,* vol. 3, p. 8.

427   Emerson never did meet: Nathaniel Hawthorne, too, was invited to meet Dickens at a dinner organized by George Hillard at Papanti's Hall in Boston on February 1, 1842. Dickens was to speak in favor of an international copyright agreement. Chary of large social gatherings, Hawthorne accepted the invitation but did not attend. *The Letters, 1813-1843,* p. 608n.

"Let there be rotation": Richardson, *Emerson: The Mind on Fire*, p. 370.

"bold bible for the Young America": Richardson, *Emerson: The Mind on Fire*, p. 335.

Emerson would write fifty-three: Richardson, *Emerson: The Mind on Fire*, p. 377.

"petty literary patriotism": Richardson, *Emerson: The Mind on Fire*, p. 376.

"grinding out of *Dials*": RWE quoted in Joel Myerson, *The New England Transcendentalists and the* Dial: *A History of the Magazine and Its Contributors* (Rutherford, Madison, and Teaneck, N.J.: Fairleigh Dickinson University Press; London and Toronto: Associated University Presses, 1980), p. 97.

"agent of Heaven": SAP to Mary Wilder White Foote, July 5, 1842, SAH Papers, Stanford.

"sister": Paula Ivaska Robbins, *The Royal Family of Concord: Samuel, Elizabeth, and Rockwood Hoar and Their Friendship with Ralph Waldo Emerson* (Xlibris, 2003), p. 106.

"a good neighborhood . . . depression of visitation": journal entry of May 6, 1842, *JMN*, vol. 8, pp. 172–73.

428   "Those of us who . . . may consist of such": RWE to Charles Newcomb, May 7 and 8, 1842, *Letters of RWE*, vol. 3, p. 51.

"I like him well": Robbins, *The Royal Family of Concord*, p. 151.

"You will find him more *mellow*": MF to RWE, June 23, 1842, *Letters of MF*, vol. 3, p. 70.

"pleased with the colony": Brenda Wineapple, *Hawthorne: A Life* (New York: Alfred A. Knopf, 2003), p. 160.

"that profound retreat": SAP to Mary Wilder White Foote, July 5, 1842, SAH Papers, Stanford.

"antique . . . we wanted it": *AN*, p. 315.

"savory": *AN*, p. 345.

429   "to remove everything . . . in marble": NH to MF, August 25, 1842, *The Letters, 1813–1843*, p. 647. Hawthorne issued this statement to Fuller in response to her suggestion that he and Sophia take in her newlywed sister and brother-in-law, Ellen and Ellery Channing, as boarders at the Old Manse.

"with such a world . . . identical in all": SAP to Mary Wilder White Foote, July 5, 1842, SAH Papers, Stanford. For much of the information on the Old Manse and its surroundings I am grateful to Joan Goodwin and her *Remarkable Mrs. Ripley: The Life of Sarah Alden Bradford Ripley* (Boston: Northeastern University Press, 1998).

430   "penetrated with joy": SAP to MF, May 11, 1842, MF Papers, MS Am 1086 XVI-30, Houghton. Sophia must have attended at least some of Fuller's Conversations; she became so enamored of Fuller that she wrote a sonnet in her honor, titled "To a Priestess of the Temple not made with hands," praising her "golden-cadenced intuitions." MF Papers, MS Am 1086 XVI-29, Houghton.

"injunction": NH to SAP, February 27, 1842, *The Letters, 1813–1843*, p. 611.

"doubtless . . . suit of black!": NH to SAP, January 20, 1842, *The Letters, 1813–1843*, p. 605.

"strange reserve . . . show it to them": NH to SAP, February 27, 1842, *The Letters, 1813–1843*, p. 611. In his biography of his parents, Julian Hawthorne (*Nathaniel Hawthorne and His Wife* [Hamden, Conn.: Archon Books, 1968, reprint of 1884 edition], vol. 1, pp. 196–98) offers this reason for his father's secrecy about his engagement. It is an outlandish tale, but worth reporting here because elements have been incorporated into other accounts of the secret romance, despite a complete lack of contemporary evidence corroborating the story:

A strict secrecy was maintained by them respecting their engagement during nearly the entire three years of its continuance; and the reason of this concealment was a somewhat singular one. Enough has been said about the extreme impressibility of Madame Hawthorne; and it appears that her son was led to imagine that the news of his relations with Miss Sophia would give her a shock that might endanger her life. What, then, was Madame Hawthorne's objection to Miss Sophia supposed to be, since, as has already been shown, she was personally very fond of her? It was owing to what was assumed to be the latter's hopeless state of invalidism. Madame Hawthorne (her son was assured) could never endure the thought of his marrying a woman who was a victim to constant nervous headaches; and were he, nevertheless to do so, the most lamentable consequences were to be anticipated. Now, any other conceivable obstacle than this would have influenced Hawthorne not a whit; but he was not prepared to face the idea of defying and perhaps 'killing' his mother ... But who put it into his head to think that his mother would adopt this attitude? I fear it must be confessed that the Machiavelli in question was none other than his own sister Elizabeth. This bright-eyed and brilliant little lady saw plainly enough how matters were likely to go between her brother and Miss Sophia, and was resolved to do what she could to prevent it. She was quite sincere, moreover, in her belief that Sophia would never be strong enough properly to fulfil the duties of married life; and this added substance to the dislike she felt to the idea of her brother's marrying at all.

430   "we do not live": Norman Holmes Pearson, "Elizabeth Peabody on Hawthorne," *Essex Institute Historical Collections*, July 1958, p. 267.
        "something wrong ... to any body!": NH to SAP, February 27, 1842, *The Letters, 1813-1843*, p. 612.
        "Nothing like our story": NH to SAP, January 3, 1840, *The Letters, 1813-1843*, p. 398.

431   "what a cloudy veil ... not they with me": NH to SAP, February 27, 1842, *The Letters, 1813-1843*, pp. 611-13.
        "external pledge": NH to SAP, April 28, 1840, *The Letters, 1813-1843*, p. 452.
        "It is a happiness ... without thee": NH to SAP, February 27, 1842, *The Letters, 1813-1843*, pp. 611-13.
        "This yearning ... I live": NH to SAP, April 6, 1842, *The Letters, 1813-1843*, pp. 620-21.
        "We have left expression ... better language": NH to SAP, January 20, 1842, *The Letters, 1813-1843*, p. 606.
        "My breast is full ... ourselves only": NH to SAP, April 6, 1842, *The Letters, 1813-1843*, p. 620.
        "Some person betrayed ... officially announced": SAP to Mary Wilder White Foote, April 1842, Friday AM, postmarked April 22, 1842, Berg.

432   "I heard a rumor": Benjamin Merrill to Leverett Saltonstall, April 25, 1842, Saltonstall Family Papers, MHS.
        "the accomplished Miss Peabody": NH to SAP, May 19, [1842], *The Letters, 1813-1843*, p. 623.
        Could his mother and sisters: Indeed, on Hawthorne's next visit to Salem, his mother admitted that she "had seen how things were, a long time ago." NH to SAP, June 9, 1842, *The Letters, 1813-1843*, p. 628. In this same letter, Nathaniel told

Sophia that "almost every agitating circumstance of her life had hitherto cost her a fit of sickness; and I knew not but it might be so now"; little wonder that Nathaniel knew so well how to care for his future wife, about whom the same could be said.

"affair . . . from us so long": Elizabeth Manning Hawthorne to SAP, May 23, 1842, Berg.

"hideous": SAP to EPP, May 2–3, 1838, Berg.

"Consult your own comforts": Elizabeth Manning Hawthorne to Una Hawthorne, July 10, 1873, HM 42658, Huntington.

433   "hard hearted": Elizabeth Manning Hawthorne to Una Hawthorne, March 20, 1864, BANC MSS 72/2362, Bancroft.

"severest critic": Elizabeth Manning Hawthorne to Una Hawthorne, March 1, 1865, BANC MSS 72/2362, Bancroft.

"most beautiful . . . to love with": NH to SAP, May 27, 1842, *The Letters, 1813–1843*, p. 626. Sophia's letter does not survive.

"very cold . . . much depended upon me": Elizabeth Manning Hawthorne to SAP, June 15, 1842, Berg.

"the world found out": Wineapple, *Hawthorne*, p. 139.

"it is not what thou dost": NH to SAP, August 12, 1841, *The Letters, 1813–1843*, p. 557.

"this arrest . . . nervous fever?": SAP to Mary Wilder White Foote, July 5, 1842, SAH Papers, Stanford.

434   "like a rising Phoenix . . . noble": SAP to Mary Wilder White Foote, July 5, 1842, SAH Papers, Stanford.

"lingering here . . . the night before": NH to SAP, June 30, 1842, *The Letters, 1813–1843*, p. 634.

"all new & bright": Goodwin, *The Remarkable Mrs. Ripley*, p. 194.

"the execution": NH to Louisa Hawthorne, July 1, 1842, *The Letters, 1813–1843*, p. 636; also NH to Louisa Hawthorne, July 10, 1842, *The Letters, 1813–1843*, p. 639.

"in a trance . . . polished emerald": SAH to Mrs. EPP, July 10, 1842, Berg.

" . . . These and more July": poem dated July 3, 1842, unsigned but likely written by Elizabeth Hoar, SAH Papers, Stanford.

"Adam and Eve . . . perfect Eden": SAH to Mrs. EPP, July 10, 1842, Berg.

"my wonderful cure . . . perfection every day": SAH to Mrs. EPP, July 15, 1842, Berg.

435   "toasting in West Street . . . no centre here": MTP to SAH, n.d., Monday Eve, [early July? 1842], Berg. My date: [July 11, 1842].

"chamber, studio & boudoir": SAP journal beginning October 1832, Salem, entry of October 22, 1832, Stanford.

"they will read & get civilized": MTP to SAH, July 17, 1842, Berg.

"*the great work is done!*": HM journal, vol. 1, entry of March 3, 1842, HM Papers, MHS.

"We will make something . . . men & angels": HM to Samuel Gridley Howe, March 17, 1842, HM Papers, MHS.

"submit . . . public opinion": HM journal, vol. 1, entry of July 3, 1842, HM Papers, MHS.

"on the Eve . . . *men must come to*": EPP to William Wordsworth, May 7, 1842, Margaret Neussendorfer, ed., "Elizabeth Palmer Peabody to William Wordsworth: Eight Letters, 1825–1845," *Studies in the American Renaissance 1984* (Charlottesville: University Press of Virginia), pp. 206–207.

If Elizabeth had known of Wordsworth's dim view of Transcendentalism, she might have felt less confident about sending Alcott his way. "Where is the thing which now passes for philosophy at Boston to stop?" Wordsworth had written to his American editor the year before, after receiving a copy of Emerson's *Essays* from Elizabeth. Wordsworth dismissed Emerson along with his English friend Carlyle as "our two present Philosophes, who have taken a language which they suppose to be English for their vehicle." Neussendorfer, ed., p. 205.

435   "a heart troubled . . . his genius": EPP to William Wordsworth, May 5, 1842, Neussendorfer, ed., "Elizabeth Palmer Peabody to William Wordsworth: Eight Letters, 1825-1845," pp. 206-207.

436   "In looking round . . . no real mother to me": EPP, "Mr. Parker and the Unitarians," p. 208.

"new turn": William B. Sprague, D.D., *Annals of the American Pulpit; or Commemorative Notices of Distinguished American Clergymen of the Various Denominations* (New York: Carter and Brothers, 1865), vol. 8, p. 382.

consider having herself baptized: I am grateful to Joan Goodwin, the biographer of Sarah Alden Bradford Ripley, for bringing this information to my attention. I am relying on her typescript of a letter from Samuel Ripley to Mary Moody Emerson, dated August 5, 1842, present location of the manuscript unknown: "I do not wonder at your surprise at the course E.P.P. has adopted—everybody is surprised—Her conversion is too sudden to suit me. And so I believe Dr Sharp thinks, for we hear that he demurs about baptizing her not having faith in the soundness of *her faith*, knowing full well how far removed she has been from what he & other serious Ctns [rest of passage excised]."

annotating tales from Vishnu Sarma's *Hitopadesa: JMN*, vol. 8, p. 490.

"make me partner . . . *first* right?": *Rem of WEC*, p. 449.

"philosophy of religion": Sprague, *Annals of the American Pulpit*, vol. 8, p. 382.

nine out of ten: Mary Kelley, ed., *The Power of Her Sympathy: The Autobiography and Journal of Catharine Maria Sedgwick* (Boston: Massachusetts Historical Society, 1993), editor's introduction, p. 22.

In Boston, however, single women had plenty of company. The 1845 city census showed that one-third of female residents were unmarried. Joan von Mehren, *Minerva and the Muse*, p. 169.

"at the period of life . . . entirely despaired": EPP quoted in Nancy Craig Simmons, "Margaret Fuller's Boston Conversations: The 1839-40 Series," *Studies in the American Renaissance 1994* (Charlottesville: University Press of Virginia), p. 215.

"there came a time": MF quoted in Simmons, "Margaret Fuller's Boston Conversations," p. 215.

"then it was": EPP quoted in Simmons, "Margaret Fuller's Boston Conversations," p. 215.

437   "Ah woman is still": EPP journal, following entry of Friday, [August 10, 1838], MVWC, p. 389, MHS.

"take the facts & make": MTP to SAH, n.d. [September 1842], Berg.

"Dr. Howe will offer up": MTP to SAH, n.d. [October 5?, 1842], Berg.

"abomination of visiting": SAH to Mrs. EPP, October 9-[October 10], 1842, Berg.

"enjoy each other": SAH to Mrs. EPP, July 15, 1842, Berg.

"many pictures will come": Caroline Sturgis to SAH, July 28, [1842], SLU.

"Were you in my place": SAH to Caroline Sturgis, August 28, 1842, Sturgis-Tappan Family Papers, Smith.

"polished man": [Mrs. EPP], "Seduction," *Christian Examiner*, no. LIX, New Series no. XXX, November 1833, p. 163.

438   "I shall be too ... deep and equal": SAH to Mrs. EPP, August 30–[September 4], 1842, Berg.

"ugly as sin ... still remaining in him": *AN*, p. 353.

"down upon the carpet ... that of our pulses": SAH and NH journal, vol. 1, SAH entry after July 9, before August 5, 1842, MA 580, Morgan.

"the Cliffs ... Hawthorne": SAH to Mrs. EPP, September 29, 1842, Berg.

"it might be a sin ... world were Heaven": *AN*, p. 334.

"our domestic harmony": SAH to Mrs. EPP, October 3, [1842], Berg.

"the Cachucha, Cracovienne": SAH to Mrs. EPP, August 11, 1842, Berg.

"I deserve John": SAH to Mrs. EPP, August [5], 1842, Berg.

"originals ... pathway of life": *AN*, p. 357.

"beloved woman": *AN*, p. 335.

"gets into the remotest recesses": *AN*, p. 349.

"the first time ... love and tenderness": *AN*, p. 362.

439   "gurgling purling ... succeeded very well": SAH to Mrs. EPP, October 3, [1842], Berg.

"I still held ... wet with tears": Sprague, *Annals of the American Pulpit*, vol. 8, p. 383.

"the only visit I ever had from him": *Rem of WEC*, p. 449.

"I had ceased to think": Sprague, *Annals of the American Pulpit*, vol. 8, p. 384.

"inspired expression": Jack Mendelsohn, *Channing: The Reluctant Radical* (Boston: Unitarian Universalist Association, 1979), p. 281.

"crowds of images ... spiritual life": Mendelsohn, *Channing: The Reluctant Radical*, p. 282.

"so gently ... tortured by poor": MTP to SAH, [October 5?, 1842], Berg.

440   "come nearer to me ... always transcended": Sprague, *Annals of the American Pulpit*, vol. 8, p. 383.

"That there is ... *within*": EPP to MTP, [week of May 16, 1836?], Berg.

"clear new life": SAH to Mrs. EPP, July 10, 1842, Berg.

"Paradise": SAH entry of August 20, 1842, in SAH and NH journal vol. 1, MA 580, Morgan.

"absorbed into another being": SAH to Caroline Sturgis, August 28, 1842, Sturgis-Tappan Family Papers, Smith.

"*half life* ... too much effort": SAH to Mary Wilder White Foote, April 6, 1843, SAH Papers, Stanford.

"above the region ... beyond the grave": EPP to MTP, [week of May 16, 1836?], Berg.

PAGE   *Epilogue: May 1, 1843*

441   "it would be too painful": HM journal, vol. 1, entry of March 26, 1843, HM Papers, MHS. Another reform-minded American couple, Henry and Elizabeth Cady Stanton, had spent their honeymoon attending the World's Antislavery Convention meeting in London in June 1840. Gerda Lerner, *The Grimke Sisters from South Carolina: Pioneers for Woman's Rights and Abolition* (New York: Shocken, 1977), p. 296.

"It cannot be otherwise ... bless you": HM journal, vol. 1, entry of April 30, 1843, HM Papers, MHS.

"the sacred words": MTP and EPP to Rebecca Pennell, May 1, 1843, HM Papers, MHS.

"the hour of *ratification*": MTP to SAH, April 30, [1843], Berg.

442   "the greatest adornment . . . heartrending to see": MTP and EPP to Rebecca Pennell, May 1, 1843, HM Papers, MHS.

"the illuminated countenance . . . as I did": EPP to Miss Rawlins Pickman, May 1, 1843, HM Papers, MHS.

"beautiful . . . as ever shone": HM to Rebecca Pennell, May 15, 1843, HM Papers, MHS.

"A floating palace . . . saloon" and other details of the *Britannia's* construction: See Stephen Fox's excellent account in *Transatlantic: Samuel Cunard, Isambard Brunel, and the Great Atlantic Steamships* (New York: HarperCollins, 2003), p. xiv.

"all in fixtures . . . in *the room*": MTP and EPP to Rebecca Pennell, May 1, 1843, HM Papers, MHS.

"but the third stuck": HM to Rebecca Pennell, May 15, 1843, HM Papers, MHS.

443   "full of courage . . . all-sustaining motive": HM to Rebecca Pennell, April 30, 1843, HM Papers, MHS.

"When I was being married . . . very quietly": MTM to EPP, May 30, 1843, HM Papers, MHS.

"so rejoiced . . . out of *our house*": MTP and EPP to Rebecca Pennell, May 1, 1843, HM papers, MHS.

"We parted with smiles": EPP to Miss Rawlins Pickman, May 1, 1843, HM Papers, MHS.

"nod our heads . . . 'And I as you!'": SAH entry of June 6, 1843, in SAH and NH journal, vol. 1, MA 580, Morgan.

"promised child": *AN,* p. 366.

"time will bring to light": NH to MF, February 1, 1843, *The Letters, 1813–1843,* p. 670.

"The longer we live . . . conditions of marriage": *AN,* p. 366.

444   "the gorgeous . . . terrible as Power": EPP, "A Vision," *The Pioneer,* vol. 1, no. 3, pp. 96–100.

445   "The world is always a new world": MTM to SAH, [1852], HM Papers, MHS.

"is a becoming": EPP to Mary Moody Emerson, ca. 1843, *Letters of EPP,* p. 265.

"mystagogues": In an 1840 letter to J. G. Palfrey, "Pope Andrews" Norton wrote that, if not checked, "[Ripley] and Brownson and Miss Fuller and Miss Peabody, with occasional aid from Dr. Channing and others, will become the mystagogues of one knows not how large a portion of the community." Kenneth Sacks, *Understanding Emerson: "The American Scholar" and His Struggle for Self-Reliance* (Princeton, N.J.: Princeton University Press, 2003), p. 95.

"only live lady . . . roll and pitch": HM to Rebecca Pennell, May 15, 1843, HM Papers, MHS.

446   "wealth and accomplishments . . . charity work": HM journal, vol. 2, entry of May 16, 1843, HM Papers, MHS.

"fields so monotonously green": HM journal, vol. 2, entry of May 18, 1843, HM Papers, MHS.

"I have not felt myself . . . ears all the time": MTM to SAH, [late May 1843], Berg.

"the whole of West Street": MTM to EPP, July 10, 1843, HM Papers, MHS.

"you could stow away": MTM paraphrased by Dr. NP in Dr. NP to Francis Peabody, June 21, 1843, Dartmouth.

"rose like an incense": MTM to EPP, May 30, 1843, HM Papers, MHS.

"with an earnest oath . . . infanticide": MTM to EPP, June 19, 1843, HM Papers, MHS.

"his strange ambition": MTM to EPP, June 15, 1843, HM Papers, MHS.

"Nahant rocks": MTM to EPP, June 27, 1843, HM Papers, MHS.

447   "ten holy years": MTM, "Estimate of HM," entry of January 24, 1860, HM Papers, MHS.

"all I could do": MTM to SAH, October 17, 1859, HM Papers, MHS.

"betrayed": MTM, "Estimate of HM," entry of January 24, 1860, HM Papers, MHS.

"Never be afraid ... *proof* of Immortality": MTM, "Estimate of HM," entry of January 24, 1860, HM Papers, MHS.

first coeducational institution: Antioch and Oberlin vie for the distinction of "first coeducational college." While Oberlin held the first coeducational classes, Antioch was first to admit female students, although women studied in separate classrooms at first.

Mary finally became a writer: Mary Mann, *The Life of Horace Mann* (Boston: Walker, Fuller, 1865); Sarah Winnemucca Hopkins, *Life Among the Piutes,* Mary Mann, ed. (New York: G. P. Putnam's Sons, 1883)—for this early "as told to" autobiography, Mary did much of the writing; Mary Mann, *Juanita: A Romance of Real Life in Cuba, Fifty Years Ago* (Boston: D. Lothrop, 1887). Mary also wrote articles and shared authorship with Elizabeth on books about kindergartens, a cause they shared. She contributed an article defending coeducation in colleges to Julia Ward Howe's *Sex and Education: A Reply to Dr. E. H. Clarke's 'Sex in Education'* (Boston: Roberts Brothers, 1874). And she became the American translator and champion of the Argentine reformer, revolutionary, and president Domingo Faustino Sarmiento, an admirer of Horace Mann with whom Mary maintained ties after her husband's death.

"bowed down ... old world": *Boston Post,* June 19, 1843.

448   "strangers": Dr. NP to Francis Peabody, June 21, 1843, Dartmouth.

"Let it rise": Daniel Webster's speech of June 17, 1825, quoted in *Boston Evening Transcript,* June 16, 1843.

"monument to the past ... orator of the occasion": *Boston Post,* June 19, 1843.

"defection ... Congress": Robert D. Richardson, Jr., *Emerson: The Mind on Fire* (Berkeley: University of California Press, 1995), p. 396.

"disunion": *Boston Post,* June 19, 1843.

"vain, and wishes to be more": MF, "The Great Lawsuit. Man *versus* Men. Woman *versus* Women," Joel Myerson, ed., *Transcendentalism: A Reader* (Oxford: Oxford University Press, 2000), p. 396.

"beings of affection": Myerson, ed., *Transcendentalism,* p. 411.

"self-dependence": Myerson, ed., *Transcendentalism,* p. 412.

"civilized ... but in thought": Myerson, ed., *Transcendentalism,* p. 405.

"partners in work": Myerson, ed., *Transcendentalism,* p. 408.

"never likes anything ... character": Joan von Mehren, *Minerva and the Muse: A Life of Margaret Fuller* (Amherst: University of Massachusetts Press, 1994), p. 171.

449   "What do you think . . . rights of woman": Julian Hawthorne, *Nathaniel Hawthorne and His Wife* (Hamden, Conn.: Archon Books, 1968, reprint of 1884 edition), vol. 1, p. 257.

"How is it ... as never man spoke": Julian Hawthorne, *Nathaniel Hawthorne and His Wife,* vol. I, p. 258.

"intellectual companionship": Myerson, ed., *Transcendentalism,* p. 406. According to the biographer Joan von Mehren, *Minerva and the Muse,* p. 184, "the Hawthorne marriage met Margaret's criteria for the highest type of marriage: two accomplished artists dedicated to the development of each other's aspirations in a peaceful home."

"serenest and most resolute ... modelling": MF to NH, January 16, 1843, *Letters of MF,* vol. 3, pp. 115, 117.

449   "a sweet return ... look like thee!": SAH, entry of July 9, 1843, in SAH and NH journal, vol. 1, MA 580, Morgan.

450   "triune ... suffering": SAH to Ellen Sturgis Hooper, December 10, 1843, MA 5015, Morgan.

"silent ministry of pain": SAH to EPP, May 14, 1865, MA 3400 (SH 39), Morgan.

"hate[d] to think ... hills & slopes": SAH to Mrs. EPP, [ca. summer 1843], box 1, folder 1, SAH Papers, Stanford.

"The faults of fashionable girls ... mantuamakers": Mrs. EPP to MTM, n.d., Monday morning, [January 1845?], HM Papers, MHS. My date: [April 1845].

"the whole W[atertown] concern": Mrs. EPP to [MTM or EPP], May 6, 1852, Straker typescripts, p. 1693, Antiochiana.

"cultivate ... Queens": Mrs. EPP to MTM, n.d., Monday morning, [January 1845?], HM Papers, MHS. My date: [April 1845].

"*aesthetic* culture ... personal character": NCP to EPP, July 29, 1850, Straker typescripts, p. 1515, Antiochiana.

451   "acquainted with every ... earth ever saw": EPP to Richard Henry Dana, Jr., n.d. [August 1843?], Dana Family Papers, MHS.

"very soon": EPP, *Last Evening with Allston* (Boston: D. Lothrop, 1886), p. 12.

"majestic ... holding a pencil": EPP, *Last Evening with Allston*, p. 14.

"What was he thinking": EPP, *Last Evening with Allston*, p. 15.

"the moon ... load of sorrow": EPP, *Last Evening with Allston*, p. 19.

"perfecting ... my child!": EPP, *Last Evening with Allston*, p. 18.

"bound up in that": Annie Adams Fields unpublished memoir of SAH, quoted in Rita Gollin, *Annie Adams Fields: Woman of Letters* (Amherst and Boston: University of Massachusetts Press, 2002), p. 105.

452   "an ideal being": MTM, "An Experience," n.d., HM Papers, MHS.

❧ INDEX ❧

Page numbers in italics refer to illustrations.